The Middle East & South Asia

Malcolm B. Russell

The World Today Series

2014–2015

48th Edition

Malcolm B. Russell . . .

Vice President for Academic Affairs at Union College, Lincoln, Nebraska. Columbia Union College (B.A., History); School of Advanced International Studies, the Johns Hopkins University (M.A.; Ph.D.), with emphases in Middle East Studies and International Economics. A Fulbright Fellowship allowed him research opportunities in Egypt, Syria, Jordan and Lebanon, and resulted in *The First Modern Arab State: Syria under Faysal, 1918–1920* (Minneapolis, MN: Biblioteca Islamica, 1985), as well as papers at a number of professional societies. Born in Beirut, after a childhood spent there and in Egypt, he attended high school in India and later traveled widely in the Middle East. He speaks Arabic and French.

Adapted, rewritten and revised annually from a book entitled *The Middle East and South Asia 1967*, published in 1967 and succeeding years by

Stryker-Post Publications
An imprint of The Rowman & Littlefield Publishing Group, Inc.
4501 Forbes Blvd., Suite 200, Lanham, MD 20706
www.rowman.com

International Standard Book Number: 978-1-4758-1235-0

International Standard Serial Number: 0084-2311

Library of Congress Catalog Number 2011932747

Cover design by nvision graphic design

Cartography by William L. Nelson

Typography by Barton Matheson Willse & Worthington

CONTENTS

Door to the Ka'aba, the sacred shrine of the Great Mosque in Mecca

The Middle East and South Asia Today

For at least the past quarter century, I have edited this volume optimistic about events in the Middle East and South Asia. I believed it was my responsibility to explain its challenges as well as to interpret the vital events in the recent national histories. Readers were invited to enjoy learning more about vital geographic regions whose populations were gaining education, wealth, and understanding. There were so many indications that better times lay ahead: the end of the Iran-Iraq War (1988), the Oslo process for a Palestinian homeland (early 1990s), the defeat of naked Iraqi aggression in Kuwait (1991), greater political stability in Turkey, Israel's withdrawal from Lebanon (2000), followed by Syria's a few years later, Dubai's rise as a great world trading center. The grounds for optimism seemed significantly greater than the indications of failure.

During the last two years that optimism has been destroyed. Three Arab countries—Iraq, Syria, and Yemen—qualify as failed states, as may Pakistan. Lebanon totters, an occasional battlefield for sides in the Syrian conflict, and incapable of electing a president on time or setting the rules for parliamentary elections. Despite impending departure of U.S. and NATO forces, the Afghan government proved incapable of conducting an honest election for president. Most discouraging of all, *al-Dawlat al-Islamiyya,* known in English as *The Islamic State* and often abbreviated as *ISIS,* has wreaked violence and horror on untold innocents in Syria and Iraq. Symbolically, it recently claimed to establish a caliphate, attempting to create a formal political structure for a jihadist group.

Nevertheless, this volume depicts a region where hopes surge in the hearts of millions who seek dignity as humans, respect from their governments, and recognition of their national ideas. Certainly, those hopes do conflict, between Israelis and Palestinians certainly, but within societies as well. In South Asia, the great discontent over corruption signals the same human desire to be treated honestly and with dignity in India, Pakistan, and other countries.

These events reinforce the view that the Middle East and South Asia together form a most interesting and strategically important region. Beginning where the peaks and rainforests separate Southern from East Asia, it includes the Indian sixth of humanity. Its northern limits touch China and republics formerly part of the Soviet Union. The Muslim countries of Iran and Turkey for centuries bordered Russia and blocked its access to warm-water ports.

At least four straits in the region (the Bosporus, Tiran, Bab al-Mandab and Hormuz) play pivotal roles in world commerce and military strategy. Threats over each of them and the Suez Canal have raised tensions or even precipitated wars in the last century. Underneath the waters of the Gulf (variously titled as Arab or Persian) and the surrounding sands lie roughly two-thirds of the world's oil deposits. Thus, far beyond its size or wealth, the region bears strategic value and importance to trade routes. It was more than a coincidence that the term "Middle East" was popularized by a geo-strategist, Alfred Mahan.

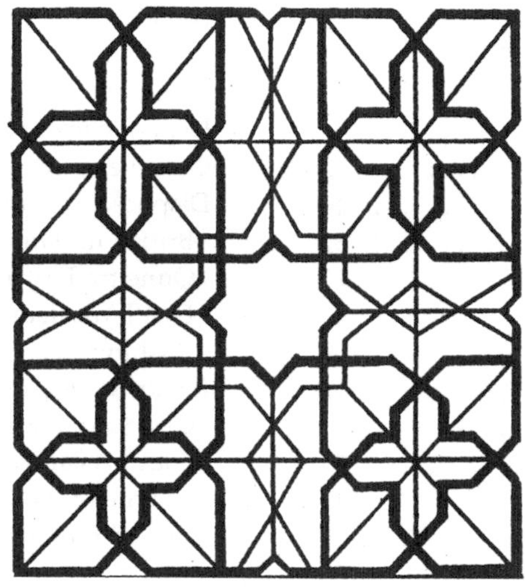

The consistent goal of this series of books is an appreciation of the peoples and governments largely from their own perspectives but moderated by the viewpoints of the author. In the many conflicts, I hope to show the claims and charges of each side, to help the general reader understand the reasons for attitudes and actions of people and governments. Doing this risks accusations of partiality, but I firmly hope that readers will share my respect for these peoples and lands, and an understanding of, if not always sympathy for, their states and political actions.

Sympathy, however, ought not excuse, even in Western societies that tolerate so much. The following pages draw attention to the plight of children, bonded into labor for the parents' debts, and to women who apparently disappear before census-takers arrive. Female circumcision—really several forms of genital mutilation—sometimes kills young girls in parts of Africa, including Egypt. Moreover, though crime rates in most countries of this volume are relatively low, the treatment of suspects and political rivals can descend from public humiliation to horrifying depths of brutality. Aside from the few democracies represented in this volume, most governments can expect, should they lose office, only the worst from their political opponents. Beyond individuals and ideologies, the rivalries of communities over relatively small parcels of land involve passions that Westerners, accustomed to moving from suburb to suburb, cannot fathom.

Technicalities: A few technical comments may help the serious reader. Except for Syria and Yemen, where crises disrupted statistical reports, this volume provides GDP and population estimates from the International Monetary Fund for 2014, the GDP at both market exchange rates and purchasing power parity equivalent (PPP). Magnified by both U.S. inflation and the U.S. dollar's declining international value, the latter estimates sometimes shock—does the average Egyptian really enjoy an income equivalent to $6,400, or the average Qatari $105,000? Certainly not, but countries are commonly compared by Gross Domestic Product, not national income, and there is value in recognizing that the average Qatari probably enjoys an income more than ten times higher than the average Egyptian's. For smaller countries, the figures are particularly imprecise when population projections vary significantly.

Another issue requires a brief comment. Arabic sounds are transliterated into English by a variety of systems, and multiple spellings are common. The Egyptian leader of the 1950s was Gamal Abdul Nasser to the press, but Jamal 'Abd al-Nasir to serious scholars. In general, this volume retains the common English spellings for well-known personalities but adopts specialized spellings without diacritical markings otherwise. Thus, the late King Hussein ruled Jordan; his great-grandfather was Sharif Husayn. Outside the Arab world, the national transliteration of Muslim names applies, the founder of Bangladesh being Mujibur Rahman, not Mujib al-Rahman.

Last but not least, I am very thankful for the corrections, clarifications, and other suggestions contributed by Joellyn Sheehy, who demonstrated uncommon abilities in thinking and writing before graduating from Union College. Certainly, any and all errors are mine, but without her thoughtful assistance, this volume would be much the worse.

M.B.R.
Lincoln, Nebraska
July 2014

The Arab Spring: Birth of a New Era?

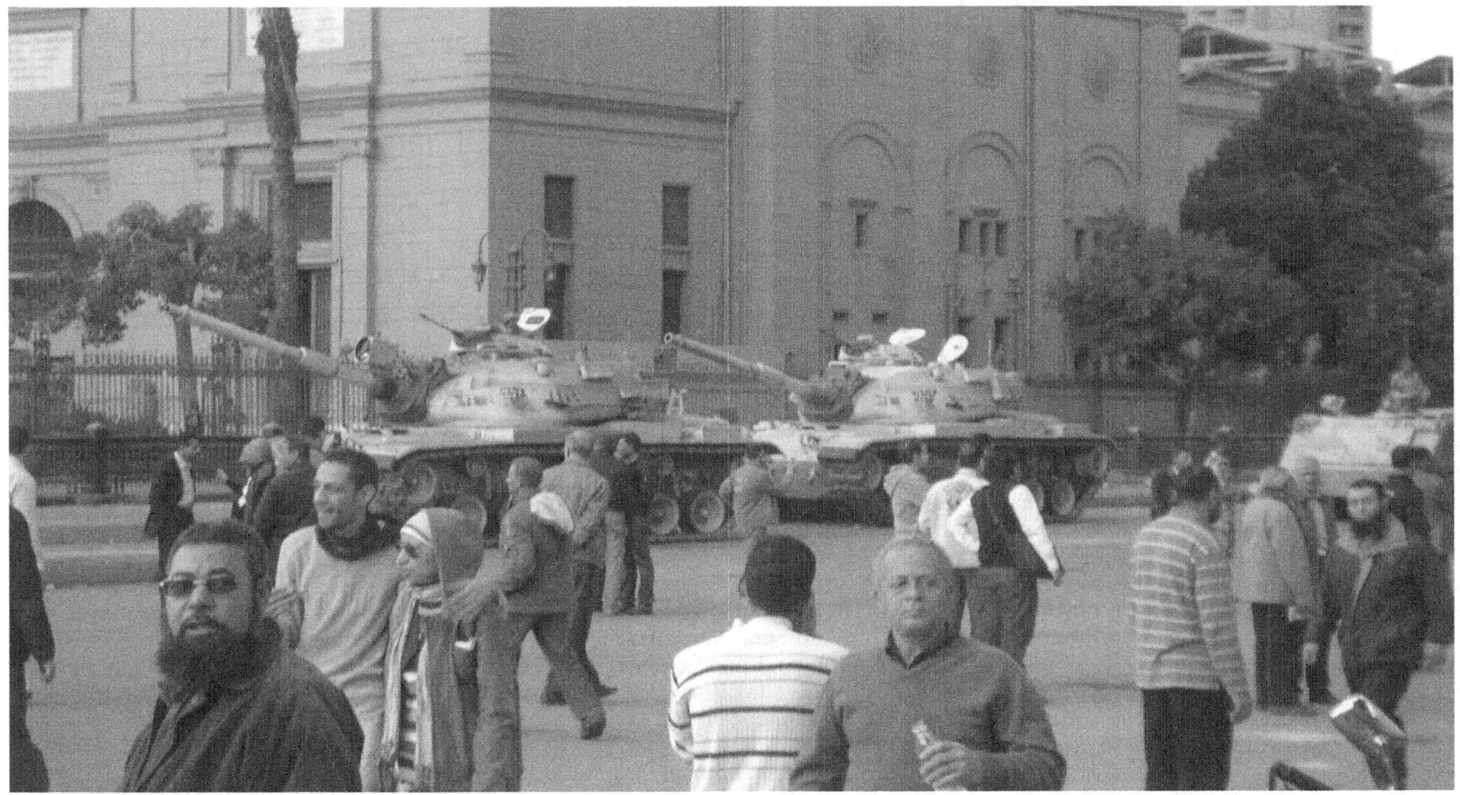

ARAB SPRING — Tank crews ordered into Tahrir Square wait outside the Egyptian Museum. Egypt's military identified its interests with the national good, not President Mubarak's.
Photo courtesy of Jim Neergaard

On December 17, 2010, a Tunisian policewoman helped herself to apples being sold by an unlicensed street vendor, Mohammed Bouazizi. He protested the theft, and in the scuffle that followed, she and two other officers tackled him to the ground. Then, according to his family's account, she slapped him across the face and spat on him.

Humiliated, Bouazizi sought to complain at city hall, but found no one to listen. Distraught, the 26-year-old quickly decided to protest the injustice and corruption by setting himself on fire. Within an hour, he had poured gasoline over himself and applied the match. Badly burned, he survived in a coma until January 4, 2011.

A simple man who lost his father when he was three, Bouazizi could never have imagined that news of his own fiery death would inflame public opinion across the entire Arab world. Within two weeks, demonstrations inspired by his fate overthrew his own president, and then a month later, Egypt's. By contrast, in the previous 30 years, only two of the 13 Arab states treated in this volume witnessed a change of ruler outside the immediate ruling family or party. The two exceptions were Lebanon, torn by civil war and foreign invaders, and Iraq, where the U.S. invasion ousted Saddam Hussein.

Laying Arab Exceptionalism to Rest: Democracy and liberty spread almost worldwide in the 1980s and 1990s. One great exception was the Middle East, and for nearly two decades political scientists, historians and commentators sought to explain why authoritarian regimes continued to dominate that region. Their analyses often concluded that Arab societies and politics were similar to one another, but very different from the rest of the world. Hence the scholars coined the term "Arab exceptionalism."

Some important theories explained the region's stable authoritarianism on the past, particularly Islamic culture or the legacies of colonialism. Other theories emphasized the present—U.S. and European support kept rulers if they adopted the desired foreign policies. Whatever the causes, though, there was consensus that Arab countries missed the forces creating an increasingly democratic world.

Suddenly, almost without warning, in early 2011 the Arab world convulsed as demonstrators in their thousands and even hundreds of thousands defied their governments and filled public squares to demand "Irhal!" ("Go!"). What had so inflamed public opinion, and created citizens brave enough to risk arrest, torture, and possibly death by publicly demanding their rulers' ouster?

Multiple explanations for what caused the previously sullen Arab populations to suddenly demand change rapidly flooded the media. One false claim merits quick rebuttal. The Arab Spring did not begin as an Islamic revolution, though some American commentators, Libya's Muammar Gaddafi, and Syria's Bashar al-Asad alleged that *al-Qaeda* and other radical Islamists ignited the protests. Those in the streets quite obviously represented a much wider segment of the region's population, from the wealthy to the urban poor, from the well-educated and more westernized to the more traditional.

On the other hand, deeply cognizant that Islamic revolts would worry the ever so influential West, demonstrators in Cairo's Egypt's Tahrir Square and elsewhere went out of their way to reinforce a more secular nationalist tone rather than a more public Islamic aspect. Clearly, everyone involved well understood that the world was watching. In most countries Muslim groups did

Table I. Social Indicators Suggesting Popular Distress in 2011

	Population (millions)	Median Age	Jobless Rate	Below Poverty Line (%)	Internet Users (m)
Algeria	34.5	27.1	9.9%	23.0%	4.7
Egypt	80.5	24	9.6%	20.0%	20
Jordan	6.4	21.8	13.4%	14.2%	1.6
Lebanon	4.09	29.4	na	28.0%	1.0
Libya	6.4	24.2	30.0%	33.0%	0.35
Morocco	31.6	26.5	9.8%	15.0%	13.2
Saudi Arabia	25.7	24.9	10.8%	na	9.6
Syria	22.1	21.5	8.3%	11.9%	4.4
Tunisia	10.5	29.7	14.0%	3.8%	3.5
Palestinian Territories	2.5	20.9	16.5%	46.0%	1.3
Yemen	23.4	17.9	35.0%	45.2%	2.2

Sources: BBC, IMF, CIA Factbook

not plant the seeds of revolution nor cultivate its early growth—indeed, in Egypt the *Muslim Brotherhood* leadership initially opposed the protests. *However, Islamic groups were the best-organized to reap their harvest.*

There were as well long-term signs of general economic distress. Arab societies suffered high poverty and unemployment rates. On the personal level, male university graduates in their twenties were commonly unable to obtain jobs paying well enough to start a home and family, thus finding themselves unable to marry (see Table I).

That was true for women as well as men. Though the culture traditionally depicted a woman's place in the home, the Egyptian TV program "I Want to Get Married" portrayed the resulting anguish and humor from a woman's point of view. It became a hit. Its political significance, largely overlooked, was the existence of a large pool of university graduates either poorly employed or jobless, with time, the internet, social media and dissatisfaction on their hands. Indeed the very useful American radio podcast *America Abroad* had highlighted the problem in a series of reports on the growing distress among Arab youth in the months just leading up to the explosion.

Moreover, economies that had adopted free-market doctrines and opened to international trade proved quite defenseless when prices rose sharply worldwide. Popular opinion often blamed the International Monetary Fund (IMF) and prime ministers sympathetic to it. Social distress also rose in other respects. Inadequate low-income housing, insufficient public transportation, and poor government services made daily life difficult for the lower classes. Oil money or not, the region was filled with obviously frustrated youth sleeping late and spending their afternoon hours sitting in the streets, the young men especially.

Unemployment and continuing poverty were certainly significant challenges, and labor protests had intensified in Egypt. More immediately, the recent hike in food prices around the world certainly affected countries in the region. Given the large proportion of typical family spending on food, the price increases provoked simmering discontent in the months before January's 2011's "Arab Spring" began.

Nevertheless, simple socio-economic distress fails to fully explain the protests.

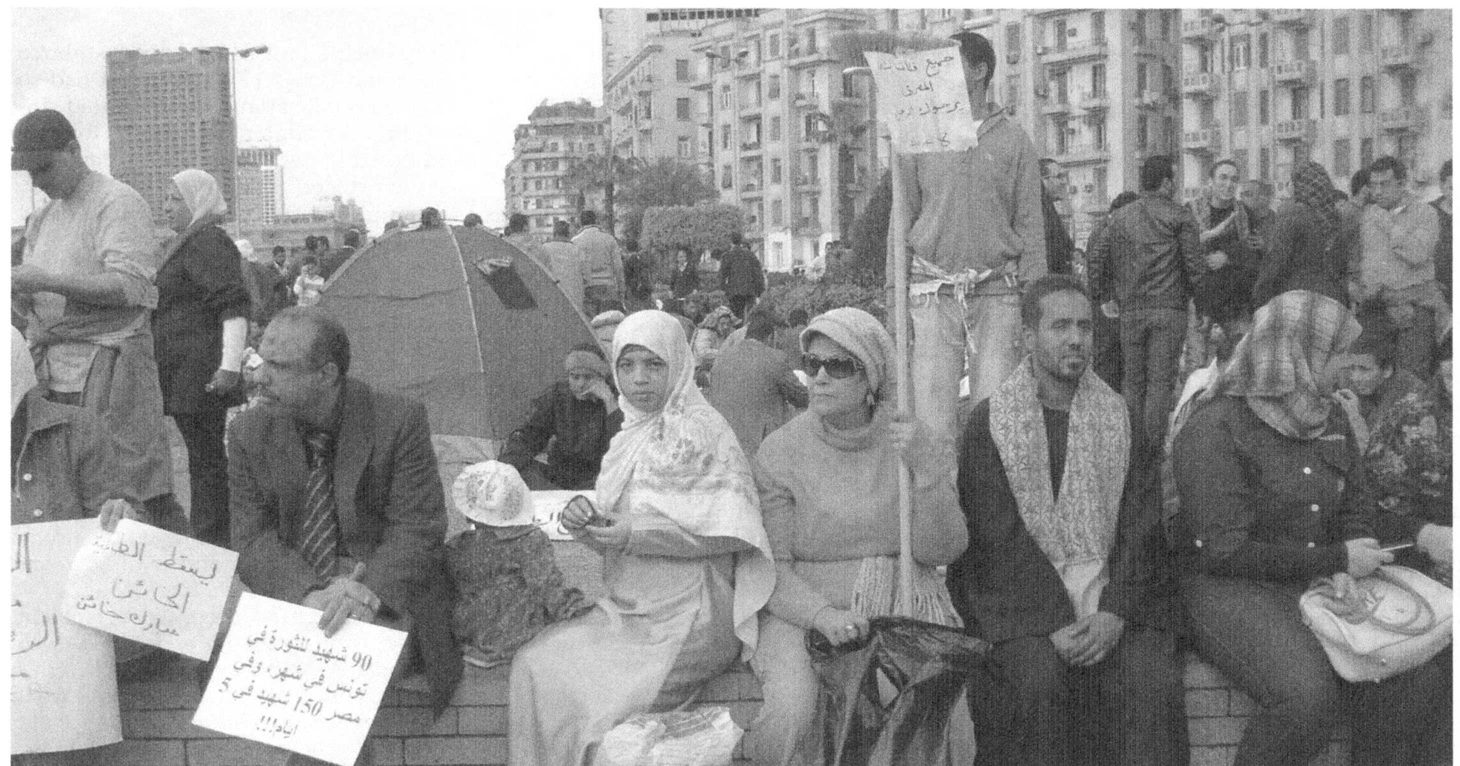

Though first sparked by technology-savvy young activists, individuals from many walks of life and socio-economic classes often joined the protests. Note the variety of clothing styles, often an indication of profession, lifestyle and attitude.

The Arab Spring: Birth of a New Era?

The revolution began in Tunisia, statistically one of the better-off countries. In Egypt, unemployment was a problem but not to the point where it might have provoked the overthrow President Mubarak. When the "Arab Spring" formally began the slogans and signs in Tunisia and Egypt's Tahrir Square were not about the price of bread. Clearly, there was more to the explosion than economic distress.

Given the fawning government media so traditional in the region, it seems plausible to conclude that that the protests could begin partly because electronic communication—Al-Jazeera on television, and the social media quartet of Facebook, YouTube, texting and Twitter—told truths and provided images about societies that governments could not control.

Repression, corruption and nepotism had become endemic; now the public could visualize them, sometimes with graphic pictures of a victim of police torture. This was not new, of course. Indeed, images from Iran's post-election demonstrations in 2009 had already shown what influence the new media could have on community organizing and activism.

While new social media increasingly allow people around the world easier ways to circumvent local domestic censors, the ability of Al Jazeera, Twitter, Facebook and YouTube to highlight events in neighboring countries was probably even more significant than focusing attention domestically.

Crucially, the social media contributed one other essential element. They enabled a small number of young organizers who were inspired with passions for freedom and rights to call for demonstrations in ways the regimes could not easily repress. As it happened, these youthful activists had already studied the tactics of nonviolent civil disobedience that successfully overthrew Serbia's Slobodan Miloševiç, tactics apparent to those who watched developments in Tahrir Square. Thus, in the broader perspective, the Arab Spring represents one element in a broader globalization of politics.

The bloodstained clothing of martyrs—the men and women slain while demonstrating—provided vivid evidence of their willingness to risk life for reform and change.

Photo courtesy of Jim Neergaard

Themes from Egypt's Tahrir Square: Perhaps most of all, the protest calls resonated because the organizers combined a simple message about change with human rights issues, not the complexities of constitutional reform. At least in Egypt, this was a middle class revolution, as evidenced by the clothing worn by many demonstrators. Avoiding the extreme mantras of Islamists and the radical demands of leftists, the protest organizers publicized a patriotic movement that could unite ordinary citizens.

To a surprising degree, their slogans reflected the perspectives and even the humor of individual Egyptians. "Mubarak: Game Over" came naturally to sports fans. "Hosni (Mubarak), hurry up, my left hand's getting tired" (of holding up this sign) no doubt earned chuckles from passers-by. But considered on a deeper level, such posters reflected the unconscious collapse of fear about the police state.

For the future, probably the most significant posters read *"al-sha'b yurid isqat al-nizam,"* generally rendered as "The People Want to Overthrow the Regime." Though doubtless a strong statement, that translation ignores subtle implications of the Arabic. *Al-sha'b* means "people" in the sense of "folk" and "nation," and carries patriotic overtones missing in synonyms that imply humanity in general. It is also singular, so the phrase should be translated "The People Wants." In a region so often divided and ruled from above, and splintered by sects and tribes from the past, the phrase marked hopefully the self-conscious birth of a people.

Likewise, *nizam*, the word translated "government" actually connotes broader concepts: order, system, and regulation as well as the individuals who actually govern. Thus the entire slogan was—and remains—an explosive phrase expressing the desire to transform society and the state's regulation of daily life. This was the slogan that teenagers in the southern Syrian town of Dar'a painted as graffiti. Their boldness, and subsequent imprisonment, touched off the revolutionary protests across Syria.

Initial Success and Subsequent Repression: Tunisia's President Zine al-Abidine Ben Ali fled to Saudi Arabia after widening protests. In Egypt, President Hosni Mubarak resigned after 18 days of public demonstrations (see **Egypt: history**). In February, 2011, the Arab Spring seemed powerful enough to overthrow other geriatric Arab rulers, many with less sophisticated methods of governing than Egypt's or Tunisia's. Elsewhere, however, opposition protests often ended in violence. The patterns of revolutionary success and failure are complex, and many demonstrate the old slogan that all politics is local.

- In both Tunisia and Egypt, the military withdrew support for the president. This precipitated an orderly departure of the head of state, but little change of government. The same prime ministers continued in office, and military leaders showed every desire to maintain the same basic system. But while Tunisia quickly held elections and clearly changed its rulers, for more than a year democracy remained a promise rather than a reality in Egypt.
- Years later, the euphoria of February 2011 seems somewhat naïve, though understandable. Though Mubarak himself fell from power, the Egyptian

The Arab Spring: Birth of a New Era?

In Egypt, both the youthful activists and the Muslim Brotherhood proclaimed the unity of the two major religious groups, evidenced by the joined symbols.

Photo courtesy of Jim Neergaard

military dominance—often termed the "deep state" established by the 1952 revolution remained intact. But one crucial change did take place: civilians continued to demonstrate in Tahrir Square to obtain justice, like the dismissal of policemen who had brutalized protesters, and the ouster of cabinet members tied to Mubarak's rule.

- Tunisia and Egypt are ethnically and religiously quite homogeneous societies. When a change occurred at the top, no tribe or sect felt threatened. Significant symbols in Tahrir Square combined the cross and the crescent, thus attempting to calm Christian fears that instability might result in an Islamist takeover.

By contrast, in other countries ruling minorities clung to power:

- In Bahrain, activists from the *Haqq Movement for Liberty and Democracy* and the *Bahrain Center for Human Rights* drew on a history of confrontation over reforms and experience with election boycotts. Inspired by events in Cairo, they held marches and eventually assembled crowds at the Pearl Roundabout, the capital's most prominent traffic circle. Initially hesitant, the Sunni royal family and ruling elite eventually ordered the security forces to crush the largely Shi'a demonstrators. They succeeded, but fired on sleeping civilians, killing several and creating martyrs. As the situation deteriorated and other Gulf rulers pressed for action, the government blamed Iranian instigators and called in Saudi troops.

  Because the government alienated the protest movement, later promises of reform largely failed. The largest legal opposition societies, *al-Wifaq* and *Wa'ad*, found it difficult to accept the Crown Prince's call for national dialogue, especially given their small representation at the talks. Though the regime enjoys significant support from Sunnis and wealthier, more secular Shi'a families, the activists and opposition political societies probably represent a majority of the population.
- The only other Gulf state where significant protest activity occurred was Oman. Sultan Qabus responded with financial benefits and the dismissal of allegedly corrupt and ineffective officials. At least initially, his actions succeeded: while low levels of dissent remain, regime-threatening demonstrations were avoided.
- In Libya, another oil-producing country, Muammar Gaddafi's regime struck back fiercely at the initially peaceful demonstrators, especially in Benghazi. The army had been organized not so much for national defense as for regime protection. As a result, there was no independent military high command to usher Gaddafi into retirement when orders came to shoot civilian demonstrators. Instead, brigades commanded by Gaddafi's sons and trusted insiders attacked cities that had fallen to the opposition, until NATO's intervention in the skies froze the combat lines of a civil war and destroyed the military's command structure and any armor that moved. With the population divided by tribal and regional loyalties, the regime mustered shows of popular support while devoting its military and security forces to repression. However, after rebels broke through to Tripoli in August, 2011, the regime collapsed quickly. Gaddafi was caught outside Sirte and executed.
- The regime of President 'Ali 'Abdullah Salih in Yemen had already met many characteristics of a failed state, with the region's worst poverty, simmering rebellions in the north and south, and an active resident terrorist group, *al-Qaeda in the Arabian Peninsula*. Initially, Salih fended off the domestic protesters—including modern women and traditional tribal rivals—with false promises, manipulation and force exercised by a presidential guard commanded by his son. Though his wounds from an assassination attempt required treatment abroad, he demanded an orderly transfer of power, one that also provided him with immunity from prosecution. Again, in the short run, an attempted Arab Spring revolution halted when an elite military unit turned its weapons on its own unarmed citizens, but eventually an autocrat was forced from power.
- The Arab Spring came later to Syria than to most affected lands. Only in March did the use of fatal violence against protesters in Dar'a ignite widespread demonstrations. Bashar al-Asad's regime claimed to support reform by offering some concessions like ending the decades'-old emergency laws. Simultaneously, it portrayed the demonstrations as an armed insurrection by foreign Islamic extremists and others. After military units and pro-regime thugs descended on town after town, government media duly displayed the bodies or funerals of dead soldiers and police

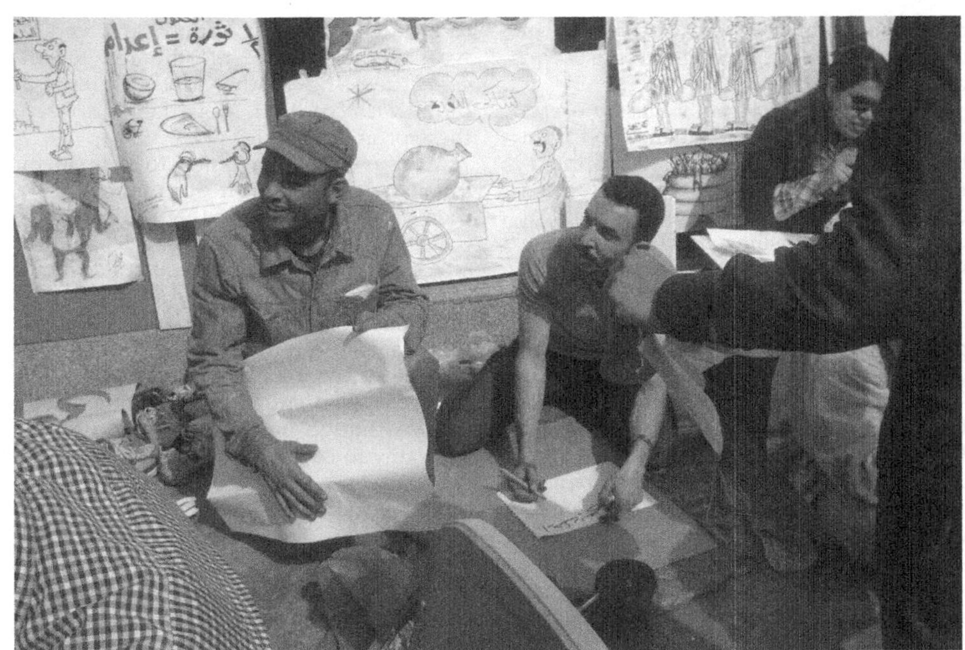

The outpouring of personal emotions took visual form in placards and posters, here produced by specialists. Photo courtesy of Jim Neergaard

as evidence. Activists and their pictures told a different, darker story: unprovoked shootings of demonstrators by the security forces and the Shabiha militia, followed sometimes by the executions of soldiers who refused to shoot civilians.

Once again, a country's sectarian diversity advantaged its rulers in the face of widely felt desires for reform. So did family-controlled military units like the 4th Division commanded by Maher al-Asad, the president's younger brother. Though the economic and governing elites included members of other religious faiths, members of al-Asad's own Alawi community recognized that his loss of power likely meant retribution by those whose families and cities had suffered long decades of repression. While other members of the elites might have supported reform and change, the minority Alawi population seemed ready to die opposing it.

- In contrast to the bloodshed in so many countries, Jordan's police initially responded to protesters by handing out bottles of water. Even before the events in Tahrir Square, economic protests and riots had shaken the regime's southern heartland, while the traditional opposition groups of leftists and Islamists certainly could adopt the demands and slogans of the Arab Spring. In response, King Abdullah's security forces avoided creating martyrs, while he sacked his prime minister and promised reforms. A bizarre attack on police by Jordan's own *Salafist* extremists no doubt reinforced the king's argument that stability depended on the monarchy. While King Abdullah remains very much in power, in the face of popular demands he has voiced support for reforms that if implemented should make Jordan a democracy ruled by parliament.

For the Longer Run: Years after it began, pessimism about the Arab Spring seems commonplace. The events that followed the first rush of enthusiasm teach three very fundamental lessons often ignored in 2011.

1. Revolutions may still shed a great deal of innocent blood. Perhaps those who remembered the popular excitement at fall of the Berlin wall assumed that authoritarian Middle Eastern rulers would confront their citizens no more forcefully than had the hardened communists of Berlin and Moscow. But bloody revolts and revolutions litter the pages of history, and some Arab rulers showed few qualms of conscience over shooting demonstrators, if necessary to continue the regime.
2. Certain cultural traits helpful to successful democracies seem less common in Arab and perhaps Muslim society. Very possibly the willingness to view political power as something one wins—and then loses—is less common south and east of the Mediterranean Sea. Another cultural difference is perhaps a weaker instinct to seek unity.

   Such traits, if they indeed exist, might be blamed on colonialism's legacy. However, they seem more deeply rooted in social relationships that foster patron-client politics, where the typical citizen supports a local leader in return for favors rather than rights. Such relationships, common in the region, are often effective in local government. However they seem to hinder the rise of competing national parties. The result is often parliaments so divided that forming an effective government becomes a nightmare. Fracturing also seems more frequent other parts of society, including religion.
3. To quote Thomas Friedman, the world may be flat. But authority and the willing respect that it evokes do matter. Regimes and opposition groups both struggle at gaining the deference of the population.

In retrospect, the Arab Spring proved deficient in each of these lessons. One result was the slower restoration of order. Where other societies might have moved on, there remained—and remains—a high level of government crisis, botched constitutional reforms, poorly prepared elections, street demonstrations, clashes between competing groups, civil wars, extremist attacks and violence of other types. Changes do take place, but these are still early days in the Arab Spring. And the death of Arab exceptionalism has been prematurely reported.

Measured by actual changes, popular demands in 2011 overthrew four republican dictators (including Tunisia's), and left Syria's tottering. By contrast, no monarchy was overthrown, though Bahrain remains contested. Apparently, Arab citizens accepted traditional, hereditary authorities that made few claims of democracy better than they did those who presented the sham of pseudo-democratic republics.

The continuing revolutionary pressure results partly from the incomplete nature of several revolutions. Presidential palaces were vacated, but most high officials initially retained their power. Ahmad Shafiq, Egypt's last prime minster under Mubarak, placed second in that country's 2012 presidential elections. Skeptics might be forgiven for doubting that much of anything has changed in Yemen, where the vice president took office. Concerns about crime, economic hardship, and extremism may play out in ways that favor those in power.

But, autocracies do not last forever. The Arab Spring dramatically portrays a cultural region—the Arab world—in the throes of epochal changes that will affect kings and emirs as well. The legitimacy of autocratic rule has been broken, and old ideas have been discredited.

Rulers may continue to suppress popular demands and deny aspirations for freedom and human dignity, but they are running against a tide of civilian desires for constitutions that define the state and protect civil liberties. Even in the absence of a charismatic reformer, the concepts of citizenship that condemn shooting at crowds—ideas now enshrined in the young, educated, and middle classes—will grow so strong that the use of force will fail.

While ruling minorities in Bahrain and Syria may hang on, the repression they exercised after 2011 renders them more dependent than ever on simple brute force. Thus they linger in power without the comfortable assurance of stability and security enjoyed for the past three decades, including, in Bahrain's case, support from the United States.

Moreover, those months of demonstrations throughout the region frequently saw young women play activist roles that went far beyond the area's cultural experiences. That alone may prove the most long-lasting impact of era—unless, as both some local Christians and American commentators fear, Islamic extremists win elections.

In the short run, Egypt's *Muslim Brotherhood* and similar groups benefitted from their hard-won reputations for opposition to the dictators and their superior organization compared to secular political groups. Arab Muslims clearly esteem the ideals, dedication, and accomplishments of Islamic organizations. Banned as political parties, some became social agencies to provide services to the poor and victims of natural disasters.

Voters knew them, and initially trusted them. In Tunisia, the moderately Islamist *Ennahda* won a plurality, while in Egyptian parliamentary elections, the *Freedom and Justice Party* of the *Muslim Brotherhood* won a strong plurality, with the ultra-conservative Salafist *Al-Nour Party* second. In a democracy, parties with such popular support eventually form a government, alone or in a coalition.

That said, elections often draw candidates to the center, in search of votes. The *Brotherhood's* Mohammad Morsi did exactly that when as a presidential candidate he promised that Copts would have their rights and women would not be forced to wear the headscarf. Unfortunately for all concerned—Egypt, the Copts, Morsi and the *Brotherhood* itself, Morsi failed to keep these promises.

Moreover, power tends to transform idealists, even when it does not corrupt them. At least in Egypt, that did not happen. In office, Islamists failed to govern effectively, for governing requires difficult choices far beyond slogans like "Islam is the Answer." Citizen demands for jobs, schools, sanitation, water, and other urgent needs force a party to address popular needs. Consequently, in a democracy, many—though not all—Islamist parties are likely to become less rigidly ideological, and more apt to compromise. The model of future Arab politics may already exist, but it is Turkey, not Saudi Arabia. Given Morsi's ouster after only a year in office, the *Brotherhood* and its supporters are likely to claim they never had the chance.

Another longer-run result of the Spring is the changed dynamics of the Israeli-Palestinian conflict. From Egypt to Bahrain, the slogans rarely addressed such matters. Palestinian rights became second

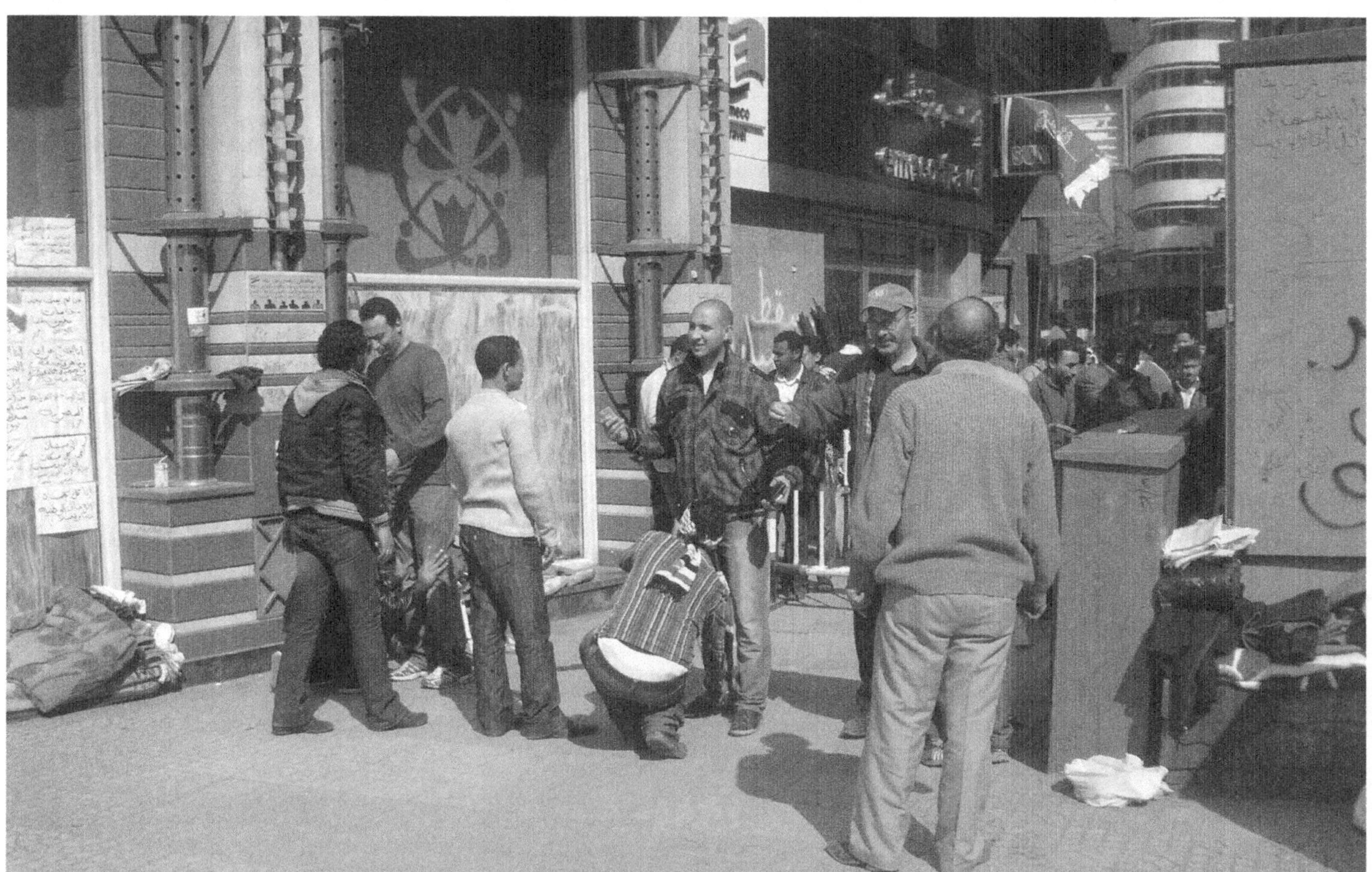

Activists frisk those joining a demonstration. Protesters regularly chanted the slogan "silmiyya" —"non-violent" — and if possible avoided violence.

Photo courtesy of Jim Neergaard

The Arab Spring: Birth of a New Era?

Map by Ray L. Cleveland

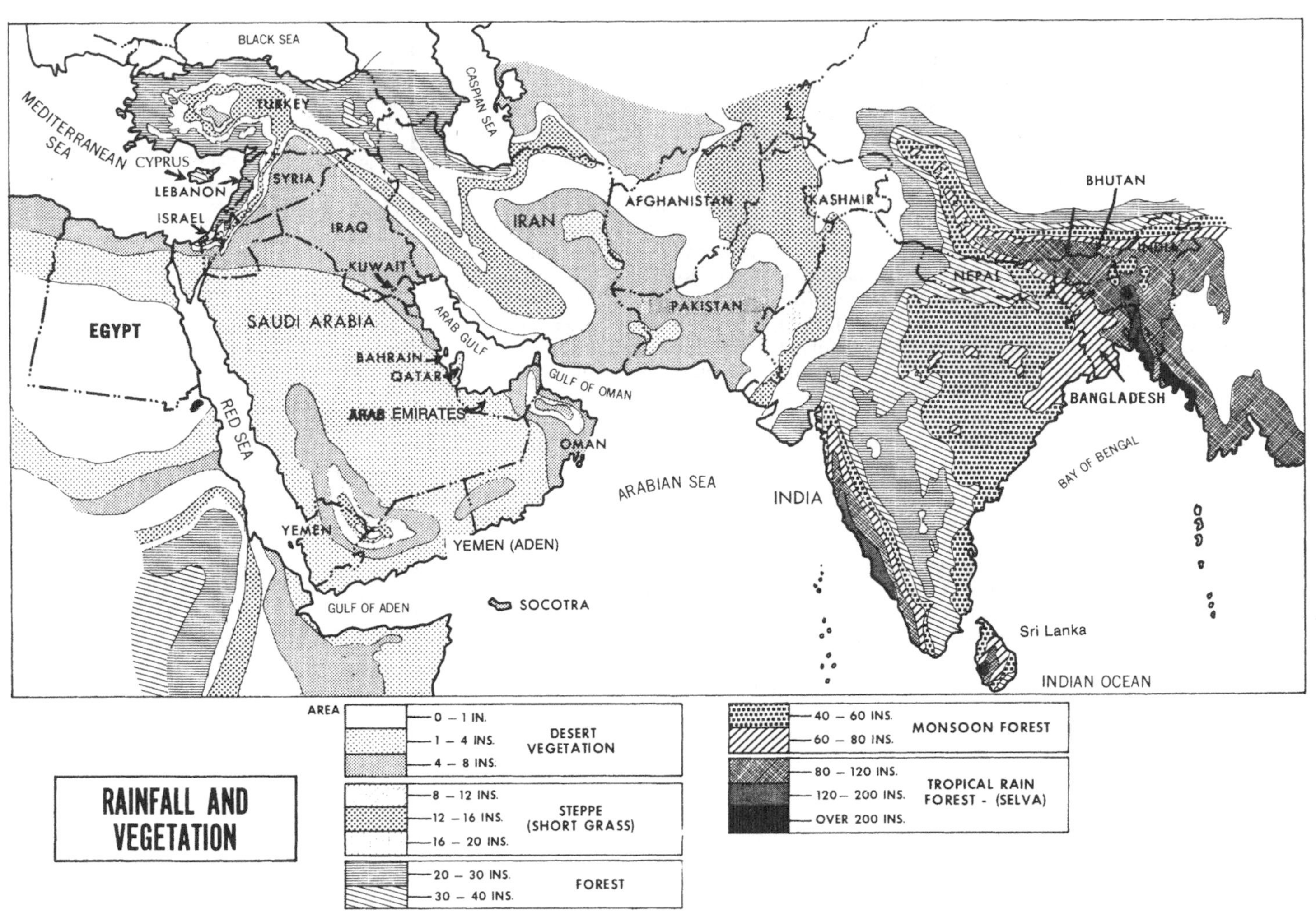

in priority to human rights within one's own nation. However, passions focused on justice and freedom at home easily influence foreign policy. When treaties or understandings with Israel seem the result of foreign manipulation rather than national interest, they will face greater criticism, whether from activists on the streets, at international gatherings, or as pressure on friendly countries.

At the same time, governments find it far more difficult to manipulate Palestinian issues for regime legitimacy while posing no direct threat to Israel. Syria portrayed itself as the heart of Arab resistance for decades, but it only challenged Israel through proxies in Lebanon and Palestine.

Faced with demonstrations in 2011, al-Assad's regime cynically attempted to create a confrontation with Israel through a civilian Palestinian crossing of the Jewish state's truce lines. The regime's cynicism resulted in more than a dozen gullible Palestinians killed, but it failed to accomplish the primary goal: reuniting the Syrian people with their ruler against an outside enemy. In fact, the cynical gesture provoked a backlash among young Palestinians who resented their manipulation.

The old politics of blaming Israel for every problem in the Arab world may thus begin to fade. But, without major progress towards peace, the Jewish state's regional isolation will likely grow.

Arab and Islamic cultures have traditionally valued human rights, but in their own terms and quite differently than does the secular West. Perhaps the most long-lasting impact of the Arab Spring will be its emphasis on human dignity, women's rights, freedom, justice, and democracy. If so, the Spring will extend beyond politics, and the blood of its martyrs will transform not just regimes but society as well.

Can Arab Islamic society make that cultural shift?

Steven Leibo, editor of the companion volume ***East and Southeast Asia*** *contributed valuable suggestions and recommendations to this piece.*

WHEN WILL THE TAPS GO DRY?

Water, like bread, comes from God
Arab Proverb

From North Africa to western India, the lands of the Middle East and South Asia receive sparse rainfall, usually far less annually than the 16–20 inches essential for cultivation. With few cloudy days and the sun blazing directly overhead most of the year, hot temperatures quickly dry the landscape even when rain has fallen. Early human settlements clustered around rivers because water was always scarce. Now, the Middle East faces a worsening crisis as individual countries attempt to claim insufficient common resources. By contrast, in the Indian subcontinent seasonal floods take hundreds of lives annually and rivers inundate productive fields, carrying their valuable silt to the sea.

For thousands of years people living in the region adapted to desert and near-desert conditions. They farmed fertile lands beside rivers, some irrigating with water from mountains hundreds or even thousands of miles away, benefiting from seasonal floods that soaked the soil and deposited nourishing silt. Less moistened lands were used to graze livestock, particularly camels, goats and sheep.

Desert societies established water rights over the scarce flow of oasis wells and springs to irrigate crops and water livestock. For transport, travelers and nomads depend on the camel, with its legendary survival without water. Their days surrounded by barren desert, nomads dreamed of rivers and greenery, even seeing them in the form of occasional mirages. Both Judaism and Islam portrayed heaven as filled with trees and water.

The modern era brought sharp changes. The technology and energy of the 20th century brought appearances of abundant water. Homes enjoyed taps and sewer connections; carefully irrigated trees lined boulevards in desert cities; and industries developed. Urban water use increased rapidly, for example, doubling in arid Saudi Arabia between 1980 and 1985. But most of all, agriculture based on irrigation fed desert nations and even provided exports of tomatoes, oranges, wheat and other irrigated crops. The desert truly seemed to bloom.

Many Middle Eastern countries literally began to run out of water by the 1990s. Some of the world's fastest-growing populations, rising standards of living, and increased agricultural production now leave Israel, Jordan, and Egypt facing difficult choices between conservation and development. Aside from Yemen, societies in Arabia already depend on non-renewable ground water and desalination. In the 21st century, water scarcity threatens bitter conflicts within and between the region's nations. Cooperation, by contrast, offers a chance to postpone water shortages, hopefully promoting peace in a region too troubled by violent conflict.

Water Resources as Threats to Peace

"River Jordan, *deep and wide*"
—Gospel song

The Biblical account of Joshua's tribes crossing the dry bed of the Jordan River to attack Jericho created in Christian imagination a mighty Jordan, deep and wide, celebrated in song and symbolizing the entrance to heaven. Reality was always different, with the Jordan's flow of 320 million cubic meters hardly more than the size of a large creek. Today the Jordan is only a narrow, salty stream, and the Dead Sea, deprived of the normal flow of Jordan River water, is drying up. Israel, Jordan, Syria, and the Palestinian Authority face questions of water use so difficult that one of them may attempt to settle issues by force. Indeed, recently Israel threatened Lebanon with war because it pumped modest amounts for local irrigation from a tributary of the Jordan.

Attempts to establish national water rights began in the 1950s, when U.S. President Eisenhower sent a special ambassador to negotiate the shares of the Jordan basin countries. At the technical level, his findings established reasonable national shares, but politically his mission failed. No international agreement yet apportions the river's waters.

With dreams of making the desert bloom, in the 1960s Israel constructed the National Water Carrier, a pipeline almost 10 feet in diameter, to bring water from the Jordan's Sea of Galilee to the coastal plain and the Negev desert. The water was vital. Arab threats to the project, by attempting to divert the Jordan's headwaters in Lebanon and Syria from flowing into Israel played a major role in the crises that led to the 1967 Arab-Israeli war. Israel's conquest of the Golan Heights and the West Bank ensured its unilateral use of the Jordan River.

Almost immediately, water from the Jordan proved to be insufficient for Israel's purposes. Along the coast and in the desert, Israeli farmers used two-thirds (now about 56%) of the nation's water for farming. To supply their fields as well as thirsty homes and factories, Israel had long pumped the Mediterranean coastal aquifer, a layer of porous rock that trapped water slowly seeping toward the sea.

When the volume of water pumped out began to exceed the rainwater trickling down into the aquifer, water levels and pressures began to fall. Salty sea water started to seep into the aquifer, reducing its water quality. By 1990 about 10% of

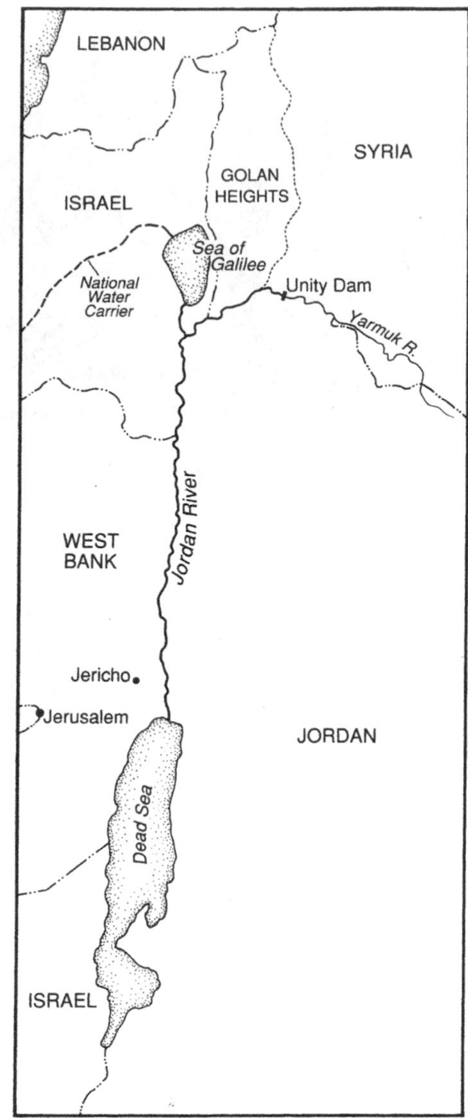

the water pumped from this resource exceeded the national limit for chloride salt. In addition, pollution increased as nitrates from fertilizers leached into the aquifer. During the winter, the Water Authority now pumps surplus Jordan River water down into coastal wells, hoping to replenish the aquifer.

The first Israeli desalination plant, completed in 2005, produces 100 million cubic meters of fresh water annually, less than 5% of the water used.

Israel's thirst also drains the separate Yarkon/Tannim aquifer. Known as the "mountain aquifer," it collects rain falling on the hilly West Bank. A few points of the aquifer extend into the 1967 boundaries, and Israel currently pumps about 20% of its water from this source. This vastly exceeds the pumping permitted the West Bank Palestinians, whose land supplies the rainfall that annually renews this resource. In addition, the roughly 300,000

Israeli settlers in the West Bank consume about as much water as the 2.4 million Arabs, whose drilling is restricted in several ways.

The creation of a Palestinian state threatens Israel's total control of the mountain aquifer. Fears of future water shortages may influence political opinion against granting concessions. The figures themselves show few alternatives: against average rainfall of 1.7 billion cubic meters, current water use reaches 1.9 billion cubic meters. Israelis consume five times as much per capita as residents of neighboring Arab nations. Because of this, the shallow wells of dozens of Palestinian West Bank villages no longer reach water. In the Gaza Strip, the contamination of water supplies has reached critical proportions.

The recent construction of the Wahda Dam on the Yarmuk River captures the flow of the Jordan's last underused tributary. The Yarmuk flows between Syria and Jordan, joining the Jordan just below the Sea of Galilee. With water resources far smaller than Israel's or Syria's, Jordan decades ago proposed building a "Unity Dam" at Maqarin to trap winter flood waters for summer use by farms, homes and industry. Israel threatened to destroy any such dam as it benefited by capturing some of the flow in the Sea of Galilee. However, its 1994 peace treaty with Jordan removed that threat.

Jordan eventually gained Syrian approval for a combined-purpose dam to provide water to Jordan and electricity to Syria, and the foundation stone was laid in 2003. However, rainfall in the Yarmuk basin falls mostly in Syria, and that country favors smaller, upstream projects within its boundaries. Such projects capture most of the run-off, and due to them, by 2005 the river's flow had fallen below the agreed level. In years of low rainfall, the Israelis, Palestinians, Jordanians and Syrians all find themselves critically short of water, a deficit that is projected to approach about 600 million cubic meters annually even with average rainfall.

One hope to relieve the water shortages is the proposed Red Sea-Dead Sea canal or pipeline. Advocates believe water from the Gulf of Aqaba would prevent the Dead Sea from drying up, generate electricity, and provide, via desalination plants, perhaps 600 million cubic meters of fresh water annually. The engineering has been possible for decades, but politics and finances proved prohibitive.

However, in 2014 Israel, Jordan and the Palestinian Authority reached agreement on a proposal to build a desalination plant in Jordan to provide water for Eilat and Aqaba. Instead of returning the brine to the sea, as an experiment to determine its environmental consequences, it will be piped to the Dead Sea to offset at least in part its drying up. In compensation for the water, Israel will share agreed amounts of fresh water with Jordan and the Palestinian Authority in the Jordan valley.

The Nile

The world's longest river, nearly 4,200 miles long, drains mountainous central Africa and the Ethiopian highlands of about 84 billion cubic meters each year, making Egypt "The Gift of the Nile." For that country and northern Sudan, no other renewable water supply exists. Survival simply depends on the Nile.

Throughout the 19th and 20th centuries, the potential for conflict over Nile River waters was very low. Ever since ancient times, Egyptian farmers had practiced "basin agriculture." Crops flourished in fields saturated with moisture from the annual summer flood and were nourished with silt that the Blue Nile had carried out of Ethiopia. Egypt's desire to capture more of the flow for year-round irrigation was reflected in the construction of barrages and small dams from the 19th century onwards. Negotiations to establish water rights followed; the first Nile Waters Agreement was signed with

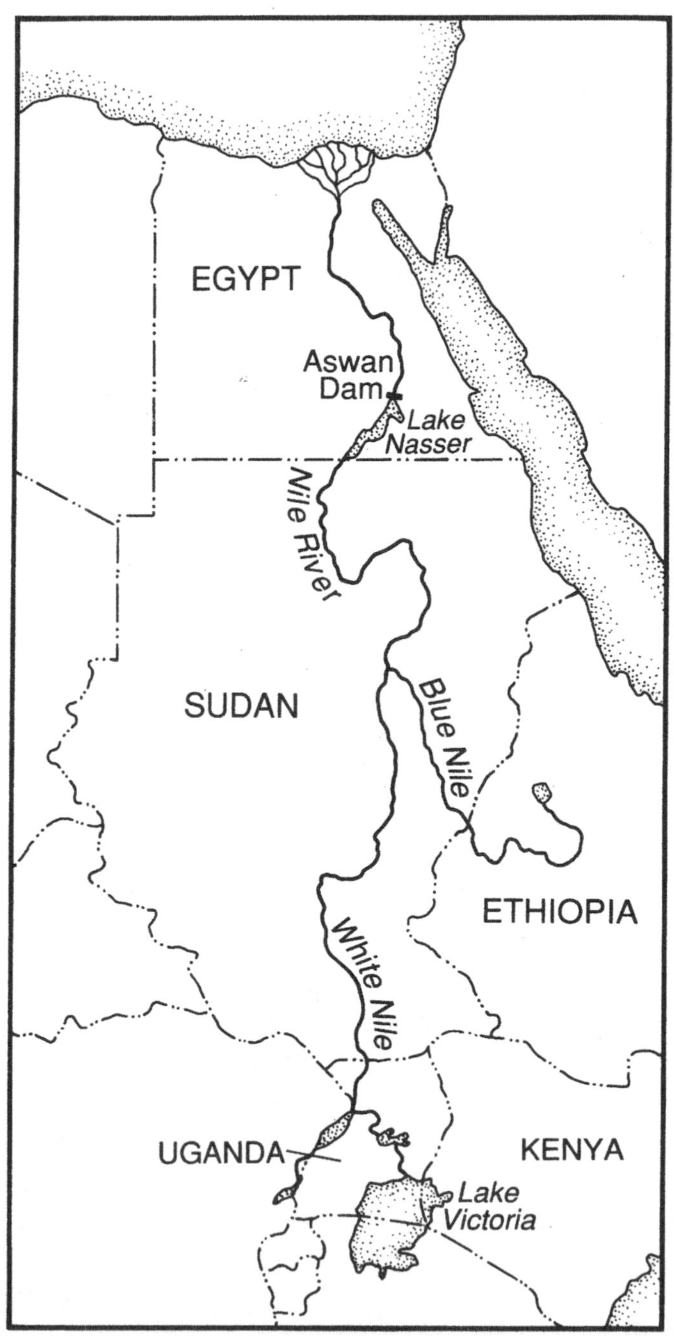

Sudan in 1929. Renegotiated in the 1950s before construction of the Aswan High Dam (see Egypt, economy), the agreement presently provides Egypt 55 billion cubic meters yearly, three times the amount allowed Sudan.

By the 1980s, severe water shortages appeared when years of drought in Ethiopia reduced the flow of the Blue Nile. Behind the High Dam, Lake Nasser dwindled. Conserving water for irrigation reduced the release of water for hydroelectric power and some years cut drastically the almost 40% of national electricity produced at Aswan.

Though rains later restored the Nile's flow, at least immediately, the crisis highlighted the inevitable future shortage of water in Egypt. Accurate figures are difficult to obtain, but one study suggested that the nation actually uses 70 billion cubic meters each year. With the population growing by one million mouths annually and the government attempting to extend cultivation, water demand will naturally increase. But Egypt's present use is only possible because Sudan fails to consume its full allotment.

Despite these dire threats, millions are not yet dying of thirst. Agriculture claims more than 80% of available water and opportunities exist for conservation. The *fellah* (farmer) typically obtains his water free, from unlined canals, and channels it to soak his fields. Free water makes sense for these poor people, whose yearly income is only a few hundred dollars; water-saving drip irrigation systems remain beyond their purchasing power. Thus, conservation will not be painless, and will impose costs, if not on very poor people, upon an impoverished government. It may also mean abandoning some lands to the insistent demands of the desert.

Until recently, it was commonly accepted that international disputes over Nile water were unlikely to end in violence. Decades of negotiation established rights and precedents. Egypt's determination to receive its historic and vital flow is firmly advertised and well-recognized by Sudan. However, the less-powerful nations upstream seem increasingly dissatisfied with their combined allocations of only 10% of the total. In 2010, Uganda, Tanzania, Rwanda and Ethiopia agreed to seek larger shares in the proposed Cooperative Framework Agreement, which Egypt has delayed since the 1980s.

Egyptian politicians reacted with shock in 2013 when Ethiopia began diverting the Blue Nile to build the Grand Ethiopian Renaissance Dam near its border with Sudan. The dam will be the largest in Africa and its reservoir will increase evaporation losses. Moreover, filling the reservoir will reduce the flow of the Nile for several years.

Egypt's President Morsi responded that "all options are open," and that he would not allow Egypt's water supply to be endangered. However, beyond economic pressures and encouraging discontent in Ethiopia, there seems little that Egypt can do. More dams will follow, some for irrigation that will divert far more water. An attack on the dams, even if a military success, would isolate Egypt and end U.S. aid. Given the region's expected population growth by 2050, Egypt will find it advantageous to conserve the Nile waters.

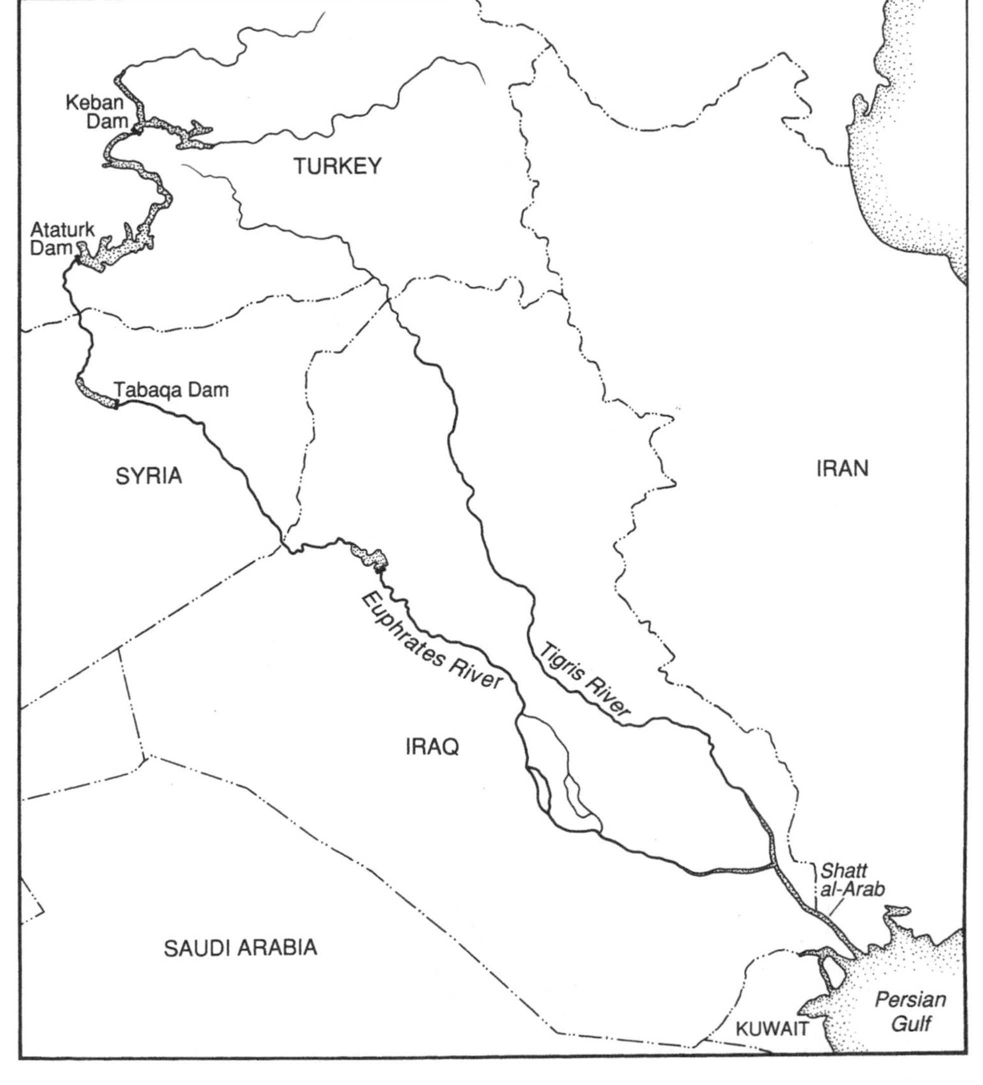

Diverting the Euphrates

To the north and east, dams on another river of Biblical fame also threaten violence. The Euphrates springs forth in the high mountains of Turkey, whose rains contribute 80% of its volume but whose rough terrain meant little was used. It flows into Syria and then across Iraq to join the Tigris at the Shatt al-Arab just before emptying into the Persian (Arabian) Gulf. Far larger than the Jordan's, the flow of the Euphrates averages 31 billion cubic meters per year. However, ambitious development plans in the three countries exceed the river's capacity by about 50%. As long ago as 1975 Iraq actually threatened war with Syria over the scanty flow below the Syria's Tabaqa Dam.

Upstream diversion of the water to fill dams and supply irrigation essentially caused the crisis, when Turkish engineers reduced the river's flow to fill the lakes behind the Keban and Ataturk dams (see Turkey, economy). The Tabaqa Dam and agricultural development project in Syria also diverted the river's flow. Alternative resources may exist for Iraq, since there is excess flow in the Tigris to the east, but development projects to use it require time and funding.

Even worse, the Euphrates and the Tigris carry a naturally high level of dissolved salts that accumulate in irrigated soils and reduce fertility. Intensive irrigation usually raises the water level in the soil, dissolving even more salts, agricultural chemicals and fertilizers. Unless drainage ditches are constructed to carry away salty and polluted waters, the land eventually becomes useless. Thus Iraq faces not only water shortages, but the danger that water quality in its major rivers will fall to levels unfit for humans and harmful for agriculture. Though in fact designed for other purposes, Iraq's man-made "Third River" may carry salty and useless water directly to the Gulf.

The nations of the Euphrates basin have not yet fought over water, but Syria and Turkey joined the anti-Iraq Coalition in the 1990–1991 Gulf War. However, in the absence of settled water rights, the potential for violence exists, and diplomatic relations remain poor.

Fighting did rage across the lower reaches of the Tigris and the Shatt al-Arab during the Iran-Iraq War of 1980–1988. That dispute had virtually nothing to do with irrigation. Iranian demands for control of the river to mid-stream, as opposed to the traditional Iraqi border on the Iranian shore, led to the crisis that produced the war. Control and navigation rights in the Shatt al-Arab remain disputed.

The Peace Pipeline

In the 1980s the Turkish government revived older ideas and proposed two "Peace Pipelines" to carry the unused flow of the Seyhan and Ceyhan rivers in southern Turkey to thirsty cities and industrial areas of Arab lands, some of them impacted by the loss of water from the Euphrates. While the proposal is intriguing, the proposed western pipeline to Jordan and Saudi Arabia is hopelessly uneconomic, due to the high elevations it must cross. The longer eastern pipeline would cross Syria and Iraq, ultimately supplying Kuwait, eastern Saudi Arabia, and several Gulf states. To date, the insurmountable obstacles of cost, national pride, and security have triumphed over good intentions. Oil pipelines across the Middle East have frequently been cut by government directive or politically—related sabotage. Would the water pipelines prove any more immune to interruption?

International Cooperation in the Indus Basin

In South Asia, two nations born in hostility faced the challenge of sharing water from the Indus River and its tributaries. By approving a technical solution, India and Pakistan brought prosperity and greater food production to the Punjab, the fertile region divided by their borders.

Simply put, the Indus is a mighty river, fed by monsoon rains and snows in the Himalayas of India and Tibet. Carrying more water than the Nile, its annual discharge reaches 97 billion cubic meters, much of it carried across the plains by five important tributaries. During British rule a system of irrigation canals was dug. After partition, India possessed the strategic advantage of controlling the head waters, but lacked economic benefit; its water was remote and difficult to use. Pakistan, in contrast, found itself farming with water from India, but strategically disadvantaged in the event India chose to divert or otherwise interfere with the flow.

A mission from the World Bank proposed in 1951 a rational solution: consider the issue a technical, not a political, problem. In effect, the key was to base water usage on irrigation potential, not nationality. Compensation for one district's use of another country's water could be made elsewhere. Despite two wars, the system has worked. Dams built with World Bank funds, plus a complex system of canals, have enabled the two countries to irrigate the Punjab, breadbasket of the sub-continent. Once again, however, increasing needs for water and power are currently leading to tension over India's planned Baglihar dam on the Chenab River.

Besides its rivers, the Punjab's other major source of irrigation is groundwater. Unfortunately, this is increasingly dangerous to the drinker's health. A 2007 study by water pollution authorities in India discovered that 80% of the samples contained mercury far above the permissible level, and that arsenic and pesticide contamination were significant as well.

If scientists' predictions prove accurate, climate change may eventually reduce the flow of the Indus more than most other major Asian rivers. According to the models, greater global warmth will melt Himalayan glaciers, initially increasing the river's flow as the vast ice fields melt. After the glaciers retreat, however, their runoff will decline in exactly the vital spring and summer periods when irrigation is most needed on the plains of India and Pakistan. Farm output would then fall dramatically, by enough to feed perhaps 26 million people.

Opposite Extremes

Bangladesh and northeastern India struggle with entirely different difficulties—seasonally. With as much as 50% of annual rainfall occurring in less than three weeks, for centuries, Bengalis reconciled their ways of life with the seasonal flooding of the Ganges, Brahmaputra, and other rivers, whose water and silt deposits nourished the soil and produced three crops per year (see Bangladesh). With few possessions and minimal homes, farmers lived knowing that floods could strike, and river channels might be altered by hundreds of yards overnight. Nevertheless, they could hope to escape with their lives and a few possessions to begin farming anew.

Such a fate hardly appealed to modernized city dwellers living in permanent homes. In 1989 Bangladesh embarked on the Flood Action Plan to build embankments to protect cities and to confine rivers to channels. Unfortunately, confining the rivers creates the danger that silt will raise the level of the river bottoms, eventually causing them to flow *above* ground-level. If this happens, one of the poorest countries in the world will have to construct and maintain a vast system of dikes for the rivers at an enormous cost, if indeed, it can be done, considering frequent devastating hurricanes and monsoons.

Even in this region of great annual flooding, periodic droughts strike during the dry season, and rival irrigation projects highlight the need for water-sharing agreements. A proposal to divert Himalayan river water to South India also looms as a threat to Bangladesh. It shares 50 rivers with India, but only one is covered by an international agreement regarding its flow.

Global warming, by changing mountain snowfall to rain, increases flooding and reduces off-season flow. As in the case of the Indus (but probably not the Ganges), the decline of Himalayan glaciers may eventually diminish spring and summer melt-water in the Brahmaputra basin. One model predicts this could reduce agricultural output by the equivalent of food for 34 million people.

Consequences of Dams and Large-Scale Irrigation

Humans first diverted rivers in the misty years of early history. However, the large dams that tower hundreds of feet above a valley or stretch miles across a lower river basin represent a triumph, however momentary, of the 20th century. First constructed in the United States and Soviet Union in the 1920s and 1930s, the dams proved valuable for flood control, hydroelectric power, recreational use and irrigation. After World War II, building dams became a worldwide fad, and 95% of all large dams date from this period.

For all their virtues, dams in the hot climates of the Middle East and South Asia involve a variety of drawbacks. An obvious one is evaporation, largely because the sun's rays strike directly and the desert air carries little of the humidity that would slow evaporation. The loss from Lake Nasser to the air is an estimated 10 billion cubic meters a year, one-fifth of Egypt's recognized portion of the Nile's flow. Serious proposals exist to cover the entire surface of Lake Nasser with small floating plastic bubbles to reduce the water's exposure to the air, a tremendous undertaking on a surface of thousands of square miles.

WHEN WILL THE TAPS GO DRY?

On many rivers, a much more serious problem is the buildup of silt in the reservoirs back of the large dams. Engineers only recently recognized how great this problem is in warmer climates. The Ganges-Brahmaputra and Indus each carry roughly 1,700 gallons of silt in each million gallons of water. Quietly, but much faster than predicted, rivers drop this sediment in the slow waters of the reservoirs.

At the Tarbela Dam in Pakistan, for example, some 2% of the reservoir fills with soil annually, and hundreds of tons of dirt settle above the Mangla Dam. Because of the silt, the Tarbela Dam may prove useful for only 40 years, a poor investment in view of its life expectancy of 100 years when built. In Sudan, the Roseires Dam on the Blue Nile ceased effective operation when deposits formed an island above the water intakes for the hydroelectric turbines.

Rapid silting not only spreads a dam's huge construction costs over fewer years, it also renders the location permanently useless as a dam. Unfortunately, projects conceived to reduce soil loss, such as planting trees, often proved less effective than projected.

As environmentalists and others have long pointed out, silt often plays important roles in nourishing fields and supporting the coastal ecosystem. Deprived of sediments, Egyptian and other farmers spread tons of chemical fertilizers on their soil, polluting the earth and rendering drainage water unfit for many uses. Coastlines deprived of silt may succumb to the sea, as has happened in Egypt and elsewhere.

Silting risks partly forced the scaling-back of the Narmada Valley Development Project in central and western India. Probably the largest single project in the world, its plans included 30 major dams, dozens of smaller ones and thousands of minor ones, constructed over a period of 50 years. The dams will supply irrigation water for millions of acres in the states of Gujarat, Rajasthan and Madhya Pradesh, and generate vast amounts of electricity for homes and industry. However, the new reservoirs also flood large expanses of tropical forest and forced hundreds of thousands of people from their homes. A series of court actions in 2000 finally lowered the maximum permitted height of one major dam, though it permitted construction to resume.

Alternatives

To supply thirsty homes and farms, nations in the Middle East and South Asia have turned to new sources. Infrared satellite pictures suggest that "fracture zones" stretching for hundreds of miles may hold billions of cubic meters of water in aquifers far below the level of traditional wells. Unfortunately, however, fossil water remains from moister climatic ages and is never replaced by nature. In a few decades these aquifers run dry. With government subsidies and assistance, Saudi farmers pumped this "fossil water" to irrigate farmland, but the project ultimately failed (see Saudi Arabia, economy).

In contrast, desalination transforms the free and limitless water of the seas and oceans into the sweet water necessary for

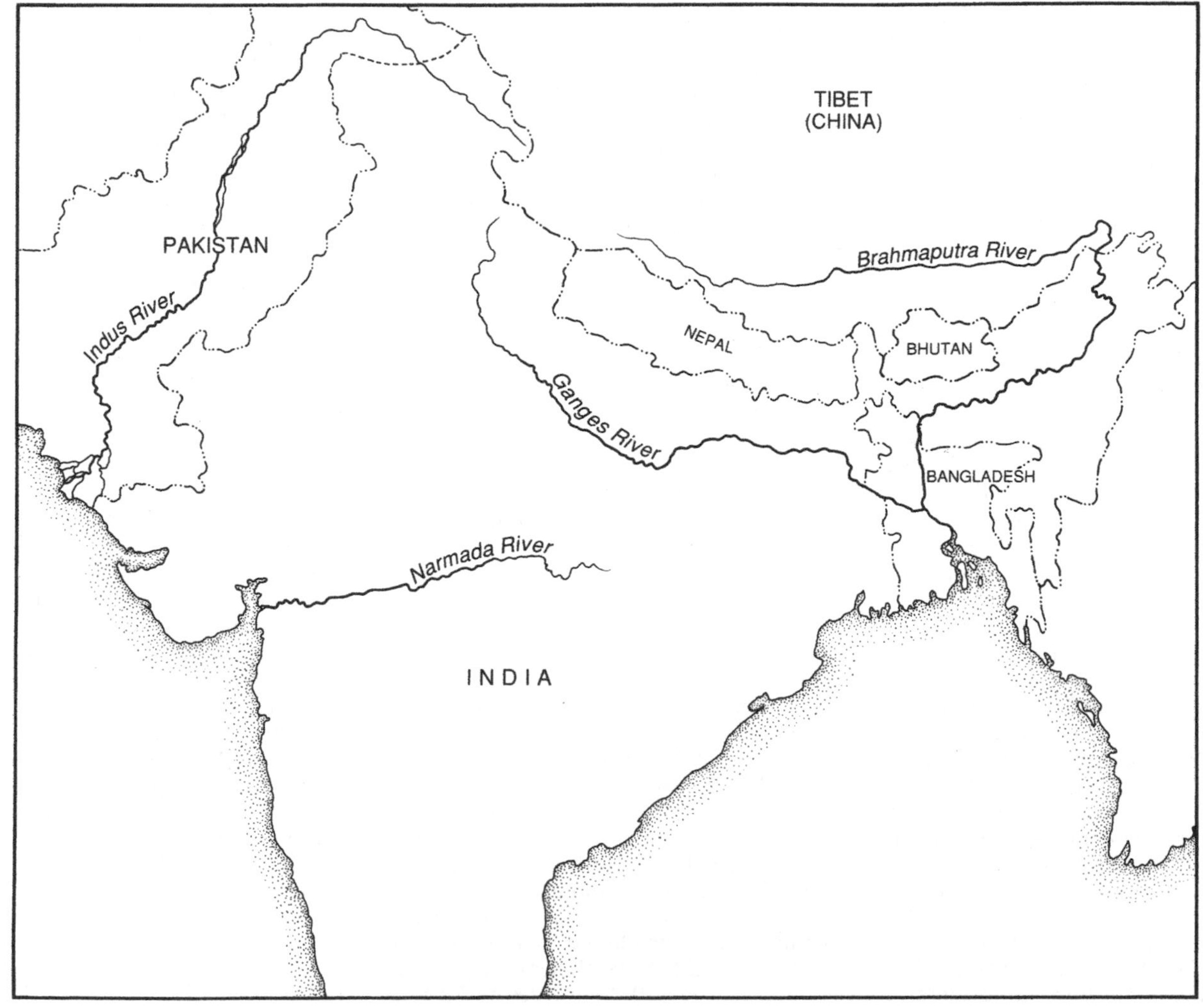

A boat bridge across the upper Indus

human life and agriculture. Despite the higher salt content of the Red Sea and the Gulf, the oil exporting nations of the Gulf lead the world in commercial desalination. Saudi Arabia alone accounts for almost one-third of the world capacity, over one billion cubic meters annually. Kuwait and the United Arab Emirates provide another fifth. While the ancients used solar power to distill water, efficient, large-scale desalination plants today employ multi-stage processes for capturing steam and condensing it into water. Costs are lowest for so-called dual-purpose plants that use relatively low-temperature waste heat from power plants. In Saudi Arabia the Ministry of Agriculture, which runs desalination plants, started generating more electricity than the Ministry of Electricity and Industry.

Despite the availability of bright, hot sunshine, it requires far higher fuel prices—or technological breakthroughs—for solar power to become economical. The most promising method uses saline solar ponds to collect the sun's energy and use it to convert salt water into usable liquid.

Desalination is now affordable for household uses in countries with high per capita incomes—at least near the coast. It remains a hope for coastal agricultural regions, but presently the process is far too expensive for irrigating crops. Other difficulties can hardly be solved by money, however. The 1990–1991 Gulf War showed how greatly Saudi Arabia and the smaller oil-producing states depend on desalination, when a massive oil slick threatened to pollute drinking water and clog equipment. To be efficient, desalination plants must be large, but large plants mean little reserve capacity and pose tempting targets for attack and sabotage.

Experiments continue in several countries using brackish water and seawater for agriculture. The goal is to discover productive plants that need little or no fresh water and then to determine profitable techniques for growing and processing them. If successful, salt water farming could revolutionize present water use patterns. Israeli enthusiasts, for example, advocate a pipeline to carry brackish, undrinkable water from desert aquifers to farms for irrigating certain crops. Results also appear promising for growing certain oil seed crops using seawater, with the added benefit of using the plants as fodder for animals. Unfortunately the application of the discoveries will be limited and will require close monitoring: salt-water irrigation contaminates permanently any fresh ground water in an aquifer below.

The recycling of sewage and other waste-water has reached the greatest extent in Israel, where some 30% of it is reused in agriculture. The potential to recycle exists in other countries as well, but the process requires well-trained personnel and careful monitoring of pollutants. Like the use of drip irrigation, higher water prices for regular water will encourage greater use of waste-water. Unfortunately, this can be dangerous: according to data from the International Water Management Institute, 85% of cities in developing nations discharge water without appropriate treatment, risking contamination of heavy metals and other pollutants.

Many novel proposals exist to meet the looming shortage. Polar ice contains about two thirds of the world's fresh water, so giant icebergs from the Antarctic could be towed to the Middle East and melted to quench the region's thirst. More conventionally, tankers might bring drinking water from European nations with excess supplies such as France and Britain. High prices might also provide the incentive to reduce agriculture in the Nile and Indus valleys, with the water thus saved piped under the sea to cities in Arabia.

Most Americans take for granted the water that simply flows from an opened faucet. By contrast, in many parts of the Middle East and South Asia there are no taps, and the assumption that sufficient water will be there in a decade or two increasingly looks risky. The area's limited water resources are already being developed and used to the maximum. For most countries this does not imply that water shortages now threaten living standards as does the devastating drought in northeastern Syria. But peaceful solutions require major changes and, above all, time.

Even with the best conservation methods, farming remains a thirsty occupation. Nations in the region value agriculture for its employment, the security of food supplies and realizing national aspirations. Rather than risk war over insufficient water supplies, Middle Eastern nations logically should develop other uses of their lands and work forces.

Unfortunately, logic frequently seems missing in matters of water management and agriculture. Given this region's shortages and its many failed attempts at peacemaking, trouble lies ahead. Water shortages in India have already led to fatal violence. Further west, in the words of Joyce Starr, founder of Global Water Summit Initiative, Middle East population growth is a "human explosion certain to ignite the issue of water."

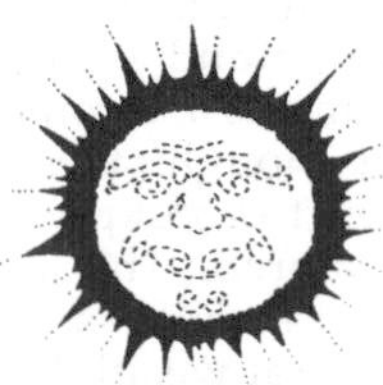

BLACK GOLD: THE IMPACT OF OIL

Petroleum refining involves precision engineering and extensive equipment anywhere on earth Courtesy: Royal Embassy of Saudi Arabia

The countries of the Middle East and South Asia enjoy few natural riches, and most of the famed mineral deposits of antiquity have been exhausted for centuries.

The great exception is petroleum. Perhaps 60% of the world's proven and probable oil deposits lie in the sedimentary basin between central Arabia and the mountains of Iran. From northern Iraq to the Strait of Hormuz, crude oil often occurs in large fields relatively near the surface. Cheap to extract, without the financial and environmental costs of drilling in deep waters or Arctic tundra, the oil is piped short distances to coastal terminals, loaded onto tankers, and shipped to refineries world-wide.

So abundant is the oil, and so efficient its production, refining and transportation, that Saudi oil probably costs under U.S. $ 0.50 per gallon to pump, refine, and transport, but it may sell for $10 per gallon in Europe and $4 in the United States. Governments and companies manage to extract enough taxes and profits from consumers to boost prices as high as other energy sources. The special physical qualities that make oil a desirable fuel also generate great wealth for those able to manipulate its price.

The Search for Oil in the Middle East

The ancients knew something about oil. Asphalt seeped to the surface in Mesopotamia. Tar paved the streets of Babylon, calked seams, and mortared bricks. Mysterious fires there and in Persia burned indefinitely, without consuming any known fuel.

Petroleum's role remained largely unchanged until the industrial revolution. By the 19th century, the new factories in Europe and the United States required great quantities of oil, for light and to lubricate moving parts. Inventors and entrepreneurs in Europe and North America dug the first wells to obtain petroleum, and after 1900 the popularity of gasoline-powered automobiles spurred demand for oil tremendously.

An integrated industry developed rapidly. The search for petroleum deposits spread to the Middle East, where prospecting began first in Iraq and Iran (then known as Persia), where the English entrepreneur William D'Arcy negotiated a concession from the Shah of Persia in 1901. After five years of disappointments, in 1908 his drillers struck the first commercial well in the Middle East, at Masjid-i Suleiman.

D'Arcy moved rapidly to exploit the find. He organized the Anglo-Persian Oil Company, which laid a pipeline to the coast and gained permission from a local chief to construct a refinery on Abadan Island at the head of the Gulf. On the eve of World War I, with the Royal Navy switching from coal to oil for fuel, Winston Churchill arranged for the British government to purchase a majority share in the company, known today as British Petroleum.

After World War I, the concessions for oil prospecting in Iraq fell to British, French and American firms who in the late 1920s formed the Iraq Petroleum Company (IPC). In the 1920s and 1930s, geologists discovered vast oil fields elsewhere in the Middle East, first in Bahrain. Then, in 1938, an American company exploring in Saudi Arabia struck commercial quantities with its seventh well. Geologists eventually recognized that quite distant oil strikes really tapped parts of one vast field, the Ghawar. Some 160 miles long, it ranks as the largest in the world, even surpassing Kuwait's Burgan field. Oil production in Qatar, the United Arab Emirates, and Oman became significant only in the 1950s and 1960s.

In contrast to plantation agriculture or modern industry, petroleum requires a relatively small but highly skilled workforce, after the initial construction of pipelines, storage facilities, loading terminals, and perhaps a refinery. Although they employed relatively few workers, the oil companies greatly affected local society. They established training programs and schools. Roads, towns, shops, medical facilities and models of new lifestyles often resulted—at least for some of the population. Another major impact was financial. Royalties, taxes, and profit-sharing flowed to the rulers, and exports supplied foreign exchange, normally scarce in developing countries.

Countries and Companies Clash over Profits

In the Middle East, land ownership of untilled areas traditionally belonged to the government, and as a result, oil companies negotiated agreements, or concessions, from governments. These stipulated the territorial limits of company operations and specified payments to the ruler.

Companies initially bargained from strength and the rulers from weakness, because the rulers needed money and neither side knew what oil wealth existed, or if it would flow in profitable quantities. The oil industry was dominated by just a few companies—sometimes titled the "Seven Sisters"—who kept prices high and maintained large reserve capacities, so their negotiations for concessions reflected such corporate strengths.

In contrast, governments badly needed money and preferred large initial payments for prospecting rights, while accepting low royalties on output that might never occur. Thus, in 1931 Iraq agreed to royalties of only four gold shillings per ton, about twelve cents per barrel. Saudi Arabia accepted the same figure two years later. Their oil companies earned remarkable profits on their productive investments, but other investments proved complete losses despite years of exploration.

Middle East nations soon felt they deserved better, that their original concessions provided too generously for the companies and failed to reflect the changed circumstances after oil was discovered. Being sovereign, they could demand revisions in what the companies considered legally binding contracts. The first important changes came with Shah Reza's Iran in 1933. Thereafter, governments repeatedly pressed for greater revenues and for minimum annual payments. By 1950, agreements often fixed payments as 50% of gross income less production expenses. However, income was difficult to determine when oil was sold to another subsidiary of the same company. Eventually, both sides accepted artificial "posted prices" to calculate the profits to be divided.

Iran's attempt to gain control of its oil in 1951 highlighted the limits that countries faced in their continuing struggles to gain greater benefits from oil. After Prime Minister Mohammad Mossadeq nationalized operations of the Anglo-Iranian Oil Company, the company increased output in Kuwait, and diverted its tankers to other sources. Anglo-Iranian halted payments to the government, and its lawyers prevented sales of Iranian oil in Western Europe. Eventually the two sides agreed that a consortium of companies would operate the oil fields for the National Iranian Oil Company. The lesson was clear: governments depended for their very survival on the tax revenues from oil, but the "majors" maintained sufficient excess capacity to meet their customers' needs without the exports of any one nation, and would lend oil to each other. Therefore, a single country lacked the power to force a major oil company to accept its terms.

In 1959, with world oil supplies plentiful and market prices soft, the major oil companies announced—rather than negotiated—a lower posted price for crude oil and thus reduced their payments to governments. In response, representatives of Iran, Iraq, Kuwait, Saudi Arabia and Venezuela met in Baghdad and established the Organization of Oil Exporting Countries (OPEC, 1960). From its inception, OPEC's goals concerned export prices, royalties, and the taxation of profits, but its members also desired that the companies train and hire their citizens.

Until the late 1950s, international oil companies treated Middle Eastern supplies as supplemental and set prices based on the U.S. market, thus keeping prices high in the U.S. Around 1970, however, American production peaked and soon began to decline, while U.S., European, and Japanese demand continued to grow rapidly. The increase could only be met from the Middle East. Its oil, hitherto excluded from the United States on grounds of "national security," became increasingly necessary for the world's largest economy.

Against this background, specific events gained disproportionate importance. The Suez Canal remained closed after the 1967 war, straining oil tanker capacity. A puncture in 1970 shut down the Saudi pipeline to the Mediterranean, and Libya simultaneously acted against some small oil companies for violating their concessions. Fears of world-wide oil shortages created the opportunity for OPEC to demand higher revenues.

The resulting 1971 Tehran Agreement between OPEC nations and the companies increased posted prices immediately (to less than $2 for a barrel of 42 gallons), and set them at $5 per barrel by the late 1970s. Hailed at the time as a major victory for the oil exporters, the Tehran Agreement raised revenues to the countries by 25%, enabling these nations to limit production and still pay their bills. The countries no longer needed to produce more to pay their bills—they discovered that at current conditions, they could reduce production but raise prices more. Future increases in demand would also allow them to force further price increases on the companies and consumers.

The 1973 Oil Embargo and Rising Prices

World politics provided the convenient opportunity. During the October 1973 War between Israel and the Arab nations of Egypt and Syria, hostility to the U.S. rose in the Arab world. King Faisal of Saudi Arabia won wide approval when he embargoed oil exports to the United States. To make the policy effective he also decreed a 10% cut in all exports.

Sensing their power, the Gulf oil exporters then broke the previous pattern of negotiated prices and set export prices without consulting the companies. Fears of shortages seized consumers world-wide, and prices on the spot market rose to $15 per barrel. Gas lines appeared across the U.S., service stations closed on Sundays, and President Nixon reduced the speed limit to 55 miles per hour. Recognizing the opportunity, OPEC met in December 1973 and raised the price countries would receive to $11.65 per barrel.

Great transfers of wealth followed the 1973 price increase. Prices doubled again during shortages created by the Iranian Revolution in 1979–1980, bringing inconceivable riches. Iran's revenues, for instance, rose almost seven-fold between 1973–1974 and 1977–1978. In 1981, Saudi Arabia received roughly $120 billion for its oil, over $12,000 per inhabitant. Massive purchases of foreign goods clogged ports throughout the Middle East. However, in just a few years conservation measures by consumers, cheating by OPEC members, and increased production outside OPEC brought prices down by about 50% (see box).

Price fluctuations in the 1990s

The rise of oil futures markets in the 1980s meant that OPEC members could not set world prices, but they could influence them. Given consumers' desires and non-OPEC production, OPEC members might collectively produce just enough to balance supply and demand at a target price. By the late 1980s, however, the cartel could not enforce the discipline. Kuwait and the United Arab Emirates overproduced, arguing that fairness should

BLACK GOLD: THE IMPACT OF OIL

Offshore drilling requires large platforms, here arriving in the Gulf
Courtesy: Royal Embassy of Saudi Arabia

link the size of the quota to oil export capacity, rather than to population or poverty. Consumers benefited world-wide from the lower prices, but revenues plummeted. Iraq, in financial desperation when prices plunged to $14 per barrel, invaded Kuwait in 1990 (see Iraq: history).

After seizing Kuwait, Iraq controlled the sources of roughly 20% of OPEC's exports. When U.N. sanctions on Iraq and occupied Kuwait blocked their export of oil, fears rose of oil shortages, and crude oil prices rapidly doubled. Industrial nations headed for recession, but despite Iraqi threats, OPEC approved extra output, and with help from oil in storage, a world-wide shortfall was averted.

By the mid-1990s, global use of oil had expanded, particularly in East Asia, while supplies from non-OPEC producers grew slowly during a decade of lower prices. Prices rose well above $20, and OPEC nations found that *they could cheat at their quotas and enjoy higher prices at the same time*. However, Saudi Arabia persuaded the cartel's members to increase the total OPEC quota from 23.833 million barrels per day (m b/d) to 26.185 m b/d (without Iraq) just as East Asia suffered economic recession. When market speculators realized that some nations, particularly Venezuela, Nigeria and Qatar, exceeded even the larger quotas, prices dropped immediately and rapidly, to levels last seen in 1973. Some experts proclaimed the death of OPEC, and argued that the rational policy for Gulf producers was to earn money from volume production, even if prices reached $5 per barrel. Such prices, after all, would render oil from Alaska and the North Sea too expensive to be profitable.

After losing billions of dollars in exports and revenues, OPEC cut quotas in 1998 and 1999. Moreover, sympathetic nations outside OPEC, including Mexico, Norway, Russia, and Oman also agreed to cut exports. After several months, the cuts persuaded the markets, and every American driver witnessed the result. Oil prices soared, gasoline prices climbed, and regular gasoline prices exceeded $2 per gallon in parts of California. So often proclaimed dead, OPEC had again revived.

High Prices since 2004: A Spike or the Future?

Oil prices rose modestly during the U.S. invasion of Iraq in 2003. This was easily predictable: the conflict halted Iraqi production and exports. Most strategists expected a rapid resumption of Iraqi exports, increasing world supplies and thus reducing prices. Instead, annual average prices climbed rapidly in 2004–05, in 2007 surpassed the 1980s peak of $85 in today's prices, and in mid-2008 refineries began to pay more than $150 per barrel.

Why?

Among many explanations, the following facts seem fundamental to any analysis:

World oil consumption rose 11%, insensitive to price: The annual price of crude oil climbed from a very low average of $12.50 in 1998 to $68 in 2007, a rise of over 400%. Economic theory suggests that consumers who face such increases would attempt to reduce consumption, but during that decade, Americans increased their consumption by almost 10%, or 1.75 million barrels per day. With the rapid spread of automobiles in China, its oil consumption rose by 84%, or nearly 3.5 million barrels per day, and other rapidly-growing Asian nations and the rest of the developing world added another 5.8 million barrels per day of consumption.

Outside OPEC, only Russia significantly increased production: Despite the high prices, U.S. crude oil output actually fell slightly, and major declines occurred in Britain (41%), Norway (18%), and several smaller producers. As a group, however, non-OPEC producers increased crude output by nearly 13%. Nearly all the increase came from territories of the former Soviet Union, and 63% came from Russia alone, as it modernized production and in 2009 overtook Saudi Arabia as the world's largest producer.

Most of OPEC pumped all it could: The 13 nations comprising OPEC lost world market share as they increased production only 7%. Nearly half the gain came from Angola, after the end of its long civil war. According to estimates of the U.S. Energy Information Administration, OPEC nations produced flat-out, with only Saudi Arabia holding any spare capacity at all (in the range of 1–2 million barrels per day). One expert, James Hamilton, disputes even this spare capacity, suggesting that the northern Ghawar field has peaked, and new projects will replace capacity, not increase it.

Seven years on, Iraqi output still lags: Sabotage, corruption, and inefficiency have combined to limit Iraqi production below 3m b/d.

Gasoline and jet fuel are not like "Coke": If the price of one brand of soft drink doubled, most Americans would switch to another brand. Because cars, trucks, and aircraft cannot readily switch to alternate fuels, and we would be horrified at reducing driving by, say, 25%, in the language of economists demand is insensitive to price, in the short run.

Speculative money flooded into oil futures: Seeking high returns when stock markets and housing loans offered modest profits, after 2000 hedge fund managers and others speculated in many raw materials, including crude oil. Given the tight world-wide supply, and the possibility that political unrest, terrorism, natural disaster, or simply bad luck could reduce that supply, speculators found many reasons to bid up prices, and little reason to fear a downward spiral.

What's next? Optimists think prices will moderate: Slower world economic growth might reduce consumption slightly, and other upward pressures may prove temporary, such as political difficulties in Venezuela and violence in Nigeria that created a "security premium." Iraq's proven reserves of 115 billion barrels, second only to Saudi Arabia's, will permit dramatic increases after peace and reconstruction. More exports might even be possible from Russia.

Finally, optimists quote figures from BP that show the global ratio of reserves to production stands at 40 years. This implies that during the last few decades, discoveries kept pace with increased production. The global ratio remained constant even in 2008, when reserves fell slightly, because production fell somewhat faster.

Pessimists point to "facts" as well: Demand is rising sharply in some countries, especially China and India, where hundreds of millions aspire to own a car. Based on trends earlier in the decade, the International Energy Agency (IEA) has predicted that global energy demand will soar by 60% by about 2030.

Though demand is rising, new supplies are not. During the last two decades, only a few very large-sized fields were discovered anywhere. Some, like those in very deep water off Brazil, will take years to develop. A decade ago, Kazakhstan and Central Asia promised "another Persian Gulf" of enormous supplies, but reality proved more modest. Excepting OPEC and Russia, reported world reserves equal only 12 times annual production. Global non-OPEC, non-Russian oil production

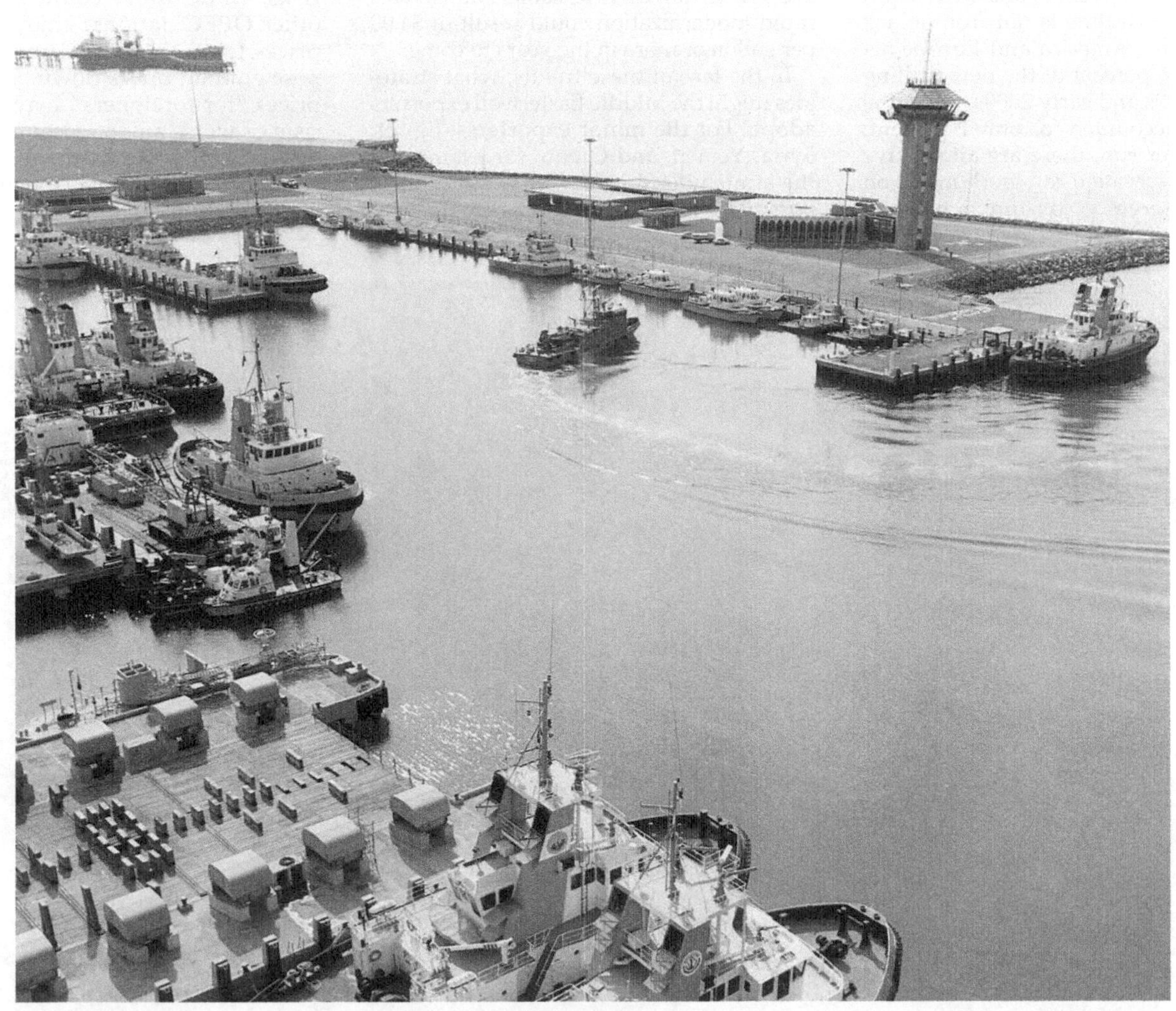

Small vessels play important roles in supply and security Courtesy: Royal Embassy of Saudi Arabia

BLACK GOLD: THE IMPACT OF OIL

Petroleum Output of OPEC Nations
(thousands of barrels per day)

	1998	2007	2011*
Algeria	820	1,370	1,240
Angola	740	1,680	1,660
Ecuador	380	510	490
Iran	3,600	3,700	3,620
Iraq	2,150	2,080	2,670
Kuwait	2,090	2,460	2,540
Libya	1,390	1,700	460
Nigeria	2,040	2,120	2,110
Qatar	660	810	810
Saudi Arabia	8,390	8,720	9,270
United Arab Emirates	2,270	2,490	2,520
Venezuela	3,130	2,300	2,380
OPEC Total	28,970	30,900	29,760

*2011 data for Iran based on secondary sources.
Source: U.S. Energy Information Agency (1998, 2007); OPEC (2011 data).
Note: Without specifying national quotas, OPEC approved a production ceiling of 30 million barrels per day in December 2011.

may have peaked in 2008, and then begin to decline. The decline is not from a lack of trying: North America and Europe accounted for 71 percent of the new drilling in the late 1990s and early 2000s, while the Middle East accounted for only 2 percent.

In the longer run, there are alternative fuels, and conservation can work magic on the ratio of reserves to consumption. However, American driving habits and China's rapid modernization could result in $4.00 per gallon or more in the years to come.

In the face of these trends, what strategies might the Middle Eastern oil exporters adopt? For the minor exporters—Egypt, Syria, Yemen, and Oman, for example—the strategy is simple: sell at the highest possible price while pumping carefully to obtain the most oil from the fields. However, Saudi Arabia, Kuwait, Iran and the United Arab Emirates possess the potential, collectively and in Saudi Arabia's case probably individually, to set production levels that will influence world prices towards the mid-$30s per barrel, or above $120 per barrel. After the sharp decline in prices in 2008, which cost Arab economies about $2.5 trillion, modest OPEC cuts were apparently designed to raise prices to roughly $80 per barrel.

Both strategic options carry risks. Higher prices encourage the development of deep-water, Arctic and other costly oilfields that would be uneconomic at lower prices. Once those wells are drilled, their extra oil production diminishes the power of OPEC. High prices also encourage alternative types of energy. Finally, hidden in the background alternatives of strategic planners is the fear that at some point, high oil prices may lead some consuming nations to "protect world supplies" by military force.

The lower-price option also carries risks. OPEC unity could split, because other OPEC nations, enjoying the high prices for their limited production, oppose guiding prices down. Second, lower prices "for foreigners" may arouse criticism or worse among a country's citizens. For example, Saudi terrorists explicitly condemned their government for selling oil too cheaply.

Off-shore loading saves time, but requires vast tank farms Courtesy: Royal Embassy of Saudi Arabia

WHY OIL PRICES PLUNGED ONCE BEFORE

When prices softened slightly in the early 1980s, OPEC's success still seemed to suggest that unlike other cartels (alliances of producers that limit production and raise prices), it could defy the laws of economics. Normally, a cartel's high prices lead customers to conserve and seek alternatives, resulting in reduced purchases. Typically, cartel producers then respond with secret discounts to lure customers, and to compete with producers outside the cartel. Eventually, according to theory, market forces—overproduction, cheating and outright defections—will destroy the cartel.

True to theory, in the early 1980s oil consumers reacted to high prices. They bought fuel-efficient cars, lowered winter thermostats and otherwise conserved energy. Oil use by the industrialized world fell by almost 20%. Producers outside OPEC greatly increased exploration, drilling, and output. However, the cartel did not collapse. Wealthy OPEC members initially could not spend all their revenues, and consequently cut production with few difficulties. This spared countries where cuts would be painful (and more likely ignored). This greatly slowed the decline of the cartel.

Over time, voluntary cuts proved insufficient to prop up prices. OPEC nations then agreed to cut production by an average of 40%. Again, the large producers with relatively small populations played a major "swing" role. Saudi Arabia, Kuwait and the United Arab Emirates accepted reductions in output of 50% or more, while Iran, Venezuela, Indonesia and Algeria, with much lower oil exports per person, escaped with far smaller cuts.

By 1985, however, the market for OPEC crude had tumbled to 15.4 million barrels per day, and many members cheated on quotas or provided secret discounts. Dropping its famous oil minister, Zaki Yamani, Saudi Arabia abandoned its role as a "swing producer" and determined to defend its market share. Crude flooded the world's markets, and prices tumbled briefly to below $9 a barrel in 1986. (Adjusted for inflation, this still represented a 40% increase over 1972 prices.) Greater OPEC discipline restored prices to about $18 per barrel in 1987, and for most of the next decade they fluctuated in the $15–22 range.

Consumers and alternate suppliers brought prices down once. Can they do so again?

The Future: Conditions seem more favorable to oil and gas consumers across the globe than they have for some years. World oil supplies should grow more rapidly than consumption, for both political and technical reasons. The effects on the environment will be mixed.

In the realm of world politics, the election of Hassan Rouhani as president of Iran provides a glimmer of hope that Iran and the powers negotiating with it can discover a compromise that ends sanctions. Promising negotiations alone might reduce the present risk premium; their successful conclusion will provide more crude to world markets fairly quickly, and more natural gas in the longer run. The reconstructed oil industries of Iraq and Libya are also likely to continue expanding crude output.

On the technical side, advances in fracking shale formations for natural gas and mining tar sands for crude oil are also boosting production. The potential scale of this change is amazing: the United States, which has imported about as much oil each year as Saudi Arabia produces, may in a decade be self-sufficient (perhaps with Canadian assistance).

The combination of greater Middle Eastern production and North American production should more than offset the upward pressure on prices from fast-growing economies like China, India, and Saudi Arabia itself.

Of course, it could all go wrong. An Israeli strike on Iran, followed by Iranian mining of the Strait of Hormuz and perhaps missile attacks on Arab oil exporters could very easily cut global supplies and push prices about $200 per barrel. This seems unlikely but possible.

In the long run, investment, technology, and conservation, might increase supplies and moderate demand so much that oil will remain abundant for several decades. However, even if that happens, Middle Eastern suppliers will enjoy low costs of production. Their huge oilfields, high output per well, and easy access to shipping make them currently the most efficient energy sources.

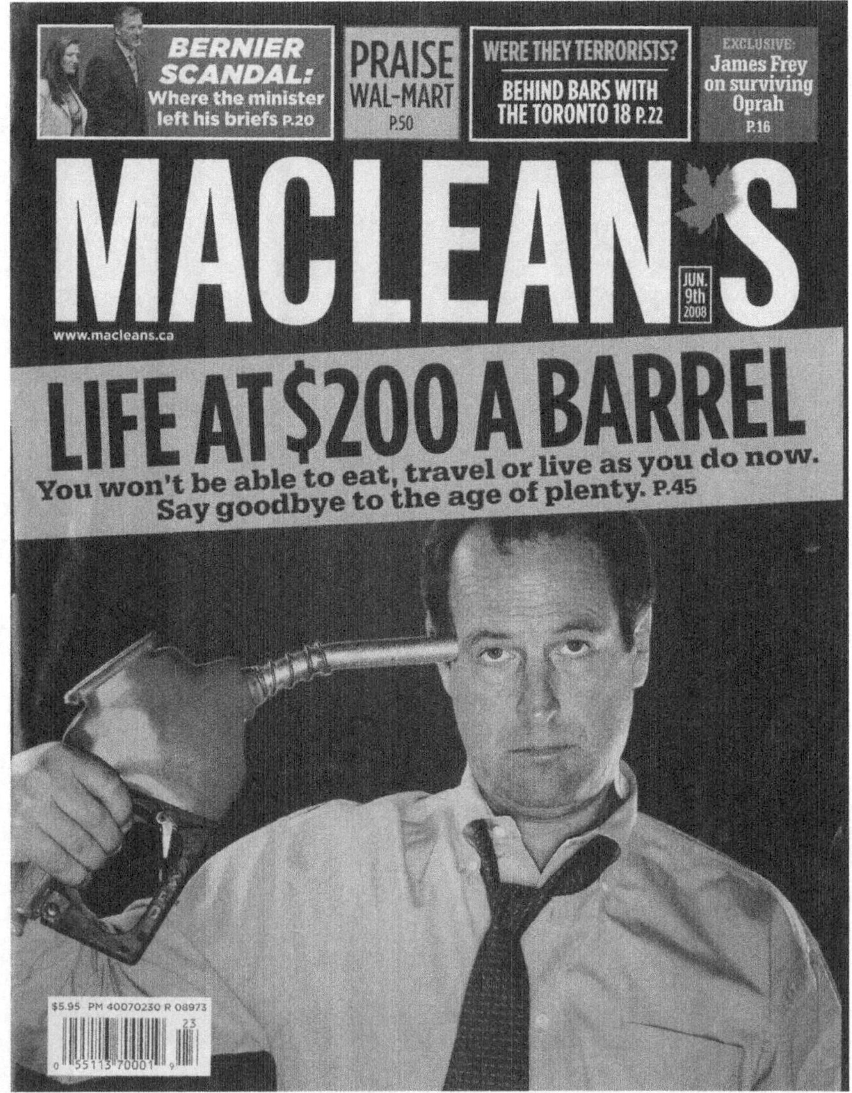

HISTORICAL BACKGROUND

The Emergence of Civilization

In the earliest stage of human history people depended for food upon hunting wild animals and gathering the edible parts of plants. For warmth they clothed themselves in animal skins, and they found protection from the weather in caves or temporary shelters. Archaeologists have found evidence for this kind of life on six continents and many islands.

Climatic changes probably played an important role in the next stage of human history, known as the Neolithic or New Stone Age. As the earth warmed after the last Ice Age, rainy weather retreated northward and to the tropics. A permanent zone of high atmospheric pressure began to dominate Southern Europe and North Africa from the Atlantic to the Middle East, and Southern Asia up to monsoon-blessed India. Under the impact of successive dry, sunny days, deserts formed where previously fishermen lived, and the hunters and gatherers were forced into confined areas, particularly along river valleys, watered by rainfall trapped by mountains and highlands often hundreds of miles distant.

Beside such rivers and streams in Southwest Asia women (more likely than men) first deliberately planted seed—barley and a variety of wheat—and cultivated land, events dated by most historians to around 8,000 B.C. About the same time, people domesticated animals: cultivation and domestication together formed the Agricultural Revolution. Initially hardly more productive than hunting and gathering, soon farmers were capable of producing a surplus over the minimum requirements of food, clothing and shelter. Such development occurred in other areas of the world, but in later periods. Once mankind had learned how to plant grain crops and raise captive animals, a much more secure supply of food was available. It was no longer necessary for small groups of people to keep constantly on the move in search of food. They planted their fields near sources of water, their numbers increased and village life developed. The sites of the oldest villages so far discovered lie in a zone stretching from southeastern Europe across Asia Minor as far eastward as the region of the middle Tigris River.

The level of technology, combined with the tasks of obtaining food, clothing, safety, and other essentials of existence must have shaped daily activities and society during prehistory. Life was short, even for survivors of infancy and childhood. Food supplies limited the maximum size of the group, for hunters and gatherers had to move further to procure food as the group rose in size. However, high mortality for children and adults—let alone infants—decreed the importance of having many women, all either pregnant or about to become so. Only thus could the existence of a next generation be expected. Lacking documentary evidence, historians can only surmise that such societies regarded highly the mighty hunter and a particularly sharp stone axe. One suspects also that they stressed communal rights and obligations in contrast to individual ones, but tempered this with the recognition that adults who could not work would not survive.

Larger communities and more efficient food production allowed—and required—increased specialization of activity; farm lands and permanent buildings required greater property rights. Rulers, warriors, administrators and priests acted to protect from invaders, settle disputes, and establish moral codes. By authority, force, and religion, these new, specialized professions appropriated much of the harvest, leaving the farmers who worked the land little beyond the minimum subsistence necessary for life. Not for the last time, therefore, improvements in mankind's ability to control nature enriched the few who took advantage of the new circumstances, but left most of society little better off than before. Nevertheless, the agricultural surplus made possible a larger population, growing slowly and settling more densely. This, in turn, made possible the early steps of civilization: cities, trade, writing, metallurgy, and the opportunity to seek beauty and truth through art, philosophy, and the early sciences.

The discovery of metals, so important for the future of humanity that historians named epochs for the predominant metal, began perhaps by accident, when rocks containing copper melted around some cooking fire. Far easier to shape than stone, copper nevertheless suffered grave defects of softness and brittleness that hampered its use in tools and weapons. With the invention of bronze around 3,000 B.C., metal became more than an ornament. So important was bronze that its era lasted until approximately 1200 B.C. in Southwestern Asia.

With the new agricultural wealth concentrated in relatively few hands, trade and the production of luxuries increased. New crafts developed and old ones expanded. Artists improved their skills, notably in sculptures and reliefs, sometimes with impressive use of gold leaf. Jewelry of gold, silver and semi-precious stones like lapis lazuli and carnelian showed great concern for personal adornment among the wealthy. For the poor, seashells, colored stone, and beads of painted pottery sufficed. With even greater visual drama, towns developed, and architects experimented with new techniques for larger and more imposing buildings. Frequently the temple of the city god became the focus of town life, and its structure was often designed as much to impress the beholder as to provide shelter for priests and rituals. Not surprisingly, temples provide some of the earliest examples of monumental architecture.

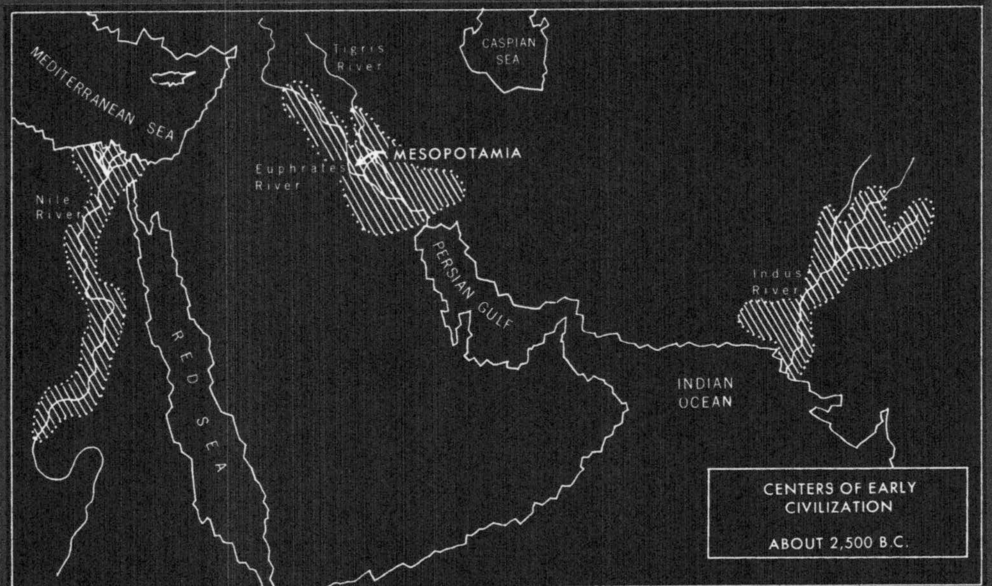

Other discoveries of the Bronze Age included improved and specialized tools, the wheel (or, more accurately, the fixed axle), and eventually the domestication of the horse. Together the last two made possible the chariot, the greatest weapon of the age. Early horses were too small to be ridden in battle, and without stirrups proved most unstable fighting platforms, but a chariot could overwhelm infantrymen. As technology armed the defenders of the river valleys with weapons superior to those of invaders from the hills, steppes, and mountains, the opportunity arose for the three great river valley civilizations to develop. Already the greatest of their achievements must have been the discovery of writing.

The Spread of Civilization

The development and spread of writing systems during the Bronze Age meant that information about business transactions, deeds of kings, and knowledge about the world could be recorded and preserved, to be read in other places and later times. Around 3,000 B.C., the first true writing appeared, among the Sumerians of the Tigris-Euphrates Plain. Their wedge-shaped characters, impressed with a reed pen on wet clay tablets, produced a script now called cuneiform. Its pictographic origins pre-dated the Sumerians, and it developed from the needs of business contracts and records in the growing cities. Cuneiform was a cumbersome and inefficient writing system, for each symbol could represent any one of several ideas or syllables, and later even sounds.

Cuneiform

Consequently, long years of training were required to become a scribe, capable of distinguishing alternate meanings. Nevertheless, cuneiform spread widely, as illustrated by one of the most dramatic recent archeological discoveries. Ebla, in northern Syria, lies hundreds of miles from Sumer. In the 1970s, archaeologists unearthed a royal library of some 16,000 clay tablets, in Sumerian and Eblian, dating from about 2,400 B.C. They provided new knowledge about the Canaanites of Abraham's time and also proof of the extent of Sumer's influence. Indeed, the writing system lingered long after Sumerian died out as a spoken language soon after 2,000 B.C., for cuneiform continued to be used for the Babylonian, Assyrian, Hittite and other languages, only dying out by the time of Christ.

Evidence suggests that writing began rather suddenly in the Nile Valley shortly after 3,000 B.C. Possibly the idea of writing, but not the system, was borrowed from Sumer. Drawings of gods, people, animals, birds and inanimate objects represented words, ideas and sounds. These so-called hieroglyphics were not a very efficient method of writing, but they were capable of recording information.

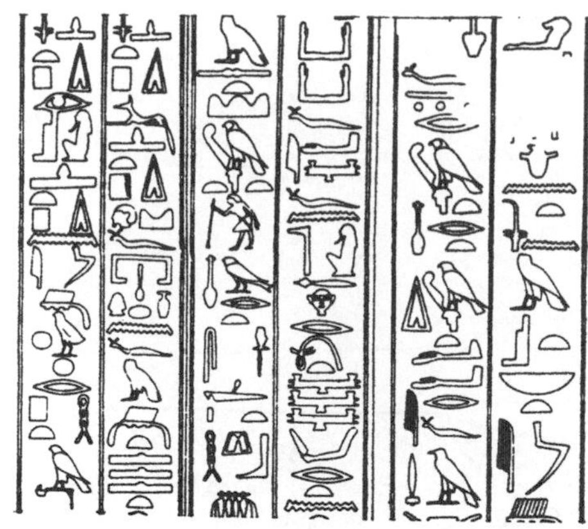

Hieroglyphics

It is not surprising that a third system of writing, the alphabet, replaced both cuneiform and hieroglyphics. Around the 12th century B.C., Canaanites living along the eastern shores of the Mediterranean assigned each symbol to represent a sound, rather than a picture, syllable, or idea. Easily applied to Semitic languages, whose words generally were characterized by three root sounds and simple vowels, the new script vastly shortened the task of learning to read and write. The alphabet thus broke the power akin to monopoly the scribes had previously enjoyed over writing. While the common man remained illiterate, merchants and officials adopted the idea of the alphabet to keep accounts and records, whatever their language.

Propelled by trade, the alphabet spread both east and west from Canaan and Phoenicia. By the 10th century B.C. it began to replace cuneiform in Babylonia, in the cursive Aramaic script whose descendants include modern Arabic and Hebrew. A century later the alphabet spread to Greece. The Greeks, in turn, used it in their far-flung trading colonies across Southern Europe, preserving in the process the name of the Phoenician city-state of Byblos, whose trade with Egypt provided Greeks with papyrus. The name remains in the English prefix *biblio* for book, and "The Book": *Bible.*

Using the Canaanite alphabet

Only after the conquest of Egypt by Alexander the Great in 332 B.C., and the rise thereafter of a great center of Hellenistic civilization at Alexandria, did the use of hieroglyphics decline. A modified Greek alphabet was devised for writing the native language, Coptic. Its use continued despite foreign rule by Greeks, Romans and Byzantines. Although after the Arab conquest, Coptic gradually fell into disuse in daily speech, it remains today in the liturgy of the Egyptian rite of Christianity, the Coptic Church.

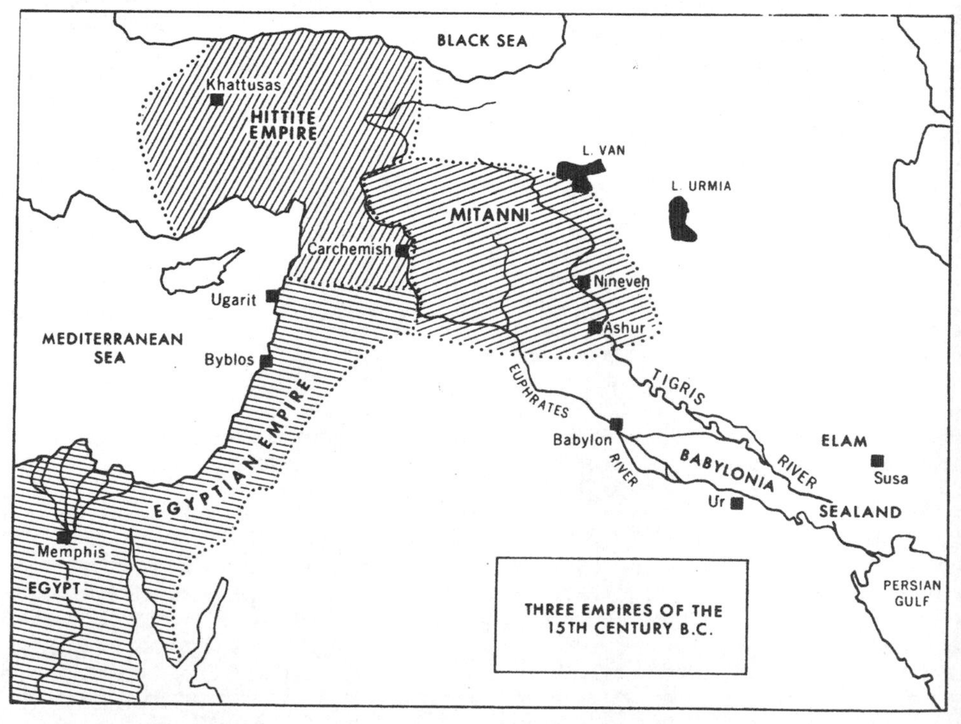

The Rise and Fall of Empires

The sport of an Assyrian king

During the many centuries of civilization's uneven advance, life for ordinary people often proved harsh. Only in the most fortunate times did the countryside and towns enjoy peace. Instead, farmers, merchants and craftsmen alike suffered interruption of work and safety because civilization provided the incentive and means for increasingly well-organized warfare.

Sometimes there were disputes over territory between neighboring communities. This led to a new dimension in fighting when one city set out to dominate others and when one little state began to subjugate others. In modern times, mechanized industrial production has permitted populations of entire nations to enjoy lives of relative comfort and convenience. In ancient times, however, production depended on human and animal energy for power and thus luxuries and comforts could be enjoyed only by small, privileged groups—and only through taking wealth from others, both slaves within society, and increasingly by conquest. Thus, the new inventions of civilization encouraged aggressive people, at first individually, then as groups and finally as nations, to reap personal benefit from the labor of others.

In the Nile Valley, where rival cities and regions had struggled for supremacy, there arose around 2850 B.C. a leader capable of unifying the distinctly separate regions of Upper and Lower Egypt (the Nile Delta). Hardly distinct from associated myths, Menes founded the first of 30 dynasties to rule Egypt. Claiming divine descent, his successors as kings or Pharaohs exerted enormous power over society. By the 26th century B.C., the pyramid age, rulers constructed enormous stone monuments as their tombs. Amazing in size and accuracy as feats of engineering, (e.g., the Great Pyramid contains 2,300,000 blocks and varies only 9½ inches on a side) they also bear dramatic witness to the organization of society and the Pharaohs' ability to extract labor and resources from the populace. However, one of the Pharaohs' greatest weaknesses was organizational: as local governors passed office to their sons, central authority weakened and the dynasty might collapse.

Although Egypt possessed then, as now, relatively secure borders against foreign attack in the form of deserts to the south, east, and west, strong Pharaohs frequently sought conquests abroad. During the Middle Kingdom (2100–1800 B.C.) and the New Kingdom (1550–1085 B.C.), Egyptian armies defeated the Nubians up the Nile and struggled for the wealth and control of Syria against both its inhabitants and powerful kingdoms in Mesopotamia. In the 15th century, Thutmose III fought seventeen campaigns and crossed the Euphrates; hieroglyphics at the Temple of Karnak in Egypt portrayed his conquests and booty.

The growth of powerful states in Mesopotamia illustrated many features common to Egypt, including the divine origin of rulers. However, geography decreed greater difficulties for those desiring to unify the land. The broader river valleys allowed city states to develop, and peoples to retain separate ethnic identities and languages. Moreover, invaders repeatedly pierced the natural barriers of desert and mountains and established new kingdoms. Thus, for most of the 3rd millennium B.C. the dominant political organization was the city-states of Sumer. In the mid-24th century B.C., however, Sargon, ruler of Akkad to the north, conquered Sumer and proclaimed himself king of Sumer and Akkad. The next centuries, marked by rivalry between the Akkadians and Sumerians as well as invading Amorites, nevertheless witnessed another great achievement of civilization: the promulgation of codes of law.

The first recorded law-giver, Ur-Nammu, was followed by the much more famous, though significantly harsher, Code of Hammurabi.

In the struggle for territory and the wealth of civilization, empires and dynas-

Ninevah: how it may have looked from ruins

ties rose and fell. Warfare took a new turn when horses were introduced into the civilized area from the northeast about 1,600 B.C. Horse-drawn chariots could crash through a line of foot soldiers. The infantry, poorer soldiers who could not afford horses and chariots, lost status in the new military organizations.

The rise of iron-smelting in Asia Minor around 1200 B.C. apparently provided an important strength for the next dominant power of Mesopotamia, the warlike and often cruel Assyrians, with their capital at Assur. Armed with iron weapons and heavy chariots, Assyrian troops proved invincible. They raided as far as the Black Sea and ruled to the Mediterranean, marching into captivity (and often extinction) skilled workmen and sometimes entire populations.

Enriched by conquests and the labor of subject peoples, the kings of Assyria adorned palaces and decorated impressive buildings with monuments and stone reliefs of colossal winged animals. The last powerful king of Assyria, Ashurbanipal (668–627 B.C.), personally directed an effort to collect the literature and learning of Mesopotamian civilizations. His royal library at Nineveh, excavated in the 19th century, acquired thousands of cuneiform tablets, including the Epic of Gilgamesh and the Babylonian Creation Epic. This single most important collection of cuneiform tablets provides modern historians with much of their knowledge of the culture and history of the Tigris-Euphrates Plain.

After the collapse of the Assyrian Empire, the center of power and wealth on the Tigris-Euphrates Plain shifted again to the city of Babylon. The neo-Babylonian (or Chaldean) Empire, which extended from the head of the Persian Gulf to the Mediterranean Sea, gathered wealth to give Babylon a final burst of glory before it gradually faded away.

The next great empire had its base in the mountains east of the Tigris River. The Medes were the first Iranian-speaking group to establish an empire. They dominated a large territory to the east and north of Babylonia. About the middle of the 6th century B.C. the empire of the Medes was taken over by their fellow Iranians and former subjects, the Persians. Under the leadership of Cyrus the Great and his successors, most of the civilized world except for East Asia and the defiant city-states of Greece, fell under the sway of the Persian Empire.

Like the Assyrians before them, the Persians did not hesitate to use force if the assigned taxes, or "gifts," were not sent by subject communities when due. On the other hand, many of the Persian rulers tried to gain voluntary submission of their subjects by showing toleration for local culture.

The vast Persian Empire was united by improved roads, a postal system for official use, uniform laws and employment of a single language for administrative purposes. The language of administration was not Persian, but Aramaic, which several centuries earlier had become dominant in business in the region between the Euphrates River and the Mediterranean Coast. The empire was divided into provinces, each with a governor *(satrap)* responsible to the Great King. Eventually the personal ambitions of these satraps contributed to the weakening of the empire. Another destructive force within the empire consisted of civil wars led by rival claimants to the throne. Each faction sought to gain power, receive honor and control the wealth produced by civilization.

The extension of Persian control over the Indus Valley had significant cultural effects. Interchange of religious and philosophical ideas was one. Another was the spread of the idea of an alphabet into South Asia, apparently in the 5th century B.C. The earliest alphabet used in the Indus-Ganges civilization preserved forms of the Aramaic alphabet used in the Persian Empire. During the period of Persian domination to the west of it, the Ganges Basin was under the control of rival minor kings. The largest of the kingdoms was that of Magadha near the mouth of the Ganges River. Meanwhile, civilization was also developing in the southern part of the Indian Peninsula.

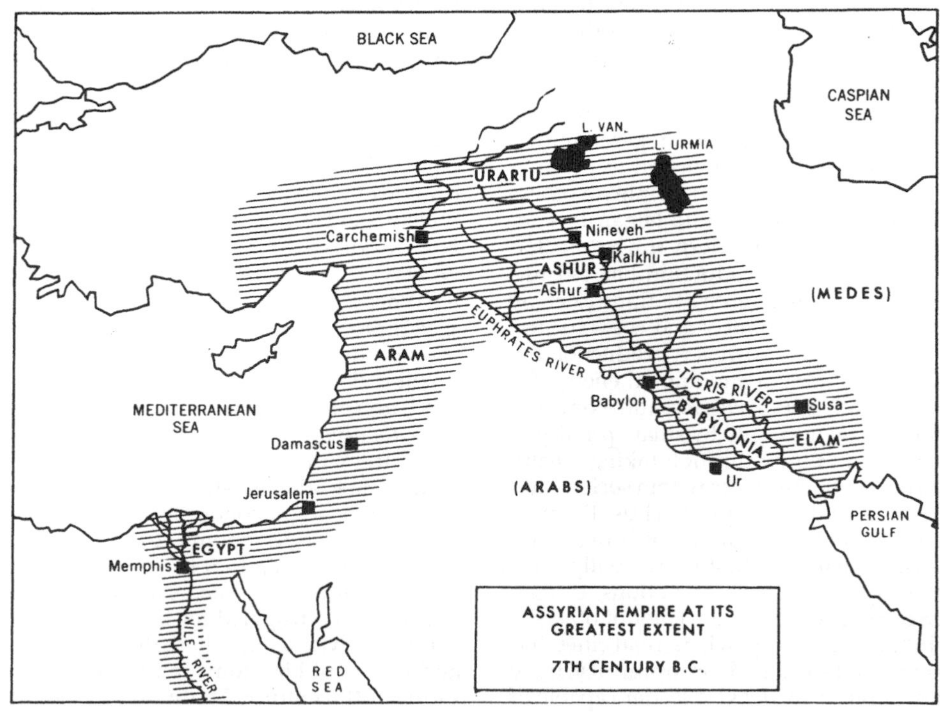

Hebrews and Judaeans

In contrast to the material splendor displayed by the great empires of the river valleys, the Hebrew tribes of the plains and highlands of Canaan gave to the world an idea, monotheism. In sharp contrast to the many gods worshipped by surrounding societies, the Hebrew prophets and scriptures proclaimed that one God, Yahweh (or Jehovah), created all; His legal code stipulated ethical and moral behavior far superior to the times. Preserved by Judaism and expanded by Christianity, the unique religion of the Hebrews has influenced European civilization more than any other cultural achievement of the ancient world.

Historical research in the 20th century lends credence to the accounts given in the Jewish scriptures, which also form the Old Testament of the Bible. The first patriarch, Abraham, claimed as ancestor by both Jewish and Arab societies, roamed Canaan with his herds, erecting in the midst of polytheism altars to Yahweh. His grandson, Jacob, also known as Israel, is generally regarded as the first Hebrew: from his sons descended the tribes of *B'nai Yisra'el*, the Children of Israel. After settling in Egypt for generations, under Moses the Hebrews escaped from captivity, to be led into Canaan by Joshua, perhaps around 1400 B.C.

Tempted by religions with visual gods—idols physically present that could be worshipped—the ancient Hebrews sometimes seem hardly distinguishable from other Canaanite tribes. They rarely ruled the entire land, and for several centuries lacked political unity even in the central highlands where their population was concentrated, running from north to south between the Mediterranean and the Jordan River. Their first king, Saul, faced invasions from the Philistines of the coastal plain and nomadic tribes to the south and east. However, after David succeeded to the throne around 1000 B.C., the little kingdom expanded in size and military prowess, reaching its zenith in peace and prosperity under David's son Solomon (961–922 B.C.), who built the first temple dedicated to Yahweh in Jerusalem, the capital.

At Solomon's death the state fractured, with the northern tribes establishing a Kingdom of Israel in Samaria. Lacking the great religious center of Jerusalem, and prey both to Canaanite religions and invasion by foreign armies, the Kingdom of Israel lasted until destroyed by the Assyrians in 722 B.C. Under the somewhat more capable kings of the House of David, the southern Kingdom of Judah survived until finally captured by the great neo-Babylonian ruler Nebuchadnezzar in 586 B.C. His troops carried off to exile in Babylon the royal family of Judah, together with many of the upper classes and skilled workers.

After Cyrus the Great captured Babylon in 539 B.C. (and in the process ended over two thousand years of Mesopotamian empires), the liberal religious policies of the new Persian Empire allowed some worshippers of Yahweh to return to the land

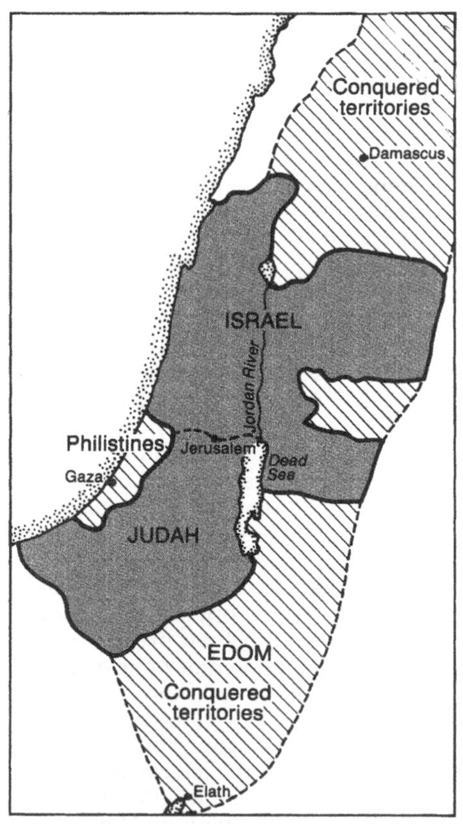

Israel and Judah under King David, c. 1000 B.C.

of their forebears, while others remained in Persia and Mesopotamia, developing a large and often prosperous center of Judaism. Despite local opposition, those who returned rebuilt the walls of Jerusalem, then the Temple itself, under tolerant Persian rule.

Far greater threats to Judaism followed the next conquerors, the Hellenistic armies of Alexander the Great in 332 B.C. Greek ideas soon came to dominate the Jewish upper classes as they discovered Greek athletics, music, and art as well as the Greek language itself. Rational religious concepts, especially about resurrection and angels, deeply impressed the wealthy, and separated them from most Jews, with their more traditional and pious values.

Direct attacks on Jewish religion and customs aroused greater resistance. When the Seleucid rulers of Syria, having captured Palestine, ordered pigs sacrificed to Zeus at the Temple, rebellion broke out. After bitter fighting, Jewish independence briefly flared anew under the Hasmonaeans, also known as the Maccabees (129–63 B.C.). Split by political rivalry, divided by religious factions and resented by non-Jewish inhabitants, the Jewish territories were easily annexed to Rome by Pompey in 63 B.C. Julius Caesar later appointed a governor named Antipater, an Idumaean from the coastal region previously conquered by the Hasmonaeans and himself possibly a descendant of the Israelites' ancient enemies, the Philistines. Converted to Judaism but opposed by the Hasmonaeans, Antipater and his sons struggled to control Judea. Finally, declared King of Judea by the Roman Senate, and aided by Roman troops, his son Herod succeeded in capturing Jerusalem (37 B.C.).

All accounts portray Herod as hated by his subjects, for many causes: a foreigner himself, a collaborator dependent on Roman rule, and a tyrant capable of killing his own sons as well as ordering the massacre of the infants of Bethlehem reported in the Gospels. Nevertheless, Herod built cities and established peace; for the non-Jews he provided festivals and Greek arts. For the Jews, he rebuilt the Temple, on a grander scale than ever before. His heirs proved less capable, and Caesar Augustus extended direct Roman rule over the area.

Increasing Jewish opposition to Rome broke into open rebellion in A.D. 66, after increasingly intolerant policies of the Emperors Caligula and Nero. Aided by rivalries for the throne in Rome, Judea became independent again, but four years later Titus defeated the Jewish armies and sacked Jerusalem after a lengthy siege. The temple, so recently rebuilt by Herod, was destroyed, and Jewish zealots holding the fortress of Masada overlooking the Dead Sea finally committed suicide rather than surrender. Again the Jewish population faced persecution and forced exile (called the Diaspora). After a second failed rebellion in 135 A.D. Rome made Judea a pagan colony, prohibiting Jews from living there, although believers survived in neighboring Galilee and elsewhere throughout the Roman Empire, as well as flourishing on occasion in Babylonia.

Solomon's Temple was made from timber brought from Tyre

A rabbi reads from the *Torah* in a synagogue

The Hellenistic Age, Roman Rule and Christianity

ALEXANDER

When the sudden and furious conquests of Alexander the Great shattered the dominance of Persian emperors in Asia, a new language and a new civilization began their lengthy domination of Southwest Asia. For centuries the city-states of Greece had learned from the older civilizations to the East. In the decades after 500 B.C. they fought off Persian invasions with difficulty, in heroic battles such as Marathon, Thermopylae, and Salamis. However, in 11 short years after 334 B.C., Alexander the Great, king of Macedonia though Greek in culture and education, captured the known world as far as India and established the greatest empire then known. This laid the political conditions for a new era of civilization called *Hellenistic*, meaning "Greek-like," in contrast to the previous Greek, or Hellenic.

Although Alexander's empire broke up after his death at the young age of 33, rival kingdoms succeeded him in Egypt (the Ptolemies) and Southwest Asia (the Seleucids). In both kingdoms Greeks and Macedonians who formed the urban upper class of rulers, soldiers, merchants and artisans mixed with the local population, in the process creating Hellenistic civilization. Trade flourished, from India and even China in the east to Italy and North Africa in the west. The growing wealth made possible great libraries at Alexandria and Pergamum as well as new cities and art. Science and learning advanced dramatically: among other achievements, scholars calculated the earth's circumference, founded geometry, and interpreted literature.

After 200 B.C., however, the Hellenistic world began to decline. Never solidly established east of Mesopotamia, the Seleucids retreated from the Iranian plateau and later from Mesopotamia in the face of Parthian invasions. Moreover, within the remaining territories, native populations increasingly rejected Greek beliefs, values, and language. With relative ease, then, the Roman general Pompey captured the remaining Seleucid territories (64 B.C.) and Egypt finally fell to Octavian (30 B.C.). However, the Romans failed to conquer either Mesopotamia or Persia from the Parthians. Moreover, within those Asian territories it did conquer, Greek rather than Latin remained the language of trade and learning. Significantly, the struggle between Hellenistic and local beliefs and culture continued, most importantly in Judea.

Into this world was born Jesus of Nazareth. Educated by his mother, rather than by either Jewish scribes or Hellenistic scholars, in adulthood he preached a message of love and obedience, of humility and enjoyment of the good. As reports of his apparent miracles spread, he rapidly gained a following of Jews and others who hoped for deliverance—divinely aided deliverance—from Rome. Nevertheless, his popularity and message threatened both the Hellenized Sadducees and the carefully traditional Pharisees. Charged by the Jewish leadership with claiming to be the Son of God, he seemed to Pontius Pilate, the Roman prefect, another agitator and resistance leader. Deserted by almost all his disciples and those who desired political revolution, he was crucified as King of the Jews. Dying at about the same age as Alexander, Jesus conquered no territories, founded no cities, and overthrew no empires.

To his followers, however, Jesus conquered much more than the world. According to the New Testament, this "Only Begotten Son" of God defeated death itself. His crucifixion made possible the redemption of mankind from sin. His apparent resurrection three days later, and subsequent return to heaven, brought the assurance of a final Judgment followed by a New Earth ruled by God. Passages from the Jewish scriptures—to Christians now the Old Testament—were interpreted to show him as the fulfillment of many prophecies of the Messiah (Greek, *Christ*). Within weeks of his death an active and growing church sprang up in Jerusalem.

Christianity first spread most rapidly among Jewish communities scattered about the Roman Empire. Within a generation, however, the preaching and writings of St. Paul rendered Christianity a world religion that promised salvation to all who believed, whether Jewish or not. Both hindered and helped by occasional persecution, Christianity spread rapidly, especially among the lower classes. By the middle of the 2nd century, the major rules of the faith had been established, the Canon of Biblical books had been largely selected, and the church had been organized into a hierarchy. When persecution by the Emperor Diocletian failed to destroy the church (303–311), the church triumphed, for his successor Constantine granted toleration and equality for Christianity while eliminating cults of the state.

In matters beyond religion, Constantine changed the face of the Roman Empire as well. In 330 A.D. he moved the capital from "heathen Rome" to Byzantium on the shores of the Bosporus. During the two centuries that followed, the eastern and western halves of the empire drifted apart, each facing invasion and struggling to maintain order and civilization in the midst of economic decay. Gradually there emerged in the east the Byzantine Empire, ruling over Greece as well as Asia Minor, geographical Syria, and Egypt. Greek in language, and Hellenistic in much of its culture, though still calling itself Rome, the Byzantine Empire mixed Christianity with the grandeur of Oriental potentates. The emperor ruled absolutely, as God's representative on earth, standing as head of the military, government, and church.

For almost a thousand years, the Byzantine Empire survived: an enormous accomplishment that contrasts with the total collapse of Roman rule in the West. During those centuries it witnessed great achievements in law, and it preserved Greek and Roman learning largely lost elsewhere. In art and architecture the stunning beauty created by Byzantine craftsmen remains at St. Marks in Venice and Hagia Sophia in Istanbul. As defenders of the faith, the Byzantine military stopped numerous invasions by infidels, and passed along to Russia and much of Eastern Europe, Orthodox Christianity and Greek-based alphabets. Nevertheless, bloodshed stains many pages of Byzantine history, and tolerance brightens few. When conflicts in theology and religion followed the same dividing lines as differences in language and culture between Greek rulers and native inhabitants of Egypt and Syria, the consequence was restlessness in those lands and weakened loyalties to the empire. When new armies appeared out of Arabia in the middle of the seventh century, Syrian, Egyptian, and North African possessions were quickly lost.

Zoroastrian, Buddhist and Hindu Cultures

When the Roman legions attempted to press eastward from Syria in the 1st century B.C., they were stopped by another military power, the Parthian Empire. This state had its origins in the 3rd century B.C. when warriors from Parthia, an area in the northeast part of the Iranian Plateau, gained local independence from Hellenistic rulers. Regarding themselves as the heirs of the first Persian Empire, the Parthians eventually expanded their control both east and west, building an empire that stretched from the Euphrates Plain to the Indus River.

Hellenistic culture declined, but was not totally eradicated, within the territory under Parthian rule. Native ideas, architecture, art and literature developed along independent lines. Although religious activity in Parthian domains is not well known, it seems that Zoroastrianism made great advances. This faith revered the teachings of Zarathustra, who lived during the 7th century B.C. In its developed form, Zoroastrianism stressed the struggle between two principal supernatural beings representing good and evil. The leading position was held by Ahura Mazda, the god of light and goodness.

About 225 A.D. the weakened leadership of the Parthians was replaced by a Persian dynasty descended from a little-known figure named Sassan. Occupying the Parthian capital of Ctesiphon on the Tigris as their own, the Sassanids presented themselves as the restorers of the purity of the first Persian Empire. Zoroastrianism took on its most highly developed form as the established religion of the government. The Sassanids increased the level of civilization in their territories by encouraging the development of cities.

The Sassanids also possessed a strong expansionist urge; this kept them in conflict with their neighbors, such as the Late Roman (Byzantine) Empire to the west, which had similar impulses. For a time in the 6th century and the first decades of the next, the Sassanid Empire was the world's leading power. In a final burst of militancy it captured Damascus and Jerusalem from Byzantium in 614, but lost them a decade and a half later. The Sassanid Empire, exhausted by the wars, succumbed to the attacks of the Muslim Arabs beginning with the fall of Ctesiphon in 637.

The golden age of Buddhism in the Indian Peninsula occurred in the state ruled by the Maurya family. At its height in the 3rd century B.C. the Mauryan Empire controlled the Ganges Basin, the Indus Valley and large regions to the south and northwest. The most illustrious ruler was Asoka (or Ashoka); during his long reign (273–232 B.C.) he turned from bloody wars of expansion to the peaceful teaching of Buddhism.

Gautama Buddha had lived several centuries earlier and it was Asoka's patronage of the Buddha's teachings which contributed greatly to the spread of Buddhism as a world religion.

Many inscribed pillars set up on Asoka's orders have been found in all parts of modern India, in Pakistan and in southern Afghanistan. These provide scholars with a picture of that early period, including Mauryan knowledge of the Hellenistic world to the west. After the death of Asoka the Great, the empire of the Maurya declined and finally ended in 185 B.C. It was replaced by many small states about which little information is available.

For nearly five centuries during which there was a notable development of trade with the outside world, attempts to build a new empire in the Indian Peninsula failed. Then in the early 4th century A.D., a territory nearly as extensive as that ruled by the Maurya was brought under the control of the Gupta dynasty. The Gupta period from the early 4th to the early 6th century is often described as the golden age of Hindu culture in the Ganges Basin, though the central and southern parts of the peninsula were to achieve their zenith of classical Hindu culture later.

The Gupta Empire reached its height from its capital of Ayodhya on the Ganges River, during the reign of Chandra Gupta II (A.D. 385 to 413). Later, particularly from about A.D. 480 to 490, Hindu civilization was badly mauled by invading Huns, who raided from bases north of the Hindu Kush Mountains. The menace of the Huns and the disturbances caused by various other peoples entering the Indian Peninsula from Central Asia did not subside for nearly a century. By then the region was again divided into a number of warring local kingdoms.

Little is known about events until the early 7th century, when a youth of only 16 years became king of a small state and attempted to build an empire. This king, Harsha, ruled well for 41 years. Not only was he a patron of art and literature, but was himself a poet and playwright. Three of his plays in Sanskrit have survived, including one called "The Pearl Necklace." With Harsha's death the last great Hindu kingdom in the Ganges-Indus region ended. Then a pattern of rival little kingdoms was a prelude to later foreign invasion.

Life-size sculpture of Buddha
Courtesy: Government of India

Muhammad and the Rise of Islam

A prayer in Tehran (late 19th century drawing)

In the rugged desert landscape of western Arabia, far from civilization's major centers, some six centuries after Christ the third great monotheistic religion arose with the preaching of Muhammad. This solemn and meditative man warned the citizens of the city of Mecca of a coming great cataclysm to end the earth, followed by a final judgment over all deeds that would grant to the righteous heaven, and to the evil, the fires of hell. From his initial messages of repentance and care of one's fellows, Muhammad's teachings expanded to fill almost all aspects of society. This religious protest first attracted a few followers, and later an entire city. Within a generation the entire Middle East lay conquered by a newly united people, and a new civilization, the Islamic, began its often brilliant rise.

Born about 572, probably after his father's death, Muhammad was orphaned as a child when his mother died. Few details of his early life are certain, but he grew up in a society undergoing dramatic social changes.

Prolonged conflict between the Sassanid Persian and Byzantine empires disrupted the traditional Mesopotamian trade route between India and the Mediterranean. One alternative route ran along the mountainous western coast of Arabia. Several Arabian tribes remained neutral in the great clash between Byzantium and Persia that stretched as far south as Yemen, and this encouraged trade. So did the religious customs that brought an annual truce to desert warfare and a pilgrimage to Mecca. Some Arab tribes, particularly Muhammad's own Quraysh, seized the opportunities, and exchanged herds for trade caravans. In the process Arab society itself changed significantly. For wealthy merchants, houses replaced tents, and the family structure strengthened as fathers viewed sons as assistants and successors. However, the increasing wealth meant greater disparities of wealth, and also a decline in loyalty to the clan and tribe. As the family strengthened, other social bonds weakened, and the poor increasingly found charity less common.

Raised by relatives and trained as a merchant, Muhammad had the good fortune to marry Khadija, a rather older widow of substantial wealth. Nevertheless, despite his financial success, he suffered inner distress over social wrongs, and meditated extensively. At the age of 40 he is alleged to have become conscious of a message from the angel Gabriel to praise the one God, Allah, as the Creator, and to care for the unfortunate.

Though living in a pagan culture, and often using the rhymed prose of common soothsayers, from his travels as a merchant, Muhammad had become familiar with the Jewish and Christian customs and beliefs. He now identified Allah as the God of their scriptures, recognized many of their prophets and considered himself the final Messenger, who recited the words sent from heaven.

Like many religious leaders, Muhammad at first appealed to relatives and friends, as well as the unfortunate. However, he aroused the hostility and anger of the leading merchants and politicians of Mecca by his vision of a dreadful judgment, by his strident demands for greater charity, and even more by his condemnation of pagan idol worship. This struck at the financial foundation of Meccan society, for pilgrimages to Mecca, with its famous black stone *Ka'aba* provided great opportunity for trade, and religion sanctioned an annual truce from raids, valuable to merchants and pilgrims alike.

Strongly conflicting with Muslim beliefs, Western scholars suggested that at one point Muhammad appeared to defuse the situation by confirming publicly that three female deities, al-Lat, al-Uzza and al-Manat, were the daughters of Allah; as such they could intercede with their Father. However, Muhammad's faithful soon recoiled at the implication of more than one god, and denounced the goddesses as mere inventions; the verses acknowledging them became the "Satanic Verses."

Muhammad and the Rise of Islam

As pressure became economic embargo and persecution, some followers fled to Ethiopia. By 622 Muhammad himself forsook Mecca for Yathrib, soon renamed Medina, "The City" of the Prophet. Celebrated as the *Hijra*, and marking the beginning of the Muslim era, the event nevertheless supports a variety of interpretations. Did Muhammad flee from persecution, or emigrate by choice? Did he fear the Meccans because of religious opposition, or Meccan opposition to his becoming the leader of a rival community strategically situated to strangle their trade route north?

Once in Medina, Muhammad became far more than a religious leader. He had come, by agreement, as the leader of the "Umma" or community: he was the primary secular authority. His Meccan followers abandoned the protection of the tribes of their birth by following him to Medina. Now they formed in effect a new tribe, and Muhammad became particularly responsible for their welfare, and that of the converts in Medina. Certainly, too, the visions continued, and included with the calls to repentance much practical material for the lawgiver of a new society.

The ten years Muhammad lived in Medina established the religion of "Islam" (pronounced like "this lamb"), or submission to God. Despite military defeats and political resistance from Jews and other non-believers resident in Medina, the Muslim ("One who submits") community grew and adopted the distinctive beliefs and practices that continue to the present. The individual Believer had five obligations. He must believe, confessing that "There is no God but Allah, and Muhammad is his Messenger," and bow in ritual prayer five times daily, prompted by the call from the minaret of the mosque. Annually, during the Islamic month of Ramadan, he must abstain from food, drink, and sex during the day. If possible, once during his lifetime he should undertake a pilgrimage (hajj) to Mecca. Finally, he must contribute annually a portion of his wealth as a charity or tax. Beyond these duties, the Muslim must accept the Quran ("Recitation") as the infallible word of God, interpreted by the consensus of the Islamic community as well as the traditions (or "sayings") of Muhammad carefully handed down over the generations.

Scholarly summaries of Islam, much like the paragraph above, rarely do justice to the combination of religious observances and custom in Islamic societies. The religion deliberately appeals to people of all languages and nations, and promises equality among the believers, who in forming the Umma attempt to have religious boundaries the same as political. For centuries the Umayyad and Abbasid caliphates achieved this in practice, as they fused subjects of varied languages and religions into a Muslim society ruled more or less within the framework of Islamic law. Despite Muhammad's condemnation of the practices of wealthy Meccans, private property is allowed, and numerous traditions report God's favor towards merchants. The payment of interest is forbidden, paralleling original Jewish and Christian views of usury.

In social aspects, Islam reinforced the position of the husband, allowing up to four wives and divorce on (his) demand, though he was urged to limit himself to one wife if he felt incapable of treating her fairly. Nevertheless, a woman retained the right to property she brought into a marriage, a privilege enjoyed centuries before Western nations granted similar property rights to women. On balance, scholars agree that Muhammad raised the status and condition of women, in part by rigidly punishing adultery as well as condemning the practice of female infanticide.

A Muslim's worship contrasts substantially with certain aspects of Jewish and Christian traditions, yet there are many similarities: sermons, ritual prayers, and reading (or recitation from memory) of the scriptures. However, singing and other music are remarkable for their absence, as are drawings, paintings, or sculptures of living things. Friday, the day of worship, is not a day of rest, and the believers commonly gather in the mosque in the afternoon, entering without shoes after washing hands and feet. Generally in Islam there is no equivalent of a priesthood: any believer may address the congregation, who stand in rows before the pulpit, with the women meeting separately. The dead await physical resurrection and the judgment, and are mourned extensively at the funeral and 40 days thereafter.

Thanks to the media, Westerners are much more familiar with more superficial regulations of Muslim society, such as amputation for certain crimes. The Quran strictly forbids wine, and by extension alcoholic drinks of any kind. Pork, carrion, and blood are forbidden, but in great contrast to the many unclean foods of Mosaic Law, Allah is thanked for the abundance of animals created to be eaten. In dress, the veil, often the trademark of a Muslim woman, in fact reflects preexisting Persian practice rather than explicit commands in the Quran or traditions of Muhammad. Instead, recognizing the power of temptation in sexual matters, Muslims must dress modestly, an injunction interpreted in some circles as requiring a woman's upper arms and shoulders to be covered. Despite the climate, men's legs are always covered.

Perhaps the Islamic doctrine most perplexing to modern, secular societies is the concept of *Jihad*, occasionally listed as a sixth individual duty. In everyday speech the term admits many meanings such as task or burden, or even one's struggle. In the context of religion, it often, though not exclusively, implied an armed struggle for the faith, to extend the boundaries of Islam or defend them from invasion by the infidel. Scholars a generation ago frequently stressed that many kinds of work for the benefit of the Umma could be considered Jihad. However, recent events, especially the rise of groups such as Islamic Jihad in Lebanon, leave little doubt that to a significant portion of the Muslim world, the struggle continues between Dar al-Salaam, the House of Peace (i.e., Islam) and the Dar al-Harb, the House of War (i.e., the unbelievers), fourteen hundred (Islamic) years after Muhammad's Hijra.

Then did Islam spread largely by conquest and forced conversions? Outside the Hijaz, only rarely: during the early conquests, Arab Muslims regarded with some suspicion those who wished to adopt the faith of their conquerors. In many places, it may have taken a century or two before the majority of the population accepted Islam. The converts' motives were mixed. To some, accepting the new religion removed discriminatory taxes. To others, a new community might bring different laws and personal advantages. Where missionary activity led to spiritual conviction, it often was the work of Islamic brotherhoods. Organized around a master, who initiated disciples in the ritual and beliefs of the particular brotherhood, these *Sufi* (from "one garbed in wool"; a holy man) orders reached beyond formal Islam into mysticism. They frequently incorporated ideas of existing religions, and this, like the missionary fervor of the members, advanced Islam as a spiritual force. On occasion, linked to Muslim rulers, Sufi brotherhoods also aided Islam as a conquering political force.

Islamic Expansion and Society: The Arab Caliphate

A new Mosque near Hofuf, Saudi Arabia combines traditional architecture with modern materials

For eight often precarious years after the Hijra, Muhammad struggled to maintain the Muslim community in the face of Meccan opposition. After 624, there were raids on Meccan caravans and battles as the Meccans counterattacked, as well as expulsions and massacres of the Jewish tribes of Medina and alliances struck with Bedouin tribes. Finally, in 630, Mecca capitulated, and the entire population converted. Almost all Arabia acknowledged Muhammad as politically supreme, though many tribes hardly accepted Islam. Two years later, however, at the height of his political power, Muhammad died. Although about 60 years of age, and too ill to worship in his last days, he left no messages about the future of Islamic society or its government.

As news spread that the Messenger of God lay dead, Muhammad's closest advisors met hurriedly to select a new leader of the community and thus avoid its disintegration under rival leaders. They settled on Abu Bakr, one of the earliest converts, and the next day the community publicly pledged allegiance to him. His position was imprecise, for Muhammad had been prophet, chief judge, supreme military commander, and sole legislator. Abu Bakr gained the vague title *Khalifat Rasul Allah:* "Successor to the Messenger of God," generally known in English as the Caliph. No prophet himself, but Commander of the Faithful, Abu Bakr led the Muslim community as Muhammad's secular successor and the sovereign in whose name the Friday prayers were offered.

Though only ruling for two years, Abu Bakr decided many of the crucial issues for the new Islamic state. When tribes admitting only political allegiance to Muhammad himself, and denying Islamic authority, attempted to secede, Abu Bakr sent armies under Khalid ibn al-Walid and other generals to conquer all Arabia. Quickly victorious, the Muslim armies established the central control of the Caliph, altering greatly the pre-existing Arab patterns of temporary alliances and confederations. Of additional importance, the apostate tribes soon were permitted to join the Muslim armies almost wholesale, thus turning energies long spent in violence between Arabs into a remarkable weapon directed by the Caliph.

The weapon quickly proved useful. Under Muhammad, Muslim raiders reached the fringes of the Byzantine Empire. Under Abu Bakr, out of the desert Arab columns appeared almost simultaneously, attacking Byzantine cities in Palestine and Persian troops in Iraq. The great mobility of their camel transport enabled them to strike far from the defending forces. At one crucial period Khalid ibn al-Walid's troops rapidly crossed the desert from Iraq to defeat the Byzantine army, leaving Palestine open to Muslim conquest.

Proclaimed caliph at Abu Bakr's passing, Umar (ruled 634–644) continued the policy of conquest. In 637 Arab armies defeated the Byzantine emperor at the Battle of Yarmuk, thus adding Syria to Arab conquests. The homeland of Christianity was lost to Christian rule, Jerusalem surrendering in 638. Meanwhile, at Kadisiya in Iraq, the Persian army was routed and Sassanid rule effectively destroyed. Soon afterwards, raiding forces unleashed by Umar on Egypt proved unexpectedly successful, and in 641 its last Byzantine city, Alexandria, surrendered. For the next century the Muslim expansion continued, to the east across the Iranian plateau into Central Asia, to the west across North Africa and into Spain and France.

To the European Christian imagination the Muslim conquests were a matter of religious crusades. Muhammad appeared as the anti-Christ of scripture; his conquering hordes offered captives the choice of conversion or the sword. Reality was somewhat more complicated, and explanations abound. Some causes lay within Arabia: possibly it was overpopulated, and now unified, its people sought living space outside it. Certainly religion played a great role in motivating individual soldiers, for death in battle to extend the boundaries of Islam brought God's mercy at the judgment and the promise of greater physical comforts and pleasures in heaven than on earth.

Other reasons for the dramatic rise lay outside the Muslim community. For the previous century in particular, the Byzantine and Sassanid empires had fought long and hard over Syria. Now both empires lay exhausted, separated by buffer states of Arab tribes unlikely to halt armies from Arabia. Under Byzantine rule, the Christian farmers of Syria and Egypt had long suffered heavy taxes, an alien language, and religious persecution over their theological interpretation of Christ. When Arab armies arrived, the vast majority of inhabitants did not resist: the Arabs offered not apostasy or death, but rather lower taxes and greater religious freedom. Likewise, in Iraq the native inhabitants had never become Persian; they too welcomed the Muslims. Only in Asia

Minor, with its Hellenic population, were the Arab invasions repulsed. In Iran, the collapse of the Sassanid dynasty enabled a rapid Muslim conquest, but it would become complicated in differing interpretations of Islam.

Administration of the new empire from Medina proved a difficult task. The caliph's share of the booty from the conquest provided great riches, but numerous problems arose. One was membership in the Muslim community, now a lucrative benefit, as the caliph's income from the captured territories was distributed among all Muslims, whose taxes in any case were minimal. Conversion, therefore, brought administrative difficulties: taxpayers became welfare recipients. To discourage them, converts had to be attached to Arab tribes. Despite Muhammad's message to all, regardless of tongue or nation, in some cases converts were not freed of their taxes on becoming Muslims. Later the contrast between religious appeal and fiscal expediency would fester and encourage the violent overthrow of one dynasty of caliphs.

Land ownership was another problem. Had Muslim soldiers received lands upon their conquest, their self-interest would have reduced the drive for further conquests. The issue was resolved in theory at least by keeping agricultural land as public land, the property of the caliph, with taxes on the harvest. Muslim troops were established in barracks cities on the fringes of cultivation, the better to keep them accustomed to a hard life and to separate ruling from ruled.

Where the local populations surrendered willingly, and possessed scriptures, they became *dhimmis*—"protected subjects." The exact rights depended on the local surrender terms, but in general, each recognized sect received religious toleration and maintained its own laws of personal status under its chief religious leader, typically a bishop or patriarch. For example, divorce, freely available to Muslim men, remained prohibited in most circumstances in the Christian communities. (A Christian desiring an additional wife, or divorce from his existing one, could usually convert to Islam.) Laws of marriage and inheritance likewise varied by religion.

Islamic toleration, though far greater than the practices in Europe of the period, did not mean freedom or equality, but limited rights mixed with discrimination. Non-Muslim testimony against a Muslim was suspect in the courts. New churches generally could not be built, nor church bells rung often, and any Muslim who adopted Christianity (unlikely though that was) risked the death penalty for apostasy. Members of the protected sects did avoid military obligations, but paid discriminatory taxes and observed separate codes of dress and behavior.

A devout man, Umar also led his community in religious matters as well as political. Many Muslims had memorized lengthy passages of Muhammad's messages, others had been written on palm-leaves, stones, and other available materials. However, renderings could differ. Therefore Umar began the collection of an authoritative book of Muhammad's recitations: the Quran. Completed and authorized by Umar's successor as Caliph, Uthman (644–656), the original *Quran* used the *Kufic* script lacking the dots that distinguish so many Arabic letters from each other. The result, not surprisingly, was variant readings, sometimes on matters of importance between Islamic groups.

The death of Uthman at the hands of assassins revealed deep rivalries within the Muslim world, rivalries of ideology and power. His rule of a dozen years illustrated the strength of the Quraysh, Muhammad's tribe from Mecca who had nevertheless been his most aggressive adversaries. Uthman appointed many Quraysh to high office, some of them close relatives newly

Pilgrims visiting the Ka'aba, sacred shrine of the Great Mosque in Mecca

acquainted with Islam. Their rule created consternation among political opponents, who saw the actions undermining Muhammad's goal of a *universal Muslim community*. Their sentiments found much satisfaction in the selection of Ali as the fourth, and final, Orthodox Caliph.

Muhammad's cousin and son-in-law, Ali nevertheless entered office surrounded by suspicions that he was an accomplice to the assassination of his predecessor, Uthman. After moving his capital from Medina to Iraq, and out-maneuvered by his opponents and facing rebellion within his own supporters over his policies, Ali was murdered in 661. His major opponent, Uthman's cousin Muawiya, became Caliph in Damascus, purchasing the acquiescence of Ali's oldest son, Hasan, and established the Umayyad dynasty of caliphs.

From their capital at Damascus, the Umayyads ruled the entire Muslim world. Attacks on the Byzantine Empire were renewed; Constantinople itself came under siege in 717. In some respects Arab, rather than Muslim, in their approach to administration, the Umayyads first used the existing Coptic, Greek and Persian administrations, ranging from coinage to provincial officials. Where necessary, as in Iraq, the Umayyads ruthlessly repressed disorder and established calm, for the first time in years. Religiously, however, by opposing Ali, and especially by defeating and killing his younger son Husayn at the battle of Karbala, the Umayyads split the Muslim world into two factions. Moreover, when they sought to rule by family descent, they introduced a fatal flaw. Those who had opposed in battle Muhammad's son-in-law and shed the blood of his grandson stirred resentments that in ninety years would overwhelm their descendants.

To the strife between Ali and the Umayyads is commonly traced the origins of the major sectarian divisions in the Muslim world. In particular, as the supporters of Ali broke away to form the *Shi'a* ("Partisans" of Ali), those accepting Umayyad rule became the *Sunni*, whose name implied orthodoxy. A number of aspects set Shi'a Islam firmly apart from Sunni practice. Its followers claim that Ali's family had been marked to lead the community from the start. Therefore even the pious caliphs Abu Bakr and Umar should be cursed; the Umayyads were clearly illegitimate. More commonly, however, the Shi'a termed those God appointed over them as Imams, or leaders, who possessed special knowledge needed to guide the Muslim community. Shi'ism commonly traces a succession of Imams, beginning with Ali. To the Imams was given authoritative understanding of the

Arab tribesmen water their horses

Quran; only traditions used by them are considered genuine.

Beginning as a political and social protest movement among Arabs, and quickly spreading to the converts, Shi'ism soon included many different groups with rival interpretations and leaders. According to most Shi'a, however, the twelfth Imam disappeared in 878. While the Imam remains hidden, the law and creed would be interpreted by religious scholars as his agents. Consequently, although Shi'a Islam originally began with stress on the rulership of the family of Ali, it has evolved to allow a greater role in political affairs for the religious establishment than does Sunni Islam. In addition, it awaits the hidden Imam, the Mahdi, who will return to save humanity.

Unsympathetic Western commentators typically note two distinct beliefs of Shi'a Islam, temporary marriage and dissimulation. Despite its obvious meaning, temporary marriage need not prove brief, though it may. Instead, it established a marriage for a period contracted in advance, frequently as long as 99 years in the case of a Shi'a man who marries a Christian woman who does not convert. Dissimulation, a practice foreign to western ethics, allows, or even enjoins a Shi'a to renounce his own religion when facing persecution or difficulty.

Beyond technical differences with Sunni Islam, the Shi'a bring to religion an emotional fervency often lacking in the more rational Sunni variety. The agony and death of Husayn at the battle of Karbala are portrayed annually at the anniversary with marches and flagellation. As their own blood streams from self-inflicted wounds, the marchers feel a unity with one who suffered 1300 years ago. For this and other reasons, many Shi'a consider life on the earth a brief interlude, and death fighting for Allah brings rapidly the joys of heaven.

The Shi'a played an important, but not exclusive, role in the overthrow of the Umayyad caliphate. After an extensive propaganda campaign concentrated among converts, in 746 rebellions broke out in the name of Abu al-Abbas, and drew support from many discontented groups in the empire. First Iran, then Iraq fell to the rebels with their standards of black, and in 750 they defeated and later almost annihilated the Umayyads. The new ruling dynasty, the Abbasid, claimed descent from Muhammad's uncle and the support of Ali's family. It ushered in a religious empire for all Muslims, in sharp contrast to the Arab kingdom of the Umayyads. Symbolizing the change, Abu al-Abbas moved the capital from Damascus to Iraq; his successor al-Mansur established the new empire along Persian rather than Arab lines, and constructed for it the magnificent capital of Baghdad. Amidst the pomp and titles, the Caliph exchanged the openness of an Arab tribal *sheikh* for an Oriental despot's glory and seclusion, complete with court executioner.

Trade and agricultural prosperity brought enormous wealth to Baghdad and its caliphs, who ruled an area larger than had Alexander the Great. Products from the Indus valley reached the Atlantic coast of Morocco, all without leaving the empire, and banks developed a widespread system of checks and letters of credit. Irrigation and drainage canals in the Tigris-Euphrates valley brought prosperity to the heart of the empire, and new foods, products and technologies spread across the vast area unified by administration, religion, and increasingly, the use of Arabic. Paper making came from China, sugar from India, and the textile centers like Damascus and Mosul enriched European languages as city names became synonymous with particular qualities of cloth (damask; muslin).

Under Harun al-Rashid, perhaps the most famous Abbasid caliph, Baghdad became the wealthiest city on earth. It hosted one of civilization's great intellectual flowerings. Scholars from a variety of ethnic backgrounds studied Greek and Hindu authors, advanced the sciences, especially optics and astronomy, adopted "Arabic" numerals from India, and invented algebra. Historians, geographers, and essayists wrote at length. In religion, Muslim scholars collected traditions attributed to Muhammad, and developed schools of law. Meanwhile, theologians disputed at length the role of logic in religion and the appropriate methods of interpreting the Quran.

From the moment they seized the caliphate, the Abbasids faced revolts and challenges to their rule, from disenchanted supporters, Shi'a splinter groups, and opportunists. In such a vast empire, control from the center often weakened along the fringes, where independent Muslim states arose. In Baghdad itself, power fell increasingly into the hands of the vizir, or chief minister, who eventually attempted to make the office hereditary. Generals intervened between rival caliphs to decide succession to the throne, and what little power remained eventually fell into the hands of the Turkish bodyguard. Although caliphs did remain, by the end of the tenth century they ceased to rule even nominally territory outside Iraq. Two hundred years after the Abbasids seized power, the reinvigorated Iranians and Turks, new to both Islam and the Middle East, came to dominate the Asian lands of Islam.

A European artist's concept of a Umayyad palace in Damascus. European reports of Arab societies often exaggerated the exotic and the sensual.

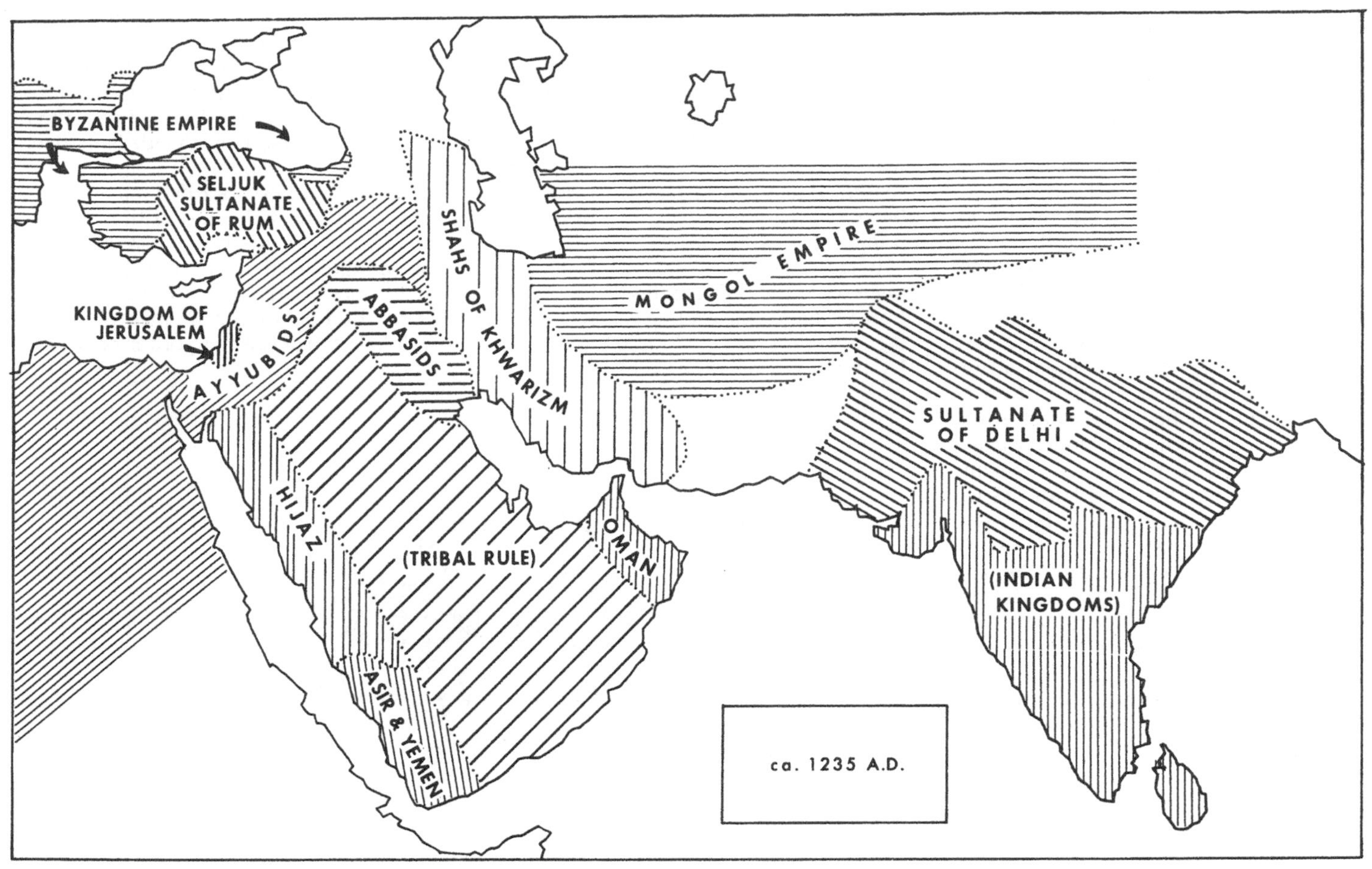

During the Middle Islamic Period (the 10th to 15th centuries A.D.; 4th to 9th centuries by the Muslim calendar) waves of invaders assaulted civilization in Southwest Asia. There was an enormous loss of human life in these invasions, as well as extensive damage to the economy. The Turkish and European inroads in this period were relatively temperate preludes to the far more destructive incursions of the Mongols and their allies.

Adventuring bands of Turks from Central Asia began arriving in Southwest Asia in the 10th century. Soon they started establishing themselves as a kind of military aristocracy, and by the 12th century various regions from Asia Minor to the Ganges River had overlords of Turkish origin. While introducing a new military fierceness into society, the Turkish rulers patronized writers, poets and learned men, especially Persians. They readily adopted Islam with their own modifications.

The rapid influx of Turks into Iraq in the 11th century led to the establishment of a vast empire stretching from Central Asia to the Syrian coast. This was ruled by Toghril, of the Seljuk (Saljuq) clan, who made himself Sultan in Baghdad in 1055 while reducing the Abbasid Caliph to the status of a spiritual figurehead without power. A decade and a half later, one of Toghril's nephews, Alp Arslan, defeated the Byzantine army and made the emperor a prisoner. This victory opened Asia Minor to Turkish immigration; in 1078 these newcomers established the Seljuk Sultanate of Rum. (*Rum,* pronounced like "room" in English, was the Asian name for the Byzantine Empire, which was still called Rome).

Seljuk attacks on the Byzantine Empire and interference with European pilgrims to Jerusalem helped inspire the Pope in 1095 to proclaim a Holy War to recapture the Holy Land. The soldiers of the First Crusade had to fight their way through the Seljuk Sultanate of Rum in order to reach Jerusalem and wrest it from the garrison placed there by a Muslim government based in Egypt. These Europeans joined in the turmoil and warfare of the Eastern Mediterranean, inflicting and receiving great loss of life. On capturing Jerusalem in 1099, the Crusaders set about an indiscriminate massacre of Muslims and Jews, but in general they were neither more nor less cruel than their foes.

The Latin Kingdom of Jerusalem was established to govern the Holy Land. It lost Jerusalem to the Muslims under the leadership of Salah ad-Din (Saladin) in 1187, but regained it again after his death. The Crusader kingdom finally lost the Holy City in 1244, but held coastal enclaves until near the end of the century. At times, the Crusaders had Muslim allies against other Muslim armies, so confused were the times and intense the political rivalries.

Seljuk power was not permanent, and rival Turkish leaders displaced them. In Iran, a line of rulers known as the Shahs of Khwarezm (Khwarizm) became prominent in the 12th century, but their power was too fragile to protect the region against new invaders.

Turks also established kingdoms in Buddhist and Hindu lands. Although there had been earlier Muslim raids into the Indus Valley, the main Muslim conquerors in the northern Indian Peninsula were Turks. The rival Hindu *Rajputs* (princes) were unable to provide a unified defense against the Turkish warriors.

In the second half of the 12th century, Turkish warriors led by the Sultan of Ghur wrought great destruction on Indian civilization. Their mounted archers swept down the Ganges Valley. Hindu temples were made into mosques and attempts were made to force people to convert to Islam. Buddhism in its stronghold in Bi-

The Barbarian Invasions

har had its monks massacred, its books burned and its temples destroyed. Buddhism was virtually extinguished and Hindu rule was ended in northern India. From that time onward, Muslim ruler and Hindu subject were always aware of belonging to different orders.

Muslim rule in India, established following the conquests by the armies from Ghur, took the form of the Sultanate of Delhi. In 1206 a Turkish general (and legally a slave) seized the opportunity created by the murder of the Sultan of Ghur and proclaimed himself Sultan of Delhi. Although hampered by frequent struggles over the succession, the Sultanate expanded, and reached its greatest extent in the early 14th century, when it ruled nearly all of the Indian Peninsula. In some ways, the Sultanate flourished, for despite severe taxation of the largely Hindu peasantry, great prosperity developed in trade and the production of textiles in Bengal, Lahore, and Kashmir. Nevertheless, decay set in rapidly, and during the later 14th century the Sultanate of Delhi ruled only Northern India.

Southwest Asia began to feel the full force of the Mongol Empire in 1219 when an army of some 100,000 led by Chingis Khan (Genghis Khan), invaded Iran. Seeking vengeance against the Shahs of Khwarezm for their early cruelty against Mongol subjects, the invading Mongols looted, destroyed and massacred as they advanced. Tens of thousands of people were slaughtered, while only the craftsmen were spared for use as slaves in Mongolia.

Part of Chingis Khan's hordes turned south to ravage the Indus Valley and Punjab. Delhi became a refuge for Muslims escaping from Mongol terror. Suddenly, for no apparent reason, the Mongol hordes turned back for the long journey home, laden with the wealth of the devastated lands through which they had passed.

Again in 1227 the Mongols and their allied hordes returned to plunder. For ten years they could not be withstood by any force in Iran or in the Tigris-Euphrates Valley. Of all the great Muslim centers of civilization, only Cairo escaped entirely unscathed and the Mamluk rulers of Egypt gained much prestige for defeating a Mongol force in Palestine. By the middle of the 13th century, much of Southwest Asia was either ruled by Mongols or paying tribute to them. However, the next generation of Mongol rulers adopted Islam. Soon the empire began to break up into small states and the way was open for another empire builder.

Claiming to be a descendant of Chingis Khan, Timur Lang (Tamerlane) looms prominently in the Mongol tradition. He rose to power in the second half of the 14th century, using a dubious devotion to Islam for his political purposes. On the one hand, he may be pictured as a fierce warrior on horseback, wielding a bloody sword as he leads his hordes of Mongols and Turks over civilized areas which have no power to resist. On the other hand, he may also quite accurately be visualized seated in a splendid palace, surrounded by poets and admiring rare works of art, in his capital at Samarkand.

Before his death in 1405, Timur conquered the Tigris-Euphrates Plain and all of Iran. He raided the leading cities of his time, including Damascus, Moscow and Delhi. Upon the last-mentioned, he poured such destruction that a century was required for it to recover. In the very last years of his life, he defeated the rising Ottoman Empire in battle, took its Sultan prisoner and seized control of Asia Minor. Using the wealth of his vast domains, Timur made Samarkand a center of civilization.

Timur's successors ruled a smaller territory until near the end of the 15th century. They presided over a mixed Turkish-Mongol-Iranian culture which created many masterpieces of art and literature. With the end of the invasions of Central Asia hordes, a new order could take shape.

Gustave Doré's drawing of the Crusaders storming the walls of Antioch in 1098 on their way to liberate Jerusalem from the Muslims

The Safavid, Ottoman and Mogul Empires

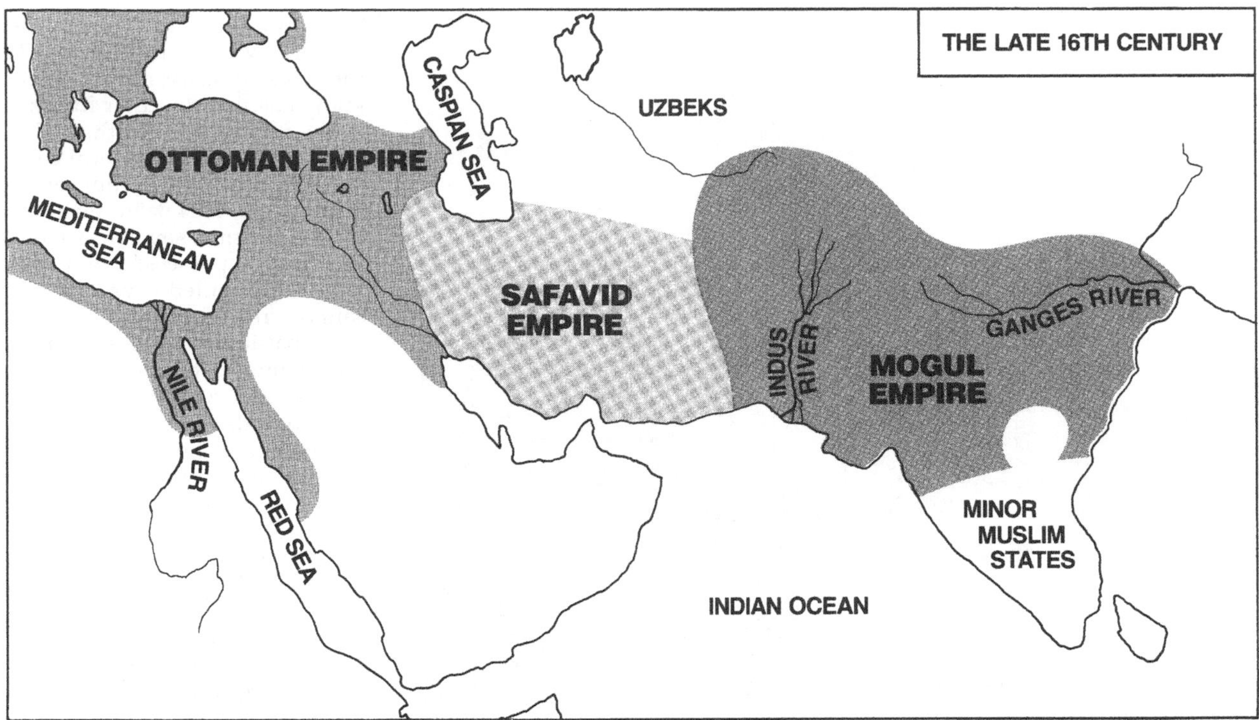

In many ways, Islamic civilization reached its height in the 16th century. Vigorous and ambitious, its religion and rulers dominated southern and western Asia, southeastern Europe, and all North Africa. It also swept south across the Sahara and through the savanna as far as the fringes of the rainforest. The caliphate, by now only an empty title in Cairo, failed to unite the Muslim world, and numerous independent Muslim states existed along the fringes. Nevertheless, the heart of the Muslim world divided into three major Islamic empires, each centers of an important culture.

In the middle, centered on the Iranian Plateau, the Safavid Empire split the Muslim world, for its strongly Shi'a Islam contrasted with the Sunni views both in the Mogul Empire in India and the Safavids' bitter rival to the west, the Ottoman Empire.

The provinces of Iran had witnessed numerous struggles for power after the rapid collapse of Timur's empire, especially among the Turkmen tribes of the north and west. In 1503, Ismail Safavi, a youth merely sixteen years old but hereditary leader of a Shi'a religious order, proclaimed himself *Shah* and Shi'ism the sole religion. Offering all the choice between conversion to Shi'ism or death, Ismail rapidly united the Iranian peasantry, urban classes and Turkish warriors into a new society and state. In time, Iranian civilians replaced warriors in the administration and central authority replaced mystical adoration of Shah Ismail as the basis of government.

From its very beginning, the Safavid state struggled with the Ottoman Empire to the West, for it appealed to Turkish tribesmen with Shi'a leanings. Nevertheless, in battle the swords, arrows, and light firearms of Shah Ismail's warriors proved no match against Ottoman muskets and artillery. After losing much of Asia Minor, and then Iraq, the Safavids in the 17th century accepted a border between Iran and Iraq that largely remains today.

In retrospect, Shah Ismail attacked the Ottoman Empire during the zenith of its 600-year-long history. It began inconspicuously around 1299, when a Turkish warrior named Osman (Arabic *Uthman;* to Europeans, *Ottoman)* proclaimed himself sultan in northwestern Asia Minor. Welcoming all who would fight Byzantium, he allied his dynasty with *Sufi* brotherhoods and merchant guilds, and adopted Byzantine administrative techniques. Steadily the Ottoman forces advanced against Christian Byzantium. By the middle of the 14th century, permanent forces had replaced mere raiding groups across the Bosporus, isolating Constantinople. The capital itself lingered for nearly a century, spared by Timur's crushing defeat of the Ottomans in Anatolia (Asia Minor). Finally, in 1453, Sultan Mehmet II massed his armies against the Byzantine capital and captured it, ending a millennium this "Rome" had ruled Eastern Christendom. Under its Turkish name, Istanbul, the city flourished as the Ottoman capital. Sultans and leading officials adorned the city with palaces and mosques, changing the skyline. Meanwhile, the conquests continued; a century later, the Balkans conquered, Ottoman troops unsuccessfully attacked Vienna.

The Ottoman Empire drew its strengths from many sources. To the uncommon valor and wisdom of the first ten sultans must be added the willingness to adopt new skills and technology. The *devshirme,* in effect a tax on Christians paid in young boys who were enslaved and educated into Islam, provided both soldiers for a standing army and administrators single-minded in devotion to the Sultan and lacking family loyalty. Financially, conquests in Europe produced great loot and tribute; in turn they enabled further aggression against Christian states. Only after 200 years did the sultans attempt significant conquest of Muslim territories. Then, under Selim I (1512–1520) dramatic conquests brought under Ottoman rule much of Anatolia and Iraq, as well as Syria, Palestine and Egypt. Under Suleyman I ("Suleiman the Magnificent"), known to his subjects as "The Lawgiver," the empire reached the height of its power and grandeur.

In contrast, by the 17th century the Ottoman Empire illustrated many signs of decay. At first Austria, then Poland and Russia pushed back the Sultan's armies in the Balkans, recapturing Hungary and parts of Yugoslavia. In the Mediterranean,

The Safavid, Ottoman and Mogul Empires

"The Golden Horn"—Constantinople in the days of yore

the Ottoman navy had suffered decisive defeat. Within the empire, anarchy spread as local administrators attempted to maintain their positions, and the sale of offices became a regular practice. The *devshirme* collapsed, and troops garrisoned in many cities rebelled. Although the capable Korprulu family *vizirs* restored administration, the Ottomans increasingly lagged behind Europe in scientific pursuits and modern learning, with unsurprising consequences for military technology. As the center of world trade shifted to the Atlantic following the discovery of the New World and sailing routes to India, the Ottoman Empire increasingly stagnated economically as well. If diplomacy and European rivalries slowed the loss of territory, the descent nevertheless seemed certain to most observers.

A Muslim Empire in India

The Mogul Empire did not rise immediately out of the ruins of the Sultanate of Delhi which had ended with a period of peace, prosperity and construction of public works, such as new irrigation canals and dams. The last important ruler let authority slip into the hands of local officials. This meant that there was no unified resistance to the hordes led by Timur Lang into the Indus-Ganges basin in 1398. Some 90,000 horsemen killed and looted without restraint, and it is said that when Timur's army returned to Samarkand, there was not a man who did not take at least twenty Indians home as slaves.

So complete was Timur's destruction of the Sultanate of Delhi that another great state did not arise in the area until the Mogul Empire was founded in about 1525. In the interim, a number of kingdoms with Muslim rulers flourished. These sultans, mainly of Turkish origin, were in general more tolerant of the culture of their Hindu subjects than the sultans of Delhi had been. Learning and the arts developed a distinctive style in this period of Islamic history in the Indian Peninsula.

The only Hindu state during the period was Vijayanagar, a name meaning "City of Victory," located on the southern tip of the Peninsula. For some two centuries after its establishment just before the middle of the 14th century, Vijayanagar defended itself against Muslim encroachment from the north and carried on Hindu cultural and artistic traditions. The combined forces of three Muslim states in the central plateau of the Peninsula finally defeated Vijayanagar in 1565 after its aged ruler was unexpectedly captured in battle and beheaded. The city of Vijayanagar was sacked by Muslim forces while many Hindus and their temples were destroyed. The fall of this state marked the end of Hindu political power.

Just after 1500, a new Islamic state was founded in Afghanistan by Babur, an adventurer from Turkistan far to the north. Barely twenty years old, and a man of taste and letters as well as the power to unite his soldiers, he claimed descent from Timur and thus the right to rule as king. Mongol by proclamation, but Turkish in race, his dynasty nevertheless became known as the Mogul or Mughal. Invited to the plains between the Indus and the Ganges by disaffected local chiefs willing to replace their own king with another, beginning in 1524 Babur invaded northern India. His army, small in size but compact and united, possessed two great advantages: unequalled cavalry, and superior cannon from Turkey. In 1526, in a single great battle outside Delhi, he destroyed the enemy military, comprised mostly of Turkish and Afghan foreigners like himself. No national movement resisted his advance, and he found himself master of a personal domain across the plains of northern India as far east as the borders of Bengal.

Plunged into disorder on the early death of Babur, the Mogul Empire finally took shape under his grandson, Akbar. Only thirteen when he came to the throne, Akbar proved a superb general, moving armies rapidly and conquering all but the southern quarter of India. Much more than a soldier, however, Akbar established stable government that would last a century. He reached beyond mere military power to become the accepted ruler of most of India, most importantly by incorporating the Rajput chiefs, though Hindu, as governors and military commanders. Indeed, he even married a Rajput princess. As a result, the Hindu community largely accepted Akbar's empire as their own. Open-minded in religious matters, he welcomed Zoroastrians and Jesuits to his court as well as Hindus and Muslims; there was also an attempt to develop an eclectic cult centered on himself.

His successors lacked both his power and his wisdom; the empire inevitably declined. The decay came gradually, and the Moguls sponsored learning through libraries and schools, and in art perfected a distinctive fusion of Persian and Hindu styles in the Taj Mahal. However, the sixth Mogul ruler, Aurangzeb (1658–1707) proved a zealous Muslim whose limited toleration of non-Muslims increased Hindu dissatisfaction and contrasted sharply with the policies of Akbar. A man of battle for much of his long reign, Aurangzeb attempted to unite all India, fighting Muslim states as well as Hindu ones in the south.

By the time of his death, the merchant vanguard of the next wave of foreign invaders of India had appeared, not in the traditional invasion route in the northwest, but in important ports along the coasts. After decades of disorder, British rule would replace Mogul, though the dynasty nominally ruled in Delhi until abolished by the British in 1857.

European Expansion into the Indian Ocean

Until the end of the 15th century, the direct routes from Europe to the East and its lucrative trade were blocked by the Ottoman Empire and Egypt. Europeans finally overcame the obstacle by outflanking the Muslims entirely, sailing boldly around the southern tip of Africa. When the Portuguese navigator Vasco da Gama reached the Indian Ocean by this route, his tiny fleet opened up a new era. First, only patterns of trade were altered, but in later centuries the total political organization of Southwest Asia was affected. Aggressive Europeans, possessing increasingly superior weapons and better-trained soldiers, gradually made themselves masters of the vast region.

When the first Portuguese reached the Indian Ocean in 1498, they sought only to monopolize sea trade, not to rule a land empire. By 1509 they had put an end to Arab sea power. Portugal then began building a maritime empire. Alfonso Albuquerque, who had become governor of the Portuguese settlements in India in 1509, carried forward the program of building forts at strategic locations on the coasts of India, Persia, Arabia and Africa. His fleet also continued to prevent native ships from carrying items so profitable in European markets. His nation thus gained almost a monopoly on trade in these goods, and required their transport in Portuguese ships, in keeping with the economic theory of mercantilism. Albuquerque on occasion treated with extreme cruelty rebellious subjects or Asian merchants attempting to compete with the Portuguese monopoly.

For over a century the Portuguese remained the chief traders across the Indian Ocean. By concentrating their activities on the sea and a few ports in regions without strong governments, they did not affect significantly the history of the nations of Asia, though colonies in East Africa eventually spread inland. By the end of the 16th century, however, other Europeans, eager for a share of the trade, began forcing their way into the Indian Ocean. Later, in 1650, the Portuguese position further declined after evacuation of the Arabian port of Masqat (Muscat) with accompanying loss of control of the Persian Gulf.

The 17th century belonged predominantly to Dutch merchants and sea power. They left less of a mark on Southwest Asia than had the Portuguese traders, for the Dutch preoccupation was with the spice lands farther east. The 18th century was characterized by rivalry between French and British interests seeking control of India and the approaches to it. In the end, Britain dislodged France from all but a few small enclaves, similar to those retained by Portugal.

The governments of the Netherlands, France and Britain played only secondary roles in this commercial expansion. Companies chartered by the respective kings were the leading agents. The Dutch East India Company, chartered in 1602, achieved remarkable success. With fortified trading depots at two places in Sri Lanka (Ceylon) and a number on the coasts of southern India and Southeast Asia, the company flourished during the 17th century. With aid from the strong Dutch fleet, it captured the spice trade from Portugal, despite British and French competition. When the demand for Asian spices fell, it encouraged the production of coffee, tea, and cocoa. Over two hundred years, its annual dividends reportedly averaged 18%.

The British East India Company, chartered in 1600, became even more important, both as one of the first permanent joint-stock companies and in the English company allowed in the region, it received authority to administer government where it operated. Concentrating on India, while the Dutch withdrew to the Spice Islands (Indonesia), the British East India Company established itself first at Surat on the west coast of India, with the Mogul permission. Surat rapidly developed into the most prosperous trading center in the country. Later posts followed at Bombay, Madras, and Calcutta, each to become a center of British influence. The East India Company traded especially in indigo, saltpeter, textiles and spices, often purchasing goods of greater value from India than it could sell there, and supplying silver to make up the difference.

During the 18th century the French Company of the East Indies (founded 1664) slowly emerged as the chief European rival to the British East India Company in both commerce and political influence. When the two nations fought in Europe, competition between the two companies became military in India. The British East India Company won the struggle and limited French influence to several small ports. They only rejoined India after the subcontinent's independence in 1947.

The Creation of the British Raj

George III (1738–1820)

A consistent theme in the history of the Middle East and South Asia from the late 18th century until 1947 was the expansion and strengthening of British colonial rule, often described by the Hindi and Urdu word "Raj", meaning "sway" or "rule." Beginning in Bengal, in eastern India around 1750, its encroachment elsewhere often followed the desire to protect existing possessions and trade routes.

By the mid-18th century, India lay ripe for foreign intervention. In the north, the Mogul Empire had reached a state of advanced decay, both in quality of rule and defeats by Indian and foreign enemies. Particularly threatening were the Marathas, a Hindu people adept at warfare and distinguished by their own language. They lived along the western coast and in central India, but spread across the sub-continent. In a series of wars with the Mogul Empire they exhausted its resources, but in the process the Maratha kingdom itself broke up into a loose confederation of states. While they dominated central India, they failed to establish firm central government. Henceforth the Marathas became raiders known for their rapacity and ruthlessness, plundering widely and feared by Hindus as much as by Muslims.

Then, in 1739, the Persian ruler Nadir Shah captured Delhi, plundering the treasury and Peacock Throne, and massacring the city's inhabitants. In a little more than a decade, it was the Afghan army's turn. Finally, in 1761, the Maratha army attempted to stop a renewed Afghan invasion in a battle near Delhi. The decisive defeat of the Marathas and the deaths of many of their leaders appeared to place India within the Afghan king's grasp. At this crucial moment, his troops mutinied. Thus India broke up into many smaller states, divided and lacking in direction just when Europeans sought control.

Learning from its French rival, by the 1740s, the British East India Company began to strike alliances with Indian rulers. Its weapons included interfering with the succession of Indian princes and bribery. Granting military aid to favorites often proved very effective, for European weapons and techniques increasingly outpaced local ones. With the Company's victory at Plessey in 1757, it effectively conquered Bengal, and British territorial rule began in India.

Circumstances encouraged the British domain to expand. Native attacks on Indian allies led to the retaliation and conquest. War with France in Europe led to conquest in India. Reports of great wealth in the hands of native rulers encouraged Company officials to conquer. That they succeeded so easily also was the result of the caliber of a number of Company officials who possessed the vision of conquest along with exceptional talents and freedom to operate. However, their harsh treatment of the Indian populations led to interference by Parliament in London, culminating in the India Act of 1784. This placed British rule in India under a governor-general, appointed not by the Company, but by the British government. Ironically, it was Lord Cornwallis, loser of Britain's American colonies at the Battle of Yorktown, who preserved those in India as the new governor-general.

Imperial Rule: The Raj at Its Height—and Fall

Warfare against Napoleon, in Egypt and in Europe, combined with circumstances in India to encourage the last great expansion of British rule. The British conquests were swift. In hardly more than twenty years after 1795, large territories fell: Mysore and Hyderabad in the south, the Marathas in the center, and finally the remaining Rajput states in the west. British India more than doubled in size, and unity of the peninsula within its natural boundaries became an appealing goal. Unity would end foreign intrigue and permit British commercial expansion at minimal defense costs. Moreover, ending the virtual state of anarchy in parts of India would bring peace to the inhabitants. The East India Company had traded with Indians for a century and a half before warring with them; for almost another century and a half the British would rule India.

The British Raj brought many advantages, including peace after the ravages of lengthy wars. Physically the country changed with the construction of harbors, railroads, and irrigation projects. Colleges and universities educated an Indian elite in science and medicine, and the administration became more regular and less arbitrary. *Suttee,* the practice of burning widows on the funeral pyres of their husbands, was banned. In general, though, the British granted religious toleration in areas they ruled directly, and in the many princely states allowed traditional dynasties to continue, whether Muslim or Hindu.

On the other hand, much was not well. Indian handicrafts suffered from cheap cloth manufactured in England. Each improvement in transportation rendered the competition worse, while British policies retarded the development of Indian industry. High taxes rendered the peasants impoverished tenants, and few schools served the masses. Moreover, in Indian eyes British rule involved westernization to an unsettling degree, and in 1857 the introduction of rifle cartridges greased with animal fat offended Muslim troops (over lard) as well as Hindu (over cows' grease). The Indian Mutiny of 1857–1858, at times savage and repressed sternly, brought the attention of London and reforms. The East India Company, long stripped of its trade monopoly, was dissolved. The British Raj now meant authority lay with Parliament and monarch in England.

Possession of India encouraged further British imperial expansion, for both strategic and commercial purposes. After the defeat of Napoleon in 1815, Britain's great European rival became Tsarist Russia, whose expansion towards both India and the Middle East seemed threatening. Recognizing that the traditional invaders' route to India came from the northwest, British officials extended their rule in that direction, adding the Punjab and Kashmir, then later Baluchistan (bordering Iran), and finally the North-west Frontier Province (1901). By then, only a thin, very mountainous portion of Afghanistan separated Russia from India, but in three different wars the Afghans proved far easier to influence than to conquer. Afghanistan became, in effect, a buffer state for India, as did Bhutan, Sikkim and (much earlier) Nepal (1816). Another direction of British expansion from India lay to the east, and Burma became a province of India in 1886.

Commercial conquests took place in the west. A naval force from India in 1820 forced Bahrain and rulers in Trucial Oman (now the United Arab Emirates) to recognize British authority. In the latter case, the British strongly desired to end trade in slaves and raids on shipping. At the other end of the Arabian Peninsula, British forces seized the port of Aden in 1839. Administered by the Government of India, it became an important coaling station for British ships.

Developments in Egypt inspired far greater British attention to the Middle East. The Nile Valley produced fine cotton needed by the mills of Britain, and in Egypt cotton provided government revenues. The ambition and determination of Muhammad Ali (1811–1847) so threatened the Ottoman Empire that it required careful European diplomacy, and on occasion Great Power military action to maintain the Ottoman Sultans. Under Muhammad

Victoria (1819–1901)
First Empress of India

Ali's successors, Egypt also provided an opportunity for European loans, to the ruler as well as to ordinary farmers. Finally, as overlord of the Sudan, Egypt inevitably played an active role in attempts to eliminate the slave trade from Africa.

Each of these reasons for British involvement, however, seems inconsequential beside the construction of the Suez Canal on French initiative. Already British passengers to India had reduced the long journey around Africa by using overland transportation across Egypt to the Red Sea. The canal, by enabling vessels and heavy freight to use the route, quickly became "the lifeline to India." British strategic policy in the region focused on the canal, and the Egyptian shares in the Suez Canal Company were purchased. When Egypt nevertheless went bankrupt and both anti-European riots and a nationalist uprising broke out, British troops landed in 1882 and restored order, defeating nationalist troops. Lightly disguised by diplomatic formalities and the almost total withdrawal of British troops, Egypt became a sphere of British influence though nominally part of the Ottoman Empire.

Its conquests during World War I brought the British Raj to its greatest extent in the Middle East and South Asia. When the Ottoman Empire entered the war as a German ally, Britain quickly annexed Egypt and Cyprus. Shortly thereafter, troops from India landed in southern Iraq, and despite setbacks began the slow conquest of that land. After repulsing Ottoman Turkish attacks on the Suez Canal, British, Australian, and Indian troops moved forward from Egypt into Palestine, capturing Jerusalem in 1917. When Ottoman Turkey appealed for peace in October 1918, these forces and their Arab allies had captured all of Syria as well. From the Nile to the Ganges, and between the Mediterranean and China, no European power rivaled British influence. British goals dominated the postwar assignment of mandates of Syria and Lebanon to France and Palestine and Iraq to Britain.

Nevertheless, as the Raj reached its greatest extent, the forces of its future downfall became evident. In Egypt the 1919 Nationalist Revolution led to the creation of an autonomous kingdom three years later. Arab nationalism, the ideology of only a handful of inhabitants of the Ottoman provinces in 1912, spread rapidly with the imposition of European mandates by force of arms in Syria and Iraq, as well as Zionist immigration into Palestine. In Iran, popular opposition blocked an attempt to establish a veiled British protectorate, and Afghanistan undertook its War of Independence. In India, nationalism had showed itself a potent force, and its repression at Amritsar produced one thousand dead and wounded. Under the leadership of Mohandas Gandhi, the struggle for self-determination was becoming effective.

Thus from west to east the British Raj tottered seriously in 1919–1920. Twenty-five years later the Second World War left Britain, though armed with weapons of greater sophistication than ever before, too enfeebled to maintain the empire. In 1947 the Raj formally ended for India, though it continued for another generation on the fringes of Arabia, where ironically formal British intervention always had been smaller.

George VI (1895–1952)
Last Emperor of India

The Kingdom of Bahrain

Downtown Manama, capital city

Area: 277 square miles (717 sq. km.).
Population: 1.2 million, 30% expatriate.
Capital City: Manama (pop. 148,000 city, 2008; metro 340,000, est.).
Climate: Extremely hot and humid except for a short, moderate winter. There is very little rainfall.
Neighboring Countries: Saudi Arabia (West); Qatar (Southeast).
Time Zone: GMT +3.
Official Language: Arabic.
Other Principal Tongues: English, Farsi (Persian), Urdu.
Ethnic Background: About 75% Bahraini and other Arab, with Indians, Iranians, and Pakistanis forming the largest groups of foreign workers.
Principal Religion: Islam, perhaps 60% *Shi'a* and 40% *Sunni.*
Chief Commercial Products: Petroleum products, aluminum, ship repairs, liquid natural gas, financial services and transportation services.
Major Trading Partners: Saudi Arabia, India, U.S., Japan, and Singapore.
Currency: Bahraini Dinar (1 BD = 1,000 fils).
Former Colonial Status: British Protectorate (1861–1971).
Independence Date: August 15, 1971.
Chief of State: Hamad bin 'Isa Al-Khalifa, King.
Head of Government: Sheikh Khalifa bin Salman Al-Khalifa, Prime Minister.
National Flag: A serration divides a white band at the pole from the remaining field of solid red. After Bahrain became a kingdom in 2002, its flag gained a gold crown.
Gross Domestic Product (GDP): $33.5 billion (at current prices); $43 billion (Purchasing Power Parity).
GDP per capita: $36,000 (PPP).

The land of two seas, as its name implies in Arabic, Bahrain consists of a group of islands located off the coast of Arabia between the Gulf of Bahrain and the Persian (Arab) Gulf. The main island, some 30 miles long and 10 miles wide, is largely desert, but springs fed by sources originating on the mainland water some gardens and groves near the northern coast. By the 2001 decision of the International Court of Justice, the island of Hawar near the Qatar coast also forms part of the country.

History: Bahrain's long history stretches back as far as Dilmun, a prosperous trading center that flourished some 4,000 years ago. Well placed to trade between Iraq and India, Bahrain played a role in Arab commerce during the Middle Ages, and the inhabitants became Muslims. The Portuguese conquest of the 1500s led in turn to Persian rule, but in 1783 the Arabian Al-Khalifa family, which had earlier established itself at Zubara on the Qatar coast, conquered Bahrain, seeking to gain control of its valuable pearl fishing industry. In a series of treaties beginning in 1820, rulers of this family allied themselves more closely with Britain, on occasion seeking aid against Persian claims and local threats. In 1861 it became a British protectorate.

Independence came in 1971 when Britain withdrew its forces from all the Gulf states, and Bahrain decided not to join the proposed union of Arab emirates. A constitution issued in 1973 created a National Assembly composed of the appointed cabinet and 30 elected members. Two years later, the assembly was dissolved for interfering with government, and for the next quarter century, the ruling family exercised power with a mixture of benevolence and the repression and alleged torture of political opponents during political unrest and rioting. Given the divide between the largely Sunni elite and the poorer Shi'a majority, the police and intelligence services—often employing foreigners—have remained alert for subversive activity.

In 1981 security forces discovered an Islamic plot to overthrow the government. The plot reflected both Iran's long-standing claims to Bahrain under the deposed shah and the Islamic Republic's desire to export its revolution. Unrest continued to fester, and in the late 1980s police foiled a plot directed at oil installations, but by the 1990s, Iranian sympathy with opposition movements was largely limited to refuge, funds and propaganda.

When Iraq seized Kuwait in 1990, Bahrain's government joined with other Gulf

Cooperation Council member states (see Regional Organizations) in condemning the invasion and supporting the multinational force. During the Gulf War that followed, Bahrain provided airbases and ports for U.S. and British forces. Though no military action occurred on the island, the massive oil spill released by Iraq during the fighting directly threatened water intakes for drinking water and industrial use, and risked long-term devastation of the local fishing industry.

Reflecting the greater spirit of democracy after the liberation of Kuwait, in 1993 Sheikh 'Isa bin Salman appointed 30 "elite and loyal men" to form a new council, the *Majlis al-Shura*. These wealthy merchants and patriarchs of notable families possessed no real powers, but provided the Emir with advice.

Resentment over the lack of personal rights and political freedoms led prominent Sunni and Shi'a Bahrainis to petition in 1994 for the reinstatement of the 1973 constitution. The government responded firmly, arresting several hundred and deporting Shi'a clerics who preached democracy. Demonstrations alternated with repression, and in 1996, a wave of protests left 30 dead, including police.

Ominously, the discontent became strongest among the Shi'a majority, whose resentment was fueled by their perceptions of poverty, unemployment, lower-class standing and discrimination. Behind the Shi'a demands, Prime Minister Khalifa bin Salman particularly discerned "outside meddling" (code for Iran). Despite a minor cabinet reshuffle, riots and sabotage continued, along with hundreds of arrests. The regime chose not to concede reforms, though they might have divided moderate democrats from radical Islamists.

When Sheikh Hamad ascended to power in 1999 on the death of his father, Sheikh 'Isa, hopes rose that calm might be restored. The new ruler released a major opposition figure from prison, and changed policies to increase employment. Under the slogan "Building a New Bahrain," he proposed a referendum on a "National Charter," a proposal to establish limited democracy and constitutional monarchy.

Sheikh Hamad's proposals initially aroused suspicions. The exiled *Bahrain Freedom Movement* considered the proposed parliamentary powers weak and opposed any referendum while hundreds of men and some women remained imprisoned or exiled for political offenses. However, Sheikh Hamad dramatically responded to the criticism by promising real authority for parliament and pardoning about 1,000 political prisoners.

In an atmosphere of euphoria, most Bahraini men and women actually voted on the National Charter in 2001, and they granted it overwhelming (98%) support. Soon afterwards, despite his reputation as an opponent of democracy, Prime Minister Sheikh Khalifa suspended the notorious State Security Laws that had permitted detention without trial. The pace of reforms continued with municipal elections in 2002, when women voted and (unsuccessfully) ran for office.

His Majesty Hamad bin Isa Al-Khalifa

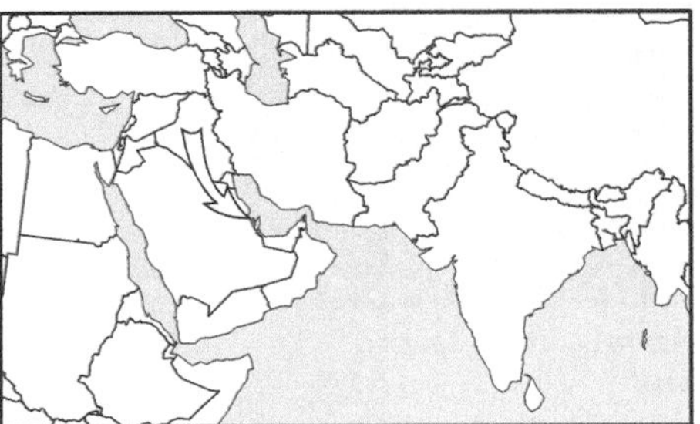

Another change that same year promoted Sheikh Hamad from hereditary prince to king. The change brought neither wealth nor additional domestic power to the ruling family, but it distinguished the Kingdom of Bahrain from the emirates around the Gulf, not all of them independent.

For the next decade, politics was dominated by the struggle between Shi'a opposition groups and the ruling family. The regime's critics were not united: some desired an Islamic state or the overthrow of the al-Khalifa family, while constitutional democrats sought changes like removing parliament's appointed (and powerful) upper house. Other opposition groups concentrated on human rights issues. In response, King Hamad took some conciliatory actions, like dismissing a minister who acted against anti-U.S. protests or appointing an occasional Shi'a activist to the cabinet.

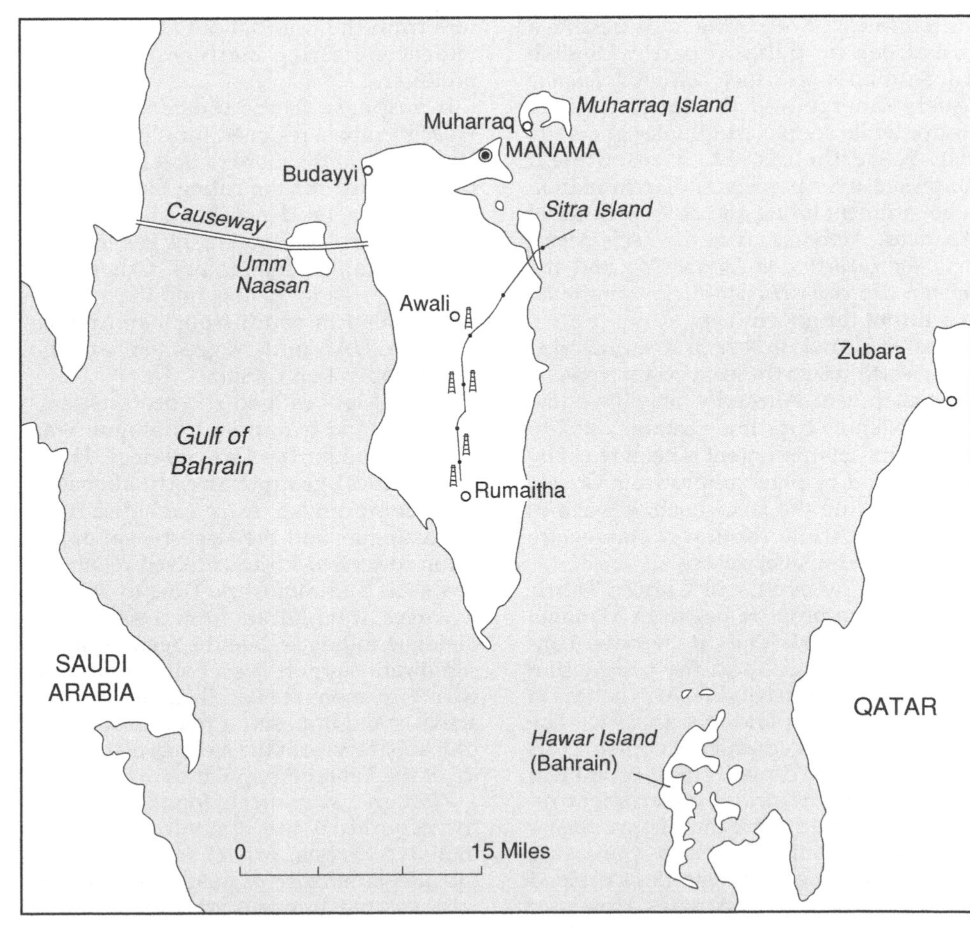

Bahrain

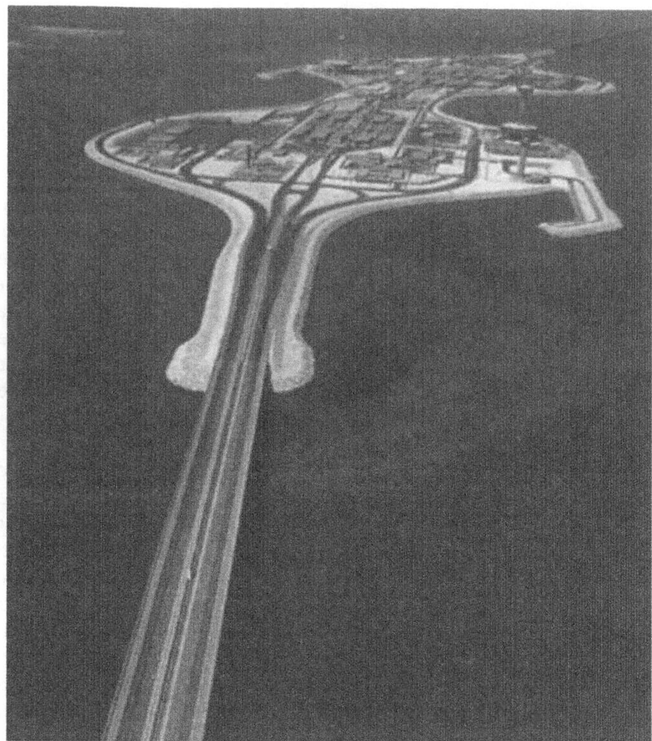

King Fahd Causeway leading to Immigration Island between Saudi Arabia and Bahrain.

Courtesy: CALTEX Petroleum Corporation

During the 2006 elections, Shi'a opinion shifted in favor of voting, and despite a formal ban on political parties, Sheikh Ali Salman's *al-Wifaq National Islamic Society* emerged as the largest single group, while secular candidates generally lost. Nevertheless, Shi'a resentment continued over perceived discrimination in government hiring and other prejudicial practices. Activists from the *Haqq Movement for Liberty and Democracy* and the *Bahrain Center for Human Rights* continued to confront the government.

Small-scale riots in several areas indicated dissatisfaction with the loss of open coastline to development. Allegedly, only 3% of the desert island's coastline remains open to the public. This discontent is heightened by poverty, and by photographs from Google Earth showing the large enclosed estates of the elite, while the lower classes are crowded into smaller spaces.

Inspired by events in Cairo's Tahrir Square, large protests began in Manama in February 2011. They demanded constitutional changes and the resignation of Prime Minister Khalifa Al Khalifa, in office since independence in 1971. The demonstrators eventually occupied Pearl Roundabout, the capital's most prominent traffic circle. The initial government responses wavered, for example promising financial handouts while also sponsoring large, pro-regime demonstrations derided by critics as luxury car parades. However, the security forces also forced demonstrators from the roundabout at night with violence, creating martyrs of the slain protesters.

In response to the police attacks, *al-Wifaq* members resigned from parliament. Supporters of the more radical groups like *Haqq* chanted for the ruling family to go, and their leaders demanded a republic. As the situation deteriorated, the government blamed Iranian instigators. Other Gulf rulers pressed for action, and the government called in Saudi troops and police from the UAE under agreements of the Gulf Cooperation Council.

Martial law calmed the protests temporarily, and a national dialogue was proposed under the Crown Prince. However, radical groups, already alienated from compromise, were excluded from the dialogue, and the largest legal opposition society, *al-Wifaq,* received relatively few seats and almost no time to present its views. It withdrew from the so-called dialogue in July. While the regime enjoys significant support from both Sunnis and wealthier, more secular Shi'a families, the activists and opposition political societies probably represent the feelings of a majority of the Bahraini population.

Western governments found it difficult to respond to the crackdown, which included arrests, prison sentences, and the alleged torture of hospital personnel who treated injured protesters. While sympathetic with some demands for reform, the U.S. valued the kingdom as the home of the U.S. Fifth Fleet and as an ally against the spread of Iranian influence. The U.S. Secretary of Defense did criticize "baby steps" to reform, but did not hint that like Egypt's President Mubarak, King Hamad should resign.

The continuing clashes, imprisonments, and injustices served to radicalize—and fracture—both the Shi'a opposition and the Sunni community. Some twenty major Shi'a opposition leaders were jailed; one of them, Abdulhadi al-Khawaja, conducted a lengthy hunger strike that aroused wide media attention. Military courts often overlooked expected rights when convicting civilians, among them physicians and nurses. These procedures were condemned by the UN Secretary-general and major human rights organizations. The Bahrain Independent Commission of Investigation into the protests, appointed by King Hamad, concluded that the security agencies had conducted illegal arrests, forced confessions, and systematically used torture.

Angered by their treatment, young Shi'a activists demanded the ouster of the king, far surpassing the call for an elected and governing parliament made by Sheikh Ali Salman, the leader of *al-Wifaq*. Rarely united, the Shi'a community increasingly fractured, though generally supporting protests against holding the Bahrain Grand Prix, a Formula One race that the regime values as a symbol of normalcy.

Similarly, among Sunnis opinion divided among those who support the king and crown prince in negotiating a compromise settlement, and those backing hardliners, whose slogan became "No dialogue with traitors."

Culture: The country's first written constitution, made public in 1973, proclaims Bahrain to be an Islamic state. A majority of Bahrainis are *Shi'a* Muslims (see Iran: Culture for details). The remaining 30% of Bahrainis, including the ruling family, are *Sunni.* Opposition groups allege the regime encourages Sunni immigrants to boost that portion of the population. Bahrain's culture includes Persian and Indian influences, but is not generally distinct from that found in other Arab Gulf states.

The kingdom has a relatively high literacy rate with universal education for all children. In addition to teacher-training colleges and various institutes, the Gulf University was established in Bahrain, sponsored by the smaller states of the Gulf. With facilities larger than its enrollment, it became a refuge for faculty and students from Kuwait who fled the Iraqi occupation.

The civilization of Dilmun left behind on the main island the heaviest concentration of prehistoric burial grounds anywhere on earth, some 80,000 mounds that once covered 5% of the island. Fewer than 6,000 sites remain, but officials hope tourists will be attracted to them, as well as the National Museum, the gold souq (market), portrayals of Arab nomadic lifestyle, and water sports along the coast.

Economy: Drillers struck the first successful oil well on the Arab side of the Gulf in 1932, initiating the development of a petrochemical industry and the modern economy. However, the country's reserves of oil remain small; at present production levels they will be exhausted soon. In 1996 Saudi Arabia allocated its revenues from a shared off-shore field, and the large oil refinery processes Saudi Arabian crude as well as local production. Oil thus remains vitally important directly, as well for revenues from the important oil refinery.

Recognizing its limited petroleum reserves, Bahrain has attempted to diversify its economy. Government policies encourage companies to invest outside petrochemicals, including low-interest loans, tax waivers, and duty-free imports of raw materials and machinery. Plans call for the expansion of small and medium-sized industries, in part to absorb a rapidly growing workforce. The country is considered one of the most liberal and least regulated in the entire region.

Bahrain became the first Gulf state to negotiate a Free Trade Agreement with the U.S., in 2004. Such agreements provide tariff-free access for products of one country in the other, and thus, the agreement should cut the price of U.S. air conditioners in the country and Bahraini aluminum in the U.S.

Fishing employs only small numbers, and agriculture faces an uncertain future because irrigation water pumped from the aquifer is turning brackish.

Abundant natural gas provides energy for the region's first large aluminum smelter, Aluminium Bahrain, which opened in 1972. Later expansion projects increased capacity to 860,000 tons, making it one of the largest in the world, with exports mostly to East Asia. The dominant U.S. producer, Alcoa, negotiated a major stake in the company in 2003.

After years of modest operations, the Arab Shipbuilding and Repair dry-dock began to flourish after the end of the Iran-Iraq war in 1988. Formerly, shipping companies and their insurers had sought to remove damaged tankers as quickly as possible from the zone of conflict.

Improving economic conditions in the Gulf help Bahrain's substantial offshore banking operations (the accounts of people living elsewhere), which suffered during Iraq's wars. By 2014, despite competition from Dubai, some 400 firms were licensed, many of them specializing in Islamic finances. Other services also play a role in the local and regional economy. The small stock exchange opened in 1989 and initially listed 30 companies, mostly in banking and insurance.

The construction of a 17-mile (27 km.) causeway connecting Bahrain with Saudi Arabia offers other opportunities for development. Over one million people used the causeway in the first year after its opening, most of them weekend tourists from Saudi Arabia, coming as families and interested in shopping and amusement parks. These visitors doubled hotel occupancy rates, and the young men among them frequented the island's nightclubs and bars. However, many of the service jobs thus created in retail, tourism, and entertainment seem undignified to conservative Bahraini citizens.

Prospects of encouraging tourism from Japan, Europe, and North America improved with the expansion of the airport and with every regional cease-fire in recent decades (Iran-Iraq War, 1988; Iraqi-Kuwait War, 1991, Gulf War, 2003). However, prospects diminish with regional turmoil and religious-based terrorism. Although Bahrain permits the importation of liquor and taxes it highly, western and East Asian tourists could easily upset conservative Muslims with demonstrations of contemporary lifestyles and entertainment. From a practical standpoint, too, non-Arab tourism also requires simple and rapid immigration procedures and inexpensive air fares, both now lacking. Most of all, of course, tourism requires political stability in the region—something far beyond the control of Bahrain.

A young population is rapidly joining the labor force, and unemployment is expected to rise significantly during coming years among Bahrain's youth. Although about 60% of the existing workforce is foreign, many of the jobs they perform will hardly attract the country's ambitious and generally well-educated youth.

The Future: Faced with protests sparked by the 2011 Arab Spring, time is slowly running out for King Hamad. Certainly, the police can force youthful Shi'a radicals off the streets, but the deep sense of injustice felt by nearly all Shi'a make a larger confrontation between them and the Sunni community almost inevitable. Concessions demanded by Shi'a moderates, such as reforming parliament, political freedoms, and releasing political prisoners, are necessary reforms. They would probably take place if the ruling family did not feel threatened by the sectarian divide. They are also not considered crucial by the U.S., which is focused on its naval base, nor by international businesses. Meanwhile, pro-republican sympathizers grow in number and intensity with each claimed brutality.

An event to watch: the proposed October 2014 elections. If the regime can compromise enough to avoid a boycott by *al-Wifaq* and other Shi'a groups, honest elections and a high voter turnout could lend international legitimacy to King Hamad. The resignation of the prime minister and heightened role of the crown prince would be favorable omens

Bahrain at night Courtesy: Royal Embassy of Saudi Arabia

The Arab Republic of Egypt

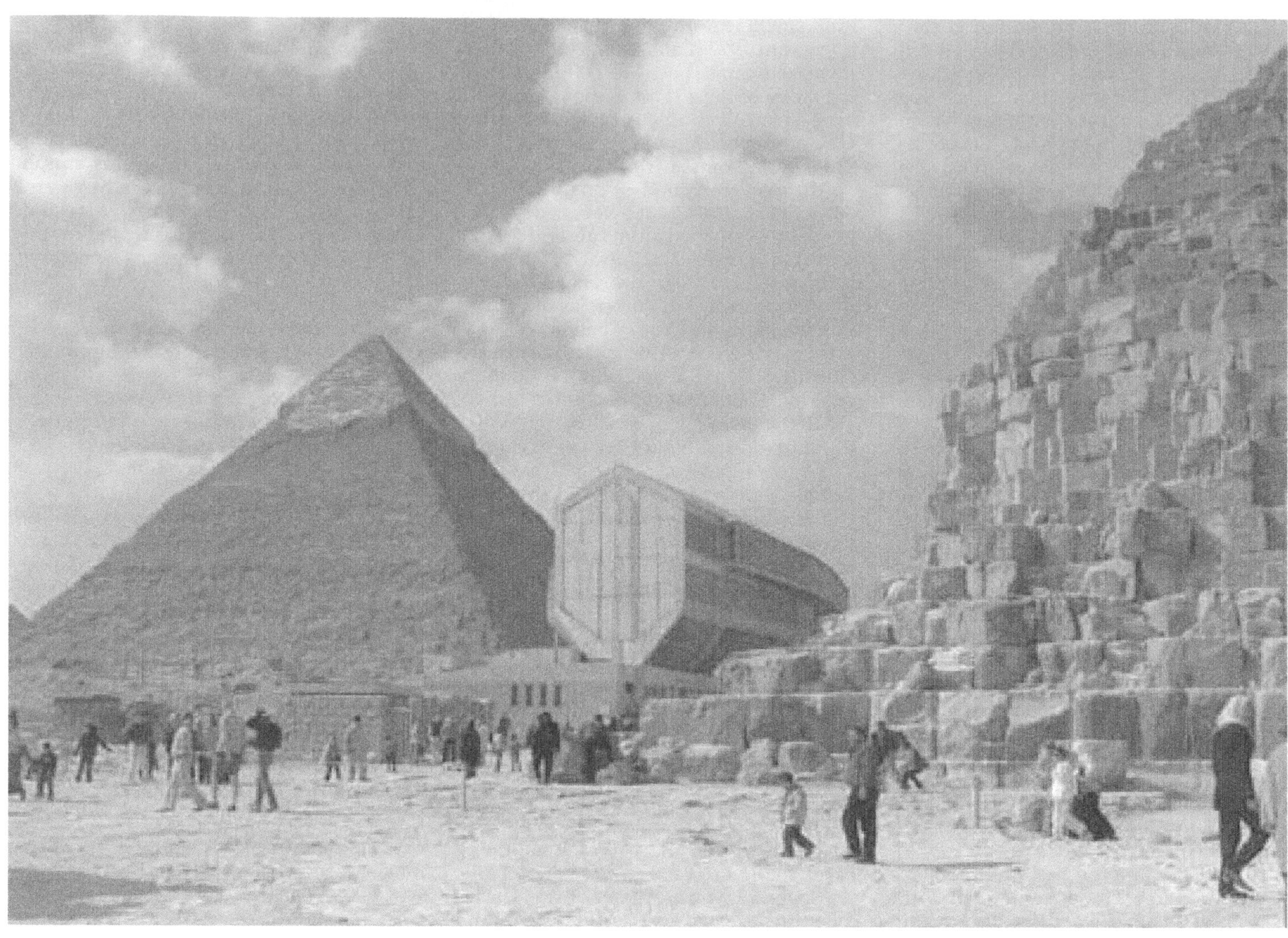

Area: 386,873 square miles (1,002,000 sq. km.), of which only about 3.5% is arable—in the Nile Valley, the Delta and a few oases.
Population: 86 million (est.).
Capital City: Cairo (7,450,000; 10,800,000 metro).
Climate: Hot summers, humid along the coast but dry in the south. Winters are cool with some rain along the northern coast, but drier and comfortable inland. Occasional strong winds intensify the winter chill and the summer heat.
Neighboring Countries: Libya (West); Sudan (South); Saudi Arabia (East, across the Red Sea); Israel (Northeast).
Time Zone: GMT + 2 (+3 in summer). At noon in New York it is 7:00 P.M. in Cairo.
Official Language: Arabic.
Ethnic Background: Their physical appearances vary, but nearly all consider themselves Arab and Egyptian, except a few Berbers from the western oases.
Principal Religion: *Sunni* Islam (over 90%) and Coptic Christianity.
Major Trading Partners: U.S., Italy, Germany, Japan, South Korea, Greece.
Chief Commercial Products: Tourism, Suez Canal usage, petroleum and refined products, military equipment, cotton yarn and textiles, light manufactures.
Main Agricultural Products: Cotton, sugar, rice and other grains, tomatoes, watermelons, onions, vegetables, dates, animals and flowers.
Currency: Egyptian £ (popularly the ghinnayh) = 100 piasters.
Former Colonial Status: British control, though still part of the Ottoman Empire (1882–1914), then a "protectorate" of Britain (1914–1922). Britain exercised political influence until the 1952 military *coup*.
National Day: July 23.
Chief of State: Abdul Fattah al-Sisi, President (2014).
Head of Government: Ibrahim Mahlab, Prime Minister, 2013.
National Flag: Three horizontal stripes of (top to bottom) red, white and black. The eagle of Saladin in gold is centered on the white stripe.
Gross Domestic Product: $286 billion (at current prices); $574 billion (Purchasing Power Parity)
GDP per capita: $6,695 (PPP).

Strategically located at the junction between Africa and Asia, Egypt holds the rank of the most populous Arab state and the center of Arab culture and entertainment. Most of its territory lies in Africa, forming the northeast corner of the great Sahara Desert. The stark desolation of gravel, sand and rock is interrupted by the Nile River, which flows from south to north for 750 miles in a valley cut through the desert. Yet for most of its length the valley floor varies in width from a mere few hundred yards to a maximum of 14 miles. Within the valley, agriculture is possible.

About 100 miles before reaching the Mediterranean Sea, the Nile divides into branches that spread out over a broad alluvial plain reaching a width of 150 miles along the sea coast. Because this triangle of fertility resembles the form of the (capital) letter *delta* in the Greek alphabet, since ancient times it has been called the Delta. The metropolis of Cairo lies at the southern tip of this Delta. At the northwest is the port city of Alexandria, named after Alexander the Great, who founded it following his conquest of the country in 332 B.C. About a quarter of the people of Egypt live in these two cities. They work as shopkeepers, government employees, in manufacturing, or at the many other jobs associated with urban areas.

Most of the remaining three-quarters of the population live in some 4,000 villages and towns scattered in the Delta and up the length of the Nile Valley. Most of them are directly or indirectly connected with agricultural production. A few people live in a half dozen remote oases in the desert west of the Nile Valley, while an insignificant and dwindling number of nomads wander with flocks of goats and camels in the desert regions that comprise about 96% of the country. There are no grasslands or forests. The highest point in Egypt, Jabal Katrina (Mt. Catherine) reaches 8,652 feet in the Sinai Peninsula, but overlooks barren rock and sands. There is total contrast between the barrenness of the desert (called "the Red Land" by the ancient inhabitants) and the tropical growth of the valley floor and Delta ("the Black Land" of the ancients).

The English name *Egypt* is derived from the ancient Greek name Aiguptos, an approximation of Hikuptah, one of the names of the ancient capital of Memphis, whose ruins are near modern Cairo. The Arabic name of the country, *Misr*, introduced with the Arabic conquest of the 7th century, originated in an ancient name used in Semitic languages. In the hieroglyphics of antiquity, the country was sometimes called "the Two Lands," referring to Lower Egypt (the Delta) and Upper Egypt (the narrow valley south of Cairo, known as *Sa'id* in Arabic).

History: The shadows of an extremely long early history lie across the modern land of Egypt—of the mighty pharaohs claiming to be gods, of Hellenistic civilization that flourished at Alexandria and especially of the brilliant Islamic civilization centered on Cairo. Yet the modern state of Egypt cannot be traced back beyond the early 19th century. Then it began to take shape under the dynamic rule of Muhammad (Mehmet) Ali, an ambitious Ottoman soldier who was neither Egyptian by birth nor a proponent of (not-yet-existent) Egyptian nationalism.

Pre-Christian civilization in the Nile Valley made enormous contributions to the development of human skills and knowledge. In fact, that civilization is considered the heritage of all humanity. Later ages also influenced the world. Roman Egypt was one of the first fertile grounds for the spread of Christianity, and its thinkers and leaders played important roles in the history of the Christian Church. The Christians of Egypt adopted a modified version of the Greek alphabet to write their language, Coptic, the latest form of the old Egyptian language earlier recorded in hieroglyphics. The Coptic Church still plays an important role in contemporary Egyptian society.

In the early 7th century, Muslim armies from Arabia spread their rule to Egypt, little opposed by the Coptic subjects of the Byzantine Empire (639–642). During the following centuries, both the Arabic language of the new rulers and their Islamic faith were adopted by most Egyptians. When the Abbasid caliphate in Baghdad lost control of distant provinces, Egypt fell under the rule of local governors, and then Turkish dynasties, including the Tulunids, whose mosque remains impressive today.

Further elegant buildings, and achievements in the arts and learning followed under the Fatimid Caliphs (969–1171), including the founding of the University of al-Azhar, one of the oldest in the world. Claiming descent from Fatima, the Prophet Muhammad's daughter, these caliphs espoused Shi'a Islam but maintained contact with the rest of the Muslim world. Sometimes they ruled much of it, but weak rulers and dependence on foreign slave-warriors eased Egypt's capture by Salah al-Din al-Ayyubi, known to the European Crusaders as Saladin. His Sunni descendants in turn lost authority to the Mamluks (pronounced Mam-*luke)*, warrior slaves often of Turkish or Circassian origins, by the middle of the 13th century.

The most important Mamluk sultan, Baybars, checked the expansion of the destructive Mongol armies in Syria (Ayn Jalut, 1260), and defeated the remaining Crusaders as well. But despite their glories on the battlefield, and their lavish spending on works of art, the Mamluks brought few advantages to the native Egyptians. Generally foreign born, the Mamluks oppressed the Egyptians harshly, and by their intrigues and rivalries brought disorder rather than peace. After the Ottoman Sultan Selim I defeated the Mamluks and conquered Egypt in 1517, the country witnessed frequent struggles between the government in Istanbul and the remaining Mamluks, who dominated Egyptian society.

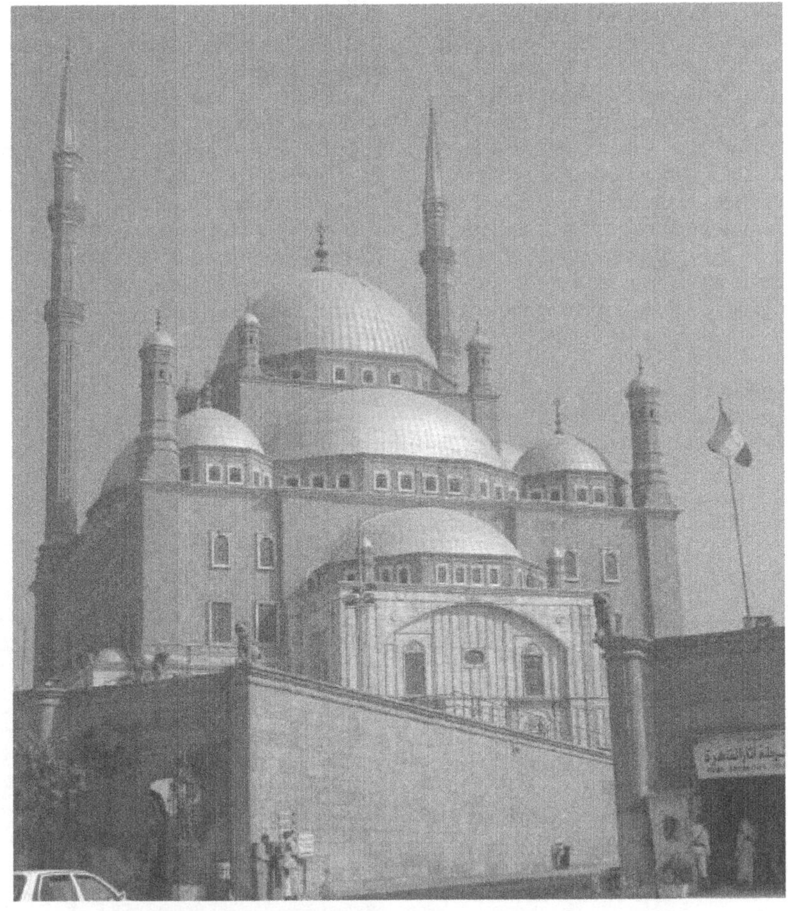

Built within Salah al-Din's Citadel, the Mosque of Muhammad Ali dominates Cairo's southern skyline.

Egypt

Napoleon's conquest and the French occupation (1798–1801) proved a vital turning point in the creation of modern Egypt. European ideas spread. More important, Muhammad Ali, an Albanian officer in the Ottoman army sent to evict the French, skillfully played off his rivals and seized power for himself while paying lip service to Ottoman rule. In 1806 the Ottoman Sultan recognized him as Pasha of Egypt.

Despite a barren treasury, Muhammad Ali set about building a modern state. After drastically reorganizing the land taxes, he established schools, founded a government press, and attempted to industrialize Egypt with imported equipment, all without borrowing funds abroad. His trade monopoly failed, but he encouraged agricultural improvements and seized vast domains from delinquent taxpayers. Considered "The Founder of Modern Egypt," he separated it from the rest of the Ottoman Empire as a self-governing region.

His successors proved lesser men. His son Sa'id Pasha greatly increased Egypt's strategic status in 1856 when he gave a Frenchman, Ferdinand de Lesseps, a concession to build a canal from the Mediterranean to the Red Sea. The Suez Canal became Britain's "lifeline to India," because it enormously reduced the length of the sea voyage from Britain to the Indian Ocean.

Sa'id's profligate successor, Ismail, borrowed large sums from European bankers for a few good reasons, and many poor ones: mostly to finance his high living and elaborate, often unsound, development schemes. Ismail bankrupted the state, and in 1875 he sold Egypt's share in the Suez Canal to Britain and accepted foreign financial advisors. He was finally forced to abdicate.

The British Occupation

After rioters killed several Europeans and others associated with the strict financial administration, in 1882 Britain landed troops in Alexandria. The wealthy, landowning elite, many of them Turkish-speaking, failed to unite and oppose the British, though most Egyptians rallied to support a nationalist colonel, Ahmad Urabi (Arabi). At the battle of Tall al-Kabir, British troops demonstrated an overwhelming supremacy, killing some 10,000 Egyptians while losing fewer than 80 men. The khedive became a British puppet, and the British Consul General, Lord Cromer, became a virtual dictator for over 20 years (1883– 1907), although Egypt formally remained part of the Ottoman Empire until World War I.

Despite Wilson's 14 Points and successful national struggles elsewhere, Britain still sought to dominate Egypt. A long-time nationalist, Sa'd Zaghlul, and his colleagues sought to form a delegation ("wafd") to attend the 1919 Paris peace conference, but they were arrested instead. An insurrection then spread to all parts of Egypt. Unsuccessful at repression, Britain offered a very restricted "independence" that retained British bases. When Zaghlul and his *Wafd Party* ensured that no Egyptian would sign such a treaty, Britain simply declared Egypt independent, with conditions, in 1923. Sultan Fu'ad, became king, but proved inept in politics. Raised in Italy, he was scarcely able to speak Arabic.

Under its monarchs (1923-1952), the country saw few positive developments, though some progress in individual freedom. The government was rent by continuing rivalry by three contending forces: the weak monarch, interfering British officials, and an ineffective parliament dominated by the increasingly corrupt and self-interested *Wafd Party*. Politicians manipulated the poor for their own ends, but did little to improve their lot. King Farouk, whose reign began in 1937, became a symbol of a system that failed to meet the aspirations of ordinary Egyptians. Opposition to the monarchy mounted after the Egyptian army's loss to Israel in 1949, and the fundamentalist *Muslim Brotherhood* became increasingly active and engaged in assassinations.

Military Rule and Republic

In 1952, a group of reformist army officers seized control and exiled King Farouk. The self-styled Free Officers sought not merely to change the ruler; they wished to revolutionize the country. Modernists at heart, they believed that an independent, honest and sincere government could reduce poverty, increase education, strengthen the armed forces and bring dignity to the average Egyptian. In keeping with these aims, they set up the *Revolutionary Command Council* (*RCC*) to handle affairs of state. The real leader in the *RCC* was, Colonel Gamal Abdul Nasser (or Jamal Abd al-Nasir), a tall, imposing orator with an interest in ideas. In 1954, he became president in name as well as fact.

Nasser made an enormous impact upon Egyptians, other Arabs, and people throughout the colonies and newly independent nations of the developing world. The wealthy and ethnic minorities aside, Egyptians loved him. When army officers overthrew monarchies in Iraq, Yemen and Libya, they modeled revolutionary councils after the one in Cairo. On the world stage, Nasser became a prominent spokesman at conferences of Third World nations, notably in 1955 when he, Nehru of India, and Zhou Enlai of China established the Nonaligned Movement of countries neutral in the struggle between the Soviet Union and the West.

The idealistic young officers of the *RCC* seized aimed to bring progress and greater opportunity for the poor and middle classes through education, public health, and other welfare programs. Lacking experience and finding few advisors, they gradually formulated principles for building a new society, defined as "Arab Socialism." They also desired land reform, to redistribute to the *fellahin* (farmers) the large estates of the rich. As moderate socialists, but not communists, they favored government control of international trade, industry, and banks. Their policies developed some industries, but stagnated much of the economy (see **economy**).

In the 1950s, Egypt dominated the Arab world. Its population far exceeded those of other Arab states; it boasted the larg-

Monumental architecture started here: the step-pyramid of Pharaoh Djoser

est (if not the toughest) military, and its achievements in the arts and culture ranged from universities to movies. Inevitably, once Nasser espoused a Pan-Arab policy that blamed Arab weakness on imperialism and dynasties that divided one true Arab nation, Egypt began to champion the interests of the Palestine Arabs and to oppose Israel.

Access to weapons proved the crucial. The Western allies who had dominated arms supplies to the region, agreed to limit combined Arab armaments to the level possessed by Israel, thus preserving indefinitely the Israeli military superiority. In a decisive stroke to escape from Western limitations, in 1955 Egypt purchased arms from communist Czechoslovakia. The move dramatically increased Soviet influence in the Middle East.

When the United States reacted to the arms sale by withholding aid for a proposed high dam at Aswan in southern Egypt, Nasser obtained Soviet assistance for the dam as well, and then in 1956 seized the Anglo-French Suez Canal Company to pay for the arms and to finance development projects like the dam.

Amid great international furor, Israel, Britain and France secretly plotted an invasion. Israel hoped to defeat Egypt before the new Soviet arms rendered it strong, and then to force it to sign a peace treaty. In late 1956, Israeli forces opened the Suez War, quickly defeated the Egyptian army, and occupied the Sinai Peninsula. Britain and France then used the fighting as a pretext to take control of the Canal Zone. Public opinion almost everywhere condemned this reversion to power politics, and at the UN, a motion demanding a withdrawal won support from the U.S. and the U.S.S.R. alike. Nasser emerged from this episode as a hero, though subsequent attempts at unity with Syria (1958-61) and intervention in Yemen (1962) were not successful.

The Six-Day War, June 5–10, 1967

In the spring of 1967, Nasser allied publicly with Syria and eventually Jordan against Israel over water rights to the Jordan and Israeli reprisal raids. When radicals criticized Egypt for talking tough but sheltering behind borders pacified by the UN observers, he ordered out the observers and then announced a blockade of the Straits of Tiran, Closing the straits threatened to deprive Israel of all direct trade with East Africa, Southern Asia and the Far East. Israel publicly considered the action a cause for war, and formed a war cabinet, while Nasser moved troops into the Sinai and delivered bellicose speeches. But with many troops in Yemen, Egypt otherwise failed to prepare for battle through military incompetence, miscalculating Israeli strength, or presuming the United States would restrain Israel from invasion.

Sudden Israeli attacks on Egyptian and Syrian air bases marked the beginning of the Six-Day War. In a few hours, the Arab air forces effectively ceased to exist. Control of the skies ensured victory on land, as Israeli tanks and infantry swept across the Sinai, reaching the Suez Canal, then turning back to trap retreating Egyptian units in the Sinai passes. Nasser accepted responsibility for the defeat, and dramatically resigned, but emotional demonstrations in Cairo led him to return to power almost immediately. Other consequences of the defeat proved longer-lasting. Egypt lost the Sinai's recently-discovered oil fields and the Suez Canal remained closed, The Israeli occupation of Sinai impoverished Egypt's economy and soon led to a war of attrition, a period of intense shelling and air raids along the Canal.

From Attrition to Peace

When he died unexpectedly in 1970, Egypt's leaders turned to former Vice President Anwar Sadat, one of the few original Free Officers who remained in public life. As president (1970–1981), he discarded the socialist ideology of the previous decade. Hoping to lure American and other foreign investment, Sadat's government lifted many, but by no means all, restrictions imposed during Nasser's era. However, the reforms largely failed to spur prosperity, but did contribute to influence peddling and profiteering by politicians, military officers and their relatives. The perennial problems of unemployment, inefficient industrialization and overpopulation worsened, and the resulting dissatisfaction found both political and religious expression.

Initially, Sadat adhered to Nasser's foreign policy, and continued the War of Attrition along the Suez Canal. Despite frequent warlike rhetoric, however, in 1973 Egypt dismissed the many Soviet military advisors and other personnel.

Suddenly, in October, the Syrian and Egyptian armies attacked Israeli forces occupying their territory. Egyptian troops successfully crossed the Canal and advanced into the Sinai. There, protected from Israeli bombing by anti-aircraft missiles, they fought monumental tank battles with the Israelis.

Within days, however, the tide of battle shifted. A U.S. airlift massively resupplied the Israel Defense Forces with sophisticated weapons. In a daring operation,

Egypt

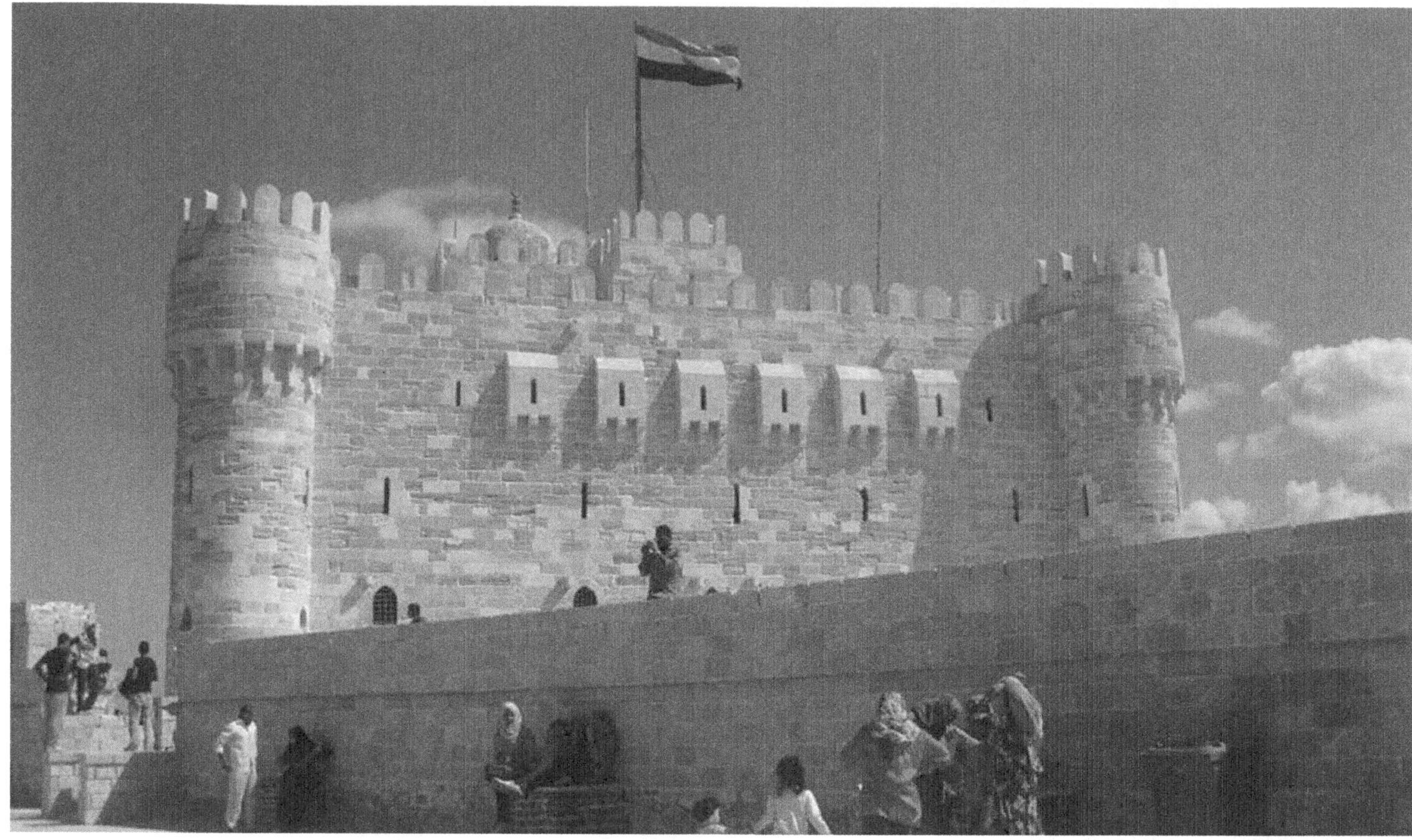

Constructed in 1477, the citadel of Qait Bey guarded the harbor of Alexandria for centuries. Photo by the author

some Israeli units crossed the Canal—into Africa, threatening Cairo and encircling large Egyptian armies. Given the risks of warfare, and its enormous human and material costs, Sadat and his advisors concluded that further confrontation with Israel was not only harmful to Egypt but also futile. Egypt accepted a truce.

After the war, Sadat's policies changed dramatically. He restored diplomatic relations with the United States, whose Secretary of State, Henry Kissinger, negotiated the return of both the Suez Canal and Sinai oil wells to Egypt. Domestically, Sadat invoked Egyptian rather than Pan-Arab nationalism. Nevertheless, while oil exports and Suez Canal tolls provided foreign exchange, and trade increased, prosperity hardly trickled down to the masses. Likewise, peace remained only a hope.

In a dramatic gesture, in 1977 Sadat flew to Jerusalem and addressed the Knesset, offering to accept the legitimacy of Israel in exchange for its withdrawal from territory seized in 1967 from Egypt, Jordan and Syria. When diplomacy seemed to falter in 1978, President Jimmy Carter invited both Sadat and Israeli Prime Minister Menachem Begin to Camp David, the U.S. presidential retreat in Maryland. Isolated from the press and their domestic political pressures, the two leaders reached the terms of a peace settlement.

The Camp David Accords signed in 1979 fell far short of peace, Sadat's initial goal. Israel retained all the territory captured from Jordan and Syria, and Palestinians received only the promise of a distant and vague autonomy. Egypt, however, regained all the Sinai. Diplomatic relations were established in 1980, and Israeli troops withdrew by 1982.

The Camp David agreements aroused widespread Arab condemnation. Without settling the basic problems resulting from Israel's creation, the agreements established peace with Israel, and thus left the Jewish state dominant militarily. In response, Arab nations broke diplomatic relations with Egypt, and financial aid from oil exporters dwindled. Many Egyptians also viewed the accords with misgivings, and disliked having diplomatic relations with Israel, especially during periods of bloodshed between Israelis and Palestinians. Nevertheless, given Egypt's poverty and military weakness, the accords seemed necessary.

When Anwar Sadat was assassinated by religious zealots in 1981, there was little spontaneous outpouring of grief such as marked Gamal Abdul Nasser's death. Vice President Muhammad Husni Mubarak was sworn in as the new head of state. Yet another military officer, he generally pursued the liberalizing economic policies of his predecessor. Major attention was directed toward organizing the economy productively and every effort was made to present an image of stability and moderation. Mubarak also released from prison many (though not all) of Sadat's political opponents and Islamic fundamentalists. Eventually their places would be filled by Mubarak's own opponents.

Persistent Islamic Opposition

Throughout his presidency, President Mubarak felt most threatened by the same broad movement whose militants had assassinated Anwar Sadat. The revival of Islamic values stretched from peaceful calls of professional groups to adopt Islamic law, the *Shari'a* (see Historical Background), through the *Muslim Brotherhood,* to extremist and violent groups such as *al-Gama'a al-Islamiyya* (the Islamic Group).

Because the government effectively banned the Islamists from contesting elections, opposition took the form of demonstrations and protests, as well as arson and murder. Feeding on popular dissatisfaction with inflation, food shortages, unemployment and Israeli actions in the

Palestinian territories, the militants came to pose a shadowy yet significant threat to the regime. In 1992 alone, some 70 people perished in Islamist violence. Intellectuals, Coptic Christians in Upper Egypt, government officials, and the police themselves suffered fatal assaults. By 1995, terrorist attacks on buses, boats and trains had left tourists dead and injured; more than 600 Egyptians died. As travelers avoided Egypt or stayed fewer days, the tourist industry's earnings slumped badly.

Some critics feared that the harsh government response to militant Islamic groups might heighten their appeal. Repressive measures by the police and military included widespread arrests, and rough treatment of suspects, allegedly even torture. The government also attempted to take control of all mosques in the country, a task as impossible as it was undemocratic.

To some critics, these desperate measures reflected the government's inability to strike at the poverty, corruption and social distress that fostered religious extremism. However, the revival of Islamic sentiment reached far beyond the unemployed. Candidates supported by the *Muslim Brotherhood* captured the leadership of the Bar Association, while Islamic charities won recognition for responding effectively to a Cairo earthquake that killed hundreds and left tens of thousands homeless.

In response, the government struck repeatedly at the nonviolent *Muslim Brotherhood*. Though technically banned, the *Brotherhood* had been tolerated for years, while it constructed a network of charities and businesses. Eventually the government attempted to crush all Islamist opposition, with little distinction between non-violent critics and those who attempted to assassinate Mubarak himself. Police detained hundreds of activists. Scores of leaders were sentenced to hard labor for belonging to a banned organization.

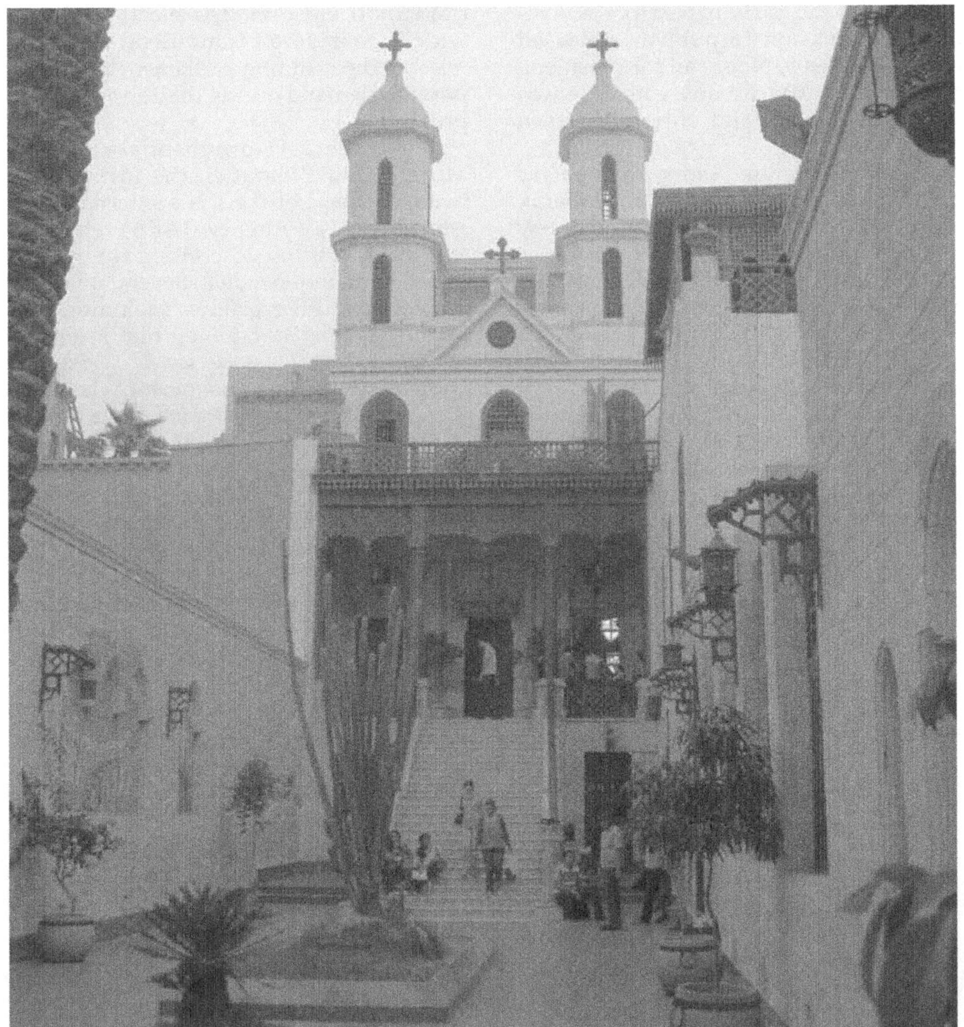

Coptic Christians often worship in churches of great antiquity, such as the "Hanging Church" of St. Mary, built in the 600s on an even older church and Roman walls.

Photo by Author

Former President Husni Mubarak

Al-Gama'a al-Islamiyya and its offshoots undoubtedly invited repression. Its extremists murdered tourists, including a massive attack in 1997 that killed 62 near Luxor. Weakened by both repression and public revulsion at the bloodshed, the militant organizations apparently lay shattered. *Al-Gama'a al-Islamiyya* called for a ceasefire, and violence declined even in Upper Egypt. The next year hundreds of imprisoned Islamists were released, and leaders publicly urged a non-violent struggle for their aims. Later attacks seemed the work of small, free-lance groups. However, they killed Egyptians and tourists alike—and their very disorganization represented a tremendous challenge to the security forces.

The attitudes of some Islamists contributed to worsening Muslim-Christian relations, as do any forceful Christian assertions, such as a church drama about a sinful Copt turned Muslim or attempts by converts from Islam to record themselves as Christian on their identity cards (the reverse is not an issue). In these circumstances, permits for church construction or alterations become impossible to obtain, and Copts increasingly feel discrimination in employment. In 2009, the government's brutal attempt to slaughter all of Egypt's pigs (kept only by Christians) on the pretext of protection against the swine flu epidemic also raised protests and resentments, by animal rights advocates as well as Copts working as refuse collectors.

Worse violence came on New Year's Eve in 2010, when a massive explosion killed 21 Coptic worshippers in Alexandria. The police issued conflicting statements about both the source of the explosion and the alleged perpetrators, raising suspicions of government incompetence or worse. Even after the Tahrir Square revolution, many Copts deeply worry about violence as well as discrimination, fears strengthened by the army's apparently unprovoked shooting of Christian demonstrators at Maspero Square in 2011.

Egypt

Regaining International Prestige

In the late 1980s Egypt emerged from the isolation that had followed its signing the Camp David Agreements. Symbolically, it returned to the Arab League in 1989, and a high-ranking Egyptian official was elected its Secretary-General in 1991. The greater prominence resulted from Egypt's support for Iraq during its war against Iran and President Mubarak's backing for Yasir Arafat and the *Palestine Liberation Organization*. After Iraq's invasion of Kuwait, Egypt joined the anti-Iraqi coalition and dispatched 35,000 troops to defend Saudi Arabia, the third largest foreign force there. President Mubarak came to play a crucial role for the Western-led alliance as an Arab leader who supported the integrity of Kuwait. This weakened Iraqi attempts to portray events as a struggle between nationalist and Muslim Arabs on the one side, and foreigners and their puppet monarchs on the other.

Domestic Economic and Political Stagnation

By the turn of the millennium, the regime seemed to have lost its sense of purpose. Its privatization program faltered, leaving suspicions that favoritism had lined the pockets of some investors in profitable companies, while the many money-losing government firms continued to require subsidies. The exchange rate was controlled, then devalued, leading many investors to flee from Egypt. The stock market and economic growth slumped, even before the disastrous impact of the September 11 attacks on Western tourism. Unemployment climbed, and probably exceeded 20%. For a variety of reasons, the economy had failed to grow and produce the necessary jobs for the 800,000 new workers annually.

Politics under Mubarak: Under the constitution of 1971, a strong president dominated the Advisory Council and People's Assembly (parliament). Except in 2005, the president was the single nominee of the People's Assembly, who was subsequently approved by a popular referendum.

Political realities tainted elections to the People's Assembly, despite the democratic claims of the constitution. The ruling *National Democratic Party* always won overwhelming victories. Official pressures, from publicity and the use of influence through police intervention to some outright rigging, ensured a majority so large the legislature served as a mere rubber stamp.

Despite obstacles, opposition parties did exist, some legalized by a parliamentary committee dominated by the *NDP*, others technically illegal. The small *New Wafd Party* traced its origins to Zaghlul and the 1919 *Wafd*. Other minor groups included the small centrist *Liberal Party*, and several left-wing parties that reflected varying viewpoints. These parties commonly demanded an end to the state of emergency (which banned unapproved meetings of more than five people), a halt to torture, and a new constitution. However, the small parties seemed more suited to permanent opposition than to governing. The *Muslim Brotherhood*, technically illegal and much more than a party, ran candidates under cover, sometimes from the socialist *Labor Party*.

The fate of only the third new party legalized in 25 years, *Hizb al-Ghad (Party of Tomorrow)*, symbolized the plight of the opposition. Ayman Nour, its founder, was jailed over alleged false signatures on the party's application, although the signatures were not necessary and Nour himself had not gathered them. While in jail awaiting trial, his leadership of the party was challenged, perhaps by government agents, and the party newspaper was refused permission to publish. Released from jail in 2005, Nour ran for president, but failed to attract many votes. He was later jailed again, and only released in 2009.

When presidential and parliamentary elections approached in 2005, Mubarak reshuffled the cabinet, bringing in a new prime minister and several younger, reform-minded ministers with business experience. Others were known as associates of Gamal Mubarak, the president's son, who favored a free economy and was suspected of high political ambitions.

As the election approached, opposition groups formed, were prohibited, and reformed. Students protested the emergency regulations. In response, hundreds of *Muslim Brotherhood* activists were arrested, but the government also instituted direct presidential elections. For the first time, ordinary Egyptians faced a ballot with more than one presidential candidate. However, with many voters skeptical, changing the process failed to affect the result. Husni Mubarak won 88% of the vote from the small percentage of the population who actually voted (about 25%).

Handwriting on the wall: Religion to God and the Country for All.

Photo by the author

Reforms, world attention, and careful judges had more effect on parliamentary elections. Held over several weeks, they showed increasing victories for the *Muslim Brotherhood*, though its members still ran as independents. As the size of their victory increased, so did reports of intimidation, fraud, and violence. Again, the *National Democratic Party* won an overwhelming majority—over 70% of the vote. But the real election news was the *Muslim Brotherhood's* 88 seats, and the pitiful showing of secular opposition parties.

In 2010, the *NDP* and its allied independents won 93% of the seats, after opposition voters were sometimes prevented from voting and their parties boycotted the runoff election. The elections were widely considered fraudulent, and dismissing the resulting parliament became a popular demand during the Tahrir Square protests.

Before the 2011 presidential election, Muhammad ElBaradei, the former Director-General of the UN's International Atomic Energy Agency (IAEA) returned to Egypt, willing to contest the presidency as an independent. Several political parties and other groups, including the *Muslim Brotherhood*, joined him in forming the *National Association for Change*, a "non-party-political movement." Though the government press depicted him as out of touch with Egypt, younger citizens relished the prospect of a civilian candidate free of corruption. His supporters turned to Facebook and other social media, a portent of what would follow.

Tahrir 2011: The Downfall of Mubarak

Frustrated by economic stagnation and political repression such as the recent death of Khalid Said, an activist beaten to death by police, and inspired by the ouster of Tunisia's president, the *April 6 Youth Movement* announced plans to protest in Tahrir Square on January 25, 2011; ironically, a national holiday celebrating the police. In a country of aging, often self-interested politicians, the *April 6 Youth Movement* itself was unusual: its three co-founders included two twenty-something activists concerned about the working class. The *Movement* rapidly became the largest political social media discussion group in the country, with over 70,000 members, most of them also young, democratic, fairly well-to-do, and critical of corruption and economic stagnation.

The activists' messages, like the video by Asmaa Mahfouz, stressed abstract themes like freedom, dignity, and honor, while denouncing corruption. They shamed those who sympathized but failed to participate. In Tahrir Square and outside the *NDP* offices nearby, the slogans included "Down with Mubarak" or simply "GO!" Demonstrations broke out in Alexandria, Suez, and other cities as well.

The government responded by arresting hundreds and blaming the *Muslim Brotherhood*: who else could organize such numbers? When the protests continued, Mubarak refused to step down himself, but dismissed his cabinet and for the first time appointed a vice president, Omar Suleiman, the long-serving intelligence chief. Perhaps Mubarak sought to reassure foreign governments who sought stability, but within the country Suleiman's agencies were regarded as instruments of repression and torture.

Its gestures failing, the regime tried brute force. Criminals were released from prison to vandalize homes and businesses in an attempt to discredit the demonstrators. In Tahrir Square, with obvious police consent or support, thugs mounted on horses and camels and armed with swords and clubs attacked demonstrators in the legendary "Battle of the Camel." The attacks proved a turning point: despite hundreds of wounded and some deaths, the protesters held their ground, and ordinary Egyptians distinguished between criminals and protesters.

In sharp contrast to the police, when ordered into the square, the army did not attack demonstrations, though it allowed thugs that did so through its ranks. It protected buildings like the Egyptian Museum and fraternized with activists. Nevertheless, many of protesters slept around and even underneath tanks to ensure they would not be used.

Another crucial event was the dramatic TV interview with Wael Ghonim, a young Google executive who returned to Egypt to participate in the protests. Obviously fatigued and emotional after days blindfolded in police detention, he denied that the demonstrators were traitors and proclaimed that the goal was human rights, not a settling of scores. Ghonim's interview revived the protests by inspiring non-political citizens, many of them never acquainted with Facebook, to support and even participate in the demonstrations.

His financial system tottering, Western support crumbling, the new cabinet of the same old faces discredited, and abandoned by the military, on the 18th day of the protests, Mubarak resigned. The nation rejoiced.

The victory belonged to the protest movements, including those associated with Muhammad ElBaradei and the *April 6th Youth Movement*. Social media—especially Facebook and Twitter—provided near-instant communication that overwhelmed the snooping abilities of the secret police. Wael Ghonim correctly argued that without the social media, the protests would have failed.

However, the youthful leaders of the protests also connected with labor movements and the concerns of those too poor to use the internet. They contrasted starkly with traditional politicians interested in perpetual questions such as the role of Islam, fair elections, or seats in the National Assembly. The protesters' focus was ethical and abstract, concerned with human rights, personal dignity, and fairness, combined with a dominant slogan: "The People Desires the Fall of the Regime."

Perhaps, too, the protest movements tapped resentment at the web of dishonesty spread by the regime. For example, when four regional leaders walked the red carpet at the White House, the official photo showed the young, basketball-playing President Obama leading his guests and an aging President Mubarak trailing. But *al-Ahram* altered the picture to show Mubarak ahead of Obama. When the official media lied in matters so apparently trivial, its statements about so much else, from the deaths of individuals in police custody to the threats presented by the *Muslim Brotherhood* could no longer be trusted.

The traditional political opposition, dominated by the *Muslim Brotherhood* and a few small middle-class parties, had always failed to turn regime weaknesses into irresistible force. Mubarak's resignation was not their success.

Protesters like this woman illustrate the success of youthful activists in reaching the general public. Photo courtesy of Jim Neergaard

The Struggle to Shape the New Egypt

Mubarak's resignation proved only the beginning of a revolution, a reshuffling of military rulers forced by public opinion. The Supreme Council of the Armed Forces (SCAF) took control, headed by Mohammad Hussain Tantawi, defense minister and military commander for two decades. The council retained the cabinet, dissolved parliament, suspended the constitution, promised to honor foreign treaties, and pledged to remain in office no longer than six months.

Nevertheless, general intimidation continued. Justice was delayed for victims of police repression: there were almost no convictions. Despite the prominent roles of women in the protests, the army conducted virginity tests on some of those arrested. One general publicly approved the practice, and sexual harassment and groping became nearly universal humiliations. Elections were manipulated: a referendum freer from intimidation than any in decades approved a constitutional amendment. However, the ballot's circle for "Yes" was printed in bright green and that for "No" in ordinary black.

The military clearly retained control, but with a constitution and elections ahead, other groups sought to influence political decisions. Attention naturally focused on the expected role of the *Muslim Brotherhood* in a democratic system. Its critics feared the largest and best-organized opposition group to Mubarak would swiftly win elections and impose conservative Islamic values. Given the fractured opinions of *Brotherhood* members, a variety of worrying quotations might be found to substantiate the critics' worst fears.

The *Brotherhood* initially acted with great caution. It pledged to limit the number of its parliamentary candidates and not to contest presidential elections. However, facing competition from *Salafists* who campaigned to impose Shari'a law and the caliphate, as well as moderate Islamists, it soon violated both promises; indeed, it even ran members for the non-partisan seats in parliament. With the non-Islamists disunited in elections for the People's Council (the lower house of parliament), its *Freedom and Justice Party* swept to victory (36%), followed by the *Salafists* (24%).

The youthful activists behind the Tahrir protests joined with leaders of some secular political parties to form a second, weakly organized group. Consistently in opposition and unable to unite for the elections, their influence was felt particularly through demonstrations that forced SCAF and others to change policies and bring presidential elections forward.

Many demonstrations passed peacefully, but some activists attacked property, and police and soldiers on occasion assaulted demonstrators, at times clearly shooting to kill. Political violence took a tragic turn at the Port Said soccer stadium, when supporters of the visiting al-Ahly team, known as "Ultras" and recognized for supporting the revolution, were attacked and 70 massacred in the melee while the police (intentionally?) watched rather than acted.

Judges and officials clearly formed other important centers of power. For example, the Supreme Constitutional Court decreed the parliamentary elections invalid because both the *Freedom and Justice* and the Salafist *al-Nour* parties had run candidates for seats reserved for non-party independents. The SCAF immediately dissolved the National Assembly and decreed that new elections must wait for a constitution. Likewise, the presidential election commission excluded several candidates, most prominently the *Salafists'* Hazem Abu Ismail (his mother once took out US citizenship) and Khairat al-Shater of the *Brotherhood's Freedom and Justice Party* (he had a recent criminal conviction).

Given the strong Islamic victory in the parliamentary elections, the results of the first presidential round proved surprising.

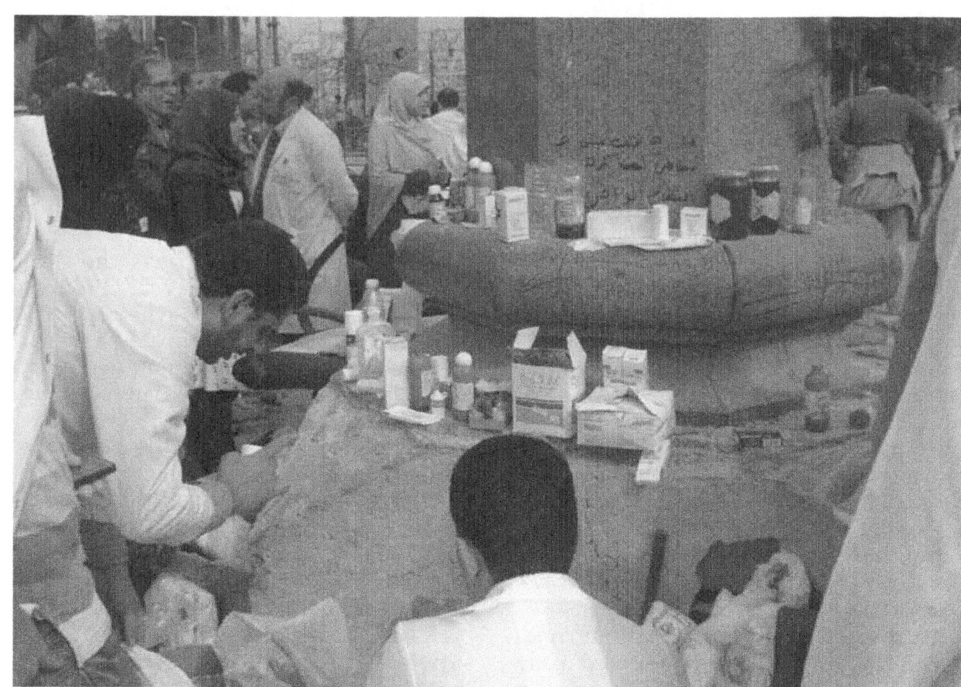

Medics treat injuries with simple supplies. When pro-Mubarak thugs attacked the demonstrators, even simple emergency care became important.

Photo courtesy of Jim Neergaard

In a large field, Mohammed Morsi, the replacement candidate of the *Freedom and Justice Party*, won 24% of the vote. However, Ahmed Shafiq, the former air force commander and briefly Mubarak's prime minister, came second (23%) on a platform of stability and order. Hamdin Sabbahi, who appealed to Nasserites, leftists, and some centrists, came third (almost 21%).

Political loyalties thus divided into three distinct groups: loyal Islamists backing Morsi, Shafiq's law-and-order-and-not-the-*Brotherhood* supporters, and the very divided supporters of one democratic candidate or another who backed Sabbahi. But in the second round, dismayed democrats faced the alternative of two disliked candidates.

Morsi won the runoff with nearly 52% of the vote, a narrow yet democratic victory. He took office promising to serve as the president of all Egyptians, and proposed to appoint a cabinet with a Christian and a woman as vice presidents.

Egypt under Morsi: all-powerful and incredibly calculating or a stooge

Mohammed Morsi represented the democratic will of the nation, having narrowly won a contested election. Nevertheless, he took office without a constitution to define his authority or a parliament to draft laws. Facing enormous, often conflicting, demands for rapid change he attempted much, failed often, accomplished little, and antagonized millions. Given the country's revolutionary change, some failures were inevitable, but the direction of the government's policies rightly worried women, the youth movements, civic organizers, the political opposition, and non-Islamists of many varieties.

In some ways a naïve college professor thrust by events into the highest office, Morsi often acted on impulse without recognizing the likely consequences. He promised that during the first 100 days he would tackle the nation's perpetual, but worsening traffic congestion, remove rubbish from the streets, improve security, and overcome shortages of bread and fuel. In fact, these challenges to daily life seemed to worsen. The only realistic improvements would have been rapid imports of flour and fuel, but too few funds were available. Once in power, the *Brotherhood's* economic policies seemed capitalist, opposing progressive taxation and constraining labor unions.

One particularly ill-conceived action was his declaration in late 2012 of wide-ranging executive powers. In effect, these powers placed him above any oversight, including the law (or at least the judges).

Morsi's narrow, partisan focus on the *Brotherhood's* agenda led to flawed actions elsewhere and charges of "creeping Islamization." The constituent assembly appointed to draft the new constitution was stacked with Islamists; a better-balanced membership would have calmed the nation and produced a less-flawed docu-

Serving and waiting: Protesters rest in the shade, ensuring that this tank does not move.

Photo courtesy of Jim Neergaard

ment. Though approved in a low-turnout referendum, the constitution's sections regarding basic freedoms— speech, religion, assembly, and equality—were sometimes vague and contradictory. They worried moderate Muslims; secularists and Christians feared them.

Some of Morsi's decisions that alarmed his critics suggested he cared little for their opinions. He apparently ignored the increasingly violent sectarian strife that included the killing of Copts within their Cairo cathedral. Instead of symbolically addressing Christian suspicions, he declined to attend the enthronement of Coptic Pope Tawadros II, though certainly other Muslim rulers had done so. Morsi also failed to order a serious response to attacks by militants in the Sinai, and initiated better relations with the *Hamas* rulers of Gaza.

One of the most absurd decisions was the appointment of a member of *al-Gama'a al-Islamiyya* as governor of Luxor. Its members had launched many attacks on foreign tourists, the bloodiest being the murder of nearly 60 near Luxor itself in 1997. While the group later renounced violence, the governor's appointment offended the tourist industry, the military, and many others. The minister of tourism resigned.

Despite the frequency of flawed decisions, Morsi could claim credit for some accomplishments. An early move settled relations with the military. It transferred the powers of SCAF to the presidency and thus placed civilian control over the armed forces for the first time in the republic's history. He also forced General Tantawi's resignation and appointed an apparently pious and sympathetic young officer, Abdul Fattah al-Sisi, as military commander and defense minister.

The government also succeeded in raising some vitally-needed funds abroad. With tourism collapsing, industrial output suffering from strikes and inflation, and demands for fuel that exceeded production, Egypt seriously lacked foreign exchange to finance imports. Fortunately, Qatar lent $3 billion and promised to provide natural gas supplies, badly needed for both households and power plants. However, negotiations with the IMF for a $4.8 billion loan proved inconclusive.

In 2013, Ethiopia announced the start of construction on the Grand Ethiopian Renaissance Dam on the Blue Nile, despite a 1929 treaty that nearly all Egyptians trust to limit upstream diversion of Nile waters (see "When Will the Taps Go Dry, p.10). Although the dam's purpose is hydroelectric rather than for irrigation, other dams are planned, and Egypt's military lacks the power to enforce the treaty. Nevertheless, Morsi responded with the threat "all options are open."

When the first anniversary of President Morsi's taking office approached in June 2013, popular agitation swept the country. A new activist group, *Tamarud*, launched a campaign to gather 15 million signatures calling for Morsi's resignation. The organizers eventually claimed 22 million, more than one quarter of the nation's population.

Tamarud reflected many of the original organizing groups behind the 2011 Tahrir Square demonstrations, including *Kifaya*, the *April 6 Movement*, the *National Salvation Front*, and several smaller parties. Ahmad Shafiq, Morsi's unsuccessful rival in the presidential elections, also supported *Tamarud*, as did, conditionally, the Salafist *Nour Party*. Thus the movement included most of the country's political spectrum, including former supporters of ex-president Mubarak, excepting, of course, the *Muslim Brotherhood.*

Whether by pre-arrangement with *Tamarud* or from a sense of national duty, the military commander, General Abdul Fatah al-Sisi, demanded that for the good of Egypt, Morsi and his critics should reach a compromise. However, in key televised addresses, Morsi remained defiant. He admitted that he had made mistakes, but also accused his opponents of trying to "sabotage" democracy: "The enemies of Egypt have not spared effort in trying to sabotage the democratic experience."

With millions demonstrating for Morsi's ouster, in smaller cities across the country as well as in Cairo, *Muslim Brotherhood* supporters turned out to support the legally-elected president. Violence occurred, and a crowed attacked and burned the *Brotherhood's* headquarters. Al-Sisi declared the nation was in danger and imposed a 48-hour deadline for Morsi to share power, or the military would impose a "roadmap for the future." As the crisis worsened, government power slipped from the hands of the president, with state-owned TV channels and newspapers demanding change.

Military Intervention & Presidential Elections

On July 3, 2013, al-Sisi announced that the Egyptian people had called on the

Ex-president Mohammed Morsi

military for help, "not to hold the reins of power, yet to discharge its civil responsibility." He suspended the constitution, granted the Chief Justice presidential powers, and pledged an interim government of technocrats until early presidential elections. Mohammed Morsi and other leading members of the *Brotherhood* and its political wing, the *Freedom and Justice Party*, were arrested. Its television channel went off the air.

While many foreign governments struggled to respond to the ouster of a legitimately elected president, pro-Morsi demonstrators came under fire by the military, who claimed they had suffered the initial attack. The initial 50 deaths, plus hundreds of injured, strengthened suspicion within the *Brotherhood* that in Egypt democracy would never offer Islamists a fair opportunity to rule. This verified *al-Qaeda's* traditional arguments that had been used to condemn the *Brotherhood's* involvement in politics. However, violence came not only from the military. In reprisal, Islamists attacked Christian churches and schools, some businesses, police stations, museums and other government facilities. For six weeks, Morsi supporters gathered at protest sites, the largest outside the Rabaa al-Adawiyah mosque in Cairo, where militant speeches advocated revolution. The sometimes-violent standoff ended weeks later, when the security services attacked the Islamists and cleared the protest sites. Hundreds were killed; the *Brotherhood* was banned and eventually termed a terrorist organization. Its leading members were arrested, and numerous charges were brought against Morsi.

While analysts and foreign governments deliberated over the appropriate reaction to the ouster of an elected government and the bloody repression of its supporters, evidence from the streets showed that many Egyptians had quickly tired of *Brotherhood* rule. For the short-run, most citizens either accepted the law-and-order of a military-backed regime or, if

The New Egypt: An unmarried Muslim couple enjoys time together, in public.
Photo by the author

President Abdul Fattah al-Sisi

opposing the regime, limited protests to brief affairs.

Against this background, a new constituent assembly re-wrote the Morsi constitution in ways that reflected the interests of the military and its non-Islamist allies. Significantly for a country with millennia of history with strong executive rule, the presidency emerged potentially weaker. Not only can a two-thirds vote of parliament initiate a referendum over holding early elections, but the prime minister appointed by the president must also carry the confidence of parliament. While the president must be a civilian, military influence is secured by the requirement that for the next 8 years the defense minister must be an officer approved by SCAF.

Other articles guaranteed freedom of faith, especially belief in the "heavenly religions of Islam, Christianity, and Judaism." The proposals prohibited political parties based on religion, though Islamic law is "the principal" source of legislation. Women's rights were better protected, as were children (the *Brotherhood* had feared that a ban on human trafficking might lead to the courts ruling against child marriage). Freedom of expression was enshrined, and the ministry of information dissolved. The constitution also dropped one of the more manipulated features of previous eras: influenced by marxist/socialist ideas, some parliamentary seats had been reserved for worker and farmer "independents," but after their election most displayed loyalty to the ruling party. The constitution was approved by a national referendum.

The next step towards a formal return to democracy was the 2014 presidential election. Al-Sisi, whose supporters had apparently used the resources of the "deep state" to popularize him as the nation's natural leader, resigned as military commander to run as a civilian. The banned *Brotherhood* urged its supporters to boycott the election; so did some moderates and liberals opposed to a military presidency. Promising expensive projects and a changed society, Al-Sisi won the election with 22 million of the 23 million votes cast, more than had Morsi two years earlier, though critics dismissed the win as relatively meaningless due to low voter turnout. His first cabinet was composed primarily of those who had held positions previously, including Prime Minister Ibrahim Mahlab.

Facing all the problems Mohammed Morsi had on taking office, plus the antagonism of political Islamists, Mahlab recognized great efforts were needed. Symbolically, one of his first decisions was to expect ministers to arrive at work by 7:00 am.

With parliamentary elections due in fall 2014, politicians must organize themselves to face the new realities. With the Brotherhood's Freedom and Justice Party dissolved, no party reflects the desires of a strong minority of voters, let alone a majority. Instead, multiple parties compete across the spectrum from moderate Islamic to Nasserist, socialist/labor, free-enterprise, and more, often based on the personalities of their leaders. For example, the Independent Current coalition pledged to support the president is composed of some 40 parties, many of them new. Other politicians formed alliances around Wafd, though not necessarily sharing its principles. With no party dominant, the key to success is likely the electoral alliances a party makes.

Culture: Perhaps no other country in the world is so overshadowed in the popular mind by the monuments, buildings, ruins and tombs of an ancient civilization as is Egypt. Only a few miles separate the incredible traffic jams and skyscrapers of modern Cairo from the great pyramids at Giza on the edge of the desert. Yet the modern culture of the country has little to do with ancient civilization. New religions, crops, and ways of living largely obliterated the customs of ancient times. Even the agricultural cycle for the Egyptian farmer—known as the *fellah*—has weakened, for the Aswan High Dam prevents the Nile from flooding his lands and depositing nourishing silt for the next year's crops.

Islamic values run deep in Egypt, particularly among the impoverished masses, but also among students and some professionals. In contrast, growing numbers of the middle and upper classes, both Muslims and Coptic Christians, blend traditional and western lifestyles, though most remain somewhat faithful to religious customs. The broader culture probably differs from western values most clearly in matters of gender and sexuality. An unmarried couple caught kissing passionately in public, for example, was sentenced to one year in jail.

The most delicate difficulty that tradition presents Egypt's government and society is female circumcision, a range of procedures often involving removal of the clitoris. Defended as an Islamic solution to avoid female immorality, the practice seems largely African, rather than Islamic; Coptic Christians continue it. Given its intimate nature, little is known about its effects on women (for example, does it render a woman uninterested in sex or increase the search for satisfaction?). It kills girls every year and leaves women maimed, but most Egyptian mothers apparently desire to have their daughters circumcised, despite a (poorly enforced) government ban on it since 1996.

Conservative social values create difficulties and obstacles for women in other ways as well. Physical abuse becomes more acceptable when, as survey data indicate, over 80% of young and middle-aged women consider wife-beating justified under certain circumstances. Most women report sexual harassment even when attired in Islamic modesty. Despite the efforts of non-governmental organizations, legal equality remains distant. In contrast to fairly rapid divorce procedures when requested by a man, a woman seeking to end a marriage must either spend years in the courts, or accept a no-fault divorce that leaves her without any financial assets from the marriage.

While society frowns strongly on premarital sexual activity, economic change and education increasingly bring single men and women together. Young couples unable or unwilling to have a formal wedding sometimes turn to "urfi" marriages, traditional but unregistered marriages often kept secret even from family. If the arrangement should break down—for example, if the woman becomes pregnant but the man does not wish to be bound by his commitments—the consequences fall most heavily on the woman.

Statue of Umm Kahlthoum, Egypt's great 20th century singer

Symmetrical and graceful beneath dramatic cliffs, the Temple of Hatshepsut

Literary Culture and Education

Though relatively poor, Egypt in many respects remains the cultural center of the Arab World, known for its novelists, short story writers, dramatists and poets. Indeed, in 1988 Naguib Mahfouz, known best in the English-speaking world for *Midhaq Alley* and *The Beginning and the End,* won the Nobel Prize for Literature. The first Arab writer to receive the honor, Mahfouz borrowed liberally from the traditions of European literature in his realistic novels of life in Cairo, because Arabic lacked a literary tradition in fiction. However, international recognition revived criticism of his work as blasphemous for portraying irreligious individuals who questioned Islam and his brave condemnation of Ayatollah Khomeini's death sentence on Salman Rushdie. Though in his 80s, Mahfouz barely survived an assassination attempt, but after recovering resumed walking the streets and alleys of his beloved Cairo until his death in 2006.

Though they lack the broad vision Mahfouz portrayed, a generation of sometimes angry young authors recently won widespread acclaim and even sales. The best known in translation is Alaa Al Aswany's *The Yacoubian Building* (2002), which reveals a society where the political corruption, sexual repression, and religious extremism flourish.

Founded in 988, the mosque school of al-Azhar in Cairo is one of the oldest universities in the world. Traditionally its professors sat at the base of one of the mosque's pillars, lecturing to students who came from many lands. There were no official examinations, but when the faculty considered a student proficient in a subject, they issued him a license to teach. Modern changes include formal diplomas, branches in medicine and other non-theological disciplines, and a women's program. The Grand Imam of al-Azhar remains an important spokesman for Sunni Islam, and offers guidance to believers on many theological issues.

For decades education for all remained a dream rather than reality. However, the government built thousands of new schools in the 1990s, for the 90% of young boys and 80% of girls who enroll. Adult literacy climbed from 40% in the 1970s to 60% by the end of the century. However, with their salaries as low at $35 per month, teachers have encouraged the practice of guiding the best learning in private tutoring sessions, and classroom study often decays into rote memorization. Not surprisingly, many children drop out: the law requiring nine years of school cannot be enforced. After just three or four years inside a classroom, many children begin working, even in agriculture and building construction, because of family poverty.

Egypt has lost its lead among Arab states in education, because of financial limitations and perhaps politically-appointed administrators as well. As in most professions, teachers in Egypt receive pitifully small salaries, so many of the best qualified have been lured to more prosperous countries to work at much higher remuneration. The quality of education at the University of Cairo and the half dozen other universities in Egypt is generally good, though in common with other Less Developed Countries, Egypt turns out too many liberal arts graduates, who fill (often needless) government positions or seek work abroad. In contrast, the country needs scientists, and especially skilled manual workers and technicians.

Two new cultural events promise to enrich the country during the coming years. In Alexandria, home in ancient times of a famous library, funding from UNESCO, the government, and other sources provided a $200 million library and conference center. The international competition to design the library drew over 500 entries, and the winning entry symbolizes Egypt's ancient heritage. The disc-shaped building slants with one side in the earth, the other elevated, recalling the ancient Egyptian sun-god.

The second cultural landmark, in Cairo, recalls the Islamic heritage in its dome, geometric windows, and marble colonnades. The New Opera House on the island of Gezira replaces the 19th century landmark gutted by fire in 1971. Built with Japanese assistance as an educational and cultural center, it offers the potential of becoming much more than a mere stage for musical and other art forms in Western languages.

Health services vary greatly according to family income and education. Although the universities train doctors to world standards, poverty prevents adequate medical services for many. Sanitation is often deplorable. In Cairo, some two million people live in areas without sewers. Preliminary construction of a new sewer system for the city began in early 1985. Years will be required to complete this project which is an urgent matter of public health. The press of millions of poor makes Cairo one of the world's most crowded and noisy cities. Indeed, a survey reported that 60% of Cairenes had used sedatives at least once against the noise and stress.

A Cairo street scene

Popular Culture and Sport

On the popular level, Cairo's constant flow of new films and television dramas makes it the Hollywood of the region. Plots frequently dramatize the sufferings of life, particularly marriage and family problems set against a background of conflict between traditions and modern individuality, as well as the persistent issue of class-consciousness. Difficulties sometimes arise with Islamic conservatives. In one example, a film about Joseph (*Al-Mohager*, "The Emigrant") was banned for showing a prophet on the screen.

Egypt's pre-eminence in Arabic film, television drama and music made the distinctive Cairene accent familiar, throughout the Arabic-speaking world. Other Arab countries attempted to develop their own television programming, but the arrival of music videos and satellite TV reinforced Egyptian dominance, as did the construction of Media Palace City (1995), an attempt to create a "Hollywood of the East" production center.

Egyptian musicians also dominate popular music and videos from Oman to North Africa. The "golden voice" of Umm Kalthoum captivated hearts across the Arab world during a career of six decades, and her recordings continue to sell well. By the 21st century, the country's music scene had developed a wide diversity of styles, from traditional songs and instruments to Arabic Pop, typically a fusion of traditional Arab styles and instruments with Western influences. Like popular music everywhere, romantic themes dominate, but despite the suggestive clothing of female pop stars, explicit references to sexuality are rare and would be censored, as would references to alcohol and politics.

Many Egyptians are passionate about soccer. Indeed, after Egypt lost a World

Cup qualifying match to Algeria in 2009, fans stirred by media coverage rioted in Cairo and attacked the Algerian embassy. While rarely successful in World Cup competitions, the Egyptian national team, nicknamed The Pharaohs, won the African Nations Cup in 2010 for an unprecedented third year in succession. Within the country, two teams traditionally vie for championship of the football league, Zamalek and Al-Ahly, the latter with over 40 million fans.

Economy: Although systematic efforts to modernize began two hundred years ago, personal incomes remain low. A rapidly growing population, misfortune in war, misguided government economic policies and a tradition of government regulation all reduced opportunities in the past 50 years. In addition, natural resources are few. There is no timber, no coal, and outside the Nile Valley, almost no water. Mineral deposits provide little wealth for a population so large, and are limited to modest oil deposits, natural gas, salt and manganese.

Camel market in Cairo

Visual evidence of the mixture of poverty and progress strikes even the casual tourist, in the form of barefoot children, simple farming methods, and the ever-present unemployed. Also obvious, the gap between the poor and the rich is enormous, the latter receiving incomes some 500 times the former. Though it has fallen from 3% in the 1980s, the population growth rate still requires feeding more than one million additional mouths food every year. Almost all live in the 4% of the country's territory comprising the Nile Valley and Delta. Egypt's population is roughly seven times that of New Jersey, but lives in only twice as much territory. Moreover, because one-third of the population is rural, average farms measure only a few acres. This overwhelms the ability of the fertile soil and warm climate to provide either sufficient food or a good standard of living.

Traditionally, agriculture formed the basis of the Egyptian economy. Famous for its desirable long-staple cotton, Egypt also produced and sometimes exported grains such as wheat and rice, as well as sugar, oranges, dates and tropical mangoes.

Before the 1952 Revolution, much farmland belonged to absentee landowners whose domains included entire villages. Under Gamal Abdul Nasser, the government attempted significant land reform, in part to break the political power of conservative landlords through limiting ownership to a maximum 50 acres in traditional farming areas. Irrigation schemes brought large tracts of desert under cultivation, and the Aswan High Dam (see page 58) provided more areas with successive crops per year. Public health and education improved in the villages.

Unfortunately, government regulations offset much of the progress. Investment in agriculture came low on the list of government priorities, while the new landowners lacked credit ratings to borrow. They of-

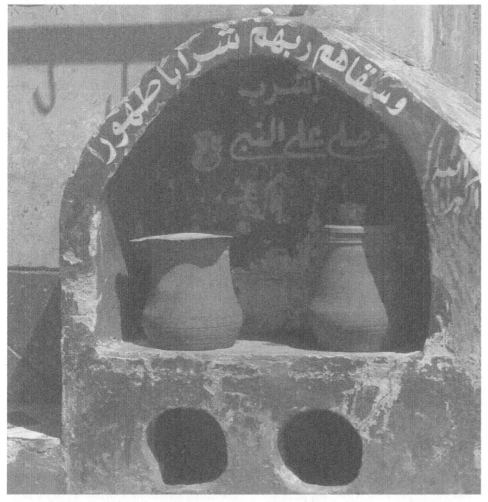

Caring for the needy: water pitchers placed for thirsty passersby in Upper Egypt

ten lacked formal education and technical training as well, both required to benefit from scientific advances in agriculture.

Recent reforms show the potential for substantial improvements in farm production and income. The output of deregulated crops has risen substantially. New policies towards reclaiming the desert stress the importance of research-intensive, low technology solutions, including the use of genetics to obtain salt-tolerant plants.

Effects of the Aswan High Dam

Above all else, Egypt under Nasser trusted the Aswan High Dam to solve poverty and raise farm output by storing the Nile's summer floods in the largest man-made reservoir in the world and then providing year-round irrigation for many areas and water for thousands of acres of desert. A great technical achievement as well as a foreign-policy success, the dam at its completion in 1971 met these goals, and its massive turbines once generated half of Egypt's electricity.

For all its benefits, however, the High Dam also brought problems. Across Egypt, the underground water table rose, threatening historical sites, and year-round irrigation spread bilharzia and other parasitic diseases, as well as obnoxious water hyacinths. Rising soil salinity and the loss of silt that enriched the soil, require expensive drainage systems and chemical fertilizers. World environmental issues pose other, less certain, risks to Egyptian agriculture. The low-lying Delta and coastal cities face inundation from the sea if the more alarming predictions of Global Warming prove true. Air pollution around Cairo poses a threat to plants and animals as well as humans. However, solutions to environmental problems sometimes benefit society. Alexandria's sewage, now flowing out to sea with harmful results, may be treated on land less expensively than in a new treatment plant for sea disposal. As a bonus, the nutrient-rich waste water will irrigate desert areas.

Industry: Industrial production began modestly in Egypt. After World War I some factories began to process food and cotton textiles, logical industries given the lack of coal and iron ore. The officers that led the 1952 Revolution desired to industrialize the country, motivated by socialist ideas that encouraged national self-sufficiency and equated modernity with heavy industry. However, socialists also loathed foreign investment and discouraged capitalists. As a result, the state nationalized a number of industrial companies, eventually controlling 85% of manufacturing assets. Those that remained suffered paralyzing regulations and red tape that hampered almost all trade and commerce.

Attempts to produce a complete range of manufactured goods within the country, from appliances to cars, provided expensive products of poor quality that required high tariff protection to compete against imports. (In contrast, the rapidly growing countries of East Asia follow the opposite policies, encouraging exports and foreign trade.)

Egypt's leadership in the Arab world also slowed economic growth. Opposing Israel militarily meant five wars (including the War of Attrition) in 25 years between 1948 and 1973. Besides the human costs of a large military force and several generations of weapons largely destroyed on the battlefield, the damage included Israeli attacks on economic targets and the devastation of cities along the Suez Canal. In addition to untold sums owed the Soviet Union for arms, the country purchased military hardware on credit from the United States, ironically during a period of peace with Israel. In contrast to past military expenses and losses, Egypt today has become a substantial and presumably profitable producer of weapons. Military exports have ranked alongside cotton as a major export. Although still dependent on imports for aircraft, electronics, and other sophisticated items, reports indicated Egypt had become self-sufficient in light anti-aircraft guns, armored trucks, rockets, bombs, and towed artillery.

Four Uncommon Assets in Change

For its past growth and modest prosperity, Egypt relied on four uncommon assets: oil, tourism, the Suez Canal, and earnings from Egyptian workers in other countries. Each provided foreign exchange, vitally important for a country perpetually short of money to purchase goods from other countries. Oil exports and canal revenues also provide alternatives to taxing citizens.

Exports of petroleum products once provided the largest foreign exchange earnings. Although not a member of the Organization of Petroleum Exporting Countries (OPEC), Egypt once exported larger quantities than some OPEC members. However, as fields matured in recent years, oil production fell, despite exploration for new deposits. By 2010, rising domestic demand for oil exceeded supply, and Egypt became an oil importing nation.

Fortunately, discoveries of natural gas deposits around Suez, in the Nile basin, and in the Western Desert created a surplus of that clean fuel, providing both alternatives to petroleum and supplies for export. The first natural gas export pipeline reached Jordan in 2003; the completion of liquefied natural gas "trains" enabled a greater volume to be shipped. However, rising domestic demand for natural gas resulted in legal limits on exports, and by 2013 Egyptian exporters met some obligations by shipping LNG from Qatar.

For two thousand years travelers have marveled at the Pyramids. A century ago, the wealth and beauty of Tutankhamun's tomb rendered a minor Pharaoh a household word. For the present era of mass tourism, Egypt possesses some of the world's most spectacular archaeological treasures and monuments. Other attractions exist as well, often inexpensive and rarely spoiled by rain. They range from sandy beaches along the Mediterranean to relatively unspoiled fishing and diving in the Red Sea. They include Mt. Sinai, where Jews and Christians traditionally believe God gave Moses the Ten Commandments. Arabs from oil states often seek culture and entertainment in Cairo, while visitors from West and East seek bargains in the city's *souks* (or suqs, pronounced like "duke") or enjoy luxury cruises on the Nile. Despite attacks by Muslim militants and visits cancelled during political stress, the industry earns billions during prosperous years, and its employees support some one million people.

One unique Egyptian economic benefit comes from the country's location connecting Asia and Africa. Cut through the Isthmus over 10 years, at a cost of perhaps 100,000 lives, the Suez Canal reduces greatly the distance ships must travel between Europe and the Indian Ocean. Tolls from the 18,000 ships that annually make the 15-hour journey through the 100-mile long canal exceed $500,000 per trip for the largest vessels able to use the waterway. These tolls provide a very important source of foreign exchange, exceeding $4 billion annually. Further earnings come from the "Sumed," the parallel oil pipeline from Suez to the Mediterranean.

At present, the very largest tankers (Ultra Large Crude Carriers, over 300,000 dead weight tons) are unable to use the waterway. Somewhat smaller vessels would strike bottom when loaded, given its depth of only 58 feet. As a result, some loaded tankers sail around Africa to markets in Europe and the U.S., but then return, empty, to the Persian Gulf through the canal. Thanks to this practice, more vessels use the canal going southbound than northbound. Dredging to widen, deepen, and straighten the canal continues, with the goal of eventually permitting passage by any vessel. Many Egyptian nationalists care passionately about the canal's nationalization in 1956, and successful operation since 1975.

The Pyramids attract all nationalities Courtesy: Juliet Bunch

No longer the most important source of foreign currency, remittances sent home by more than two million Egyptians working outside the country still play a very important role. Millions of Egyptians—almost all male, mostly young, and often educated—work abroad, primarily in the Gulf, as teachers, doctors, and other professionals but some as unskilled laborers. They sought foreign jobs, some of them dangerous, difficult or dirty, because remaining at home meant unemployment or low wages. They often planned to return in a few years, with funds saved for marriage and the purchase of a little land, a house, or perhaps a business. With pay abroad often 10 times the Egyptian rate, four years hard work might equal the gain of 20 years at home.

Reforms and Continuing Challenges

Though often seeming piecemeal and halfhearted, the economic reforms of the 1990s created an environment for sustained economic growth. Difficulties like the budget deficit, inflation, and the balance of payments deficit that had plagued the country for decades diminished when the government, hesitantly and slowly cut subsidies and controlled its spending.

The subsidies had distorted prices badly—kerosene, for example, had cost only $.20 per gallon, and legends describe farmers feeding bread to their animals, since it was cheaper than grains. Removing the subsidies encouraged more efficient use of resources, but Egypt's poor and middle classes found holes in their economic safety-nets. Afraid of popular backlash—in 1977 rioters had chanted at President Sadat, "Hero of the Crossing (of the Suez Canal), Where is our Breakfast?"—the cuts were scheduled gradually, and subtly. Rather than raise the price of bread, for example, the government cut the size of the pita-style loaf.

Cutting the government's large payroll and privatizing the companies it owned proved a more difficult task. In 1990, nearly one-third of all employed Egyptians worked for the government and its companies, far more than needed. A major purpose of the privatization drive was to provide jobs for the roughly 800,000 new job-seekers annually, but many legal, political and practical complications slowed the sale of government firms to private owners. Fortunately, new private companies flourished as the government removed regulations. By 1999 only about 20% of output came from government firms while the government's share of the workforce had fallen to 25%.

Some factories proved particularly difficult to privatize, particularly in textiles, where workers understood that secure lifetime employment offset low wages. Strikes spread across the Delta's textile industry in 2006–07 over rising prices, lagging wages, and broken promises by management, idling some of the largest factories in the world. Given higher inflation world-wide, living conditions have often declined for industrial workers, resulting in strikes and labor disputes after the breakdown of authoritarianism in 2011.

The Future: Mohammed Morsi failed as president of Egypt. Yet his removal and the subsequent bloody suppression of his supporters are longer-term tragedies for the country, and indeed, for the wider Arab and Islamic worlds. For almost 70 years, despite being banned, harassed, and often persecuted, the *Brotherhood* has reflected the desires of millions of Egyptians. The ouster of a legitimately elected *Muslim Brotherhood* president will strengthen its extremists who believe that democracy is not an option, that power must be seized. And justice is hardly seen to occur when a judge sentences more than 500 people to death for a single murder, as recently happened. Twice.

For many Egyptians and foreign commentators, the election of an immediate past military commander as president confirms that Egypt's recent protests and elections meant very little: beyond the public charade, the "deep state" composed of the military, state-owned firms, wealthy private business interests, and their sympathetic politicians and judges really control the nation. If so, then expect a return to moderately veiled military rule, continued corruption, and political stagnation.

However, Abdul Fattah al-Sisi may prove more than just another youthful (aged 59 at his inauguration) Mubarak. Raised in a pious home, he clearly values Islam in his personal life. His wife dresses in Islamic modesty. He apparently cares deeply about Egypt's role in the world. His support for a constitution that modestly increased parliamentary powers at the expense of the presidency indicates that his concept of the nation extends beyond the military parade grounds.

Like the country's many rulers before him, his challenge is to restore confidence in the economy and the Egyptian pound, increase imports of petroleum products and natural gas to end the shortages, and guide the economy to provide jobs, especially for the 40% of young adults who are unemployed. If the coalition of forces that brought down Mohammed Morsi in July 2013 continues to support him, there is hope. If not—and the Islamist *al-Nour Party* will play a crucial role in coming months—the dangers of chaos in the rest of Egypt will resemble the anarchy now threatening the northern Sinai. Amidst the tragedy, there are grounds for hope.

The Islamic Republic of Iran

Supporters of former President Muhammad Khatami celebrate his victory in 1997. The flowers faded. AP/Wide World Photo

Hoping for flowers again: Celebrating the election of Hassan Rouhani, 2013

Area: 636,313 square miles (1,648,043 sq. km.).
Population: 78 million.
Capital City: Tehran (pop. 7.4 million, with suburbs, over 10 million).
Climate: Arid, except for regions of moderate to heavy rainfall in the northwest. Temperature changes are extreme, from cold winters of the central plateau and northern mountains to the intense heat of the humid southern coast
Neighboring Countries: Armenia, Azerbaijan, Turkmenistan (North); Afghanistan (East); Pakistan (Southeast); Iraq (West); Turkey (Northwest)
Time Zone: GMT +3 hours, 30 minutes
Official Language: *Farsi*, or Persian.
Other Principal Tongues: Kurdish, Baluchi, Luri, Armenian, Turkish, Shushtari, Azeri and Arabic.
Ethnic Background: People are identified mainly according to language (about 80% Persian or Iranian), but also according to tribal group or religion.
Principal Religion: Shi'a Islam (89%), Sunni Islam (10%), Baha'i (1%).
Chief Industrial Products: Petroleum and petroleum products, carpets, iron and steel, light manufactured goods, vehicle assembly.
Agricultural Produce and Livestock: Wheat, barley, pistachios, rice, sugar beets, sugar cane, potatoes, sheep, goats, cattle and chickens.
Major Trading Partners: Japan, Germany, Italy, France and the United Arab Emirates.
Currency: Rial (10 rials = 1 toman)
Former Colonial Status: Under influence of Russia and Britain (1907–1923); occupied by Soviet and British troops (1941–1945).
National Day: February 1.
Chief Executive: Hassan Rouhani, President (2013).
"Head of the Revolution" and "Supreme Leader": Ayatollah Seyyid Ali Khamenei.
National Flag: Three equal horizontal stripes of (top to bottom) green, white and red. The edges of the green and red stripes carry 22 repetitions of the words *Allah-o-Akbar*, "God is Great." A red emblem symbolizing the Islamic Republic is centered in the white stripe.
Gross Domestic Product: $405 billion (falling); $974 billion (PPP).
GDP per capita: $12,500 (PPP).

The heart of Iran is neither picturesque nor fertile. Occupying more than half the country, the center is a bleak, windswept combination of desert and salt-flats—scorching hot in summer days and freezing cold during winter nights. However, the outlying mountains and watered plains support large populations, making Iran one of the three most populous Middle Eastern countries.

The least typical region is the coast of the Caspian Sea, which lies below sea level. Created by abundant rainfall and warm weather, this garden of Iran is the most densely populated area of the country. Several million people also live in the extreme northwest province of Azerbaijan, a land of mountain forests, cultivated valleys and good rainfall. Tabriz, once Iran's second largest city, is the center of this province. Other important populations of farmers and herders live in the mountainous regions along the border with Iraq on the west, and east of the Caspian Sea near Turkmenistan.

The rest of the country is largely uninhabited except for nomads who make great seasonal wanderings from north to south. The elevation of the central plateau (3,000 to 6,000 feet) produces great extremes of temperature; 110° or 115° (F) during the day in the summer contrasts with sub-freezing temperatures of the winter nights. The southern coast and neighboring areas are the hottest regions of Iran; frost is unknown there. Light rainfall provides sparse pasture for livestock.

Tehran has grown in two centuries from a village to a huge city and the seat of a highly centralized government. Railroads, roads and trade center on it; industry is concentrated there. The other major cities are Tabriz and Isfahan, both of them commercial and handicraft centers with long histories.

Geologically, the country sits uneasily atop seismic zones where the Arabian and Eurasian tectonic plates meet. As the plates press against each other, they generate more earthquakes than any in any other country, with small quakes striking daily. Except for Isfahan, all major Iranian cities lie in zones of high or very high seismic activity. Deprived of timber, Iranians construct homes out of concrete block or bricks, and when powerful earthquakes strike, the loss of life is often catastrophic. For example, the relatively small city of Bam in eastern Iran lost 30,000 dead in December 2003.

History: Civilization stretches back thousands of years in Iran, whose name means "Land of the Aryans," and its Indo-European peoples formed several of the notable kingdoms of ancient history (see Historical Background). Later invaders added Arab Islam and Turkish warriors to Iranian society.

So ancient is the history of Iran—or Persia, as it was traditionally known—that the modern period began hundreds of years ago, with the Safavid dynasty in the 16th century and the widespread adoption of Shi'a Islam (see Historical Background). The Safavid Empire reached its greatest power and extent under Shah Abbas (1587–1629), after whose death it declined. By the early 18th century, Persia was threatened by Turkey on the west, Russia on the north and the Afghans on the east.

After an Afghan invasion ended the Safavid dynasty, Nadir Shah (1736–1747) restored much of the country's unity and conquered additional territory. Famous for his military exploits and adventures, he returned from invading India with incredible wealth and the famous Peacock Throne, but he failed to found a dynasty. The peaceful reign of Karim Khan Zand (1750–1779) was followed by the establishment of the Qajar dynasty. Though often beset with tribal revolts and bloodshed over the succession, the sometimes—brutal Qajars maintained power until 1925. Shah Agha Mohammed Khan made Tehran his capital in 1788.

Under Qajar rule, Persia fought unsuccessful wars with Russia, the Ottoman Turks and the Afghans, and lost territory to each. Under sometimes capricious rulers, domestic politics often stagnated at best, and the country failed to advance with the times.

Rivalry between the Russian Empire and the British Empire often focused on Persia. Russia sought to expand to the warm water ports of the Persian Gulf, while Britain was concerned primarily for the security of India. Russia enjoyed more influence in Persia, though the British worked to gain favor through agents in Tehran. Finally, in 1907 Russia and Britain arrived at an agreement—without any consideration of Persian desires in the matter—providing Russia a "sphere of influence" in the north, and Britain one in the south. A strip of less important territory in the middle was left as a neutral zone.

Dissatisfaction with foreign influence and the ineffectiveness of the monarchy in resisting it grew stronger in the late 19th century, symbolized by disapproval of granting British companies a tobacco monopoly in 1890. This produced protests and a ban from the clergy on using tobacco.

Partly influenced by Western ideas of political freedom, in 1906 groups of merchants, religious leaders and reformers compelled the shah to grant a constitution and allow a parliament, known as the Majlis. Known as the Constitutional Revolution (1905–1911), these changes began an era of numerous struggles between the monarchy and the Majlis over control of the government.

During a decade and a half of struggle, marked by several closures and re-openings, the Majlis and its reformers had no

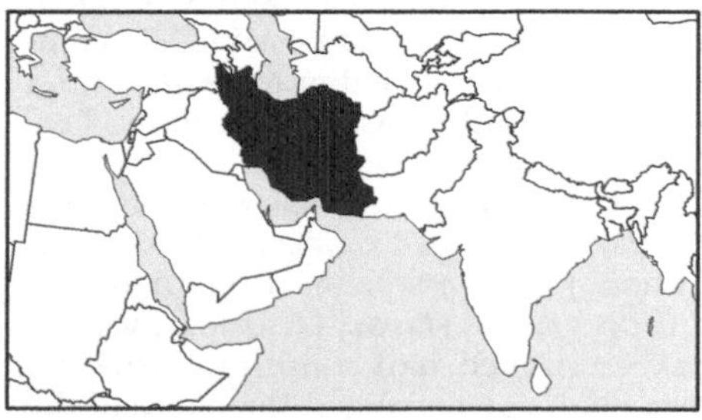

Iran

A map of Persia from a 1560 atlas

more success in strengthening the country and reducing foreign influence than had the monarchy. Central authority collapsed almost entirely during World War I, as Ottoman, Russian, and British forces and puppets occupied parts of the country. This set the stage for the rise of a dictator. In 1921 Reza Khan, deputy commander of the Cossack Brigade, joined a *coup d'état.* After creating a national army to replace various foreign-influenced units, in 1923 Reza compelled the shah to appoint him prime minister. The shah then left for exile, and in 1925 Reza Khan had the Majlis depose the Qajar dynasty. Later that same year he proclaimed himself Reza Shah Pahlavi, taking the ancient name Pahlavi from Persian history because he, a commoner, needed a dynastic name.

A man of action rather than theories, Reza Shah improved and enlarged the army—then he used it, sometimes harshly, to establish obedience and order in every part of the country. He worked to gain full independence, to make himself the nation's master, and to make it as much like modern Europe as possible. He commanded the construction of roads, and a railroad from the Caspian Sea to the Persian Gulf. He introduced new secular laws and moved away from Islamic religious law. He encouraged modern technical education, forced people to dress more like Europeans, and started factories. By 1942, they employed half a million workers. Reza Shah even changed the name of the country from Persia to Iran to impress the world that things had changed. Moderate but steady income from oil exports produced by the Anglo-Iranian Oil Company financed the new projects.

After the German invasion of the Soviet Union in 1941, Soviet and British troops occupied Iran to prevent Reza Shah from allying with Nazi Germany, and to secure the country's oil and transportation routes for Allied use. Reza abdicated and went into exile, where he died.

When the Allied troops began to withdraw from Iran after the end of the war, the new shah, young Mohammed Reza faced wide opposition. Factions of many sorts, previously repressed by his determined father, vied to control the government. Great landowners, who paid nearly no taxes, attempted to dominate politics. Nomadic chieftains sought to free themselves and their tribes from Reza Shah's central authority. Shi'a religious leaders denounced secular government, and elderly politicians schemed for office. In the streets, the Communist-leaning *Tudeh Party* held sway, and foreign powers courted ethnic minorities.

In these circumstances, the Soviet Union attempted to form an autonomous Communist regime in Azerbaijan, the Turkish-speaking northwestern province. However, the United States and Britain stood by the shah, and Soviet troops withdrew in 1946. The Iranian army dealt severely with the separatist leaders.

In response to the dire economic conditions, a seven-year plan won approval from the Majlis in 1949. Because the plan's projected expenses exceeded local taxes, Iranian politicians sought what they considered a fairer share of income from oil exports. When Anglo-Iranian refused higher payments, in an atmosphere of emotional nationalism the Majlis in 1951 nationalized the entire petroleum industry. The elderly politician who had championed the bill, Mohammed Mossadeq, became prime minister. His government found itself unable to produce and market oil in the face of an international boycott organized by Britain, and during the next two years the country became poorer and suffered serious political disturbances. However, Mossadeq firmly refused any compromise, and demanded full national economic independence, meaning Iranian control of its oil.

President Hassan Rouhani

The shah dismissed Mossadeq in mid-1953, but the prime minister refused to leave office. Lacking authority and fearing mobs and riots in Tehran, the shah and his queen fled the country. Iran tottered, near financial collapse and anarchy as Mossadeq attempted to seize more power. However, urged and financed by the U.S. CIA, forces loyal to the monarchy took to the streets, and the army arrested Mossadeq and restored order. The shah returned, and the United States provided an emergency grant to begin the country's recovery. Large-scale military and technical assistance was promised, and in 1954 a compromise agreement on the oil industry permitted exports to flow and provided fees and royalties. Thus, linked to America, the shah began to dominate the political scene in alliance with the army.

Because he faced continued opposition from such groups as wealthy landholders, extreme religious elements, politically active students and politicians of various ideologies, the shah developed several methods of maintaining his authoritarian rule. The National Security and Intelligence Organization (SAVAK) was created in 1957 to control political activity and the press. Through arbitrary arrests and torturing of prisoners, SAVAK came to possess great power, though it made many enemies for the shah's government. While effective for a decade at suppressing Islamic fundamentalists, SAVAK also divided the modernized middle class and left it suspicious of the shah.

To win the support of peasants and moderate reformers, and decrease the appeal of leftist revolutionaries, Shah Mohammed Reza proclaimed a "White Revolution" in 1963. Two aspects of it, land distribution and greater rights for women, aroused the fierce opposition of many Shi'a clergy. They considered that the changes in the role of women threatened family morality, and the distribution of land to the peasants from vast religious foundations endangered the substantial revenues they received as administrators. While a national referendum overwhelmingly approved the reforms, they turned religious leaders such as Grand Ayatollah (Shi'a clergy's highest rank) Ruhollah Khomeini into irreconcilable enemies.

To support his government, the shah rewarded the upper ranks in the civil service and army with good incomes. Thus, he gained support from a small elite, but the almost ubiquitous bribery and other forms of dishonesty among officials contributed to the hostility of others. Increasingly, the shah proposed grand projects, and emphasized his imperial title. In 1971 when he spent millions of dollars celebrating the 2,500th anniversary of the founding of the ancient Persian Empire. To prevent opposition in the Majlis and yet maintain a form of representative government, the shah sponsored a royal political party, while other parties were outlawed.

Though failing, perhaps unavoidably, to meet the needs and desires of most citizens, the government attempted to assert Iran's role as a regional power with large and well-equipped military forces. This power influenced neighbors. After decades of tension, in 1975 Iran and Iraq agreed to move their border from the Iranian shore of the Shatt al-Arab to midchannel. Because the river connects the oil center of Abadan with the Gulf, Iran gained long-sought benefits. In return, Iran halted supplies to Iraq's rebellious Kurds.

Vast increases in oil revenues during the 1970s enabled the government to rush development at home while purchasing the latest U.S. weapons such as the F-15 fighter. The guns-and-butter approach created wealth for many Iranians, but the lower classes gained little prosperity, suffered high inflation, and resented the corruption and westernized lifestyles of the rich. In between, the middle class found few legal political opportunities. With the parliamentary opposition stifled, illegal left-wing parties and Islamic groups widened the appeal of extremists.

Riots in the religious city of Qom and in Tabriz in early 1978 showed deep popular dissatisfaction. In response, the army fired on the mobs, killing many. These deaths triggered further riots, and despite official bans, demonstrations spread to Tehran and elsewhere. Massacres by loyal troops ended all pretense of popular support for the shah, and the bloodshed united the rival opposition groups in the single goal of ousting the monarch. Despite his age (76) and long years of exile (14), Ayatollah Khomeini assumed leadership of the movement.

After months of strikes and confusion, with oil production and exports halted and the economy in chaos, Shah Muhammad Reza left the country in early 1979. As a concession, he placed the government under a long-time critic. However, the concessions came too late. Khomeini quickly flew home to a triumphant welcome in Tehran, and appointed Mehdi Bazargan prime minister. Despite the lavish attention the shah had paid it, the army abandoned its struggle against the revolutionaries. Voters overwhelmingly approved the creation of the Islamic Republic of Iran; it became official on April 1, 1980.

The Islamic Republic immediately faced major problems. Restive ethnic minorities, many of them Sunni rather than Shi'a, threatened rebellion. The economy required emergency measures, but was largely ignored. Rival groups and individuals who had united against the monarchy now struggled violently for power. To maintain power, self-appointed "revolutionary courts" began imposing long

Ayatollah Ruhollah Khomeini

Iran

Iran's Imperial Family in exile, Panama (1980).

prison terms or death sentences on former officials, accused wrongdoers or "sinners." By mid-1979 some 200 executions had been carried out—often within hours of arrest. Opposing groups began political assassinations, and Khomeini had ordered the establishment of a special militia for his *Islamic Revolutionary Council*.

When militants seized the U.S. embassy in Tehran in 1979 and took 63 hostages, they won wide approval in the streets. Many political leaders approved the illegal action, but the Bazargan cabinet resigned almost immediately because it had no effective authority. Khomeini then directed the *Islamic Revolutionary Council* to take control. International pressures on Iran to release the hostages proved useless, and an American attempt to rescue the hostages in 1980 ended unsuccessfully in the Iranian desert. After the deposed Shah died in Egypt, the hostages finally were released in 1981, a gift for Ronald Reagan's inauguration.

Against this chaotic background, a plebiscite overwhelmingly approved a new constitution. Besides the typical democratic institutions of the elected Majlis (parliament) and president, the Islamic Constitution established two novel centers of power. First, the Supreme Leader (or faqih) is the chief theologian, appointed by the 86-member Assembly of Experts. He interprets religious law and acts on behalf of the Hidden Imam who disappeared in 878. The second unique source of authority is the Council of Guardians, an appointed committee of 12 clergymen charged with ensuring that proposed laws conform to Islam. Given these two innovations, supreme authority lies in Islamic law as interpreted by religious scholars, rather than in the nation's (un)sovereign people. For the first decade of revolutionary Iran, Ayatollah Khomeini held the position of Supreme Leader.

The relatively moderate Bani Sadr won the 1980 presidential election, but by 1981, facing impeachment, he fled the country. The clergy's *Islamic Republican Party (IRP)* then completely dominated government, but faced an uprising by the secular and socialist *Mujahedin-e Khalq*. The regime suppressed the uprising with great brutality and torture, executing tens of thousands of alleged *Mujahedin*, who for their part turned to bombings and assassinations, and decimated the *IRP* leadership in a single blast.

The War with Iraq, 1980–1988

Considering Iran weakened by a deteriorating economy, political tensions and international isolation, Iraq invaded its oil-rich southwest in 1980, capturing border cities and driving miles into the country. Within months, however, Iranian troops had reorganized and obtained supplies for its U.S.-made weaponry, some obtained from Israel and financed by oil sales to the "Great Satan," the United States. Revolutionary Guards counterattacked, and largely regained the border by 1982.

Despite major offensives, Iranian forces failed to cross the marshy terrain into southern Iraq. To compensate for Iraq's superior weapons, Iran began human wave attacks with poorly-trained teenagers. Nevertheless, Iraqi tanks, aircraft, helicopter gunships, and even poison gas effectively stalled both conventional attacks and the human wave onslaught.

Despite the casualties and growing war-weariness, Khomeini rejected any peace that kept the Iraqi president, Saddam Hussein, in office. Desperate, the government secretly worked to release American hostages seized by pro-Iranian groups in Lebanon in exchange for arms and intelligence. Thus equipped, in 1986 troops and the Revolutionary Guards crossed the Shatt al-Arab waterway below Basra and occupied the Faw peninsula, Iran's most successful offensive during eight years of war.

Although Iraq seemed on the verge of collapse, Iranian dominance rapidly faded. Rivalries between the Revolutionary Guards and the military ended their effective cooperation. After the Iran-Contra scandal broke, the U.S. halted vital supplies.

Iraq responded to its loss of Faw by widening the conflict. It bombed oil export centers at Khark Island and tankers hauling Iranian crude oil. When Iranian forces then attacked tankers carrying crude oil from Arab nations, the Western nations became involved and destroyed most of the Iranian navy.

By 1987 defeats followed disasters. Tehran and other cities suffered missile attacks and bombing raids, and Iraqi troops quickly recaptured the Faw peninsula. The Iranian *Mujahedin-e Khalq* "liberated" bits of Iranian territory. Meanwhile, an obvious Iranian role in hijacking a Kuwaiti airliner isolated Tehran in world affairs. When a U.S. cruiser mistakenly shot down an Iranian airliner, Iran failed to gain a UN condemnation.

At last, the leadership recognized that continuing the war threatened the Islamic Revolution itself and Iran quickly accepted a ceasefire (1988). However, the ceasefire did not ensure peace. Disputes remained over the Shatt al-Arab, and the repatriation of POWs was soon halted. Some unfortunates lingered in captivity for about 20 years.

Domestic Issues under Khomeini

The war with Iraq overshadowed almost eight years of the Islamic Revolution's first decade. After the guns fell silent the next year, debates raged within

Iran over the future of the Islamic Revolution. In defeat, its leaders lashed out at possible rivals. Thousands of opposition supporters were probably executed, the savage response by a divided government to opposition viewpoints and the *Mujahedin-e Khalq's* invasion. Facing violent insurrection against the Islamic Revolution, the *Islamic Republican Party* had appealed to religion, ruled by repression, and tortured rivals. Because the *IRP* opposed any alternative loyalties, the pro-Moscow *Tudeh Party* joined the *Mujahedin* as victims. Nevertheless, the often-distorted formalities of a democratic system continued.

Single-party elections to the Majlis brought fewer clergy and other significant changes to its membership. However, the very conservative Council of Guardians repeatedly blocked significant changes, deeming them contrary to Islamic principles. The Council of Guardians also gained a major role in elections through its power to disqualify candidates.

Bitter struggles also deepened within the political elite. "Hardliners," those determined to spread the Islamic Revolution, supported the overthrow of unsympathetic Arab regimes. They also waged a vitriolic struggle against Israel and the United States. By contrast, "pragmatists" wished to use worldwide horror at Iraq's use of chemical weapons to gain closer ties with Western Europe and even the United States, and thus hasten reconstruction.

The scope for rebuilding was vast. A quarter million had died, and tens of thousands were maimed for life. Important cities and industries lay devastated, including one of the largest oil refineries in the world. Contemporary estimates placed the probable cost of reconstruction at $200 billion.

The publication abroad of the novel *The Satanic Verses* strengthened the hardliners. For a variety of reasons, all Muslims found the book offensive. Its author, Salman Rushdie, lightheartedly portrayed the Prophet Muhammad's reference to three idol goddesses as the daughters of Allah (see Historical Background) as a deliberate attempt to compromise, not a mistaken vision. In addition, Muhammad appears unable to recognize changes his secretary makes to the wording of the angelic message—but to believing Muslims, the *Qur'an* is the Word of God, dictated word-by-word to Muhammad and memorized by his followers.

When Ayatollah Khomeini sentenced Rushdie to death—a response likely considered appropriate by many religions before the modern era—he strengthened Iran's hardliners at home. However, the death sentence isolated Iran internationally: any Western sympathy with the anguish of devout Muslims rapidly disappeared in the face of death threats against an author.

In 1989, Ayatollah Ruhollah Khomeini died, just weeks after he disowned his heir-apparent. Nevertheless, the succession flowed smoothly. The Assembly of Experts appointed President Ali Khamenei as Supreme Leader. For good measure, given his modest clerical rank, he gained the rank of ayatollah as well. This appointment preserved the unity of mosque and state, at the cost of appointing a low-ranking clergyman who had succeeded in politics to the highest theological position.

Weeks later, with significant rivals blocked from nomination, the speaker of parliament, Ali Akbar Hashemi Rafsanjani, handily won the presidency. The voters also approved constitutional reforms that gave the president control over the cabinet and military.

A shrewd politician, Rafsanjani drew power into his own hands. His priority was reconstruction, and thus an end to Iran's isolation. He negotiated the purchase of Soviet factories and electric generating stations in return for natural gas. He encouraged the release of American hostages in Lebanon, and announced that Iran would not export its revolution. He removed several powerful hardliners from the cabinet. However, the regime balanced friendly gestures towards the United States with fiery denunciations of the "Great Satan," and crackdowns on the opposition.

Despite its dramatic impact on politics and the position of women, during the 1990s the Revolution remained incomplete. There were successes, especially the roads and electricity that reached many more villages, and higher rural standards of living. However, income inequality had widened. The poorest 40% of the population shared only 2.9% of national income, and the top 1% received 22% of it. Socially and politically, the country stagnated. Despite scheduled elections, the regime limited freedom. It punished journalists and artists whose independent views became too strident. For example, Professor Abdol Karim Soroush was forced into exile for suggesting that the clergy's involvement in politics might harm religion.

Soroush was fortunate. Thousands faced charges of drug offences, many trumped-up or resulting from confessions extracted by torture. Executions continued, often secretly, to complicate information-gathering by human rights groups. A Baha'i who converted to Islam but then reverted to his former faith was sentenced to death. Five authors and politicians were murdered in Tehran within a few weeks. "The work of foreign powers," claimed Supreme Leader Ayatollah Khamenei, but the evidence implicated agents from the Intelligence Ministry.

Khatami and the False Dawn of Reform

Against this background, in 1997 Mohammad Khatami, the relatively tolerant Minister of Islamic Guidance in the 1980s, upset the analysts' calculations and challenged the leading conservative for the presidency.

Even outwardly, Khatami symbolized the changes in society, for he wore both fine European-style clothes and the black turban that designates descent from the Prophet Muhammad. No secularist, his book *Fear of the Wave* proclaimed Islam superior to the West. However, from a study of philosophy, Khatami gained an appreciation of the role of freedom, the benefits of justice, and the importance of civic responsibility. Campaigning on these themes, he attracted wide support: the middle classes, the young who resented personal restrictions, women, and advocates of greater economic freedom. Leftists who desired state control over the economy supported him also, mostly to defeat the conservatives.

The election results were astonishing, particularly in the countryside, where some rural clergy had openly forbidden their followers to vote for Khatami. He won there decisively as well.

Though the conservatives lost the presidency by a landslide, they did not fall from power. The Supreme Leader and other conservatives allied with fundamentalists (those who favored Islamic law) to block change. Conservatives vetoed reformist nominees to the Assembly of Experts, and several student demonstrators were sentenced to death, without any evidence of a trial. On the streets, fundamentalist toughs attacked political rallies by moderates.

The most decisive battleground took place in the press. Brash reformist newspapers sprang up and attacked individual officials and narrow-minded policies. For example, *Neshat* questioned the role and authority of the Supreme Leader, Ayatollah Khamenei. Another paper mocked a conservative reappointed to direct the national TV network by publishing a cartoon showing a TV set as a toilet.

The police and conservative judges, beyond President Khatami's control, reacted to the explosion of criticism by arresting editors and closing papers. The leading reformer, Abdollah Nouri, was fined, sentenced to 74 lashes with a braided leather whip, imprisoned for five years, and barred from writing or publishing. Such judgments shocked reformers, but apparently most people cared little.

In 1999, police responded violently to student protests, raiding a dormitory at

Tehran University, killing one student and injured many. This provoked student demonstrations in Tehran and Tabriz; when suppressed by police and fundamentalist gangs, the students turned to riots. Though the students had strongly supported Khatami's reform policies, he could not condone violence, and condemned the rioters.

Political activity exploded during the Majlis elections of 2000. For the first time, identifiable political parties appeared, rather than factions of the clergy. The most prominent of the reformist alliance was *Mosharekate* (the *Islamic Iran Participation Front*) headed by Reza Khatami, the president's brother. Election day provided reformers a two-thirds majority in the Majlis.

However, the reformist victory again aroused conservative militiamen, judges, and other government employees outside the president's authority. With the backing of the Supreme Leader, the police closed every reform newspaper and arrested many journalists. The courts convicted reformers of crimes against Islam that the Majlis could not overturn.

Although his reform program had already failed in many areas, in 2001 Muhammad Khatami won re-election, and once again, his victory strengthened the conservatives' determination to enforce strict Islamic rule. Secret trials convicted journalists, old-time nationalists, and even members of parliament for opposing the Islamic Republic. Hardliners attacked peaceful reformist rallies and infiltrated student organizations. Judges sentenced young men to public whippings for drinking alcohol or making social advances at women, heedless of the danger of alienating public opinion.

Ex-president Mahmoud Ahmadinejad

The reform era effectively ended with the 2004 Majlis elections. The Council of Guardians blocked most reformist candidates, and thus guaranteed conservative victories for nearly half the seats before a single ballot was cast. Along with some other reformist parties, *Mosharekate* chose to boycott the election. The reformers' defeat left President Mohammad Khatami an isolated lame duck.

Ahmadinejad's 2005 Victory

The unexpected victor of the 2005 presidential contest was Tehran's relatively inexperienced mayor, Mahmoud Ahmadinejad, a former member of the Revolutionary Guards. A populist, he won the election by appealing to the poor, the unemployed and others struggling with the weak economy—individuals particularly upset by corruption and possible cuts in subsidies. His other themes, including defiance of Western demands over Iran's nuclear program and opposition to Western culture, also won votes. The appeal of social liberalization proved to be limited to a relatively small, well-off, university-educated class.

In office, Ahmadinejad proved wildly popular with the rural poor, but dangerously incompetent in matters of state. He nominated an oil minister rejected by the conservative Majlis, twice. He proposed admitting women to soccer games, and earned a decisive rejection from religious conservatives, worried about allowing women to view male legs and hear the spectators' profanities.

On the streets, yet another crackdown on morality (or, rather, women showing hair and ankles) pleased fundamentalists but angered many university students. Given the president's view of reality, he perhaps feared a cultural "soft revolution" that would weaken the purity of the Islamic Republic. If so, the fear was strengthened by American policy, including $75 million to strengthen democracy in Iran. Several Iranian-American scholars visiting Iran were arrested and released only months later, while a U.S.-born journalist was tried and convicted of spying, but was released. Paranoia became both politics and policy; Baha'is and others were targeted.

Ahmadinejad's populist economic policies proved particularly bizarre. Though benefiting from high international oil prices—oil revenues reached $50 billion in 2006–07—his administration spent even more lavishly, and paid the bill partly by raiding the Oil Stabilization Fund, set aside by law for years of low prices. In addition, the central bank allowed the money supply to grow at 40% per year, stoking inflation.

Severe consequences appeared: by 2007 housing prices had doubled, and there were shortages of some foods, particularly meat. Inflation reportedly climbed to 30%, but government figures showed less. Gasoline rationing was imposed, despite violent protests. During the cold winter of 2008, natural gas and electricity ran short, apparently due in part to unpaid bills for gas imports. The government's responses included contradictory policies like decreeing interest rates below the rate of inflation, and selling shares of government corporations to the poor for a fraction of their value. Politics apparently replaced the laws of economics, at the cost of enormous subsidies.

By 2010, with oil prices at half their 2008 peak, Ahmadinejad struggled with the Majlis to reduce $40 billion of the $100 billion cost of annual energy and food subsidies, with the president arguing, bizarrely, that doing so would cut inflation. Recognizing that such cuts would

Presidents Rafsanjani and Gorbachev in Moscow, June 1989 AP/Wide World Photo

raise inflation and probably ignite social unrest, Parliament hesitated. However, the monthly ration of very cheap gasoline (under US $0.40/gallon) was cut from 20 gallons to 15 per vehicle, saving money on imported gasoline.

Foreign Relations: Risking Peace and Prosperity

In foreign affairs Ahmadinejad's populism proved dangerous, not merely bizarre. Republican Iran had historically opposed the West. It had condemned peace moves between Israel and the Palestinians and sympathized with suicide attacks on Israeli civilians. Iran trained fundamentalists in terrorism, and aided Lebanon's *Hizbullah*. Consequently, Iran has remained isolated.

Ironically, the U.S. and Iran sometimes shared common interests. Both countries faced a common enemy to Iran's east—the Taliban regime in Afghanistan—as well as one to the west, Saddam Hussein's Iraq. Iran openly permitted U.S. relief supplies for Afghan refugees to cross its territory. Secretly, both countries aided the Northern Alliance.

After September 11, 2001, even the hardline Supreme Leader condemned terrorism. The U.S. invasion of Iraq in 2003 benefited Iran so greatly that some analysts suspect that Tehran planted evidence to spur the U.S. actions. The invasion ousted a hated dictator who had attacked Iran, ended the persecution of Iraq's Shi'a, and brought them to power. However, Iranian policymakers felt threatened by the presence of U.S. ground forces to the east and the west and an American fleet concentrated off the coasts. Tehran therefore acted very cautiously. Surprisingly, relations between the U.S. occupation authorities and Iran proved workable. Many Iranians undertook pilgrimages to shrines in Iraq.

Matters turned far worse with the election of Ahmadinejad. He increased the pressure and the tension, out of conviction as well as to secure popularity among the Iranian masses. He wrote U.S. President Bush a long letter that was dismissed in Washington as nothing new, but made good propaganda on Muslim streets. The Revolutionary Guards and other organizations armed Lebanon's *Hizbullah* with the missiles that it showered on northern Israel during their 2006 war. Although Ahmadinejad was once a teacher, he repeatedly denied that the Holocaust ever took place, thus proving to the world a disregard for reality. He also promised that Israel would soon disappear (though perhaps he meant Israel as a political state rather than the annihilation of its Jewish citizens).

Ambitions for Nuclear Weapons?

Evidence of Iranian duplicity at the nuclear facilities in Arak and Natanz surfaced in 2003, thanks to evidence supplied by an Iranian opposition group. The International Atomic Energy Agency (IAEA) then inspected the facilities. It discovered that in the early 1990s, Iran had launched a secret project to enrich uranium, using Pakistani guidance and equipment from North Korea, China, and elsewhere. The project repeatedly passes uranium hexafluoride gas through centrifuges to concentrate the radioactive U-238.

The tomb of Darius I, who reigned 521–486 B.C. The ancient kings of Persia had their tombs carved into cliffs so high that they could only be reached by ropes and, thus, could not be burst into to plunder.

The Nuclear Non-Proliferation Treaty permits enrichment for peaceful purposes such as low-enriched nuclear fuel (3.5% enriched) and research purposes (20% enriched) but not high-enrichment for nuclear weapons (90%). Iranians of all political groups passionately defend their country's right to enrich uranium for fuel. However, nations are obligated to notify the IAEA of enrichment activities, and Iran failed to do this. Moreover, the program hardly seemed peaceful. Its facilities were secret, carefully dispersed, sometimes duplicated, and occasionally built deep underground, obviously to discourage attacks on them. The production of weapons-grade fuel would certainly become a possibility, and Western intelligence analysts speculated that left undisturbed, Iran could soon complete an atomic bomb.

Facing Western demands to avoid producing weapons-grade uranium, before leaving office President Khatami attempted compromise and diplomacy. Iran halted enrichment during negotiations with European powers, but talks repeatedly floundered. In 2005, President Ahmadinejad authorized resumed enrichment, claiming that Iran gained nothing from negotiations. Soon afterwards, Iran's technicians achieved success with cascading centrifuges, operating some 3,000 simultaneously. They planned for perhaps tens of thousands more. Although a U.S. National Intelligence Estimate concluded in 2003 that Iran had abandoned nuclear weapons production, many Israelis, Western governments, and Arab states continued to distrust Iran's intentions.

Despite these world-wide anxieties, Ahmadinejad refused to enter serious negotiations. The UN Security Council twice imposed sanctions, overcoming Russian and Chinese reluctance. Concerns grew further in 2009, when reports speculated about advanced work that might produce a warhead small enough to fit inside the existing Sahab-3 missile. Iran declared—tardily—that it had begun work on an additional enrichment plant at Fordo, near Qom. Creative negotiations followed, but failed to produce a breakthrough partly because Iran's domestic politics were too weak to reach an international agreement.

As negotiations floundered, Israel's Prime Minister Netanyahu openly threatened a military attack, even though it seems clear that a military strike could only delay a weapon, given a determination to build one. Moreover, a strike could plunge the region from Israel to Afghanistan into conflict. In both Israel and the U.S., the highest levels of military officials have warned against an attack, though some politicians and interest groups continue to advocate an attack before Iran achieves actual nuclear weapons

The United States, while not ruling out the military option, led other Western powers in applying increasingly stringent economic sanctions, which proved surprisingly effective in both the banking and oil sectors. The sanctions did not halt the economy—their impact was uncomfortable rather than unbearable—but they contributed to a rapid depreciation of the rial, growing inflation, and rising unemployment.

Tehran's determination to continue a suspicious program also led to covert attacks, presumably the work of Israeli and perhaps U.S. intelligence agencies. Some physicists disappeared; others were assassinated. Explosions occurred at sensitive military installations. Beyond the physical violence, e-warfare attacks included Flame and Stuxnet, the latter an elaborately complex electronic worm designed to target industrial operating systems, and likely engineered by foreign governments.

Against this background, Iran resumed nuclear talks in 2012. With its nuclear negotiator, Saeed Jalili, seeking the presidency, Iran was reluctant to take difficult decisions, and did not.

A Stolen Election and Sanctions

The 2009 presidential election campaign witnessed novel political practices, including surprising media freedoms and real 1-on-1 TV debates. Mir Hossein Mousavi, an early revolutionary who served as prime minister in the 1980s, emerged as the strongest rival to Ahmadinejad's reelection. Mousavi greatly expanded political discourse. He broke tradition by appearing publicly with his wife, Zahra Rahnavard, an accomplished academic, and even demonstrated affection in public by holding her hand. This appealed to women of all ages, and youth were courted by a combination of Iranian and Islamic themes, including revolutionary-era songs, mixed with Obama-style internet-based campaigning. Mousavi's campaign platform demanded social reform and changes in the economy.

Nada Sultan, shot dead while joining protests against the 2009 elections

A high turnout on election day suggested that Mousavi had either won or forced a run-off. However, despite the complication of hand-counting over 40 million paper ballots, Ahmadinejad was declared the winner even before the polls closed. Given his strength in the countryside and among the poor, Ahmadinejad might have won a fair election. However, the evidence is strong that a group composed of the president's circle, the Revolutionary Guard leadership, and the interior ministry feared a "velvet revolution," one that without violence would reform or even overthrow the Islamic Republic. To defend it, they apparently stuffed the ballot boxes. Clearly, some ballot boxes literally had more votes than their precincts had registered voters, and Ahmadinejad's vote totals were statistically improbable in a number of locations.

Claims of fraud brought large demonstrations in the streets, often including women, using the color green (the Prophet Muhammad's color as well as the environment's). In reprisal, the Basij militia attacked dormitories at Tehran University and protestors on the streets, killing Nada Sultan among others. Gradually, after the Supreme Leader declared the election results were divinely inspired, the Revolutionary Guards and other right-wing Islamic elements of the government re-asserted control, arresting hundreds or even thousands and blocking texting services to disrupt planned demonstrations.

Feeroozah bazaar in downtown Tabriz, especially noted for the sale of handwoven rugs.

Courtesy: Faranak A. Benz

Show trials followed the clampdown, as did reports of the torture, rape, and even the deaths of some prisoners. When later public holidays and the death of Grand Ayatollah Hoseyn Ali Montazeri were marked by new demonstrations, some officials made explicit death threats against Mousavi. His nephew was murdered. During the subsequent presidential elections four years later, Mousavi remained under house arrest, hundreds of political activists remained in prison, and those behind the killing of protesters remained free.

Ahmadinejad's second term demonstrated the presidency's weakness within the political system. The conservatives who dominated the Majlis generally disrespected the populist and quirky president, who prophesied that Venezuelan President Hugo Chavez will be resurrected alongside Jesus Christ and the hidden imam of Shi'ite Muslims. The Supreme Leader repeatedly intervened to block Ahmadinejad's policies, and publicly forced the resignation of Esfandiar Rahim-Mashaei, whom Ahmadinejad had appointed senior vice president.

Other presidential protégés were arrested on corruption charges. Saeed Mortazavi, a former Tehran prosecutor himself and ally of President Mahmoud Ahmadinejad, was charged as an accessory to the murder of anti-government protesters.

The conservative political establishment clearly acted as part of a deeper struggle for power. The conservative *United Front of Principalists* won a strong majority over Ahmadinejad's *Resistance Front* in the 2012 Majlis elections, and its leaders aimed to weaken the president's influence over the 2013 elections. Ayatollah Khamenei eventually intervened in the conflict, ordering the Majlis to stop summoning the president for questioning that might benefit foreign enemies.

As the 2013 presidential elections approached, American and other western nations' sanctions became increasingly effective. Oil exports fell because of U.S. diplomatic pressure on nations like Japan and India, as well as Europe's own sanctions on imports. The economic warfare continued with prohibitions on insuring cargoes of Iranian oil even to neutral nations, while banking regulations forced banks to choose between obeying U.S. sanctions or risking serious penalties.

The sanctions effectively cut off Iran from the SWIFT system for electronic payments. Money exchangers in Dubai, the transit point for many Iranian imports, became reluctant to trade the rial because American regulations banned payments in them. Some foreign companies ceased operations in the oil fields as Iran struggled to pay for imports, and oil companies found it difficult to pay for Iranian crude oil with international currencies. By some estimates income from oil exports fell over 60%.

The rial slumped in value against the dollar, falling by 90%. Never stable but always growing, the projected budget deficit reached more than $60 billion in late 2012, or 45 percent of the country's budget.

To keep the economy from slowing severely, the central bank "printed money," thus raising the inflation rate, already under pressure from the much higher costs of imports. Food prices, a politically-sensitive measure, climbed 60%, and led to street protests. The expressions of discontent widened, with former president Rafsanjani speculating that "I don't think the country could have been run worse."

Days before the election, thousands attended the funeral of Ayatollah Jalaluddin Taheri, a dissident cleric. It was the country's biggest anti-government protest for years; some even dared to chant slogans against the Supreme Leader, calling him a dictator.

A Centrist Wins, 2013

Ahead of the elections, the Guardian Council performed its usual task of removing the most threatening or objectionable candidates from the ballot. This time they disqualified Rafsanjani, all women, a protégé of President Ahmadinejad, and many others. Six candidates remained, four of them hardline conservatives, one reformer, and a long-standing official, Hassan Rouhani, 64, who proclaimed himself a centrist.

Just days before the election, the reformist candidate withdrew on the advice of former president Khatami and threw his support for Rouhani, the result of reformist surveys that indicated Rouhani was more likely to win. At the same time, Western pundits worried that Saeed Jalili, the inflexible nuclear negotiator and rigid conservative, would likely prove successful. This apparently assured conservatives that their candidate would win—and among moderates it aroused the reaction "Anyone but Jalili!"

As polls indicated Rouhani's growing strength, many of those intending to boycott the election decided to give even limited democracy another chance. In heavier than expected turnout, Rouhani won just over 50% of the vote, thus avoiding a runoff. Jalili was humiliated, placing third with only 11%.

A cleric with a doctorate from a Scottish university and moderate in both his religion and personal style, Rouhani had been a trusted insider. He once headed the Supreme National Security Council, and continued as a member. During Khatami's second term, he served as the chief nuclear negotiator, winning respect from European powers and the U.S. Nevertheless, as a long-time insider he was distrusted by skeptical foreign commentators who discerned a crafty plot by the conservatives to foist their own safe candidate on the country with the support of gullible moderates and liberals.

Hundreds of thousands of Iranians felt otherwise. They took to the streets on news of the victory, many wearing purple, Rouhani's election color. Others dressed in reformist green.

During his first months, President Rouhani symbolized his slogan, "Hope and Prudence," as he addressed the nation's problems. He apparently gained Ayatollah Khamenei's permission to conduct serious negotiations over the nuclear program, and promised to resolve the issue within a year. An interim deal, reached quickly, provided reductions in enrichment activities and a modest decrease in sanctions. Israel called that a "historic mistake," but almost exactly one year after Rouhani's election, diplomats begin work on the text of the final accord, although recognizing that significant differences remain. The publicly quoted deadline for the document was July 2014.

Other foreign policy initiatives included a visit to Oman and assurances to Saudi Arabia and other Gulf Arab states that Iran hoped for good relations. Similar prudence seemed reflected in Tehran's response when Sunni militants seized much of northern Iraq from its Shi'a-dominated government. Iranian troops would not fight with the Iraqi army, but if necessary volunteers would help defend the Shi'a holy places.

At home, Rouhani moved cautiously, in a contrast to Muhammad Khatami's first term. He reframed the political debate with the slogan "Moderation is revolutionary, extremism is reactionary." He spoke at Tehran University about the importance of faculty freedoms, and promised the nation that prosperity was beginning to arrive. Nevertheless, although his opponents within the government and political system are divided, major challenges remain: the release of political prisoners, upholding many civil rights, strengthening respect for women, and tackling an economic system bloated by ex-president Ahmadinejad's appointments of thousands of his supporters.

Culture: More than half the population lives in the 25 largest cities. An increasing number of urban men work in industry and government, a contrast to the past when most were merchants, craftsmen or casual laborers. Despite the restrictions placed on them, many women also find employment, and there is even a taxi service in Tehran by women for women. Life in the towns and cities is generally crowded, and wages for the less skilled cover little more than life's necessities.

Most of the rural population lives in small communities, whether peasants who farm in the Elburz and Zagros Mountains, or nomads who live in goat-hair tents that are carried from place to place as they wander in search of pasture for their flocks. These people are as hardy as their life is hard, and generally as hospitable as their environment is inhospitable.

Except for the Kurds of the Zagros Mountains, nearly all Iranians follow the *Shi'a* sect of Islam, which Ismail Shah imposed in the 16th century. Historical and theological differences divide *Shi'a* Muslims from the orthodox, or *Sunni*, Muslims who form the great majority in the Islamic world. Relations between Iran and Afghanistan, for instance, are tempered by the fact that most Afghans are *Sunni* Muslims.

Although *Shi'a* Muslims make pilgrimages to Mecca as do other Muslims (see Saudi Arabia: Culture), they also have important shrines in Iran, particularly at Meshed, where their eighth Imam, Ali Reza, was buried. Many also journey to Najaf and Karbala in Iraq, holy cities sacred by virtue of the association with Ali, the first *Shi'a* Imam (and the Sunni's fourth Caliph), and his two sons. The division of Islam between *Shi'a* and *Sunni* goes back to a dispute over whether Ali and his sons, or the Umayyad clan (see Historical Background) were the rightful successors to Muhammad as rulers of the Muslim community.

A religious hierarchy dominates *Shi'a* Islam. Simple teachers and the preachers at Friday prayers in rural villages form the bottom rank. Above them are judges of religious law, then mujtahids who interpret the law, ayatollahs, and grand ayatollahs. At the top, the Shi'a Imam has remained hidden for a thousand years, although Ayatollah Khomeini's followers applied the term to him.

Iran is a country famous for its architectural monuments, some in ruin, like those of the Achaemenid Empire, but some still standing, such as the mosques of Isfahan. Museums have also been established to display the antiquities which represent every period of the country's history.

During the 1970s, the monarchy funded a rapid expansion of colleges and universities. However, the quality of education declined, as new institutions struggled to develop traditions, and students valued degrees for job placement rather than learning. Iranian education also suffered widely from a unique defect. Students who demanded high grades threatened professors by hinting at connections with *SAVAK*, the shah's dreaded secret police.

After Khomeini came to power, although *SAVAK* was demolished, the decline in education gathered speed. The Revolution shut some schools, closed the universities, and banned women from many teaching positions (and from much of public life in general). Few students could study abroad, and the lower curriculum reduced to reading, writing, arithmetic and religion. Many teachers with good training fled the country; some who stayed were executed. In 1982 the medical schools in Tehran and Shiraz were reopened because of practical needs, and the universities followed. The education crisis is now acute, as the large generation born after the revolution seeks university education.

During the Pahlavi era, many middle- and upper-class Iranians adopted external aspects of Western culture, from stylish clothing to skiing, parties and rock music. Religious conservatives and the traditional poor opposed and resented these changes; with the Islamic Revolution, such Western customs ended, at least in public. Most obviously, new laws forced women to wear *hijab* attire, notably the *chador*, or headscarf, but a much larger realm of Western culture was suppressed, including magazines and music. Khomeini approved instrumental music only just before his death, so symphonic music may now be enjoyed, but many clergy consider rock music or female vocals sinfully enticing. Other regulations prohibit unmarried men and women from walking or dining together in public. While two girls may hitch rides from passing automobiles, unmarried couples ought not ride alone in a car, especially after dark.

Living their entire lives after the revolution, many young people now dislike these strict social controls. Risking heavy penalties if caught by revolutionary committees, some students and other young adults enjoy parties and dancing with members of the opposite sex. Pale lipstick worn by coeds in university classes, colored headscarves, and brightly colored track shoes likewise suggest widening desires for a relaxation of social regulation. There are risks: in one month an estimated 1,000 women were arrested for offenses like failing to cover their ankles or wearing too much makeup.

Advancing technology presents fundamentalists with additional targets. Parliament debated banning video-recorders, until it became obvious that leading politicians and clergy found them useful. When a western company began broadcasting TV programs to Iran by satellite, in 1995 the government banned satellite dishes, thus placing would-be TV addicts at the mercy of inspectors from the local revolutionary committees. In recent years, Iran has tried to jam satellite broadcasts, and under President Ahmadinejad the government cracked down on illegal dishes.

Drug Addiction

Probably the most severe and growing social difficulty is the swelling population of drug addicts. The numbers are frightening, and on a percentage basis place Iran as the highest in the world. Approximately 20% of all adults and teenagers probably use hashish or narcotics in one form or another, more than one million of them using opium and heroin. Given its culture and lengthy borders, Iran had a drug problem before the Revolution. In the 1980s the problems worsened, with heroin largely replacing opium, and the number of addicts growing rapidly.

As addicts lost the label "miserable persons" and became "enemy infiltrators in society," officials predictably blamed the problem on the American Central Intelligence Agency and the Mafia. Possession of more than 30 grams of heroin became a capital offense; hundreds were executed. All addicts were required to register, and many were dispatched to labor camps in distant desert regions to break the habit. Drug-related convictions accounted for 70% of Iranian prisoners. These harsh measures failed, and with an additional 600,000 users each year, *three-fourths of them women*, a variety of social agencies provide counseling, assistance, and methadone.

Such large-scale use of narcotics points to more than cheap supplies from Afghanistan. Like the riots that followed World Cup soccer games, narcotics usage indicates a society whose young are unemployed and bored. Lacking jobs and entertainment, many have lost faith in the future, a truly astounding phenomenon for a religious republic.

Youthful Rebellion & Temporary Marriage

Traditionally, Iranian families arranged marriages for their teenaged daughters and provided a dowry of furniture for the new household. In the 1980s, reflecting revived Islamic cultural values and the regime's desire for more children, the birth rate approached world record levels and population grew at 4% annually. However, planners convinced Ayatollah Khomeini of the enormous economic and social pressures such growth would create. He approved family planning shortly before his death, and in 1989 Ayatollah Khamenei declared that birth control was not against Islam. By the mid-1990s all forms of contraception (but not abortion) were available—and free. Family benefits now end with the third child. As a result, the rate of population growth fell to less than 2%.

Today society faces the challenge of educating, employing, marrying, and otherwise incorporating the children of the 1980s into adult society. Young and restless, these adults tend to present challenges to the hardline populism of President Ahmadinejad. In response, one suggestion is "make love, not dissent," that young Iranians contract temporary marriage, long-established as a Shi'a practice. However, virginity is prized in brides of permanent marriages, so families will probably oppose a daughter's temporary marriage.

Economy: With a large population and fertile lands, thanks to its abundant and varied mineral deposits Iran possesses great industrial potential. It also benefits from large oil resources, and natural gas deposits so vast they rank second only to Russia's. The earliest crude oil producer in the region, in recent years it ranks as the second largest oil exporter in the Middle East, after Saudi Arabia.

Not surprisingly, economic policy in the country revolves around two issues: first, the policy over petroleum, the greatest producer of foreign exchange, and second, agriculture.

Agriculture always played an impressive role in Iranian history. The farms vary greatly, from the well-watered lands near the Caspian Sea to plots in the mountains and plateau that depend for irrigation on systems of underground channels.

Generally, life for farmers meant working another's land. Until Shah Muhammad Reza's land reform program in 1963, some 10,000 of the country's villages had belonged to landlords each owning five or more villages. Indeed, a few families and religious endowments dominated the lives of farmers across the country. While unsuccessful in satisfying the hopes of the peasants, the shah's land reform broke the power of the large farming families. It improved the supply of credit, seeds and agricultural techniques. Dams permitted the irrigation of additional lands, and new roads reduced transportation costs. These changes encouraged large-scale commercial agriculture, especially near rivers in the west.

All land reform proposals in Iran face a difficult choice, between equality and economic growth. Because only some 10% of Iran can be farmed, redistributing the land to all existing peasants would create miniscule, inefficient farms. But without redistribution, the great differences in wealth cause political stress, and industry and the services are not growing enough to absorb the thousands who leave farms every year.

Although demands for land reform had played a major role in the Islamic Revolution, initial attempts to seize the larger landholdings were blocked by the Council of Guardians, whose conservative clergy believed that the Qur'an upheld private property rights. Only 3% of the nation's farmland was distributed during the republic's first decade. However, feeling threatened by calls to seize their lands, the owners of large farms cautiously stopped investing in irrigation and equipment, or even repairing the vital irrigation channels.

Predictably, farm output fell. At the same time, the population rose by 3%–4% per year, one of the highest rates in the world. Until 1970, Iran had exported surplus food, but during the last years of the

Demonstrators of all ages proclaim that victory belonged to Mousavi, Tehran, June 2009

war, Iran spent over one-third of its oil earnings to *import* food. Millions of refugees from Afghanistan and Iraq added to the shortages.

Fishing is a substantial industry in the Persian Gulf and Arabian Sea. However, it is sturgeon from the Caspian Sea whose eggs, caviar, carry the epithet "black gold." Unfortunately, pollution in the closed sea, combined with legal and illegal over-fishing, threatens the long-term future of this delicacy. Despite the annual release of over 20 million young fish, Caspian sturgeon may become extinct by about 2020.

The country's non-petroleum mineral resources include lead, chrome and turquoise, which are exported, while coal and iron are mined for domestic use, along with some sulfur and salt.

Although handicrafts are losing importance, Isfahan, Tabriz and other cities remain famous for their metalwork, carpets, ceramics and textiles. The best carpets come from the Safavid period, but those of recent manufacture deserve fame—and after oil are often the most important export.

Under the Shah's rule, Iran followed a policy of rapid economic expansion and industrialization. It exported vast quantities of oil to pay for large development projects as well as consumer goods and sophisticated weapons. Using its oil revenues on a massive scale, Iran contracted with foreign companies to build and operate entire factories. A number of different cars and trucks were assembled in the country, and dozens of other industries were founded. By 1978, the number of industrial employees reached two million. Iran's first modern steel mill was constructed in Isfahan, with technical assistance and a large loan from the Soviet Union. By the mid-1990s the country actually exported significant quantities of iron and steel.

The policy achieved one of the world's highest rates of economic growth, and the middle class prospered. Other results included inflation and resentment by the unskilled urban poor and landless peasants, who migrated to the cities in search of work.

The Economy after 1979

Despite many hopes, the Islamic Revolution provided little economic progress, though it greatly changed business conditions. It quickly nationalized the oil industry completely, thirty years after Mossadeq's failed attempt. It also took over many large manufacturing firms, and the entire banking and insurance industries, partly because many owners had fled.

However, because of their divisions over the role of private property, especially in agriculture, the ruling clergy failed to establish the economic rules of the game. Leftist clergy advocated socialism, and blamed inflation and shortages on hoarding by private businessmen. Conservatives claimed that Islam protected private ownership. The government simply intervened to suit the needs of the moment. Investors, fearing eventual confiscation, avoided long-term projects and favored trade. For those with access to foreign exchange, it became far more profitable to import than to manufacture in Iran. The result was devastating: manufacturing output fell to only 40% of capacity.

Oil policy changed significantly in the Islamic Republic. Initially, the revolutionaries favored only small quantities of exports, thinking that imports implied dependence on Western nations and Japan, and encouraged imitation of their lifestyles. However, the need for revenue for the regime, the military, and economic development reversed that perspective.

One particular difficulty facing the oil industry is U.S. sanctions, with some in effect for many years. Sanctions block foreign subsidiaries of U.S. oil companies from assisting Iran's industry or providing American technology. They also penalize any foreign company that spends significant funds to develop Iran's petroleum resources. In step with Iran's nuclear enrichment, the U.S. increased its sanctions activities, and by 2007 several major projects languished, with foreign companies negotiating for future options but avoiding involvement now.

No major foreign investment has taken place since 2002, and the development of liquefied natural gas exports depends entirely on it. Moreover, the present oil production level of nearly 4 million barrels per day will gradually fall by as much as 40% without further major investments. One major unknown is the role of China, whose need for imported oil is growing faster than any other country, and whose government does not seem to base its foreign policy on human rights issues or worry overmuch about nuclear weapons development elsewhere.

After 2003, world oil prices set new records almost annually, and the country's petroleum industry operated at full capacity. The resulting earnings greatly benefited the budget, and the national economy grew at rates of 5% or more annually, twice the rate of population growth and fast enough to begin to provide jobs for the millions of unemployed. Moreover, the Majlis finally enacted economic reforms. It slashed some business taxes and simplified the foreign investment law. Iran also announced a unified foreign exchange rate. As confidence in the economy expanded, wealthy Iranians living overseas invested again in their homeland, even though many fundamental issues remained unsolved. The stock market rose rapidly.

After the election of Mahmoud Ahmadinejad, smart money feared foreign controls or other difficulties ahead and it flowed out of the country. Economic policies took several bizarre turns, including interest rates below the inflation rate. Prosperity languished, just as populism gave millions of people hope for a better life.

High oil revenues may even change the level of urban air pollution. For decades, the standard Iranian car was the Peykan, a British-engineered, 1950s-era subcompact that lacked pollution controls. However, its production finally ended in 2005, and that year the country's two major auto firms, Iran Khodro and Saipa, produced nearly one million vehicles between them, of recent French, Japanese, and Korean designs. However, polluting Peykans will remain on the roads for years to come.

The Future: Hassan Rouhani's defeat of the hardliners changes the landscape of Iran's future. Given the shambles he has inherited, all indicators suggest improvements of some sort. This being Iran, progress in which directions and for how far is hard to predict.

There are grounds for anticipating a successful conclusion of the nuclear negotiations. Reiterating Ayatollah Khamenei's decree banning the production and use of nuclear weapons, Hassan Rouhani has clearly indicated that Iran rejected acquiring them based on moral principles. Furthermore, he has argued, if the threat of mass destruction was necessary, chemical and biological weapons would serve the purpose with far fewer difficulties. Despite bellicose statements from Jerusalem, the likelihood of war over the nuclear enrichment program is diminishing.

For the medium term, Iran might be considered an "island of stability" in a Middle East torn by sectarian Islamic conflict. Members of the younger generation, who comprise more than half the population, interpret Islam—and its ceremonies—quite differently than the aging veterans of the Islamic Revolution and the war with Iraq. While the political pendulum will continue to swing between moderates and conservatives, the scale itself seems to be shifting away from rigid fundamentalism.

Expect a thaw in relations with America, slowed by the bitter antagonism in each country of those who consider that the other nation held them hostage.

The Republic of Iraq

In April 1995, Iraqis protested the proposed UN Oil for Food Program. The next year, they celebrated it.

Area: 169,235 square miles (438,317 sq. km.).
Population: 35.8 million (estimate).
Capital City: Baghdad (pop. 7 million, est. 2012).
Climate: Extremely hot in summer, moderately cool in winter; rain is limited, falling in winter. The northern mountains are colder, with snow in winter.
Neighboring Countries: Iran (East); Kuwait (Southeast); Saudi Arabia (South); Jordan (West); Syria (Northwest); Turkey (North).
Time Zone: GMT +3.
Official Language: Arabic (and in northern districts, Kurdish).
Other Principal Tongues: Farsi (Persian) and English (as language of education).
Ethnic Background: Mixed; mostly Arab (80%) or Kurdish (nearly 20%), plus some Chaldeans and Persians.
Principal Religions: Shi'a Islam (55–65%), Sunni Islam (30–35%), Christianity (under 3%; mostly Chaldeans and Assyrians), some Yazidis, and a very few Mandeans.
Chief Commercial Products: Petroleum, natural gas, petrochemicals, textiles and cement.
Main Agricultural Produce and Livestock: Wheat, barley, rice, tomatoes, watermelons, grapes, dates, rice, cotton, sheep, goats, cattle and chickens.
Major Trading Partners: (pre-war) Japan, Germany, Italy, Great Britain, France, U.S., Brazil, Turkey and India.
Currency: The New Iraqi Dinar (2004).
Former Colonial Status: British occupation and Mandate (1918–1932)
Independence Date: October 3, 1932; U.S. returned sovereignty, June 28, 2004.
National Day: Republic Day, July 14 will probably remain a holiday.
Chief of State: President, TBD. (Jalal Talabani, incumbent, ailing abroad)
Head of Government: Prime Minister, TBD (Nouri al-Maliki, caretaker, June 2014)
National Flag: Three equal horizontal stripes of (top to bottom) red, white and black, with "Allah Akbar" (God is great) on the white stripe in Kufic script. Parliament removed three stars in 2008 as allegedly Ba'thist.
GDP: $229 billion (current prices, 2013); $273 billion (PPP, 2013)
GDP per capita: $7,400 (PPP, 2013).

Iraq (pronounced *Ee-rock*, not *I rack*) is about two-thirds the size of Texas. Modern Iraq stretches across the birthplace of human civilization. Ancient Mesopotamia, the land "between the rivers," flourished because the Tigris and the Euphrates provided water. Without the rivers, nearly the entire country would be desert. About 18% of the land is under cultivation.

The two rivers flow southeast across an alluvial plain, between the rocky desert of the southwest and the Zagros Mountains along the northern and eastern borders. Except on the slopes of the mountains there is little annual rainfall, ranging from 6 inches in the south to 15 inches in the northern plains. Most of the water in the rivers comes from rain or melting snow in the mountains of northern Iraq and southern Turkey.

The people differ as much as the land. A handful of Arab nomads *(badu)* still roam the deserts. In the southern marshes upstream from Basra a few *Ma'dan* remain. Known as the Marsh Arabs, they inhabit reed huts, raise water buffalo and travel by boat. In most of central Iraq farmers live along the rivers, their tributaries and canals, while Kurdish mountain villages dot the heights and valleys in the north.

In recent decades people from all parts of the nation have migrated to Baghdad in search of work in that rapidly expanding city. They represent all the linguistic, religious and social variety of the country. It is this nationwide diversity which makes political agreement so difficult in Iraq.

Iraq

History: The creation of a single, united government over the region is a modern innovation. In this land of the two rivers, some of the first cities—and city-states—evolved, and writing was first invented. Here the caliphs of Islam heard the *Arabian Nights* (see Historical Background). After serving as the capital of a vast Islamic empire, Iraq suffered invasions, the worst of all by the Mongols. In 1258, they devastated Baghdad, and most of its population was killed or forced into exile. Untended irrigation canals silted up; equally seriously, drainage canals that remove salt deposits from the fields disappeared. Today, over two-thirds of the irrigable land lies idle, sparkling in the sunshine but barren because of the high salt content of the soil.

For four centuries the Ottoman Empire ruled the region (1554–1918), and after decades of intermittent warfare, it established the border with Iran. It administered Iraq as the three provinces of Mosul (or Musil), Baghdad, and Basra. Beyond controlling the main towns, the governors attempted to maintain order among the often unruly and usually autonomous tribes. As European nations seized control of trade in the Indian Ocean and the Far East, commerce through Iraq stagnated, and little development took place. Located on the fringe of the empire, the provinces generally received few improvements. Modern schools, hospitals, and newspapers only began to appear around the turn of the 20th century, and steamboats then began regular service on the Tigris.

When the Ottoman Empire entered World War I as a German ally, British Indian troops landed in Basra and slowly moved inland. They found the population generally unsympathetic or even hostile. Politically conscious Arabs, Kurds, Turkmen and others commonly supported the Ottoman Empire or desired greater autonomy within it. Iraq as a nation—or even as a notion—did not exist. However, a small number of army officers promoted the newly-conceived idea of an independent Arab nation encompassing the Ottoman-ruled areas of Mesopotamia, Syria, and Palestine.

By the end of the war in 1918, British troops occupied most of the country, and

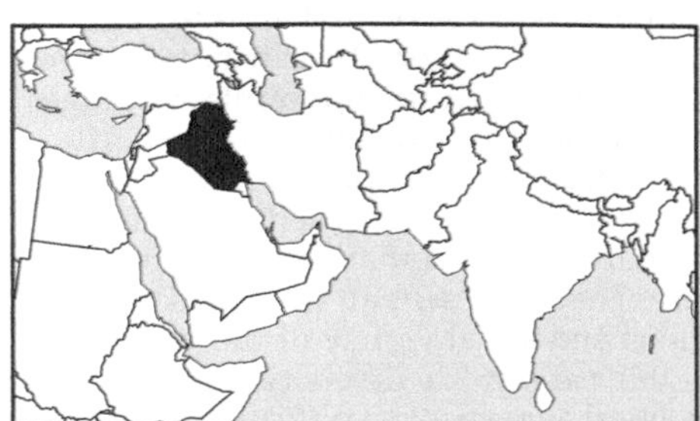

King Faisal I (1885–1933)

shortly afterwards added the province of Mosul, valuing it and the region around Kirkuk because of their oil deposits. The future was uncertain: in the secret Sykes-Picot Agreement and other negotiations, France had pledged to support British rule over Iraq. However, Britain also had promised to recognize the independence of Arab lands, except the Syrian coast and Basra.

After most inhabitants rapidly recognized that Britain meant to rule the territories under the guise of a mandate from the League of Nations, a nationalist, anti-British uprising spread rapidly. To quell the rebellion, Britain sought a political solution as well as military victory, and it successfully supported Prince (Amir) Faisal, son of Sharif Husayn and commander of the Arab forces who had fought in Syria, to become king.

The new nation adopted the Arabic name for the southern part of the country, al-'Iraq, for the entire nation. The state's inhabitants, however, were not solely Arab. Kurdish tribesmen dominated the northern mountains, where Britain desired influence because of oil deposits.

As a Hashemite, King Faisal traced his descent from the Prophet Muhammad through Hasan, son of Ali, the fourth Caliph (and first *Shi'a* Imam). He therefore brought a semblance of unity to the Arab population with its *Shi'a* majority but *Sunni* ruling class. Having learned from

the loss of his throne in Syria in battle with the French, Faisal worked to gain independence by compromise with Britain. In 1932, Iraq received its formal independence and became a member of the League of Nations.

The Kurdish Problem

Even before it received formal independence, Iraq faced rebellion from the Kurds. Hardy and brave, but isolated from commerce and education, Kurdish tribes for centuries had maintained dialects of their Indo-European language. Lacking sea access or rail transport, and little influenced by democracy and nationalism, Kurds populated the eastern lands of the Ottoman Empire as well as western Iran. The Kurds had the misfortune to inhabit the region where three great civilizations (Arab, Persian, and Turkish) came together. Their own identity and achievements mattered less. Ruled lightly from distant capitals through tribal leaders who often challenged each other, the Kurds received little attention. They were simply Muslim tribesmen in Muslim Empires. After they adopted *Sunni* Islam, their very names often became Islamic or Arab.

Because of Britain's desire to control the oil-possessing regions of Kirkuk and Mosul, after World War I these areas were joined to Iraq despite their Kurdish majority. Although Turkey and Iran each contained more Kurds than did Iraq, its Kurds formed a large and distinct community that dominated the hills and mountains, with the Arabs centered on the plains.

In every country where they formed a significant group, the Kurds revolted, starting with the British in Iraq in 1923. A major Kurdish uprising lasted from 1930 to 1933, coinciding with Iraq's independence. Its leaders were later confined to non-Kurdish parts of the country, or fled to the Soviet Union. During World War II, a second rebellion was briefly successful. After the war, its leader, Mustafa Barzani, continued the struggle for Kurdish independence by creating, with Soviet sympathy, a republic around the city of Mahabad in Iranian Kurdistan. After years of exile in the Soviet Union, Barzani led later revolts against Iraqi regimes and died in exile supported by the U.S.

Foreign governments often sympathized with Iraq's efforts to transform its Kurdish population into orderly civilians. However, granting Kurdish demands would have threatened oil revenues, and growing nationalism blocked any government in Baghdad from ceding its territory. On the other hand, Iraq generally lacked the military force to control a fierce and individualistic people living in rugged mountains with few roads. Periods of calm and order, therefore, proved the exception.

An Independent State

After the formalities of 1932, many Iraqis recognized that they were not really independent. British military bases remained, British and French companies controlled the Iraq Petroleum Company, and British advisors played very influential roles in government. Restrictions on free elections always seemed to favor those Iraqi politicians closely tied to Britain. On the other hand there was the beginning of a modern school system. Iraqis also gained experience in the affairs of state, in politics, administration, and in modern military practices. A modern economy began to develop beside the traditional crafts and agriculture, aided significantly by exports of oil after 1934.

Military coup d'état followed attempted coup between 1936 and 1941. The final attempt to seize power was led by Rashid Ali Gailani, a bitter opponent of Britain and Nazi sympathizer during World War II. With the help of the Arab Legion from Transjordan, Britain quelled the revolt and reinstated friendly officials. The new government declared war on the Axis in 1943 and thereby became a charter member of the United Nations.

Nationalism developed even more during the post-war years with the spread of education. During the 1940s and 1950s, a veteran Arab nationalist, Nuri Said, generally controlled parliamentary affairs on behalf of the throne—and in the opinion of many Iraqis, on behalf of the British. The rising popularity of Egypt's President Gamal Abdul Nasser and Arab nationalism isolated Nuri, as did the monarchy's policy of investing oil revenues in long-term projects that favored wealthy landowners.

On July 14, 1958, a day regarded by many Iraqis as their real day of independence, a lightning but bloody revolution by Iraqi army units overthrew the cabinet, the monarchy, and foreign influence. King Faisal II and dozens of hated officials, among them Nuri Said, were killed by troops and mobs. The new Republic of Iraq turned sharply neutralist in international affairs and renounced treaties with Britain.

The leader of the revolt, General Abd al-Karim Qasim, soon emerged as dictator and proclaimed Iraq democratic and united with the Arab world. A political amnesty allowed exiles to return, including the Kurdish leader Mustafa Barzani. Land reform began. However, Qasim soon clashed with his fellow revolutionaries, especially those who desired rapid unity with Syria and Egypt under Gamal Abdul

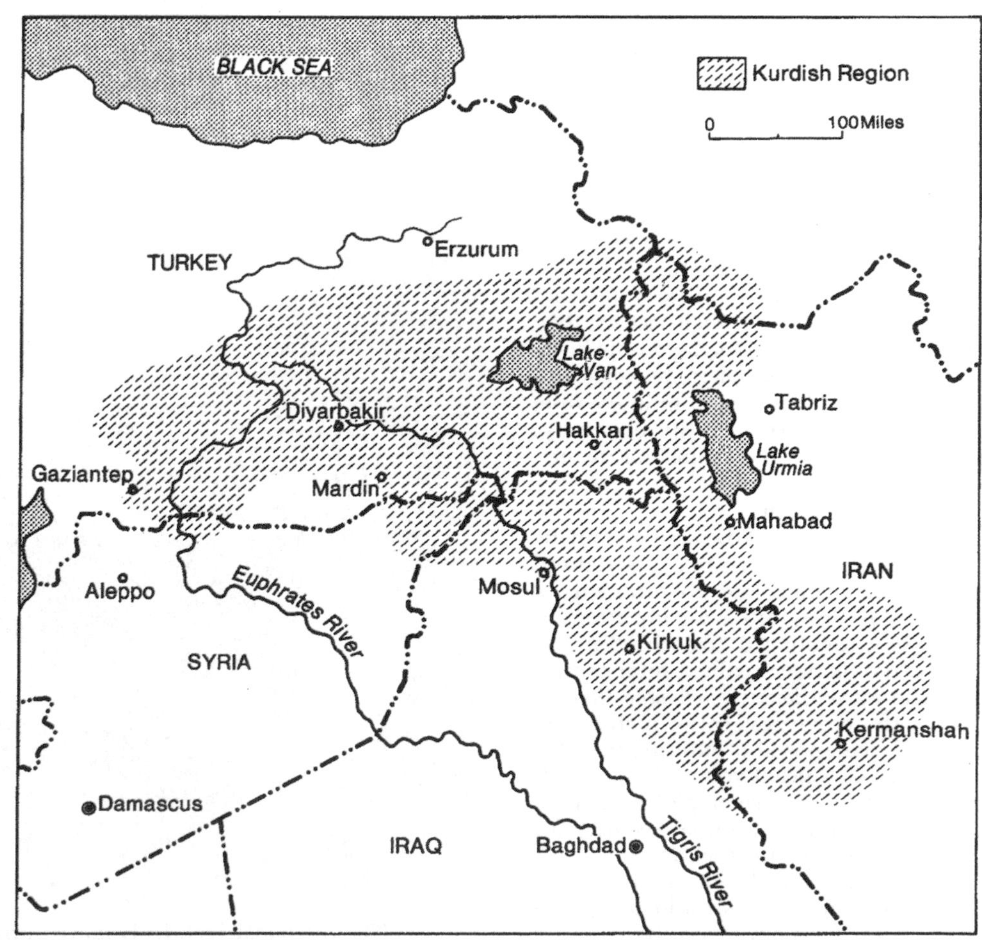

Iraq

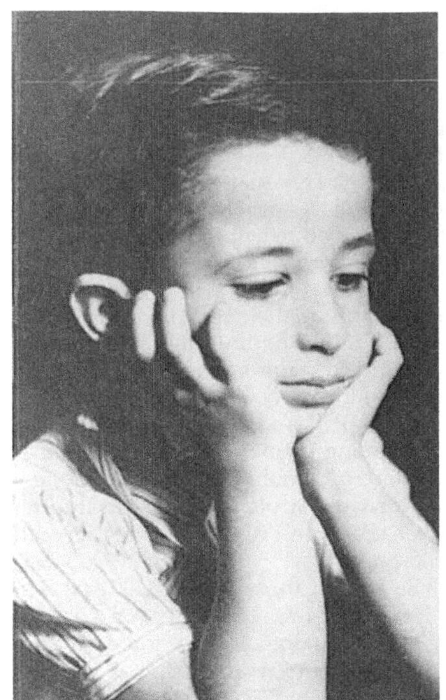

King Faisal II (1935–58)
The six-year-old monarch, 1941

Nasser. Thus, instead of uniting Iraq with other Arab states, the revolution created new rivalries between it and Egypt.

Faced with assassination attempts and an army mutiny, Qasim turned for help to the Soviet Union and the *Communist Party of Iraq*. However, Qasim grew isolated, though remaining popular among some of the poor for his spending on housing. He also decreed the equality of women before the law, thus initiating great improvements in women's status.

In 1963 nationalist military officers seized power. To prove their victory, they executed Qasim and displayed his body on television. Nevertheless, his legacy to republican Iraq remained: military rule, government control of the economy, Kurdish rebellion, and claims to Kuwait.

Iraq under the Ba'th

In 1968, one year following the dramatic Israeli military victory that discredited many Arab armies and governments, a nearly bloodless military coup brought the *Ba'th* (pronounced "Ba-ath") *Party* to power. Its members gained total control over the *Revolutionary Command Council (RCC)*, the chief governing institution. Generally composed of officers, the *RCC* included a significant young civilian, Saddam Hussein. A former plotter against Qasim, he directed internal security for the party and now the regime.

Socialist and Arab nationalist rather than communist in its philosophy, the *Ba'thist* government strongly opposed the United States because of its support of Israel. It also regarded pro-American Iran as a prospective enemy, because Iran claimed the eastern half of the Shatt al-Arab waterway near Basra.

The new government dealt harshly with individuals and groups remotely capable of rivaling the regime, often discrediting them as alleged agents of foreign countries. Accusations of espionage flowed freely. Among those executed publicly were Jewish leaders, Islamic fundamentalists and even communists. Fierce disputes between the *Ba'thists* ruling Syria and those in Iraq increased the natural rivalry of the two countries. Nevertheless, in 1973 Iraqi tank units joined Syrian troops fighting Israel on the Golan Heights.

In 1979 Saddam Hussein, for years the real center of power, became simultaneously President, Chairman of the Revolutionary Command Council, and Secretary-General of the *Ba'th Party*. Saddam considered his clan from Tikrit the only trustworthy group. Some clansmen held high office; others played key roles in the country's several secret police and intelligence services. Rivals within the party were purged (and often murdered), while the public suffered kidnappings and assassinations.

Despite the dictatorship, oil revenues meant economic progress. After decades of production-disrupting disputes with foreign oil companies, Iraq gained total control of its oil production in 1973. Later that year, OPEC raised the price of crude oil four-fold (see Black Gold: The Impact of Oil). Petroleum revenues financed both economic prosperity and military equipment. Living standards rose, education expanded, and new industries and housing multiplied. Young Iraqis flocked to cities for jobs in industry and government offices.

In 1975, a compromise with the Shah of Iran moved the southeastern boundary to the center of the Shatt al-Arab, the normal international custom, instead of the traditional eastern shore. In return, Iran ceased supplying the Iraqi Kurds, who once again had risen in revolt under Mustafa Barzani. The rebellion rapidly collapsed amid deportations and executions.

A second difficulty with the mosaic of Iraqi's ethnic groups arose with the *Shi'a* population, concentrated in the south. Though Arab, and in fact the majority population, they identified strongly with many religious values of Iran (see Iran: Culture). The Iraqi *Shi'a* had never played a political role appropriate to their numbers, even before independence. Thereafter, *Sunni* officers dominated the army, the focus of political power during both monarchy and republic.

The secular and strongly pan-Arab *Ba'th Party* evoked particularly little support among the *Shi'a*. *Ba'thist* governments, largely military and *Sunni*, traditionally

The Mustansiriyah University during the socially more liberal 1970s

spurned issues cherished by the *Shi'a*, and the absence of democracy left the largest community in the country marginalized and often repressed.

Rivalry with Iran brought particular tension for the *Shi'a*. To oppose the modernizing Shah, the *Ba'thists* accorded refuge to his dedicated enemy, Ayatollah Khomeini. Such support was intended as only tactical, as the Iraqi regime allowed less religious influence on politics than did Iran, and dissatisfaction arose among Iraq's *Shi'a* as well as Iran's. In 1977, demonstrations and riots broke out in the holy cities of Najaf and Karbala. When civil disturbances in Iran threatened an Islamic revolution against the shah, Saddam Hussein expelled Ayatollah Khomeini.

After their Islamic Revolution, Iranian religious leaders, now under the charismatic Khomeini, called on the Muslims of Iraq to revolt. Disturbances in Baghdad and elsewhere resulted in stern repression. Ayatollah Muhammad Bakr Sadr, a prominent *Shi'a* leader, was executed in Baghdad for subversion. Amid such turmoil, controlled elections to the powerless National Assembly meant little.

War with Iran

Angered by Iran's calls for an Islamic revolution, Saddam Hussein sensed an opportunity to weaken a divided and internationally isolated Iran and therefore invaded in 1980. Iraqi troops captured Khorramshahr and pushed into oil-rich regions beyond.

Despite early victories, the president miscalculated. By advancing broadly, Iraqi forces failed to deliver a fatal blow. The war united Iranians against an ancient and often despised foe. By 1981, Iraq had lost the initiative and faced the onslaught of religiously-inspired and often fanatical Iranians determined to obliterate the *Ba'th* regime in Baghdad. Iranian naval and air attacks destroyed tanker facilities on the Gulf near Faw, and Kurdish groups rebelled in the north, supported by Iran.

To defend itself, Iraq drafted almost all able-bodied men. Aid from other Arab governments, fearing that a victorious Iran would export its Islamic Revolution, sustained Iraq's survival. Arab oil states "lent" an estimated $35 billion, and Egypt alone supplied over one million workers. Alone among Arab nations, *Ba'thist* Syria supported Iran. It halted the flow of Iraqi crude oil through Syrian ports, thus closing the last export route for the crude.

Massive Iranian attacks against Basra in 1984 and 1985 inspired Iraqi soldiers with the will to resist, aided by chemical weapons illegal under international law. The destruction of life and property in Basra, a largely Shi'a city, also weakened sympathies of Iraqi Shi'a for Iran.

Largely stalemated on the ground, the war took other forms, including a "Tanker War" when Iran attacked vessels carrying oil from Kuwait and Saudi Arabia. Eventually the U.S. and other nations sent naval units to escort shipping and clear the Gulf of mines. In 1987 missile and bomb attacks on Tehran and Baghdad caused civilian casualties and created fear.

Saddam Hussein al-Takriti

Iraqi forces finally gained the initiative in 1988. They recaptured the Faw Peninsula—Iraq's access to the Gulf—and attacked across the border. Isolated and lacking heavy weapons for defense, Iranian resistance collapsed and Tehran finally sued for peace (see Iran: History).

On the verge of military victory, Iraq engineered a crime against humanity. Some Kurds had allied with Iran and "liberated" Kurdish territory. In response, the military and police brutally evicted thousands of mountain villagers, demolished their homes, and buried some alive. Survivors were exiled to the hot deserts. Perhaps 180,000 died, mostly unnoticed by the world press. However, a poison gas attack on the town of Halabja gained world-wide TV coverage of the massacre. More than 50,000 Kurds, mostly women and children, then sought refuge in Turkey.

After the ceasefire, military industrialization remained a priority. Popular generals and other officers were arrested or disappeared. Secrecy cloaked normal public information, such as the budget, trade, and social characteristics. Torture extended to executing children, to persuade their parents to confess.

Believing himself the embodiment of the Ba'thist slogan "One Arab nation with an eternal mission," Saddam Hussein thought himself the liberator of Arabs everywhere from their princes, kings, and presidents. Hence he had ordered massive programs to develop chemical and biological weapons. He recognized that if Arab unity involved conquest, the collapse of the Soviet empire meant it must come quickly, and the U.S., traumatized by Vietnam, continued to sell his government subsidized rice and wheat despite

City Street in Karbala Photo by William Parker

the chemical attack on Halabja. Luckily, the closest target ranked among the richest.

War over Kuwait

In 1990, Iraq provoked a diplomatic crisis with Kuwait, demanding border concessions, payment for Iraqi oil allegedly pumped by Kuwaiti wells, and billions to compensate Iraq for low world oil prices resulting from Kuwait's production beyond its quota. Suddenly, Iraq broke off negotiations. Hours later its troops swiftly conquered all Kuwait.

Iraqi rule proved brutal. Officials and troops systematically looted museums, libraries, warehouses, hospitals, and offices to benefit Iraqi hospitals, universities, and government offices. The Central Bank yielded foreign exchange and gold worth billions. Soon Baghdad's civilians could purchase, cheaply, consumer goods long denied them. Sharing in the booty made accomplices of thousands of otherwise honorable civilians.

Responding to the unprovoked aggression, the UN Security Council imposed an economic boycott. The Gulf Cooperation Council enabled Saudi Arabia, protector of Islam's greatest Holy Places, to accept a defensive international Coalition force. U.S. and other NATO forces arrived, Egypt and Syria pledged troops, and smaller Gulf states provided bases and token units. Careful diplomacy by U.S. President George H. W. Bush built international support.

Isolated from the Western world, Saddam Hussein apparently believed that Muslim protests and American anti-war emotions would deter any sustained U.S. attacks. He therefore refused to back down. One day after the U.N. deadline, Coalition aircraft and missiles began massive attacks on military and economic targets. Precision weapons reached their targets with relatively few civilian casualties.

For 38 days and nights the aerial campaign pounded weapons depots, communication links, bridges and highways, water and sewage treatment plants, refineries and factories, and the national electric power grid. Military units, especially the better-equipped Republican Guard divisions, suffered intensive bombing by B-52s. To avoid arousing Muslim and anti-war sentiments, the Coalition kept secret the casualty estimates.

To widen the war and thus split the Coalition, Iraq fired Scud missiles at Israeli targets (see Israel: History). Israel did not retaliate, and Baghdad's appeal for a Holy War failed.

Striking swiftly, Coalition ground forces punctured the dreaded Iraqi defenses with surprisingly few casualties. Tanks and airborne units swept around Iraqi de-

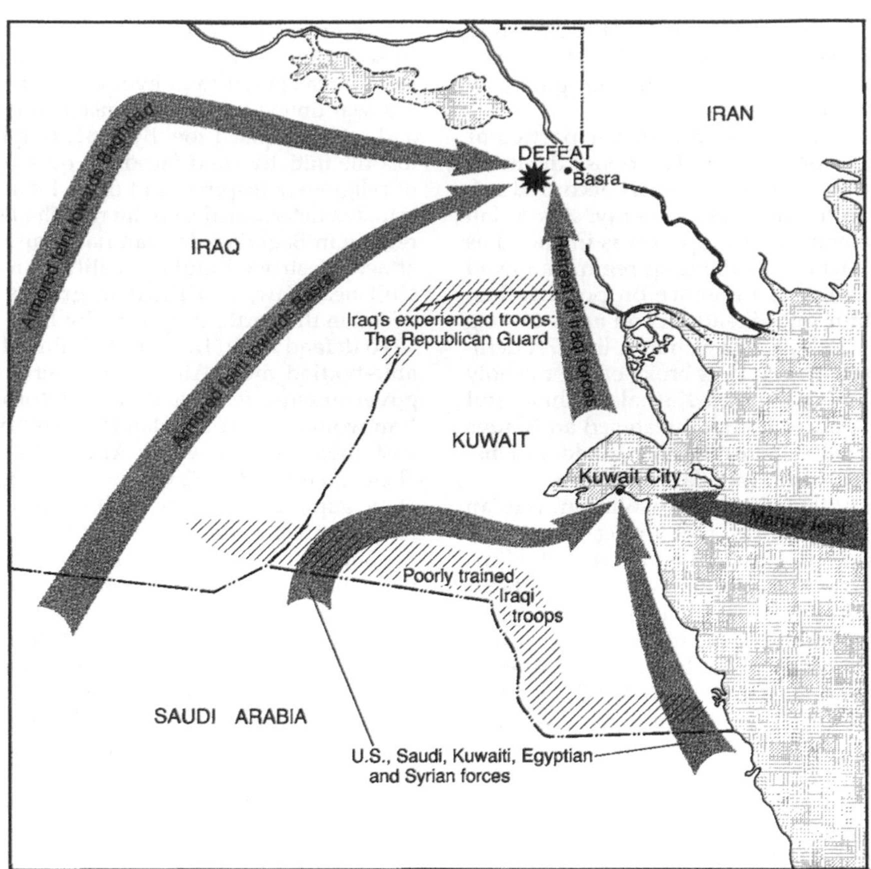

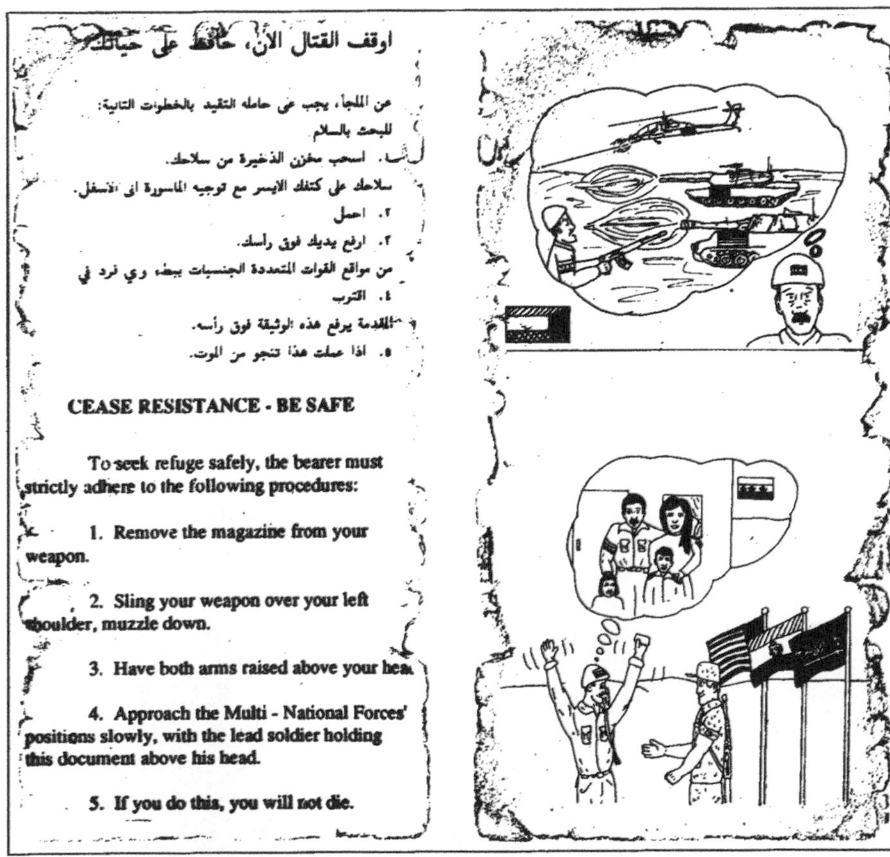

One of thousands of leaflets dropped on Iraqi troops during the Kuwait War

fenses from the west, cutting off an Iraqi retreat, while others struck at Republican Guard divisions north of the Iraqi-Kuwait border (see map). Egyptian, Syrian, and other Arab troops joined U.S. Marines to push northwards to Kuwait City.

After just 100 hours of ground fighting, President Bush announced a cease-fire. Iraq lost an estimated 10,000–30,000 dead, most of its air force, and some 3,700 tanks. The physical destruction cost scores of billions of dollars.

The cease-fire did not bring peace. In Basra and other cities, despondent troops and Shi'a militants seized power from officials and the *Ba'th Party*. The revolt became a bitter civil war in southern Iraq. Kurdish *pesh merga* guerrillas soon revolted in the north. Iraq appeared to be disintegrating along ethnic and religious divisions.

To face the crisis, Saddam Hussein charged Ali Hasan al-Majid, who had earlier "pacified" the Kurds, with restoring control. After the U.S. refused to intervene, Iraqi troops moved methodically from city to city in the South, pounding rebel areas relentlessly. Mosques were not spared, nor the families of those resisting. The rebels lacked an over-all command, and despite fighting desperately, the Islamic revolutionaries lost Basra, the Shi'a holy cities of Najaf and Karbala, and many smaller towns. Perhaps 30,000 died in the fighting. Thousands of others were executed. Refugees flooded into U.S.-occupied territory and Iran.

After subjecting the South, the Iraqi military moved north, and their overwhelming superiority in armor and helicopter gunships defeated the Kurdish fighters who had captured Kirkuk. The resulting flood of Kurdish refugees into Turkey presented Coalition leaders with a dilemma. To do nothing would arouse a sense of moral injustice: two million Kurds seemed worth defending as much as 600,000 Kuwaitis. More practically, two million refugees staying indefinitely in remote regions could create political and economic difficulties. However, any military assistance for the Kurds violated Iraqi sovereignty. This was only a technicality, but an independent Kurdish state might destabilize both Turkey and Iran. Consequently, with UN cooperation, Coalition forces forced Iraqi troops to withdraw, and then erected refugee camps inside Iraq. A Kurdish alliance took control of northern Iraq, about 10% of the country.

Post-War Difficulties in Arab Iraq

In central Iraq, Saddam Hussein and the *Ba'th* party retained power, despite military conspiracies and popular dissatisfaction. To ensure the destruction of Saddam's biological, chemical and nuclear weapons program, the UN established economic sanctions. These rapidly took bitter effect. Although they permitted imports of humanitarian goods like food and medicine, they banned the oil exports necessary to pay for them. Moreover, food for civilians was not the government's priority. So effective were the sanctions that the dearth of spare parts and raw materials reduced industrial production to one-tenth of capacity. Dire shortages of insecticides, herbicides and seeds depressed farm output, and prices rose rapidly.

To shift the blame for inflation, the regime arrested dozens of merchants and executed them for profiteering. Public works projects, from palaces to the "Third River" (designed to drain salty run-off and other pollutants), helped lower unemployment, but popular frustrations rose as family savings disappeared and heirlooms were pawned. Monthly salaries that had once provided middle-class living standards fell to $40 in 1991; by 1999 a public school teacher's monthly salary was the equivalent of only $2.

Any open expression of discontent, however, risked severe punishment. Few places on earth exhibited official brutality at the Iraqi level. Penalties initially included amputating the limbs of profiteers or farmers who hoarded their harvest, and removing an ear or tattooing the forehead of military deserters.

The Highway of Death—The scorched remains of both civilian and military vehicles litter the main highway leading from Kuwait City to Basra and Baghdad. The vehicles were destroyed in allied bombing raids against the retreating Iraqi army.

Iraq

Slowly, UN inspectors discovered evidence of a vast prewar operation involving over a dozen factories that might produce, eventually, an atomic bomb. By 1993, Iraqi cooperation replaced confrontation, and the UN established a vast monitoring system involving planes, helicopters, ground inspectors, tagged equipment, sensors and video cameras.

In 1995, biological experts from UNSCOM, the special commission of inspectors, discovered that prewar Iraq had imported vast quantities of growth media for toxic bacteria, far more than necessary to culture and identify hospital germs. Evidence mounted that despite Iraqi denials, a large germ warfare program had existed, aiming to produce anthrax, botulinum toxin and aflatoxin.

Very possibly, the inspectors' discovery of the project caused the man ultimately responsible for it, Saddam Hussein's son-in-law, Hussein Kamal, to flee to Jordan with his wife, children, and documents. Upstaging any evidence he might give, Baghdad released further evidence of the construction of biological missile warheads and spray containers for pilotless aircraft. However, Iraqi officials claimed that these had been destroyed (contrary to agreements) soon after the Gulf War. For his part, Hussein Kamal returned to Baghdad, where he and his young sons were shot days later.

Despite the inspectors' suspicions of hidden weapons, the Iraqi people's desperation won public sympathy in many countries. Rather than lift the sanctions, the UN Security Council approved a strict "Oil for Food" program. It allowed $2 billion (later, $5.2 billion) in oil exports every six months, to pay for food, medicine, and vital equipment, plus contributions for war victims, weapons inspectors and the Kurds.

Oil for Food funds did not eliminate poverty; but they stabilized diet and improved public health. Gradually the death rate of some 6,000 children per month fell. These "silent" deaths, largely unreported by the world's media, occurred largely because of impure water supplies, open sewage, past malnutrition and poorly functioning medical facilities. However, the government manipulated the system, extracting bribes from some, and favoring sympathetic countries and companies.

Amid the popular suffering, the country's fortunate few lived well. A new luxury resort opened at an artificial lake near Baghdad in 1999, with nearly every brick carrying Saddam's initials in the manner of Nebuchadnezzar, the ruler of ancient Babylon. New presidential palaces arose across the country, and statues or portraits of the president littered almost every significant intersection.

Kurdish Autonomy in the North

Protected by a U.S. no-fly zone over Northern Iraq, in 1991 the three million Kurds found themselves free from Iraq—but short of fuel, food and the supplies needed to reconstruct hundreds of entire villages destroyed by the Iraqi army. Kurdish leaders formed their own administration, eventually known as the Kurdistan Regional Government.

Separated by geography, dialect, tribal affiliation, and personal ambitions, the Kurds were divided into two major political groups. Masoud Barzani's *Kurdistan Democratic Party (KDP)*, strongest in northern and western Kurdistan, reflected the spirit of his late father, Mustafa, the legendary hero of the independence struggle. The *KDP* cooperated with the Islamic Republic of Iran. Jalal Talabani's *Patriotic Union of Kurdistan (PUK)* drew its strength in southeastern Kurdistan.

Uniting these two parties proved impossible, despite their promises to share public office between themselves. Disputes over taxes, property ownership and other matters set one party against another. In 1994, the *PUK* evicted Barzani's followers from Arbil (Erbil), the Kurdish capital, and in 1996 the *KDP* invited Iraqi troops to capture Arbil from the *PUK*, in the process discovering sensitive CIA operations. However, aid from Iran enabled the *PUK* to regain some lost territory, and U.S. and Turkish pressure eventually led to a formal cease-fire. Only the rough rule of Barzani and Talabani limited the zone's descent into anarchy.

Legally part of Iraq, the Kurdish zone traded with the rest of the country and suffered UN sanctions aimed at Saddam's regime. Factories closed for lack of supplies and customers, and trade languished. The major source of taxes and trade was the (sanctions-busting) re-export of Iraqi oil and diesel fuel. Kurdistan also endured sabotage and terrorist attacks by Iraqi agents, and the zone survived largely on sanctions-busting and aid handouts.

The guerrilla war for independence launched by the *Kurdistan Workers Party (PKK)* against Turkey (see History) complicated matters greatly. The *PKK* sought refuge in Iraqi Kurdistan, and gained some freedom of action by threats to attack trade. In return, Ankara launched major invasions that inevitably destroyed homes and villages but rarely destroyed small *PKK* units in mountainous terrain.

In 1998 the two rival parties divided the territory, and formed two administrations. The *KDP* dominated the capital, Arbil, and the vital road between Iraq and Turkey through Dohuk, with its trucks carrying cheap sanctions-busting oil to Turkey. The *PUK* capital was Sulaymaniyah, a large and vibrant city despite its location outside the U.S.-imposed no-fly zone.

Despite a legacy of poverty and anarchy, by 2003 new roads crossed the land, satellite TV broadcasts communicated in local dialects, and apartments housed refugees previously living in tents. New universities were established at Dohuk and Sulaymaniyah in addition to Salahad-

School yard in Karbala Photo by William Parker

din University in Arbil. The UN's Oil for Food program deserved much credit for the stability and progress. It distributed Kurdistan's share of oil revenues, and did so quite effectively.

When the U.S. sought Kurdish assistance against Iraq in 2003, Kurdish leaders feared punishment or genocide if the proposed invasion of Arab Iraq failed. They clearly desired to add the city and oil fields of Kirkuk to the Kurdish zone, but they also recognized that Turkey considered Kurdish control over Kirkuk as a reason to invade. Might they lose autonomy if they were outmaneuvered in the peace settlement?

War over Saddam's Alleged Weapons

For many reasons, it was no surprise that President George W. Bush quickly abandoned the traditional U.S. policy of "containing" Saddam Hussein. His new goal became "regime change." Unable to arrange a successful military coup d'état, or unite Iraqi opposition groups to overthrow Saddam Hussein in a civil war, the U.S. determined to invade Iraq.

Especially after September 11, 2001, the U.S. focused world attention on Iraq's alleged weapons of mass destruction, worrying that these might somehow reach Islamic extremists. At the UN, President Bush claimed that such weapons threatened civilization itself. However, the "evidence" of Iraq's alleged weaponry proved flimsy or false, allegations to win public opinion rather than foundations of a policy. Furthermore, no evidence emerged of an alliance between the Iraqi regime and extremist groups like *al-Qaeda*. Historians will judge the weapons issue as merely a negotiating argument and patriotic rallying cry, rather than genuine misjudgment. In any case, the U.S. raised the issue of weapons inspections at the Security Council, which unanimously voted for the inspectors to return to Iraq.

Facing united world opinion, Saddam Hussein yielded. Very quickly the new inspectors confirmed that Iraq was nowhere near producing atomic weapons, but they discovered some minor violations, such as missiles whose range extended a few miles beyond the limits. When no evidence appeared of biological and chemical weapons, the Bush administration strongly criticized the UN.

Diplomatic efforts to destroy Iraq's alleged weaponry ended when the U.S. and Great Britain failed to overcome threats of French and Russian vetoes, or even to gain a "moral majority" for a resolution authorizing war.

Some American "experts" (most of them civilian ideologues) argued that a small invasion force with massive air support would suffice, because Iraqis would dance for joy at their liberation. However, the regional commander, Army General Tommy Franks, desired much larger, more heavily equipped units. Because Jordan, Saudi Arabia, and eventually Turkey refused to allow use of their territories for the invasion, American and British units assembled in Kuwait and invaded from the south. Only U.S. Special Forces and the Kurdish *pesh merga* operated in the north.

The war began in March 2003, with air attacks. There was never any doubt that the only superpower would defeat the ill-paid, badly-equipped, and poorly led Iraqi forces. Unlike the 1991 conflict, no sustained bombing preceded the ground invasion, but intense raids destroyed defensive units. While some units stood and fought—often being destroyed by cluster bombs and other hi-tech weapons—many soldiers simply vanished into the population.

Because the U.S. and British planners wished to avoid casualties, the invasion tended to bypass southern cities, which were sometimes defended with determination by militiamen and irregulars. Baghdad, however, fell quickly just three weeks into the campaign, and Tikrit's surrender soon afterwards marked the end of Saddam's rule. In the north, supported by U.S. bombing, Kurdish fighters seized control of Kirkuk, long desired for its historical connections and oil wealth. At the behest of Turkey, the *pesh merga* were soon replaced by American forces, but Kurdish families began to return to homes they had fled a decade earlier, sometimes evicting their Arab residents.

From Liberation to Occupation

There were few scenes of jubilant Iraqis rejoicing at the largely American victory. Iraq's Shi'a apparently remembered the high price they had paid in 1991. The tumbling of one of Saddam's statues in Baghdad reminded foreigners of the fall of the Berlin Wall, but it proved to be a photo op by the U.S. military just outside the media's hotel, before only a few hundred onlookers. The occupation rapidly cost many more American lives from terrorism and guerrilla tactics than had the entire invasion. What went wrong?

First, popular opinion soon linked the U.S. "liberation" with the looting and destruction of stores, homes, hospitals, oil facilities, electrical generating plants, transmission lines, universities, the national museum, the national library, and much else. Priceless objects were stolen, as well as items of practical value. Some hospital equipment was even seized from the patients using it. Things too large to move were smashed or burned.

The looting, often conducted by gangs, usually occurred *after* U.S. and British forces had seized a locality. Iraqi security forces would have executed such criminals on the spot. As the occupying power, the Coalition forces were responsible for maintaining public order, yet they did so very selectively. American troops garrisoned the petroleum ministry but ignored pleas for protection from the national museum nearby.

The looting and general lawlessness were entirely predictable. Despite the sanctity of property in Islam, Iraqis had looted Kuwait in 1990. They looted again during the Shi'a rebellion of 1991. Their brutal mob violence extends back at least to the 1958 murder of the king. The U.S. command should have instituted a curfew and required all troops and police report to barracks, partly to keep armed young men off the streets. It did not issue such orders partly because of ideology (Iraqi troops and police were often Ba'thist), partly to show the world a peaceful population that delighted at its liberation, and partly because there were too few American troops to maintain a curfew.

Dismissed in Washington as merely the "untidiness" inevitable at the end of a dictatorship, the looting and lawlessness caused great and serious harm. Professors, hospital workers, private businessmen, and other professionals sympathetic to western-style democracy witnessed the destruction of their lifework, and sometimes their private property as well. Freed from Saddam's thugs and secret police, they now lived in fear of random arson and violence. Afraid of personal attacks, women moved about much less freely, at work or at study.

There were improvements, notably the religious freedom enjoyed by Shi'a believers to perform ceremonies connected with mourning the death of Husayn ibn 'Ali, grandson of Muhammad. Just days after their liberation, hundreds of thousands walked to Najaf in processions long banned by secular-minded Ba'thists, who feared the political potential of such gatherings and regarded the displays of emotion and self-flagellation as backward.

Bloodshed in Occupied Iraq

To the world outside, the chief feature of the occupation era was the violence and callous disregard for human life. The insurgency began with selective murders and attacks on American troops, probably by former intelligence agents and demobilized troops. However, peace did not follow the destruction of many Ba'thist cells, the deaths in battle of Saddam's sons Uday and Qusay, and the capture of Saddam himself. Instead, Islamic extremists and unidentified but sinister groups joined the resistance. The country became a cauldron of anti-American violence that attracted Sunni Islamists, occasionally

Iraq

LATE SPORTS

Masters goes on today
Tiger eyes third title; protests planned. Preview, 1, 10-11C

NO. 1 IN THE USA

Battles still rage in the north

Kurdish fighters, above, join U.S. troops in the field, 5A

Thursday, April 10, 2003

Baghdad falls

Why capital fell so quickly, 2A

Jubilant crowds swarm U.S. troops as 3-week war topples regime; 'Game is over,' Iraqi diplomat says

History in Iraqi capital: A U.S. soldier watches and Iraqis cheer Wednesday as a 20-foot high statue of Iraqi President Saddam Hussein is pulled down in a central Baghdad square. A U.S. armored vehicle pulled it down.

Newsline

News ■ Money ■ Sports ■ Life

North Korea terminates non-nuclear treaty ties

Today, North Korea becomes first country to pull out of 33-year-old Nuclear Non-Proliferation Treaty, an ominous move. 10A.

Mystery illness is testing Canada's medical system

Even so, Canada is at forefront of trying to contain deadly SARS as the U.S. Department of Defense leads search for a treatment. 1D.

■ **Money: DirecTV deal**

Pending approval, News Corp. will obtain coveted foothold in USA's satellite TV market. 1, 3B.

■ **Sports: Auto racing extra**

Catching up with Matt Kenseth and NASCAR's other top drivers in full page of racing news. 12C.

■ **Life: Foot help is here**

Get soothing, expert advice today: 1-800-422-8728. 10D.

By John O. Buckley

Crossword	11D	Marketplace	11D
Editorial	14-15A	State-by-state	11A
Lotteries	15C	Stocks	4-5, 8-12B

'There is no government left,' U.S. general says

World marvels at celebration that war's architects had predicted: Iraqis dancing in the streets, embracing allied soldiers, reveling in newfound freedom

By Gregg Zoroya and David J. Lynch
USA TODAY

BAGHDAD — Saddam Hussein's government lost control of Iraq's capital Wednesday as U.S. forces extended their reach deep into the city. Jubilant crowds tore down a 20-foot statue of the Iraqi leader and dragged its head through the streets in a scene reminiscent of the fall of the Berlin Wall in 1989.

U.S. officials declined to declare victory and warned that days of fierce fighting may lie ahead. But in three weeks, the war to remove Saddam from power appeared to have reached the "tipping point" that the campaign's architects had hoped for — the moment when the Iraqi people would realize his brutal, 24-year dictatorship had ended.

"We have been in all the government buildings, and there is no government left to speak of," said Maj. Gen. Buford Blount, commander of the Army's 3rd Infantry Division. "I think we have defeated Saddam militarily." In New Orleans, Vice President Cheney said, "We are seeing the collapse of the central regime authority."

Wednesday produced the scenes of joyous Iraqis that Cheney and other Bush administration officials had predicted months ago. Iraqi citizens ransacked and looted government buildings. In a highly symbolic act unthinkable during Saddam's reign, a statue of the Iraqi leader in al-Firdos Square, which is at the center of Baghdad, was toppled with the help of a chain and a U.S. Marine tank recovery vehicle.

Cover story

As the statue — which had been surrounded by 37 ornate white columns, each bearing Saddam's initials, to mark his 1937 birth date — fell, some Iraqis threw shoes and slippers at it, a terrible insult in the Arab world. "This was the turning point," Marine Lt. Col. David Pere said.

Marines had briefly covered its face with a U.S. flag — then replaced it with the red-black-and-white Iraqi flag — before it was toppled. "We are playing down this whole concept of American flags," Marine Lt. Gen. James Conway said. "I'll allow American flags inside the camps but not on the roads because this isn't about advancing America into the heart of Iraq. This is about liberating the Iraqi people and getting their flag back where it needs to be."

State-run radio continued to broadcast patriotic

Please see COVER STORY next page ►

What's the status of regime's inner circle

From Saddam and his sons to Tariq Aziz, 4A

Bush certain to reap benefits of liberation

Victory to strengthen hand in Congress, 5A

In Arab world, relief and disappointment

Cheers for "new era"; shock over speed, 10A

Allies' checklist for victory shows much work remains

Military, political goals not yet met

By Mark Memmott
and Bill Sternberg
USA TODAY

Even as many Iraqis celebrated Wednesday in Baghdad, tough questions remained unanswered, including a basic one: how to know when the war is over.

Secretary Donald Rumsfeld said.

Last week, White House spokesman Ari Fleischer said, "Victory is when the president announces it." Wednesday, the commander of Marine Corps forces in Iraq said he didn't know whether there would ever be a traditional surrender by the Iraqi government. "I don't think we know who's calling the shots, if anyone is," Lt. Gen. James Conway said.

Even amid talk of victory, many of the coalition's objectives have been seen since a U.S. bomb attack Monday aimed at a building they were thought to be in, but there was no firm evidence that they were killed or injured. Rumsfeld described Saddam as "not active." It was not clear Wednesday when U.S. forces could safely reach the neighborhood in Baghdad where the bombs hit.

► **Securing the north.** Key cities in northern Iraq, including Saddam's ancestral hometown of Tikrit, were not under coalition

weapons of mass destruction. The war was premised on disarming Iraq of banned weapons. Several suspicious sites have been investigated, but there was no conclusive proof Wednesday that Iraq possessed chemical, biological or nuclear weapons.

► **Restoring law and order and civil authority.** As coalition forces raced to Baghdad, a tide of thievery, violence and recrimination swept in behind them. Now, U.S. and British forces are trying to

fields. Only Saudi Arabia has more known oil reserves than Iraq, and 40% of Iraq's reserves are in the northern half of the country. Many are believed to have been wired for destruction, as was the case with southern fields.

► **Locating U.S. prisoners of war.** There are seven American POWs from this war, and 10 other U.S. troops are missing in action. One American pilot from the 1991 Gulf War, Lt. Cmdr. Michael Scott Speicher, is still listed as missing.

some Shi'a radicals, and Muslim extremists from other countries.

In 2005, the Iraqi government estimated the number of insurgents at 40,000 hard-core fighters and perhaps 150,000 supporters and part-timers. A Jordanian linked to *al-Qaeda*, Abu-Musaib al-Zarkawi, became the symbol of the Islamic resistance. He and his group were specifically blamed for bombings of Shi'a gatherings and the murder of prisoners through beheading or slitting throats.

Unsuccessful against the firepower and tactics of U.S. troops, the rebels turned to terrorism against soft targets. One suicide bombing destroyed the UN mission, costing dozens of lives; another, the Red Cross offices. Many Western civilians left the country, or retreated to the fortified "Green Zone," Saddam's former palace area turned into the U.S. headquarters. Iraqis employed by the occupation were less fortunate: thousands died, many of them policemen and soldiers. Even in the relatively safe Kurdish zone, the major political parties suffered direct attacks.

Anti-American attitudes and attacks were, until 2007, fiercest in the "Sunni triangle," the region north and west of Baghdad. The resistance there reflected its Ba'thist past, and the privileges the region had enjoyed under its native son, Saddam Hussein. The cities of Falluja and Ramadi particularly became centers of the insurgency and illustrate the great suffering of the region. Early in the occupation of Falluja, as on occasion elsewhere, U.S. troops mistook (allegedly innocent) rifle fire in celebration of a wedding as an attack. The return fire killed civilians; demonstrations later followed. Gunmen hidden among the protesters fired at troops, who in turn shot several demonstrators.

Following the murder and dismemberment of four U.S. civilian security guards, U.S. Marines besieged the city and attempted to subdue it. After significant casualties on both sides, and widely televised pictures of civilian suffering, a political solution was found: the creation of a "Falluja Protection Force," headed by a former Republican Guard general. The novel arrangement brought temporary peace, but Falluja fell under the control of militant clerics and became a center of the resistance. The Marines renewed the invasion in 2004. Working with mainly-Shi'a units of the new National Guard, they then conquered the city, but hundreds died and nearly every building was damaged.

Large-scale Shi'a resistance came in 2004 from the *Mahdi Army* of Muqtada al-Sadr. The charismatic son of an ayatollah murdered by Saddam's regime, Muqtada appealed to the poorest sectors of society, and his fiery populism combined anti-American nationalism with Islam and socialism. After he was charged with the murder of a Shi'a cleric and his newspaper was shut for vitriolic denunciations of the occupation, the *Mahdi Army* seized parts of Baghdad and the shrine cities of southern Iraq. However, Muqtada's followers wore out their welcome. Pressured by the Shi'a leadership, especially Grand Ayatollah Ali Sistani, Muqtada accepted a political solution and his fighters were replaced by police.

Photographs of tortured and disgraced prisoners held by American troops for interrogation at Baghdad's infamous Abu Ghuraib prison deeply offended Iraqi sensibilities. Such non-lethal but nonetheless degrading and inhuman torture—or worse—was common in Abu Ghuraib during Saddam's era. But the U.S. had justified the war partly to bring human rights. To many an Arab mind, any moral superiority vanished.

Greater Roles for Iraqis

Clearly acting with insufficient forethought, the U.S. Defense Department established the Coalition Provisional Authority (CPA) to govern for several years while creating democracy and a new constitution. The CPA laid ambitious plans for reconstruction, and planned a rigidly free-market economy with some of the world's lowest taxes. It quickly spent uncounted billions of U.S. tax dollars and Iraqi oil revenues on contracts to well-connected U.S. companies, some without bids, and on Iraqis, often without receipts. As anti-American violence grew, the CPA administrators and military leaders concentrated in the tightly guarded "Green Zone" of western Baghdad.

The CPA reacted slowly to shortages of public services, particularly water, sewage, electricity, and fuel. Power plants, water treatment facilities and similar installations had not been targets of U.S. bombing, but looting harmed a fragile infrastructure that had suffered 13 years of sanctions. Pumping water and sewers required electricity; this in turn required generating plants that used fuel oil or natural gas. By the summer of 2004, electrical blackouts halted air conditioning and widely depressed morale. Individual acts of good will and reconstruction by U.S. troops and civilians often seemed to matter little.

Nevertheless, the CPA improved life in significant ways. It cut import tariffs from 400% to essentially nothing, enabling merchants to fill the markets, stores, and auto dealerships with new merchandise (though destroying Iraqi competitors). It granted press freedoms, and hundreds of new papers appeared, advocated conflicting viewpoints. It repaired and re-opened schools, and revised school textbooks. It paid veterans, and continued Saddam's massive food distribution policies that meant survival for over half the population. It issued a new currency, and raised wages.

Nevertheless, it was not Iraqi. Within months, American influence began to diminish. Popular demands for greater Iraqi decision-making were not satisfied by the appointment of exiles to administrative positions.

After violence rose sharply, a new Iraqi army was created and the police force expanded, both with American advisors. On June 28, 2004, sovereignty was publicly transferred to the interim government.

In Saddam's former Green Zone palace, the largest American embassy anywhere replaced the CPA. It supervised—and subsidized—the country. The new Governing Council selected 'Iyad Allawi, a Shi'a neurologist and businessman, as Prime Minister. While the new leaders thanked the U.S. for liberating Iraq, they also demanded genuine sovereignty, including the right to demand the withdrawal of occupation forces.

Constitution and Government (2005–06)

Yielding to Shi'a demands for elections, the CPA's transitional laws stipulated elections for a National Assembly that would select a government, draft a new constitution, and hold further national elections, all within a year. Besides this challenging schedule, the CPA prescribed one of the purest forms of democracy: national proportional representation, combined with the requirement that a 2/3 "supermajority" approve the cabinet, thus precluding a Shi'a-only regime.

This ideologically pure democracy encouraged politics to focus on religious or ethnic groups. The national electoral district—26 million inhabitants (more than Texas)—prohibited local notables from running independently, and reduced discussion of local issues. Political parties recognized the importance of a national presence, and as a result, they merged into "lists." In the Shi'a community, the larger religious-based parties, *al-Da'wa* and the *Supreme Council of the Islamic Revolution in Iraq (SCIRI)* formed the *United Iraqi Alliance (UIA)* with several smaller groups. Its rival for Shi'a support was the secular *Iraqi List* of 'Iyad Allawi, the interim prime minister. The major Kurdish parties, the *KDP* and *PUK*, set aside their own rivalries to establish the *Kurdistan Alliance*. However, the largely Sunni insurgency denounced elections, and few Sunni politicians dared to run.

As expected, Iraqis voted their religious and ethnic identities. The *United Iraqi Alliance* won 140 of the 275 seats. To gain the required "supermajority" it formed a coalition with the 77 deputies of the *Kurdistan Alliance*. By contrast, voters decisively rejected Allawi, who gained only 14% of the vote.

However, a system cleverly intended to reward communities that voted backfired in the Sunni provinces. Only small minorities of those eligible cast their ballots, and Sunni Arab candidates, representing a quarter of the population, won only 6% of the seats. Thus the National Assembly clearly failed to include reasonable representation of all Iraqis, a particular challenge when framing the constitution.

Immediately after the elections, the level of violence fell. The voters—58% of those registered—had spoken, and they directly rejected the insurgency. However, the coalition of just two parties took two months to select Jalal Talabani of the *PUK* as president, and three months to form a cabinet under Ibrahim al-Jaafari of *al-Da'wa (UIA)*. Much of that time was consumed by negotiations over the Sunni representatives. Meanwhile, violence returned to higher levels.

Ironically, the U.S. had sponsored the Iraq's most freely contested election in decades—to the benefit of Iranian influence. President Talabani's *PUK* had often sought military supplies from Iran, and used them to recover lost territory from the *KDP* in the 1990s. Prime Minister al-Jaafari had lived in exile in Iran and Britain. His party, *al-Da'wa*, had long contacts with Iran. The deputy Prime Minister, Ahmed Chalabi, had been identified as an Iranian spy just a year earlier. Behind the scenes, other Iranian links included Grand Ayatollah Ali Sistani, who was born in Iran, speaks Arabic with an accent, and heads charitable foundations across the border.

The Jaafari cabinet ruled ineffectively during perilous times. It confronted the insurrection by incorporating Shi'a fighters from the *Badr* and *Mahdi* militias into the police. While willing to fight, these militiamen in police uniform reportedly abducted, tortured, and massacred Sunnis. Al-Jaafari's cabinet also earned a reputation for corruption. Oil exports fell, and reconstruction stagnated.

Nevertheless, the cabinet succeeded in two important tasks. It drafted a constitution, and held parliamentary elections that were truly national, for they included wide Sunni participation.

The constitutional debate focused on three issues: the role of Islam, the degree of regional autonomy, and control of oil revenues. Article 2 of the draft constitution recognized Islam as the religion of the state, and "a (rather than "the") fundamental source of legislation." It also prohibited any law that contradicted Islam's "undisputed" decisions.

Given the devout population, a formal Islamic role was inevitable, as was a retreat from gender equality imposed by secular Ba'thists. However, some clauses of the constitution left wide room for later disputes. For example, Article 2 prohibited laws contrary to democracy or human rights, and Article 14 granted all Iraqis equality. Elsewhere, women were guaranteed 25% of parliamentary seats.

Demands for regional autonomy proved an even more vexing issue. Sunnis desired a unitary state, ruled from Baghdad, but Kurds insisted on either their self-government within Iraq—or independence. Some Shi'a leaders also desired autonomous Shi'a regions in the south. Unable to compromise, the National Assembly approved a federal system, but left some details for later decisions.

For good measure, at least to the Kurdish interpretation, the constitution allocated oil revenues from existing fields to the central government, but those from new fields to the regions. Since the major oil deposits lie in Kurdish and Shi'a areas, Sunnis naturally opposed a clause that suggested their future impoverishment.

After a bitter six-week campaign, Iraq's voters ratified the constitution with 78% approval. However, two Sunni provinces (Anbar and Salahuddin) overwhelmingly opposed it. Voters in Nineveh also rejected it, but by only a 55% majority.

Over two hundred parties contested the 2005 elections for a permanent parliament, the Majlis. Sunni groups joined the contest, implicitly recognizing that the opportunity to participate in government outweighed the risk of insurgent opposition. This time, the Shi'a *United Iraqi Alliance* included Muqtada's *Sadr Organization*, but it lacked Ayatollah Sistani's open support.

Once again, the elections proved that voters cherished ethnic and sectarian identity above ideology and political platforms. As expected, the *UIA* (128 seats) fell short of a simple majority, and with the *Kurdistan Alliance* still lacked the 2/3 supermajority required to approve a cabinet. Sunni groups gained significant representation, with the *Iraqi Accord Front* receiving 44 seats. The major losers were secular Shi'a groups. Chalabi's alliance even failed to enter parliament.

Due mostly to rivalries within the *UIA*, it took five months of bargaining, rising violence, and American pressure before a "supermajority" emerged. Eventually, the *UIA* proposed Nouri al-Maliki, deputy leader of *al-Da'wa*, as prime minister. Al-Maliki gained both Kurdish and Sunni approval and formed his cabinet in April 2006.

From any perspective, Prime Minister al-Maliki faced immense challenges. The explosions that destroyed the golden dome of the Askari shrine in Samarra had unleashed a savage reprisal by Shi'a militiamen, with hundreds of dead in Baghdad alone. Though not formally at civil war, the country suffered deadly sectarian cleansing. Thanks partly to the rapid hiring of Shi'a militiamen as government employees, some soldiers, police, and guards engaged in organized kidnapping, torture, and murder—even in Basra, where few insurgent attacks had occurred.

The UN estimated that 34,000 civilians were killed in 2006, and the International Red Cross learned that mothers deeply hoped for someone to collect the bodies from the streets before their children went to school. *Nearly 20% of the population became refugees.* Two million wealthy enough to do so moved abroad, and as many more fled to safer neighborhoods. Their homes were usually looted and then occupied by families from the locally dominant sectarian group. As the professional and business classes began to disappear, hospitals and clinics lost staff. Only the bravest university professors continued to teach; over 200 were assassinated. The Western nations most responsible for the conflict—the U.S. and Britain—accepted only a few Iraqi refugees, while Syria and Jordan hosted roughly one million each.

Non-Muslim minorities continued to face particular violence. Christian leaders were assassinated, and the laity threatened with death if they did not flee the country. Yazidis (inaccurately) face charges of worshipping Satan. The Mandaeans, followers of one of the oldest religious traditions in the world, fear extinction, because Islamic extremists in Iraq are trying to wipe them out through forced conversions, rape and murder.

In 2006, Saddam Hussein was convicted by an Iraqi court for the killing of 148 Shi'a from the town of Dujail following an assassination attempt. A trial over the Kurdish massacres was also sought, but he and a few aides were rushed to execution.

Despite other successes, such as the death of Abu Musaib al-Zarqawi, who had led of one of the most fanatical insurgent groups, *al-Qaeda in Iraq*, violence against civilians increased in 2006–07. Suicide bombings, sectarian reprisal killings, improvised chlorine gas bombs and ambushes of police units proved deadly. Attacks on U.S. troops featured increasingly sophisticated weapons, particularly roadside bombings by "explosively formed projectiles" (EFPs), complex devices that even pierce armored vehicles.

The "Surge" Succeeds

After the Iraq Study Group warned of a slide toward chaos and government collapse, President Bush rejected calls for an American withdrawal. Instead, he ordered an increase in the U.S. military forces in Iraq to provide more troops in zones of conflict. This "surge" was expected to reduce the violence while politicians in Baghdad reached the compromises necessary to attract Sunnis and radical Shi'a groups.

The surge gradually reached in its military goals. Initially, with more American troops on patrol, their casualties climbed to some of the highest levels of the war. Some of those casualties, inflicted by EFPs supplied by Iranian groups, came from Shi'a militiamen unwilling to accept the limitations of law and order on their ethnic attacks on Sunnis. Nevertheless, violence declined in Baghdad, temporarily increased in Diyala and other provinces as insurgents found easier targets, then declined there as well. In Anbar province and elsewhere, tribal leaders who had tired of the harsh fanaticism of many insurgents formed tactical alliances with the U.S. military in return for arms and money. Mosul became the last insurgent stronghold.

With the decline in violence, many refugees began to return to Baghdad and elsewhere, in some cases only to find their homes occupied by others. Many returnees were women; like those who had remained, they found conditions worsening for women and girls. Their discouragement over the availability of jobs or fear of violence was expected. However, over three-quarters of those surveyed reported that their daughters were not allowed to attend school, a shocking outlook for the future.

Slow political progress accompanied the security surge. Parliament only tardily addressed legislation crucial to attracting Sunni support, such as reversing aspects of de-Ba'thification, the distribution of oil revenues among the regions, and possible regional units of a federal nation. Muqtada al-Sadr withdrew his party first from the cabinet, then from the *United Iraqi Alliance*. However, he proclaimed a cease-fire by his militia, the *Jaish al-Mahdi*, and asserted control over at least some of its rogue elements.

In 2008, Prime Minister al-Maliki suddenly ordered the army and police to crack down on militia activity in Basra some months after the British withdrawal. In practical terms, this meant assaulting al-Sadr's *Jaish al-Mahdi*. It successfully fought back; hundreds of troops and police deserted; even air support proved insufficient for a clear military victory. The fighting spread to Baghdad, but thanks in part to Iranian advice, al-Sadr agreed to a cease-fire. Thereafter, police and military patrols and roadblocks gradually asserted law and order. Al-Sadr's followers were not defeated, but stood down.

By 2009, both Basra and Baghdad had become much calmer, with some barriers down and social life resuming. On June 30, U.S. troops formally withdrew from Iraqi cities. Hailed by the Iraqi government as a huge victory and celebrated as "National Sovereignty Day," the withdrawal was possible only because of the increased professionalism of Iraqi forces and the war-weariness of the nation. While suicide bombers later managed to devastate government ministries in Baghdad and kill scores elsewhere, the trend of violence was clearly downward, and the attacks did not ignite sectarian reprisals.

The politicians of democratic Iraq move slowly. Legal changes for the 2010 parliamentary elections involved repeated delays, and the elections themselves were postponed for two months without a solution to a major contentious issue, the status of Kirkuk.

The election confirmed political fractures within sectarian groups as well as between them. The Shi'a religious parties that had united in 2005 as the *Iraqi National Alliance* fractured when Prime Minister al-Maliki formed the *State of Law* coalition, clearly hoping to benefit from the improved security. Despite being officially secular and less pro-Iranian, it appealed mostly to Shi'a groups traditionally loyal to the *Da'wa Party*. The other significant Shi'a parties, including the *Iraqi Islamic Supreme Council* and the *Sadrists*, formed the *National Iraqi Alliance*, and split the votes of conservative, religiously-oriented Shi'a. By contrast, former interim Prime Minister Allawi's *Al-Iraqiyya (Iraqi National Movement)* appealed to Sunnis as well as some Shi'a.

To some surprise, *Al-Iraqiyya* carried every Sunni Arab province and won 91 seats in the 325-member assembly, two more than the *State of Law* alliance. Despite al-Maliki's charges of voting irregularities and an appeal for a recount in Baghdad, the two-member plurality held. However, with fewer than 30% of the seats, *Al-Iraqiyya* could not govern alone.

Al-Maliki concentrates power

During Iraq's violent history, compromise often proved dangerous, a lesson learned well by present political leaders. Unable to work together, Allawi and al-Maliki sought allies, particularly after the Federal Court ruled that the largest coalition rather than the largest party should have the first opportunity to propose a government. The ensuring contest established a new world record for the longest time between election day and the formation of a new government, but finally the *Sadrists* agreed to join al-Maliki's coalition.

Many Iraqis soon considered that government had failed them. Inspired by the Arab Spring demonstrators, protestors attempted to publicize their demands for an end to corruption, action on unemployment (probably near 30%), improved government services, and transparent security forces rather than perceived repression. Al-Maliki denounced the planned demonstrations as inspired by either the *Ba'thists* or *al-Qaeda*, which was largely nonsense. Across the country at least twenty died—a figure not that different from the early days in countries ruled by dictators.

The government maintained unity, and reduced violent attacks, by withstanding Washington's pressures to accept a long-term U.S. military presence of several thousand troops. This rejection publicly humiliated the U.S., though most Americans, glad to be out, cared little.

The moment that the last American troops departed their last base, however, political unity fractured publicly. Claiming that the prime minister sought to monopolize power, the *al-Iraqiyya Bloc* walked out of parliament. Days later, its leading official, Vice President Tariq al-Hashimi, was charged with murder. The Vice President fled to the Kurdish zone, then abroad, and was tried in absentia, mostly on evidence supplied by arrested bodyguards.

Though many accused al-Maliki of pursing a sectarian or pro-Iranian agenda, more than anything else he used his second term to consolidate his personal power. He retained personal control of the defense and interior (police) ministries, and reportedly micro-managed them. Court rulings granted him control of previously-independent ministries and confined the ability to propose laws in parliament to the government.

Vindictive by nature, al-Maliki brought charges very selectively against those who displeased him. For example, Faraj al-Haidari, who as head of the independent electoral commission rejected al-Maliki's attempt to disqualify some *al-Iraqiyya* votes, was charged with corruption. The head of the Central Bank was arrested on similar charges. TV stations that broadcasted unflattering news faced temporary closures or worse.

Many government ministries perform poorly, and in material respects such as private car ownership, the country is worse off than in 2003. By 2013, criminal gangs and terrorists had raised the death toll to nearly 1,000 per month, despite, or because of, al-Maliki's personal responsibility for public security. Iraq's ranking in the corruption index from Transparency International reached the fifth worst in the world in 2012.

Given all these strains, national politics fractured further. To concentrate power in himself, al-Maliki used prosecutors

Prime Minister Nouri al-Maliki and President Bush

Courtesy of the White House

and the courts to harass his opponents. One example was his use of the judiciary to eliminate opponents from running for office. Iraqi law permits the exclusion of candidates who lack a "good reputation." The electoral commission interpreted that as barring individuals convicted of criminal offenses. The ministry of justice, by contrast, selectively blocked candidates who had received an arrest warrant, something it could arrange.

His Shi'a rivals attempted, but failed, to displace him with a vote of no confidence in 2012, but the strongest opposition came from Sunnis. The arrest of the Sunni finance minister prompted mass protests in Anbar Province and other Sunni Arab areas; the demonstrators also condemned the general repression of their community's leaders and the arrest of women for the alleged offenses of their husbands and sons. The demonstrations became continuous when a protest camp was established in Ramadi.

Relations between Baghdad and the Kurdish Regional Government (KRG) also deteriorated greatly and in 2012 nearly led to armed clashes over territory. The long-running dispute between Baghdad and the KRG continued over contracts for oil exploration in Kurdish areas and the KRG's agreement with Turkey to pump crude directly to Turkey.

Personal animosities compounded inherent differences, symbolized by the words of Masoud al-Barzani, the Kurdish president: "The F-16 must not reach the hand of this man (al-Maliki)." Barzani, like the fugitive Vice President al-Hashimi, warned that without power-sharing by the Shi'a ruling clique in Baghdad, Iraq might break up.

The ISIS Conquest

Months before the election, and possibly to enhance his stature, in late 2013, al-Maliki ordered the arrest of a Sunni MP and the closure of the Ramadi protest camp as a "terrorist site." In response, fighters of the extremist *Islamic State of Iraq and [Greater] Syria* (also translated *Levant; ISIS or ISIL)* an offshoot of *al-Qaeda,* struck at police and army units in Ramadi and Falluja, the main urban areas of Anbar province. Despite support from some Anbar tribesmen, government shelling and air attacks were unable to repulse the rebels, whose strength the prime minister blamed partly on missiles and other weapons from Saudi Arabia (probably a lie, but effective electioneering?).

In June 2014, *ISIS* suddenly launched an unexpected offensive against the northern city of Mosul, the country's second-largest. Rather than fight, police and soldiers frequently abandoned their positions; within hours, the city fell. Following accounts of brutality and bloodshed, thousands fled the city for the nearby Kurdish territory. *ISIS* forces looted millions of dollars from banks: their rebellion seems financed very effectively.

From Mosul the fighting spread further east and south. Joined by discontented Ba'thist sympathizers and others angered by al-Maliki's policies, the rebels isolated and captured Iraqi units that failed to retreat in time, sometimes evidently massacring prisoners of war to enhance Shi'a fears and hatred. The Kurdish *pesh merga* halted the *ISIS* advance outside Kirkuk; otherwise all other significant cities and towns in the north and west fell to the rebels within two weeks, except for the oil refinery at Baiji and the Shi'a shrine at Samarra.

Within the country, the rebel successes intensified the sectarian divide. Arab Sunnis demanded an inclusive, national government. Kurdish forces used the collapse of authority to extend their control over areas they had long claimed. The perspective of Nechirvan Barzani, prime minister of the Kurdish region, seems decisive: "If we think that Iraq will go back like before Mosul, I don't think so—it's almost impossible."

Threats against Baghdad and Shi'a led al-Sadr's *Jaish al-Mahdi* and other Shi'a militia groups to parade their weapons, and in some cases to fight alongside the military. However, several top Shi'a clergy adopted a more balanced approach, and Grand Ayatollah Ali Sistani called for a government representing all groups, a pointed criticism of al-Maliki's practices.

Internationally, the successes of *ISIS* horrified western politicians and policymakers, as did the gruesome pictures and videos of executions that *ISIS* used to boast of its conquests and strike fear into its enemies. When *ISIS* symbolically flattened borders and denounced the Sykes-Picot Agreement, it struck at the century-old settlement of World War I that established the states of the modern Middle East. Abu Bakr al-Baghdadi, the group's leader, announced as Ramadan began in 2014 a change in name and title. The *Islamic State in Iraq and Syria* was now simply *The Islamic State,* and al-Baghdadi became Caliph Ibrahim, to whom all true Muslims owe allegiance.

Culture: As Muslim Arabs, Iraqis share major cultural features with other peoples of the Middle East, ranging from the father's authority to food and religious holidays. The family remains the basic social unit, with parents, children, and grandchildren often forming a single household. Though their education may postpone it, girls usually marry young, by arrangement between her family and the groom's, and soon bear the first of many children. Large families have been encouraged by both traditional values and government policies. Consequently, the population has grown rapidly, and about half the population is less than 15 years of age.

Before the 1958 Revolution, most Iraqis lived in rural areas, typically in small, mud-brick houses except in the north, where the climate required stone. Agriculture occupied perhaps three-quarters of the population. Their living conditions were simple or even harsh, with diets restricted to bread, rice, lentils, beans, onions, occasional mutton and dates. As oil revenues provided prosperity in the cities, they attracted a great migration, until by 1990 some two-thirds of the nation lived in urban areas, usually in neighborhoods of people from the same rural district. Agriculture, often neglected though still important, proved unable to feed the nation during the UN embargo.

After two decades of war, sanctions, and occupation, these are not ordinary times. Poverty and inadequate food rations discouraged parents from having many children. Though the family remains the basic social unit, marriage has become far more difficult, and reportedly there are now at least one million single women aged over thirty-five. Few men can afford the traditional dowry or furnish a home, while many educated women seeking a successful career preferred to remain single, at least during the last years of Saddam's rule.

Sixty years ago, large Bedouin tribes like the Shammar roamed the deserts. However, the number of nomads has dwindled to insignificance due to motor transport, resettlement programs, education, and easier sedentary life.

Modernization most visibly affected the large cities of Iraq, as the government constructed roads, shopping centers, and large buildings. The modern homes and apartment houses in the better suburbs contrast with the narrow streets of older sections. Poor migrants, on the other hand, find temporary shelter on the outskirts, often of reed matting and mud.

Formal culture in Iraq, like most other Arab countries, stresses achievements in poetry and learning, while sculpture, painting, music and drama received less interest. The great recent exception proved the rule, as the population defaced or destroyed the many statues and pictures of Saddam Hussein.

Few of the older generation of Iraqis formally entered school, but in recent decades the government vastly extended the educational system. Primary education is compulsory, and schools now dot villages and cities alike; their renovations are one achievement of the U.S.-led occupation. A modern curriculum with post-war textbooks replaces the Quranic emphasis of the kuttabs, or mosque schools.

Beyond secondary education, universities in the major cities offer instruction in most disciplines. Although the role of women remains less public, until 2003 all schools and universities were coeducational, though this may change in the democratic post-Saddam era. Another threat to higher education comes from the killing of nearly 200 professors and other academics during the first three years of the occupation.

During the *Ba'thist* era, readership of the press remained low, a function of its predictable propaganda. However, one positive result of the U.S. occupation is a vibrant press. Over 100 papers have appeared, with titles like *New Era, Dawn of Baghdad,* and *The New Iraq,* reflecting popular desires for a better future. Daily concerns like insufficient clean water and electricity receive extensive coverage. Some private TV and radio stations compete with the government's broadcasting services and those of the two Kurdish parties.

By the 1980s, many urban men and some women selected Western styles of clothing, though the traditional gowns for men and the voluminous black *abayas* for women remained widely used, and dominated rural areas. Rural Kurds wore distinctive clothing, the men in baggy pants and women in long gowns over pants.

After 2003, Arab women generally returned to traditional dress and headscarves, to avoid harassment, certainly, but also for their own safety after at least three students in Basra were killed for their failure to do so. During the height of the insurgency, men also faced strict demands for modesty: in 2006, the coach of the national tennis team and two players were taken from their car and shot—apparently for wearing shorts.

The Marsh Arabs

For centuries, the Marsh Arabs, known also as the Ma'dan, formed a sharp contrast to the traditional image of Arabs as herders of sheep and goats in a desert landscape. Inaccessible except by canoe, the Marsh Arabs inhabited a world of water, surrounded by vegetation and living in reed houses with high, arched ceilings. Some homes were even built on artificial islands constructed of reeds. All this was made possible by the flat terrain between the lower Tigris and Euphrates rivers, where the annual flow and flooding of the rivers created an area of permanent and seasonal marshes, lakes, and waterways that stretched across 10,000 square miles. Invaluable for fish and migrating birds, the marshes also provided an environment for rare species of otter, lizards, wild boar and other animals.

Shi'a by religion, the Marsh Arabs lived by fishing, herding water buffalo, and weaving reed mats. They preserved several unique customs and except for limited trade, they mixed little with outsiders, rarely marrying them. During the war with Iran and later over Kuwait, military deserters sought sanctuary amidst the isolation of the marshes.

In response, the Iraqi government determined to control the region. Because irrigation and dams upstream diminished the flow of the rivers and ended the seasonal floods, some areas became accessible by roads. Later, the "Third River" drainage project diverted water to regions below the marshes. By the mid-1990s, the marshes effectively ceased to exist, and most of the Marsh Arab population had fled to refugee camps in Iran. After the fall of Saddam, efforts are being made, with international support, to restore this unique environment. However, regional drought and dams upstream in Iran, Turkey, and Syria as well as Iraq divert too much water to maintain the full scale of the marshes.

Economy: Agriculture and livestock-raising dominated the economy before the construction of a modern oil industry in the 1930s. Iraq once grew 70% of the world's dates, mostly along the rivers and marshes of the south, and wool was a significant export. Today, wheat and barley are the main winter crops of the rain-fed north, while rice and cotton grow in irrigated areas in the south. Sheep, goats, cattle and water buffalo are raised for meat, milk and hides.

Agriculture improved markedly between 1958 and the 1980s as a result of irrigation schemes and the introduction of scientific methods. After 1990, failing irrigation pumps and sanctions on pesticides, equipment, and fertilizers combined to reduce output by at least 30%. Because pesticides could not be imported, the date groves became infested with insects, and harvests fell to a small fraction of the 1980s.

The English adjective "muslin" reflects the traditional textiles of Mosul. Present industrial production includes cement, leather, shoes, cotton textiles, beer, and household articles such as matches. Small shop or home manufacturing is still important, especially for homespun woolens, rugs and reed mats.

Economic sanctions imposed after Iraq invaded Kuwait distorted Iraq's development in almost every regard. UN sanctions after 1991 essentially halted all business investment, but the era of American rule through the CPA witnessed a remarkable reduction in personal and corporate taxes. It also abolished all tariffs and permitted 100% foreign ownership of firms (aside from oil production). Iraqi-owned companies felt unprotected, but this offered foreigners a "capitalist's dream" of purchasing Iraqi land and firms exceptionally cheaply. Should these free-enterprise policies remain when peace and order eventually return, Iraq's business climate will contrast sharply with the rest of the entire region.

Insurgency, crime and corruption greatly slowed recovery from the economic collapse of 2003. Unemployment neared 50% at mid-decade, and the country desperately needs economic growth. Unemployed men become available for desperate actions, including terrorism.

Petroleum: Since the 1930s, oil exports have provided the major source of government revenue and as much as 95% of foreign exchange earnings. Iraq's proven reserves are vast; over 100 billion barrels, second-largest in the world and about 10% of the global total. Nevertheless, petroleum output has rarely reached a level appropriate to the deposits. Besides wars, friction between the Iraq Petroleum Company and the government often limited exploration and production. Geography was also a major impediment.

Reaching overseas markets from an almost land-locked country proved difficult from the start. The initial oil deposits in the northeast lay almost as far from Iraq's few miles of southern shoreline as from the Mediterranean. Therefore, a pipeline was constructed to Palestine before World War II, but it proved useless when Israel won independence in 1948. Another line to ports in Syria and Lebanon depended on their goodwill and security, and Syria interrupted exports for decades. After the discovery of oil in the south, newer technology permitted offshore loading terminals for the export of southern crude. However, that route depended on freedom to navigate the Gulf and the Strait of Hormuz, and the facilities also lay uncomfortably close to Iran and Kuwait.

Seeking other export routes, in 1977 a new pipeline was completed to the Turkish port of Ceyhan, a new direct access to the Mediterranean that did not cross Syria. Iraq also arranged construction of a pipeline across Saudi Arabia to the Red Sea, capable of raising the export capacity above the country's OPEC quota. However, both the Turkish and Saudi lines were closed after the invasion of Kuwait, and sanctions greatly hampered investment in the industry for over a decade.

While the real role of Iraq's oil in leading the U.S. to invade may never be known, some Washington think-tanks publicly advocated breaking up the government oil monopoly into smaller units that would compete with each other and hopefully destroy OPEC. After the occupation, Iraqi public opinion strongly opposed doing so, but the country lacked the ability to restore production rapidly. In 2009, Iraq auctioned production contracts for about half the country's oilfields, and Britain's BP and China's CNPC agreed to develop and service the giant Rumaila field in the south.

In 2013 the petroleum exports are expected to average 3.6 million barrels per day, the third highest in the world after Saudi Arabia and Russia. Optimists hope to expand production to possibly 12 million barrels per day, earning revenues of perhaps $200 billion per year.

The Future: Can Iraq be saved? Even before the *ISIS* conquests of 2014, the country suffered relentless suicide bombings, political assassinations, arbitrary arrests of opposition leaders, and a corruption ranking among the global worst.

Almost all Iraqis are decent folk who wish to set conflict behind them and enjoy peace and prosperity. So the real question to ask is "Can Iraqi citizens and their politicians find sufficient strength of character to form an effective *national* government that can defuse sectarian rivalries, deter violence, and use oil revenues to society's benefit rather than its corruption?"

For the near future, the answer is no. Revived tribalism encourages voters to support persons rather than parties, and as a result at least 24 parties or coalitions won at least 2 seats in parliament. The smallest number of parties that can form a government is four, but without including Al-Maliki's *State of Law*, a ruling coalition must have at least 22 partners.

Should a country that fractured survive? Many world leaders might wonder, but strategic reasons of state usually lead them to favor present arrangements. When Israel's Netanyahu announced that the time for Kurdish independence had come, the U.S., Britain, and Turkey all pledged support for a united country. Nevertheless, Masoud Barzani, the Kurdish Regional Government president, announced an independence referendum would be held.

It's hard to imagine how Iraq can hold together as anything except a loosely-linked federal state, with the KRG keeping Kirkuk and the impoverished Sunni Arabs deprived of most oil revenues.

No cross zone in Karbala

Photo by William Parker

The State of Israel מדינת ישראל

Theodor Herzl

Introduction: Whether for its heroism during the War of Independence (1948–49) or later conflicts, its farming that "made the desert bloom," its democracy, the achievements of its citizens in music, science, or its military prowess, no other nation of the region captured the imagination of the Western world like Israel. Its immigrants from around the globe provide a more diverse culture than any other nation, and it remains a special focus even of Jews who live elsewhere by choice.

Area: 8,017 sq. mi. (20,700 sq. km.) within the Armistice Demarcation lines effective 1949–1967. In addition, since 1967, the West Bank (of the Jordan River), the Gaza Strip and part of Syria have been under Israeli military occupation and subject to Israeli civilian settlement.

Population: 8 million (75% Jewish), including Jewish settlers in Golan and the West Bank

Capital City: Jerusalem (pop. about 750,000), more than two-thirds Jewish. Few nations recognize Israeli sovereignty over East Jerusalem (captured in 1967) so most maintain their embassies in the Tel Aviv metropolitan area (pop. 3.2 million, 2008).

Climate: Summers are hot and dry, winters mild with moderate rainfall, except in the arid south part of the country.

Neighboring Countries: Egypt (Southwest); Jordan (East); Syria (Northeast); Lebanon (North).

Time Zone: GMT +2 (+3 in summer).

Official Languages: (Modern) Hebrew and Arabic.

Other Principal Tongues: English, Yiddish, Ladino, Polish, Russian, Persian, German, French, Hungarian, Bulgarian and Romanian.

Ethnic Background: European, North African and Asian.

Principal Religion: Judaism (83%), Islam and Christianity.

Chief Commercial Products: Computer software and high-tech applications, armaments, aircraft and aircraft servicing, military electronics equipment, chemicals, cut and polished diamonds, agricultural products.

Main Agricultural Produce and Livestock: Oranges and other fruit, vegetables, wheat, potatoes, poultry, sheep and cattle.

Major Trading Partners: U.S., Japan, Germany, U.K. Switzerland, France, Italy, Hong Kong and Belgium.

Currency: New Israeli Shekel (= 100 agorot).

Former Colonial Status: Britain conquered the territory now controlled by the State of Israel from the Ottoman Empire during 1916–1918 and held it until 1948.

Israel

Independence Date: May 14, 1948. Like all holidays, Independence Day is celebrated according to the Jewish calendar, and it varies from late April to May.
Chief of State: Reuven Rivlin (2014)
Head of Government: Binyamin Netanyahu, Prime Minister (2009).
National Flag: White field with a broad blue horizontal stripes near both the top and bottom; centered between the stripes is a large blue "Shield of David," that is a cut-out six-pointed star.
Gross Domestic Product: $305 billion (current prices); $286 billion (PPP)
GDP per capita: $35,600 (PPP).

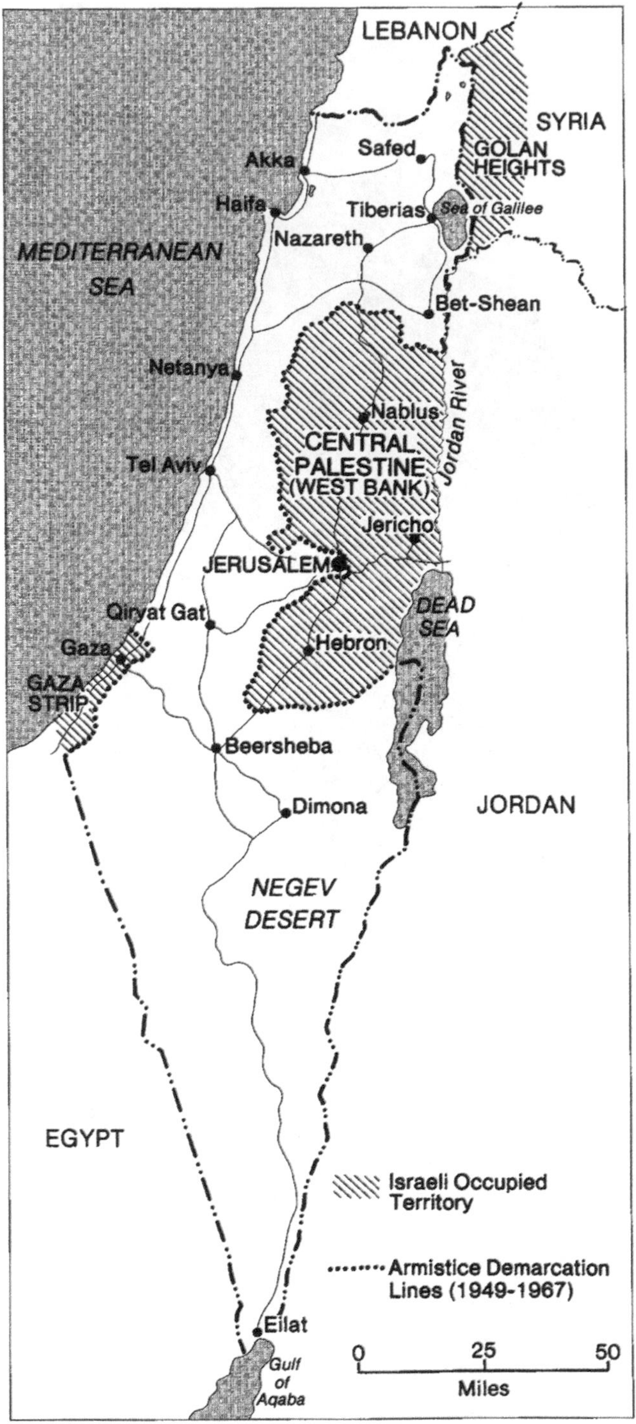

Lying on the coast of the Mediterranean Sea with the Arabian Desert at its back door, Israel has considerable variety in climate and geography. The northern part enjoys good rainfall, sometimes as much as 40 inches in a winter, but the southern part is arid desert of gravel and rock. Summers can be unpleasantly warm throughout the land, but winters are not severe, though chilly at higher elevations.

The Mediterranean seaboard is bordered by a coastal plain averaging about ten miles in width and broken only by a ridge extending northwest from the West Bank to a promontory just south of Haifa. Much of this plain is under cultivation, as it has been for many centuries. A central ridge runs south from the border with Lebanon through Israel and the West Bank, and then fans out in Israel's southern desert. The rainfall caught on the western slopes of these central hills allows a variety of fruit trees to flourish, as well as small fields of grain and vegetables. The Hula Plain north of the Sea of Galilee has been partly reclaimed from marshes. A fertile plain lying to the southeast of Haifa has been a source of grains and other foods since ancient times.

Flowing from sources on the slopes of Mt. Hermon and the Golan Heights, the Jordan River provides the major source of fresh water in the region. South of the Sea of Galilee the Jordan Valley lies entirely below sea level, and at the Dead Sea it reaches the lowest point on earth (about 1300 ft. below sea level, and falling). South of the Dead Sea, the deep valley rises gently to the Gulf of Aqaba and Israel's southern port, Eilat.

History: Proclaimed independent on May 14, 1948, Israel represents the triumph of modern Zionist dreams for a Jewish state. Its origins reach back for centuries, to the Roman Empire's expulsion of the Jewish population after their revolts in the first and second centuries C.E.

Despite ravages of Muslim conquests, Crusaders, the Black Plague, famines, and rival rulers, the Jewish communities survived. They strengthened after 1492 with a rapid influx of Spanish Jews expelled from their homeland, but Ottoman rule (1517) decayed relatively quickly, and many Jews left to avoid the subsequent instability. By 1800 the Jewish presence in Palestine had dwindled to the lowest level for centuries. Events took an unexpected turn a century later: , Zionism infused the Jewish world with the idea not merely of Jewish settlements in the Promised Land, but of a *Jewish state* there.

ZIONISM: For centuries Zionism reflected the yearning of Jews to return to Zion, meaning the citadel at Jerusalem, and even the entire Holy Land. After increasing nationalism in Europe, Theodor Herzl and others transformed cultural and religious Zionism into a political ideology. It holds that Jews everywhere form *one people,* whose protection requires a Jewish state.

The Birth of Political Zionism

The origins of Zionism lay far from the traditional and pious Jewish settlements in Palestine. Persecutions (pogroms) in Eastern Europe, especially in Czarist Russia and Poland, led Leo Pinsker to demand a home for oppressed Jews in 1882; a colonization society sprang up. By 1900 thousands of Jews fleeing the anti-Semitism of Eastern Europe entered the Holy Land to pioneer new settlements with the goal of developing a self-supporting economy based on agriculture. The number of Jews in Palestine thus increased to an estimated 45,000.

Against the backdrop of this often religious migration, the concept of political Zionism arose, the belief that the Jews scattered across the world constituted a single nation, that their right to liberty and independence—perhaps even their survival—included a return to the Promised Land and the establishment there of the State of Israel. Its best known early advocate was Theodor Herzl, who published *The Jewish State* in 1896 and organized the movement with the first Zionist World Congress of 1897 in Basel, Switzerland. Under the influence of European anti-Jewish persecution and discrimination, he envisioned "the establishment for the Jewish people of a home in Palestine."

Only accepted by a handful at first, this application of 19th century European territorial nationalism to Jewish existence began to grow steadily. Eventually the main ideas of political Zionism included (1) the concept of "a Jewish People," not merely various communities following the religion of Judaism; (2) the inevitable recurrence of anti-Jewish persecution; (3) the impossibility of Jews living full and complete lives outside a distinctive and territorial state; (4) the historic right of "the Jewish People" to *Eretz Yisrael*, the Land of Israel (see Historical Background) and (5) the duty of all Jews everywhere to support the national cause. These ideas formed the basic ideology in building the State of Israel and in its history to the present.

Before World War I, the desire Land of Israel was part of the Ottoman Empire. Most Ottoman authorities did not favor the Zionist immigration and land procurement because of local Arab opposition, but they were only partly able to resist external European support for Jewish immigration, as well as internal subterfuges and bribes that provided land to Jewish settlers, if expensively.

The vigor and ideals of a new generation of Zionist immigrants, known as the Second Aliyah, influenced deeply the founding of modern social institutions by 1914: they established newspapers, trade unions, and political parties. Hebrew became the language for Jewish schools, the first secondary school started, and land was purchased for a university. Moreover, the character of Zionist settlement had been formed. The native Jewish settlements were primarily urban, and other Jewish immigrants lacked a clear philosophy of purpose, some producing wines for export using French experts, Arab labor, and Baron Edmond de Rothschild's subsidies. In contrast, socialists within the Zionist organization sought to build a society of collectives where Jews worked together at even the most menial tasks and refused to employ (cheap) Arab labor. By the beginning of World War I, about 100,000 Jews lived in Palestine, compared to roughly 550,000 Muslims and 70,000 Christians.

World War I proved a major turning point for Zionist hopes. The persuasive influence of a prominent scientist, Dr. Chaim Weizmann, led on November 2, 1917, to the Balfour Declaration. It promised British favor for the establishment of a "national home for the Jewish people" in Palestine, although it expressed support for the civil and religious rights of the non-Jewish populations. Most Pales-

Entrance to the Dome of the Rock, a sanctuary erected in the 7th century by Muslims on the site of the Temple of Solomon and the Second Temple, then in ruins. This is one of the most sacred of all Islamic shrines. Photo by Linda Cook

1947 UN Recommendation

tinians opposed the declaration and testified their opposition to the American King-Crane Commission during the peace talks. Nevertheless, incorporated into the 1920 San Remo Agreement that divided the Middle East, the Balfour Declaration formed part of Britain's Mandate for Palestine in 1923. Unlike Arab mandates, it did not prescribe a constitution and eventual independence.

Jewish Achievements during the Mandate

With the end of war and a sympathetic nation in control, Jewish immigration rapidly expanded, with predictable Arab reactions. In 1920 serious rioting broke out, as it did frequently during the Mandate. Jewish immigration rose sharply after Hitler gained power in Germany. By 1939, despite Arab riots and consequent British reductions in permitted immigration, nearly one-third of the population was Jewish. The relative prosperity of Palestine also attracted Arab immigrants, though those numbers are poorly documented. In any case, Zionist leaders could plan for the day when Jews formed a majority of the total population. Until then, Jewish organizations bought land, settled it, and established industry.

Jewish land purchases provided a major source of Arab resentment. Fertile, watered farmland rarely lay vacant, and it frequently cost far more than similar land in the United States. Although many acres remained idle, their cultivation was handicapped by qualities the twentieth century would change: the low level of agricultural technology and education, the absence of engine-powered pumps, incursions by Bedouins, expensive animal transportation, and blocked foreign markets.

Against this background, the Jewish National Fund purchased farmland from Arab landlords. The land had rarely been owned by those who farmed it, however. Significant purchases came from absentee landlords residing in Syria and Lebanon.

With the change of ownership, any Arab tenant farmers became dispossessed, for whether a communally-run *kibbutz* or a *moshav* with private ownership, a Jewish settlement stressed the dignity of Jewish labor. Moreover, once purchased, the land became the inalienable property of the Jewish community. Superior in education, technical knowledge, machinery and incentives to the Arab tenant farmers they replaced, the Jewish settlers often succeeded in bringing the desert to bloom. Indeed their example influenced the remaining Arab farmers, whose production increased substantially. Jaffa's oranges won fame as Jewish exports, but Arabs had cultivated them for centuries and still accounted for about half of all orange exports in the 1930s.

The social development of the Jewish community continued apace before World War II. The Hebrew University was founded in 1918, and universal elementary education was achieved in the 1930s. The Jewish Agency was established in 1929 to assist in fostering the immediate goals of immigration and the acquisition of land, as well as the promotion of religion and the use of Hebrew. The Jewish Self-Defense Force, the *Haganah*, developed in secret, coming to possess a strong organization and significant weapons.

Nevertheless, the Jewish community was not united. One minority, firmly orthodox, feared that the nationalism of Zionism destroyed the religious basis of Judaism. At another extreme, the Revisionists led by Vladimir Jabotinsky demanded the immediate fulfillment of the Jewish national home on *both sides* of the Jordan River, thus including the East Bank or Transjordan.

The War for Independence, 1948–1949

With the Western world aghast at Hitler's Holocaust, after the war skillful Zionist leaders in America, cooperating with David Ben-Gurion, managed simultaneously to uphold U.S. limitations on Jewish immigration, and to encourage President Truman to urge it publicly for Palestine. No longer a great power, and no longer valuing the Suez Canal as a route to India, Britain found the difficulties of ruling Palestine too great and turned the problem over to the new United Nations. The Zionists won a major legal and psychological victory in late 1947 when the General Assembly voted by a narrow margin to recommend the political partition of Palestine. It assigned about 60% of the territory to a "Jewish State" although the Jewish settlers comprised only a bare one-third of the population. The Security Council did not endorse this recommendation nor did it provide any enforcement. As Britain had announced its plan to withdraw from Palestine by May 15, 1948, the issue was left open to resolution by force.

Within Palestine, force pitted the Arab majority against the Jewish minority. The latter were organized militarily into three groups. Representing the mainstream Zionist movement, the *Haganah* counted some 60,000 fighters, armed even with a few tanks and backed by a supply system that smuggled arms from Europe. In contrast, the Revisionists of the 1920s influenced the two right-wing and smaller groups, the *Irgun* of Menachem Begin, and the *Stern Gang*. Sabotage of British military and transport installations already showed their capabilities. The *Irgun* and *Stern Gang* in particular adopted methods which today are considered terrorist. In one of the most daring examples, in reprisal for British arrests of Jewish leaders, the Irgun blew up the British headquarters at the King David Hotel, killing 91.

The Palestinians, by contrast, organized no comparable military force, but counted on help from the surrounding states. As the British forces withdrew, Syrian volunteers and army officers entered Galilee (January 1948), and an Arab Liberation Army formed, financed and supplied in part by Egypt and Iraq. By April 1948 full-scale war broke out on many fronts, as both sides fought for as much land as they could obtain, regardless of the UN partition plan. Jewish forces quickly gained the Galilee region and Haifa, according to the partition part of the Jewish state. In addition, they captured Jaffa and Akka (Acre), allocated to the Arab state.

The fighting involved entire communities, and descended quickly to brutality. The *Irgun* attacked the Arab village of Deir Yasin, near the vital road to Jerusalem, and massacred some 250 people, many of them women and children. In response, Arabs attacked a convoy headed for the Hebrew University and Hadassah Hospital outside Jerusalem; 77 professors, students, and medical personnel perished. Thereafter, hundreds of thousands of Arabs fled from exposed villages and cities captured by the Zionists, in fear, to escape the fighting, or pressured by Jews. The Jews had nowhere to flee and fought rather better.

As the Mandate drew to a close, on May 14, 1948, in Tel Aviv David Ben-Gurion proclaimed the establishment of the State of Israel, and won immediate recognition from the United States. The next day, backed by resolutions of the Arab League, armies of Egypt, Iraq, Transjordan, Syria and Lebanon entered the war. The first war between Israel and the Arab states began, with the Israelis fighting for their independence and very existence as a separate state. The Israeli army outnumbered the Arab forces in Palestine and soon gained the offensive, striking at enemy targets in turn. Poorly coordinated on separate fronts, their equipment often obsolete or defective, the Arab armies also failed to evade a United Nations arms embargo successfully. Like the four major wars that followed, this ended in Israeli victories almost everywhere, though one Jew of every 100 in Israel died.

The boundaries of the various armistices of 1949 found Israel much enlarged from the partition plan, with about 70% of the mandate's territory. The highlands of the West Bank remained largely Arab and controlled by the Arab Legion of Transjordan, except for a Jewish sector including part of Jerusalem. The other portion of Palestine not under Israeli rule

Prime Minister David Ben-Gurion signs the independence declaration, May 14, 1948
AP/Wide World Photo

was the Gaza Strip in the southwest, inhabited mostly by wretched refugees and administered by Egypt. Equally important for the future, 700,000 Arab refugees fled what was to become the State of Israel.

Building the State of Israel

Independence meant a national government. Chaim Weizmann was elected to the largely honorary position of president in 1948, while the next year elections were held to the *Knesset*, the national parliament, whose majority leader is the prime minister. Israel's electoral system is one of the fairest in the world at translating preferences for political parties into seats in the legislature. With only one electoral district (the entire country), and proportional representation, each party's number of seats in the 120-member Knesset reflects very closely its percentage of the national vote.

Many parties sought the electoral system's opportunities in 1949. David Ben-Gurion headed the largest, *Mapai*, (the core today of the *Israel Labor Party*), but although it dominated every cabinet until 1977, it never won a majority in the Knesset. Governments have always been coalitions, in the early years largely between *Mapai* and the *National Religious Party*. The need to form a parliamentary majority usually gives small parties disproportionate weight in forming the coalition's policies.

Besides the burden of defense, the government budget faced enormous costs of absorbing Jewish immigration. One of the first enactments of Israel, the Law of the Return, granted citizenship to all Jews who landed in Israel. In the first four years of independence, some 700,000 responded, many of them relatively poor and less-educated from Arab countries such as Morocco, Yemen, and Iraq. In contrast to the Eastern European *Ashkenazi* Jews who had dominated the Zionist movement and Israeli society, the new immigrants were overwhelmingly *Sephardic* Jews, with differences significant for Israeli politics and society (see Culture). Another important project was the Israel National Water Carrier, a system of canals and pipelines bringing water from the Jordan River to the coastal plain and then the Negev desert for irrigation.

The Arab Minority

For the Arabs who remained, Israeli rule brought the second-class citizenship of a discontented and distrusted minority. The symbols of state reminded them that they had lost: the Star of David on an alien flag and an official language they could not speak. Israeli development often removed all traces of previous Arab habitation, even buildings and cemeteries, so Arabs witnessed the destruction of the memories of their past. The annual commemoration of Land Day (March 31) protests the confiscation of Arab land.

Less educated and relatively impoverished, with a high birthrate, Arab towns often failed to develop municipal services in a country where welfare came from charitable organizations more than from the state. Except for members of the Druze community (see Lebanon: Culture), Arabs are relieved of military service and thus of veterans benefits. Nevertheless, their economic progress generally exceeded that of most of the Arab world. Israeli Arabs also enjoyed the right to vote in genuine multiparty elections, in contrast to most Arabs' lives under dictatorships and authoritarian rulers.

After living on the margins of national life for decades, in the late 1990s many Israeli Arabs became more assertive, electing Arab members of the Knesset rather than voting for *Labor*. They joined the protests that initiated the *"al-Aqsa Intifada"* in 2000, and suffered pillage and vandalism by Jewish mobs. The police shot Arab demonstrators, but put their weapons away when facing Jewish mobs. Further Arab-Jewish riots rocked Acre in 2008.

Triumphant Wars: 1956, 1967, and 1973

Armistice agreements—truces between hostile nations—were negotiated with neighboring states in 1949 through UN mediation. Nevertheless, despite the efforts of the UN Truce Supervision Organization, armed Palestinians launched attacks across the borders, sometimes killing civilians. In the long run, these raids enabled Israel to expand well beyond the 1949 armistice lines through three connected wars.

In 1953 the cabinet adopted a policy of "retaliatory" military responses, raids that destroyed property and civilian lives on the Arab sides of the demarcation line. Consequently, ten times as many Arab civilians died as did Israeli civilians through armistice violations. Nevertheless, increasing tensions and rapidly expanding Egyptian armaments led Israel to launch a massive surprise attack across the Sinai Peninsula in October 1956, seizing the Straits of Tiran at the entrance to the Gulf of Aqaba which threatened Israel's maritime route to East Asia. France and Britain had secretly joined the aggression (see Egypt); they then invaded the Suez Canal Zone. However, the United States, the Soviet Union, and most democracies condemned the invasion, President Eisenhower demanded Israel's withdrawal, and the UN halted the fighting. A UN Emergency Force took up positions on the Egyptian side of the frontier to prevent incidents, and the Straits of Tiran remained open for Israeli shipping.

Israel

Partly a consequence of intense political rivalries, in 1964 the Arab states voted to strengthen their armed forces and divert their major tributaries of the Jordan River. This threatened Israel's major source of fresh water. Palestinian guerrilla raids also increased. Then, in early 1967, President Nasser of Egypt ordered the UN Emergency Force to leave, moved troops into the Sinai, and announced the closure of the Straits of Tiran. In response, Israel demanded that the Straits remain open, world diplomacy sought to relax the tensions, and Jordan and Syria formed a united front with Egypt.

In June, Israel launched a new war in full force, though disguising its origins as an Egyptian attack. After a few hours, the Arab air forces lay destroyed. Israeli tanks again swept across the Sinai to the Suez Canal. Because Jordan and Syria had joined the conflict, by the end of fighting Israel had also occupied the Old City of Jerusalem, the West Bank, and a strip of Syria's Golan Plateau about 20 miles wide.

Israel's victory gained much, at a small cost in lives, wounded and finances. Given pre-war Arab belligerency, the U.S. did not force a return to the 1949 boundaries. The new ceasefire lines stretched fewer miles but encompassed three times the territory of 1949. As important, the Jewish Diaspora again felt its deep attachment to Israel. Thousands came to fight or replace men and women called to battle; funds flowed to aid society and government. Often discouraged and worried about emigration before the war, Israelis found their self-confidence returned with victory.

Diplomatic wrangling delayed until November 1967 the UN Security Council's formal conditions for peace. Bland in its wording, Resolution 242 masked strong divisions of interpretation. Israel stressed the need for peace and its right to sovereignty. Thus, withdrawal "from territories occupied" meant withdrawal to secure boundaries. To Arabs, however, it meant the evacuation of *all* territories occupied. The words "a just settlement" of the refugee problem held no common meaning, and Palestinians resented being classified merely as refugees deprived of a nation.

Israel moved quickly to incorporate East Jerusalem into Israel itself. Within the Old City lies the Wailing Wall, remaining from the Second Temple and the most sacred Jewish shrine. Greatly complicating the achievement of peace, the Wailing Wall borders the Haram al-Sharif, one of the holiest Muslim shrines, containing the Dome of the Rock and al-Aqsa Mosque. Prohibited from worshipping there during Jordanian rule, the Israelis rapidly bulldozed neighboring houses for better access. Reconstruction of the old Jewish quarter commenced, and the city administration of Jewish Jerusalem stretched east.

Unlike events in 1956 and 1967, the third war was not Israel's choice. While Israel observed *Yom Kippur*, the Day of Atonement, in October 1973, surprise attacks by Egypt and Syria opened the war. Though initially successful in crossing the Suez Canal and advancing on the Golan, the Egyptians and Syrians never reached Israel. Rather, they attacked Israeli forces on their own national territories.

Mobilizing rapidly, the Israel Defense Force (IDF) counter-attacked, and the intense tank battles destroyed perhaps 2,000 tanks and 500 aircraft. Benefiting from advanced arms and technical superiority, units led by General Ariel Sharon crossed the Suez Canal into Egypt itself, encircling an entire Egyptian army and leaving Cairo almost defenseless. The Syrians likewise retreated, but the enormous cost of the war convinced many on both sides of its futility. Henry Kissinger, the American Secretary of State, mediated disengagement agreements that withdrew Israeli troops from the Suez Canal and oil fields used since 1967, and returned a narrow portion of the Golan Heights to Syria, including the devastated town of Quneitra. Egypt allowed non-military cargoes for Israel to pass through the newly-reopened Canal.

Peace with Egypt and Camp David

When elections approached in 1977, the *Labor* government disintegrated under charges of mismanagement and corrup-

SPECIAL DOCUMENT

UN Security Council Resolution 242

On November 22, 1967, the Security Council of the United Nations unanimously approved—and has subsequently reaffirmed—a resolution outlining the basis for peace between the State of Israel and the Arab countries with which it is in conflict. The United States, Israel and Egypt, in the Camp David accords of September 1978, specifically endorsed the implementation of this resolution "in all its parts." The following is the text of that resolution:

The Security Council,

Expressing its continuing concern with the grave situation in the Middle East,

Emphasizing the inadmissibility of the acquisition of territory by war and the need to work for a just and lasting peace in which every state in the area can live in security,

Emphasizing further that all member states in their acceptance of the Charter of the United Nations have undertaken a commitment to act in accordance with Article 2 of the Charter,

1. Affirms that the fulfillment of Charter principles requires the establishment of a just and lasting peace in the Middle East which should include the application of both of the following principles: (a) Withdrawal of Israel armed forces from territories occupied in the recent conflict; (b) Termination of all claims or states of belligerency and respect for and acknowledgment of the sovereignty, territorial integrity and political independence of every state in the area and their right to live in peace within secure and recognized boundaries free from threats.

2. Affirms further the necessity: (a) For guaranteeing freedom of navigation through international waterways in the area; (b) For achieving a just settlement of the refugee problem; (c) For guaranteeing the territorial inviolability and political independence of every state in the area, through measures including the establishment of demilitarized zones.

3. Requests the Secretary-General to designate a special representative to proceed to the Middle East to establish and maintain contacts with the states concerned in order to promote agreement and assist efforts to achieve a peaceful and accepted settlement.

4. Requests the Secretary-General to report to the Security Council on the progress of the efforts of the special representative as soon as possible.

tion. Supported strongly by Sephardic Jews, *Likud* triumphed, and ended *Labor's* unbroken hold on government. Menachem Begin, who had led *Irgun* fighters against the British and long opposed returning any occupied territory, formed a coalition of religious and right-wing parties. Rejecting socialism, the government raised taxes, devalued the currency, and reduced subsidies. The labor unions went on strike.

That same year, President Sadat of Egypt offered to visit Jerusalem in quest of genuine peace. For the first time, an Arab ruler publicly met with Israel's prime minister and talked directly to Israelis in their own country. Sadat offered full peace. In exchange, he asked for the principle of withdrawal from the occupied lands and the right of their Palestinians to determine their own future.

Sadat's dramatic moves posed a difficult choice for Jerusalem: between territory and peace. After weeks of equivocation, Prime Minister Begin responded that his government could not give up "Judea and Samaria" (to others, the "West Bank"); they formed part of the "historic land of Israel." Instead he offered Palestinians "living in the Land of Israel" civil autonomy under Israeli control.

Terrorist attacks by Palestinians and an Israeli invasion of southern Lebanon further jeopardized diplomatic progress, until President Carter invited the Israeli and Egyptian leaders to Camp David. Secluded from the press and political pressures, Menachem Begin and Anwar Sadat negotiated the agreements finally signed at the White House. Israel obtained a major policy goal: peace with Egypt, the most powerful Arab state, at the cost of returning the militarily-valuable Sinai. However, a wider peace was not achieved. Though yielding four Jewish settlements in Egypt, Begin and *Likud* pledged that no other settlements would ever be removed, effectively ruling out exchanging other occupied territories for peace. Therefore, while Camp David assured Israel's conventional military superiority, it was followed by more wars.

With Palestinians increasingly restive in the West Bank and Gaza, the Begin cabinet worried about the growing Palestinian military in Lebanon. Under secret plans drawn up by Defense Minister Ariel Sharon, in 1982 Israeli forces used a pretext to launch a massive invasion of Lebanon. The IDF eventually reached Beirut's suburbs and linked up with the Maronite Christian enclave (see Lebanon: History). Outside Beirut, Israeli casualties began to mount, eventually making the invasion of Lebanon Israel's most costly foreign war, measured in lives. Moreover, Israeli troops permitted Maronite militiamen to enter captured Palestinian camps, where they massacred nearly 1,000 men, women, and children. Israeli opinion grew increasingly divided. Many citizens, including some officers, demonstrated for a withdrawal from Lebanon; the *Peace Now* movement reflected such concerns.

Soviet Immigrants Change the Demographics

Jewish immigration from the Soviet Union and the Palestinian *intifada* combined to challenge Israel's occupation, politics and society in the early 1990s. Aided by changes in Soviet society, tens of thousands of Jews and their spouses emigrated from Russia to Israel. This massive population transfer touched the very basis of Zionism. Soviet immigrants boosted the productive population, and they postponed the threatened Arab majority for decades. Further immigrants were airlifted to Israel from Ethiopia in 1991. In time, the immigrants changed Israeli society, with Russian newspapers and even Orthodox churches appearing. Politically, the new immigrants generally opposed withdrawal from the occupied territories, and their politicians initially allied with *Likud*. They later supported the secular nationalist platform of *Yisrael Beiteinu*, "Israel is our home."

The West ("Wailing") Wall within Jerusalem where Jews pray. Tradition is that the wall was partially built of materials from Solomon's temple. Photo by Linda Cook

Consideration of a Palestinian State

The first twenty years of Israeli's occupation of the lands captured in 1967 brought few serious challenges. However, the seven years from 1987 to 1994 changed the entire focus of Israeli-Palestinian relations.

The strikes, civil disobedience, rock-throwing and other violence of the first Palestinian *intifada* began in late 1987. Coordinated in secret, it took Israeli leaders by surprise. The *intifada* marked a distinct change from the physical threats posed by Arab armies in past wars. Because the *intifada* stressed defiance, not attacks on Israel, it contrasted sharply with attacks by Palestinian guerrillas. Indeed, only 15 Israelis died in its first year, compared to more than 360 Palestinians.

Crushing the uprising meant using one of the world's most highly rated war machines against teenagers throwing stones and Molotov cocktails. Annual reserve duty was extended, and troops adopted lethal tactics. Nevertheless, military force did not crush the political uprising: rather, the *intifada* focused world attention on the Palestinians. The U.S. attempted a peace shuttle, and officially accused Israel of violating human rights and inflicting "many avoidable deaths." Yasir Arafat, Chairman of the PLO, successfully used world concern over the *intifada* to win UN General Assembly approval of an international peace conference which would grant Palestinians "official observer" status. The *Likud* resistance to land for peace had lost its foreign support: the United States seemed to change sides, and many American sympathizers and major Jewish groups supported Israel-PLO talks under certain conditions.

Israeli opposition to a Palestinian state includes many strands. The 1967 West Bank threatened vital highways and Tel Aviv's suburbs, while the Jordan River provides the shortest and most defendable border. Another strategic argument holds that any Palestinian state would sometime fall to extremists. Continuous occupation may be less damaging in Israeli lives and world opinion than terrorist raids and reprisals.

Other reasons to keep the territories lie in ideology. Revisionist Zionists, from Jabotinsky in the 1920s to ultra-Orthodox Jews today, stress that Israel must occupy the whole of the Biblical Promised Land. Over Jerusalem the refusal to withdraw becomes almost universal. Arab East Jerusalem physically forms part of a city almost all Jews promise never to divide. Moreover, Judaism's most sacred shrine, the Wailing Wall, lies within the largely-Arab Old City.

Political reality presents another major hurdle. The policy of "creating facts" involves the settlement of 500,000 Jews in the West Bank and East Jerusalem. Though numbering fewer than 10% of the electorate, these settlers form a major political force with one over-riding issue: "No withdrawal." Finally, there are economic reasons to hold the West Bank, among them the vital water surplus it provides for Israel itself.

Presidents Sadat, Carter and Prime Minister Begin, September 17, 1978, at the White House

Courtesy: Jimmy Carter Library

Pressures do exist for compromise. One is the difficulty of indefinitely occupying a land and depriving its inhabitants of self-determination. Ruling the restive population requires military control, and increases military influence in public and private life. Moral questions arise also, because without ethnic cleansing, the greater Arab birthrate will soon provide more Arabs than Jews living between the sea and the Jordan River. The occupation therefore means permanently depriving another people of self-determination, and inevitably complicates foreign relations.

General Rabin & Negotiation from Strength

Iraq's seizure of Kuwait in 1990 seemed a grave threat to Israel's security, because Saddam Hussein claimed a war over Kuwait was actually a war for Israel. The government issued gas masks, and hours after coalition forces attacked Iraq in 1991, the first Scud missiles landed in Tel Aviv, destroying and damaging homes in a residential area. Scores of injuries and a few deaths resulted from the attacks. Remarkably, Israel did not retaliate: a general Arab-Israeli conflict would have benefited Iraq but not the United States or its Arab allies. Patriot missile crews arrived to defend Tel Aviv, and U.S. aid covered missile damage, military expenses, and economic losses such as the decline in tourism.

For the 1991 elections, *Labor* selected Yitzhak Rabin as its leader. A tough general, he nevertheless favored Palestinian autonomy and peace through concessions. After *Labor* won a decisive victory, Rabin halted the construction of new communities in the Occupied Territories. This won American loan guarantees for housing construction within Israel and raised hopes at the peace talks. Rabin's negotiators even conceded a possible withdrawal in the Golan Heights in return for peace with Syria.

The *intifada* proved the most pressing and increasingly lethal problem (see Palestine: History). Finally, Rabin closed Israel to the 60,000 workers from the Occupied Territories, thus halting most contacts between Israelis and Palestinians. As calm returned, most Israelis favored a permanent ban. On the deeper level, many also recognized that the practical separation of the Territories made some later withdrawal more likely.

After secret negotiations in Oslo with the PLO produced a Declaration of Principles for an eventual peace agreement, Prime Minister Rabin and PLO Chairman Yasir Arafat publicly shook hands at the White House in 1993. The declaration stipulated a withdrawal from most of the Gaza Strip and Jericho and the creation of a Palestinian Authority to administer them. It also specified later Israeli administrative and military withdrawals from much of the West Bank.

The Oslo Accords were clearly not a peace agreement. They deliberately left many matters undecided. Very difficult issues, such as borders, Palestinian refugees, and East Jerusalem (claimed as the Palestinian capital) remained for the final agreement, to be reached after confidence-building measures provided greater trust between the two sides. Radical Jewish and Arab opponents of peace sought to destroy the peace process through violence that often took the lives civilians and children. Each unfortunate case required revenge that in turn incited reprisals that continued the cycle of violence. However, "Oslo" had established a timetable, and after last-minute bickering, in 1994 the Israeli flag was lowered over Gaza and Jericho.

The withdrawal brought neither economic bonanza nor safety to Israel. Suicide attacks by *Hamas* and the *Islamic Jihad*, particularly against buses, killed scores of Israelis. In response, the cabinet again sealed the border with Gaza and the West Bank and halted the agreed release of prisoners. Fearing for the safety of isolated settlements, the cabinet halted further withdrawals.

Despite mixed success with Palestinians, the Oslo Accords brought welcome progress towards peace with some Arab states. Morocco established diplomatic relations. More dramatically, Jordan signed a peace treaty, after settling its demands for water rights and the small occupied territory (145 square miles) along the border. Visionaries predicted broad trade and development links, as well as hydroelectric and desalination schemes at the Dead Sea. Peace with Syria proved more difficult, given the domestically hazardous issue of the Golan Heights. Syria demands the entire territory. However, Golani settlers vote *Labor*, and many Israelis fear losing important strategic advantages from a withdrawal. Repeated negotiations have accomplished nothing—but occasionally provided a distraction when a prime minister needs relief from domestic pressures.

The Assassination of Yitzhak Rabin

Despite vicious attacks by right-wing extremists, including posters depicting Prime Minister Rabin as a Nazi, in 1995 the cabinet approved a withdrawal from several West Bank cities as a prelude to Palestinian elections. Two months later, after the usually unsmiling Rabin celebrated at a peace rally in Tel Aviv, a fanatical Orthodox law student shot him

THE JERUSALEM POST
INTERNATIONAL EDITION
The perfect gift for your friends and relations overseas

FREE COPY

THE JERUSALEM POST

Vol. LII, No. 15711 Sunday, September 16, 1984 • Elul 19, 5744 • Zi al-Hija 20, 1404 IS200

DON'T MISS THIS COPY
The Economist
September 15, 1984
★ COVER STORY:
EVERYTHING ABOUT ISRAEL
SOLE DISTRIBUTOR
BRONFMAN

The cabinet

Shamir determined

Unity terms

Histadrut 'won't accept' C-o-L reduction

The "government of national unity," September 1984

in the back. The assassin murdered, he said, because Rabin had negotiated away Israel's God-given land and endangered settlers' lives.

Immediately after Rabin's death, the vast majority of Israelis supported the peace negotiations. However, once again suicide attacks, targeted assassinations and an economic closure weakened advocates of peace on both sides. Israelis buried the dead while elections approached.

Stagnation, not Peace

The forceful and telegenic Binyamin "Bibi" Netanyahu of *Likud* won the 1996 elections after he accepted Oslo, promising to win a more secure peace in a last-minute gesture that clinched his victory.

In reality, stagnation resulted, not peace. Construction of the Jewish settlement of *Har Homa* on Arab land between East Jerusalem and Bethlehem completed the Jewish encirclement of Arab East Jerusalem. When the bulldozers moved in, Palestinian leaders halted the peace negotiations.

Serious fractures appeared within domestic society. Russian and Ethiopian immigrants demanded spending to meet their needs, while many Sephardim (descendants of Middle Eastern Jews) sensed the Ashkenazi (European-descended) elite looked down on them. Students struck for lower tuition, and government workers for higher pay. The divide between religious and secular Jews became a greater issue than peace, and the resulting emotions challenged the integrity of government. When the Supreme Court ended the draft exemption for the Orthodox and allowed farms to operate on the Sabbath, a mass rally attacked the court. Secular Jews objected to the automatic draft deferments for ultra-Orthodox *(Haredim)* students in yeshivas.

Ehud Barak: Worthy Goals Unfulfilled

After Netanyahu's government collapsed of its own instabilities, elections brought *Labor's* new leader, the much-decorated General Ehud Barak, to power with a coalition government.

Against the background of an increasingly harsh culture war between secularists and practicing Orthodox and ultra-Orthodox Jews, the cabinet tackled difficult and divisive issues. Barak moved to end the abuse of draft deferments by ultra—Orthodox men. Yossi Sarid, the minister of education, changed the history curriculum to reinterpret the War of Independence and admit Israeli mistakes. Through its brinkmanship over the budget, *Shas* retained large subsidies for its badly-run school system.

The difficult work of government reform seemed overshadowed by scandals. President Ezer Weizmann, accused of receiving illegal payments, fell from office, as did the deputy prime minister, over allegations of sexual assault. Binyamin Netanyahu was blamed for corruption and misuse of gifts he received as prime minister, though the charges were dropped. During the next decade, President Katzav was charged with rape, resigned in disgrace, and eventually imprisoned. Further from politics, financial irregularities in some *yeshivas* vied for publicity with the national soccer team. Its players lost a match after a pre-game visit to a brothel.

In foreign affairs, Barak sought solutions to all remaining conflicts. He negotiated with Syria, and bluntly accepted an eventual Palestinian state. Overcoming right-wing criticism, he opened a 27-mile route connecting the Gaza Strip with the West Bank. Ten unauthorized Jewish settlements on the West Bank were closed, though dozens remained.

Although Barak often proved a tough defender of Israel's interests, his reputation came to rest on the withdrawal from South Lebanon. Unable to negotiate a departure from territory occupied for two decades, the IDF withdrew under pressure in 2000. Its local militia, the *South Lebanon Army*, collapsed, and even Hebrew papers noted parallels with Vietnam.

Failure at Camp David

With the deadline looming to complete the Oslo Accords, President Clinton summoned both Prime Minister Barak and Chairman Arafat to Camp David in 2000. Removed from the media spotlight, Clinton attempted to resolve the outstanding issues: borders, settlements, refugees, and East Jerusalem. Conceding what no Israeli leader had yielded previously, Barak offered Arafat a Palestinian state with a capital in the Jerusalem suburbs, some local control in Arab districts of the city, and possible international sovereignty over the Muslim Holy Places (the Haram al-Sharif). A small number of refugees would be reunited with families in Israel.

This offer defied the almost universal Israeli desire for a united Jerusalem. It outraged the settlers, *Likud*, and most religious parties. Vague talk of treason and assassination prompted increased security for the prime minister. But Yasir Arafat rejected the proposal because it failed to meet one minimum Palestinian demand: Arab sovereignty for Arab Jerusalem. (This outright rejection was a grave practical mistake. Immense suffering and thousands of dead since then have failed to produce so favorable an offer.) On his return, Barak resigned, forcing an election only for the office of prime minister.

Sharon Dominates Politics; Oslo Collapses

Likud's nominee was the portly party leader, General Ariel Sharon. Sharon's aggressive career had contributed to the deaths of many Arab civilians, and his recent visit to the Haram al-Sharif, asserting that the Temple Mount was not negotiable, set ablaze passions already very hot. A new *intifada* broke out, this one much more violent. Without a proposed peace agreement, the election failed to offer voters a referendum on peace. Instead, it focused on personalities and approaches. Sharon won a landslide, and formed a government of national unity, including *Labor* leaders in sensitive positions.

The new *intifada* brought the Oslo peace process to collapse, and violence escalated on both sides. In response to terror attacks, Israeli troops surrounded Palestinian-controlled areas, blocked travel and trade, and squeezed them economically. Targeted assassinations killed dozens of alleged terrorist leaders, and often innocent bystanders. Palestinian security forces became frequent targets. Yasir Arafat was limited to the city of Ramallah, then, after renewed Israeli occupation of much of the West Bank, to two rooms in his headquarters (see Palestine), until Israeli troops withdrew under U.S. pressure.

American, Egyptian, European and other mediators vainly tried to calm the crisis, but found themselves blocked by the interplay of Palestinian attacks and Israeli intransigence. Sharon's cabinet refused to talk peace during violence, and demanded seven days of calm before opening talks or implementing peace proposals. But Sharon excluded from "violence" Israeli assassinations of Palestinian leaders. Historians may well conclude that Prime Minister Sharon bore significant responsibility for the hostilities; at least since 1982, he had carried a personal grudge against Yasir Arafat. Sharon gave Israeli troops great freedom to attack Palestinian suspects, and eyewitnesses claimed the killing of men and boys sleeping or otherwise unarmed. Nevertheless, Sharon frequently faced harsh right-wing critics whose solutions often included ethnic cleansing.

Objectively, Sharon had promised peace, but blood flowed in Jewish streets. The economy had nosedived into recession, and 20% of the population lived in poverty. A poll found that most Israelis felt they had never had it so bad. Serious cuts in government services were likely. Media accounts of financial sleaze reached all the way up to Sharon himself, for past violations of campaign finance laws.

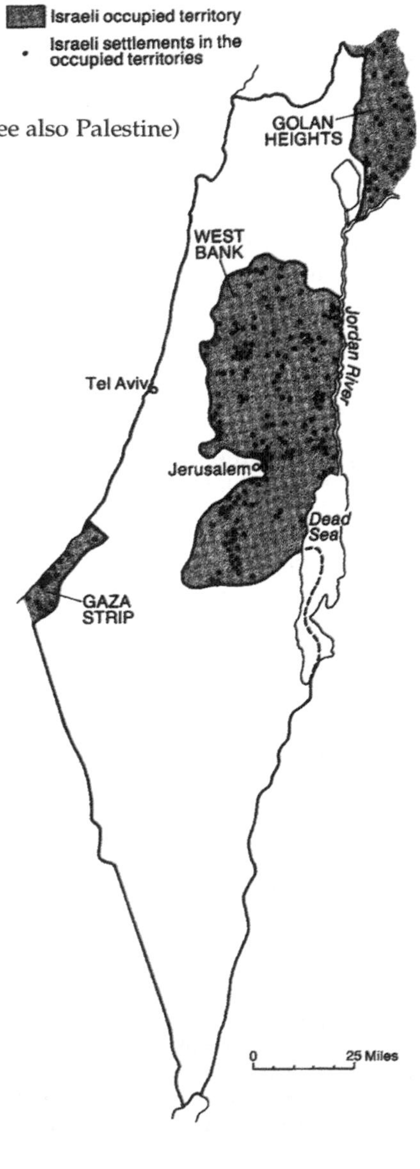

(See also Palestine)

Nevertheless, Sharon and the *Likud* easily won the 2003 elections, while the left-wing of Israeli politics—*Meretz*, and *Labor* itself—fell badly, as did *Shas*. *Likud* almost doubled its seats in the Knesset. Clearly, Israelis had reacted to the suicide bombings by blaming *Hamas* and other Palestinians, not the grandfatherly general who was doing as well as anyone could expect. Many Israelis deserted the parties inclined to compromise for peace.

The Roadmap, Gaza, and Kadima

Peace gained further importance because of a "roadmap" developed by the U.S., the UN, the European Union, and Russia. Backing a two-state solution, the roadmap proposed a provisional Palestinian entity by 2003 and a complete agreement by 2005. The roadmap reflected Israeli and American rejection of Yasir Arafat as a trustworthy Palestinian leader, but it clearly accepted a Palestinian state. This dismayed many settlers, other right-wing Israelis, and their American fundamentalist supporters, whose typical solution is an ethnic cleansing of Judea and Samaria by removing all Palestinians to Jordan. Despite their warnings, President Bush backed the roadmap. Prime Minister Sharon initially refused to accept the plan, but eventually his cabinet bowed to foreign pressure and did so—by a narrow majority, with 14 reservations.

The roadmap's first steps included, on the Israeli side, withdrawal from the recently occupied towns and cities, a halt to settlement activity, and the dismantling of illegal (by Israeli definition) and some legal settlements to permit contiguous Palestinian areas. For their part, the Palestinians needed to achieve political reform (including elections) and end the violence.

Ariel Sharon had always backed Jewish settlements. For decades his vision of a Palestinian state had been Arabs densely packed into several small clusters with municipal self-government but not much else, divided from each other by corridors of Israeli roads and military posts. Sharon's approval of the roadmap was likely a momentary acquiescence to be followed by later obstruction. Certainly, he remained committed to building homes in West Bank settlements, despite U.S. objections.

Nevertheless, Sharon's ideology split from the hardliners because he recognized that the Arab population of Gaza was too dense and crowded for Jewish settlements to succeed, while the price for holding Gaza was continuing casualties. *Sharon realized the impossibility of Israel's long-term control of Palestinian cities.* As he told the UN General Assembly in 2005, "The Palestinians will always be our neighbors.

THE JERUSALEM POST

SECOND EDITION

VOLUME LXIII, NUMBER 19113 | SUNDAY, NOVEMBER 5, 1995 • HESHVAN 12, 5756 • JAMAD 12, 1416 | NIS 4.20 (EILAT NIS 3.60)

RABIN ASSASSINATED

Peres pays tribute to longtime rival, partner

DAVID MAKOVSKY, BATSHEVA TSUR and agencies

AN empty chair draped in black marked Prime Minister Yitzhak Rabin's place at the cabinet table as the nation's leaders met in emergency session and declared a transition government hours after he was assassinated at a peace rally.

Ministers wept while acting Prime Minister Shimon Peres paid tribute to his long-time political rival and partner in forging peace with the Palestinians.

"He was a rare leader in Jewish history...in the last three years as Israeli prime minister he effected a revolution in the positive sense in the Middle East," Peres said in televised remarks.

"I asked myself if this happened to me, what would I want to happen later," Peres

(Continued on Page 12)

A black day for the whole Jewish nation

EDITORIAL

THE shock is universal. No Israeli, no Jew, no decent human being anywhere can help being shaken to the core, shattered to the depth of his and her soul by the news of the assassination of Prime Minister

Pronounced dead at 11:15 p.m. after being shot

RAINE MARCUS, SARAH HONIG and ALON PINKAS

PRIME Minister Yitzhak Rabin was assassinated last night by a 27-year-old Herzliya law student, who fired three bullets from a pistol at him at point-blank range. Rabin was felled as he was entering his official car at 9:50 p.m. at the conclusion of a massive pro-peace rally in Tel Aviv's Kikar Malchei Yisrael attended by some 100,000 people.

Rabin was pronounced dead at 11:15 p.m. by doctors at Ichilov Hospital, where he had been brought with wounds to his back, abdomen, and chest. He died on the operating table from massive hemorrhaging and heart failure, without regaining consciousness.

The prime minister was not wearing a bullet-proof vest, that he "did not regret his deed," which he said was "planned for some time."

A police source said that Amir had twice before attempted to assassinate Rabin, but no more details were available. In the two previous attempts, said the source, Amir tried to get close to the prime minister and was armed both times.

Amir was apprehended immediately after the shooting by police and pressed up against a cement wall, as dozens of policemen surrounded him.

Eyewitnesses reported seeing Rabin collapse. His bodyguards pushed him into the car and whisked him off to Ichilov Hospital, some 500 meters away. One of Rabin's bodyguards was also wounded by bullets.

Health Minister Ephraim Sneh told reporters at midnight that Rabin sustained bullet wounds in

We respect them and don't aspire to rule over them. They also deserve freedom and a sovereign national entity in their own country."

His solution was to withdraw from the entire Gaza Strip, unilaterally, and for good measure, also from four unofficial West Bank settlements. The roadmap was incidental: other settlements would remain. Most Israelis backed the withdrawal, but, the settlement movement bitterly attacked it, and their vigorous campaign led *Likud* to reject it. The prime minister won cabinet approval for a modified plan, but his coalition frayed.

The Gaza plan represented a one-sided solution to the Israeli-Palestinian conflict. Its logical outcome was not a negotiated permanent peace, but an Israel beyond Palestinian violence, leaving the Palestinians to live in poverty and, if they were inclined, even anarchy. The same philosophy motivated construction of a 300-mile barrier to separate the Arab West Bank from Israel—comfortably encircling major Jewish enclaves at Palestinian expense. It cuts off considerable Arab land (by one estimate this exceeds 40% of the West Bank) and some homes. UN reports condemned it and the International Court of Justice, in an advisory opinion, claimed it illegal.

To deter any boasts that Israel had been forced out of Gaza, as had been claimed for South Lebanon, IDF raids destroyed the infrastructure and workshops of *Hamas* and the *Islamic Jihad*. An invasion of the Jabaliya camp in northern Gaza killed more than 100 Palestinians. Success for a unilateral withdrawal also meant the targeted assassination of extremist leaders, most prominently Sheikh Ahmad Yassin, the so-called "spiritual leader" of *Hamas* and its unifying figure.

On schedule in 2005, Israeli troops smoothly removed the 8,500 settlers who clung to the 21 small colonies of Gaza. Building on success, Sharon overturned the political landscape by abandoning *Likud* and forming a new, centrist party, *Kadima* ("Forward"). A veritable tidal wave of leading politicians, including Shimon Peres, abandoned their parties and joined *Kadima*, destroying decades-old political and social boundaries. Competitors fumed that *Kadima* lacked ideology and was dominated by one man.

Months before the 2006 elections, a massive stroke struck the 77-year-old prime minister. The shocked nation compared Sharon's fate with the assassination of Yitzhak Rabin a decade earlier. Once again, a traditionally hawkish leader was struck down on the verge of dramatic actions for peace. Some radical settlers quietly gave God the credit for both incidents.

The deputy prime minister, Ehud Olmert, assumed control of both government and party. He maintained *Kadima's* unity and rallied the nation around Sharon's legacy. The other parties fared less well. The electorate remembered that *Likud's* nominee, Binyamin Netanyahu had vacillated over Gaza and had clung to his cabinet post. *Labor* managed to present a thoughtful campaign, concentrating on domestic issues.

Kadima won 29 seats, and became the Knesset's largest party. *Likud* tumbled to apparent insignificance, with about 10% of the vote, similar to the Russian émigrés' hardline *Israel Beiteinu*, and *Shas*. Within weeks, Ehud Olmert negotiated a coalition with *Labor, Shas*, and the *Pensioners' Party*. However, the press savaged several appointments, and the cabinet's lack of military expertise. One opinion poll suggested half the population had misgivings about the new prime minister.

The War with Hizbullah, 2006

Hizbullah guerillas crossed the Lebanese-Israeli border in July 2006, attacked an isolated patrol, and captured two Israeli soldiers. The raid apparently sought hostages for bargaining and to embarrass Israel's newly-formed coalition. The Olmert cabinet, determined to rescue the captives, escalated its response to the

Former Prime Minister Ehud Olmert

raid into a war to destroy *Hizbullah*. The IDF attacked *Hizbullah's* military positions, and bombed widely. It also targeted non-*Hizbullah*-Lebanon: Beirut's airport, vital road bridges, gasoline service stations, factories, and road traffic far from battlefields.

Hizbullah responded by launching missiles—several thousand of them—far deeper into Israel than ever before. They reached Haifa and most of northern Israel. It also fought the poorly-executed Israeli ground assault well enough to boast of divine victory. In any case, *Hizbullah* was not destroyed. The fighting finally ended when the Security Council established a ceasefire (see Lebanon: history) in a conflict whose human cost was heavy for Israel (40 civilians, 112 military personnel).

The Israeli public quickly concluded that the war had been bungled by an incompetent cabinet and military. Commissions investigated the failures, and resignations followed. Combined with missile attacks on southern Israeli towns from Gaza, the war led many Israelis to question the very possibility of a two-state solution. After all, *Hamas* and *Islamic Jihad* on the southern border and *Hizbullah* along the north rejected Israel's very right to exist. Will any Israeli borders ever achieve moral significance to them?

Olmert Stumbles, Launches Gaza War

A man known to appreciate luxuries, over the years Ehud Olmert had received funds from questionable sources, and had been investigated, but charges were dropped. This time an American businessman testified that he had passed envelopes stuffed with cash for the prime minister's political campaigns. The claims threatened the ruling coalition. Polls indicated that nearly 70% of Israelis desired Olmert to step down, and *Labor* threatened to withdraw from the cabinet. Olmert agreed to go, but remained in office pending Knesset elections in early 2009. National security issues dominated his last months in office.

After *Hamas* gunmen gained control of Gaza in 2007, the territory provided a base for missile and other attacks on Israel, but lacked a government willing to negotiate with Israel, or that Israel could recognize. The simple, home-made Qassam missiles fired by *Hamas* and *Islamic Jihad* at the closest town, Sderot, and the city of Ashkelon did not constitute a strategic threat, but they inflicted casualties. They also posed the eventual risk of longer-range missiles with larger warheads. Ariel Sharon's entire policy of disengagement/unilateral withdrawal collapsed.

In response, the Olmert cabinet declared the Gaza Strip a "hostile entity," and to pressure *Hamas* to halt the attacks, it restricted deliveries of fuel, electricity, and almost all supplies, eventually including food. This effectively crushed the territory's economic life. Virtually the entire population came to subsist on international assistance (see Palestine: history). A truce negotiated in mid-2008 reduced the rocket fire significantly, but the border blockade remained. The truce broke down in response to an Israeli attack on an alleged tunnel from Gaza into Israel, and was not renewed.

Striking by surprise in December 2008, the Israeli air force opened the Gaza War when it attacked Gaza, demolishing *Hamas* militia bases, rocket launching sites, police facilities, and government offices. Civilian locations were also targeted—homes, mosques, hospitals, schools and others, on grounds they were used by *Hamas* fighters or stored weapons. After a week of aerial bombardment, the Israeli army invaded the Strip, eventually entering parts of the city of Gaza itself.

After three weeks of fighting, Prime Minister Olmert declared a unilateral ceasefire and promised a withdrawal from the Strip if rocket attacks ended. With the Gaza Strip bisected and most Palestinian population centers surrounded, the major objectives had evidently been achieved. Soon after, *Hamas* also ended its major hostilities, though in the months following some rockets were fired at Israeli towns.

The Gaza War was planned months before the pretext for launching it, and its major goal was to deter possible future attacks by any enemy, by demonstrating the power and effectiveness of the military's response. Despite *Hamas* claims, this was largely achieved, as evidenced by the vastly different casualties suffered by each side. Although precision weapons were often used by the Israeli forces, the fighting claimed the lives of hundreds of *Hamas* combatants as well as hundreds of civilians. By contrast, just three Israeli civilians and 10 soldiers were killed. Critics claimed that Israel had committed war crimes, including the disproportionate use of force, and the U.N. Human Rights Council demanded a credible investigation of charges of war crimes. However, disproportionate force is fundamental to an effective deterrence.

Netanyahu's Isolation and the Flotilla Attack

The Gaza invasion was scheduled by politics: it was to end before the inauguration of President Obama in January

Bitterness and frustration: Palestinian youths defy the Israeli army

ISRAELI SETTLEMENTS AND THE SEARCH FOR PEACE

From its 19th century origins, Zionism stressed settling the land. After the 1967 war, however, the English term "settlement" came to apply to Jewish groups establishing communities beyond the 1967 boundaries: within East Jerusalem and the Golan Heights, both considered by Israel as legally annexed, and the West Bank, where they now control 40% of the land. Over a half-million Jews live in these areas, including 250,000 residents who encircle Arab Jerusalem, and the numbers increase at a faster rate than the national population. The UN, the International Court of Justice, human rights organizations like Oxfam and Amnesty International, and most nations regard the settlements as illegal under international law. Israel and a number of scholars disagree.

Support for settlements arose from three distinct sources. Devoted Zionists desired to re-establish, after 1967, specific communities that had been evicted from Arab areas in 1948–49 or earlier. Some of their re-established Jewish communities are located in the heart of dense Arab populations, for example in Hebron. By contrast, the strategic and military settlements along the Jordan River or other border areas generally avoided population centers. Most settlers, however, live in new communities established from the broad Zionist motive to settle all the land of Israel. The communities range in size from outposts of a few mobile homes in remote areas to cities of 30,000 inhabitants near the 1949 armistice lines. Most settlers evidence a strong religious motivation for their choice of residence, and they endure greater risk of Palestinian attacks than do Jews living in Israel itself. The low cost of housing in the settlements also provides an inducement.

The very existence of the settlements "creates facts" that make it very difficult for Israel ever to relinquish control over them. *An attempt to remove many settlers, let alone all, would invite civil war.* Conveniently, the settlements and their access roads (which Palestinians may not use) divide the Palestinian population into very small townships, facilitating total control of their access to the wider world.

As is evident from the Sasson Report commissioned by then-Prime Minister Ariel Sharon in 2005, settlement activities, both illegal and legal, benefitted from a variety of informal government assistance, including the transfer of private or communally-held Palestinian land. Even outposts technically illegal under Israeli law often received government-provided infrastructure such as paved roads and power lines.

Several Israeli groups, particularly *Yesh Din, Peace Now,* and *B'Tselem,* attempt to halt the expansion of settlements by providing information about them. *B'Tselem* has even supplied cameras to Palestinians, to provide photographic evidence of violations of their property or dignity. The U.S., European Union, and other foreign nations have also demanded a halt to the growth of settlements, a matter often complicated by an Israeli defense of their "natural growth." All attempts to halt settlement growth have been unsuccessful, and during the past decade their populations grew about three times the rate of Israel proper.

For Palestinians, the settlements constitute a disaster. The long list of harmful results includes isolation, prohibitions on new constructions though settlers build nearby, dry wells from a lowered water table, and pollution from the untreated sewage of illegal hilltop settlements. *Peace Now* reported that in the years 2000–07, 18,472 homes were built for Jewish settlers, but only 91 permits were granted against 1,624 Palestinian requests for a population five times as great.

2009, but occur close enough to Knesset elections to impress public opinion with the cabinet. Two ministers, Tzipi Livni (foreign affairs, *Kadima*) and Ehud Barak (defense, *Labor*), were party candidates for prime minister. However, the war failed to bring either political victory, although *Kadima* won the most seats. The greatest beneficiaries of the violence were extreme right-wing parties whose nationalism opposed any Palestinian state.

With effort, Binyamin Netanyahu of *Likud* formed a coalition with *Yisrael Beiteinu*, *Shas*, smaller right-wing partners, and *Labor*. The most contentious appointment was the foreign minister, Avigdor Lieberman of *Yisrael Beiteinu*. His party's electoral slogan, "No loyalty, no citizenship," heightened tensions within the country over the Arab minority. He rejected U.S. calls for a halt to the growth of settlements and his hard line on negotiations created difficulties with the U.S. and the E.U.

The Prime Minister himself deftly attempted to deflect U.S. demands for a two-state solution by announcing his support for a demilitarized Palestinian state. However, embarrassed by new settlement housing announced during the visit of Vice President Biden, the U.S. demanded a real halt to settlements, including in East Jerusalem. Netanyahu did halt a temporary freeze to additional new home construction, but he did not apply it to existing construction or municipal buildings. After the freeze ended in 2010, the peace talks collapsed. Most international political leaders except in the U.S. Congress felt Netanyahu's cabinet was most responsible for the collapse.

By contrast, a group of former military, security and intelligence chiefs and officials proposed to restart the talks by offering to recognize a Palestinian state in almost all the captured 1967 lands, with border adjustments to retain the larger settlements. Without such an initiative, one leader warned, Israelis risked the label "peace refuseniks."

Israel's international reputation worsened in 2010 when its commandos seized the *Mavi Marmara*, a Turkish ferry used by pro-Palestinian human rights activists who challenged the blockade of Gaza. When they attempted to deliver supplies of cement, paper and water purification tablets, commandoes boarded the vessel in international waters, in the process killing nine Turkish citizens.

World opinion overwhelmingly condemned the operation, which brought far more attention to the plight of Gaza than any Palestinian public relations campaign had ever done. Enraged by "state terrorism" against its vessel and the killing of its civilians, the Turkish government halted military cooperation with Israel. The raid thus cost Israel its one allied Muslim state and weakened other relations. Embarrassed by attention to its own blockade of Gaza, Egypt permitted individuals to cross the border. President Obama called the plight of Gaza unsustainable.

With broad Western support, the embargo was initially imposed to block weapons shipments to terrorists. It had also served to pressure the *Hamas* rulers of Gaza by depriving residents of life's necessities and luxuries. The passing years provided more rationales: it was maintained partly to secure Gilad Shalit's release after that soldier's capture in 2006.

The government appointed its own limited inquiry into the *Mavi Marmara* affair, partly to forestall international investigations. More immediately, Israel relaxed the embargo on items such as food, clothing, and toys, and also announced that supplies for UN agencies would be permitted.

The arrival of the "Arab Spring" of 2011 harmed Israel's interests in the short run and possibly for longer. Egypt's President Mubarak had cooperated with Israel and the U.S. for decades, permitting natural gas shipments, adopting a hard line against *Hamas* and blocking trade with Gaza. His fall led to a modest reopening of the border. Mubarak was ousted, and Jordan's King Abdullah, the other Arab ruler with a treaty with Israel, found himself denounced by demonstrators. Even Syria under the Assads, long regarded as the most resolute Arab regime, seemed preferable as an authoritarian state that enforced border calm rather than a democracy awash with popular emotions.

On the ideological level, the Arab Spring awakened waves of protestors who chanted "The People Demands the Fall of the Regime," using Arabic words that emphasized the desire for great change to the system. On the larger scale of Middle East international relations, Israel was considered to run the system.

The slogans and emotions strengthened a broad international movement to delegitimize Israel as long as it failed to negotiate. The movement argues that the settlements contravene international law; some participants boycott goods from the settlements. Others prefer the benefits gained through supporting the Arab and Muslim worlds rather than by alliance with Israel. Given President Obama's statement of support for the 1967 borders as the starting point for negotiations, Netanyahu's policies failed to maintain the confidence of Israel's closest ally.

Massive middle-class demonstrations shook the country during 2011, complete with protesters' camps. The cause was neither foreign policy nor the culture wars between secular and observant Jews. Rather, it was the high cost of living. Professionals complained that their salaries failed to cover food, housing, child care and other elements of modern life. The protests diminished during the winter, but suggested rising popular concerns about domestic issues.

Recognizing that his coalition was fraying over disputes on domestic issues, Netanyahu conducted dramatic midnight negotiations with *Kadima* and established the largest coalition in Knesset history, claiming 94 of the 120 seats. *Kadima's* presence in the cabinet could restrain the excessive special interest demands by some long-standing coalition partners over issues like subsidies to religious groups and the controversial Tal Law that exempted the ultra-orthodox from military service. The grand alliance also provided Netanyahu the symbolic strength of a united country as he condemned Iran's nuclear enrichment program at the U.N. It reduced domestic criticism when he openly supported Mitt Romney for the U.S. presidency.

2013 Elections Strengthen the Center

Lauded in the press as "an authoritative, experienced statesman with no viable replacement," Netanyahu soon switched policies again. He called for elections in January 2013, a year early. To fight it, he formed an electoral alliance between *Likud* and *Yisrael Beiteinu*, the far-right nationalist party headed by Avigdor Lieberman despite, or possibly because of, Lieberman's legal difficulties.

The short, swift election campaign proved that a significant number of Israelis desired domestic change. New faces mattered: nearly half (53) of the members of the new Knesset had not served in the previous one. *Yesh Atid* ("There is a Future"), a new party created by the TV news presenter Yair Lapid, adopted a just-left-of-center platform. It won 14% of the vote and emerged as the second largest party.

Former Prime Minister Sharon

On the further right, Naftali Bennett, a software multi-millionaire and the new leader of *Jewish Home* (*HaBayit HaYehudi*) party addressed everyday domestic problems—including high prices and the ultra-Orthodox avoidance of military service. *Jewish Home* placed fourth, with 12 members, some of them settlers.

By contrast, voters abandoned *Kadima*, that collection of familiar faces recycled from other parties. It fell from 28 seats to just two. The *Likud-Beiteinu* alliance also fared far worse than expected, losing 11 of its previous 42 seats.

The four right-wing and religious parties had won a bare majority, just 61 seats. Any attempt to form them into a coalition risked immediate failure, because *Shas* and *United Torah Judaism* desired privileges over the draft and education that Bennett's *Jewish Home* would not accept. After weeks of negotiations, Netanyahu formed a coalition of four parties, his *Likud-Beiteinu* and *Jewish Home* on the right, and *Yesh Atid* and *Hatnuah* (composed mostly of ex-*Kadima* progressives) on the center-left.

Cooperation between Yair Lapid and Naftali Bennett proved crucial to forming the coalition. The two new leaders shared a commitment for a smaller cabinet, for budget cuts, for work and military service for ultra-Orthodox men, and for educational reforms including modern subjects in ultra-Orthodox schools. The stranglehold of the settlers and religious right over cabinet decisions was thus broken. Despite protests by the ultra-Orthodox, in 2014 the Knesset voted to end the

View of the Sea of Galilee

Photo by Eugenia Elseth

THE JERUSALEM POST

There's no such thing as hard to reach
177-100-2727
AT&T

VOLUME LXIII, NUMBER 19216 MONDAY, MARCH 4, 1996 • ADAR 13, 5756 • SHAWAL 14, 1416 NIS 4.20 (EILAT NIS 3.60)

Hamas suicide bomber kills 18 in Jerusalem

Peres: We are at war with Hamas

BILL HUTMAN

PRIME Minister Shimon Peres declared that Israel is at war with Hamas, following yesterday's deadly suicide bus attack in Jerusalem.

A Hamas suicide bomber blew up a No. 18 Egged bus on Jaffa Road in Jerusalem yesterday morning, killing 18 and seriously wounding seven, exactly a week after another suicide bomber took 25 lives on the same line.

An angry Peres listed new security measures to be enacted, and declared his commitment to "separation" between Israeli and Palestinian peoples. (See story below).

The bomb was similar to the ones used in last week's attacks in Jerusalem and Ashkelon, a senior police source said.

"The evidence points to the same hand being involved in all the attacks," the source said. In all the attacks, 15 kg.-20 kg. of TNT were used and metal scraps, in

Security and medical personnel run for help immediately following yesterday's deadly bus bombing. (Brian Hendler)

Bodies were flung into the air, and glass flew everywhere," he said.

"The rescue work was finished within minutes," Amit said. "It's sad to have to say that we have become experts in dealing with this type of event."

Light rain began to fall after the injured had already been evacuated, and did not appear to affect the police work.

Several police officers commented that the location of the attack, even if coincidental, near the police station and City Hall, made it that much more enraging.

Prime Minister Shimon Peres came to the scene about two hours after the attack to see the devastation first-hand. There were a few anti-government calls from the crowd during the short briefing Peres received from Amit and Inspector-General Assaf Hefetz.

Amit and Hefetz later met with Peres at the Prime Minister's Office, where they discussed the government's planned security moves, including beefing up police and army presence in the capital.

There were brief pushing and shoving matches between police and the crowd of several hundreds onlookers, including many who openly expressed their outrage by chanting "Death to Arabs," and "Peres go home."

Amit said police were bracing for demonstrations and possible attempts by Jewish extremists to carry out revenge attacks on Arabs. Dozens of protesters chanting "Death to Arabs" rushed toward the Old City in the afternoon, but were halted by police.

Mayor Ehud Olmert called for restraint from the crowd. "I understand that people are angry, but this type of behavior is not helpful at this time. It only makes

draft exemption for students at religious seminaries.

No agreement was reached over the most enduring issue of foreign affairs: peace with the Palestinians. Agreement on this issue seems impossible, but averting a cabinet breakdown was easily accomplished—by simply waiting. The parties on the right basically oppose a two-state solution, and their members advocate a goal of one million settlers in Judea and Samaria. Such settler numbers would render any Palestinian state impossible. By contrast, Yair Lapid favors the immediate resumption of negotiations with the Palestinians. The leader of *Hatnuah*, Tzipi Livni, is even more insistent on a settlement.

Like most recent U.S. presidents, during his second term Barack Obama determined to pursue peace in the Middle East. In 2013 Secretary of State John Kerry strongly engaged Israeli and Palestinian leaders, holding 34 meetings with Palestinian President Mahmoud Abbas and about 60 with Prime Minister Netanyahu. Kerry achieved a resumption of peace talks and a commitment that the negotiators for each side, Tzipi Livni and Saeb Erekat, would complete the draft of a final treaty by April 2014.

A final treaty must include agreement over these core issues, besides many more detailed ones:

- Jerusalem: Israel has proclaimed the undivided city its capital. But Jerusalem—or at least its eastern portion—also remains sacred to Palestinians as their capital.
- Borders and settlements: Many and perhaps most Israelis desire to keep major Jewish settlements. Palestinians demand the pre-1967 armistice lines but accept some land swaps.
- Palestinian refugees: Israel rejects any "right of return" by Palestinians, but the "Right to Return" is an article of faith in refugee camps.
- Security: Palestinians wish their homeland free of any Israeli military or police presence, while many Israelis consider the occupation of strategic locations near the Jordan River essential to security.
- A Jewish state: *Likud* and several other parties desire Palestinian recognition of Israel as a "Jewish state." In Palestinian opinion, this would compromise the citizenship of Muslim and Christian Arabs living in Israel.

Although some construction permits for settlement housing were placed on hold to facilitate the negotiations, the U.S. initiative failed. Palestinian attempts to gain international standing by signing treaties angered Netanyahu, and Kerry's mediation faltered. Then, as the deadline approached, the two rival Palestinian political parties, *Fatah* and *Hamas*, agreed on a transitional administration pending elections. Netanyahu then rejected further negotiations.

Although receiving fewer headlines, progress has been made in recent years on increased water desalination projects. A continuing drought that began in 1998 led to the creation of the Water Desalination Administration in 2000. Its latest project, the Sorek Desalination Plant near Tel Aviv, became operational in 2013. With a capacity of 150,000 cubic meters of water per year, the plant is the largest in the world. Although Sorek's water costs about $0.50 per cubic meter to produce, perhaps twice the average of natural sources, at least two more such projects are planned by 2020.

Desalinating water consumes substantial amounts of energy. Fortunately for Israel, the offshore Leviathan natural gas field is likely to commence commercial operation in 2016, avoiding an increased need for imported energy.

Culture: As the Zionist settlers of the pre-independence period were mainly Europeans, their culture has tended to dominate, with attempts to Europeanize the later waves of immigrants from Persian, Afghani, Kurdish, Yemeni, Iraqi or North African backgrounds. These Sephardic Jews now outnumber European Jews, and they increasingly assert their own cultural values.

Israel in fact enjoys cultural diversity as great as that found anywhere, because its people have come from the symbolic four corners of the world. Approximately half of all Israelis were born in some other

The Knesset Political Spectrum, 2013

4	Hadash	far left, mixed Arab, Jewish
6	Meretz	left-of-center
15	Labor	center-left
19	Yesh Atid	center-left
6	Hatnuah	center-left
2	Kadima	center
31	Likud-Yisrael Beitenu	right
12	HaBayit HaYehudi	far-right religious
7	United Torah Judaism	religious—ultra-Orthodox
11	Shas	populist; religious—Sephardic
4	United Arab List	Arab nationalist
3	Balad	Arab nationalist

Former President Shimon Peres

land, and they brought a variety of cultures with them. Though Jews, they neither act alike, nor think alike, nor look alike, though most now wear European style clothes.

The non-Jewish minorities are almost entirely Arabic-speaking and comprise about 750,000 Muslims, 150,000 Christians and 60,000 Druze (see Lebanon: Culture). In general these minorities suffer lower standards of living, and receive less education. One recent study found 48% of Israeli Arab families living below the poverty level, and the high school dropout rate was 50%. However, there was not much benefit to remaining in school: in one sample, educated Arabs suffered 33% unemployment.

The complex educational system includes both state and private schools, but even the private schools are partly subsidized and controlled by the government. Within the state schools there are three systems: secular, religious, and Arabic-speaking. Secondary schools receive no direct public financing, but the government helps pay the fees for qualified students on the basis of need.

Of the several institutions of higher learning, the oldest and most prestigious is the Hebrew University of Jerusalem. Many faculty members have been educated in Europe or North America, and there is significant interchange with universities on those continents. In terms of its research accomplishments, publications, and student quality, the university outranks all others in the Middle East. However, between 2001 and 2005, the Israeli government cut its funds to higher education by about 15%, leading to student strikes supported by academic administrators who feared that further cuts could cause the system to collapse. Strikes by professors and others marred the 2007–08 academic year.

At independence, Orthodox Judaism became the established religion of the state. Religious holidays and Sabbath observance marked the nation; in Orthodox and ultra-Orthodox areas, stores close and public buses ceased operating on Saturdays. Until 2012 only Orthodox rabbis were paid by the government, and even now, only Orthodox weddings are legally binding. Secular couples therefore submit to Orthodox rituals many find sexist, or marry elsewhere. Each year, over 25% of all Jewish couples who marry do so outside Israel, often in Cyprus.

Today, a minority of Israeli Jews adheres to this branch of Judaism. Others consider themselves secular, or worship at Reform synagogues, but the fastest growing congregations are the ultra-Orthodox, a term applied to a number of black-clad groups, including the Hasidim of European origin and Sephardim from the Middle East. Collectively they are known in Hebrew as the Haredim, "those who tremble before God."

Culture Wars and the Roles of Women

Religious and ideological differences between different groups have led to sharp social and political disputes, sometimes labeled the culture wars. At one extreme, secular Jews may define a Jew as anyone who considers himself or herself such, even though an atheist. In contrast, many Orthodox and ultra-Orthodox hold strict expectations of converts, even desiring to exclude converts according to Reform, Conservative, and Reconstructionist Judaism for citizenship under the law of return. Many also consider secular Jews responsible for the loss of Jews through assimilation in other societies. Some are not Zionists, believing that the Messiah's return should precede the establishment of Israel, and a few equate secularism as a loss to Jewry equivalent in numbers to Hitler's exterminations. Ultra-Orthodox vandals recently defaced the Yad Vashem Holocaust memorial in Jerusalem with graffiti denouncing Zionism.

The most perplexing conflicts usually involve the ultra-Orthodox or Haredim. They formed just a few small communities at independence, when David Ben-Gurion offered them subsidies and exemption from the military draft. In sixty years the Haredim population grew to about one million, initially through immigration, then through early marriages and many children. Although women may be employed outside the home, many Haridim men devote themselves to study of the Torah. Most avoid both military service and work. Their unemployment rate hovers around 60%.

Prime Minister Binyamin Netanyahu

The combination of refusing military service and declining work, while accepting government studies and averaging six or eight children per family, upsets many others in society. They fear that future prosperity will suffer from the rapidly growing, but poorly educated and economically unproductive Haredim population.

The conflict between secular rights and divine commands often leads to bitter language. Rabbi Ovadia Yossef, spiritual leader of the Sephardic party, *Shas*, claimed in 2006 that God helped soldiers when they "believe and pray" and so they did not get killed. In fact, many observant soldiers had been killed in Lebanon. Some years earlier, a *Shas* cabinet member called a fellow minister a "Satan to be wiped from the face of the earth."

Perhaps the sharpest disputes revolve around the role of women, their place in society, and their right to be visible in public. Following the Talmud much as very conservative Muslims follow the sayings of Muhammad and rulings of Shari'a law, Haredim men argue that to preserve the purity of their thoughts, women must be covered—and out of the public eye. The resulting restrictions render women second-class citizens when not entirely invisible. For example, the national bus company, Egged, has designated "modesty buses" that separate the men (in the front) from women (to the rear, of course). Religious extremists spat on an 8-year-old girl, Naama Margolese, as she walked to school, because they considered her clothing immodest. Professor Channa Maayan, receiving a health ministry award for her book on hereditary diseases frequent among Jews, discovered at the awards ceremony that she and her husband would have to sit apart—and that since women were not on stage, a male colleague must receive the award for her.

Many Israelis feel that the character of the nation is at stake.

In the first decades of Israeli statehood, citizens bonded together from the shared experiences of the Holocaust and winning independence. Zionism unified diverse populations, and the socialist ideology minimized differences of wealth and income among the population. Concern with morality delayed the introduction of television to Israel.

As Israeli society matured, individualism played a greater role, and great distinctions grew between economic classes. Now income equality is lower than almost any other developed nation except the United States, with the top 10% receive 31% of net income.

Given social change and economic disparity, in common with other developed societies, Israel's crime rate has risen. The more common criminal acts range from fraud and corruption to burglary, and reach from high government officials to youths from the less prosperous *Sephardic* Jewish and Arab communities. In addition, the occupied territories continue to witness high levels of crime, including murder, often between Israeli settlers and Arabs.

Economy: During the first two decades of its existence, Israel enjoyed one of the fastest rates of economic growth of any country, despite insignificant oil, natural gas, and coal deposits. Following a basically socialist pattern, the government established new towns for immigrants and subsidized worthy essentials like bread and milk. Extensive medical care and other benefits came through the widespread system of labor unions. Some of the highest taxes in the world accompanied these social advantages, with rates as high as 70% on upper middle class income. Not surprisingly, budget deficits, inflation, and trade deficits accompanied the rapid growth.

During the oil shocks of the 1970s and 1980s, most non-oil economies suffered stagflation—the combination of high inflation and high unemployment. Israel also suffered the heavy burden of defense spending (24% of GDP in 1984) and the marriage between socialism and Zionism that produced a bloated bureaucracy, extensive government regulations, and heavy taxation.

International factors and deliberate political choices played major roles in enabling the highly-educated workforce to achieve its present success. Rigid control over the money supply, just as world oil prices declined and then plummeted, broke inflation. Though occurring slowly over a number of years, the privatization of industries, the nation's shipping firm and the national airline, *El Al*, increased competition and efficiency.

During the 1990s, three further factors contributed to economic prosperity. One million immigrants from the former Soviet Union brought education and skills, and strengthened demands for pro-business legislation.

Simultaneously, the Oslo Accords reduced political tensions. The moves towards peace also weakened the Arab boycott of Israeli goods, and the secondary boycott of companies doing business with Israel.

Finally, a great inflow of foreign investment, particularly in electronics and telecommunication, provided prosperity and foreign exchange. Because scientific and technological research occurs at one of the highest rates in the world, major firms like Microsoft and Intel frequently sought and bought out local startups. This contributed to the prosperity of the banking, acquisitions, and venture capital markets as well. Solar energy, the medical sciences, genetics, and engineering firms also attracted foreign interest.

In 2010 Israel gained recognition as a developed economy, when it was admitted to the Organization for Economic Cooperation and Development. The country generally ranks as one of the top 30 in per capita income and foreign exchange reserves, and in recent years boasted an unemployment rate below the U.S. and European Union. Despite the prosperity, about 20% of the population lives below the poverty line. Two population groups account for much of the poverty: the Ultra-Orthodox Haredim, whose menfolk traditionally study rather than work, and Arab citizens.

Two international developments in the mid-1990s offered greater opportunities for the Israeli economy. First, the Arab boycott of companies doing business with Israel, a form of secondary boycott illegal in many countries, shuffled towards final collapse when the Gulf States abandoned the boycott. Second, the Free Trade Agreement between the United States and Israel came into full effect in 1995, and included Israeli agricultural products excluded by the Free Trade Agreement with the European Union.

Agricultural output has expanded enormously since 1948. The introduction of new crops, chemical fertilizers and irrigation systems increased production more than 500%. Sparse grazing lands turned into farms, thanks to irrigation from the Jordan River and the most advanced dry-climate agricultural cultivation methods. Israel imports basic foodstuffs, including beef, but exports high-value and out-of-season fruits and vegetables to Europe and even the U.S.

For a small country, Israel produces a wide variety of industrial products, from simple furniture to cut diamonds to satellites. The armament and related service industries employ over 10% of the national workforce, and produce a leading category of exports. These have included guided missiles, artillery, and fighter aircrafts as well as the most famous, the Uzi submachine gun. Customers range from the United States to Taiwan, South Africa, and a number of Latin American nations. Israel typically ranks as one of the world's larger arms exporters, with India the largest customer.

Israel Aircraft Industries had hoped to become a major producer of high-technology fighters, but financing failed. While planes are serviced and executive jets are built, the pride of the aviation industry is missiles. The Arrow missile system, one of the few anywhere that intercepts ballistic missiles, is now operational. The Iron Dome anti-missile system reportedly

Panoramic view of Tel Aviv Courtesy: Embassy of Israel

proved very effective against short-range missiles from Gaza during the 2012 fighting there. Iron Dome batteries were also moved north during the worsening Syrian civil war, amid fears that one side or the other might lob conventional or chemical weapons at Israel's cities.

The recent discovery of major off-shore natural gas deposits about 50 miles from the Mediterranean coast suggests major financial improvement for a land poor in natural resources. Gas started to flow from the Tamar field in early 2013; its output will eventually exceed national needs. The Levant Basin also includes the Leviathan field, farther out and considerably deeper. It was only discovered in 2010 and is also under development. The production companies have suggested exporting the gas as LNG, possibly to Korea, but yielding to consumer pressure, proposed regulations will cap exports at no more than 40% of production, to ensure sufficient supplies for domestic use at low prices.

Another prominent industry in terms of foreign exchange earnings is tourism. Jerusalem contains the holiest shrines for both Jews and Christian pilgrims. Numerous Biblical and historical sites elsewhere also attract visitors, and there are beaches and other attractions both scenic and cultural. Understandably, tourist arrivals suffer from fears of terrorist attacks; in 1991, the Gulf War discouraged tourists whose idea of pleasure did not include gas masks. Tourism fared better with the peace treaties, however, and reached 2.7 million visitors in the year 2000. By the following year, many hotel rooms were empty again, a byproduct of the renewed *intifada,* but by 2011 foreign visitors exceeded 3.5 million.

THE FUTURE: Israel is an amazing place. Despite Prime Minister Netanyahu's warning some years ago that the unacceptable—its strategic enemy's completion of an atom bomb, whose logical destination is Tel Aviv—was just months away, citizens and foreigners alike continue to invest in the economy, and the hot topics in the last Knesset election were domestic ones.

One oft-forgotten key to understanding this enigma is that Israelis are realists. Rather than expecting peace—a goal that has proved impossible for nearly a century—they seek to space out limited wars that demonstrate the superiority of the Israel Defense Forces and deter any sustained aggression.

Thus, few Israelis seem concerned that Washington's latest peace initiative is dead or that the viability of a two-state solution declines each year.

For the short- to medium-term, then, expect much of the same. With discussion of peace terms averted, the present *Likud-Beitenu* coalition with *Jewish Home, Yesh Atid,* and *Hatnuah* should last its term.

There are longer-term implications from the direction of American Jewish society. The successful integration of American Jews into the dominant Protestant society has reduced anti-Semitism and encouraged evangelical support of Israel. However, Jewish influence over U.S. policy might diminish from the broad changes taking place in American demographics (reflected by the election of Barack Obama). Moreover, the low fertility of non-Orthodox Jews, combined with their intermarriage with Gentiles, suggests a much diminished community. At the same time, ultra-Orthodox populations are growing, but many of them reject the intellectual foundations of Zionism. Their concerns are concentrated on their own community needs, and their influence on mainstream America is far less.

The Knesset through Palombo Gate

The Hashemite Kingdom of Jordan

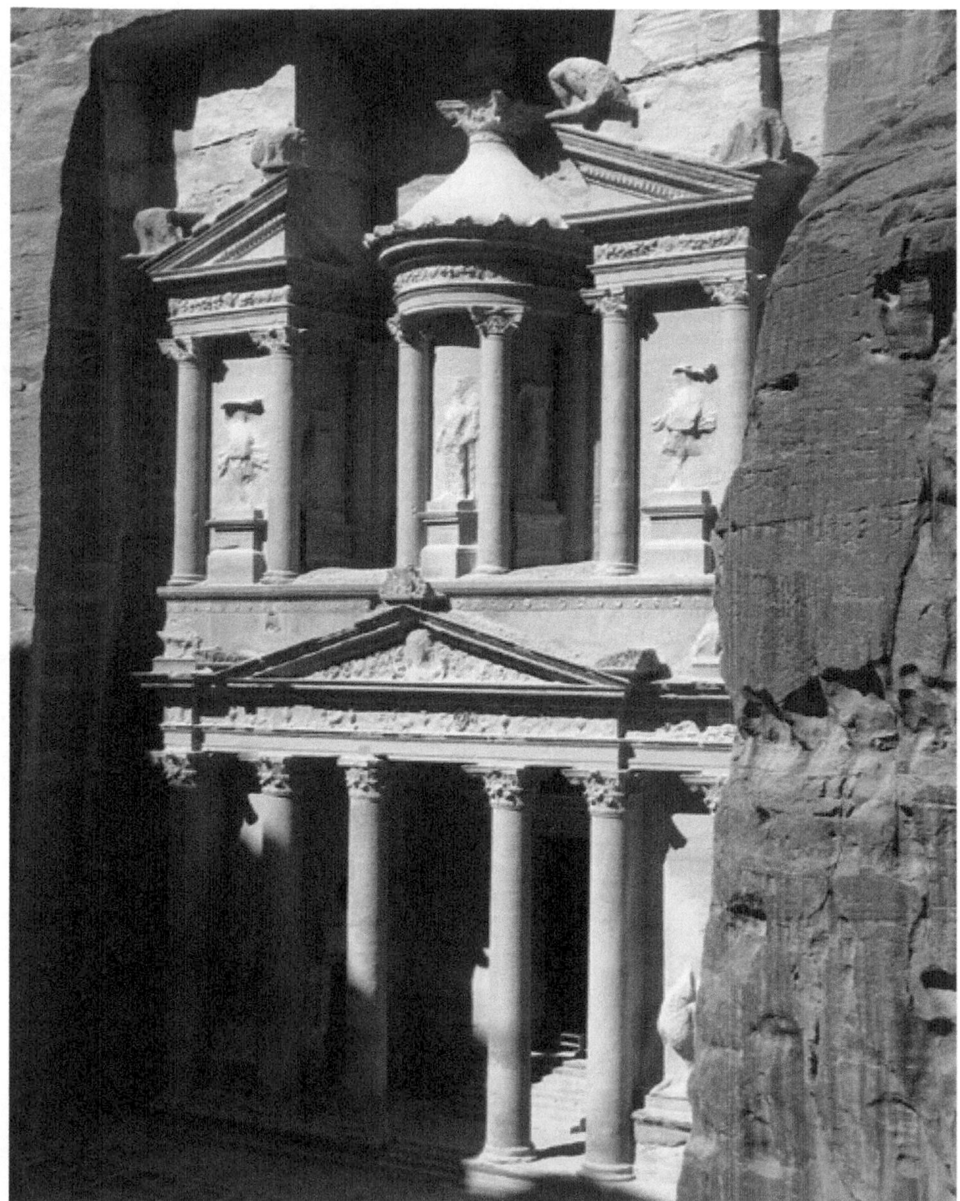

Carved from the multi-colored sandstone cliff, the Treasury at Petra symbolizes the ancient Nabataean center of trade and wealth. It creates a dramatic impression on visitors emerging from the long, narrow entrance gorge known as the Siq. photo by the author

Area: 34,495 square miles (89,342 sq. km.).
Population: 6.3 million (plus ~ 800,000 Syrian refugees).
Capital City: Amman (pop. 2.6 million).
Climate: Hot and dry in the summer, but winter can be cold with moderate rain and even snow in the northwest. The Jordan Valley and Aqaba area are warmer. The eastern and southern regions are desert.
Neighboring Countries: Syria (North); Iraq (Northeast); Saudi Arabia (Southeast); Israel and Occupied Territories (West).
Time Zone: GMT +2. When it is noon Pacific Standard Time it is 10:00 P.M. in Jordan.
Official Language: Arabic.
Other Principal Language: English is widely used.
Ethnic Background: Arab except for small Circassian communities; a majority originally Palestinian.
Principal Religion: Sunni Islam (about 91%) and Christianity.
Chief Commercial Products: Phosphate, olive oil, tomatoes, wheat, barley, figs, lentils, tobacco, sheepskins, hides, cement, salt and refined petroleum products.
Major Trading Partners: Saudi Arabia, U.S., Germany, Iraq, Japan, U.K., Syria and India.
Currency: One Jordanian Dinar = 100 piasters.
Former Colonial Status: Under British control (1918–1946).
Independence Day: May 25, 1946.
Chief of State: Abdullah II (Abdullah ibn Hussein al-Hashimi), King.
Head of Government: Abdullah Ensour, Prime Minister (2013).
National Flag: Three horizontal stripes of black, white and green and a red triangle at the pole bearing a white seven-pointed star.
Gross Domestic Product: $36 billion (current prices); $42 billion (Purchasing Power Parity).
GDP per capita: $6,300 (PPP).

The borders of Jordan, like those of many other countries drafted by colonial powers, often fail to reflect either natural features or differences in populations. In the years immediately following World War I, the boundaries were drawn to suit British policy, and they have been modified little since. The country takes its name from the Jordan River, which with its tributary, the Yarmuk, is the only real river in the area, and provides the only natural boundary.

The Jordan River, deprived of an estimated 95% its fresh water by diversions, is only a small stream when it empties into the salty Dead Sea, the lowest body of water on earth. Its surface lies more than 1,300 feet below sea level. Because the Jordan's scanty flow falls short of the very rapid evaporation caused by the heat and solar rays in the depression, the Dead Sea is drying up, the water level falling about 3 feet per year. About 50 miles long from north to south just a generation ago, as shown on the map, it has lost the southern third. However, the sea will not quickly disappear: its maximum depth reaches about 1,300 feet. The salt concentration is almost ten times that of ordinary sea water. This great density allows bathers to float easily and in fact to read the newspaper while sitting afloat, but they suffer stings at every scratch on their skin.

Immediately east of the Jordan Valley the land rises steeply to the edge of a high plateau. The strip along the edge of the plateau, wider in the north, receives moderate rainfall (about 25 inches annually). As the plateau drops in elevation to the east and south, rainfall diminishes rapidly to nothing. Only the hardiest *Bedouin* nomads wander out into that area in search of a livelihood.

Amman, the capital of the country, lies on the plateau, spread onto the sides of several converging valleys. In 1925 it was only a small Circassian village built among the ruins of ancient Roman Philadelphia. Since

Jordan

The Royal Family of King Abdullah II

then, Amman has grown into a large, modern, and fairly comfortable city.

History: Although the high plateau was farmed extensively during the Roman and Byzantine eras, and Umayyad caliphs built palaces in the desert, for most of the last thousand years Bedouins dominated the country. During the 19th century, settlement increased, as did Ottoman control, and the Hijaz railroad was built through the territory from Damascus to Medina a decade before World War I. During that conflict, the troops and Bedouin allies of the Arab Revolt fought against the Ottoman forces along the railroad, and the port of Aqaba became the first important Arab conquest outside the Hijaz. Under Emir Faisal, and supported by British supplies and advisors such as T.E. Lawrence (Lawrence of Arabia), the Arab forces used their mastery of the desert to outflank the Ottoman forces, tying down large numbers of them in garrison duties.

After the war, Jordan fell under Arab rule from Damascus, and thus in 1920 part of Faisal's Kingdom of Syria. However, French forces soon marched on Damascus, ousted Faisal, and subjected Syria to the French mandate. Jordan, though the southern portion of Syria, lay in territory that by Anglo-French agreement fell under British influence. Hence France did not occupy it. Weeks later, Faisal's brother Abdullah arrived in Amman from the Hijaz, hoping to regain all Syria for Arab rule, but only minor raids took place against the French.

Acting on the wishes of Britain and France, the League of Nations granted Britain control over the territory within the Palestine Mandate (the term "Jordan" then referred only to the river and valley). However, conditions contrasted greatly between the two banks of the Jordan River. The western territory had cities and towns, settled farmers, and Zionist immigrants.

The East Bank resembled a frontier society. There were no cities, a mere scattering of towns, and only the skeleton of modern government. Tribes of nomads and semi-nomads raided each other and the few settled farmers. For the practical reason that Abdullah already ruled the area as Faisal's replacement and as a reward for his family's alliance, Britain formed the Emirate of Transjordan for Abdullah. Claiming descent from the Prophet Muhammad's family, and thus a Hashemite, Abdullah eventually gave his family name to the state.

Aside from settled areas around the towns of al-Karak, al-Salt, Ajlun and Irbid, nomadism remained the dominant way of life. Abdullah selected Amman as his capital. An impressive city in ancient times, it was located on the Hijaz Railway, and a few Circassian refugees from Russian expansion in the Caucasus had settled nearby. During the 1920s Emir Abdullah attempted to establish law and order, protect the frontier, settle nomadic tribes, and undertake the beginnings of modern government.

The military, known as the Arab Legion, became the instrument that brought order to the countryside. Composed of Arab soldiers with British officers, during World War II it also fought for the Allies in Syria and Iraq. As the Emir's government showed more competence, the treaty with Britain was revised several times, each revision giving his officials more authority. Finally, negotiations in 1946 led to a treaty recognizing the independence of Transjordan, and Abdullah proclaimed himself king. A mutual defense treaty permitted British troops to remain in the country, and British officers technically under Abdullah's orders commanded the Arab Legion.

When the United Nations voted in late 1947 to partition Palestine between Jews and Palestinians (see Israel: History), King Abdullah saw the opportunity to realize one step in his cherished dream of ruling a kingdom of "Greater Syria," including Transjordan, Syria, Lebanon and Pales-

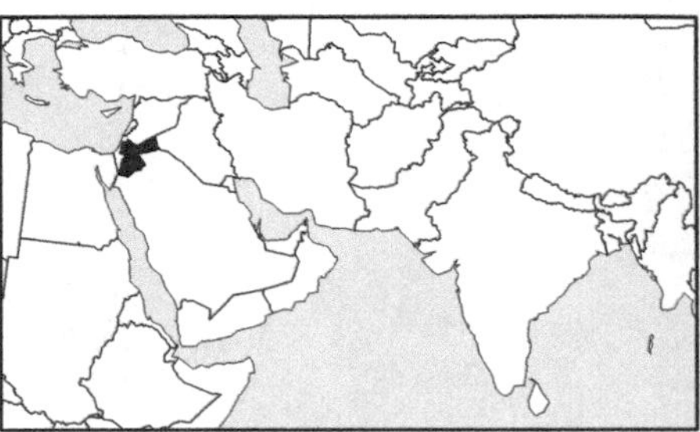

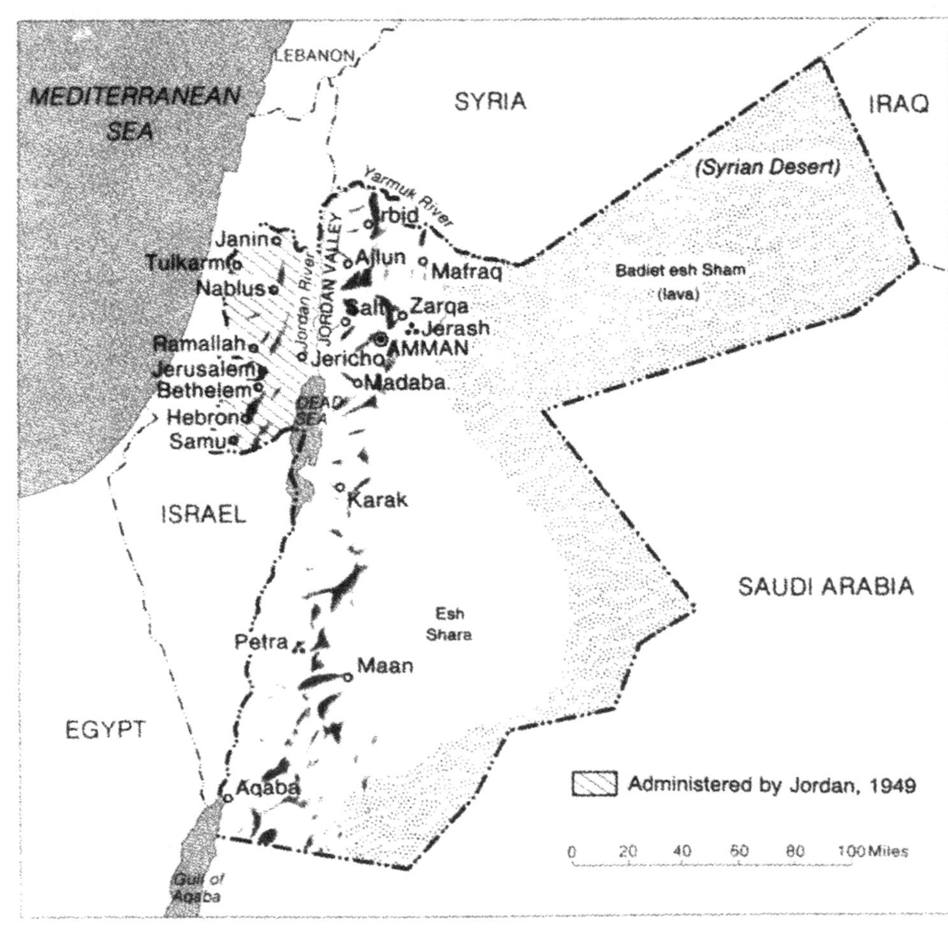

King Abdullah of Jordan (1882–1951)

tine. When Britain's mandate over Palestine expired, he sent the Arab Legion to fight the newly proclaimed state of Israel. Other Arab states acted likewise, but in the War of Israeli Independence (1948–49) Arab armies suffered defeat. Israeli forces occupied areas reserved by the United Nations partition plan for the Arab state. The Legion fared better than most Arab forces, capturing the Jewish section of Jerusalem's Old City, but before the final armistice, it was forced, by Israeli ultimatum, to pull back elsewhere.

Most Palestinians thought King Abdullah had intervened in Palestine as much for dynastic gain as to repulse the Israelis. As the fighting ended, he secretly met Israeli officials to assure them of his limited intentions. Later he convened a congress of Palestinian notables that proclaimed him King of all Palestine; in 1949 he annexed formally the central portion that his troops controlled. Except for Gaza, all Arab Palestine became the West Bank of the Hashemite Kingdom of Jordan, and Abdullah came to rule the holy places in Jerusalem, Bethlehem and Hebron.

However, Jordan also gained a large and restive population, including several hundred thousand refugees on both sides of the river. They widely opposed Abdullah as an agent of Britain and a traitor to the Palestinian cause. Furthermore, because of their greater achievements in education, larger population, and greater sophistication, Palestinians considered Transjordan as backward. Not surprisingly, tensions arose between the Palestinians and the Transjordanians.

In 1951 a Palestinian assassinated King Abdullah as he walked in Jerusalem. His young grandson, Hussein, then became king, although guided by a regency council until he turned 18 in 1953.

At first, Hussein permitted political activity and allowed parties to organize and govern through parliament. Most politicians were extremely nationalistic and anti-Western, critical of the roles played by Britain, France and the United States in the creation of Israel. In a showdown in 1957, King Hussein, dissolved parliament, arrested the cabinet, ended the Anglo-Jordanian defense treaty and dismissed Glubb Pasha, the long-serving British commander of the Arab Legion.

These events marked the young king's assumption of personal authority. To replace British aid, he sought financial, military and technical assistance from the United States. Nevertheless, following the Iraqi Revolution in 1958 that overthrew and murdered Hussein's cousin, Faisal II, British troops returned to Jordan to uphold the monarchy.

Between War and Peace with Israel

Given Israel's military strength, Jordan recognized the importance of preserving the 1949 armistice agreement with Israel. However, most Palestinians, especially those exiled from homes in Israel, wanted Jordan to join other Arab nations in a military confrontation against it (see Palestine). Tensions between several Arab states and Israel led Egypt's Nasser to deepen the crisis in May 1967 (see Israel: History). King Hussein was drawn unwillingly into a military treaty with Egypt, and then into war with Israel in June.

In four days of fighting, the vastly superior Israel Defense Forces crushed all Jordanian units west of the Jordan River, and seized the richest portion of the kingdom. With nearly half the population lost, and economic benefits from the major tourist locations around Jerusalem ended, Jordan faced great economic, political, and social difficulties.

Nearly 400,000 Palestinians fled to Jordan, creating a new wave of refugees, adding to the large communities of displaced Palestinians from 1949 around Amman, at Zarqa and elsewhere. New camps were set up with international aid, to provide food and shelter for the flood of persons crossing the river. The burden of the refugees stretched Jordan's finances; their numbers swamped the available jobs.

Both old and new camps became fertile recruiting centers for *al-Fatah* and other guerrilla groups linked to the *Palestine Liberation Organization (PLO).* Claiming they would succeed against Israel where the combined Arab armies failed, these groups launched attacks against Israel and Israeli-occupied areas. Israeli reprisals turned much of the Jordan valley into a zone of sporadic battles, but at Karamah in 1968 the guerrillas held their positions against an Israeli raid, consequently gaining fame and support in the Arab world (see Palestine: History).

The late King Hussein of Jordan

After first permitting the guerrillas to operate in its territory, Jordan feared both their growing power as a "second government" and Israeli reprisals for guerrilla raids. The government therefore attempted to curtail the armed groups. Finally in "Black September" 1970, King Hussein ordered his army to crush the guerrillas. Perhaps 10,000 people, most of them Palestinian, died in Amman during the fighting; much of the city was heavily damaged. A tank invasion by Syrian-based units of the Palestine Liberation Army met defeat from Jordan's small air force, while troops set free Western passengers hijacked by Palestinian radicals.

The firm suppression of the fashionable guerrillas evoked fierce hostility from Palestinians and other Arabs, but after sometimes bitter fighting the military had regained control everywhere by 1971.

The widespread nationalist uprising *(intifada)* that began in 1987 in the Israeli-occupied territories showed again that the inhabitants of the West Bank considered themselves Palestinians, not Jordanians. The 1974 Arab summit had proclaimed the *PLO* to be the only representative of the Palestinian people, thus denying Jordan's claim to the West Bank. However,

Jordan

Jordan continued to pay the salaries of some civil servants in Palestine. As the *intifada* gathered strength, however, such links aroused widespread criticism from Palestinians and other Arabs. Consequently, in 1988 King Hussein dramatically recognized the Palestinians' wish to form their own country.

Iraq's invasion of Kuwait in 1990 plunged the Jordanian economy into a major depression. UN sanctions halted the transit trade and Jordan's own exports to its main customer, Iraq. Some 200,000 Jordanian workers returned from the Gulf states, reducing the annual remittances sent to families, and raising the unemployment rate to nearly 30%.

In the aftermath of the war, King Hussein ended martial law imposed in 1967. He issued a "National Charter" that re-established multiparty democracy and secured allegiance to the king. Prime ministers followed in rapid succession, and some 15 political parties, including the *Islamic Action Front* of the Muslim Brotherhood, contested the 1993 elections. However, the new and sometimes uneven electoral districts weakened parties, by allowing voters just one vote even if there were multiple candidates in the district. This helped independent candidates from traditionally important families, nearly all of them the king's supporters. The largest group, the *Islamic Action Front* led the opposition of Arab nationalists and leftists.

In the shadow of the Madrid and Oslo peace processes between Israel and the Palestinians, quiet and symbolic diplomacy tackled and resolved the major disputes with Israel. In 1994, a peace treaty formally ended 46 years of belligerence, and regained some small bits of land (totaling 145 square miles) occupied by Israel, although the *kibbutzim* cultivating them leased some property back. More importantly, the treaty also restored water rights in the Jordan and Yarmuk valleys, and the U.S. promised to waive repayment on loans of nearly $1 billion. Jordan gained a privileged role at Muslim sites in Jerusalem, though it promised to turn them over to Palestinian authorities once Israel withdrew.

Peace required Jordan to amend its anti-Israeli laws and permit trade with Israel. However, popular opposition made this difficult. Some professional associations banned their members from dealing with Israelis. Islamic, leftist and Pan-Arab parties demanded that the treaty be scrapped. The opposition gained strength because the first visible benefits seemed limited to short-term tourists bound for Petra. However, critics failed to anticipate the opportunity for exports of light manufactures to the U.S. under the accompanying free trade agreement. By 2002 the U.S. had become Jordan's largest export customer though the products were largely assembled by Asian temporary workers, not Jordanians.

The last months of King Hussein showed again that real power in the country lay not with parliament but with the royal family. Stricken with cancer, Hussein left his treatment at the Mayo Clinic in 1999, to fly home to Amman, where he very publicly designated his eldest son, Abdullah, as heir, in place of his brother, Hassan, the crown prince since the 1960s. Days later, after final medical efforts at the Mayo Clinic failed, King Hussein returned home to die.

Hussein had ruled Jordan for nearly 47 years, many of them tumultuous, and he cut a much larger figure on the world stage than his country's population and wealth merited. A vast assembly of world leaders gathered for the funeral—the only significant absentee seemed to be Saddam Hussein of Iraq.

Jordan under King Abdullah II

The son of Hussein's British second wife, Abdullah had spent almost his entire life in the military, eventually commanding the special forces. Educated in Britain and the U.S., he had long accepted his uncle as the next king. Nevertheless, commentators commended the initiative and energy he displayed as monarch.

Amman, a city built on seven hills. Against the slope of one is this large Roman amphitheater now restored and being used for performances as it once was almost 2,000 years ago.

Wadi Rum drivers taking a break Photo by Susan L. Thompson

He quickly visited most Arab rulers and improved relations with political opposites like Syria and Kuwait. During trips to Western capitals, he sought economic concessions, particularly debt relief.

In Amman, Abdullah proved adept at popular symbolic gestures, and over the years appointed a succession of new prime ministers. However, the cabinets often failed to move as quickly as the king desired, and hopes for substantial change remained unrealized.

Overdue elections in 2003 reestablished parliament, and expanded it, after two years of rule by royal decree. Voters of the newly designed districts overwhelmingly favored independent candidates, a goal of the electoral system. The *Islamic Action Front* won only 20 seats, and both women and leftists failed to win a single contested seat. However, women had been guaranteed nine seats by recent reforms and could be appointed.

Coordinated attacks on three foreign-own hotels in Amman killed dozens of Jordanian wedding guests, and a few foreigners in 2005. King Abdullah rallied public opinion in the shocked nation against Abu Musaib al-Zarqawi, the Jordanian leader of *al-Qaeda in Mesopotamia,* who claimed responsibility for the attacks. The televised confession of an Iraqi woman whose explosives failed to detonate strengthened the king's claims, and increased popular opposition to terrorism. No doubt the public support will be appreciated. Jordanian intelligence agencies keep close track on Jordanian activists and plotters, but identifying foreign terrorists becomes a difficult challenge.

By definition, faithful conservatives supported the king's rule and avoided stringent criticism over the peace treaty with Israel. However, that same conservatism opposed important elements of the king's reform agenda. Apparently unhappy with the failure of parliament to enact desired legislation, in 2009 the King Abdullah again dismissed parliament, and in typical style used the year before the next election to initiate some reforms, most prominently economic liberalization. The results of the 2010 elections demonstrated that as expected, the modest changes in the electoral system reserved six more seats for women, but changed little else, except that the *Islamic Action Front* boycotted the vote over the reforms.

Even before the Egyptian protests at Tahrir Square, unrest over corruption and unemployment began in Jordan's conservative south—the heartland of the king's support. Leftists, Islamists, and other traditional opposition groups joined these Friday demonstrations, calling for reforms and democracy. Significantly, they did not espouse revolution against the king, but demanded that parliament choose the prime minister.

In contrast to other Arab rulers, King Abdullah initially defused the protests. Very likely, the security services hacked into dissident blogs and closed websites, but the police treated protestors carefully—handing out water bottles rather than beating them. Abdullah met with the *Muslim Brotherhood*, and dismissed the prime minister, commonly considered too close to corruption and the IMF.

The king apparently yielded to one of the opposition's chief demands—that democracy meant the people, through parliament, should choose the prime minister, not the king. However, Abdullah left plenty of room to retreat, stipulating that a functioning three-party system (left, center, and right) would be necessary, and would take years to become effective. Cynics noted that the monarchy's electoral system, so often modified, is deliberately designed to weaken political parties.

A violent protest by Islamist *Salafists* in Zarqa certainly reminded the general population of the dangers posed by some opposition groups. Waving a sword in front of the media's cameras, the group's leader demanded the release of prisoners, including the mentor of the slain leader of *al-Qaeda in Iraq*, Abu Musab al-Zarqawi. When police attempted to break up the protest, they were attacked by *Salafists* wielding swords, clubs, and clubs.

The king later proposed reform measures, and parliament approved them, including a provision that enabled electors to vote for both the local representative and a vote for the 27 nation-wide seats distributed by proportional representation. This modest reform failed to meet opposition expectations, since gerrymandered districts remained, and the powers of the lower house of parliament were limited. It would not choose the prime minister, formulate the budget, or even introduce laws. After protests, parliament postponed consideration of a proposal to criminalize allegations of corruption, but journalists were arrested for reporting

The 1989 elections in Jordan demonstrated vividly the deeply-held differences between Muslim fundamentalists and women influenced by Western concepts of equality and women's rights.

In her campaign for parliament, the TV personality, Toujan al-Faisal, raised a number of social issues, including child abuse, polygamy, and wife-beating. For this, she was charged in Islamic court by two Muslim radicals, one a deputy to the Mufti (legal scholar) of the military, on grounds she had "defamed Islam." As punishment, her critics demanded the court declare her legally incompetent, dissolve her marriage, remove her children, and grant immunity to anyone who shed her blood.

The Islamic court dismissed the case, possibly at the urging of the royal palace. Neither Toujan al-Faisal nor any other woman won a seat in the elections, but soon after King Hussein did appoint Layla Sharaf the first woman in the Senate.

Ms. al-Faisal later became the first woman elected to parliament, but after she posted an article on the internet that accused the prime minister of corruption, she was imprisoned. Toujan al-Faisal was pardoned by King Abdullah in 2002, but remains banned from parliament for life.

that the king intervened in parliament's investigations.

The small weekly protests by Islamists continued and grew dramatically when the cabinet withdrew subsidies on bottled gas, necessary because of attacks on the pipeline bringing cheaper Egyptian supplies. Some demonstrators even dared to blame the king himself for the financial difficulties. Foreign observers worried that the January 2013 election, if boycotted successfully by the *Muslim Brotherhood's Islamic Action Front*, trade unions, and leftists, could discredit the entire reform project and provoke widespread protests.

On election day, Jordanians voted at a slightly higher rate than in past elections—at 56%, just over half the electorate. Perhaps conscious of the political and economic difficulties in Egypt, Yemen, and Syria, they chose tribal and business independents sympathetic to the king. After consultation with parliament—for the first time—Abdullah appointed a reformer, Abdullah Ensour, as prime minister.

As the Syrian civil war worsened, Jordan played an increasingly important role as a conduit for supplies and weapons to militias fighting against the Assad regime in southern Syria. Hundreds of thousands of refugees fled the opposite direction. The fortunate could afford to rent modest apartments in cities; some 120,000 impoverished others crowded into the Zaatari Refugee Camp, becoming, in effect, Jordan's fifth-largest city. The Syrian conflict also led to the temporary posting of American troops and aircrafts.

Two happier events in the summer of 2013 united nearly all Jordanians except the strictest fundamentalists. Mohammed Assaf, a young Palestinian singer from Gaza, won the Arab Idol contest in a gentle assertion of Palestinian identity that won millions of non-Palestinian votes.

On the playing fields, the national women's soccer team, "al-Nashmiyyat" ("The Brave"), representing many of Jordan's ethnic and religious divisions, achieved an unthinkable 21–0 victory over Kuwait to qualify for the Asian Cup for the first time ever. A week later, the men's team, "al-Nashama," beat Oman 1–0 in a must-win battle to remain a contender for the World Cup. Though Jordan failed to play in Brazil, such events helped unite the nation. Moreover, the population was drawn to the monarchy through the efforts of the president of the football association, King Abdullah's brother Ali.

Sluggish economic growth in the kingdom received a significant boost with the Abdali Project, a joint venture between the government and the Lebanese billionaire and politician, Sa'id Hariri. The project is a mixed-use community envisaged to become Amman's new downtown. Envisaged to include hotels, retail outlets, offices, and residential apartments totaling over 20 million square feet, the development opened its first major component in 2014 and employed over 5,000 workers.

T. E. Lawrence described Wadi Rum as "vast and echoing and God-like."

Photo by Susan L. Thompson

King Abdullah II

Culture: Antiquities lie strewn profusely across—and beneath—the landscape of Jordan. Perhaps as many as 500,000 identifiable archeological sites exist, and teams of workers from many lands descend annually to discover remains dated from the Paleolithic to the Ottoman periods. In years of good fortune, they unearth seals, broken pottery, and occasional pieces of jewelry. In the popular imagination, however, the foreigners must come for gold. As a result, archeological pillaging constitutes a widespread crime.

Although desert palaces of the Umayyads and the Byzantine mosaics at Madaba constitute a priceless treasure, the most impressive ruins date from the Roman era. Now the scene of a cultural festival, the columns, buildings, streets and amphitheater of Jerash rank as one of the Empire's best preserved cities outside Italy. By contrast, Semitic Nabateans carved residences and tombs in the nearly vertical limestone cliffs of a narrow gorge. The home of enterprising merchants, Petra flourished for about 200 years after 100 BC. Already in decline by the Arab conquest, it became a lost city, rediscovered only in the 19th century. Tourists today endure sand and sunshine to marvel at the intricately carved columns, the splendor of sunlight on rose-colored sandstone, and carved channels that brought water from a distant spring.

Universal, compulsory education through six elementary and three preparatory ("junior high") years has almost been attained, partly due to facilities provided for children by the UN Relief and Works Agency for Palestine Refugees. The quality of instruction tends to be good, if traditional, in Arabic language and literature, as well as in mathematics, where Jordanian test scores approached U.S. levels.

The University of Jordan opened on the outskirts of Amman in 1963, and remains the most prestigious in the country. Yarmuk University was established at Irbid in 1976, while the 1980s saw the beginnings of Mu'ta University in the south. In the 1990s, numerous private colleges and universities sprouted across the landscape, often to serve students whose families had lived in the Gulf States.

The modern culture of Jordan is essentially similar to that found in Syria and parts of Lebanon, with stronger nomadic and Saudi influences in the eastern and southern deserts. Nevertheless, observers often notice differences in Jordan, including greater respect for standing in line and obeying traffic regulations.

For most inhabitants, entertainment means spending time with friends and relatives, typically in segregated circles of men and women, drinking coffee and tea. Entertainment may also mean watching television; some Bedouin tents even boast a set. One key difference from American customs is the relative absence of single men and women mingling together. Romances are rarely conducted openly, and few girls or women would consider going to the movies without a group of relatives or friends. A wide variety of sports attract some enthusiasts, but in a small country there are no professional teams. Soccer is played at the high school level and by some men's teams.

Hospitality in a Jordanian family.

Economy: A century ago life in Jordan revolved around nomadic and semi-nomadic herding and farming, with a handful of small towns. Today, some herders do remain, and Prince Hasan bin Talal's Badia project attempts to encourage ecologically sound ways of life. Where rainfall and irrigation permit, settled farmers cultivate a variety of crops, ranging from grains and other staples to tomatoes, melons and warm-weather vegetables. Agricultural exports account for around one-fifth the total, but many foods must be imported. The climate and soil usually ensure that farmers, some of them tenants paying one-third of the crop to the landlord, achieve only a modest standard of living. After independence the government undertook a series of irrigation projects and other assistance for agriculture, particularly the East Ghor Project to use water from the Yarmuk River for farms in the Jordan Valley.

Water Shortages

Given the frequent pattern of several consecutive years of low rainfall, Jordan often faces prolonged and devastating droughts. Wheat and other crops that depend on rainfall fail, and many herders lack water for their flocks to drink and stubble for them to eat. Piped water in Amman becomes highly contaminated with bacteria and smells foul. Even parts of the capital city receive tap water only one day per week during the summer

In the short term, little can alleviate a water shortage shared with neighboring countries. Irrigation-based agriculture, which accounts for 75% of water use, may need to be curtailed. In King Abdullah's words, "Drinking water remains the most essential."

For the longer term, the Wahdah Dam project with Syria on the Yarmuk River may provide the expected 50 million cubic meters of water to Amman and to agriculture in the Jordan valley, but it will not satisfy the country's needs. Indeed, small Syrian dams upstream threaten to divert much of the expected flow. The Disy aquifer deep in the southeastern desert has been tapped, but it is a non-renewable resource.

Proposals exist to desalinize seawater in the valley south of the Dead Sea. However, that source of fresh water will be distant, expensive, and possibly nuclear-powered. It will also require international cooperation. Under the auspices of the World Bank, Jordan, Israel and the Palestinians signed an agreement in 2013 to construct a desalination plant near Aqaba, partly to supply Israel's city of Eilat. In return, far to the north Israel will transfer water to both the Palestinian territories and Jordan. To test the effects of replenishing the Dead Sea with water from the Red Sea, brine from the desalination plant will be piped to the Dead Sea.

Unlike its Arab neighbors to the northeast and south, Jordan contains no significant oil deposits. The country plays a modest role as a regional trade and commercial center, partly because its drier, cooler climate contrasts favorably with the Gulf, partly because Westerners find their lifestyles less restricted and Jordanians hospitable.

Besides encouraging trade and tourism, economic development projects have included exploiting the phosphate deposits that account for about 25% of the nation's exports. Ambitious plans also exist to exploit the Dead Sea for potash.

The economy has alternately suffered and prospered because of international events. Disputes with Syria often cut access to the Mediterranean. War with Israel in 1967 inflicted 400,000 new refugees, the collapse of tourism, and the loss of the most highly-developed portion of the kingdom, which accounted for 40% of GNP. Financial aid rewarded Jordan's rejection of the Camp David Agreement (1978), and the economy grew at 10% annually. While many Jordanians (330,000 in 1988) worked abroad, often as skilled professionals in oil-exporting countries, some 200,000 other Arabs filled low-paying jobs in Jordan.

The collapse of world oil prices in 1986 initiated an era of economic retrenchment. Aid from Arab oil exporters fell, and job prospects weakened abroad. Interest and repayment on the foreign debt soared, and foreign exchange reserves fell. The dinar fell steeply against the dollar, losing as much as 50% of its value in one year. Thus, by early 1989 several economic difficulties hit simultaneously: lower aid, debt repayment, precarious reserves, inflation, rising imports, and a budget deficit surpassing 20% of GNP (the U.S. then: 2–3%). Clearly Jordanians had lived beyond their means, and could no longer borrow to do so.

Although the government responded with economically-reasonable measures such as higher indirect taxes, cuts in subsidies, and canceling new weapons purchases, popular resistance led to riots and political change (see History). Friendly Arab nations responded with promises of modest aid, and rescheduled debt repayments. The cabinet cut spending for investment projects, and devoted more to debt repayment. In these ways the country survived the immediate crisis, only to suffer lost subsidies and disrupted trade during the Gulf War.

Flooded with hundreds of thousands of new Palestinian refugees, this time from the Gulf, the economy recovered surprisingly rapidly after 1991. Construction boomed, as former workers in the Gulf invested their savings in homes, offices, and apartments. Foreign exchange reserves rose, the economy briefly grew rapidly (over 5% per year), and yet inflation remained modest.

For the medium-term, however, Jordan lost its major export market, Iraq, to UN sanctions. The lost transit earnings themselves reached billions of dollars. Despite fanfare and hopes, peace with Israel brought no great economic dividend. In the late 1990s the country entered a significant recession. Unfortunately, economic policy could not be used to restore output. Fiscal policy was immobilized: massive budget deficits, covered partly by foreign aid, marked good years as well as bad. Monetary policy was equally ineffective: a rapid increase in the money supply would lead the wealthy to send it abroad, before the *dinar* fell in value. As an importer of natural gas and petroleum, the country suffered again when oil prices rose in 2008, requiring 20% of GDP to pay for energy imports.

With a rapidly-growing workforce, the economy must grow by 5%–7% annually to create the number of jobs needed for those newly seeking work. However, after 1996, the population grew faster than the economy, and by 2002 total unemployment perhaps reached 25% of the labor force, and then remained very high.

A free trade agreement signed with the U.S. provides easier access for Jordanian goods, especially textiles produced in Qualified Industrial Zones using some Israeli inputs. In recent years these exports grew rapidly, and the zones employ 35,000 workers. However, Jordanians apparently lack the skills or the desires to work in textile factories, and about 75% of the employees come from South Asia and China.

The recent discovery of substantial uranium deposits in the desert south of Amman offers the possibility of creating a nuclear industry that could generate electricity, power desalination and irrigation projects, and export nuclear fuel. However, the U.S. generally opposes the spread of nuclear enrichment facilities, and Israel may also raise objections behind the scenes to the construction of civilian nuclear power plants.

Arab hospitality quickly means hot tea. Photo by Michael Russell

The Future: Effective and likable, King Abdullah rules with the assistance of trusted friends, through a parliamentary system that magnifies the votes of sympathetic communities and minimizes votes cast for opposition parties. Aspiring to lead a country that is "secure, stable, and prosperous," he taps the fears of middle-class Jordanians who fear the disorder of the Arab Spring.

The young and often unemployed protesters make three crucial demands: jobs, ending corruption, and an elected prime minister. Given world economic conditions, the political and economic reforms necessary to meet those demands will block the aspirations of the monarchy's traditional supporters.

The conflict in neighboring Syria may paradoxically unite Jordanians of many reluctant ideologies behind its moderate monarch. The costs of revolution are visible in the death and destruction of the nightly news, prompting many who might otherwise desire radical change to find comfort in security and stability. Once again, an international crisis has strengthened the domestic role of Jordan's king.

As a former special forces commander, King Abdullah recognizes the dangers posed by the regional goals of al-Dawla al-Islamiyya fi al-Iraq wa al-Sham, known variously in the West by the initials *ISIS (Islamic State in Iraq and (Greater) Syria)* or *ISIL (Islamic State in Iraq and the Levant)*. Infamous for its war crimes in Syria and rapid conquest of most of Sunni Iraq, ISIS clearly considers Jordan a part of its realm. Expect Jordan to halt any attacks on its territory promptly and vigorously.

The State of Kuwait

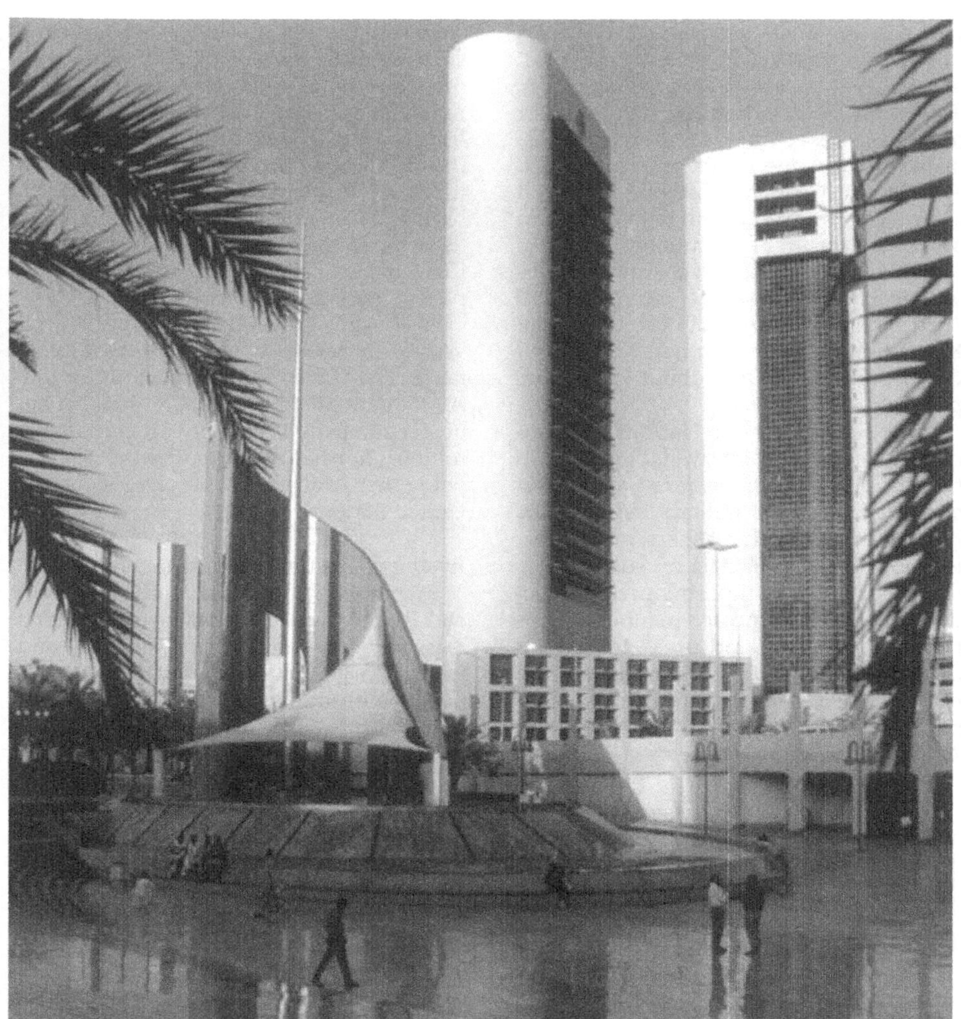

Luxury Hotels in Kuwait City

Area: 6880 sq. mi. (17,819 sq. km.; estimates differ).
Population: 4 million (under 40% native Kuwaiti).
Capital City: Kuwait City (1.7 million).
Climate: Very hot except for a short comfortable winter, which usually brings a few inches of rain.
Neighboring Countries: Saudi Arabia (South) and Iraq (North).
Time Zone: GMT +3.
Official Language: Arabic.
Other Principal Tongues: Persian and English.
Ethnic Background: Overwhelmingly Arab, with communities of Persians, Indians and Pakistanis.
Principal Religion: Islam.
Chief Commercial Products: Crude oil and refined products.
Major Trading Partners: Japan, U.K., U.S., Netherlands, Italy, Germany, South Korea and Singapore.
Currency: Kuwaiti Dinar (= 1000 fils).
Former Colonial Status: British Protectorate (1914–1961).
Independence Day: June 19, 1961.
Chief of State: Sheikh Sabah al-Ahmad al-Sabah, *Emir,* or Ruler.
Head of Government: Sheikh Jaber Al-Mubarak Al-Sabah, Prime Minister (2013).
National Flag: Three horizontal stripes of green, white and red, with a black trapezoid at the pole.
Gross Domestic Product: $185 billion (at current prices); $161 billion (Purchasing Power Parity).
GDP per capita: $40,200 (PPP).

Kuwait (pronounced *Kwait*) is a tract of flat desert at the head of the Arab (Persian) Gulf. There are only a few natural oases in the country and no significant supply of fresh water for the city of Kuwait, which gave its name to the state.

Most of the population lives in the modern suburbs, a vivid change from the old town of mud houses that existed a generation ago. The wealth produced by oil attracted hundreds of thousands of immigrants, who with their descendants amount to over 60% of the population. The Arab world, especially the nations from Egypt to Syria, provided teachers, engineers, doctors, office staff, and skilled workers. Sharing language (but not dialect), culture and usually religion with native Kuwaitis, before 1990 these immigrants formed a majority of the population.

Aside from some Iranians, the other immigrants present a physical contrast. Indians, Pakistanis, and other Asians fill service jobs, and even build *dhows,* the boats that for generations established Kuwait as a trading center and base for pearl diving. The few European and American expatriates work in the oil industry and hold scattered positions in finance and commerce.

History: Although ancient ruins on Failaka island show human settlements thousands of years ago, for centuries the inhabitants were essentially nomadic. Then, in 1756, Bani Utbah families of the Aniza tribe from central Arabia settled and built a fort where the city of Kuwait now stands. In Arabic, Kuwait means "Little Fort," and the little collection of mud huts, benefiting from a natural harbor, grew into a trading outpost and pearl-diving center. It eventually came to possess a defensive wall.

The ruling family of Kuwait descended from the first ruler, and carries his name, al-Sabah (pronounced es-sabah). Though formally titled emir (prince), the ruler and other important members commonly use the honorary Arab title of sheikh. Arab custom and a tradition of consultation limited the sheikh's autocratic powers, and senior men in the extended family selected the most appropriate successor. Because the early emirs proved to be long-lived, there was less opportunity for interference by the swiftly-growing Ottoman Empire, which claimed the territory as part of the province of Basra.

At the end of the 19th century, Emir Mubarak faced a critical decision. Fearing the increased ability of the Ottoman Empire to rule its distant territories, in 1899 he negotiated a secret treaty with Britain that placed Kuwait under its protection. Then, when the Ottoman Empire entered World War I in 1914, Britain easily declared Kuwait a protectorate. The Sabah family retained internal authority over the town, which remained an uninviting and lonely little trading center.

On the death of Sheikh Mubarak in 1915, the succession passed to each of his sons, Jabir and Salim. This established a pattern of the succession, alternating between their two families. Thus, until 2005, a "crown prince" was not the son of the current emir, but rather a cousin who

Kuwait

The late Sheikh Jabir al-Sabah

traced his paternal ancestry through a different line.

As geologists searched for oil deposits near the Gulf, British and American companies formed the Kuwait Oil Company and received a concession from the Emir. The company began drilling for oil in 1936, and soon discovered some of the richest deposits in the world. Exports began after World War II, and oil production and revenues soon made a startling impact on the dusty little town as it began the awkward change into a large, modern city.

Sheikh Abdullah al-Sabah became ruler in 1950. A benevolent monarch, he presided over the early period of economic growth. He initiated the policy of using the fabulous oil revenues for the benefit of all through a program of public works. In spite of this, much of the money was squandered.

The British protectorate ended in 1961, when Kuwait became independent. President Qasim of Iraq immediately claimed the state, threatened to invade, and blocked Kuwait's membership in the UN. However, Britain remained an ally, and its troops returned quickly, until Arab League forces replaced them. After the overthrow of Qasim in 1963, the *Ba'thist* government in Iraq recognized Kuwait's independence, reportedly in an arrangement involving money. Several treaties followed between the two states. One difficulty remained the boundary. The 1932 demarcation agreement between (British-protected) Kuwait and (British-influenced) Iraq contained neither map nor detailed descriptions, so that Kuwaiti territory began "south of the southernmost palm tree at Safwan."

After independence, Kuwait moved towards democracy. Elections in 1961 selected twenty men to serve with members of the ruling family in a Constituent Assembly that would draft a constitution. Their 1962 Constitution retained the Emir as the chief executive of government, assisted by a prime minister and cabinet. An elected National Assembly received the power to make recommendations and serve as a forum of discussion. The electorate, however, extended only to males whose family possessed citizenship in 1920. The Constitution even prohibited Kuwaiti-born males of a non-Kuwaiti father from voting. Only about 10% of the population could vote.

In its early years the National Assembly worked reasonably well. However, in the late 1960s the ruler, faced a series of difficulties—foreign military tensions, the hijacking of Kuwaiti airliners, and terrorist violence. He reacted by suspending the Assembly and imposing press restrictions. This halted inconvenient criticisms from its members, and press censorship discouraged unflattering commentary by journalists. Kuwait reverted to government by decree, in common with the other Arab Gulf states.

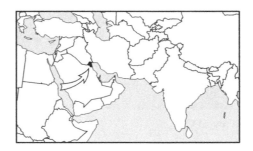

During the 1980s, the war between Iran and Iraq pitted two ideological opponents of monarchy against each other: socialist republican Iraq against Islamic republican Iran. Fearing Islamic revolution more than the traditional threats of its large Arab neighbor, Kuwait loaned more than $10 billion to Iraq interest-free, and sold oil on its behalf against promise of repayment. Kuwait also allowed Iraqi military supplies to pass through its territory.

When the combatants attacked neutral vessels in the Gulf, Kuwait sought assistance. The U.S. provided naval protection. After an Iranian missile attack on the main oil terminal in 1987, Kuwait purchased military hardware and sought closer ties with other Arab Gulf states, Egypt and the United States.

Invasion, Occupation and Liberation

After the 1988 cease-fire between Iran and Iraq, popular protests swelled among Kuwaitis anxious to end censorship and restore parliament, suspended since 1986. Some politicians even questioned the royal family's role in a stock market crash. At this, Sheikh Jabir balked, and police used unexpected violence on the wealthiest demonstrators in the world. In 1990 he ordered elections for a *Shura*, a consultative council rather than the legislature. Members of the former Assembly boycotted the elections, complaining that the *Shura* "lacked teeth," and condemned the arrest of critics.

In July 1990 President Saddam Hussein fiercely denounced Kuwait, warning that "cutting necks is better than cutting the means of living." Iraq complained, first, that Kuwait had exceeded its OPEC quota

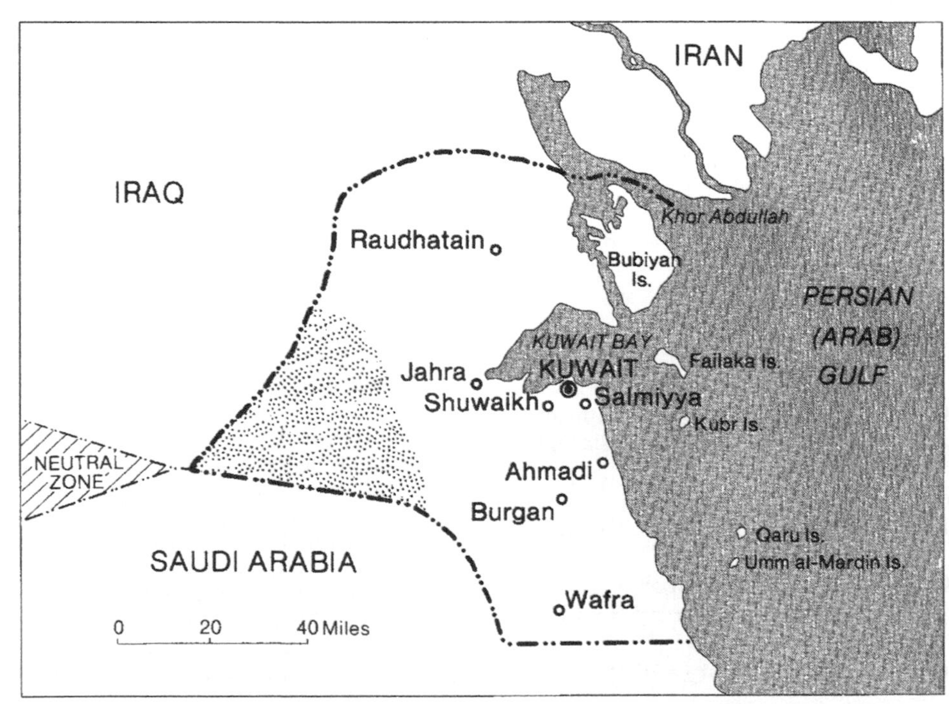

Kuwaiti women weep at the graves of relatives killed by the Iraqi army during the 7-month occupation

AP/Wide World Photo

and thus (possibly) drove down oil prices. After the long war with Iran, Iraq could not afford the loss.

Second, Iraq demanded money: billions in aid besides writing off the wartime loans, plus compensation for $2.4 billion worth of Iraqi oil allegedly pumped from the Rumaila field that straddles the border. Finally, Iraq demanded long-term leases on the islands of Bubiyan and Warba, to protect its naval base and access to the Gulf.

Hours after Saddam's diplomats suspended negotiations, Iraqi forces attacked Kuwait. By nightfall, Iraqi troops had crushed all opposition. Sheikh Jabir and the crown prince barely escaped; other members of the ruling family were arrested.

Initially Iraq claimed it had acted to support Kuwaiti revolutionaries. However, courageous Kuwaiti opposition leaders refused to collaborate. Deprived of any Kuwaiti authenticity, Iraq annexed Kuwait six days after the invasion (see Iraq: History).

In exile, the government reformed. The Kuwait Investment Office and other resources in London funded the government and hundreds of thousands of exiled citizens. The government lent to Kuwaiti banks, preserving them from default, and promised $5 billion to the coalition forces gathering against Iraq. Further billions were pledged to countries suffering severe hardship from the invasion and economic sanctions against Iraq.

To unite Kuwait's citizens, Sheikh Jabir met with opposition figures, and the crown prince pledged trust in the 1962 Constitution and parliament. For its part, the opposition agreed to support the dynasty.

Meanwhile, Iraqi forces plundered Kuwait: gold and foreign currency worth billions, truckloads of consumer goods, cars stolen from the streets. Hospital equipment and library books disappeared; even traffic lights were stolen, along with cadavers from the medical school. Iraqi university officials apparently divided the academic spoils before shipping them home. The vast booty depressed prices in Baghdad.

Such pillage greatly encouraged resistance by the 200,000 citizens who remained. Government employees stopped work, and at night, defiant women shouted "Allahu Akbar" from rooftops, implying that Allah, not Saddam Hussein, was great. A resistance movement helped subvert Iraqi rules and aided foreigners sought as hostages by the Iraqis. Equally important, it maintained morale and social order.

In response, the Iraqi forces deported thousands; other thousands were executed and apparently buried in mass graves. Several hundred deportees remained missing two decades after the conflict.

As coalition forces neared victory in the 1991 war to liberate Kuwait, Iraqi forces deliberately sabotaged industry and the environment. Eight million barrels of crude oil were dumped into the Gulf, creating one of the greatest oil slicks in history. A decade later, local coral reefs had still not recovered.

Iraqi units also set afire 732 of the nation's 950 oil wells. The fires burned up to 6 million barrels of oil daily, about 10% of all petroleum consumed world-wide, and their smoke damaged neighboring countries with soot, acid rain, and other pollution. Led by the legendary Red Adair, teams from nine nations extinguished the fires far ahead of schedule. However, the escaping oil reduced underground pressure in the oilfields, thus permanently reducing the nation's oil potential.

Liberated by coalition forces, Kuwaitis rejoiced. However, their euphoria soon yielded to concern. Destroyed water mains and electrical generating plants took time to repair, despite stockpiled equipment and parts. Within days, leaflets condemned the government for the lack of food and utilities, apparently delayed because of bureaucratic fumbling. Critics demanded the ending of martial law, a broader-based cabinet, and restoring the Constitution. In response, Sheikh Jabir promised to restore the National Assembly.

Searching for Security: Foreign Relations

After 1990, Kuwait's search for security surpassed many traditional concerns. The post-war demarcation of the border placed several oil wells, a ship channel, and the major Iraqi naval base within Kuwait. Though approved by Saddam Hussein's rubber-stamp parliament in 1994, international disputes over the new border seem inevitable.

Sheikh Nasser Muhammad Al-Ahmad Al-Sabah, Prime Minister 2006–12

Copyright: Brian McMorrow

After its liberation, Kuwait spent more per capita on arms than any other country. Defense spending exceeded 20% of the total budget, but it will take time for troops to master the tanks, aircraft and missile boats.

Seeking allies from outside the Gulf region, Kuwait signed a defense pact with the U.S. in 1991 (renewed in 2001) that covers joint training and military exercises, as well as U.S. stockpiles of equipment. Similar arrangements provide French and British support in time of conflict.

In a rare move for an Arab country, during a 1998 crisis over UN inspection in Iraq, Kuwait agreed to let UN forces use its airbases. After U.S. and British bombers used those bases to attack Iraq in 1999, Saddam Hussein denounced Kuwait's sovereignty. However, threatened by a U.S. invasion, in 2002 he softened this stand and even returned some of the seized National Archives.

Alone in the Arab world, Kuwait publicly backed the U.S.-led attack on Iraq in 2003. Most Kuwaitis delighted in the destruction of Saddam Hussein's regime in Baghdad, but the thousands of foreign troops passing through the emirate presented targets for international terrorists and grounds for Islamic criticism. In 2005, several fatal shoot-outs occurred as security forces attempted to capture Muslim militants, some of them foreigners. Partly in response, the government announced moves to curb militancy by removing intolerant school textbooks and closing unofficial mosques.

The U.S. defeat of Saddam Hussein's Iraq ended the constant threat of an Iraqi invasion and promised international calm if good relations can be maintained with Iran. This may reduce the need to host U.S.

troops and thus ease the tensions that inevitably occur when American troops, and their families, live in a strict Muslim state.

Domestic Politics after Liberation

The 1992 National Assembly elections proved honest and even festive. Given the few thousand male voters in each two-member district, the numerous candidates met the electorate at *diwaniyas* (see Culture) to chat about politics and society. Lacking political parties, voters could choose between candidates sympathetic to the ruling family or opposition candidates reflecting three broad groupings: the *Democratic Forum* (secular liberals), Islamists, and traditional politicians. During the following years, this "Opposition," proved to be little more than unstructured and shifting alliances. Though it represented a majority on some issues, it could not form the government, and its options were, and remain, limited: the grilling of an unpopular minister, and even voting no-confidence in the individual.

As a result of the system, in practice, the Assembly has proved a debating society incapable of effective action. It debated but could not remedy challenges common to many Gulf states: severe budget deficits in years of low oil prices ($5.6 billion in 1994, some 20% of GDP), an over-large bureaucracy, and inefficient government-owned companies. It delayed approving the vote for women until 2005. However, it could attempt a motion of no confidence because free copies of the *Qur'an* had been distributed despite a missing verse. (Muslims believe the book is the uncreated Word of God, so such an error is more significant than, say, a printer missing a few verses of the Bible).

In 2006, Sheikh Jabir died. The planned succession faltered when the crown prince proved too ill to recite the oath of office. After a few days of uncertainty, both a family majority and the National Assembly elected Prime Minister Sheikh Sabah, the younger half-brother of Sheikh Jabir, as emir. He in turn chose his brother, Sheikh Nawaf, as crown prince, and his nephew, Sheikh Nasser, as prime minister. These appointments destroyed any semblance of alternation between the al-Ahmad and the al-Salem branches of the family.

Reformers in the Assembly and Kuwaitis in general welcomed the promise of a more active leadership. However, within months the long-simmering demands for electoral reform suddenly caught the public's attention. Reformers claimed that, in the absence of political parties, the system of 25 two-member electoral districts encouraged corruption, exaggerated tribal influence, and favored local notables, "service politicians," concerned with petty local issues. Both the government and loosely-linked opposition recognized the need for reform. The cabinet favored 10 districts, the opposition, just five.

Adopting the slogan "5 for Kuwait," young and educated activists launched a campaign of public protest to demand change. Focusing on just one issue, the activists communicated by text messaging and blogs, and cut strips of orange cloth for sympathizers to wear. Night-time demonstrations outside the National Assembly surprised the nation. Orange-clad protestors filled the Assembly's visitor galleries. Emboldened, the Assembly demanded, without precedent, to question the prime minister, and opposition members walked out. A constitutional crisis threatened. To defuse it, in 2006 Emir Sabah called early elections. For the first time women, could vote and run for office.

The results disappointed women candidates. Women's issues such as the financial problems of divorcées, widows and children, the unequal treatment of women married to non-Kuwaitis, and health care, received less attention than redistricting and alleged government corruption. Not a single woman won.

Sheikh Nasser, the emir's nephew, again formed a cabinet and accepted the proposed five electoral districts, but within months conciliation failed on other issues. The Assembly's opposition members continued attacks on the government, but the emir and crown prince were constitutionally protected from criticism. Rather than face questions about the economy and corruption, the prime minister resigned again.

The 2009 elections provided a substantially different set of victors. Dr. Maasouma Al-Mubarak, the first woman to hold a cabinet position, received the most votes in the first district, and three other women—all holders of doctorates from

> At first sight, the emir's "one-man, one-vote" decree seems reasonable. Indeed, many well-educated Kuwaitis defend it as the sort of practice common in democracies. However, because Kuwait does not have single-member constituencies, the similarities are misleading.
>
> Each of the country's five electoral districts selects 10 members of the National Assembly (or parliament). By allowing voters only one vote in an election for 10 seats, the emir's decree clearly minimizes tactical voting. It also prevents election alliances that resemble political parties. Less evidently, the single vote encourages corruption among the lower tiers of candidates, where an extra million funneled to the right candidate to spend on receptions and posters might mean ninth place instead of eleventh. Under the guise of innocent democracy, then, the single-vote decision gravely harms the development of a functioning democracy.

KUWAIT'S 4 WOMEN ELECTED TO THE NATIONAL ASSEMBLY

Dr. Maasouma Al-Mubarak

Dr. Rola Dashti

Dr. Salwa al-Jassar

Dr. Aseel al-Awadhi

A Kuwaiti oilfield worker kneels for midday prayers near a burning oil well
AP/Wide World Photo

U.S. universities—also won seats in the Assembly. Their gains came at the expense of Islamic conservatives. For the first time, this parliament succeeded in grilling the prime minister.

Denunciations of corruption and mismanagement exploded in 2011 when newspaper accounts alleged payments—apparently bribes—deposited in the bank accounts of some members of parliament. The amounts were substantial: two members reportedly received $92 million between them. Protestors stormed parliament, and its members scheduled a grilling of Sheikh Nasser about the allegations. Recognizing the need for change, the emir appointed another relative as prime minister, Jaber Al-Mubarak Al-Sabah. However, with the opposition sensing victory and power, his first months in office proved difficult. Once again the emir, Sheikh Sabah, dissolved the legislature.

With corruption and government failure so obvious, the campaign for the 2012 election was filled with invective and hate. The opposition triumphed, winning about two-thirds of the seats. Islamists captured some previously-Shi'a seats and defeated every single woman. Both groups had previously been considered too sympathetic to the ruling family. Islamists then began enacting legislation for their preferred causes, such as amending the constitution to make the Shari'a the only source of Kuwaiti law, establishing "morality police" to regulate public behavior, and setting death as the maximum penalty for blasphemy.

Within months, the constitutional court ruled the February 2012 elections illegal on a technicality, and restored the previous parliament. However, its members could not establish a quorum, and Sheikh Sabah called new elections for December 2012—the second within the calendar year. In the absence of parliament, he also decreed a single choice for voters "to preserve national unity" (see box).

Angered by the single-vote decree, protests flared. Between 50,000 and 150,000 demonstrators attempted to march on government buildings; police required stun guns and tear gas to block them. The former opposition MP who had received the most votes nationwide, Musallam al-Barrak, warned Sheikh Sabah that he would not be allowed to "take Kuwait into the abyss of autocracy." Opposition leaders decided to boycott the elections; Al-Barrak, strongly Islamist in his politics, was later arrested for threatening the emir.

The election results proved about as expected. Due to the boycott, with under 40% of the electorate bothering to vote, Sunni Islamists lost nearly 20 seats, which went to Shi'a lawmakers, women, and independents sympathetic to business. The National Assembly became less contentious, although some ministers were grilled. Prices on the stock exchange climbed, buoyed by expectations the cabinet might actually address long-standing financial problems.

However, for the second time within a year, the constitutional court declared the most recent election unconstitutional, and also confirmed the legality of the Emir's "one-man one-vote" ruling. Islamists and liberal therefore boycotted the new election, which took place during Ramadan/July 2013. Surprisingly, despite the boycott, 52% of the electorate voted, choosing a new assembly that contained many new faces, among them a number of liberals and tribesmen loyal to the regime. Days later, Sheikh Sabah initiated improved relations when he pardoned those convicted of insulting him. The era of good relations lasted most of a year, when some parliamentarians demanded to question the prime minister over corruption. Little progress was made on the 2010 development plan.

In 2014 a video circulated that allegedly showed former senior officials and one member of the Sabah family plotting to overthrow the government. Although the speaker of the National Assembly denounced the video as a forgery, it was referred to the public prosecutor and discussed in a closed session of parliament. Discussion of the matter was forbidden by both the public and social media.

Culture: Kuwait shares the basic culture of its neighbors. Until the affluence resulting from oil production, its population of less than 100,000 wandered with flocks, engaged in trading in the town, or worked as seamen on the sailing vessels that plied as far as India and East Africa. Its culture was indistinguishable from that of southern Iraq or eastern Saudi Arabia. Some of its inhabitants were the *bidoun*, literally, "those without," desert Arabs whose families wandered across national boundaries in the region. The *bidoun* lacked citizenship because ancestral residence could not be proven.

Oil wealth following World War II changed the face of the town and the people. The poverty-stricken *badu* virtually disappeared, as did the Kuwaiti sailors, while poor shopkeepers became wealthy businessmen. Mud huts gave way to air conditioned houses, often of palatial proportions. Kuwaitis often hold the world's top ranking in ownership of many consumer items, from cars to boats to electronics.

Non-Kuwaiti professionals and even workers have benefited from free medical service, educational facilities and other welfare programs. The educational system in Kuwait is the best financed in the world; students are not only provided with free education, including books and other equipment, but are given at least one free meal a day. Secondary school students receive living allowances.

The University of Kuwait, founded in 1966, grew to be one of the best in the region, with the pre-war student body numbering over 10,000. About half of the students came from Kuwait, a quarter from other Gulf states and the rest from various Asian and African nations. The faculty was drawn from Egypt, Syria, Iraq and other Arab countries. In recent years, a number of private colleges and universities have been established, some with American links.

For the past twenty years, women have formed a majority of the graduates at the University of Kuwait. This achievement reflects the surprising roles held by women in the country's liberal professions and business community, and provides the educated women who enable that role to continue. Kuwaiti women drive, shop, and otherwise play a much more public role than women in other Gulf countries, and in 2009 the constitutional court ruled that married women may obtain passports without the consent of their husbands.

In a society without alcohol or nightclubs, and with social restrictions separating men and women, *diwaniyas* play an important role in Kuwaiti society. Held in the relaxed atmosphere of private homes, with segregation by gender, these evening gatherings bring together the relatively small number of citizens. In recent years they provided forums to discuss political and social issues, and increasingly seem to take the function of political parties, which are banned.

Economy: Eighty years ago Kuwaitis earned their living by pearling, nomadic herding, and trading with sailing vessels. By 1990, they became the first country in history whose earnings on foreign investments exceeded those of trade. The key to the transformation was petroleum. After reconstruction, it regained its position as the source of almost all (roughly 95%) exports, nearly half (45%) of the GDP, and most government revenue.

Despite its small size—about that of New Jersey—Kuwait sits atop the Burgan field, one of the largest oil fields in the world. The country traditionally ranks fifth in world oil reserves, about 10% of the total, slightly below Iran and the United Arab Emirates. Given the small population, a very modest share of global oil output provides one of the highest per capita incomes.

Oil revenues allow Kuwaitis to live in substantial comfort despite the climate. In a desert land, they each consume an average of 22,000 gallons of fresh water annually. While some springs have been tapped, five giant desalination plants provide most of the flow. Brackish water from springs serves for street cleaning, livestock watering, and when mixed with fresh water, for irrigation.

That any agricultural production takes place is surprising, given wealth and climate, and government aid is critical. Besides an annual stipend, farmers receive interest-free loans, seeds and other supplies at 50% of cost, and subsidies for drilling wells.

After immediate development needs were cared for, in 1966 Kuwait established the Reserve Fund for Future Generations. Its income from oil revenues was to be invested but not consumed until the 21st century. In 1990 its assets approached $60 billion, or over $100,000 per citizen. Additional government funds brought total assets to roughly $100 billion. So large were the accounts that the Kuwait Investment Office (KIO) found it difficult to invest the money abroad without arousing opposition. For example, in 1988 it purchased nearly 22% of the shares of British Petroleum, but was forced by the Thatcher government to reduce its holding to less than 10%.

The Iraqi occupation in 1990–1991 imposed enormous economic devastation on the small country. Wartime expenses, subsidies to Coalition allies, and the costs of reconstruction cost about $50 billion. Deliberate sabotage damaged the entire oil industry, including all three refineries and almost every well. Seeping and burning wells destroyed an estimated $20 billion of crude petroleum. However, reconstruction moved rapidly, and both refining and

oil exports resumed in 1991. The pace of reconstruction surprised the experts, and the next year oil production rose to its pre-invasion quota. By 1993, other OPEC nations, who had waived Kuwait's quota, demanded output cuts in an effort to balance world supply and demand.

Revenue from oil sales helped fund reconstruction costs, estimated at $20 billion rather than the initial $60–$100 billion. By 1994, many major rebuilding projects had been completed and refinery capacity had climbed to 800,000 barrels per day. However, despite its greater OPEC quota, and oil revenues exceeding $10 billion annually, the government had to borrow massively to fund subsidies, the bureaucracy, and military rearmament.

The occupation raised anew the question of the economic future of Kuwait, and it cast doubt on its ability to survive as a workplace for foreigners (82% of the workforce). If the government reduces the number of foreigners permitted to work, citizens will then have to survive with fewer employees and servants. Kuwaiti women face traditional cultural objections to their working, but they now form about one-quarter of the indigenous workforce.

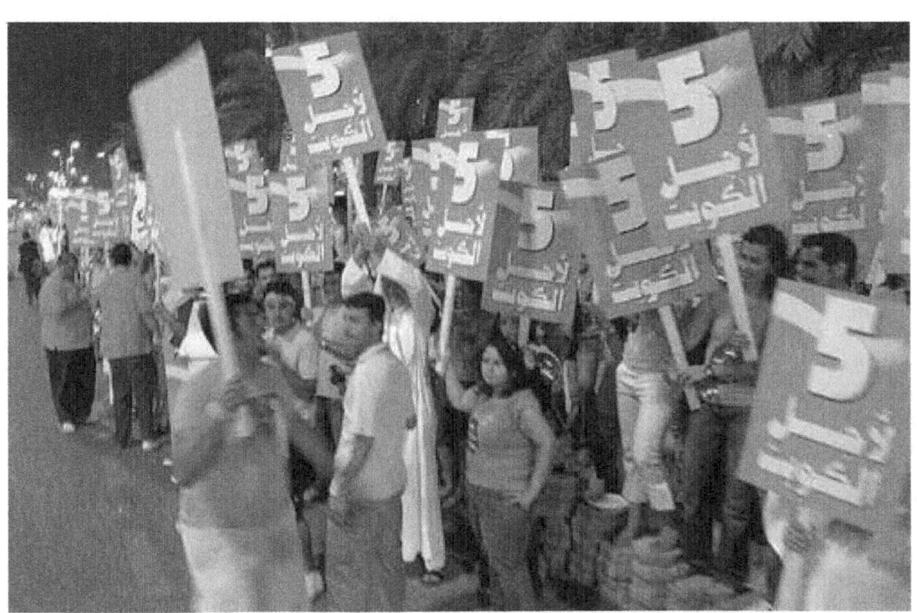

Dressed in orange and carrying signs proclaiming "5 for Kuwait," demonstrators pressured the cabinet to resign and call early elections, 2007.

The Future: News of a video of former senior officials plotting the government's overthrow greatly increases the level of political instability, just when a favorable National Assembly had reduced legislative demands for change. More than the balance of power between ruling family and legislature could be at stake if family members or trusted advisors appear among the plotters.

Expect to hear more from the traditional opposition, whose leaders no longer participate in parliament. The Opposition Coalition of Islamists, some liberals, and youth activists recently launched a "political reform project" that, while not demanding the ouster of the regime, seeks deep changes.

Given an aging ruler in neighboring Saudi Arabia, and a tottering cabinet in Iraq, perhaps the most appealing matter in foreign affairs is Iranian President Hassan Rouhani's desire for good relations with the Gulf's Arab states.

The Republic of Lebanon

The Souk al-Nasr, a colorful Beirut market, with beautiful materials, sacks of flour, exquisite handicrafts, and fresh vegetables.
AP/Wide World Photo

Area: 4,036 square miles (10,452 sq. km.).
Population: 4.5 million, including about 450,000 Palestinians but excluding 1 million Syrian refugees. Last census: 1929.
Capital City: Beirut (pop. about 1.6 million, plus suburbs).
Climate: Summers are hot and humid on the coast, cooler and drier in the mountains. Winters are mild on the coast, but colder and snowy in the high mountains. Rainfall is normally plentiful in winter, but rare in summer.
Neighboring Countries: Syria (North and East); Israel (South).
Time Zone: GMT +2. When it is noon Central Standard Time in the U.S., it is 8:00 P.M. in Lebanon.
Official Language: Arabic.
Other Principal Tongues: French, English and Armenian.
Ethnic Background: About 93% of the people are Arab, based on language. The largest cultural minority is the Armenians, who comprise about 6% of the population.
Principal Religions: Islam (more Shi'a than Sunni), Christianity (mainly Maronite and Greek Orthodox) and the Druze faith.
Chief Commercial Products: Citrus fruit, apples, olives, wheat, potatoes, tobacco, leather goods, vegetable oil, cotton textiles, cement and chemicals.
Major Trading Partners: Italy, United States, United Arab Emirates, France, Germany, Syria and Switzerland.
Currency: Lira or pound.
Former Colonial Status: French Mandate (1920–1943).
Independence Date: November 22, 1943.
Chief of State: None; Parliament is unable to elect a successor to Michel Suleiman.
Head of Government: Tammam Salam, Prime Minister (2013).
National Flag: Three horizontal stripes, with a green cedar tree centered on the wider central white stripe between two red ones.
Gross Domestic Product: $45.5 billion (at current prices); $68 billion (Purchasing Power Parity).
GDP per capita: $15,100 (PPP).

The smallest mainland nation of southwest Asia, Lebanon historically connected the interior of the *Fertile Crescent* with lands across the Mediterranean Sea. Over the centuries, ideas, (including the alphabet), the military (the Persian fleet against Greece) and a variety of products made the journey in one direction or the other. After World War II, Lebanon became an intellectual and commercial center for the entire Arab world, but disputes among its peoples—disputes that involved how closely it should link with the West or East—plunged the nation into a civil war that nearly destroyed it.

Four geographical zones run the length of the country from north to south and resemble layers of a sandwich. First, a narrow plain hugs the coast; the largest cities are all located in this zone. Moving inland, the slopes of Mount Lebanon (a range rather than one mountain), with peaks exceeding 9,000 feet above sea level, comprise the second zone.

On the inland side of the Lebanon range lies the third zone, the *Biqa'* (or Biqaa) valley, a plain up to 15 miles wide. Its rich soil and flat fields provide most of the country's grains and vegetables. The Litani, the only significant river entirely in Lebanon, flows southward through most of the plain before turning sharply to the west to empty into the Mediterranean. The Orontes River begins in the northern part of the Biqa' Plain and flows north into Syria.

The last and easternmost division is the Anti-Lebanon Mountains; these form the border with Syria on the east. Near the southern end of this range is Jabal al-Sheikh or Mount Hermon, a snow-capped peak visible in clear weather from the tropical Jordan Valley to the south. Lebanon has no desert.

Winter and early spring constitute the rainy season. Much of the country receives at least 30 inches of precipitation annually, some areas much more. Snowfall is often heavy in the higher mountains, making the area suitable for winter sports.

In their physical appearance, culture and linguistic dialects, the inhabitants resemble those of neighboring Syria. In both cases, the vicissitudes of history have left a variety of traits.

History: Homeland of the ancient Phoenicians, its strategic location made Lebanon a battleground in ancient times. Inscriptions at the Dog River commemorate conquerors ranging from Egyptian pharaohs and Babylonian kings to Roman emperors. The territory fell to the Ottoman Empire in 1516.

Given its rugged terrain, Mount Lebanon traditionally provided a haven for persecuted minorities, who often gained autonomy under their local leaders. Three religious communities dominated the mountains. The Maronite Christians in the north eventually linked with Roman Catholicism. In the center, the secretive Druze split from orthodox Islam in the Middle Ages. Like the Maronites, the Druze were uniquely Lebanese (see Culture). In the south and east, Shi'a Muslim villagers shared religious ideas and practices with fellow Arab Shi'a in Iraq.

During the 17th Century the powerful Druze chieftain Fakhr al-Din extended his control beyond Mount Lebanon to parts of Syria and Palestine, but conflict with the Sultan in Istanbul led to his execution. After years of little change, the 19th Century witnessed greater trade and missionary activity, especially schools. A decade of Egyptian occupation brought greater rights for Christians as well as (hated) conscription. After communal violence in 1860, to protect the remaining Maronites from further massacres and mistreatment, France landed troops, and forced the Ottoman Sultan to grant Mount Lebanon a special legal status under a Christian governor.

As European nations sought zones of influence in the Ottoman Empire, France's traditional protection of Roman Catholic Christians naturally led it to expand its contacts in Lebanon.

When Ottoman Turkey allied with Germany in World War I, its officials seized French documents that compromised many leading notables, both Christians and Muslims, and several were executed. As a further punishment, the Ottomans prohibited the transport of grain into Mount Lebanon, and thousands starved to death, particularly after an attack by locusts.

Secret wartime negotiations between Britain and France, formalized as the Sykes-Picot Agreement, assigned the coast and the Syrian interior to France. Thus, soon after British forces liberated the inhabitants from Ottoman troops in 1918, a French detachment landed in Beirut and occupied the coast and Mount Lebanon. However, they did not take control of the Arab-ruled Biqa' valley and Anti-Lebanon mountains until 1920, when a French invasion defeated the nationalist government in Damascus.

While the League of Nations prepared a mandate for the region, in 1920 the French High Commissioner divided Syrian territory into four districts. "Greater Lebanon" included the coast, Mount Lebanon itself, and the entire Biqa' plain. Nearly twice the size of Ottoman Mount Lebanon; its

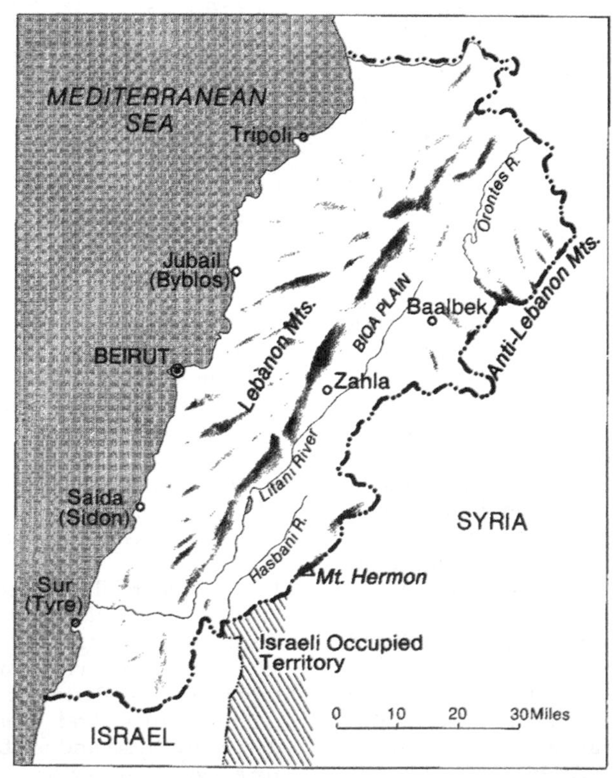

The cedars of Lebanon

population was evenly divided between Christians and Muslims. In 1926 France proclaimed this the Republic of Lebanon.

Public opinion divided sharply over the new state. Many Christians favored a separate Lebanon under French protection, thinking it would provide them political power and safety. However, most Muslim Lebanese opposed the mandate. Between 1926 and 1939, the occasional outbursts of violence against French rule proved local affairs, discouraged by concentrated French military forces in the country. The Lebanese government received internal autonomy subject to veto by the French High Commissioner, while France continued to control international relations.

After France surrendered to Nazi Germany, British and Free French troops invaded Lebanon and Syria in 1941, and the Free French commander afterwards proclaimed the two countries independent. However, in 1943 the French arrested the elected Lebanese president and his cabinet. This united Christian and Muslim politicians in favor of independence, and pressure from Great Britain and the United States forced France to free the officials and grant independence.

Traditional political leaders began maneuvering for the interests of their communities even before the French withdrew, and formalized the agreement as the National Pact. Broadly revered as the unwritten constitution, this stipulated a *Maronite* president, a *Sunni* Muslim prime minister and a *Shi'a* Muslim speaker of the parliament. Citizens of the various smaller religious groups were thus barred from the highest offices (see Politics). Unfortunately, Bishara al-Khuri, the first president after independence, manipulated the political system for corrupt ends. He was forced from office.

During the presidency of his successor, Camille Chamoun (1952–1958), Arab nationalist ideas associated with Egypt's President Nasser further stirred the tensions in Lebanese society. The champion of conservative Maronites who insisted that the Lebanese were not "Arabs," Chamoun sought support from the U.S. and from monarchial Arab regimes trying to stop Nasser's radical ideology from spreading.

With foreign money, some reportedly from the CIA, Chamoun organized the election of sympathetic candidates in the 1957 elections, filling the Chamber of Deputies with his men. He then proposed to change the constitution so he could have a second six-year term. This would have allowed him to orient Lebanon to the West, strengthen Maronite supremacy and subdue the opposition.

1958 Disturbances

Dissension caused by the president's actions led to a restrained civil war in 1958. This divided both the country and the capital city into zones controlled by local political bosses and their private armies. Muslims sympathetic with Pan-Arabism and Nasser fought Maronites sympathetic to Chamoun. The national army remained neutral, and used its strength to police danger zones and minimize conflicts.

After a revolution overthrew the pro-Western king of Iraq, at Chamoun's request U.S. Marines landed at Beirut, ostensibly to support Lebanon's independence from communist threats. Chamoun's attempt to garner further American support for his power play failed, however, and he left office when his term ended.

The crisis of 1958 settled none of the basic issues facing the country. When the Chamber of Deputies met to select a new president, opinion overwhelmingly favored Fu'ad Chehab, the army commander. A neutral and less partisan figure, Chehab's presided over the country's brief golden age of progress and tolerance. However, during the rule of his successors in the late 1960s and early 1970s, dissatisfactions smoldered, factionalism persisted, the gap between the rich and poor widened, and animosities grew. Handicapped by a lack of consensus regarding national goals and the virtual monopoly on power held by a few communal leaders, governments rarely acted positively or decisively.

Necessary steps were not taken. Lebanon was unable to impose fair taxation or finance free public education. Attempts to build a strong, unified army were blocked by leaders fearful that such a force might override their individual communities. In time, solutions might have been found, but regional issues forced their way into Lebanon, and its governments could never formulate a widely-accepted policy toward Palestinian activity within Lebanon.

Neutrality

After playing only a nominal role in the 1948 war with Israel, Lebanon's small military avoided the 1956 and 1967 conflicts. Soon afterward, however, the country became the hapless victim of Israeli reprisal raids against Palestinians who launched guerrilla raids into Israel from Lebanon (see Palestine: History). Both Palestinians and Israelis resorted to tactics directed at civilian targets, including an Israeli raid on Beirut airport that destroyed many of Lebanon's civilian airliners. Concerned about the reprisals and national sovereignty, but pressured by Arab states and political opinion among the growing Muslim majority, the government proved unable to assert control over the Palestinians.

By 1975, both society and government exhibited classic signs of failure. Assassinations and small-scale violence erupted between rival groups. Journalists were kidnapped. Armed Palestinian units operated freely in parts of the country, scrutinizing—and sometimes seizing—Lebanese travelers at checkpoints along roads and streets. In the atmosphere of lawlessness and disorder, frustration mounted. Slogans of the 1960s, suitably adapted, appeared on the walls, among them, "Lebanon: Love it or Leave it."

Militia and Proxy Warfare

As tensions rose, Maronite militias trained for battle, and political rallies featured armed supporters. Most Maronite leaders hoped to regain Maronite supremacy, restore order, and rid the country of all Palestinian fighters. In early 1975 Maronite militiamen attacked a bus loaded with Palestinians. Palestinian forces retaliated, and for 19 months, war engulfed the country and especially its capital region.

Described abroad as a struggle between Christians and Muslims, the fighting was not purely sectarian. Palestinian and leftist groups joined together and though overwhelmingly Muslim, they included a few Christians. Nevertheless, many civilians were murdered or maimed solely because of their religious identity, obvious usually from names and certified by the national identity card.

Foreign involvement added further complexity. Weapons, supplies, finances and advice fueled the conflict. Besides representing a struggle for power in Lebanon, the war served as a battlefield for the Arab struggle with Israel. To accomplish their national aims, first Syrian (1976), then Israeli (1978) troops invaded parts of Lebanon. Syria initially invaded to limit the Palestinians and Lebanese leftists, and relieve the Maronite forces. Other foreign troops played a peace-making role, with the United Nations (UNIFIL), in the South and the Arab League. Neither proved successful. By the early 1980s, however, violence became more infrequent, crossing the previously-deadly Green Line that divided Muslim and Christian Beirut became more common, and some attention focused on reconstruction.

Israel's War in Lebanon (1982)

Chaos returned, however, when Israel again invaded in 1982, publicly to gain "peace in Galilee" but actually to implement General Ariel Sharon's secret plans to destroy Palestinian military forces and create a zone of influence in Lebanon. The massive assault occupied the southern half of the country and besieged the capital. Saturation bombing ahead of the Israeli advance kept Israeli casualties to a minimum, but killed over 15,000 civilians. Material devastation was extensive; nearly a quarter of all buildings in Beirut were damaged. However, West Beirut did not fall. As its siege stalemated, international pressures grew on Israel, and negotiations enabled Palestinian forces to evacuate the city rather than surrender.

Through war and occupation, Lebanon's politicians struggled to function. With elections due for a new president, the Chamber of Deputies met, surrounded by Israeli soldiers and Maronite militiamen. Its members elected Bashir Gemayel, head of the right-wing *Phalangist Party* as president. Before he could take office, however, a massive bomb killed him at his headquarters, the work of one or more of his many enemies, Lebanese or foreign. Parliament then selected Bashir's brother, Amin, as president, though he lacked Bashir's political and military authority.

In response to Bashir's assassination, Israeli forces extended their control around Beirut. Fatefully, they allowed pro-Israeli Christian militiamen into the Sabra and

Beirut "Paris of the Middle East" before the ravaging civil war

Stylish, bustling Beirut in times before invasion and civil war Credit: National Council of Tourism in Lebanon

Chatila Palestinian refugee camps south of the city. There the militiamen sought revenge for their past losses by murdering about 1,000 civilians while the Israeli military ignored the gunfire.

It took U.S. and European troops to restore order from the chaos. They maintained public order as Israeli units withdrew; they then helped reorganize the Lebanese army. Soon, however, the army joined the political and sectarian fighting, and the peacekeepers' role became partisan. After a suicide truck bomb killed 241 U.S. Marines in their barracks, the remaining American forces withdrew, and Lebanon returned to its usual wartime patterns. The president governed the palace, but the rest of the country fell under the control of local militias or foreign troops. Some technical departments still attempted to function.

The worst violence continued in the south, where forces within the Palestinian, Druze, and Shi'a communities fought each other and the Israelis. In central Lebanon, the *Lebanese Forces* collected taxes and imposed some order and administration on East Beirut and the surrounding countryside, while near-anarchy prevailed in West Beirut.

Final Events of the Civil War

Parliament failed to select a successor to President Gemayel in 1988, and minutes before his term expired, he appointed General Michel Aoun, Commander-in-Chief of the (divided) Lebanese Army, as prime minister. This placed a Christian in the highest office reserved for Sunni Muslims; the incumbent prime minister and cabinet refused to resign.

A straightforward general determined to reunite Lebanon and expel all foreign troops, Aoun blockaded small ports used by militias to import military supplies and often to export illegal drugs. As a patriot, Aoun led his forces into intense battles with Syrian troops, who replied with indiscriminate shelling of civilian targets. One million fled; hundreds died, and survivors spent days and nights underground, often without electricity, fuel, or running water. Industry ground to a halt, and most factories were damaged.

Civil War Zones, 1983–1990

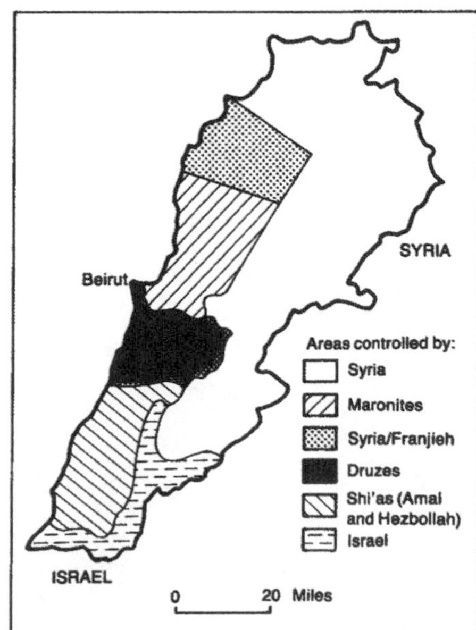

Unable to force a Syrian withdrawal, Aoun hoped for foreign pressure to remove them. But no nation intervened when Syrian troops attacked his headquarters in 1990, the last major action of a civil war that officially claimed over 144,000 dead, another 17,000 missing, and 184,000 wounded.

Under pressure from Saudi Arabia, in 1989 most Lebanese parliamentary deputies met in Taif, Saudi Arabia, and hammered out a new constitutional arrangement (see Politics). The deputies also accepted the Syrian occupation, at least temporarily.

After their first choice as president was assassinated, the deputies elected Elias Hrawi, a Maronite, to the post. He quickly recognized the prime minister and gained support from important Maronite elements, including the *Phalange Party* and the *Lebanese Forces* militia. Hrawi asserted control over East Beirut and began to destroy the many walls dividing Lebanon. Daily life improved, business activity strengthened, funds flowed into the country and schools reopened.

The army moved to regain control of South Lebanon in 1991. Troops entered Sidon and Tyre to public cheers, and they defeated *PLO* units that refused to yield their heavy weapons. However, possibly under Syrian influence, the army did not move against *Hizbullah* units, which continued to attack Israeli troops and the *South Lebanon Army* in the Israeli Security Zone. Israel retaliated. Despite worthy attempts and the release of Western hostages, sovereignty and peace proved elusive. Car bombings occurred even on the American University campus.

Deep controversy arose over elections scheduled for 1992, and, indeed, all elections that have followed. Until the Syrian withdrawal in 2005, critics—including the Maronite patriarch—faulted elections held under foreign occupation. On the practical level, hundreds of thousands of refugees could not return home safely to vote. True to tradition, political parties did not dominate the results, but *Hizbullah* consistently proved the strongest party, typically gaining 12 seats of the 128 only because it did not contest more. Its victories reflected Shi'a communal identity, popular appreciation the party's social welfare programs, and support for its attacks on Israel.

By contrast, in the twenty years that followed, the Maronite community struggled with its loss of primacy and rarely achieved its aspirations. The Maronite leadership fractured, and some Christian seats were captured by pro-Syrian figures elected by Muslims.

Rafiq Hariri was appointed prime minister in 1992, and he would dominate Lebanese politics for the next thirteen years. Born in Sidon to a family of very modest means, like many Lebanese he sought fortune abroad, in his case, construction in Saudi Arabia. Eventually becoming a close friend of the king and a billionaire, he nevertheless maintained close ties with Lebanon and provided scholarships to thousands of Lebanese. As a man expected to give Lebanon far more than he might (corruptly) take, his appointment as prime minister won support even from traditional Maronites.

Hariri aimed to fight corruption and cut the bloated bureaucracy He desired to restore government schools, hospitals, electricity, water utilities and telephones. He sought foreign aid and extended army control to the Shi'a suburbs south of Beirut. However, *Hizbullah* retained considerable freedom to strike at Israeli forces and the *South Lebanese Army* in the Israeli-occupied territory.

The prime minister's efforts to build national unity and restore government authority clashed with attempts by Syria, Israel, Iran and other countries to manipulate events for their own purposes. Thousands of Syrian troops remained. Critics condemned them as occupiers, but to their supporters, they were peacekeepers. They assisted *Hizbullah*, and they provided an excuse for Israel to occupy the south as a "security zone."

Treaties signed in 1991 linked Lebanon to Syria politically and diplomatically. By prohibiting media attacks on Damascus, the treaties clearly violated the traditional freedom, bordering on license, exercised by the Lebanese press. The Syrian link alienated most Maronites, who perceived political discrimination in many ways, including selective prosecution of Christians for violent crimes.

Lebanon's recovery from the devastation of nearly two decades of war proved uneven and slow. Annual economic growth rates reached as high as 7%, but though they were impressive as statistics, they failed to bring the expected prosperity to the middle and lower classes. International aid came only in trickles. Tax revenues reached only 50% of expenditures, and exports only about 10% of imports. Government salaries fell behind the comparable private sector, and teachers went on strike.

The focus of Hariri's reconstruction effort was Solidere, a $1.8 billion company given great powers to seize property and rebuild the heart of Beirut. Funds poured into real estate development, and hundreds of buildings were torn down. As the bulldozers moved in, archaeologists found remarkable ruins from almost every era of history, adding another complication to reconstruction.

Rebuilding central Beirut was largely complete by the late 1990s. However, broad-based prosperity still eluded the country, and the political system faltered, unable to select a new president when the incumbent's term ended. Corruption worsened, and critics often blamed Hariri.

Bleeding Beirut: bomb blast killing 30 people, July 1986 AP/Wide World Photos

The South Liberated

After nearly 20 years of occupation, *Hizbullah's* attacks on Israel's self-proclaimed security zone and northern Israel sharpened in 1996. Israel responded with large-scale bombardments from land, sea, and air on both military and economic targets, including a water reservoir and an electricity installation in Christian Beirut. Deliberately or carelessly, Israeli gunners also shelled civilians sheltered at the UN post at Qana, killing about 100 and drawing international condemnation. Tel Aviv and Washington had initially proposed peace terms that disarmed *Hizbullah* "terrorists." After the slaughter at Qana, "terrorist" hardly seemed a label for one side alone.

Continuing casualties, sometimes reaching as many as 30 Israeli soldiers killed annually, led Ehud Barak to promise during an election campaign to withdraw from Lebanon. The difficulty, as always, was security: Lebanon and Syria refused to guarantee of the safety of northern Israel. While *Hizbullah* attacks continued, morale declined in the *South Lebanon Army* (*SLA*) and among Israeli troops. Slowly disintegrating, the *SLA* retreated from the Christian town of Jezzine in 1999. The collapse of the *SLA* forced a rapid retreat that saved Israeli lives but meant abandoning supplies and equipment. Abruptly, Israel withdrew from the entire zone in 2000, months ahead of Barak's deadline. *Hizbullah* had forced an Israeli retreat; the war for Lebanon seemed the only Arab victory in a century-long struggle.

The Faraya ski resort—a far cry from the desert heat found in neighboring nations.

One significant border dispute remained: the Shabaa farms region on the slopes of Mt. Hermon. Only a few hundred acres, they were claimed by Lebanon historically, but occupied by Syria and captured by Israel in 1967. The UN considers them part of the occupied Golan Heights. Death stalks within the Shabaa farms, and *Hizbullah* has ambushed Israeli soldiers in operations designed to gain counter-hostages for the dozens of Lebanese imprisoned in Israel.

Despite predictions of a bloodbath for collaborators, when the *SLA* collapsed completely, its soldiers typically were sentenced to short prison terms. Others former members fled to Israel with their families. South Lebanon remained calm under *Hizbullah* control; Lebanese administrative control only gradually returned.

Continued Occupation and the Cedar Revolution

Gerrymandering, manipulated regulations, and intimidation marked parliamentary elections held after the Israeli withdrawal in 2000. Nevertheless, in a political system where personalities matter more than parties, voters decisively favored candidates linked to Rafiq Hariri. Despite the personal animosity between the two men, President Lahoud reappointed him.

In fact, the campaign rhetoric overshadowed the actual winners. Some candidates openly raised the issue of foreign—meaning Syrian—domination. Walid Jumblatt, the Druze leader long close to Damascus, called for a new relationship between the two countries. Clearly, Lebanese across most of the political spectrum felt that the end of Israeli occupation removed one rationale for the Syrian occupation as well.

In response, Damascus withdrew its troops from Beirut in 2001, removing an eyesore. However, strong Syrian influence remained, exercised through the Lebanese intelligence services, political manipulation, and some 25,000 troops in the north and east. To counter any sense of declining Syrian prestige, the security forces (rather than Lebanese police) arrested hundreds of Maronites on flimsy charges. Although most were soon released, several prominent personalities, including international journalists, were charged with treason for communicating with Israel. Such maneuvering further weakened any desires for reconciliation.

Before President Lahoud's six-year term expired in late 2004, Syria summoned the Lebanese cabinet to Damascus. On its return, it proposed a constitutional amendment to extend the president's term by three years. Despite opposition, parliament agreed. However, the UN Security Council, led by the U.S. and France, voted for the withdrawal of all foreign (i.e., Syrian) troops, the disarming of all militias (*Hizbullah;* Palestinians in camps), and fair elections. Rafiq Hariri resigned, and formed an anti-Syrian alliance with traditional Maronite politicians and the Druze leader Walid Jumblatt, thus uniting three of the country's four sectarian groups.

On Valentine's Day, 2005, a massive suicide bomb killed Hariri and dozens of others. The very sophisticated assassination plunged the country into crisis. Many Maronites and Druze condemned the Syrian and Lebanese intelligence services directly. Others blamed the security forces' failure to protect an obvious target after opposition politicians had warned of death threats against them. In sharp contrast, most Shi'a suspected that Israel or the U.S. had engineered a murder that would damage Syria's reputation. A leaked UN report later claimed that Syrian President al-Assad had threatened Hariri, that top Syrian intelligence officials were implicated, and that Lebanese authorities had utterly failed to conduct a competent investigation. Everyone but the security services, it seemed, had heard of threats against Hariri. Eventually the UN's report changed, and Hizbullah officials were formally charged.

As protests mounted in central Beirut, political opinion swung strongly against Syria. Perhaps 25% of the country's entire population massed in Beirut's central square on March 14, 2005 to demand justice and the complete withdrawal of Syrian troops. Its participants called this the "Cedar Revolution."

To the surprise of many, Syria responded by withdrawing all its troops from Lebanon. However, many blamed Syrian intelligence and its Lebanese allies for continued bombings in Christian areas and the murders of prominent journalists and politicians critical of Syria.

As Lebanon prepared for elections under a gerrymandered system that most Maronites opposed, the Hariri-Jumblatt-*Lebanese Forces* alliance took the label "March 14" forces. The election results showed a starkly divided country. Saad Hariri's alliance carried all of Beirut's seats, and did well in the north and east, while the rival *Hizbullah-Amal* coalition took every seat in the south. In Mount Lebanon, Jumblatt demonstrated his wide support from the Druze community.

Maronite voters, however, sharply rejected Hariri's *Lebanese Forces* allies in favor of the populist General Aoun, the former ruler during the Civil War who had returned from exile to contest the elections. A decade earlier, Aoun's defiance of Syria had cost the lives of hundreds of soldiers and perhaps thousands of civilians. Now he formed pragmatic alliances with pro-Syrian politicians. The elections thus emphasized the sectarian nature of Lebanese society, with each sectarian group's heartland uniting behind one leader.

Despite his solid majority, Saad Hariri refused office, and his alliance nominated Fouad Siniora as prime minister. Siniora formed a unity cabinet that included pro-Syrian representatives from *Hizbullah* and Aoun's *Free Patriotic Movement.*

The Year of Lebanese Turmoil (July 2006–07)

Breaking six years of relative calm along the internationally-recognized Israeli border, in 2006, *Hizbullah* guerillas captured two Israeli soldiers and killed several others. Besides hostages for bargaining, the guerillas likely sought to embarrass Israel's newly-formed cabinet, and to divert attention from Iran's nuclear processing.

Israel's inexperienced cabinet under Ehud Olmert seized the opportunity to turn the border raid into a war, aiming to free its soldiers, crush *Hizbullah's* military force, and perhaps demonstrate Iran's inability to protect its ally. The Israel Defense Forces (IDF) launched a missile and bombing blitz of *Hizbullah's* military in the South, its offices and television station in Beirut, and even the home of Hassan Nasrallah, its leader. Non-Shi'a Lebanese often thought this appropriate retaliation for a reckless provocation, though unfortunate in the civilian casualties.

When Israel held Lebanon directly responsible for the fate of the soldiers, it ignored the common Lebanese distinction between *Hizbullah's* territory and sovereign Lebanon. Long powerless over *Hizbullah,* Beirut also proved powerless when Israel attacked businesses, Beirut's airport, vital road bridges, gasoline service stations, and even individual commercial trucks. A raid on Beirut's generating station created an enormous slick of heavy oil—one of the Mediterranean's worst. An air and sea blockade halted the economy and caused several billion dollars in damages. *Hizbullah* retaliated by launching missiles far deeper into Israel than ever before, reaching Haifa, then further south. The missiles, supplied by Iran through Syria, killed over 40 civilians and wounded scores more. By contrast, Lebanese civilian casualties from Israeli fire exceeded 1,000 dead, plus thousands injured. Nearly 25% of the population fled their homes.

After weeks of air strikes, the IDF launched ground assaults into South Lebanon. However, by the standards of past Israeli triumphs, the troops were unprepared, or the plans were flawed, and *Hizbullah* fighters inflicted unexpected casualties. The world clamored for a ceasefire, but in hopes that Israel would destroy *Hizbullah,* the U.S. obstructed a Security Council decision. After a month of fighting, with no Israeli victory in sight, the Security Council finally voted Resolution 1701. It called for the return of the two captured soldiers, the disarming of *Hizbullah,* government control over the Lebanese south, and a strengthened UN presence.

Having battled to perhaps a draw, *Hizbullah* rapidly won the post-war public relations victory. Its officials poured a "river of green" on Lebanese eager to rebuild their destroyed homes, $12,000 in cash, with virtually no paperwork. *Jihad al-Bina',* the party's construction arm, quickly cleared ruined apartment blocks. In a play on Hassan Nasrallah's name, the party posted signs proclaiming "Divine Victory;" in Arabic "Nasr min Allah."

By contrast, the widespread attacks on Lebanon weakened the democratic and anti-Syrian government. With U.S. diplomatic backing, Israel had devastated a pro-Western country, but left untouched Syria and Iran, *Hizbullah's* key suppliers. This strengthened Syrian sympathizers in Lebanon, and Islamist extremists worldwide. *Hizbullah* and its allies left the national unity cabinet, leaving it short of any Shi'a minister, and then declared the government illegal. Whether to block the UN tribunal over Rafiq Hariri's assassination, or to extend its own power, *Hizbullah* demanded a unity government. It sponsored months of demonstrations in central Beirut, including a protest camp outside Parliament.

The aftermath of the war proved particularly discouraging to the Lebanese, who had long hoped for prosperity and development. Bombings and assassinations targeted anti-Syrian figures, members of parliament and leading journalists—men with names like Gemayel (Minister of Industry) and Tueni (MP and respected journalist), whose fathers and grandfathers were pillars of Lebanese society. A brave TV anchorwoman, May Chidiac, survived an assassination attempt that cost her arm and leg. The assassins were never found.

President Lahoud's extended term expired in 2007 with Parliament immobilized, and the country began a period of anxious uncertainty. Nearly all political groups accepted the military commander, General Michel Suleiman, as a compromise candidate, but the election was held hostage until *Hizbullah* had gained several wider goals.

After months of crisis, in 2008 the cabinet attempted a show of authority. It dismissed the military commander of Beirut airport and declared *Hizbullah's* land-line telephone system illegal. *Hizbullah's* response was firm: its militiamen seized Sunni sections of West Beirut, demonstrating their military superiority over Sunni militias. The military maintained its unity by taking no action, though it threatened to do so if gunmen did not leave the streets.

In Washington, President Bush proclaimed, "The international community will not allow the Iranian and Syrian regimes, via their proxies, to return Lebanon to foreign domination and control." However, the U.S. had no proxies to support its allies. Outmaneuvered, the cabinet backed down. In response, *Hizbullah* reopened roads and the international airport. Even more important, both government and opposition accepted an invitation backed by the Arab League for talks in Qatar.

With diplomacy and arm-twisting by Sheikh Hamad bin Jassim, the Prime Minister of Qatar, the two sides agreed a major political compromise. Presidential elections would be held, almost immediately. The new cabinet would include a blocking minority from *Hizbullah* and its allies, with the remainder appointed by the new president. Re-drawn parliamentary districts would concentrate sectarian voters, strengthening their ability to elect their own, and no group would be allowed to use arms to settle disputes. Finally, the opposition promised to disband the protests that had paralyzed downtown Beirut for months.

After 19 failed attempts, the Chamber of Deputies met and quickly elected Michael Suleiman president. The next day he took office, and reappointed Prime Minister Siniora.

Successful Parliamentary Elections, 2009

Many Western commentators interpreted the 2009 election of a new parliament in geo-strategic terms, portraying Lebanon's vote as a contest between the pro-American, anti-Syrian March 14 bloc and the pro-Iranian/anti-Israeli/Muslim extremist *Hizbullah* bloc. Though partly true, that explanation ignored local realities, personal rivalries, and *Hizbullah's* desire to avoid direct control. It also neglected the powerful role played by fear. After the 2008 fighting in the streets of Beirut, Sunnis felt apprehensive of Shi'a encroachment. Shi'a opinion feared the government's alignment with the West would leave Lebanon weakened in another war with Israel. Many Christians feared becoming insignificant.

In almost any democratic election, *Hizbullah* could easily win about 40 of the 128 seats in parliament, so strong is its hold on Shi'a loyalties. However, it has consistently avoided such an overwhelming victory. In 2009 it nominated only 11 candidates of its own. In fact, there were no close contests for about 100 of the 128 seats. The remaining seats were mostly Christian, and fear of Hizbullah deterred enough voters from supporting General Aoun so that Christian candidates aligned with the March 14 alliance gave it a national majority.

Lebanon's government is a rarity among nations: the political opposition often has insisted that democracy means power-sharing, so the cabinet should reflect all factions country without giving the victors too much power. After months

Prime Minister Tammam Salam

Sidon: Temple of Eshmoun. Mosaic of the four seasons. Courtesy: CNT/Yetenekian

of bargaining, Saad Hariri formed a cabinet of 30 members, divided 15 for the victors, 10 for the opposition, and five loyal to the president.

The cabinet started to act on the backlog of needed decisions, for example, it voted the first budget in five years. However, Hassan Nasrallah, *Hizbullah's* leader, denounced the UN's Special Tribunal for Lebanon (STL), which indicted party members for the murder of Rafiq Hariri, and warned the government not to cooperate with the STL, which had been created to bring his father's murderers to justice.

Sensing the rising influence of the *Hizbullah*/Syrian alliance, Walid Jumblatt, leader of the Druze *Progressive Socialist Party*, withdrew from the March 14 alliance. Hariri's cabinet then collapsed.

Careful once again to avoid formal responsibility for governing, *Hizbullah's* March 8 coalition selected Najib Mikati, a Sunni independent, as prime minister. A billionaire and the richest man in Lebanon, Prime Minister Mikati represents a world far from the Shi'a suburbs of Beirut. A graduate of the American University of Beirut, he studied management at both Harvard and INSEAD. While his interest in serving all Lebanese must be considered genuine, it is surprising that the cabinet fails to contain a single woman. Iran and Syria cheered his appointment, while Israel and the United States worried that he might be influenced too heavily by his allies.

The deepening political crisis and bloodshed of the Arab Spring in Syria is gradually drawing Lebanon into the abyss of sectarian conflict. Many clergymen take political sides, even if their own confessions are not directly involved. For example, the Maronite patriarch, Beshara al-Rai, told an interviewer "The closest thing to democracy [in the Arab world] is Syria," because Islam was not the state religion. Frequently, Lebanese consider fighting for their sectarian allies in Syria more important than obedience to Lebanon's laws and neutrality.

Hizbullah views the conflict as a foreign policy matter: an attempt by the U.S., Israel, and their conservative Sunni allies to fracture the Iran—Syria—Hizbullah axis. After all, if the Syrian rebels win, they will cut off the Lebanese party and its militia from Iran, its military supplier. Sectarian concerns also lead Hizbullah to fight alongside Assad's largely Alawi Syrian military.

By 2013 it was clear that *Hizbullah* fighters played an increasing and sometimes decisive role in the Syrian regime's successful offensives, first by protecting Shi'a shrines in Damascus. Then, from bases in Lebanon, the fighters, assisted by Syrian troops, recaptured the pivotal town of Qusair from the rebels. *Hizbullah* units now reportedly fight in other critical battlegrounds in Homs, Damascus, and Aleppo. This intervention arouses bitter criticism by those who feel it will bring the war to Lebanon. By contrast, Hassan Nasrallah claims that by winning in Syria, his militiamen defeat threats to Lebanon.

Militant Sunni fighters, many of them from Tripoli, have also joined various rebel brigades in the civil war and smuggle arms to them. Clearly, Lebanon is failing to enforce its neutrality; inevitably, the sides fighting each other in Syria sporadically battle in Lebanon as well. Clashes have repeatedly broken out in Tripoli between the pro-Assad Alawi district of Jabal Mohsen and the neighboring Sunni quarter of Bab al-Tabbaneh.

In response to Lebanese joining the mayhem of Syria's civil war, both the Syrian government and the Islamist rebels carried the fighting back to Lebanon. Car bombings killed scores at a Sunni mosque; suicide bombers also targeted Shi'a and *Hizbullah* neighborhoods. Given the porous borders, Lebanese security proved unable to deter all the planned attacks.

The violence imperiled the country because its political system was already overloaded. Prime Minister Mikati resigned in March 2013. Within two weeks Tammam Salam was designated his successor by agreement with the major factions, but he could not form a cabinet until the following February. Meanwhile, parliament proved utterly unable to approve a voting system for the 2013 elections, though the deputies were able to find a majority to vote an extension of their terms for 18 months.

With the legislature tottering, the government frequently failed to accomplish its tasks. Decisions as vital as selecting the new army commander could not be made. The public considered that corruption seemed worse; beyond the usual tales of public sector squandering, scandals in medicine and food safety went uncorrected. In addition to the many accumulated problems that only government could solve, the presence of one million Syrian refugees gathered in perhaps a thousand informal camps demanded exceptional measures. The government could not act decisively, and the world community proved reluctant to disburse funds through it.

When Michel Suleiman's term ended and he vacated the palace in April 2014, the presidency collapsed. Disputes between (and perhaps within) the two major blocs, *Hizbullah's* March 8 coalition and the March 14 alliance of Sunnis and Christians prevented the Chamber of Deputies from even achieving a quorum to elect his successor. His final year of office was marred by political and regional events far too great for the Lebanese presidency to resist. One of the few good turns of fortune was Saudi Arabia's donation of $3 billion to re-equip the army.

Politics: Dating from the French mandate, the Lebanese constitution stipulates a Chamber of Deputies (parliament), and a president elected by it for a single term of six years. The president is the most powerful authority, for he selects and may dismiss the prime minister, subject to parliamentary approval.

Representative democracy really means representation of religious groups. The *National Pact* of 1943, an unwritten amendment to the constitution, reserves the presidency to a Maronite Christian, the premiership to a Sunni Muslim, and the speaker of parliament to a Shi'a Muslim. Similar sectarian restrictions apply elsewhere, so that the army commander must be a Maronite. Christians historically dominated the Chamber of Deputies by a 5:4 ratio, but the 1989 Taif Accord equalized the membership of the 128 deputies. The accord also determined the number of seats for the country's six districts based on political compromise, not the actual number of residents.

In practice, the formal democracy becomes a feudal system based on traditionally important families, sometimes abetted by voting practices that trespass on the secrecy of the ballot. Voters support a local leader, known as a *za'im*, from an important family of their own faith. Once elected, a *za'im* develops a patron-client relationship, using the political system to obtain benefits for his district and his family, a sometimes foggy distinction. While they cling to privileges for their commu-

Former President Michel Suleiman

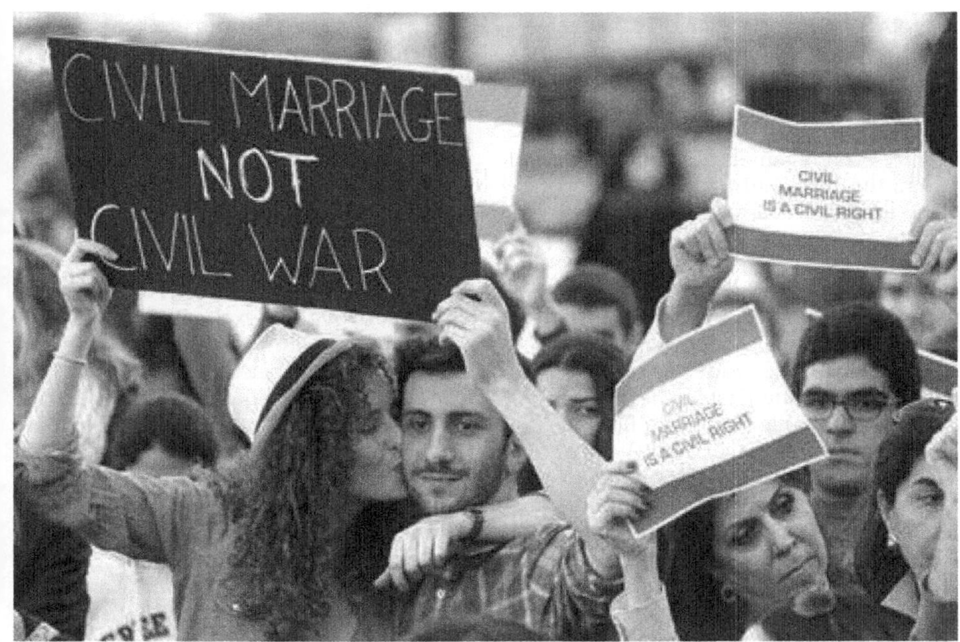

These Activists in Beirut say it all.

nities, *za'ims* recognize the benefits of cooperating with leaders from other sects, who often share their economic wealth. Alliances might even be formed across the sectarian divide against rivals of the same faith.

Thanks to this system, there are no significant national parties. Ideology and typical political issues are diminished as sons—Chamoun, Jumblatt, Karami, and many others—replace fathers in politics and often in parliament. There is never a landslide that "throws the rascals out" no matter how disillusioned the voters.

At one time the size of the Maronite community justified its dominance. But Maronites emigrated more often than Muslims, and as they became wealthier more quickly, they preferred fewer children. By the 1970s, Maronites (probably) fell to third place demographically, but they refused to relinquish the presidency and command of the army, for they remembered past Muslim domination and persecution.

Long the country's neglected community, the Shi'a community's rise to greater recognition followed the replacement of feudal Shi'a *za'ims* by *Hizbullah.* Because it supported Palestinian groups that murdered Israeli civilians and maintained links with suspected hijackers and the 1983 Marine barracks bombers, *Hizbullah* is often derided in the U.S. as merely a group of terrorists.

But in today's Lebanon, the *"Party of God"* runs schools, dispensaries, and public works projects. It provides fertilizers and agricultural advice to thousands of farmers, and clean drinking water in slums. With 11 representatives in parliament, the effectiveness of its organization far exceeds any other political group in the country, possibly including the government bureaucracy. Across the Arab world it was hailed for liberating South Lebanon and defeating Israel (i.e., holding its own) in 2006. These achievements render *Hizbullah* too strong for the Lebanese government to challenge, regardless of U.S. desires to freeze the organization's financial assets as a terrorist group and the UN vote to disarm it.

In a related matter, the party's political strength led the Hariri government to support the right of the "resistance" against Israel to maintain arms, contrary to U.N. decisions. While the *Party of God* undoubtedly possesses thousands of rockets, contrary to Israeli claims it probably is not armed with SCUD missiles, if only because the older, liquid-fueled weapons are too large to hide and too cumbersome to use.

Culture: Though often Western in dress, material possessions, and television, most Lebanese naturally retain their own social values. A more traditional life and dress is found in small towns and villages, especially in those inhabited by Shi'a Muslims. The traditional culture differs very little from that of Syrians and Palestinians.

The Maronite (Arabic *Maruni*) Church is unique to Lebanon. Formed as a distinct group in Syria about the 6th century, the Maronites have preserved many ancient customs in the mountains. Arabic and Syriac are both used in the liturgy. The marriage of priests is permitted, but the Maronite Church has been in communion with the Roman Catholic Church since the First Crusade. In recent centuries, Maronites have been rivals with the Druze for control of the Chouf Mountains overlooking Beirut. In 1860, when Maronites suffered defeats at the hands of their enemies there, French soldiers intervened on behalf of the Christians. Many Maronites, including monks who own some of the best land, still believe that Western Christians have a duty to help the Maronites gain victory over their non-Christian rivals.

Long before the Israelis adopted the argument, Maronites presented themselves as isolated defenders of the "values of Western Civilization" among unruly Arabs. However, the continued bloodshed typical between rival Maronite factions indicates a perverse understanding of "western values." For example, in 1988 presidential bodyguards killed two officers of the *Lebanese Forces* over some petty dispute. Four days later, two of the president's supporters were murdered in retaliation, following the age-old principle of the vendetta.

The Druze (Arabic *Duruz)* form a cohesive community whose origins lie partly in Shi'a Islam. Several Christian ideas and practices have also been incorporated into the sect along with unique beliefs and interpretations belonging only to the initiated. Besides their stronghold in the Chouf southeast of Beirut, they are also found in Jabal al-Druze in southern Syria.

Traditionally inhabiting the southern mountains and the *Biqa'* valley, the Shi'a often suffered exploitive landowners and received few government services. In the 1970s and 1980s, their towns and villages suffered Palestinian occupation and then Israeli invasions. Less educated, the Shi'a formed the poorest religious community, but after they migrated to Beirut's southern suburbs, they gained significant military and political clout, especially with the formation of *Hizbullah.*

Nearly all Lebanese value education very highly. Thanks to its mixture of state, private and church-supported schools and universities, the country long enjoyed the distinction of some of the finest education in the Arab world. The American University of Beirut attracted students and faculty from many lands; so did other colleges and universities, helping to maintain Beirut's status as an intellectual center. However, while the government developed a public school system after independence, its teachers or facilities often lack the qualities and advantages of the better private schools.

For many years, the highlight of Lebanese cultural activities was the summer Baalbeck Festival. World-class orchestras, pop stars, and dramatic groups performed against the imposing backdrop of some of the greatest Roman-era ruins. A wartime casualty, the festival returned to the hearts of Lebanese when Fairouz, one of the Arab world's most famous singers, returned to the stage in 1998. During the civil war, she had refused to perform anywhere in Lebanon, and though a Christian she had remained a national symbol. Thus her return to Baalbeck represented the return of normalcy.

Younger Arab men and women often prefer the sounds—and gyrations—of the rock stars of music videos, and Lebanon's Nancy Ajram and Haifa Wehbe attract a large following in the region while scandalizing Middle East conservatives. Members of Bahrain's parliament nearly unanimously sought to ban what they imagined would be a sexually provocative concert—despite Wehbe's promise to cover up. The incident provided many Lebanese, more worldly-wise, respite from the immorality of communal bloodshed.

Another cultural challenge is the recovery of antiquities looted from museums or kept privately, contrary to the law. Officials have seized thousands of works, including mosaics and sarcophagi, and recently even regained full control of Beit al-Din, the 18th-century capital and one of the most famous historical sites in the country.

Economy: In the first decades of independence, many Lebanese prospered from their country's role as a center of international banking and trade. Beirut became the natural Middle Eastern headquarters for many companies. Tourism flourished, transit fees on Iraqi and Saudi Arabian oil helped meet the government's budget, and Lebanon visibly achieved the highest Arab standard of living outside the oil states.

Two decades of civil and international war destroyed much of the formal economy. Artillery salvos gutted banks and factories, the transit trade collapsed and government revenues plummeted as militias collected customs duties for themselves in the many small ports. Once aspiring to a moderately wealthy standard of living, many Lebanese faced destitution.

The collapse of the Lebanese Lira symbolized the wider economic catastrophe. The lira initially maintained its value remarkably well. However, sometimes the government printed money to pay its bills, especially after 1986. The resulting inflation drove the exchange rate so low that one lira became worthless. Money, in fact, became cheaper than wallpaper. The human effects of inflation were often disastrous. It wiped out the lifetime savings of many people, and because wages failed to rise equally with prices, impoverished most others.

The chaos of civil war provided a little-noticed example of the unacceptable face of unregulated capitalism. An Italian company, Jelly War, shipped thousands of barrels of toxic waste to Lebanon, burying the containers in the mountains or near the sea. Complaints led the Italian government to repossess much of the material, but Greenpeace claimed that several thousand barrels remained.

The task of reconstruction was enormous. Wartime destruction and neglect particularly devastated the networks of electric and telephone cables, water pipes and sewer lines. Enterprising Lebanese often coped by makeshift arrangements that conveniently avoided payment for the erratic services, but massive rebuilding was required. In the late 1990s government reconstruction funds had reached about $20 billion, and a construction boom brought new housing as well as roads and commercial buildings. Most construction workers were not Lebanese, but Syrians and other Arabs, who formed roughly 20% of the workforce. After 2006, they were needed again, for reconstruction after Israeli attacks.

The Future: A bit more than usual, intertwined domestic and regional crises threaten the collapse of its governing system. Parliament's term of office, already extended, will expire in months. While another extension might be arranged, the presidency is vacant, teachers and other special interest groups threaten strikes over higher pay, and suicide bombings render life uncertain. A million Syrian guests depress earnings for the lower classes and raise rents for nearly all.

Will the country bounce back once again? Can the Lebanese unite enough to select a president? As long as their political groups willingly serve as proxies in regional rivalries, expect the country to teeter close to open conflict, its factions too often manipulated by foreign powers.

Lebanese rock star Nancy Ajram

The Sultanate of Oman

Small village in the interior of Oman

Area: About 119,500 square miles (309,500 sq. km.).
Population: 3.3 million, including 400,000 South Asians.
Capital City: Muscat (pop. 800,000).
Climate: Extremely hot and dry except for the short winter season which is comfortable in most areas, cool in the mountains. Winter normally brings adequate rainfall at higher elevations.
Neighboring Countries: United Arab Emirates (North); Saudi Arabia (West); Yemen (Southwest).
Time Zone: GMT +4.
Official Language: Arabic.
Other Principal Tongues: Baluchi and languages of the Mahri group.
Ethnic Background: Predominantly Arab, with significant African and Asian inter-marriage. Small communities in Dhofar preserve the remnants of older linguistic and ethnic groups.
Principal Religion: Islam.

Oman

Chief Commercial Products: Petroleum, dates, dried fish, grain, pomegranates, limes, goats, cattle and camels.
Major Trading Partners: Japan, United Arab Emirates, U.K., U.S., West Germany, Netherlands.
Currency: Rial (1 rial = 1000 biaza).
Former Colonial Status: Independent but under British influence, mid-19th to mid-20th centuries.
Chief of State: Qabus bin Said, Sultan.
National Flag: At the pole there is a vertical stripe of bright red bearing the national emblem (crossed swords behind a broad dagger on a belt) at the top; the remainder of the flag consists of three horizontal stripes, white, red and green, top to bottom.
Gross Domestic Product: $82 billion (current prices); $100 billion (Purchasing Power Parity).
GDP per capita: $30,000 (PPP).

One of the hottest and driest countries on earth, Oman lies on the southeast corner of the arid Arabian Peninsula. Facing the Gulf of Oman to the northeast and the Arabian Sea on the south, it extends along 1,000 miles of coast. It is the oldest independent Arab state.

Stretching from Sur at the eastern tip on the country toward the northwest, the Hajar Mountains form one of the major geographical features of Oman. The highest part of the range, with peaks rising more than 9,000 feet, is *Jabal Akhdar*, the "Green Mountain." Average annual rainfall on the upper slopes is a modest 20 inches per year, far exceeding the country's typical precipitation of only 3"–4" annually. By contrast, then, the mountains are green.

Between the Hajar Mountains and the sea from just north of Masqat to the UAE border beyond Sohar lies the Batina Plain. Watered mostly by mountain rainfall that flows underground toward the coast, its inhabitants mostly depend on water raised from shallow wells. Nearly all sedentary Omanis live on the Batina Plain, in Masqat or its twin city Matrah, or on the eastern slopes of the mountains.

The remaining three-quarters of the country is mostly arid steppe, with no standing water. The scant pasturage for goats and camels is found in river valleys. One unusual climatic feature helps a few varieties of wild animals survive in otherwise uninhabitable regions. Sea breezes moving inland bring fog and dew. To survive without streams or drinking holes, animals must lick the moisture off the leaves of plants. In one such area conservationists are attempting to reintroduce the locally-extinct Arabian oryx with animals bred in captivity in the United States.

In the southwestern corner of the kingdom lies the smaller coastal plain of Dhofar, with the town of Salala. Rising behind it, the Qara Mountains receive enough moisture during the summer monsoon to support cattle and goats. In ancient times, Dhofar flourished as a supplier of frankincense, the fragrance famed in the Biblical story of the Three Wise Men. In the late 1990s, the moist climate of Salala began to attract Arab tourists who found vacationing in clouds and rain cheaper and more congenial there than in Europe.

History: Before the 19th century, the history of Oman was largely a series of tribal wars, peaceful interludes under powerful rulers, and foreign invasion from other parts of Arabia or Persia. Saif bin Sultan, who died about 1711, extended Omani control over ports of East Africa and Zanzibar, establishing an empire.

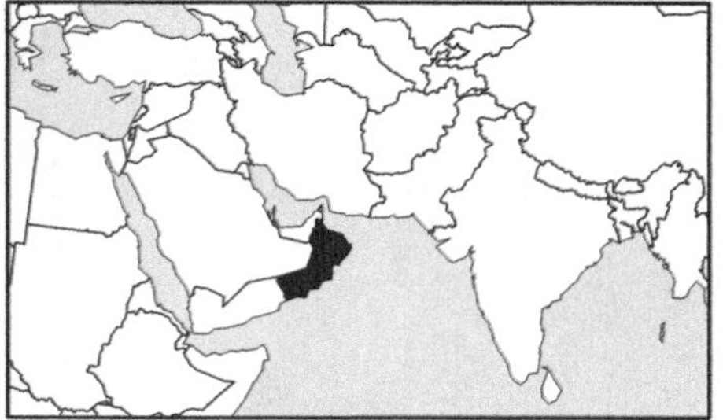

The present line of rulers, who belong to the Al Bu Said family, was established about 1744 with the expulsion of the Persian invaders from Masqat and other coastal towns. The reign of Said the Great (1804–1856) saw Oman as the strongest native power in the Indian Ocean. The newly established cloves plantations on Zanzibar and the slave trade—until curtailed by the British—accounted for Said's wealth, along with his active fleet of sailing craft. When he died, his empire was divided between two sons. One took Zanzibar (now a part of Tanzania), where his descendants ruled until deposed in a 1964 revolt. The other received Oman, then of much less international significance. Gradually, Oman came under increasing British influence, though it retained its legal independence.

In 1932, Said came to the throne on his father's abdication. Said took to the job readily, but after two decades of uneventful rule largely hidden from the outside world, he faced two crises. The first was a dispute over Buraimi Oasis, which Oman shares with Abu Dhabi (see United Arab Emirates). Saudi Arabian soldiers occupied this collection of villages in 1952, and a Saudi governor took up residence. Eventually, after several years of adverse publicity, Sultan Said reoccupied the villages

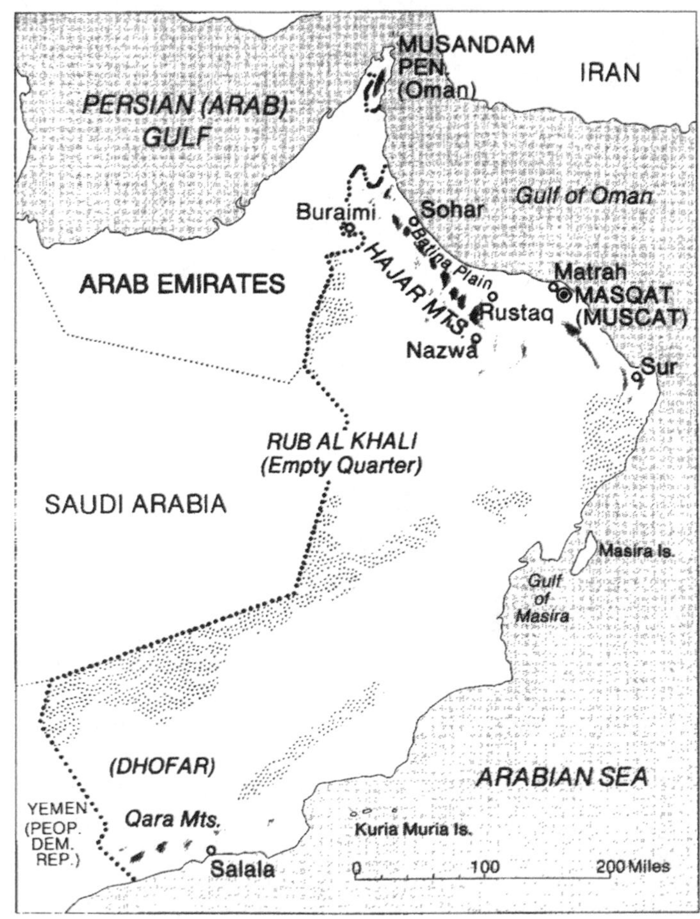

A young couple in traditional dress

he claimed with the aid of British-trained and British-led soldiers from Trucial Oman (now the United Arab Emirates).

The second major crisis was an armed rebellion (1957–1959). Ghalib bin Ali claimed both the religious title of Imam and an independent state in the interior, with its capital at Nazwa. Ghalib's followers received weapons and training in neighboring Saudi Arabia. Returning to Oman, they seized control of Nazwa before the Sultan had time to act. The rebellion was suppressed with the aid of British soldiers and aircraft after a few months duration.

A palace coup deposed Sultan Said in 1970. His only son, Qabus (also spelled Qaboos) swiftly seized power and quickly began careful modernization. To symbolize his new policies, he changed the name of the Sultanate from "Muscat and Oman" to simply "Oman."

The scope for social reforms was vast. Committed to preserving the traditional lifestyle, Sultan Said had failed to spend the new revenues from oil exports. The country's sole hospital had 12 beds, and only six miles—10 kilometers—of road had been paved. Fewer than 1,000 students attended primary school; no high school existed. Communications languished, with only 550 telephone subscribers, and the ports, airfields and public utilities remained primitive. The new sultan's government attempted to develop all these areas, as funds permitted.

Under Sultan Qabus the country also began to emerge from diplomatic isolation. It joined international organizations and allowed foreigners to enter. Oman was admitted to the League of Arab States and the United Nations in 1971. That same year, diplomatic relations were established with Saudi Arabia, the most important neighbor and a past supporter of rebel movements in Oman.

The first six years of Sultan Qabus' reign fell under the shadow of the Marxist-oriented rebellion in Dhofar, which his father had failed to restrain. Supported by the People's Democratic Republic of Yemen, the leaders of the rebellion ultimately aimed to overthrow all the conservative rulers in Arabia and thus control vast oil-producing regions. Advised by British officers and aided by Iranian units supplied by the Shah, Omani forces claimed victory in 1976. This freed the government's attention for economic development.

In the 1980s relations between Oman and South Yemen improved, and Oman came to play an important role in the Gulf Cooperation Council, though it frequently follows its own foreign and defense initiatives. It joined the war against Iraq over Kuwait (1991), and U.S. and British forces use its military bases.

Widening its diplomatic contacts substantially, in 1994 Oman hosted Israel's Prime Minister Yitzhak Rabin for discussions, the only known visit by an Israeli leader to a Gulf state. Radical Palestinian groups and Iran strongly condemned the visit. However, Oman cooperated with Iran in developing joint oil and gas fields, and has sent observers to Iranian military exercises. It essentially seeks peaceful relations in the region.

Seeking to modernize the government as well as the economy, Sultan Qabus gradually increased popular participation in political decisions. In the early 1990s he established a Consultative Council (Majlis al-Shura) free of official appointees, and thus more open to citizen viewpoints. Voting was limited to selected tribal sheikhs, religious leaders, and businessmen voted to select the Council members.

In 1996 Sultan Qabus extended the reforms by decreeing a "Basic Law" that created a supreme court and added an upper house, named the Council of Oman. However, Qabus apparently sensed that the political elite seemed more interested in personal success than the national good. In response, he reshuffled the cabinet to involve more reformers, and appointed women to both houses of the Council.

For the first time, all adult Omani citizens held the right to vote in the Council's 2003 elections, and a woman was appointed a cabinet minister. Despite these formal changes, some analysts suggest that many Omanis have felt apathetic towards an advisory group that could not address issues like defense, foreign policy, or other matters declared sensitive.

Conceivably the Sultan, born in 1940, plans to lead the country towards representative government in his lifetime. However, the Omani public seems to prefer his benevolent though autocratic rule to most alternatives.

The succession is not clear: Sultan Qabus never married and never named an heir. The Basic Law stipulates that male members of the ruling family determine the succession within days of his death. If no agreement is reached, Qabus's secret nominee will be designated. Meanwhile, the security forces maintain close watch over potential trouble-makers, arresting alleged Islamic extremists in 2004 but releasing them the next year.

His Majesty the Sultan Qabus

Oman

A desert country whose scant rainfall falls partly in scattered summer thunderstorms, in 2007 Oman unexpectedly suffered the most severe storm ever recorded to hit the Arabian peninsula. When Cyclone Gonu, a category 3 hurricane, passed along the eastern coast, its winds, waves and rainfall killed over forty people, knocked out power in Muscat, and flooded roads, homes, and cars.

The government reacted effectively to the disaster. It evacuated people from flood areas, closed shops ahead of time, and ordered everyone indoors. Repairs to roads and electric systems began almost immediately, and both of Muscat's water desalination plants returned to operation a few days later. Despite economic losses estimated at about $1,500 per inhabitant, Sultan Qabus politely declined offers of aid from Gulf nations and the U.S.

Inspired in part by events in Tunisia and Egypt, protests and a sit-in erupted in Oman in the spring of 2011, with some initial violence. The demands were typical: additional jobs, dismissal of corrupt officials, and greater freedoms. Sultan Qabus responded by relaxing limits on the media, promising to involve the Council in decisions, and dismissing 12 cabinet ministers. He raised the minimum wage, initiated unemployment benefits, and pledged to create 50,000 new jobs. Funding for the additional spending will come from the $10 billion in assistance from the Gulf Cooperation Council.

The protests largely subsided, but some activists continued critical blogs and writings, until a sharp crackdown in 2012 led to the arrests of dozens of critics. However, Sultan Qabus did not follow the stern example of other Gulf rulers and order trials and harsh punishments. Instead, within a year he issued a blanket pardon of his critics, leading to rare praise from Amnesty International for an Arab ruler.

The 2011 protestors demanded an end to corruption, not the region's worst (61st of 155 countries) but recognized by Transparency International as significant. At the Sultan's orders, the state auditor and prosecutors investigated contracts and payments; this resulted in criminal convictions of several highly-placed officials. A former minister of commerce, for example, had paid a bribe to win a contract for the airport's expansion, and the CEO of the state oil company received a twenty-year sentence for bribes and money laundering. Prosecutors were reportedly astounded by the extent and scope of the corruption. The level of business investment seemed to falter: no doubt many executives worried about past arrangements as well as what rules would be enforced in the future.

Opportunities for corruption frequently result from conflicts of interest when government officials, including cabinet ministers, legally maintain business interests in firms seeking government contracts. Oman has failed to sign the OECD Anti-Bribery Convention.

Culture: Oman has one of the highest percentages of nomads of any country in the world. Over half its people spend most or all of the year wandering with their herds. The remainder of the population is divided between farmers and townspeople. In the principal ports of Masqat and Matrah, many Baluchis and Indians work respectively as laborers and merchants.

The highway at Matrah

Most Omanis follow the teachings of the *Ibadhi* sect of Islam, whose origins lie in the *Khawarij*, a faction that disagreed with Ali, the fourth Caliph of Islam. Many traditions and rituals found in Sunni and Shi'a Islam are not followed by the *Ibadhis,* who stress the importance of proper belief, righteous conduct and the supreme authority of the Qur'an.

Through much of *Ibadhi* history, a leader called the *Imam* led the community in both religious and secular domains. He was selected in theory by all believing males, but in practice by tribal leaders. His duty was to rule the true Muslims, i.e., the *Ibadhis,* and force heretics—Sunni or Shi'a—to follow him. Outside Oman, there are only scattered *Ibadhi* communities in North Africa, India and Pakistan.

Dhofar is administered separately from Oman itself, and has communities that are distinct from other Arabians. Most important among them are the *Qara* people, who speak their own Semitic language and give their name to the mountains in which they live. The Qara dress distinctly, and follow different social habits from most Arab tribes. They are the only Arabians who depend primarily on cattle rather than on goats and camels for a livelihood. Their cattle are very small, about half the size of usual breeds.

One of the most important recent developments in Oman has been the expansion of educational facilities. In 1970 there were scarcely half a dozen schools. Today, hundreds of schools, with thousands of foreign teachers, many of them Egyptian, enroll over 300,000 students, more than half of them girls. Evening classes provide learning for adults.

Sultan Qabus University opened in 1986 with a largely Western curriculum. In common with many other Arabs, Omanis find the study of the humanities, Islamic studies, and the behavioral sciences more appealing than technical skills, engineering and the physical sciences. Around one-half of the university students enroll in the former programs, although the country needs technicians and scientists. The expansion of education now includes a university at Nazwa.

Thanks to the classical music tastes of its sultan, Oman boasts the only professional symphony orchestra of the entire Arabian Peninsula. When the Royal Oman Symphony Orchestra was founded by the Sultan's decree in 1986, there were no pianos or violins worth mentioning in the entire country. No Omanis had studied music, and the first high school was only a decade old. British instructors conducted a talent search and identified musically talented children. Now aged twenty-something, these young Omanis form the national orchestra. Its performances, though considered surprisingly good by Western critics, lie outside the country's culture and tastes, so Omanis generally ignore them.

Economy: Unlike the smaller, oil-rich nations of the Arab Gulf, Omanis acquired a strong agricultural tradition over the centuries. This provides a significant focus for economic development. Even with oil revenues, farming, herding and fishing remain vital parts of the economy; the government, however, no longer depends on taxing produce and livestock to meet its budget.

Three years after the discovery of petroleum deposits, Oman entered a new economic era in 1967, when oil exports began and revenues flowed to the ruler. After Sultan Qabus seized power, development activities increased rapidly. Agricultural projects improved water supplies and crop varieties for farmers. Investment in up-to-date shipping facilities at Matrah and an international airport improved transportation links with the rest of the world, while paved roads and airfields eased travel within the country. Electrical generating plants, housing projects, and radio stations increased the enjoyment of life, while modern hospitals and public health programs extended the lifespan.

Given these favorable conditions, private businesses also expanded rapidly, in the retail trade, services, and other areas. In 1989 the Stock Exchange opened, with 71 companies, mostly in services such as insurance and transportation. The pace of economic development attracted foreigners as well.

Like other Gulf states, Oman will face growing difficulties finding suitable jobs for its young. Half the population is 15 years of age or younger, but already some 4,000 youth graduate from high school annually. They often aspire to government jobs that, compared with private businesses, pay higher salaries, offer greater job security and require shorter hours. However, even by replacing its foreign employees, the government cannot absorb many of the job seekers. In the private economy Pakistanis and Indians accept far lower wages and often fill lower-status jobs. Legislating higher wages for Omanis, or forcing out foreign workers, will merely raise the cost of doing business.

Although income from oil constitutes about 80% of government revenues, known reserves are estimated at a modest 5 billion barrels. As a minor producer, Oman never joined OPEC. By 2006, production had fallen to 630,000 barrels per day due to disappointing declines in output. Recent efforts at steam injection, which heats oil in the rock and facilitates its flow, are among the largest in the world. By combining steam and gas injection methods (known as enhanced recovery) with other improvements, the industry hopes to raise the recoverable portion of oil deposits from 10–20% to nearly 40%. Helped by the first off-shore production, by 2013 output had surpassed 900,000 barrels per day.

Natural gas offers more promise of long-term benefit. In the mid-1990s an ambitious program to develop natural gas resources raised confirmed reserves to 25 trillion cubic feet. The government created Oman LNG, a joint venture with oil companies and private firms to build a multi-billion dollar plant to export 6.8 million tons of liquefied natural gas annually. The first shipments took place in 2000.

If the government can reach agreement with the petroleum multinational BP, development may begin soon on a shale gas project that could yield up to 30 trillion cubic feet. However, shale gas projects require very substantial amounts of fresh water for injection into the rocks.

Oman also seeks diversification outside the energy sector. Copper is mined, refined and exported, and Japan has assisted the search for further copper and gold deposits. Though encouraged, industrial output is small, and large projects to produce aluminum, fertilizers and petrochemicals remain incomplete. Oman's few manufactured exports enter the U.S. under a free trade agreement ratified in 2006.

In 1999 the Raysut transshipment terminal was opened not far from Salala. A major deep-water port costing over $250 million, the project was designed to unload the Gulf-bound cargoes of large vessels for transport into the Gulf on smaller ships. A direct competitor to Jebal Ali in the UAE, the project will only succeed if it operates efficiently and if major shipping firms prefer to avoid the sometimes troubled waters of the Gulf.

The Future: Political stability seems likely, because the Sultan continues to rule, and rule well, as evidenced by a quick and calming response to protests in 2011. However, Oman's petroleum income is far smaller than most of its neighbors. The time bomb of rapid population growth ticks away, and the problem of creating suitable jobs for the young is assuming serious proportions.

The Qurum Natural Park in the Heart of Muscat Courtesy: Royal Embassy of Saudi Arabia

The Palestine National Authority

CAN THIS FRAGMENTED HOMELAND SUCCEED?

Palestinians unite around a common flag, a common Arab culture, and a love of their ancestral homeland between the Mediterranean and the Jordan River. However, nearly two decades after the Oslo Accords promised an eventual Palestinian state, sovereignty still eludes this long-suffering people. A legal framework exists in the Palestinian Authority (PA), complete with legislature and executive. But the PA lacks a capital, governs only 17% of the West Bank, survives only on foreign assistance, and controls no borders. Its police forces—several of them—sometimes shoot each other, and the Gaza strip, controlled by *Hamas*, defies the president. Limits on media freedom come from PA censors rather than Israelis. The advances toward statehood merit the inclusion of Palestine among the formally independent states of this volume. However, the nation-state of Palestine is not an accomplished fact. Critically, popular acceptance of peace with Israel, vital to the PA's very existence, is lower today than a decade ago.

After suffering many calamitous events during the twentieth century, the Palestinians now reside in four distinct categories:

1. Palestinian Authority Territory: Gaza and most Arab areas of the West Bank

Area: Gaza: about 136 square miles. West Bank: Palestinian autonomy in a few square miles of the 2,140.
Population: 3.9 million (UN, 2007), of whom 1.5 million in Gaza
Capital City: Ramallah (legislative). The desired capital: East Jerusalem.
Climate: Mild winters; summers hot (Gaza) to very hot (Jericho).
Neighboring Countries: Israel and Egypt (west of Gaza).
Time Zone: GMT +2.
Official Language: Arabic.
Other Principal Languages: Hebrew (used by Israeli settlers); English.
Ethnic Background: Arab.
Chief Commercial Products: Citrus, including oranges; olives, grapes, figs, vegetables, flowers, grain, handcrafted items and services.
Major Trading Partners: Israel; Arab states (for oil imports).
Currency: Israeli New Shekel; dollars preferred.
Colonial Status: Still subject to Israel; previously under direct Israeli occupation (1967–1994; parts reoccupied) and rule by Egypt (Gaza) and Jordan (West Bank) (1948–1967). Britain ruled the area under League of Nations Mandate after World War I.
Official Holiday: November 15, commemorating the National Council's declaration of independence of the West Bank and Gaza, 1988.
Leader: Mahmud Abbas, President of the PA and PLO chairman.
Head of Government: Rami Hamdallah, Prime Minister (unity cabinet, 2014).
National Flag: Three horizontal stripes of black, white and green and a red triangle at the pole.
Per capita income: Less than $1,000 annually, but 60% live on less than $2 per day.

2. East Jerusalem and other Israeli-controlled areas

Area: Desired by Palestinians: about 25 square miles annexed to Jerusalem in 1967; other areas near strategic locations or Jewish settlements.

3. Israeli Arabs

Population: 1.2 million, est.

4. Refugees and Emigrants Abroad

Population: Perhaps 4 million, 10% living in refugee camps. Major concentrations live in Jordan (2,250,000), Saudi Arabia and other Gulf States (450,000), Lebanon (450,000), Syria (500,000) and Egypt (100,000). These estimates exceed UN estimates for actual refugees, and are often supplied by those with political or financial interest in the numbers.

Palestinian-administered territory lies in two portions of the ancient Biblical holy land. The smaller but more densely populated is Gaza, a narrow strip at the southern end of the coastal plain. The larger region, whose boundaries perplex negotiators, is the West Bank, located on the ridge of hills between the Mediterranean Sea and the Jordan River. The western slopes of the hills enjoy substantial rainfall that seeps into important aquifers that extend into Israel. By contrast, the barren eastern slopes and Jordan valley receive little precipitation.

History: Civilization extends back into pre-history in the land between the Jordan and Mediterranean. Jericho, for example, is one of the oldest continuously-occupied towns in the world. Given the light rainfall, most of the population herded flocks of sheep and goats outside the villages and towns. The Biblical narrative of Abraham and similar accounts in the Quran, suggest a semi-nomadic life under the authority of a family patriarch.

Some 3,000 years ago two new peoples settled among the existing Semitic Canaanites. The *Bnei Israel* (Sons of Israel) crossed the Jordan River and seized the central hill region. Their Semitic language resembled the Canaanites', but religious, intellectual, and tribal matters set them apart. The Philistines, a sea people, landed and occupied the coastal plain. Influenced by the Greeks, the Philistines enjoyed superior iron technology and sometimes physical (Goliath!) superiority, but their power eventually weakened. Nevertheless, the Philistines contributed their name to the region's Greek and Roman occupiers. Jewish revolts against Roman rule in the century following the death of Jesus of Nazareth led the Romans to expel most Jews from the territory.

The centuries following the Arab conquest of Palestine (635–638) brought major changes in religion and language. Most of the Christian majority converted to Islam. With the exception of the Crusaders' conquests, the chronological record of Palestine differed little from those of neighboring territories (see Historical Background).

Modernization impacted the region visibly during the 19th century, and the first substantial Jewish immigration took place at its end (see Israel: History). Nevertheless, the population remained largely Muslim and overwhelmingly Arab. Only about 10% of the inhabitants were Jewish when British forces defeated Ottoman armies during World War I and ended Muslim rule.

Arab nationalism grew rapidly during the early twentieth century, but Palestinian identity only came later. In 1919 most Christians and Muslims desired to form part of a united Arab state, as they indicated to the King-Crane Commission. Nevertheless, the 1923 San Remo Conference granted Britain a mandate whose terms incorporated a Jewish national home.

Both Muslim and Christian Arabs fared badly under the mandate. Misled by Hajj Amin al-Husayni, the Mufti of Jerusalem, the Palestinians failed to develop pragmatic leaders or quiet methods to influence the government in London. Their leading families considered each other as rivals, rather than as allies against foreign threats, though the struggle with Zionism did lead them to perceive themselves distinct from Arabs living in Transjordan or Syria. Arab society lacked funds for investment, and because the mandate deliberately left health and education to the communities, rather than to the government, Arabs fell further behind Zionist settlers.

Lacking a coherent ideology, the Arab population readily realized that if immigration continued, Arab Palestinians

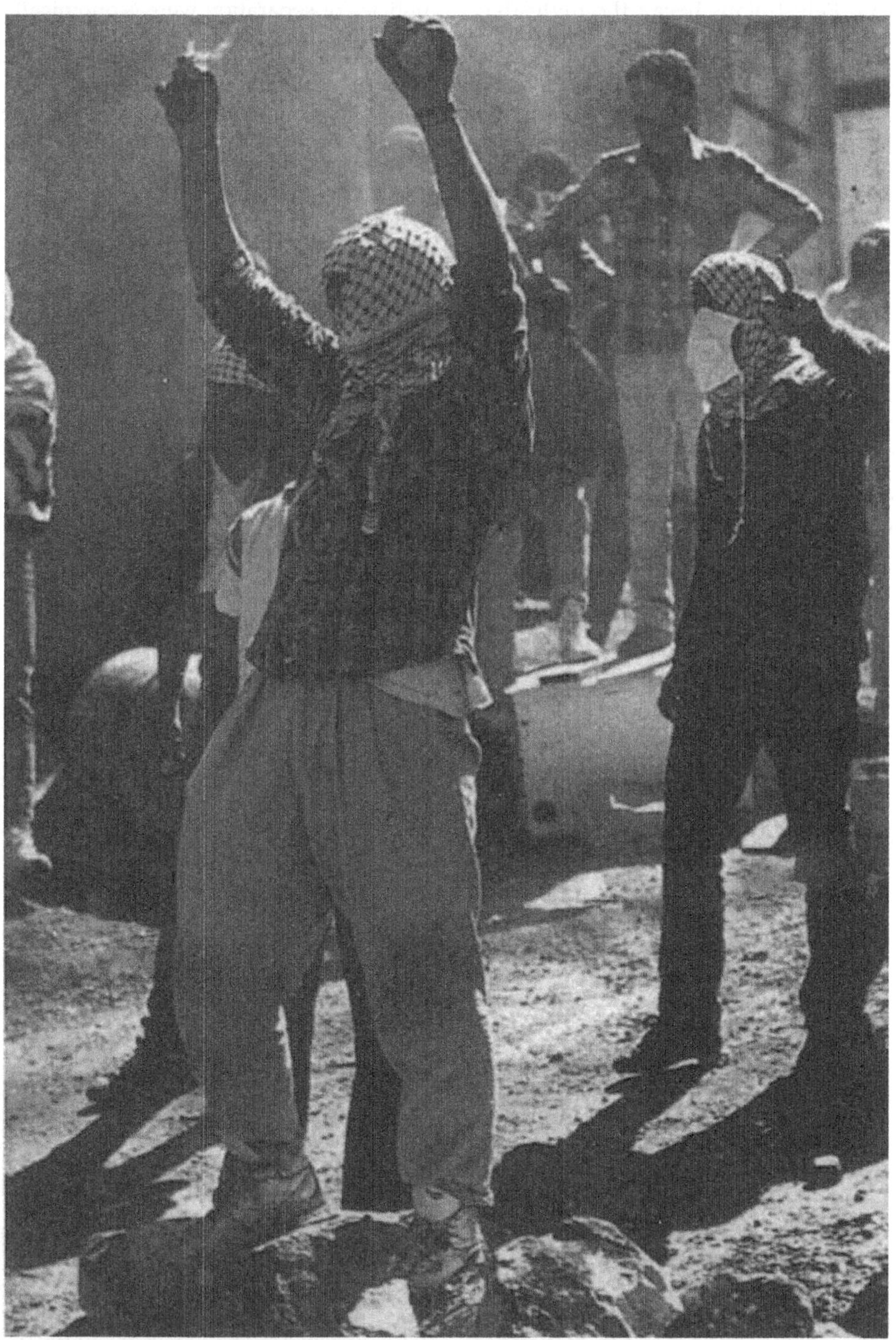

The Arab headdress—the kufiyya—served as a valued identity mask.

would eventually become a minority in a Zionist state). In desperation, Palestinians turned to large-scale communal violence in 1929 and a lengthy general strike in 1936. When a British commission proposed the partition of Palestine, virtual civil war broke out, with Arabs fighting both the British and Jews.

Origins of the Refugee Problem

After the mandate ended with partition voted by the United Nations (1947) and growing violence (see Israel: History), Palestinians began the flight that divided them into four groups. Historians continue to dispute, often very bitterly, the reasons why some 700,000 Palestinians fled their homes during the 1948–1949 Israeli War for Independence. Interpretations sympathetic to the Palestinians stress the Jewish warnings to flee, or outright expulsion. Moreover, some Arab homes were simply demolished and their inhabitants fled.

Israeli apologists sometimes accuse Arab radio broadcasts of warning the inhabitants to move from the path of advancing Arab troops. However, no credible evidence exists for this claim. The reality was complicated: clearly in some locations Israeli troops ordered the inhabitants out, but in Haifa, the Jewish mayor urged the Arabs to remain. Often, as the fighting drew near, the sight of refugees encouraged other families to seek greater

PALESTINE: Partition Plan recommended by the UN General Assembly, November 1947

safety while they awaited the verdict of battle. After atrocities such as a massacre of Arab civilians at Deir Yasin, and the reprisal murder of Jewish medical personnel on Mt. Scopus, many families on both sides must have felt their lives were at stake.

The Palestinians who fled to refugee camps were usually illiterate peasants. Deprived of farmland, they posedthey posed a significant welfare burden on newly-independent countries whose own populations were very poor. Consequently, policies of separation were economically expedient, and despite sharing language, history, and religion, most Arab states discouraged the integration of refugees. Often, Arab regimes did little but police the camps and proclaim the refugees' distress as evidence of the moral wrongs inflicted by Zionism.

The refugees themselves also rejected assimilation. They argued that they should return to homes in Palestine; some, indeed, could see their houses and lands across the armistice lines. Resettlement in other Arab countries might weaken their claim for justice. Of course, Israel consistently rejected any form of repatriation.

For over 60 years the refugees and their descendants have yearned for their day of return. While waiting, they lived first in tents, then crowded into houses of concrete block and galvanized roofs. Many lacked running water, and the buildings proved cold in the winter and hot in the summer. Often unemployed and nearly always poor, the refugees remained a fertile ground for political agitation. Minimal levels of food and clothing provided by the United Nations Relief and Works Agency (UNRWA) ensured that none starved. Ironically, UNRWA schools, employing Palestinian teachers, made the Palestinians among the best-educated Arabs. They also instilled an intense nationalism in their school children.

The West Bank

In 1949, after his Arab Legion proved at least partly effective against Israel, King Abdullah united the West Bank with his existing state of Transjordan and proclaimed the Hashemite Kingdom of Jordan. For the West Bank Palestinians, the union with Jordan proved difficult. Although the Palestinians outnumbered East Bank Jordanians and had achieved higher levels of education and political sophistication, East Bankers dominated government and the military.

Most of all, Palestinians distrusted Abdullah's moderation towards Israel. They interpreted his annexation of the West Bank as enriching his dynasty; their passion was Arab nationalism and the desire to destroy Israel. Abdullah enjoyed his enlarged kingdom only briefly, for he was assassinated by a militant Palestinian in 1951. King Hussein, his grandson and successor, continued the royal moderation; Palestinians retained their suspicions. Investment was concentrated in the East Bank, an astute policy in view of the increasing military superiority of Israel, though naturally unpopular on the West Bank.

Conditions were materially worse for the Palestinians in Gaza, a strip about 25 miles long and five miles wide administered by Egypt but not annexed. The 200,000 refugees overwhelmed the existing population of 70,000, and the dense population limited agricultural development. With its own impoverished millions, Egypt lacked funds to develop Gaza, and in fact Cairo discouraged the refugees from settling in Egypt.

Israel's conquest of the West Bank and Gaza Strip in June 1967 ushered in a new era. East Jerusalem was annexed, and its inhabitants therefore gained the vote. The rest of the West Bank fell under military administration. Absent a peace agreement, its inhabitants officially lived in occupied Jordan, but West Bankers grew increasingly separate from it despite financial aid and salaries from Amman.

Although Security Council Resolution 242 called for an Israeli withdrawal from territories occupied during the war, Israel evidently intended to remain. Israelis "created facts." They established settlements on Arab lands, particularly around Jerusalem, at strategic points along the Jordan River, and places where Jewish settlements had existed before 1948. Within 20 years, the 60,000 settlers came to control about 50% of the West Bank's land, and 34% of that in the crowded Gaza Strip. Settlers also claimed a disproportionate share of water, using almost four times as much per person as the natives. Until 1988 the occupation failed to arouse significant criticism in Israel or the United States.

Palestinians in Exile

By contrast, Palestinians abroad sensed a surge of hope after 1967. The 1964 Arab Summit Conference established the *Palestine Liberation Organization (PLO)*. Subsequently, the Palestine National Council was formed to reflect Palestinian opinion, and the Palestine National Charter formalized the PLO's goals. These called for a "One State Solution"—replacing Israel with a secular and democratic state where individuals of all religions could live together. Such phrases perhaps seem innocent, but the Charter also called Palestinians to liberate their land by force and denied Jewish immigrants a place within Palestine. Even without Zionism's emphasis on a special state for Jews, Israelis would hardly accept a solution that expelled most of them from their homes. Also in 1964, Yasir Arafat founded *al-Fatah,* the guerrilla movement whose small attacks on Israel from Syria and Jordan, actions that drew Israeli reprisals that in turn led to the June 1967 War.

That war exposed the futility of Arab military goals to defeat Israel, and it discredited virtually every Arab leader. Only the guerrillas "who sacrificed themselves," the *fida'iyin* remained. When they fought back bravely against an Israeli raid on Karameh in Jordan, they became heroes. Guerrilla groups multiplied; among the many were the *Popular Front for the Liberation of Palestine (PFLP)*, the *Popular Democratic Front (PDFLP)*, and *Saiqa*. The first two groups reflected leftist ideologies, complete with class struggles and the necessity of political and social revolution throughout the Arab world. Others were basically paid agents of particular Arab regimes.

Most Palestinians and their financial backers turned to the straightforward nationalist views of *al-Fatah*. Its founder, Yasir Arafat, became Chairman of the *PLO* in 1968 and came to symbolize Palestine as no other leader had. The *PLO*, in turn, became an umbrella organization for the various *fida'iyin*, running the refugee camps and conducting Palestinian publicity and diplomacy.

Inevitably the guerrillas disturbed Arab governments. Raids into Israel provoked retaliation, against both commando groups and economic targets in the host country. The *fida'iyin* then sought sophisticated weapons and fortified bases, and became armed units operating within an Arab state, often better paid and more glamorous than the national army. Syria quickly controlled its local guerrillas. Egypt permitted none. For Jordan and Lebanon the experience was bitter, but the refugees themselves suffered the greatest loses in inter-Arab fighting.

Its long border with Israel and large Palestinian population made Jordan a naturally desirable base for the *fida'iyin* desiring to liberate all Palestine—including freeing the West Bank from Hussein's kingdom. In 1970, the *Popular Front* hijacked Western jetliners to a desert landing strip in Jordan. In part to free the passengers taken hostage, the Jordanian army fought bitterly against Palestinian guerrillas in Amman. Thousands died, many of them civilians, and the surviving Palestinians called it Black September. (Later a secret terrorist group linked to *al-Fatah* adopted the name as a memorial.) King Hussein regained control of his capital, and after further fighting, expelled the *fida'iyin* from Jordan.

They transferred their activities to Lebanon, a country too weak to limit their activities or prevent Israel from striking at will. Scores of problems developed between the Palestinians and the Lebanese, ranging from unpaid traffic tickets and electric bills to guerrilla checkpoints and gun battles. Against a background of political wrangling between Lebanon's Muslims and Maronites, in 1975 the ambush of a Palestinian motorcade marked the beginning of the Lebanese Civil War (see Lebanon: History).

Palestinian losses were significant, and often civilians. The major refugee camp at Tel al-Za'tar fell to Lebanese Christian forces after a bloody struggle. Thousands of Palestinians and Lebanese alike perished in 1982, when a full-scale conventional attack brought Israeli troops to the suburbs of Beirut (see Israel: History). Still more civilian deaths resulted when Israeli troops allowed Maronite militiamen to enter Palestinian refugee camps outside Beirut and massacre—unopposed—hundreds of women, children, and old men.

The long years of fighting brought few benefits to Palestinians, and the hopes kindled by Karameh waned. The *fida'iyin* killed many times more Arabs—Jordanians, Lebanese, Syrians, and others—than Israelis. Likewise, the refugees suffered more deaths from Arab weapons than from Israeli ones. Despite their great popularity in some Arab and Third World circles, the *fida'iyin* had by their terrorist actions aroused intense disgust in Western public opinion. Fortunately for the Palestinians, world attention turned in 1988 from the exiled Palestinians to those living in the West Bank and Gaza Strip.

Resisting Occupation: The Intifada

The popular rebellion known as the *intifada* began in 1987. Against the Israel Defense Force, one of the world's most admired military organizations, civilians of the West Bank and Gaza used strikes, civil disobedience, rock-throwing, other petty violence and boycotts of Israeli goods. Rock and bottle-throwing youths damaged thousands of passing cars and buses; firebombs gutted others. However, the violence was not deliberately lethal, and the statistics for 1988 firmly established the one-sided nature of fatal violence: 366 Arab deaths and 11,000 wounded compared with 15 Israeli deaths and 420 injured. The *intifada* reflected a deliberate attempt to defy Israeli rule rather than to kill Jews.

The youthful activists earned wide television coverage, but the *intifada* involved many elements of Palestinian society. Middle-aged, middle-class merchants accepted repeated general strikes designed to demonstrate the authority of the resistance movement. Traditional Israeli controls—for example, smashing shutters on closed shops or welding them shut—failed to break the strikes.

Other economic actions included the boycott of Israeli cigarettes and softdrinks, and widespread resistance to taxes. The 140,000 Palestinians who provided the major source of cheap unskilled labor in Israel's construction and other industries obeyed strike calls and disrupted the Israeli economy.

The *intifada* inflicted heavy costs on the Palestinians. Besides the deaths—many of them avoidable—there were beatings, deportations, and tens of thousands of arrests. Attempting to break the uprising, Israel closed professional associations and charitable groups. It destroyed the homes of families whose teenagers were suspected of throwing gasoline bombs.

The *intifada* dramatically changed world opinion about Palestinians. They had been refugees first, then terrorists who hijacked airliners, murdered Olympic athletes, and massacred hostages. Such acts provoked outrage and extreme hostility in the Western world. After the *intifada*, they became a defenseless people, beaten and shot by alien soldiers. Even in America, the televised sufferings of Arabs eroded the prevailing belief in the moral rightness of the Israeli occupation. Closer to home, witnessing the intense nationalism, King Hussein of Jordan withdrew his claims to the West Bank.

These strengths enabled Yasir Arafat to take the diplomatic initiative in seeking an independent Palestine limited to the Occupied Territories. When the Palestine National Council met in Algiers in 1988, Arafat's carefully worded policy triumphed. Despite years of condemning it, the delegates voted to accept UN Security Council Resolution 242, linking it to the Palestinian right to self-determination (see Israel: History, Resolution 242). The resolution also implicitly abandoned the PLO's goal of eliminating Israel, and condemned terrorism of all kinds. The Council balanced these actions by declaring Palestine independent, using words that mirrored Israel's similar declaration in 1948. However, the acceptance of a state on the West Bank and Gaza—the "Two-State Solution," split the Council into moderate and rejectionist camps. It also failed to win recognition from European nations and the United States, who insisted that accepted territory and boundaries must precede formal recognition.

Soon afterwards, Arafat addressed a special session of the UN General Assembly, held in Geneva because the U.S. considered him a terrorist and refused him a visa. Posing as a statesman, he detailed the positions adopted by the National Coun-

Palestine

The first *intifada* began with protests and stones

cil, and gave away the ultimate Palestinian bargaining chip—recognition of Israel. He hoped, in response, for negotiations to free the occupied territories and form a Palestinian state. After more than two years of the *intifada*, Palestinians had restored their self-respect and unity, and gained Western sympathy. But neither the *intifada* nor Arafat's recognition of Israel had gained an inch of territory or improved the harsh military occupation. Israel's new hard-line cabinet under Yitzhak Shamir fundamentally opposed ceding any territory of Eretz Israel for peace.

Moreover, the facts on the ground worsened. In its last days, the Soviet Union reversed policy and allowed its Jews to emigrate; some one million Jewish immigrants were expected. They placed a longer fuse on the "demographic time bomb" of an Arab majority between the Jordan and Mediterranean. Settlement activities also increased in the territories, subsidized by the government despite international condemnation.

Within Palestine, the *intifada* showed signs of disintegration, as its targets became alleged collaborators or Palestinians charged with moral failures like corruption, homosexuality or prostitution. The *intifada*, itself a struggle of the weak against the powerful, was creating its own victims. To some extent, the violence between Palestinians resulted from Israeli success in rounding up or eliminating leaders and activists. Some 10% of the population suffered imprisonment, injuries requiring hospital care, or material losses such as destroyed crops or confiscated possessions.

The Price of Backing Saddam

Many Palestinians enthusiastically supported Iraqi President Saddam Hussein in 1990 when he seized Kuwait, because he then demanded a peace settlement involving Israeli-held lands. Yasir Arafat publicly embraced him. This obviously marked the triumph of emotional desperation over reason. Palestinians suffered more from the Gulf War than any nation besides Kuwait and Iraq. In Kuwait, though divided in their response to the invasion, they suffered collective reprisal. Thousands lost their jobs and life savings. Hostility, revenge, and deportations decimated the community. Palestinians in other Gulf countries found themselves under suspicion, and unable to renew visas. Losing residence and employment, they became refugees yet again.

In the West Bank and Gaza, support for the invasion cost Kuwaiti support for hospitals, schools, and the *intifada* just as Israeli curfews worsened living conditions. Gulf rulers halted aid estimated at $100 million per month to the PLO. The official PLO position swung to "neutrality," over Kuwait, but popular feeling in refugee camps and the Occupied Territories openly supported Saddam Hussein and cheered Scud attacks on Israel. It was yet another public relations disaster by a cause prone to self-destruction.

Despite their misfortunes, Palestinians won representation at the 1991 peace negotiations in Madrid because the Jordanian delegation attached Palestinian intellectuals outside the PLO. These negotiators won wide respect. Their spokeswoman, Hanan Ashrawi, presented their case to Westerners far more persuasively than Yasir Arafat ever had. Nevertheless, the discussions produced nothing of substance, partly because Israel intended to yield nothing, as its prime minister later confessed. Meanwhile, led by *Hamas* and other militant Islamic groups, Arab opposition strengthened against the talks.

After the 1992 Israeli elections, the new *Labor* government halted most new settlements outside Jerusalem. However, when the killings of Israeli soldiers and civilians continued, Prime Minister Rabin refused Palestinians entry to the Occupied Territories, even for work. Immediately unemployment soared to 50% or more in some places. The closed border carried momentous consequences. Israelis realized that they preferred life without Palestinians, and support rose for a break with the Occupied Territories.

Against this background, Israeli and *PLO* negotiators secretly met in Oslo in 1993, and agreed to create a Palestinian administration in Jericho and Gaza by April 1994. A now-famous handshake at the White House formalized the Declaration of Principles between two men who had been bitter enemies for decades, Prime Minister Rabin and Chairman Arafat.

Progress towards Palestinian Autonomy

Though the Oslo Accords won wide support in the world's press, many Palestinian groups condemned them, both on the left (the *Popular Front* and the *Democratic Front*) and the religious right (*Islamic Jihad* and *Hamas*). These groups considered two disconnected parcels of land under limited self-rule far too small a reward for ending the struggle to replace Israel with a Palestinian state. Opposition also arose within the Palestinian leadership. Calls grew for democracy, and Hanan Ashrawi chose to serve on a human rights group rather than on the administrative council.

The Oslo Accords envisaged complete agreement in 1993, followed by a phased Israeli withdrawal and elections in 1994. However, each side desired the immediate steps to reflect its vision of the final arrangements. And over the final arrangements there had been no agreement. Officially, Israel still regarded the Palestinian future as up for negotiation, and it sought to protect every Jewish settlement and access route, even those surrounded by tens of thousands of Arabs in Hebron and Gaza. In contrast, Palestinians considered their zones the embryo of an independent state, and sought the trappings of statehood: tariffs and economic regulations, currency (even if only symbolic), passports, stamps and telephone area codes. From its beginnings, the Oslo process fell behind schedule, and the slow pace of negotiations weakened support for peace.

Important forces on both sides would sabotage the peace process, and Palestinian history between 1993 and the present ultimately reduces to the conflicts these forces provoked. Unwavering in their rejection of the Oslo Accords, *Hamas* and *Islamic Jihad* launched terrorist raids that ranged from the isolated murder of soldiers to suicide attacks that killed dozens. His mentality shaped by his years as a guerilla, Yasir Arafat proved unwilling or unable to enforce the security that Israeli leaders saw as the basis of peace. On the other side, Israeli cabinets often pressed tactical demands about negotiations at the cost of setbacks to the strategic goal of peace. Border closures inflicted unemployment and other hardships that likely created additional recruits for the most militant groups. Targeted assassinations—the selective murder of militants by intelligence agents or missile strikes—often provided justification in Palestinian minds for further suicide raids.

Against this background, there were moments of achievement. In 1994, Palestinian autonomy took its first steps when the *PLO* took control of Jericho and Gaza. Middle-aged soldiers from the Palestinian Liberation Army arrived to become policemen; crowds of well-wishers cheered them. The rapid pace of events caught Palestinian leaders unprepared, but the Palestinian flag flew over Gaza and Jericho. After later negotiations, the occupiers departed Ramallah, but two-thirds of the West Bank still remained under Israeli control, including military bases, 128 settlements, and access roads, in a territory half the size of Connecticut.

Freed from the occupation, in 1996 voters overwhelmingly elected Arafat "Ra'is," or president. His supporters likewise won a majority in the Palestine National Council. Arafat then kept a very significant promise. He summoned the Council to Gaza, where after decades of exile, it met and voted overwhelmingly to delete the Charter's call for the destruction of Israel. Talks began on the final, most difficult issues: East Jerusalem, refugees, water, and settlers.

During the elections that followed the assassination of Yitzhak Rabin, Palestinian suicide bombers demonstrated the insecurity of the peace process, and thus aided the victory of Binyamin Netanyahu, whose *Likud Party* had opposed the Oslo Accords, and in fact any Palestinian state.

While Netanyahu withdrew troops from part of Hebron, he also permitted the start of a new Jewish settlement, Har Homa (Jabal Abu Ghnaim), in the vital stretch of Arab-inhabited land between Bethlehem and East Jerusalem. The Peace Process continued to disintegrate. Suicide bombings by *Hamas* in Jerusalem provoked an internal closure on Palestinian areas. This shut down travel and trade *between the individual Palestinian towns*, a blow far worse than closures Israel had inflicted before the Oslo Accords. Unemployment afflicted half the working population, and many individuals had incomes of under $2.00 per day.

The city of Hebron, the largest Arab community with nearly 100,000 inhabitants, has remained an intense source of conflict and resentment. To protect some 450 Jewish settlers and students, Israel retained 20% of the entire city, including its commercial and religious center. On the outskirts, other settlers used any available pretext to seize Arab farmlands and demolish homes built or extended without permits.

Near-success, then Diplomatic Collapse

The greatest opportunity for peace occurred in 2000. During the final days of his presidency, President Clinton invited Arafat and then-Prime Minister Ehud Barak to the Camp David presidential retreat. During intense negotiations, Barak conceded a greater Palestinian role in East Jerusalem than any Israeli leader had ever discussed in public, but he would not yield actual control over the Arab parts of the city. Mindful of both political opinion at home and his place in history, Arafat rejected the concession, insisting that "the Arab leader has not been born who will give away Jerusalem."

Months later, General Ariel Sharon's visit to the Haram al-Sharif, the Muslim holy places on Temple Mount with a security detachment of 1,000 plunged the two sides into violence. The leader of the opposition *Likud* party, Sharon had earned a reputation for aggressive behavior towards Arabs (the Qibya massacre, Jordan, 1953; ignoring a cease-fire, Egypt, 1973; permitting militiamen to enter Palestinian camps, Lebanon, 1983, where they murdered hundreds). Angry Muslims considered his visit a sacrilege and protested by stone-throwing; the police shot dead some rioters. This marked the beginning of *"al-Aqsa intifada,"* a bloody resumption of protests and violence against the occupation (see also Israel: History).

The Palestinians frequently initiated violence, but they overwhelmingly suffered the casualties. Under *Labor's* Prime Minister Barak, troops shot to kill, and half the casualties came from gunshots to the neck and head. The televised death of Muhammad Dura, a twelve-year-old boy shot while huddling with his father, won sympathy (but little else) in Arab countries and the West. Instituting a collective punishment over all the territories, Israel re-imposed its closure system, cutting the Gaza into six enclaves, and the West Bank into 24. Economic conditions, never prosperous, again became desperate. Families shared what they had, but many survived only on UNRWA food subsidies and aid from abroad (perhaps averaging $500 per person in 2001).

Seeing little progress, Palestinian popular opinion increasingly accepted the militants' argument that the Oslo peace process had created little else than a powerless and undemocratic Authority mismanaged by President Arafat. The Palestinian police even did Israel's dirty work: the occupied provided security for the occupier. Because Israel was unwilling to grant Palestinian demands, reasoned the militants, the *intifada* must continue until victory.

Yasir Arafat, alternating between his role as president and a manipulator seeking negotiating strength, permitted or (allegedly) encouraged violence if that might strengthen Palestinian interests. He possibly used terrorism to force concessions from Israel, striving to keep the territory and power gained by Oslo without delivering the promised security. Certainly

Intifada

Palestine

Likud's new Prime Minister Sharon held him personally responsible for the terrorists' bloodshed.

Whatever the initial relationships, the militants soon escaped official control. Religious and secular groups joined the armed struggle. Besides *Hamas* and *Islamic Jihad,* they included the *al-Aqsa Brigade* of Arafat's own *Fatah* movement. This placed the Palestinian security forces in impossible circumstances. Israel and the U.S. demanded that Arafat end terrorism and arrest its perpetrators before negotiations. To make those arrests required the police, but widespread public support for these groups sometimes blocked Palestinian police who attempted to arrest alleged militants. The police also became particular targets of Israeli fire, as targets in reprisal killings.

After an explosion killed 25 elderly Jews gathered for Passover in the spring of 2002, Israeli forces systematically attacked the major West Bank cities in an effort to destroy terrorist cells. Over 200 Arabs died; tens of thousands endured hardships ranging from battle wounds to confinement indoors. Government offices, police offices and stores suffered vandalism. After a carefully planned ambush in the Janin refugee camp took the lives of Israeli soldiers, the Israel Defense Forces left destruction compared by eyewitnesses to an earthquake zone. Accounts verified by Human Rights Watch suggested war crimes occurred, such as the use of civilians as human shields, or the prevention of medical assistance to the camp for five days.

In Ramallah, the Israelis deliberately spared part of Yasir Arafat's headquarters, but confined him to two rooms, and prevented him from attending an Arab summit conference. Thus imprisoned, he regained some of the respect as a leader that his inept administration had destroyed. Released after American pressure, Arafat later promised reforms and elections, the first to the legislature in six years. However, suicide bombings led Israel to seize and hold most Arab cities and towns. The elections were postponed, but Arafat probably did not desire a free vote anyway. His popularity, overwhelming while he was besieged, fell rapidly in the face of demands from nearly everyone—Palestinians of all parties, Americans, Israelis—for improved security, an attack on corruption, and the rule of law.

Fatah Fractures; Hamas Wins

Beyond symbolism, in almost a decade the Palestinian National Authority had achieved little. Israel controlled the electricity, water supply, and telephone lines, and divided Palestinian islets from one another by roads to the growing settlements. Financially, the PA depended almost completely on foreign aid. In fact, most of its own taxes are collected by Israel on trade, thus enabling Israel to block them when desired. Arafat's employees felt underpaid, and the Palestinian public resented corruption and the creation of monopolies. The heavy-handed police often acted repressively. When twenty academics and legislators signed a severe attack on the Arafat administration and called the Oslo peace process a "conspiracy" against the nation, the security forces arrested half the signatories without charging them.

The late Yasir Arafat, PLO chairman and PA President

Arafat's death in 2004 offered the possibility of a new start. Long the personal symbol of the Palestinian struggle, in Israeli and American eyes he often epitomized the causes of his political rivals, the suicide bombers. As president, he also bore responsibility for an incompetent and failing administration. His death left a nation so fractured politically that commentators speculated about the possibility of anarchy, or that Islamic militants might seize Gaza and split it from the West Bank.

In the presidential race that followed *Fatah* united around Mahmud Abbas, a long-time aide to Arafat. Despite his moderation and opposition to the violent *intifada,* Abbas won an overwhelming majority in a light turnout. He adeptly negotiated a ceasefire with Israel that required a halt to Palestinian violence. In return, Israel agreed to withdraw from some West Bank cities, stop assassinations, and release hundreds of prisoners.

Abbas fared less well with domestic politics. He failed to combat corruption effectively, or to halt the growing anarchy when *Fatah's* own multiple security forces confronted each other and those of *Hamas* on the streets of Gaza. However, he did persuade the various armed units to halt suicide operations in 2005, thus making possible the Israeli withdrawal from Gaza.

Recalling the Arab sense of victory that followed Israel's withdrawal from Lebanon, the Sharon cabinet determined to erase any doubts about Israeli power before withdrawing from Gaza. Israel Defense Forces assassinated a number of militants, notably Sheikh Ahmad Yassin, the elderly leader of *Hamas* who died in his wheelchair. After his successor was assassinated a few weeks later, *Hamas* kept its leadership secret.

Besides exterminating the militants' leadership, the Israeli military also targeted supply depots, workshops and other possible military targets. Its units inflicted such destruction on the Rafah refugee camp that the U.S. abandoned its usual veto and allowed the UN Security Council to condemn the operation.

The Israeli withdrawal initially brought a great sense of freedom to Gaza, but within months, the predictions of anarchy began to come true. Abbas's own party, *Fatah,* splintered between the Old Guard around Abbas and supporters of younger militants like Marwan Barghouti, a hero imprisoned for life in Israel for approving attacks on civilians. Without Barghouti, *Fatah* symbolized a policy blamed by the public for corruption and the economic depression. By contrast, *Hamas* decided to contest legislative elections, and it entered the contest united and disciplined. *Hamas* won decisive victories in most locations, the highest share of the national vote, and it captured 72 of the 132 legislative seats.

By exercising their democratic right to vote for the party of their choice even though it refused to recognize Israel, Palestinian voters plunged themselves into difficulties. *Hamas* found no allies; its prime minister, Ismail Haniya, immediately faced a cut-off of almost all government revenue—taxes collected by Israel, foreign aid from the U.S. and Europe, and funds from Arab states. On the surface, Israel and the U.S. refused to contribute funds to a group committed to Israel's destruction. Conveniently, this same tactic might strangle the Palestinian Authority to financial death and thus also discredit *Hamas.*

Israel could hardly be expected to finance those committed to its destruction. However, the financial strangulation carried somber consequences. Following a relatively free election, the West punished the Palestinian people for voting out a

The Palestinian Red Crescent Society offices, directly targeted (Photo by Said Abedwahed)

decrepit and divided party. Arab democracy, it seemed, was desired—but only as long as voters selected winners approved by America. Although unwilling to recognize Israel, Ismail Haniya was willing to pursue a truce with it.

The results of the financial blockade were as predictable as they were perverse. Utterly unable to pay salaries, the regime floundered. The economy continued in depression. Western nations and organizations therefore funded relief activities and even paid salary support for civil employees. In fact, *they actually spent more money on Palestinians during the blockade* than they would have without it. Arab government aid, though, could not reach Haniya's legitimately elected government.

Gaza under Hamas

In 2007 King Abdullah of Saudi Arabia pressured *Hamas* and *Fatah* to form a cabinet of national unity, in hopes of lifting the blockade and ending the frequent clashes between their militias in Gaza. However, Ismail Haniya remained prime minister, and he continued to refuse to recognize Israel, so the blockade continued. That summer, clashes between the two parties' militiamen in Gaza reached a crisis. *Hamas* rejected President Abbas's attempts to control the security forces, and arrested or killed *Fatah's* fighters in Gaza. In response, Abbas dismissed Haniya's cabinet. Almost immediately, the financial blockade was lifted on Abbas's government. Because *Hamas* members still formed the parliamentary majority, contrary to standard democratic practices Abbas governed only the West Bank. Gaza remained under *Hamas* rule.

Once *Hamas* ruled Gaza, Israeli restrictions gradually halted Gaza's economy. The level of goods entering Gaza fell to 10% of the previous level. Construction stopped completely, 90% of private industries shut down, farms became free-fire zones for Israeli tanks, and 80% of the population only survived thanks to food aid. The power generating plant failed to operate well after it was attacked, and Israel cut the levels of electricity and fuel permitted into the Strip. Hospitals fell short of medicines, but animal vaccines were rushed into Gaza, to avoid communicable diseases that might spread across the border.

In response, enterprising Gazans and *Hamas* militants built multiple tunnels where smugglers brought consumer goods—eventually, even new cars—and undoubtedly military supplies. Ironically, since *Hamas* taxed the smugglers, its control over the economy increased—it now gained revenue from trade without Israel collecting the taxes.

Soon after the 2005 Israeli withdrawal, sporadic fighting broke out between Islamic militants in Gaza and the Israeli military. A brazen raid by militants over the border into Israel captured 19-year-old Corporal Gilad Shalit, and during 2006, while Israel fought Hizbullah across the northern border, it also launched attacks on militants in the Gaza Strip. Though world attention focused on Shalit, the bloodshed proved highly one-sided. During the year after the withdrawal from Gaza, two Israeli civilians died from the militants' simple rockets. By contrast, according to the human rights group B'Tselem, the retaliatory air strikes and tank invasions killed about 400 Palestinians.

Despite foreign mediation, by 2008 neither side had gained its desired goals. A truce had committed Israel to permit in-

A wounded Palestinian being evacuated. Palestinian and Israeli accounts conflict dramatically over the identity of those killed and wounded. The lack of a uniform does not imply a civilian casualty.

creased trade, and *Hamas* to halting all attacks by all groups on Israel. But the rocket attacks never quite stopped, and trade never resumed its peace-time levels. After the formal expiration of the cease-fire, Israel launched an intensive bombing campaign followed by a land invasion of Gaza, seeking to destroy the rocket-launching capabilities, reduce or eliminate *Hamas* as an armed organization, and re-establish respect for its military after the inconclusive war against *Hizbullah* in 2006 (see Israel: **history**).

Hamas fought back with tactics borrowed from *Hizbullah* and Iran. Its fighters dispersed among the population to fight in civilian areas, with weapons stored in many homes and mosques. To avoid air attacks, fighters moved directly between homes, or used tunnels and underground command posts—one headquarters was reported underneath the largest hospital. Clearly, these tactics did not seek to minimize civilian casualties, and Amnesty faulted *Hamas* for endangering Palestinian civilians by firing rockets from residential neighborhoods. For their part, Israeli troops rarely entered houses by the door, fearing booby-traps, and they combined the use of precision weaponry with heavy, short-range firing at points of resistance. Inevitably, hundreds of Palestinian civilians were killed, some of them sheltering beside UN compounds or in a UN school. Thousands were wounded.

Charges of war crimes quickly arose against both sides. Israel received the most condemnation (e.g., from the UN, the Red Cross, Amnesty International), for its use of civilians as shields or to enter suspected booby-traps, for using white phosphorous bombs, for obstructing access to medical care, and the "wanton and deliberate" destruction of homes, businesses, and public buildings. However, *Hamas* was blamed for its rocket attacks on civilians. Israel also claimed that *Hamas* fighters abandoned uniforms to mix with the population, violated rules on the use of the white flag, sheltered behind civilians, and generally fought in ways that endangered civilians.

President Mahmoud Abbas of Palestine

The three-week war ended when first Israel and then *Hamas* independently announced cease-fires. It left enormous destruction, including neighborhoods and an industrial area flattened by bulldozers and shells. Along with other infrastructure, damaged sewer and water pipelines may take years to repair. Nevertheless, the fighting had failed to create new rules of the game. *Hamas* remained in power, the blockade continued, and the world perceived Gazans as the victims, but did little about it. Smugglers quickly resumed their trade through the tunnels, no doubt importing weapons as well as consumer goods.

Israeli missiles score direct hits on Gaza University, suspected of harboring Hamas military activities

Although the United Nations, the International Committee of the Red Cross, and other organizations long warned about the consequences of the blockade of Gaza, for three years Israel successfully defended it in Western public opinion as a necessity for security against home-made missiles. The gradual release of information about details of the restrictions failed to change perceptions. What U.S. congressman cared, for example, if mineral water could be imported but not fruit juice, or by preventing repairs to the sewer treatment plants the blockade threatened public health?

When Israeli commandos stormed the *Mavi Marmara* in international waters and killed 9 peace activists, world perceptions shifted radically. The Turkish ferry was part of a flotilla organized to challenge the blockade by attempting to carry humanitarian supplies to Gaza. World perceptions changed, and even the U.S. president recognized that conditions in Gaza had become unsustainable.

Responding to international pressure, the Israeli cabinet reduced the embargo's scope. Food, toys, and kitchen utensils would be permitted, as well as material for the UN, but sea shipments to Gaza remained prohibited. Given Egyptian cooperation, Israel retained almost total control over imports. The collective punishment of Gaza continued, though presumably less harshly. After the downfall of President Mubarak, Egypt symbolically opened the Rafah crossing, but strict controls remained, with only a fortunate few allowed to cross each day.

After repeated cross-border attacks by both sides, open warfare resumed between Israel and Gaza in November 2012, beginning with a surgical airstrike that killed Ahmad Jabari, the *Hamas* military commander. For most of two weeks the two sides conducted an aerial conflict, with the Israeli strikes on militants, *Hamas's* rocket launchers, underground tunnels, storage areas, and other facilities. In turn, *Hamas* fired some 1500 locally-manufactured short-range missiles and a few Iranian-made Fajr-5 and M75 medium-range missiles at Israeli towns and cities, some reaching the outskirts of Tel Aviv, despite the success of Israeli's Iron Dome anti-missile system.

The conflict ended through U.S. and Egyptian mediation. Israel's motives in launching the war were complex and remain murky. Rocket fire from *Islamic Jihad* and sometimes *Hamas* often provided a pretext. Two other factors may interest historians. The fighting began a few days before the UN General Assembly was set to debate the appeal of Palestinian President Mahmoud Abbas for "non-member observer state status." A war with *Hamas* might weaken the appeal. And just like the last war (of 2009) the fighting occurred just a few weeks before *Knesset* elections, a good time to remind voters of the prime minister's astute leadership via the nightly news.

Meanwhile, Israeli restrictions continue to make life "extremely hard" for Palestinians in the West Bank. Getting to school, work or hospital is often virtually impossible, and restrictions linked to Israeli settlements deprive many Palestinian farmers of their land. An estimated 50% of the West Bank's population lives in poverty.

Domestic Instability and International Stagnation

Free and open Palestinian elections are extremely unlikely, given the division between *Hamas*-ruled Gaza and the West Bank under *Fatah*. Moreover, *Fatah* is divided between those loyal to Mahmud Abbas and others seeking a new face such as Marwan Barghouti, still imprisoned. Therefore, when the already-extended presidential term neared its end in 2010, the *PLO* met the difficulty by prolonging once again the terms of the president and parliament. Predictably condemned by *Hamas,* the decision hardly strengthened popular support for the Palestinian Authority.

The post-Mubarak regime in Egypt mediated an understanding, but after just a few weeks the conflicting needs of each party overwhelmed it. After all, *Fatah* desires early elections to restore legitimacy to the presidency and legislature whose terms have expired. But for *Hamas,* early elections risk unfavorable comparisons between the economic disaster of Gaza and the modest prosperity of the West Bank.

Such domestic political shambles left the PA a poor partner for the indirect "proximity negotiations" widely considered the only route leading to a two-state solution. However, it was Israel that essentially ruptured the talks. When the Netanyahu cabinet refused to extend the settlement freeze in 2010, the Palestinian Authority halted the negotiations, as it had threatened to do.

The Palestinian Authority then sought a distinctly different path to a settlement: a UN vote recognizing independence. Several European governments seemed sympathetic, but the U.S. threatened a veto in the Security Council, and the matter was sidetracked. Then, in November 2012, with Abbas repeating his acceptance of the 1948 borders, Palestine appealed to the UN General Assembly for recognition as a non-member observer state. It was not recognition of independence, but the U.S. carries no veto in the General Assembly, and the motion passed, 138-9, with 41 abstentions. Observer state status may permit the Palestinian Authority to play a greater role in the UN's various agencies, likely embarrassing Israel. In turn, Israel responded by blocking the transfer of taxes collected on imports to Palestine, forcing the Palestinian Authority to destitution.

Other tactics undertaken to isolate the Jewish state include the commemoration of past disasters by exiled Palestinians such as Nakba Day, and organizing refugees abroad to march home to "Palestine," thus forcing Israel's military to decide whether to shoot unarmed civilians.

However successful declarations and protests might be, to live as an independent nation requires a government. A recent report by the UN special coordinator gave the PA passing marks in areas such as rule of law, health and social services, and infrastructure. The gravest difficulty has been and remains political, where opinions and decisions are constrained by Israel and other more powerful actors.

Years after his presidential term expired, Mahmud Abbas continues in office but lacks legitimacy. Though unconstitutional and often ineffective, his rule does permit far greater freedom than enjoyed in some Arab states. For example, one of

Gaza University leveled by direct Israeli attacks.

the most popular TV programs is "The President," a weekly reality show that features real politicians interviewing ordinary people willing to discuss what they would do if they took office.

Financial difficulties in Gaza, Abbas's need to demonstrate accomplishments, and U.S. pressure for serious peace talks spurred moves to end the political dispute between *Hamas* and *Fatah.* At least temporarily, the rivals overcame their internal rivalry, and after seven years of separate regimes in Gaza and the West Bank, in 2014 they agreed an independent cabinet supported by both parties. Rami Hamdallah, the incumbent West Bank prime minister, headed the new cabinet of technocrats pledged to hold elections within six months. Crowds in Gaza welcomed the news with celebrations, and Ismail Haniya's cabinet formally resigned.

The agreement to create a unified cabinet aroused intense criticism from the Israeli government. Prime Minister Netanyahu denounced any cabinet supported by *Hamas*, but failed to win much international support, even from some normally pro-Israeli commentators. As the U.S. officially commented, Palestinians had formed "an interim technocratic government" that did not include any members of *Hamas*.

Nevertheless, the unity cabinet provided the final obstacle to U.S. peace efforts led by Secretary of State John Kerry.

Culture: As Arabs, and most often Muslims, Palestinians share many cultural values of the surrounding countries. Customs regarding food, dress, and limitations on young men mixing with young women are much like those in Jordan. However, the diversity of personal experiences provides a greater variety of cultural impacts than in most Arab states. Most refugees in Gaza, for example, lack the financial sophistication of an engineer in Saudi Arabia, or the intellectual breadth of an educated woman from East Jerusalem.

Heavily influenced by Marxism and other secular ideas, the *Palestine Liberation Organization* accepted women as professionals, and many of them dressed in Western styles. With the growth of Islamist militancy, however, women in Gaza and other bastions of *Hamas* increasingly choose to wear at least a head covering, and conservatives clearly consider a woman's significance to come from her husband or family. Islamists in recent years also discouraged concerts of popular music and dancing. There is only one movie house in the entire Palestinian authority.

The most-recognized Palestinian intellectual in the Western world was undoubtedly Edward Said, the eloquent literary critic and author of *Orientalism*, a serious attack on much Western writing about the region. Far closer to contemporary passions, the feature film *Paradise Now*, a joint production of Israelis and Palestinians, portrayed the emotions of two young men recruited as suicide bombers. The movie was nominated for an Oscar in 2006 as best foreign film and it won that category at the Golden Globes.

Economic Prospects: Several recent studies attempt to predict economic conditions in the first years of an independent state. Given the high birthrate, and the possible return of some refugees, the population of the PA will climb significantly from the three million at the turn of the century. Water use for irrigation, industry, and households by such a dense population would place severe pressure on resources, and imply that current Israeli dependence on West Bank supplies must cease.

Estimates of the cost of establishing a Palestinian state exceed $14 billion, with large investment in housing, business, industry, and the infrastructure. Because independence will likely permanently reduce the number of jobs in Israel, it will require greatly enlarged economic opportunities in the West Bank and Gaza. Companies linked to Israel would need to shift to other export markets, or find alternative suppliers. Given such substantial financial burdens, an independent Palestine located between Israel and Jordan can prosper only with large subsidies from other Arab states.

The Future: Hopes might rise for improved living conditions within Palestinian-administered territory if elections can be held by the December 2014 deadline, and voters select a moderate rather than extremist majority.

But the political agonies among Palestinians are not about reducing unemployment a few percentage points and raising GDP growth. Instead, the questions are existential: will a Palestinian state exist between Israel and the Jordan River? Is a two-state solution viable any longer, given Israeli settlements scattered across much of the land? Is it acceptable in Islam to conclude peace with unbelievers who have conquered part of the Dar al-Salam? In second rank are the fate of Jerusalem, the right of the refugees to return, and whether Israel should be recognized as a Zionist state.

The U.S. likely made its last significant effort for a peace settlement with John Kerry's direct involvement in 2014. As the Obama administration is a lame duck, its ability to exert pressure for a reasonable solution has collapsed.

Expect the Palestinian population to slowly sell lands to the occupier and suffer even more difficulties inflicted by those who desire a land without its hereditary people. Very possibly, there is no happy ending for this generation or the next.

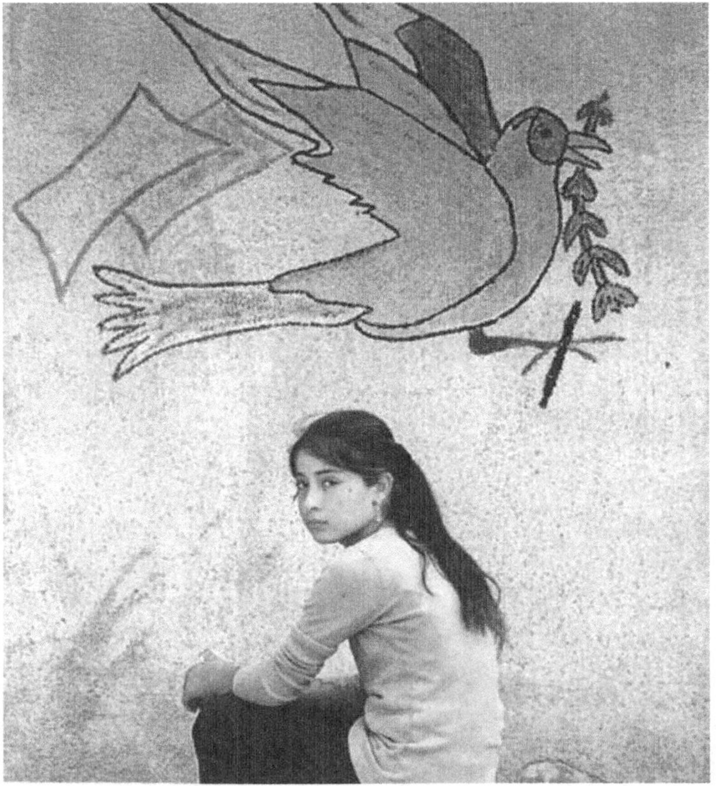

A Palestinian girl in Gaza

The State of Qatar

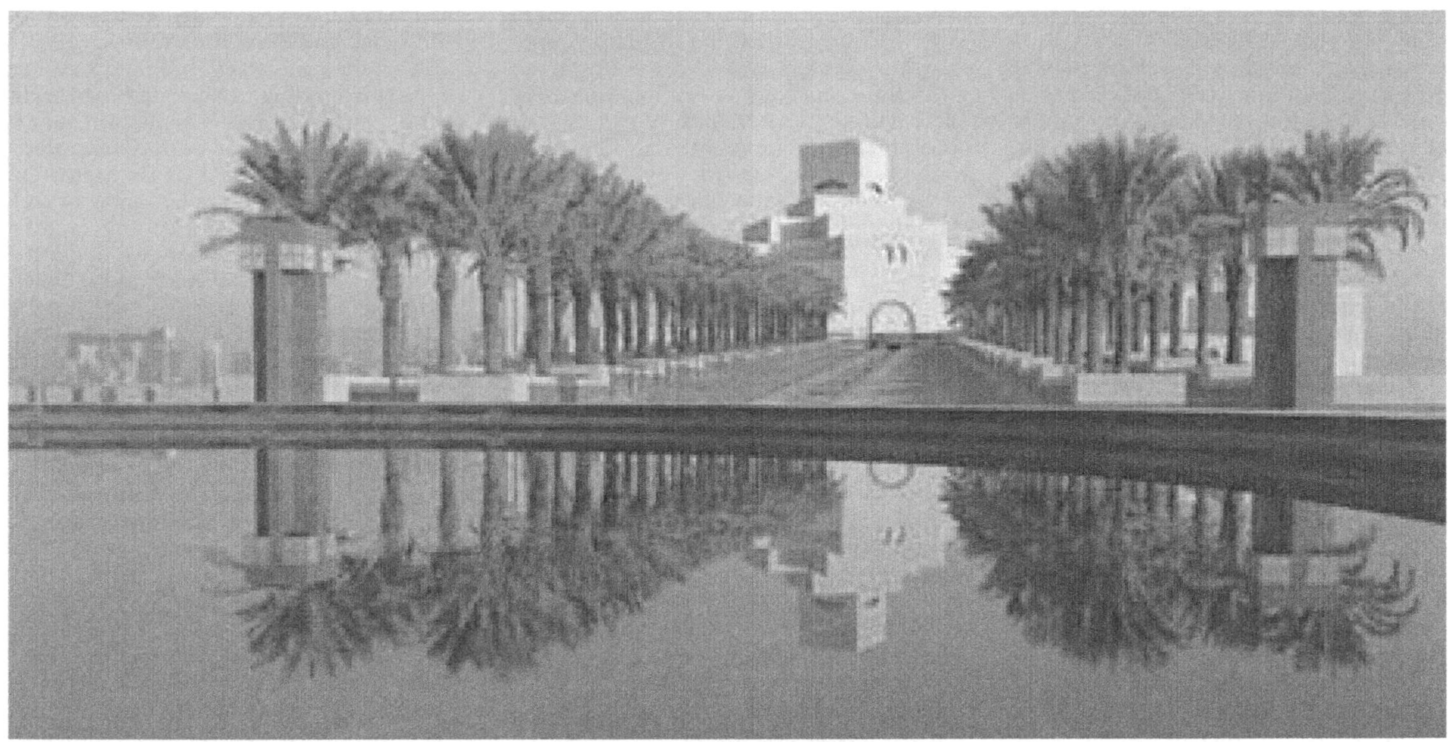

The Museum of Islamic Art, Doha, designed by I. M. Pei

Area: 4,416 sq. mi. (11,437 sq. km.).
Population: 2.2 million, fewer than 20% native Qataris.
Capital City: Doha (metro area pop. 1.0 million).
Climate: Extremely hot and humid except for moderate and dry winters.
Neighboring Countries: Saudi Arabia (South); Bahrain (off Northwest coast); United Arab Emirates (Southeast).
Time Zone: GMT +3.
Official Language: Arabic.
Ethnic Background: The Arab majority is less than half Qatari. The workforce is often Iranian or Pakistani.
Principal Religion: Islam.
Chief Commercial Products: Liquefied natural gas (LNG), petroleum and petrochemicals; iron and steel; urea and ammonia fertilizers; some vegetables during the winter.
Major Trading Partners: Japan, U.S., Germany, U.K., France, Thailand.
Currency: Riyal (= 100 dirhams).
Former Colonial Status: British Protectorate, 1916–1971.
Independence Date: September 3, 1971.
Chief of State: Sheikh Tamim bin Hamad Al Thani, Emir (2013)
Head of Government: Sheikh Abdullah bin Nasser al-Thani, Prime Minister (2013).
National Flag: An unadorned maroon field with a broad, serrated vertical band of white at the pole.
Gross Domestic Product: $214 billion (current prices) and $215 billion (Purchasing Power Parity).
GDP per capita: $97,000 (PPP).

Qatar, (pronounced *Gah*-tar, stress on the first syllable) occupies a peninsula jutting northward into the Arab Gulf from the mainland of Arabia. It is little more than 100 miles long and varies from 35 to 50 miles in width. The terrain is almost entirely a barren desert of gravel, rock and sand. Sources of fresh water are extremely scarce. Aside from a few date palms and agricultural experimental stations, the little vegetation is hardy desert scrub.

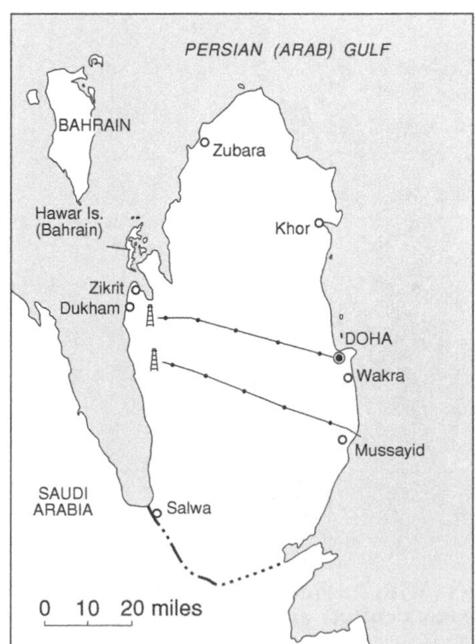

History: Two fundamentals—dependence on the sea for livelihood and a culture shared with others in the region—have influenced life in Qatar ever since the Late Stone Ages. Given its meager water supplies, Qatar played no significant role in the region's conquests, whether by Alexander the Great's navy, Muslim Arabs nine hundred years later, or occasional Persian rulers. However, archaeological remains from the Abbasid era (9th century) suggest that the inhabitants used greater wealth, perhaps from selling pearls, to construct better homes and public buildings. When the Abbasid prosperity declined in Iraq, so did the population of Qatar. By the 13th century an Arab geographer considered it just a village.

Safavid Persia claimed the area in the 18th century, and taxed coastal communities for their pearling activities. In 1795, Saudi forces captured the important fort of Zubara. The Saudis appointed a governor in 1809, but within a decade the Saudi state collapsed (see Saudi Arabia: History).

Sporadic confusion and disorder marked much of the 19th century. Raids by Gulf towns on each other and on merchant shipping led Britain in 1820 to draft a treaty that committed most Gulf ports to honor a regional truce, but Qatar lacked an acknowledged ruler to sign the document. Fighting later broke out with its traditional rival, Bahrain, whose forces razed the largest town, Doha. Following inconclusive skirmishes in 1868, Britain negotiated a settlement with Muhammad bin Thani, a leading tribal leader, whose authority gradually spread to the entire peninsula. Before the end of the century, Ottoman Turkish troops had landed, and the population had mostly embraced *Wahhabism.*

By the early 20th century, then, four outside powers desired to influence the territory: Bahrain, the Saudis, the Ottoman Empire and Great Britain. Despite the rivalries, Qatari pearling activities reached their zenith, with hundreds of pearling boats carrying nearly 13,000 crew and divers.

After World War I began, the Ottoman detachment withdrew, and the 1916 Anglo-Qatari treaty ended centuries of legal limbo. It recognized British influence as paramount, gave protection to the pearling fleet, and forbade the slave trade. Qatar was allowed to govern itself under the Al Thani (Al translates "family;" al- means "the"). Its formal society, politics and culture remained almost completely undeveloped, with virtually no medical facilities and only a solitary modern grade school.

The 1930s proved devastating. World demand for jewelry, and thus pearls, fell greatly during the Great Depression. Even worse, the Japanese discovered a method to raise cultured pearls. This created devastating competition and sharply falling prices. In 1935 another agreement with Britain granted the (British) Anglo-Persian Oil Company exclusive rights to search for oil. Commercial deposits were discovered in 1939, but World War II postponed development, and oil exports only began a decade later.

Oil changed Qatari society. The ruling family inevitably squandered some of the new wealth. Nevertheless, oil revenues financed roads, schools, and hospitals. A shortage of local labor led to a steady influx of workers and professionals from other Arab and Muslim nations. Soon Qataris found themselves a minority in their own state.

With British withdrawal from the Gulf on the horizon, Qatar considered federating with Bahrain and the seven sheikhdoms of Trucial Oman (see United Arab Emirates). However, old rivalries stirred distrust, and satisfactory terms could not be negotiated. Qatar then proclaimed its separate independence and in 1971 it gained membership in the League of Arab States and the United Nations.

As independence neared, the emir approved a basic law for the state. While no charter of democracy, this included a bill of rights and provided a Council of Ministers and an Advisory Council—both appointed by the ruler himself. Soon after independence, a more cautious and hard-working cousin, Sheikh Khalifa bin Hamad, seized power, blaming his predecessor for squandering financial resources. The ruling family and most Qataris approved the change.

The new emir energetically devoted some oil income for economic development, including steel and fertilizer projects. He appointed an advisory council in order to learn opinion outside the ruling family.

Emir Sheikh Hamad and his wife Sheikha Mozah with President and Michelle Obama in 2009. Sheikha Mozah plays a major role in Qatar's culture and education

White House photo

Internationally, he donated generously to Palestinian and other Arab causes.

Given the historically insignificant value of the surrounding uninhabited coral reefs and expanses of desert, some of Qatar's boundaries had never been demarcated. In 1986 a dispute with Bahrain heated up over Hawar Island, an outcropping of reef whose possession conferred sovereignty over potential oil deposits (see Bahrain). Failing to obtain local mediation, Qatar asked the International Court of Justice to determine its rightful owner. In 2001 the court ruled that Hawar was indeed Bahraini territory, but that the contested town of Zubara belonged to Qatar. Both sides accepted the ruling.

As a member of the Gulf Cooperation Council, Qatar joined the multinational coalition to liberate Kuwait. Its forces fought in the first ground victory of the war, defeating an Iraqi attack on the Saudi city of Khafji.

After years as the prime minister, in 1995 Sheikh Hamad overthrew the emir, his father, Sheikh Khalifa Al-Thani. Much younger than many Gulf rulers, Sheikh Hamad, assisted by his foreign minister, displayed a distinctively independent foreign policy, sometimes labeled "Brand Qatar:" spend wisely , give generously, and keep your name in the public eye. He approved military facilities for U.S. forces, and hosted visits by Israeli officials. This earned condemnation from many Arabs. However, he also expressed sympathy with Iraq and Iran.

Sheikh Hamad took initiatives in domestic politics as well. He reduced press censorship and encouraged media discussion of serious issues such as the role of women. Along with greater freedom of speech, he instituted municipal elections. This proved a success with the voters, and six women ran for office, though they did not win.

The constitution issued by Sheikh Hamad and approved in 2003 created a partly-elected advisory parliament and provided a level of democracy surpassed by only Bahrain and Kuwait on the Arab side of the Gulf. Sheikh Hamad has also emphasized the separation of family and state finance. In 2003 he transferred the designation of crown prince to a younger son, Tamim, a British-educated soldier.

During the 2003 invasion of Iraq, the U.S. increasingly used the al-Udaid military base south of Doha. It became a politically safe location because Qatar's small population seemed too rich to protest about the bases, whereas many Saudis opposed the presence of U.S. troops. The U.S. military concentrated its information activities in Doha and installed the latest command facilities at al-Udaid, which became the primary U.S. base in the region.

Qatar

An exciting and highly competitive camel race across the desert

The combination of growing wealth and Sheikh Hamad's interest in mediating thorny regional problems elevated Qatar's international influence above that expected for its population. The emir and his officials successfully mediated between Lebanese factions (2008), Sudan and the Darfur rebels (2011), and the Palestinian rivals, *Fatah* and *Hamas*. Going beyond the Arab League's call for intervention in Libya in 2011, Qatar dispatched fighter aircraft to police the no-fly zones. It also provided diplomatic support for the Syrian demonstrators, and reportedly supplied weapons to the Free Syrian Army.

In 2013 Sheikh Hamad abdicated in favor of his son, Tamim, then aged 33. By far the youngest ruler in the region, he also enjoyed the first peaceful transition of power in three generations. Educated in Britain, Sheikh Tamim developed a passion for sports that led to chairing the organizing committee for the 2006 Asian Games and serving on the International Olympic Committee. He also chaired the Qatar Investment Authority, the state's sovereign investment fund that owns Harrods, the London department store, and has major investments in Western oil and banking companies.

As the emir, Sheikh Tamim broadly supported Qatar's major domestic policies, in part because major infrastructure projects are underway and government spending is planned for years ahead. However, the new ruler quickly enforced modest spending cuts and limits on borrowing by state-owned companies. Some cuts took place in the arts, until then often lavishly funded. One program of dubious logic that was curtailed was the multi-billion dollar Qatar National Food Security Program. As its name implied, its purpose was to produce most (70%) of the country's food needs, much of it with desalinized water. The new goal became 40%, using less water and natural gas, and producing a much smaller carbon footprint.

The primary cause of the cutbacks is massive spending for the 2022 FIFA World Cup. Its eight (originally 12) new air-conditioned football (soccer) stadiums and the accompanying infrastructure—a rail system, new airport, seaport, and hundreds of miles of expressway—may cost at least $150–$200 billion, or over $75,000 per resident. Allegations that a former Qatari football official, now disgraced, paid bribes to win votes for Qatar's proposal have created some uncertainty about the entire project, but even if proven, such corruption would hardly be new to the organization.

Sheikh Tamim bin Hamad Al Thani, Emir of Qatar

The new Sheikh is considered more religiously conservative than his father, and reportedly sympathizes strongly with Egypt's *Muslim Brotherhood*. He became emir just as Egypt's President Mohammed Morsi's government was overthrown by General al-Sisi, a setback for one of Qatar's protégés. Nevertheless, backing for the *Brotherhood* continued, financially and symbolically. Sermons by Yusuf Qaradawi, a *Brotherhood* preacher, continued to be broadcast by the Arabic channel of Al-Jazeera; they sometimes attacked Gulf governments. In response, Saudi Arabia, Kuwait, and the United Arab Emirates withdrew their ambassadors from Qatar in 2014.

The frantic pace of urbanization, economic growth, and pursuit of the consumer culture have imposed significant social costs on native Qataris, as well as on the foreign workers engaged in often-risky construction jobs. In addition to the highest per capita incomes in the world, Qataris enjoy free education, free healthcare, free water and free electricity. There are job guarantees for those who studied; unemployment is the world's lowest. However, financial abundance enables a lifestyle that leaves two-thirds of Qataris, adults and children, obese. Perhaps 40% of marriages now end in divorce, and nannies from the Philippines, Nepal or Indonesia raise most children. The family unit, so vital to survival in the difficult past, is breaking down.

Culture: Qatar is the only country besides Saudi Arabia with a sizeable Wahhabi community. As most Qataris (but few of

Qatar

The ultra-modern Doha Sheraton Hotel

its foreign workers) follow Wahhabi practices, strong historical ties link the state with Saudi Arabia.

Like most Arab countries, Qatar's school system provides free education through high school. More than 50,000 children and young people enroll in this twelve-year system. There are also technical schools, a teacher-training school and a religious institute. The University of Qatar, completed in 1985, now has an enrollment of about 8,000, nearly 75% women.

The Qatar Foundation for Education, Science and Community Development opened Education City in 2001, bringing together everything from schools to graduate programs. Six prominent U.S. universities, including Cornell and Carnegie Mellon, and three European universities offer specialized programs on an impressive campus that reflects Qatar's determination to become a leading educational force in the Middle East. The curricula and textbooks are the same as the home campus, and all instruction is in English. On-campus, even the traditional gender separation is relaxed, at least in some disciplines.

The goals underlying Education City are relatively straightforward. Young people, particularly women, desire a first-rate education, but especially since 2001 are reluctant to study in the U.S. In addition, the universities attract wealthier expatriates, and hopefully students from abroad.

Qatar's Al-Jazeera satellite TV station, government-financed but operated independently, broadcasts sophisticated critiques and interviews, including some of Saddam Hussein's attacks on Arab rulers. The broadcasts occasionally lead some governments to shut down Al-Jazeera's offices, and a group of Arab governments in 2008 attempted to crack down on satellite channels that "offend the leaders or national and religious symbols" of Arab countries, or fail to "protect Arab identity from the harmful effects of globalization." Surveys indicate that audiences over most of the Middle East enjoy its fresh approach, including its persistent coverage of the protests of the Arab Spring, 2011.

In 2008 the dramatic Museum of Islamic Art opened to rave reviews of its collection of priceless objects from throughout the Islamic world. The country's cultural statement to the world, the museum is set in a building designed by I. M. Pei with influences from the Mosque of ibn Tulun in Cairo. Its current patron, Sheikha Al-Mayassa, is the emir's sister and head of the Qatar Museums Authority. In 2013 she was named the most powerful figure in the art world by *ArtReview* magazine.

Economy: Though the traditional Arab lifestyle of nomadic herding existed for centuries, locally the most important industry was pearling. In the relatively shallow waters around the peninsula, mollusks grew thickly enough to permit a flourishing trade involving, at its peak, 13,000 sailors and divers and hundreds of boats. Life aboard the pearling vessels was difficult, for the sailboats would be gone most of the summer. With no underwater supply of air, most divers sought banks of oysters at depths of about 50 feet, descending rapidly and returning to the surface within a minute. The most daring might descend 80 feet, but breathing and severe health problems were not uncommon.

The international price of pearls climbed rapidly after the 1870s, and an economic system developed to finance pearling expeditions. However, in the 1930s the Japanese development of cultured pearls undercut the industry, with devastating effect.

After the discovery of oil in Bahrain and Saudi Arabia, it was not surprising that the Anglo-Persian Oil Company (ancestor of today's British Petroleum) found modest quantities of commercial deposits in Qatar. Thanks to its deep port, Umm Said became the center of petroleum operations and industry. Although Qatar today is relatively industrialized in terms of output, industry is concentrated in a relatively small area.

The great oil price increases of the 1970s provided enormous wealth. The government bought out the subsidiaries of foreign companies producing in the country, and by 1977 all production came under its Qatar General Petroleum Company.

Recognizing that its oil deposits were fairly small, the government adopted a deliberate policy of diversification away from petroleum. By the late 1990s, exports of steel, aluminum, fertilizers and other petrochemicals based on natural gas partly offset the decline in oil revenues. Qatar is becoming the Middle East's largest producer of ammonia and urea fertilizers, with export markets in India, China and Japan.

The most important diversification was the development of Liquefied Natural Gas (LNG). Liquefaction is the only practical means of transporting natural gas to markets that lack pipelines to them, but it requires highly expensive facilities, known as "trains," to convert the gas to a highly explosive liquid at –256° Fahrenheit and only 1/600th the original volume. Specially designed ships then carry the liquid to another "train" near the consumer, which transforms it back to gas.

In 1997, Qatar shipped its first exports of LNG, and East Asia became a major market. However, in 2005 Qatar Petroleum and ExxonMobil began to build the world's largest LNG refinery at a cost of $14 billion. Its two "trains" produce 15 million tons of LNG per year, originally for the American market, but now shipped elsewhere since the great increase in U.S. natural gas output due to fracturing shale. Qatar is the greatest LNG producer in the world.

The North Shore gas field below the waters of the Gulf is enormous. Its reserves, estimated at 900 trillion cubic feet, suffice to place the country third in global proven reserves, behind Russia and Iran. Since world demand for LNG is limited mostly to electric generating plants, Qatar seeks additional uses for natural gas. A joint Qatari-South African venture opened a gas-to-liquids refinery in 2006 to produce environmentally cleaner low-sulfur diesel. However, the process is tremendously expensive, and with a competitor's plant expected to cost $18 billion, in 2007 ExxonMobil abandoned a similar project.

With both gas and oil exports immensely profitable in recent years, Qatar's per capita incomes are simply the highest in the world. The government's Qatar Investment Authority has acquired well over $100 billion in assets; its annual revenues may soon reach $30 billion. It recently purchased 20% ownership of the London Stock Exchange, and bids are expected for other prominent Western companies, though the buying spree may be reduced to pay for World Cup construction.

The Future: A small state with 15% of the world's natural gas reserves, cultural homogeneity, and careful planning will continue to flourish economically so long as its national defense is secure and international trade operates freely. The recent slow-down in Qatar's spending is likely temporary, but regional instability is certainly increasing, and Sheikh Tamim's views run contrary to those of neighboring states.

Allegations of corruption in the vote that led to Qatar hosting the 2022 World Cup will cause some discomfort in Doha, but thus far no evidence exists of government involvement in the bribes. Even if wrong-doing is substantiated, common sense suggests that it is already very late to reassign the location; a fine may be the appropriate consequence.

Qatari woman weaving intricately designed heavy rugs

Masmak Fortress Riyadh Courtesy: Royal Embassy of Saudi Arabia

Saudi Arabia

Area: About 864,870 square miles (2,240,000 sq. km.).
Population: 30.6 million.
Capital: Riyadh (pop. 5.3 million, estimated).
Climate: Very hot and dry, but humid on coasts; at higher elevations nights are cool. Rain is negligible except in the southwestern highlands.
Neighboring countries: Jordan (Northwest); Iraq (North); Kuwait (Northeast); Qatar (East); United Arab Emirates (East); Oman (Southeast); Yemen (South).
Time Zone: GMT +3. Solar time, calculated daily from sunset, is used for religious purposes.
Official Language: Arabic.
Other Principal Tongues: English, in commerce and in some schools.
Ethnic Background: Generally identified as Arab, including dark-skinned communities found in coastal towns.
Religion: Islam (officially 100%, except for foreign residents).
Chief Commercial Products: Petroleum, dates, salt, gypsum, cement, wool, grain, hides, fish, chemical fertilizers, plastics and steel.
Major Trading Partners: U.S., Japan, France, Italy, Germany, Netherlands.
Currency: Riyal (= 100 halalah).
Former Political Status: Ottoman rule in the west; British advisors in the east.
National Day: Only religious holidays are officially observed.
Chief of State: Abdullah bin Abd al-Aziz Al Saud, King and Prime Minister.
Leading Royal Aide: Salman bin Abd al-Aziz Al Saud, Crown Prince and Deputy Prime Minister (2012).
National Flag: The Islamic creed in ornate Arabic script is written in white on a green field; beneath the writing is a horizontal sword, also in white.
Gross Domestic Product: $772 billion (at current prices); $990 billion (Purchasing Power Parity).
GDP per capita: $32,500 (PPP).

Covering more than two-thirds of the Arabian Peninsula, Saudi (pronounced phonetically *Sah-oo-di)* Arabia is one of the bleakest desert countries in the world. It has no rivers, no perennial streams and no lakes. Most of its total surface is rock, gravel or sand. Less than 1% of the land has enough natural moisture for agriculture of any kind. There are no real forests; only sparse desert plants survive. Nearly one-third of the area is used seasonally as scrub brush grazing land.

From west to east, the country's terrain begins in the Hijaz, with a coastal plain along the Red Sea. A chain of mountains then rises steeply, from Jordan in the north to Yemen in the south. With peaks ranging up to 10,000 feet, the mountains in the south catch some precipitation and allow limited agriculture. Further inland, the land slopes down gradually toward the Persian (Arab) Gulf. The central region, known as *Najd* ("steppe"), receives only two or three inches of rainfall annually, while much of the southern area receives none at all in most years.

Known as the *Rub' al-Khali,* or "Empty Quarter," the south contains virtually no permanent habitation, but the largest stretch of sand in the world. It is a region of giant, seemingly endless sand dunes, often several hundred feet high and miles in length; eternally shifting, pushed by the hot desert winds. Finally, along the Gulf coast stretches the Eastern Province, Hasa, with a hot, humid climate and an abundance of oil.

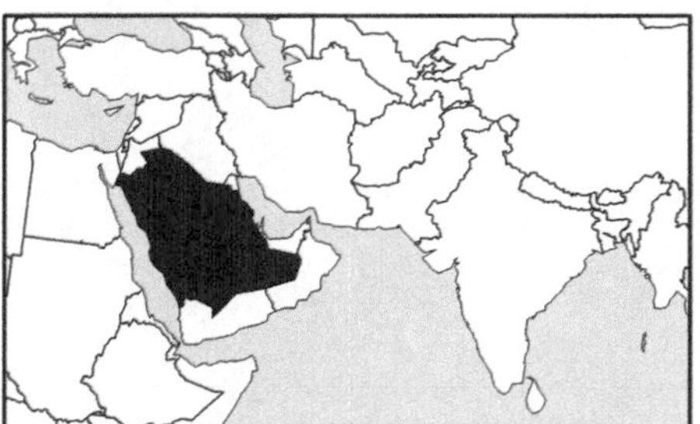

History: A land of nomadic tribes and scattered oasis settlements, Arabia was never united until Muhammad proclaimed his prophetic messages and established an Islamic government with its capital at Medina (see Historical Background). However, after Ali, the fourth caliph, moved the capital to Iraq, Arabia lost much of its political importance, though Mecca and Medina retained significant religious roles.

When the later caliphs in Damascus and Baghdad lost control of the united Muslim world, most of Arabia returned to tribal rule. Outside influence was greatest in the Hijaz, thanks to the pilgrimage and the general prestige of Islam's origins. Ottoman sovereignty was proclaimed there in the 1500s.

The origins of the Saudi kingdom lie in the 17th century, when Muhammad ibn Saud, a tribal leader in Najd, accepted the teaching of Muhammad ibn Abd al-Wahhab. After study in Damascus and Baghdad, Abd al-Wahhab had become convinced of the need to reform and purify Muslim society of pagan practices among

Saudi Arabia

Abd al-Aziz Al-Saud, King of Saudi Arabia, 1932–53

the Bedouin and philosophical and secular influences in the cities.

Strengthened by the appeal of these teachings, known to Westerners as Wahhabism, during the 18th century Saudi troops and Wahhabi believers conquered large parts of central Arabia and raided north into Syria. During the Napoleonic wars, the Wahhabis conquered the Hijaz, seizing from the Ottoman sultan the holy places of Mecca and Medina that he claimed to protect. However, the Wahhabis had overextended. Muhammad Ali, the ruler of Egypt, defeated the Saudi fighters and even destroyed their capital. Rival Arab rulers encroached on Saudi lands.

By 1902, the heir to leadership was a 28-year-old exile, Abd al-Aziz Al Saud (*Al* in Arabic means "House," or "Family;" it differs from *al-*, meaning "the"). With only a handful of followers, he undertook a daring mission to restore family fortunes, seizing Riyadh, the capital, from the rival family of Rashid.

A tall and powerful man with a natural gift for leadership, Abd al-Aziz gradually enlarged the area of his control by victories over rival tribes. In 1913 he conquered the eastern coastal district of Hasa from the Ottoman Turks, not knowing that years later the oil under its sands would make him one of the world's wealthiest men. During World War I, Abd al-Aziz promised the British that he would not join the Turks against England; for this he was rewarded with $25,000 a year.

Dominant in central Arabia by 1921, Abd al-Aziz turned against his remaining rival, Sharif Husayn (Hussein) of the Hijaz. Supported by Britain during his revolt against the Turks, Husayn was a difficult character, and harbored great ambitions. In pursuit of them, he adopted the imprecise title "King of the Arabs" and hinted at proclaiming himself caliph, thereby outraging Arabs of many different backgrounds.

Abd al-Aziz's followers, the militant *Ikhwan* ("Brotherhood") who relinquished tribal loyalties for Wahhabism, were eager to cleanse the holy cities of Mecca and Medina from what they considered sacrilegious traditions. At the end of 1924 the *Ikhwan* entered Mecca and within a year took Medina also. In 1926 Abd al-Aziz was proclaimed "King of Hijaz." After repressing a revolt by the *Ikhwan*, in 1932 he formed his various domains into the Kingdom of Saudi Arabia. Satisfied with his conquests, and blocked from further expansion by Transjordan and Iraq, King Abd al-Aziz turned to consolidating the country he ruled.

Unhampered by a constitution or democracy, his autocracy nevertheless faced limits from the Wahhabi religious leaders and from the ruling family, enlarged by his many marriages to daughters of tribal leaders. Moreover, the kingdom was poor: for many years pilgrims visiting the Hijaz were its economic mainstay.

The discovery of oil in Hasa in 1938 marked the beginning of a new era, but significant petroleum production was delayed by World War II (see Economy). By the late 1940s, oil revenues began to pour into the country, and the aging Abd al-Aziz faced the challenges of corruption common to the arrival of such wealth. His numerous sons and relatives squandered millions of dollars monthly and every transaction involved the payment of suitable bribes to officials.

Reforms under Faisal

Since 1953, Saudi Arabia has been ruled by one of the 37 sons of Abd al-Aziz. The reign of Faisal, the second to rule, witnessed gradual but limited reforms that became the pattern of nearly all subsequent changes. Faisal shared the oil wealth, but limited abuses by family members. He greatly increased the budgets for education, medical care and transportation facilities. , However, he rejected many aspects of westernization and made little effort to promote social change. He refused to allow free political expression or formal public participation in government. The traditional Saudi social system spread responsibility over a large number of relatives, and politically it provided access to the royal family for even the poorest citizen. Rather than replace these features, Faisal worked to render them more honest and efficient.

In international affairs, Faisal proved a cautious conservative willing to work quietly for his goals. He sought better relations with neighboring states, and naturally opposed any communist or other revolutionary influences in the Arab world. Only after Egypt's defeat in the 1967 Arab-Israeli War ended its revolutionary propaganda would Faisal cooperate with it.

Another pivotal Saudi issue was support for Palestinian Arabs. Faisal, and his brothers who ruled after him, considered Jerusalem to be Islam's third holiest city, and he wished to pray there under an Arab and Islamic flag, rather than a Jewish one. To that end, Saudi Arabia paid funds directly to the Palestinian leadership, to Arab countries partly occupied by Israel in 1967, and to the UN, to care for Palestinian refugees.

Like his father, Faisal worked closely with the United States. However, Saudi Arabia did join OPEC, and during the Arab-Israeli war of October 1973, Faisal proclaimed an embargo on all oil shipments to the energy-short U.S. until he was "able again to pray in Jerusalem under an Arab flag." He ended the embargo in 1974 in exchange for vague assurances concerning Israeli withdrawal from Jerusalem.

While the embargo was not fully effective, the embargo was accompanied by a reported 10% cut in oil exports. Against the background of tight world oil supplies, these Saudi moves enabled the Organization of Petroleum Exporting Countries (OPEC) to raise the price of oil about 400% (see Introduction: Black Gold). A flood of oil revenues resulted, and Faisal reaped a great increase in prestige at home and abroad.

Four years after King Faisal was shot fatally by a nephew, the government, royal family, and outside world were stunned in 1979 when Islamic extremists seized the Grand Mosque in Mecca and called for revolution. After crushing the rebellion and executing some participants, the Saudis responded with reforms, in particular for the Shi'a inhabitants of the eastern province bordering on the Gulf. The mosque's takeover emphasized the importance of maintaining the royal links with the *ulama'*, or Muslim scholars, and it also served to warn that social changes should not overtake cultural and religious values.

Invasion and the Gulf War, 1990–91

The 1990 Iraqi seizure of Kuwait placed Saudi Arabia in grave peril. The Iraqi forces in Kuwait alone numbered three times the total Saudi military (though the Saudis enjoyed vastly better equipment). Baghdad threatened to attack if its oil exports across Saudi Arabia were halted, as the UN Security Council demanded. Enormously complicated oil installations—wells, pipelines, tank farms, refineries, ports—lay within range of Iraqi missiles and bombers. Moreover, if he kept Kuwait's oil wealth, Iraq's President Saddam Hussein would control reserves and output rivaling Saudi Arabia's, upsetting the balances of power in both the Arab world and OPEC.

The political threat also seemed substantial. Saddam Hussein's invective against the Kuwaiti ruling family mocked all Gulf dynasties, including the Saudi. Demands that Arab oil wealth support all Arabs stirred popular resentment among poor Arabs everywhere and threatened isolation from the Arab world.

Acceptance of the US offer to defend Saudi Arabia and liberate Kuwait also carried risks. To many Muslims, the "Protector of the Holy Places" must not depend on "infidel" troops. Some Arab nationalists condemned an attack by Israel's ally (the U.S.) against Israel's strongest enemy, Iraq. Domestic opponents could scorn defense by "Jews and women" and religious conservatives would take offense at the display of Western lifestyles ranging from Christmas to unveiled women actively serving in the military. Hosting foreign troops also risked the presence of foreign politicians and journalists, who could and did circulate unflattering attacks on the lack of Western-style democracy.

Despite these risks, King Fahd and his government quickly requested troops from Arab, American and other nations that formed the Coalition forces. After the United Nations deadline passed for Iraq

The modern Red Sea port of Jidda

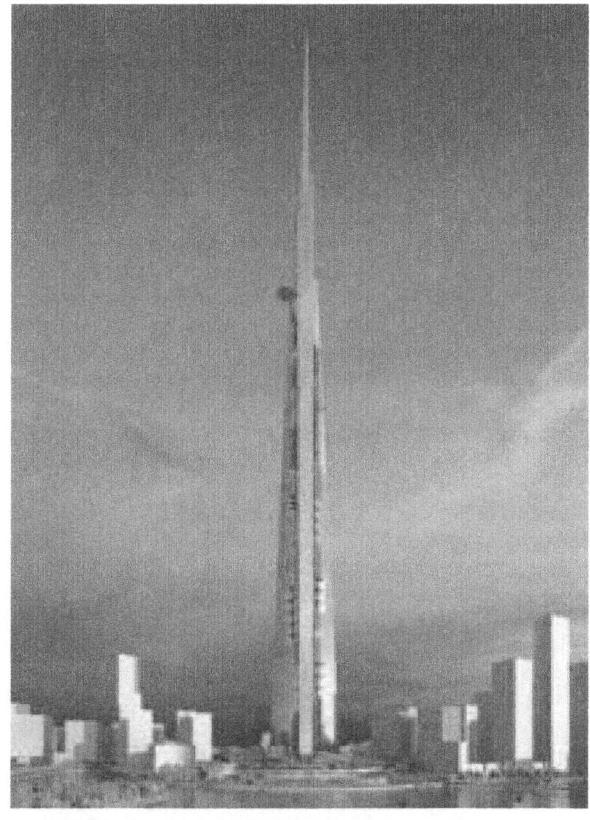

Jidda Tomorrow: The $1 billion Kingdom Tower complex is expected to soar 3,284 feet at completion in 2019.

to evacuate Kuwait (January 15, 1991), Coalition aircraft, often from Saudi bases, launched a massive destruction of Iraq's military and infrastructure (see Iraq: History). In response, Iraqi Scud missiles were targeted at Riyadh and apparently at oil and military targets in the Eastern Province. Damage did occur, notably to a Muslim religious college in Riyadh and barracks housing Americans in Dhahran. An Iraqi tank column also assaulted the city of Khafji, but was repulsed by Saudi and Qatari troops. Rather than undermine the government, the attacks generally served to increase patriotism among Saudi civilians, including the minority Shi'a of the Eastern Province. Saudi ground forces played an important role in the recapture of Kuwait City, and a Saudi pilot scored the only double kill of the war.

Like many wars, this one with thousands of foreign soldiers created expectations of reform. Partly in response, in 1992 King Fahd proposed a formal, written constitution, with a *Majlis al-Shura*, or consultative council, and he appointed the council's 90 members, but gave them no executive powers. The country was not becoming a democracy: the king remained commander of the armed forces, chief administrator, and dispenser of the royal treasury.

King Abdullah of Saudi Arabia talking with Secretary of State Condoleezza Rice.
Courtesy, U.S. State Department

Foreign Challenges & Domestic Perils after 9-11

By 2001, relations with the United States—the country's major ally—showed signs of difficulty. Most Saudis sympathized with the Palestinians, and felt that the Bush cabinet favored Israel. This sentiment led officials to call off high-level military talks in Washington just days before the September 11 terrorist attacks.

News that 15 of the 19 men identified as terrorists came from Saudi Arabia unleashed Western disparagement of nearly everything Saudi and placed the kingdom on the ideological defensive. In addition to repeating long-standing concerns about human rights violations like harsh justice and the treatment of women, critics made three particular allegations.

First, Saudi policy had created a society that encouraged radical fundamentalist religious groups. Extending its long-standing alliance with doctrinaire Wahhabi leaders, during the 1990s the state had funded a rapid increase in religious schools. A decade later, their graduates, ill-equipped for employment in business or technology, formed a pool of potential extremists.

Second, *al-Qaeda* and other militant Islamic groups had been funded, knowingly or not, by contributions to various charities. Critics suspected that the regime had reached an unspoken understanding with the religious militants. If they spared the kingdom from their violent attacks, militant organizations could raise funds for various causes.

Third, some U.S. critics claimed, the kingdom was not a genuine ally. It refused permission for U.S. bases in the kingdom to launch aircraft against the *Taliban* and *al-Qaeda* in Afghanistan. The government also rejected use of its territory for an attack on Iraq, even if the UN approved the invasion.

With limited success, Crown Prince Abdullah and others explained that the West's enemy was not Islam, but rather a few misguided individuals. In addition, they argued, Western nations' support for Israel weakened moderate Arab governments friendly to the U.S. Abdullah promised that his nation would meet any shortfall in world oil supplies. Saudi Arabia kept this promise during the Iraq War of 2003, using its spare capacity and stockpiled crude to replace Iraqi output.

Nevertheless, the monarchy found itself trapped between American policy and the Islamic and Arab values of its population. It proposed a comprehensive plan for Arab-Israeli peace, but Washington ignored the proposal and some preachers at home condemned it as compromising. The two governments announced the closure of American bases, but within a month, suicide bombers struck Riyadh anyway.

Pressures for Reform and Counter-terrorism

Confronted by declining standards of living, high unemployment, allegations of corruption, and heavy-handed policies by the justice system and religious police, many Saudi civilians strongly desire change. However, public opinion is deeply divided about the desired direction of reform. Advocates of greater personal liberty inevitably clash with preachers blaming lax morality for social decline. Because each side's essential reforms reach deep into personal lives, the pathway to reform is as dangerous as it is vital.

Often influenced by their higher education in the West, the country's few liberals advocate greater personal liberty and a softening of harsh elements of the Shari'a, including abolishing whipping and amputation as punishments. Some concentrate on economic reforms, such as wider roles for private business and reduced regulation of them. Others desire social changes, including fewer restrictions on women.

Daily events sometimes support arguments for greater liberalism. For example, 15 girls died in a school fire because the religious police refused to allow the pupils to escape without wearing their scarves and cloaks. Then, editors and authors who criticized the police actions too strongly found themselves dismissed or even arrested.

Opposition groups are illegal, and generally not tolerated. However, in 2003, several hundred Saudi intellectuals—dozens of women as well as men—signed a petition to the crown prince entitled "In Defense of the Nation." It presented the reformist argument that the lack of popular participation in government fostered extremism, and it warned that radical reforms were needed soon.

Soon afterwards, just as the government hosted the country's first human rights conference, a small but unprecedented rally in the center of Riyadh called for political reform. Although bearded men led the group in chanting "God is Great," the police broke up the demonstration and arrested many suspected participants, including some young women. The Grand Mufti condemned the gathering, claiming that "demonstrations are the behavior of non-Muslims." Perhaps this demonstration and several others elsewhere, shook the government's self-confidence.

When further petitions called for urgent reforms, the government arrested several leaders, carefully selecting members of both the liberal and the Islamic reform movements. More were arrested after the exiled *Movement for Islamic Reform in Arabia* called for demonstrations. The poet Ali al-Demaini and two other reformers who urged the government to hasten change and issue a constitution were punished by lengthy prison terms for "stirring up sedition."

Nevertheless, cabinet members discussed the possibility of electing, some years hence, some members of the Consultative Council. The first formal elections in the country's history were the municipal elections in 2004–05. However, with political parties banned, religious conservatives won most seats, and at least initially the councils accomplished little.

In 2003, simultaneous suicide car-bombers struck three residential complexes for foreigners in Riyadh, killing or wounding scores of Westerners and Saudis. The next year, terrorists struck repeatedly in Riyadh, in Yanbu, at the security forces headquarters in Riyadh, and at a luxury business and hotel complex in Khobar. Individual Westerners also became targets, a policy that could harm the oil industry.

The security situation worsened as militants murdered non-Muslims in cold blood. This shook international confidence in the government's ability to protect foreign workers. In response, Prince Nayef bin Abd al-Aziz, the minister of the interior, launched a vigorous assault on the extremists. Police hunted them in Mecca and fought several pitched battles elsewhere, eventually killing a number and seizing large caches of weapons. Some of those arrested reportedly suffered torture; those convicted of murder were publicly beheaded. By 2005, terrorist attacks had diminished, and most militants known to the government were dead or in captivity.

Nevertheless, the violence confirmed that extremists drew strength and political allure from the country's economic and political malaise. Hundreds of Saudi men a decade earlier had trained with Osama bin Laden in Afghanistan. These "Afghans" maintained loose ties, and spread their messages by fax and the web as well as sermons. Their proclamations advocated replacing corruption with morality, repression with legitimate Islamic government, and weakness with a strong military. This morally pure though perhaps impractical critique appealed to the young, often unemployable graduates of religious schools. Sensing the danger, the government attempted to reform education.

In fairness, it must be remembered that well before the 2003 attacks—in fact, even before 9-11—the regime had arrested militants, perhaps hundreds of them, for allegedly threatening national security. In response to derogatory denunciations of the kingdom, the government purged over 2,000 mosque imams of their positions, and instituted cultural education courses for hundreds who remained in office. In 2008, it announced that 40,000 clerics would be re-trained.

Abdullah Ascends the Throne

After years in declining health, King Fahd died in 2005. Crown Prince Abdullah, his half-brother, smoothly ascended the throne, having exercised power for perhaps a decade. He confirmed Prince Sultan, his half-brother, as his heir and deputy. However, the position of the second deputy prime minister—the heir to the heir—was not filled. Speculation mounted that Abdullah, recognized as something of a reformer, lacked support within the royal family to appoint another reformer, perhaps Prince Salman or, more radically, a prince from the next generation.

Abdullah did act to create a new institution to guide the succession. The Allegiance Committee, composed of sons and grandsons of Abd al-Aziz, can reject the king's nominee and thereby force discussion of other potential heirs. Regardless of family disputes, a decision will be made soon: Abdullah was born in 1924 and most surviving brothers a few years later. Two crown princes, both younger than Abdullah, died within months in 2011–12.

The evidence suggests that the king desires that his successors will continue his moderately reformist policies. Crown Prince Salman bin Abd al-Aziz, a liberal, is only 78, but he suffers from ill-health. The deputy crown prince appointed in 2013, Muqrin Abd al-Aziz, is the former intelligence chief and the youngest son of Abd al-Aziz. Perceived as liberal in some respects, he also addressed terrorism with force. Meanwhile, the growing influence of Muhammad bin Nayef, the minister of the interior who has escaped multiple assassination attempts, suggests he may be the first nominee to the succession among the 36 living grandsons of Abd al-Aziz.

Saudi government decisions are generally taken within a closed group. While the effective ruler for a decade, Abdul-

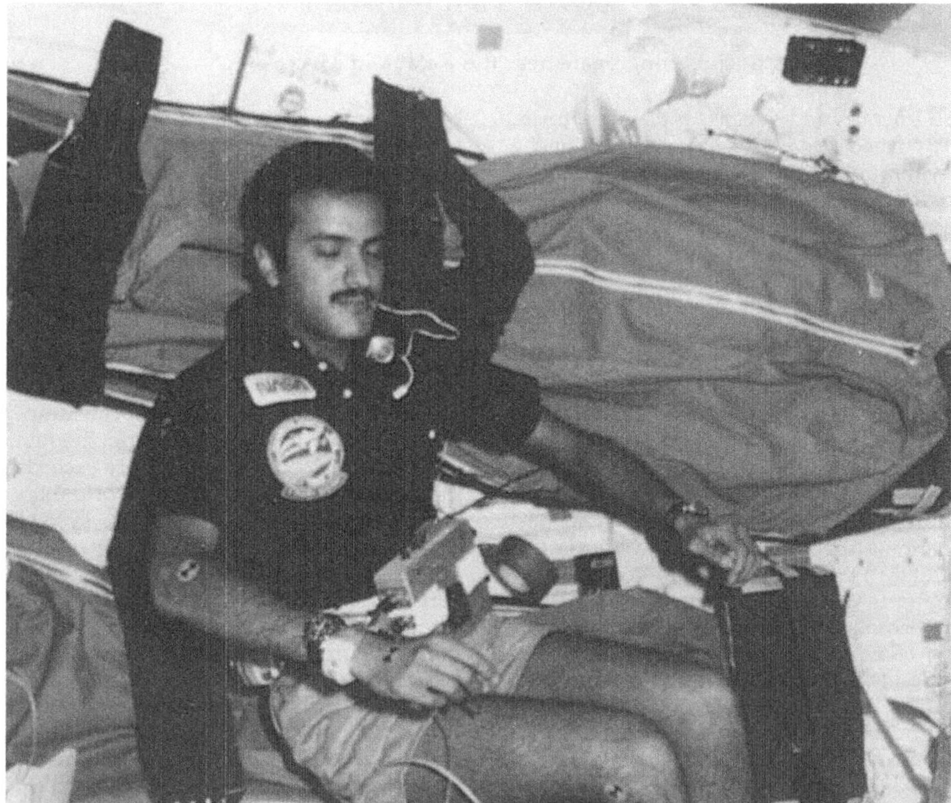

Aboard spaceship *Discovery*: Prince Sultan bin Salman during an experiment.
Courtesy: NASA

Saudi Arabia

Saudi Pilgrims congregate near the Ka'aba in Mecca

lah encouraged several types of reform. He curbed privileges for members of the royal family (such as free water, free electricity, and free tickets on Saudia, the national airline). He also favored the country's successful application to the World Trade Organization, to raise the standard of competition generally and streamline the bureaucracy. In the political realm, he championed elections for half the city councilmen, although they were won by religious conservatives and had not met months later. In 2009 his gradual efforts at reform resulted in the dismissal of both the head of the religious police and the country's most senior judge, who had earlier approved killing the owners of satellite TV channels that offered immoral content. He also appointed a woman as government minister, a first for the country. Her role as the sole high-ranking female official will certainly prove unique: within days of her appointment she announced that she would not be visiting male colleagues in their offices.

In 2013, Abdullah carried his modest reforms further by reviving the *Majlis al-Shura*, or Consultative Council, and appointing 30 women among its 150 members. Women have also received the vote for the 2014 municipal elections.

The government announced plans in 2013 to build the world's most expensive metro system for Riyadh. When complete, its six lines will stretch 109 miles, with state-of-the-art technology for trains and some stations designed by world-class architects. The $22 billion project should provide multiple benefits, including thousands of jobs during construction and a reduction in gasoline and diesel consumption. It also makes financial sense: the rate of return on the project probably exceeds that of investing oil income on world markets. Finally, a world-class metro system is the mark of an up-and-coming capital city, and Saudi policymakers apparently consider Riyadh the capital of the Gulf Cooperation Council as well as the kingdom. The first lines are expected to open in 2019.

A major public health crisis struck the country in 2013 and 2014 as several hundred individuals died from the Middle East Respiratory Syndrome, or MERS. Though related to the common cold, the coronavirus proves fatal to about 40% of those infected. The infection apparently originated when a similar virus affecting camels mutated and passed to humans, but its human-to-human transmission also proved deadly among some hospital staff. Two years after it was identified, there is still no cure for MERS.

Responding to the Arab Spring (2011)

Despite protests in the Eastern province among the Shi'a population, and liberal activists' attempts to use the social media to organize demonstrations and demand reforms like a constitution, the wave of demonstrations that swept the Arab world in 2011 largely missed Saudi Arabia. King Abdullah apparently calmed popular opinion by promising major spending increases. A half-million housing units would be built for low-income families and a minimum wage was established. Unemployment benefits would begin with a monthly stipend of $250, and some 60,000 new security jobs were promised to reduce youth unemployment. University students received extra grants, while government workers gained two months' extra pay. When the promises are delivered, they should cost an estimated $130 billion—equivalent to nearly $5,000 for every inhabitant, but with high oil prices, not particularly a challenge.

The arrests of peaceful dissidents and Shi'a protestors reinforced the powerful image of the near-absolute monarchy. Clearly, the pre-conditions for popular demonstrations like those of the Arab Spring would not be permitted. A blogger who declared May 7 "a day for Saudi liberals" was arrested and charged with apostasy, a capital offense. Among other offenses, he had apparently pressed the "Like" button on a Facebook page for Arab Christians. Though a court later refused to charge him, he remained imprisoned. Similarly, a court dissolved the Saudi Civil and Political Rights Association and sentenced its founders to lengthy prison terms.

The kingdom also moved to calm agitation beyond its borders. Grants of $10 billion each were provided Bahrain and Oman, the two neighboring countries with significant protests, and Saudi security forces entered Bahrain as its demonstrations were crushed. In general, Riyadh became known as a center of opposition to the protest movements, often linking them with Iran.

The government recently began construction of a 1,100 mile fence stretching from the Red Sea to Oman along the border of Yemen. Given the disintegration of public authority in much of that country, the fence is aimed to protect the kingdom from terrorists, drug runners, illegal immigrants seeking work, and other such undesirables. The scale of illegal immigration is surprising: in early 2014, 15,000 individuals were caught illegally crossing the Yemeni border.

King Abdullah has played a significant role in international efforts to address the civil war in Syria that began when regime forces attacked demonstrators who supported the Arab Spring. The kingdom funded opposition groups, advocated resolutions against Syria at the Arab League and United Nations, and reportedly provided military assistance in the form of light weapons and ammunition.

Involvement in Syria led to disillusionment both with the Syrian opposition and the kingdom's long-time partner, the U.S. Deprived of the anti-tank and anti-aircraft missiles necessary to defeat the Syrian military, the opposition splintered. Salafist groups such as *Jabhat al-Nusra* and *al-Dawlat al-Islamiyya fi al-Iraq wa al-Sham* (*ISIL* or *ISIS*; later proclaimed the *Islamic State*), with origins linked to *al-Qaeda*, proved the most successful on the battlefield. While to an outsider, these groups share many religious perspectives with Saudi *Wahhabism*, in reality these groups are bitter critics of Gulf rulers.

The foreign policy difficulties increased when *ISIL*, with the evident assistance of Sunni tribes, rapidly captured Mosul and large parts of northern and western Iraq in 2014. Concerned about its own restive Shi'a minority, the Saudi government naturally sympathized with fellow Sunnis in Iraq who had suffered loss of influence and repression during the long rule of Prime Minister Nouri al-Maliki. But the *Islamic State's* self-proclaimed caliphate in Iraq's Sunni Arab territory threatens the Islamic legitimacy of Arab monarchies.

Despair over U.S. policy in Syria, including President Obama's decision to set aside threatened air strikes of the government's chemical warfare sites, grew more serious with the election in 2013 of Hassan Rouhani as president of Iran. Saudi Arabia has long considered Iran a keen rival across the Gulf that divides them. The two nations pursue conflicting petroleum policies, support opposite sects in deadly disputes, and Saudis fear that Iran still desires to export the ideology of its Islamic revolution. For the future, Saudi leaders fear the "Shi'a crescent" of Iraq and Alawi-dominated Syria may become a "Shi'a full moon" as neighboring Sunni Arab regions fall under Iran's influence.

Lacking any nuclear weapons program of their own, the kingdom's leaders strongly criticized Iran's program. Were it not for the Palestinian issue dividing them, King Abdullah and Israel's Prime Minister Netanyahu might form an alliance of convenience to press for the destruction of Iran's nuclear enrichment program. Opinion in Riyadh's governing circles is therefore strongly opposed to the Obama administration's attempts to obtain a compromise over that program.

Because Egypt's *Muslim Brotherhood* has long condemned rule by kings as contrary to true Islam, the election of Mohammed Morsi as president of Egypt created a serious rift between the two countries. Riyadh therefore welcomed General al-Sisi's ouster of Morsi in 2013, and together with Kuwait and the United Arab Emirates provided billions of dollars in financing for Egypt. Saudi Arabia also joined Kuwait and the United Arab Emirates in pressuring Qatar to end its support for the *Brotherhood*, even withdrawing its ambassador from Doha.

Culture: To understand the workings of Saudi Arabia, one must appreciate some aspects of its social structure, such as the unwritten laws relating to kinship. The most important unit is the extended family or clan: all descendants from a common ancestor carry responsibilities to one another. In the era of tribal desert raids, this system protected individuals. Membership in the family system is based on male descent; a person belongs to the same clan as the father's family, but not necessarily the mother's family and clan. The House of Saud, the ruling family in Saudi Arabia, is just such a clan—these relatives have the duty of looking after their collective interests.

Groups of clans that allied together historically and believe they share descent from a common ancestor form a tribe. Until the establishment of the kingdom there was no important group larger than the tribe. They often skirmished with each other despite forming temporary alliances.

As Saudis gain more wealth, travel abroad, and study in universities, the traditionally strong family bonds are weakening. Conservative Saudis associate these weaker bonds with lowered ethical and moral standards and even illegal drugs. Naturally, Saudi leaders seek to maintain the strong sense of family loyalty and discipline, considering them to be part of Islam.

The Hajj and the Role of Islam

The Prophet Muhammad lived and recited the words of the Qur'an in the western province of the Hijaz. All Muslims, and thus about one human in six, regard the land as holy and bear the obligation to perform the Hajj, the pilgrimage to Mecca, at least once in their lifetimes. Over two million pilgrims annually perform the *Hajj*. All of them hope to spend the identical five days praying at the Grand Mosque, circling the Ka'aba with its black stone, and joining the final ceremonies on Mount Arafat, where Muhammad preached his last sermon. Transported by 10,000 buses from Jeddah to Mecca, most pilgrims sleep in a vast tent city, where they meet fellow-believers from across the globe. They slaughter half a million animals as sacrifices.

Given the size of the crowds, Saudi officials attempt to take careful precautions, screening for communicable diseases and providing the services of thousands of medical personnel, guards, food preparers and cleaners. After an inferno killed hundreds in the 1990s, the authorities supplied fireproof tents and carved large water storage tunnels in nearby mountains. They also widened passageways where a crowd might stampede. Nevertheless, disasters continue, including a stampede in 2004 that killed several hundred pilgrims.

Time in Saudi Arabia was traditionally observed beginning not at midnight, but at sunset. This meant that in spring when the daylight gradually lengthens, a Saudi day takes slightly longer than 24 hours. In the fall, of course, it takes slightly less. For obvious reasons, this system of time is not suitable for international airline schedules and many business purposes, where Arabia Standard Time (GMT +3) is observed. The construction of a giant clock tower opposite the Ka'aba has excited some to propose moving the prime meridian from Greenwich to Mecca, and thus making Mecca Mean Time the world's standard.

Although Islam teaches the brotherhood and equality of all believers, class distinctions have developed. In the old days, some tribes considered themselves more socially important and prestigious than others, and would not intermarry with them. Modernization reduces class distinctions of these traditional types, for wealth and education are becoming the tokens of status, but family prestige still matters.

Based on Islam and enforced in a traditional fashion, the legal system varies considerably from Western practices. The courts impose one of the highest execution rates in the world, for drug dealing, rape, murder, and witchcraft, though if the victim's family accepts blood money, the criminal may be released. A woman's testimony carries half the weight of a man's, the practice of non-Islamic religions is forbidden even to foreigners, and freedoms of speech and the press are extremely limited.

Lesser crimes may be punished by beating; for example, a passenger who persisted in using his cell phone during an airliner's takeoff received 70 lashes. However, the severity of Saudi sentences is sometimes offset by royal pardons, or by the substitution of payments to a victim's family.

Saudi Arabia

Courtesy: Royal Embassy of Saudi Arabia

Foreigners are sometimes surprised by the absolute ban on alcoholic beverages, in accordance with strict Islamic belief. A non-Saudi businessman found with any quantity of alcohol in his belongings is normally deported on the next available flight. Penalties for possession of narcotics are also strictly imposed, and importers of narcotics risk the death penalty. On the other hand, tobacco is allowed, and an education program warning against the health hazards of smoking is only now becoming significant.

In 2007, King Abdullah announced major reforms of the judicial system that will create a supreme court, a system of appeals courts, and courts for commercial and labor matters. Besides modernizing the system, the reforms apparently aim to reduce the wide discretion judges have had to impose their own, sometimes unique, interpretations of Shari'a law. Lacking an effective appeals process, it required King Abdullah himself to pardon "the Qatif girl," a victim of gang rape sentenced, on appeal, to 200 lashes and jail for being alone with a man when they were abducted and raped.

Reem Asaad, campaigner for women-staffed lingerie stores

The modern side of Islam is reflected in the style and substance of the "satellite sheikhs," popular preachers like Ahmad al-Shugairi or Amr Khaled who expound religious perspectives over television and the internet, often working the emotions of crowds in ways similar to American televangelists. The emotional, joyful perspectives of such preachers attract the young and relatively secular who find traditional preaching quite boring.

Other signs suggest some relaxation from the strictest Wahhabi practices. Sheikh Muhammad al-Habadan, a judge, might still claim that a two-eyed veil offered too much opportunity for decadent sensuality, and an eight-year-old bride sought an annulment to her marriage to a man in his 50s. However, more concerts and other cultural activities are reported, and the first Saudi commercial film since at least the 1970s appeared recently. Movie theatres are still prohibited.

Education's Expansion and Reform

As suggested above, education very rapidly changed life in the kingdom. In 1953 only ten junior and senior high schools offered public instruction, with a total enrollment of 1,315. By 1973, there were 573 schools at these levels with 105,853 students. During the same 20 years the number of elementary pupils increased from 39,000 to more than half a million. Access to primary education is now virtually universal, with millions of children in gender-segregated schools.

Critics of the country's schools often focus on their educational style. Thanks in part to the conservatism of the country's heavy religious influence, student learning often becomes the memorization of facts, which is much safer for teachers than the development questioning minds that think critically. Both foreign commentators and some Saudi commentators have also faulted the sometimes reactionary comments and interpretations of Islam found in a number of textbooks.

The first full institution of higher education was the King Saud University in Riyadh, dating from the 1950s. The university system expanded with the rise in oil revenues, though at the turn of the millennium, only eight public universities served a population of nearly 15 million Saudis. However, after the government the higher education budget tripled starting in 2004, more than 100 new colleges and universities opened.

The kingdom's education leadership was shocked when the country's three leading universities received low scores —or were not even rated—in the 2006 international rankings. The response was a series of successful efforts to raise quality. Research chairs were endowed, and highly-published foreign scholars recruited. All professors were encouraged to conduct research, collaborate with academics in other countries, and publish in selective journals.

The most impressive new institution is undoubtedly the graduate-level King Abdullah University of Science and Technology, which opened in 2009. Funded by $10 billion of the monarch's personal wealth, its research orientation and goal of educating women and men together are precedent-setting. It offers programs in fields like nanotechnology, water and conservation technology, the biosciences, energy and the environment, and applied computer science. This curricular emphasis is no accident. An estimated 80% of Saudi college students major in history, geography, Arabic literature and Islamic studies, but the economy generates fairly few jobs in these areas.

The Slowly Changing Status of Women

Aside from King Abdullah University, education carries the burden of separate schools and other facilities for girls and women. This is part of the struggle to prevent gender mixing (ikhtilat in Arabic). In the cause of maintaining sexual purity, Saudi women must be kept apart from men outside the family. At least to the political and religious leadership of the country—which is exclusively male—this is a matter of modesty and separation rather than inequality, but to critics it amounts to "gender apartheid." Demands from religious conservatives on occasion suggest minds possessed with a desire to root out any display of the feminine, for example by the argument that two-eyed veils promote immorality by leading women to adorn the eyes too greatly.

To Western critics, though, regulations of the status of women extend beyond Islamic concerns of morality to a desire to keep women in a "perpetual childhood" that requires male relatives to exercise "guardianship" over them. Saudi women have to obtain permission from male relatives to work, travel, study, receive health care, or even open bank accounts for their children, matters sometimes removed from sexual morality, but key elements of the social order.

The critics also find disgusting what many—but clearly not all—Saudis themselves oppose. Recently, a man in his 90s paid a dowry of $17,000 to marry a 15-year old girl, who was so frightened she locked out her husband on the wedding night and later fled to her parents. The better-educated users of Twitter and other social media condemned the incident, but thousands of girls under 14 have reportedly become brides. Leading officials do support a ban on child marriage, but conservative clergy find it difficult to prohibit behavior that the Prophet Muhammad himself followed.

That order is the strictest in the world. Vice police ensure utmost modesty in dress and brevity in contact. Cinemas and theaters are forbidden, let alone night-clubs, lest men and women meet. Unaccompanied women do not frequent shopping centers and malls. When several dozen Saudi women broke the tradition against driving and formed a procession of luxury cars in 1990, they were arrested, dismissed from their jobs, and condemned by the vice police as prostitutes. Thereafter, the law was officially changed to prohibit women from taking the wheel.

In 2007–08 and again in 2012-14, reform-minded women petitioned the king to permit women to drive for economic and practical reasons (hiring a male driver is increasingly expensive). In recent years, some women have driven, partly because King Abdullah overturned one woman's sentence of ten lashes for the offence. However, in 2014 a woman caught behind the wheel was fined.

Opposition to women's driving remains rooted in ignorance. In the words of one anti-reform religious sheikh, "If a woman drives a car...that could have negative physiological impacts as functional and physiological medical studies show that it automatically affects the ovaries and pushes the pelvis upwards. That is why we find those who regularly drive have children with clinical problems of varying degrees." (By that reasoning, apparently there are no objections if older and barren drive?)

There are strong practical reasons to permit women to drive. Many families find their finances stretched to afford a driver; letting women drive would act like a permanent tax cut. At the national level, the billionaire Prince Alwaleed bin Talal recently twitted that legalizing their driving could result in 500,000 fewer foreign workers.

For decades the vice police overlooked one peculiar mixing of men and women. Stores that carried intimate female apparel hired only male clerks. New regulations in 2006 required such stores to hire female sales clerks, but enforcement was delayed. Religious conservatives disapproved, and so do the stores' owners, who fear financial loss when replacing cheap Indian and Pakistani clerks with higher-paid Saudi women. In 2010, some women demanded a boycott of stores using male clerks. Finally, in 2012, the requirement went into effect.

Though the pace is sometimes glacially slow, broader change is occurring. Additional economic sectors may also open up for women, partly because Ghazi al-Gosaibi, the minister of labor, recognized the waste of talent and resources when women compose 55% of university graduates but only 5% of the workforce. For his part, King Abdullah decreed that women may vote and run in the next elections for municipal councils, due in 2015.

What matters most, though, is culture—and the message is mixed. In 2007 a popular Saudi TV comedy portrayed an unaccompanied woman driving her children home from the movies. But each February as Valentine's Day approaches, the religious police typically ban the sale of red roses and other items that reflect Western ideas of friendship between men and women.

Economy: Before the discovery of its oil, most inhabitants of the country's arid lands lived by herding flocks, or raised dates and a few other crops in an oasis. The yearly pilgrimage, or Hajj, to Mecca and Medina employed others, but the traditional camel trade routes of ancient times could not compete with sea freight, especially after the introduction of steam and the construction of the Suez Canal. Then came oil.

It is difficult to over-estimate the impact of oil on Saudi Arabia. It typically funds about three-quarters of the government budget, directly contributes over 40% of GDP, and provides 95% of exports. In addition, the major industry, petrochemicals, depends on oil as a raw material.

Saudi Oil Policy

Having persuaded King Abd al-Aziz to grant a concession for drilling, prospectors for a group of American oil companies struck commercial quantities of oil in 1938. After World War II, oil production by the Arabian American Oil Company (Aramco) increased by nearly 20% a year. Soon the kingdom ranked with Iran and Iraq as a leading Middle East producer. In the following decades, the search for oil, its production, and its export revenues completely transformed the Saudi economy.

From the late 1950s economic development became a priority. This created challenges, because the industry provided only a few thousand jobs. How could millions of people be transformed from a life of subsistence herding and agriculture to the levels of income and comfort enjoyed by advanced industrial nations? One answer came from Aramco, which built a hospital, clinics, schools and housing. It also provided assistance for agriculture, and lent advice for a variety of projects, including the kingdom's railroad.

The cooperation between Aramco and the government contrasted with usually bitter relations in other oil exporting nations. Nevertheless, Saudi Arabia became a founding member of the Organization of Petroleum Exporting Countries (OPEC), where it usually adopted a firm but moderate stance. Given the country's reserves and production, its opinion mattered.

By the early 1970s, with its oil sales rising at 25% per year, the country became the dominant Middle East producer, and Sheikh Ahmad Yamani, the Petroleum Minister, became a leading figure in the cartel. He played a major role in the 1973 oil embargo, and in other agreements that drove the price of oil from roughly $2.50 in 1970 to $32 in 1980. However, high prices encouraged production elsewhere and reduced consumption through conservation. When demand declined for OPEC's exports, Saudi production and oil revenues both plummeted.

During the 1970s, Saudi Aramco invested in additional pipelines to carry crude to the Red Sea, beyond the potential bottleneck of the Strait of Hormuz. Investment also increased oil production capacity to about 10 million barrels per day. During the Gulf War of 1990–91, Saudi Aramco met world oil needs while exports from Iraq and Kuwait were halted. During the next era of tight oil supplies, in 2005–08, Aramco initiated projects to raise output to over 12 million barrels per day, nearly a 25% increase.

Today's high crude oil prices bring enormous wealth to the country, but also risk longer-term harm. Prosperity makes it difficult to build a consensus supporting reasonable but unpopular measures like raising the price of gasoline or electricity.

Growth of the National Economy

From the late 1950s to the early 1970s, the government erected public buildings, paved roads and highways, and began to offer education and health services for its citizens. Oil revenues supplied foreign exchange to purchase all manner of imports from cars to cloth and even building materials. Money that found its way into private hands frequently went into large homes, as well as stores and office buildings. Reluctant to have a "Central Bank," with implications of interest payments, the nation established the Saudi Arabian Monetary Authority (SAMA) to provide modern control over national finances.

Following the 1973 spiraling of oil prices, the nation's economic development spurted to higher levels of growth. The government offered tax breaks and subsidies to attract firms in non-oil industries. Factories began to appear, sometimes joint ventures with foreign firms. The early ones typically provided consumer goods or construction materials for the building boom, such as a mill for rolling steel rods. With the decline in oil prices in the mid-1980s, government subsidies diminished.

In general, Saudi industrial projects suffer from a number of common difficulties. Lucrative profits in trade and other services also discourage long-term investment in manufacturing. Once established, local entrepreneurs, managers, and skilled workers are scarce. Until recently, inadequate financial markets made it more convenient for Saudi capitalists to buy shares in foreign companies rather than take ownership of local factories. Finally, for all its famed wealth, the country represents a relatively small market, whose consumers are fewer than those of Belgium or Illinois, and until recently much poorer. Per capita income was less than $9,000 in 2002.

The most impressive industrialization effort is the petrochemical producer, SABIC. It rapidly grew to massive size, the only Arab industrial company on the international Fortune 500. By 1988, its major plants had been constructed, and profits soared as the company turned cheap petroleum raw materials into fertilizers, plastics and other products. By 2004, SABIC held 10% of world sales of petrochemicals. It also produced a much larger proportion of specialty products like MTBE (methyl tertiary butyl ether), a gasoline additive that reduces carbon monoxide emissions and replaces lead in enhancing octane. Profits exceeded $1 billion for the first time in 1994, and privatizing the government's 70% share of ownership could provide a windfall to cushion the budget deficit. In 2007, SABIC purchased the plastics subsidiary of General Electric.

The University of Petroleum and Minerals, Dhahran

Another success is the national airline, Saudia. True to national culture, its flights begin with Muhammad's prayer for travelers, and ceiling-mounted compasses indicate the direction of Mecca for passengers' prayers. Attention to religious details did not hamper its rise to the largest regional carrier, offering service between Western Europe and East Asia.

Saudi Arabia became a major exporter of grains by the end of the 1980s. Fearing an American food embargo in retaliation for the 1973 oil embargo, the government provided extensive subsidies for grain farmers, paying the costs for wells, fertilizers and other supplies. Cultivated acreage increased tenfold, and giant green circles provided bumper crops of wheat. From a mere 3,000 tons in 1976, output climbed to 3 million tons in 1989, three times consumption. Similar subsidies raised the output of eggs, dairy products, and dates, spreading national wealth and slowing migration to the cities by keeping a quarter of the population in agriculture.

The successes were costly, and did not last long. Annual wheat subsidies of $1 billion equaled *eight times* the cost of equivalent imported wheat. By 1996 price supports had been cut 25%, and production fell to half the record of 4 million tons. After later cuts in subsidies, many small family farms collapsed. In 2008, the country again became a net importer of wheat, and the population is now 95% urban.

Nature reinforced the financial austerity. About 90% of the water supplies came from "fossil" sources, trapped far below the soil during a much wetter climatic age. In the 1990s, the nation used 18 billion cubic meters of this fossil water annually, against apparently reliable estimates of only 500 billion cubic meters in the aquifers. Desalinized water, somewhat expensive for household use, becomes exorbitant for wheat farming, raising total costs 700%. Imaginative alternative supplies—from the Nile, Turkey, Iraq, or Antarctic icebergs—are likewise prohibitively costly and uncertain. Despite its wealth, the country's future food production seems limited to drought-tolerant crops, plus fish and shrimp from the sea.

Economic and Budget Policies

When oil prices fall, Saudi Arabia suffers financial distress. If they fall sufficiently, it will face a budget deficit as well. To cover such deficits, the government borrows money, while obeying the Islamic prohibition of the payment of interest. Thus it issues "development bonds," whose payment depends in theory on the success of the project. Total indebtedness by 2003 exceeded $130 billion, a much higher level than most developed countries, but with annual oil revenues of about the same amount, it was a trustworthy borrower. Revenues hit $200 billion in 2007 but fell in 2008–09 with the decline in oil prices and the world recession.

Other revenue sources are difficult to find. Only a few acceptable taxes exist, for the wealthy and commoners alike expect government services to be financed somehow by oil. An attempt to impose income taxes on foreign workers created such difficulties that it was withdrawn. Higher tariffs on imports largely breed domestic inflation, and are no longer an option since the country joined the World Trade Organization (WTO).

Despite the boom in oil prices, foreign financing is still necessary for major electric, water, and petrochemical projects. Estimates of the funds needed by 2025 are astounding. Development of natural gas reserves will probably cost even more than the $45 billion Aramco is spending, plus the $25 billion initially agreed by several major oil companies. To meet the estimated electricity needs in 2025 will require $120 billion in new generating plants and transmission facilities, and the water industry another $50 billion. The six new "economic cities" planned for 5 million inhabitants by 2020 will cost another $100 billion, perhaps achieving the goal of being steps towards a post-petroleum era.

To meet the challenges, the government promised larger roles for private companies. However, international firms capable of billion-dollar projects, delighted to invest in projects that export oil and gas, hesitate to become involved in local utilities, given the unprofitable traditions of nearly-free water and electricity.

The Future: Optimism is tempting for a country that possesses 25% of global oil reserves, protects pilgrimage centers for one-sixth of the world population, and boasts a decades-old special relationship with the only superpower. Nevertheless, some sleepless nights should appear in the forecasts for the 7,000 Saudi princes who form the ruling elite.

Most immediately, the kingdom seems to be losing influence. As fracking releases oil in other regions of the world, OPEC's significance naturally diminishes and its largest producer's influence along with it.

In international politics, the Sunni Middle East lies in shambles, its political loyalties split between moderates and Islamists. Although the *Wahhabi* doctrine of Saudi Arabia is close to several Islamist strands, it is bitterly divided from many. No doubt King Abdullah thought Caliph Ibrahim's demand that all good Muslims support the *Islamic State* a trifle absurd, though in practice the *Islamic State* constitutes a very dangerous opponent.

One medium-run challenge is a stable succession. The older grandsons of King Abd al-Aziz are now in their 70s; soon the era of his sons' kingships must conclude. The rules of that succession are unclear.

Long-term economic challenges seem endemic: despite the vast income from oil, per capita incomes are modest, about one-fifth those of neighboring Qatar and the United Arab Emirates. Economic reforms to correct decades of paternalism and dependence on the work of foreigners will not come easily. The country is also burning oil to produce electricity when its natural gas resources would prove far cheaper.

Reforms in Saudi policies traditionally move at glacial speed, but society itself is changing rapidly. Nearly half of the population is under the age of 17, and their videos, satellite TV, and internet sites typically portray the pleasures of living now more than the blessings of worshipping Allah. Despite the kingdom's intense emphasis on the sanctity of women, some 70% of the cell phones of a sample of unruly male teenagers contained pornography. The world is breaking through attempts to isolate the younger generation.

Also threatening both the royal and religious establishments are foreign intellectual influences that consider truth—if it can even exist—to be the outcome of testing conflicting ideas. It follows that individuals will make personal choices rather than accept pronouncements from a traditional leader or book. It is impossible to know whether the real struggle will be that against *al-Qaeda* and its associated groups, or against very conservative members of the House of Saud allied with official, but reactionary clerics.

King Abdullah's great challenge is to reform quickly enough to satisfy those with modern inclinations, while avoiding changes that alienate the religious establishment and increase the allure of extremism among the devout. He is aging, and his health is faltering. At least the immediate succession seems undisputed and reforming.

King Abdulaziz Al-Saud meets with President Franklin D. Roosevelt on board the USS Quincy in the Suez Canal's Great Bitter Lake, February 1945

The Syrian Arab Republic

Desert Protector: This little-known fortress towers above the ruins of Palmyra.

Area: 71,498 sq. mi. (185,180 sq. km.).

Population: 21.1 million (2010 estimate). About 4 million are refugees abroad, and over 7 million internally displaced.

Capital City: Damascus (pop. 2.5–3 million, estimated).

Climate: Summers are generally hot and dry; winters are mild in low areas, cooler with increasing elevation. Winter brings adequate rain in the western part of the country, but the remainder is arid.

Neighboring Countries: Turkey (North); Iraq (East); Jordan (South); Lebanon (West); Israel (Southwest).

Time Zone: GMT +2 (+3 in summer).

Official Language: Arabic.

Other Tongues: Kurdish and Armenian.

Ethnic Background: On the basis of language and culture, nearly all Syrians are identified as Arab.

Principal Religion: Islam (about 82%, mainly *Sunni),* Christianity; Druze and Alawi Islamic communities.

Chief Commercial Products: Petroleum and natural gas; textiles, cement, processed food, wheat, barley, cotton, grapes, olives, sheep, chicken and other farm products.

Major Trading Partners: Germany, France, Italy, Netherlands, Greece, Russia, Lebanon.

Currency: Lira (1 SL = 100 piasters).

Former Colonial Status: French mandate (1920–1946).

Independence Date: April 17, 1946, marking French evacuation.

Chief of State: Bashar al-Assad, President; re-elected, 2014.

Head of Government: Wael al-Halqi, Prime Minister (2012).

National Flag: The flag consists of three horizontal stripes of (top to bottom) red, white and black; two green, five-pointed stars are aligned on the central white stripe. The opposition uses the pre-Baathist flag whose stripes are green, white, and black with three red stars.

Gross Domestic Product: $60 billion (at current prices); $107 billion (Purchasing Power Parity) (2010 estimates; GDP has fallen by at least 40% since.)

GDP per capita: $5,000 (PPP) (2010).

Lying at the eastern end of the Mediterranean Sea, Syria consists of two main climate zones. The western region includes the coastal mountains, the Orontes River valley, and a range of interior hills or mountains. On its eastern limits, the western zone includes Damascus and Aleppo and it provides the home of four-fifths of the population.

The eastern zone takes the form of foothills descending from an average elevation of 3,000 feet to the vast, open desert cut by the Euphrates River as it flows across Syria from north to southeast. Its two main tributaries come from the north, and they also support agriculture along their banks. Arabs invading the region called the area north of the Euphrates *al-Jazira,* "The Island," a cultivated expanse of green surrounded by desert.

Most of Syria has an average rainfall of less than ten inches a year, but the western zone enjoys more. The seaward slopes of the coastal range may receive as much as 50 inches near the crest, which in some places is 5,000 feet high. Cities such as Damascus and Homs along the eastern base of the inland range are great oases watered by springs and streams fed by the mountain rains.

History: Human civilization extends back as far in time in Syria as anywhere else. Many of antiquity's great empires occupied the country, although no Syrian dynasty arose to conquer the region, a reflection perhaps of its diversity of geography and population. For the 2,700 years between Assyrian conquest and Ottoman expulsion, Syria's history is deeply intertwined with the events related in the **Historical Background** of this book.

In the 7th and 8th centuries, Syria became host to the world empire of the Arab Umayyads, a Meccan dynasty that ruled from Damascus. The region flourished, with the construction of new cities and palaces. However, the Abbasids overthrew the faltering Umayyad dynasty in 750, and moved the capital to Iraq. As the united Muslim empire disintegrated in the following centuries, Syria's important geographical position attracted invasions from every side except the desert: Seljuk Turks, Egyptian caliphs, European Crusaders, Mongols, Mamluks from Egypt, and finally, the Ottoman Turks.

By 1900, most of the territory now included in Syria formed the two major provinces of Aleppo and Damascus. The present international borders did not exist, even as provincial boundaries. Jordan and parts of Israel and Lebanon reported to Damascus, while Antakya and some smaller regions of southern Turkey near the city of Aleppo formed part of Aleppo province.

In the late 19th century, greater education and economic development encouraged the rise of a self-consciousness of being Arab in language and culture. Partly as a result, the politically active upper class of landowners, officials and Muslim scholars demanded the greater degree of local self-government propounded by the *Decentralization Party.* Just before World War I broke out, small, secret societies of civilians and officers, *al-Fatat* and *al-Ahd,* formed to struggle for Arab independence from the Empire.

After the Ottoman Empire joined the Central Powers in 1914, these nationalists plotted with Sharif Husayn of Mecca to gain independence. They provided the details for territorial demands he made from Britain in exchange for an uprising against the Ottoman Empire. After the outbreak of the Arab Revolt in June 1916, Syrian opinion increasingly favored the Allies.

The great British victory over the Ottoman army in Palestine opened the way to Damascus. British and Arab forces raced for the city—historians still debate who conquered it—and pressed on to capture Aleppo in the last weeks of the war. Initially the Arab army administered the interior of Syria, and French troops were limited to Mt. Lebanon and the coast northward into Turkey.

In 1920, nationalists in Damascus proclaimed the independence of Syria (including Jordan and Lebanon), with Emir Faisal as king. The son of Sharif Husayn, he had led the Arab army into Damascus, but his rule was brief, ended when France invaded and imposed its rule on Syria.

Although the French mandate provided some modernization and technical progress, the French dismembered Syria into small regions that emphasized ethnic minorities, such as *Jabal Druze* in the southeast and an *Alawi* state based in Lattakia. The fertile Biqa' Valley was assigned to Lebanon, and Antakya, a region in the far northwest, was transferred to Turkey. This divide-and-conquer approach established scars that still disfigure political opinion today. Considering the territories lost parts of the homeland, nationalists often strove to dominate Jordan and Lebanon, and Damascus even refused to establish an embassy in Beirut.

The French goal was to weaken the *Sunni* majority with its nationalist ideas, but it also stirred nationalist fervor. In the mid-1920s a revolt shook much of the country, and French artillery shelled sections of Damascus sympathetic to the rebels. During the 1930s, protests and general strikes dominated political life. French troops finally withdrew after World War II.

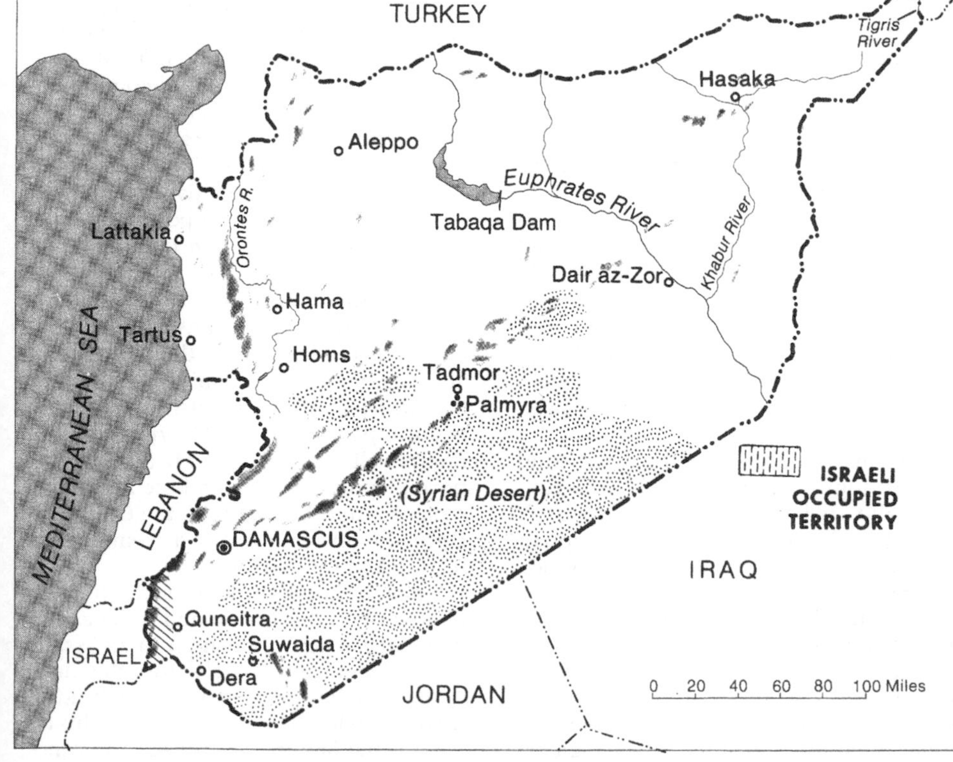

Years of Political Instability

Syrian independence came to a country uncertain of its destiny. The generation of nationalists who had opposed the French—and sometimes compromised with them—took power, but rival, more radical ideologies attracted support, especially from students and army officers. Some sought the borders of geographical Syria; others, a merger with Iraq to counter the Jewish settlement of Palestine. Socialists hoped to weaken the power of the wealthy notable families who formed the top nationalist leadership.

Increasingly, politicians appeared grasping for power. Corruption proved to be one cause among several for the Syria's conclusive defeat by Israel in 1948–49, when the army entered Palestine to attack the new Jewish state.

Against this background, Husni al-Za'im, the Chief of Staff, carried out Syria's first military coup d'état in 1949. He arrested leading politicians, banned political parties, arranged a cease-fire agreement with Israel, and reached a verbal alliance with Iraq. Al-Za'im offered to meet with Israel for peace talks, but was rebuffed. Less than five months after seizing power, another military coup led to his execution. No Syrian leader ever again offered to meet Israel's prime minister.

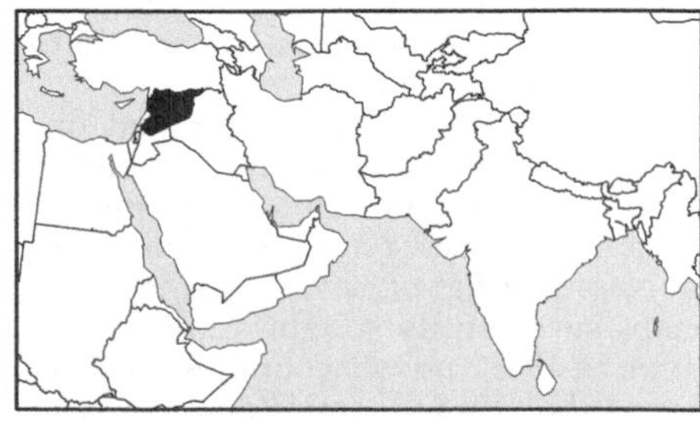

Syria

Young Syrians performing a traditional dance at a local festival

By ending ineffective though constitutional government, al-Za'im ushered in a long era of instability. For the next twenty-one years, Syrian governments proved most unstable, suffering more than a dozen military coups, some quite bloody. Elections generally showed popular support for pan-Arab and socialist politicians, whose rivals came from a small group of leading families who exercised great influence through their vast land holdings and wealth.

The *Ba'th Party* soon proved more influential than other radical ideologies such as the communists. Founded in the early 1940s in Damascus by Michel Aflaq, a Christian, and Salah al-Din al-Bitar, a Sunni Muslim, the party took its name from the Arabic word for renaissance. Highly committed to a nation uniting all Arabs and thus bringing them self-respect instead of backwardness and defeat, its ideology naturally threatened Arab states created by European agreements rather than national identity. The party's socialist goals included the creation of a classless state, and its radicals threatened a government takeover of industry and trade as well. Though the party's legality was sometimes uncertain, it attracted disillusioned military officers and spread to Jordan, Lebanon and Iraq.

By the mid-1950s, Syria lurched unsteadily leftward in its domestic politics, and received Soviet military equipment. Given the nationalist appeal of Gamal Abdul Nasser of Egypt, several leading politicians successfully sought a union with Egypt. In 1958, the two countries officially formed the "United Arab Republic" with Nasser as president and ideological source of all authority.

Economic problems aggravated by drought and friction between Egyptian and Syrian officials enabled conservative groups to organize a revolt which broke the union in 1961. Reformist politicians soon regained power, however, and in 1963, army officers favoring the *Ba'th Party* seized control in yet another coup d'état. They outlawed all rival political groups, and despite factional struggles within the party, it forced many economic and social changes, such as the nationalization of petroleum and other major industries. The wealthy and tradition-minded complained privately about the seizures of property and loss of freedoms, but they could not successfully oppose the *Ba'thist* government.

Clashes with the militarily-powerful state of Israel across the demilitarized zone frequently broke out between 1949 and the 1960s. Occasionally they flared into serious incidents with artillery and aircraft joining the battle. Several clashes followed Syria's attempts to divert headwaters of the Jordan River that had flowed to Israel.

Tensions along the Israeli border led to aircraft dogfights in May 1967, and full-scale war in June (see Israel: History). After quickly defeating Syria's Egyptian and Jordanian allies, Israeli forces stormed into Syria and up the slopes which rise to the plateau known in Arabic as *Jawlan* (pronounced *Golan* by Israelis), occupying some 1,250 square miles. Israeli troops forced nearly all the remaining civilians to leave, and they destroyed or damaged public buildings and homes in the regional capital, Quneitra. Rather than permit the Syrian refugees to return to their farms and villages in accord with a UN resolution, Israel established its own settlements on the farmlands of the ousted Syrians.

Hafiz al-Assad, an Alawi, Seizes Power

In 1970, General Hafiz al-Assad seized power from his fellow Ba'thist officers. Unlike its unstable predecessors, his regime succeeded in neutralizing all rivals, by crushing them or winning their support. Al-Assad ("The Lion") was elected president in 1971, as the only candidate on the ballot, and two years later a new constitution provided for an elected legislature, the People's Council. Formal power remained firmly with the president, a Muslim who appoints the vice president, prime minister, and cabinet. But the really important decisions in Damascus have apparently been taken in secret, by the president and a close circle of family, relatives, and army officers rather than by the civilian prime minister and cabinet.

Within the tightly-controlled country, al-Assad's government won some public acceptance for its stability, reduced radicalism, and pragmatism. The relaxation of doctrinaire socialism encouraged economic growth. Syria was not a democracy, and al-Assad always won the referendum on the presidency with an overwhelming majority; likewise, elections to the People's Council (parliament) always returned the *Ba'th Party* to power, though some independents and minor leftist parties held a few seats.

By 1980, many Syrians desired political change and the end of military rule. Like many other top officers, Hafiz al-Assad was a member of the Alawi community, an offshoot of Shi'a Islam that incorporates ideas from several other religions. Patronized by the French, but ignored after independence, the frequently-impoverished Alawis had found few opportunities open to them. As a consequence, their young men sought careers in the military, where many of them joined the *Ba'th*. As Alawi soldiers moved up the ranks, they eventually formed a majority of the officer corps, although Sunni officers initially dominated the highest ranks. *Ba'thist* military rule eventually meant an Alawi-dominated regime, although Sunnis always held important positions. By embracing *Ba'thist* socialism and linking with the *Communist Party*, the officers presented themselves as secular and modernizing.

Since Syria was a police state that prohibited open discussion and independent political parties, opposition to al-Assad's government came largely from the illegal Sunni *Muslim Brotherhood*, which advocated an Islamic state. Repressed by the regime, the *Brotherhood* turned to violence,

Syrian Army troops training for the civil war Photo courtesy of SANA

and in 1982 launched a revolt in the conservative city of Hama. In brutal fighting isolated from the news media, the military crushed the rebellion, but at the cost of perhaps 20,000 lives and great damage to an old and picturesque city. The bloodshed ended most dreams of removing the regime by force.

Syrian domestic affairs traditionally received little foreign attention, in part because the public rarely expressed itself, and the press, firmly controlled by party and government, was bland, propagandistic, and unquestioning. The regime remained in power for four decades by removing any possible alternative leaders from influential positions and independent wealth. Anyone expressing discontent was frequently arrested and detained indefinitely. In 1992 Syria still held an estimated 5,000 political prisoners; their numbers rose or fell depending on the regime's sense of security. Many political activists sought exile abroad.

International Involvement and Isolation

Despairing of diplomatic efforts to recover their lost territory, the relatively new leaders of Syria and Egypt launched a surprise offensive in 1973 in a desperate effort to drive out Israeli forces. Three weeks of intensive fighting again demonstrated Israeli military superiority, but with aid from Iraq and Jordan, the Syrian defenses did not break. U.S. mediation efforts led by Henry Kissinger in 1974 returned a small strip of territory to Syria and established a buffer zone between the two armies.

An important recurring theme in the country's recent history has been its often self-inflicted isolation. Its military intervention during the Civil War in Lebanon became brutal, and the subsequent occupation lasted decades (see Lebanon). Western nations often felt disturbed by terrorism allegedly masterminded in Damascus by Palestinian and other radical groups. The struggle to regain the Golan inevitably discouraged amicable relations with Israel's fervent allies, but intelligence services, sometimes perhaps following their own agendas, indulged in murderous exploits. Eventually, the Soviet Union, Syria's strongest ally, refused al-Assad's request for high-tech weapons because his government could not pay for them, nor his troops use them effectively, nor protect their secrets.

Within the Middle East, the revolutionary *Ba'thist* vision of a single Arab state—"one Arab nation with an eternal mission"—naturally prohibited enduring alliances with monarchies. Al-Assad's uncompromising stand against the Camp David Agreement precluded friendship with Egypt or the U.S., and quarrels with Yasir Arafat isolated Syria when the Palestine National Council and the United Nations favored Arafat's diplomatic approach.

Other Middle Eastern disputes also isolated the regime. Most Arab states feared the Iranian Islamic Revolution, and when Iraq invaded Iran in 1980, they supported Iraq. Al-Assad, already embroiled in a bitter party rivalry with *Ba'thist* Iraq and as an Alawi probably more sympathetic to Shi'a than Sunni Islam, uniquely allied with Iran. A decade later, because Iraq's seizure of Kuwait in 1990 threatened to strengthen his long-standing *Ba'thist* rival, al-Assad publicly supported the posting of American forces in Saudi Arabia, and even dispatched 20,000 troops of his own. However, popular opinion accepted such behavior only reluctantly. Syrian troops played only a defensive role and did not invade Kuwait or Iraq. President al-Assad again surprised observers—and upstaged Israel—in 1991 when he accepted a U.S. invitation to a peace conference on the Middle East. The alternative, a military re-conquest of the (Syrian) Jawlan was clearly impossible, given the end of Soviet assistance and the destruction of Iraq (often a potential ally against Israel, though daily a bitter *Ba'thist* rival).

Negotiations with Israel proved surprisingly hopeful during the *Labor* government of Yitzhak Rabin. His negotiators conceded the possibility of withdrawing from the Golan; Damascus suggested that if Israel acknowledged Syrian sovereignty, demilitarized zones and agreement over water rights might form part of the peace settlement. But neither the simplicity of the solution nor the advantages of peace brought agreement. Each side demanded conditions the other would obviously reject.

In 2007 Israeli aircraft attacked a building near the eastern town of Deir al-Zor, to muted public reaction. However, the attack eventually initiated claims that a nuclear reactor was being built with North Korean assistance. Despite Syria's denials of unapproved activities, the site was razed. Subsequently the International Atomic Energy Agency (IAEA) claimed uranium traces found at the site differed from that used in Syria's recognized research.

Syria

The late President Hafiz al-Assad

Given its own bloody conflict with Islamic groups in the 1980s, Syria's leadership privately cooperated with the U.S. in the aftermath of September 11. However, with its own Golan Heights occupied, Damascus considered national resistance against Israel "a social, religious, and legal right." It naturally proclaimed some of the most virulent anti-Israeli propaganda of any Arab state, but maintained tight security and calm along the ceasefire line. Instead, Syria used auxiliaries to exert violent pressure against Israel. It openly supported *Hizbullah's* struggle to free South Lebanon in the 1990s, and (secretly) provided the supply route for missiles used against Israel during the 2006 war. With lesser justification, Damascus hosts a variety of radical groups whose violent acts sometimes proved useful.

Faced in 2003 with President Bush's demand that Damascus "choose the right side in the war on terror," Syria voted for UN Security Council Resolution 1441, which demanded new inspections and threatened severe consequences if Iraq did not cooperate. However, Syria strongly condemned the U.S. invasion that followed. It quietly allowed Arab volunteers to pass through Damascus en route to battle. Militants continued to do so even after the fall of Saddam's regime, though a border barrier was erected and some Iraqis were arrested and turned over to Baghdad.

The U.S. occupation of Iraq threatened the near-encirclement of Syria by rival or enemy states. Moreover, U.S. critics also attacked Damascus for supporting anti-Israeli groups and its occupation of Lebanon. Congress passed sanctions that prohibited U.S. companies from trading with Syria. In response, Bashar al-Assad undertook to strengthen relations with Turkey, Europe, and other possible moderating influences on Washington.

Hariri's Murder Threatens the Regime

Nevertheless, al-Assad played directly into his critics hands, when in 2004 Syria—apparently Bashar himself—attempted to extend Lebanese President Lahoud's term of office, contrary to that country's constitution. International condemnation rapidly followed, and the Security Council unanimously voted for a free election and the withdrawal of Syrian troops and intelligence agents.

The international position worsened greatly in 2005, when an expertly executed explosion killed Rafiq Hariri, the leading Lebanese politician. Blaming Damascus, massive demonstrations in Beirut demanded an end to the occupation. Entirely isolated diplomatically, Syria withdrew its troops and known intelligence offices to the eastern Biqa' valley, and then ended 29 years of occupation with a complete military withdrawal.

Despite patriotic celebrations for the returning troops, Bashar al-Assad's regime had clearly suffered serious setbacks. Worse followed. The Syrian interior minister and former chief in Lebanon, Ghazi Kanaan, committed suicide in mysterious circumstances. Days later, the interim UN investigation into Hariri's murder named as suspects both the commander of the Syrian Presidential Guard, Maher al-Assad (Bashar's brother), and the head of military intelligence, Asaf Shawkat, Bashar's brother-in-law. One witness even reported that planning for the assassination took place in Shawkat's home.

Admittedly, suspicion is not conviction, and by 2011 the veracity of many claims were doubted, and evidence pointed to the involvement of *Hizbullah* members. Syria alternately cooperated with the UN investigation and hampered it, by creating its own investigation that kept witnesses from appearing in Beirut.

Domestic Affairs under Bashar al-Assad

After Hafiz al-Assad died in 2000, the legislature nominated his son, Bashar, to the presidency although constitutionally he was six years too young. Nevertheless, he won overwhelming (and probably genuine) support in the popular vote that followed.

In his inauguration speech, Bashar called for openness and reform. Hundreds of political prisoners were released, and the infamous Mezze prison was closed, along with the special security courts. Internet access greatly increased. On the foreign scene, relations improved with Jordan, with Yasir Arafat, and even with Iraq, which began exporting oil to Syria after Syria reopened the long-sealed border to trade. This broke UN trade sanctions, but the import of perhaps 250,000 b/d of Iraqi oil permitted a similar increase in Syrian petroleum exports.

Progress towards democracy and individual freedom encouraged Riad Seif, an independent member of parliament, to form the Friends of Civic Society. The first independent newspapers appeared since the 1960s, a satirical paper followed by a business journal. The arts reflected the greater openness, and actors enjoyed the

A covered 17th century *souk* (shopping area) in the old part of Damascus

new freedom to express on stage sentiments often felt by people on the street.

The "Damascus Spring" proved brief. Just one year into Bashar's era, in 2001, Seif was arrested, charged with trying to change Syria's constitution by illegal means, and sentenced to years in prison. Dozens more activists were arrested but mostly released a few days later. Apparently the most sensitive topics were corruption and the wide activities of the intelligence services and secret police. Attacks on them threaten the old guard and perhaps Alawi rule, thus undermining the very foundations of the regime. Despite its proclaimed socialism, the regime in Damascus feels far more comfortable with private banks than with free speech.

For a decade, President Bashar al-Assad hinted at reform, but aside from economic liberalization he changed little. Whether the result of rivalries within the elite or hesitancy by Bashar, the regime played games with activists, arresting those who pressed too hard in sensitive areas, but releasing some prisoners to win public support. After forty years of *Ba'thist* dictatorship, many Syrian opponents of the regime viewed the vacillating policies, the withdrawal from Lebanon and the UN investigation as signs of an eventually fatal weakness. A long-time vice president fled the country and publicly accused Bashar of having threatened Hariri and intelligence officials of involvement in the murder.

Feeling threatened, the regime asserted its strength by repressing intellectuals and critics, such as those who had issued the "Damascus Declaration for Democratic and National Change" in 2005. That had called for an end to emergency laws, a halt to political repression, and a national conference to move the country from a security state to a civil state. The Declaration united aging secular intellectuals, some Kurdish leaders, and a few Islamists, but most were exiles with little influence.

***Portrait of a Young Man* by noted Syrian artist Fateh Almudarres**

From Arab Spring to Civil War

The Arab Spr ing came late to Syria. Only in March, 2011, did the motto "The People Desires the Fall of the Regime" (see **The Arab Spring**) appear as graffiti in Dar'a, a disadvantaged small city in the drought-stricken south. The arrest of the graffiti-writing teenagers, and fatal violence inflicted against protesters in Dar'a, ignited widespread demonstrations that gradually spread to most of the country.

The regime initially responded with apparent concessions. A new cabinet was appointed, and the decades'-old emergency laws were formally abolished. But fundamentally, Bashar al-Assad and his ruling circle chose the wrong alternative. Rejecting serious reform, instead they trusted a mixture of nationalist appeals, financial favors, fears of sectarian chaos, and a manipulation of public opinion that extended to outright lies. Rather than dialogue with critics, the official media leveled wild accusations at the demonstrators, claiming they were Israeli agents or armed Salafist extremists. Large pro-government rallies took place in Damascus, attended by government employees, middle-class sympathizers who feared chaos, and Christians and Alawis who feared Islamist rule. However, satellite TV and the social media discredited the regime's announcements, and Syrians not tied to the regime realized that dictatorship was not the only choice.

Despite its talk of reform, the regime soon clamped down harshly on the demonstrations for change. Protestors who gathered after Friday prayers were often shot; by July over 1,400 civilians had died; by July 2012 perhaps 14,000. Given the multiple security services and intelligence agencies, responsibility was usually impossible to demonstrate. Military units and pro-regime thugs (the heavily Alawi *Shabiha*) also besieged towns where demonstrations had taken place, imposing curfews and conducting house-by-house searches for political activists. Many feared a repeat of Hama's repression in 1982, but social media made it

Syria

The village of Ma'aloula where the Aramaic language of Christ is still spoken

impossible to keep large-scale brutality a secret.

Instead, terror was unleashed on neighborhoods and small towns, with dozens killed, and sometimes the bodies burned or removed. Activists and their pictures told a story of unprovoked shootings of demonstrators by the police, soldiers, and the *Shabiha* militiamen, dressed in black.

The really enormous popular protests occurred in the strongly traditional and Sunni cities of Homs and Hama. As the conflict continued, violence spread to the northwest and Deir al-Zor in the east, where the opposition seized some neighborhoods and even towns.

Soldiers who refused to shoot civilians, or who appeared to aim off-target, were executed. Surviving deserters often joined the Free Syrian Army or one of the many opposition militias. As the violence increased, hundreds of security agents and soldiers were also killed. State media duly displayed sometimes gruesome pictures of their bodies or funerals as evidence of a violent insurrection, but to maintain morale the government ceased the daily announcements of funerals of security personnel.

Six months after the initial slogans, Syria was a country divided. Damascus and Aleppo, with their favored socio-economic classes and less traditional cultures, provided large crowds of pro-regime supporters. Elsewhere, elite army units used artillery on city neighborhoods considered sympathetic to the opposition. Homs in particular suffered a sustained and brutal shelling of the Baba Amr quarter. However, neither side in the conflict possessed the strength to dominate the country. Syria's sectarian diversity had divided the opposition and enabled al-Assad to arouse sufficient fears of chaos to defy demands for reform.

International attempts to halt the repression and fighting proved powerless. Turkey's Prime Minister Recep Erdo an warned al-Assad against repression and permitted refugees to cross the border. Turkey also hosted the opposition, which formed the Syrian National Council in Istanbul. Qatar and Saudi Arabia urged peaceful dialogue, and the Arab League proposed a halt to violence, the army's withdrawal from cities, permission for international media to operate, and government-opposition discussions. The proposal failed in practice, and the League's observer mission was soon withdrawn.

Efforts by the United Nations failed in the Security Council. Russia stoutly blocked any intervention, reasoning that regime change was not the UN's responsibility. Kofi Annan was dispatched on a fruitless mission to negotiate a cease-fire, but the Human Rights Council provided evidence that security forces had committed crimes against humanity. Its chief, Navi Pillay, called for al-Assad to be referred to the International Criminal Court.

A UN monitoring mission, accepted reluctantly by the government, was manipulated by it. Towns and city neighborhoods where demonstrators openly displayed opposition slogans were later pounded by the army's artillery: the government switched from mass arrests to collective punishment.

The UN monitors did confirm that the pro-government *Shabiha* executed most of the 108 victims of the Houla massacre, dozens of them children and women. After vehicles of the unarmed monitors were blocked and hit by gunfire, the monitors withdrew.

One significant difficulty for sympathetic nations is the fractured Syrian opposition. Ranging from western-style liberals to the *Muslim Brotherhood* and extremists linked to *al-Qaeda*, the opposition was led publicly by long-time exiles, often professors, and by members of the *Brotherhood*. These groups failed to unite effectively under their initial umbrella, the *Syrian National Council (SNC)*.

The *Syrian National Council (SNC)* failed to unite disparate groups such as western-style liberals, socialists, and the *Muslim Brothers*. Its successor, the even more encompassing *National Coalition for Syrian Revolutionary and Opposition Forces*, proved no more effective despite the quality of its individual leaders. Neither organization controlled the Free Syrian Army, and each had only limited links with the demonstrators' organization within the country: the Local Co-Ordination Committees. This gravely weakened the opposition's ability to engage in diplomacy, since the fighters within Syria might reject compromises accepted outside.

Corruption, fanaticism, and an inability to respond to the concerns of Syria's many minority groups gravely weakened both the political opposition and many militias. Most Druze and Christians preferred stability under al-Assad to chaotic change. They feared rule by Islamic extremists who might impose Islamic aw and persecute their communities. Having seized control of Raqqa, the *Dawlat al-Islamiyya fi Iraq wa al-Sham* (*Islamic State in Iraq and Greater Syria*, known in English as *ISIS* or *ISIL*) even imposed the medieval Islamic head-tax on Christians and reportedly crucified opponents. Though some individual Alawis might have wished otherwise, members of that most important minority apparently felt their safely

President Bashar al-Assad

depended on closing ranks to support the regime in what became a civil war. Bloodcurdling threats from some Islamic extremists certainly strengthened such perspectives, but even moderate rebels failed to portray a future where Alawis would remain safe.

The Syrian opposition turned to violence in defense of neighborhoods and towns. As a result, rather than a single rebel army, an uncounted number of militias grew up, some moderate and secular, others mildly or strongly Islamist. However, it was the militant Islamist groups like *al-Nusra Front*, with loyalties to *al-Qaeda*, that successfully captured much of Aleppo in July 2012.

By late that year, rebel militias controlled much of the north and northeast, including border crossings to Turkey, and threatened Damascus. Despite the regime's superiority in heavy weapons and relentless bombing and shelling, al-Assad's future seemed grim. Prime Minister Riad Hijab defected, and analysts speculated about an Alawi retreat to a state stretching from the coast to Damascus.

Facing defeat, the regime reorganized. It formed a large civilian militia, the National Defense Army, trained by Iranian experts to defend local communities. Shi'a fighters from Iraq and Iran reinforced the military. Even more important, *Hizbullah*, the Lebanese Shi'a militia familiar with guerrilla warfare, dispatched thousands of fighters to recapture Qusayr, a small city along the border. The rebels' loss of Qusayr cut their supply routes from Lebanon and simultaneously strengthened the regime's hold on territory between Damascus and the coast. By summer 2013, government forces had seized the initiative nearly everywhere.

The intensity of the fighting in Syria has shocked the world to numbness. After three years of war, more than 160,000 have been killed, with massacres, sexual violence, and other despicable acts committed by both sides. Tens of thousands may be permanently disabled. Millions have fled as refugees, either internally or to neighboring Turkey, Lebanon, and Jordan. Damage to public infrastructure alone has been estimated at $15 billion; total economic losses seem at least four times that amount.

U.S. and other Western policymakers initially hoped that humanitarian and non-lethal assistance to the rebels would somehow unite them, form an effective fighting force, defeat the regime, and establish a government of moderation. Those hopes proved false as the rebels increasingly fought each other. In particular, *ISIS* sought territory so aggressively that local moderates joined with *al-Nusra Front* and repulsed it from parts of Aleppo and surrounding territory. Given the high levels of disorganization and rivalry among the rebel militias, Western nations continue to fear that any sophisticated or heavy arms may end up in the wrong hands.

After midnight on August 21, 2013, rockets carrying nerve gases landed in at least two rebel-held suburbs of Damascus. Within hours, dozens of videos documented adults and children suffering from the nausea, disorientation, vomiting, and other symptoms of sarin. The opposition blamed the government for the deaths, their number estimated between 588 (UN) to over 1,400 (U.S.). The Assad regime denied its involvement, and claimed the rebels shelled their own suburbs to win world sympathy. However, no evidence showed the rebels possessed nerve agents or missiles of the types used to gas the suburbs. By contrast, the Syrian military likely possessed such missiles, and the angle of flight suggested they were launched from military bases overlooking Damascus.

President Obama had earlier pledged that the use of chemical weapons would cross a red line. Syria—and the world—awaited the U.S. response. In the end, given difficulties in Congress and the dangers of unexpected results from missile attacks on facilities where chemical weapons might or might not exist, the U.S. president backed down. He accepted a Russian proposal that Syria disarm its chemical weapons under the auspices of the Organization for the Prohibition of Chemical Weapons. Despite delays, all the declared stockpiles were removed from Syria by June 2014, about two months late.

The failure of the U.S. to intervene even in the face of crimes against humanity signaled that moderate rebels could not

Modern Syria

expect substantial U.S. military assistance. Since 2013, the civil war has continued without significant military breakthroughs. However, a number of cities and territories loyal to the opposition but surrounded by the military, including the Palestinian camp of Yarmouk in Damascus and the old city of Homs, negotiated surrenders in the face of starvation.

More confident on the battlefield, the government announced that presidential elections would be held in June 2014 in all areas not held by "terrorists." As expected, Bashar al-Assad won handily (88%). Except for allies such as Iran and Russia, most countries regarded the election as invalid.

Culture: Most Syrians live in cities or towns, though significant numbers live in villages or farm communities. The few nomads now form under 1% of the total population. The two principal cities are Damascus and Aleppo (Halab); each exceeds two million residents. Most industry is concentrated around those cities and at Homs.

A majority of Syrians are Sunni Muslims. The Arab Christian minority is mainly Greek Orthodox; the once-sizable Armenian community has declined due to emigration. Several other groups merit mention, including *Druze* (see Lebanon: Culture) in the southeast and *Alawis* along the Mediterranean coast and nearby mountains. Together these groups form about 16% of the population.

Developing their beliefs and ritual secretly in the rugged mountains, the impoverished and disadvantaged *Alawis* for centuries remained something of a mystery. Modern scholars, little better informed, find major *Shi'a* influences, especially the *Ismaili* variant. The Imam Ali, for example, is revered as the incarnation of God. Other beliefs and the liturgy suggest Christian and other religious influences.

Syria

Though they do not form as great a community as in Turkey, Iraq, or Iran, several hundred thousand Kurds live in the northern and eastern border areas. Though Syria provided sanctuary for Turkey's Kurdish rebels, its own Kurds enjoy no legal rights to organize. They appeared restive in 2004, rioting after a soccer match. Further riots followed the kidnapping and murder of a religious leader in 2005, this time with hints at Kurdish demands for independence rather than simply fair treatment.

The Jewish community of Damascus faces extinction. After thousands of years of vibrant life and two generations of experience surviving the Arab-Israeli dispute, by 2002 it had dwindled to about 50 members worshipping in one surviving synagogue. The demise did not result from direct persecution. Rather, legal changes permitted families to emigrate together to the West, and as the community dwindled, the U.S. seemed more appealing to the few who remained.

The *Ba'th Party* has no formal religious element to it, and was founded by both Christians and Muslims. For decades, it favored a distinctly secular society, forbidding head scarves in schools or uniformed soldiers worshipping in mosques. Sectarian differences are not recognized in the government structure as they are in Lebanon, and legal political parties were not formed along religious lines. In spite of the religious differences, until the regime's repression of demonstrators during the Arab Spring, there was little strife between communities.

Nevertheless, a growing allegiance to Islam has been evident in women's dress and men's beards. This suggests that on the popular level, secularism and pan-Arabism are being replaced by faith in Allah. The variety of expression is broad, ranging from students in Islamic schools to women's Qur'anic discussion groups and then members of the outlawed *Muslim Brotherhood.*

Like Egypt and Iraq, Syria contains numerous archaeological sites of great historical importance, stretching from recent times back to the earliest village life. The spectacular ruins of the caravan city of Palmyra lie in the middle of the desert beside the modern oasis village of Tadmur. Queen Zenobia once ruled there until defeated by the Romans and carried off to Rome as a royal prisoner.

At Aleppo, in the northern part of Syria, a great citadel of bygone days arises on a high mound in the middle of a modern city. Damascus boasts it is the oldest continuously-inhabited city, anywhere. The National Museum contains one of the finest displays of Islamic art to be found anywhere. In the city center, adjacent to the covered market known as the *Souk al-Hamidiya,* the Umayyad Mosque preserves gold leaf from the 7th century. Other museums illustrate the lifestyle of wealthy families during the Ottoman period, while in small villages outside Damascus the inhabitants still speak Aramaic, the language used by the Jews of Palestine at the time of Jesus.

Economy: Syria has a more balanced economy than most nations of Southwest Asia. One-third of the population still depends directly on agriculture. Farmers raise cotton in irrigated fields along the Orontes and Euphrates rivers, wheat and other grains on the steppe, or fruits and vegetables in oases like the Ghuta outside Damascus.

In years of abundant rainfall, Syria's farms produce grain for export, but usually the country imports food. There is great scope for improved farming methods, and experimental programs are carried on with the United Nations. Given the high cost of importing food, agricultural development is vitally important. Increases in the area of irrigated land resulting from the Euphrates dam proved much lower than expected.

The largest single industry is still textiles. Domestic cotton from the Euphrates Valley, the Aleppo Plain and elsewhere supply the mills. Raw cotton is also exported, but in lesser quantities as more and more is woven into textiles in Syria. Because of its socialist regulations, the country receives little foreign investment outside tourist projects. Because government funds rarely allow any large new development projects, emphasis is being placed on improving production levels in existing projects.

An oil pipeline from the modest deposits in the northeast to a refinery in Homs and the port of Tartus has operated since 1968. Syria's oil exports were a major earner of foreign exchange during the 1970s, but declining exports and lower prices brought a drop in this income. Promising deposits of oil east of Deir al-Zor (also spelled Dair az-Zor) reached commercial production in 1989, but whether because geology or a lack of reinvestment, they have since declined. The search for oil and its production continues, as production declines in existing oilfields. However, the country has failed to attract steady exploration activities by foreign firms, and several majors have left the country in recent years. In the near future, it could become a net importer of oil, as local consumption exceeds production.

The Future: The civil war's violence affirms the lesson that the collapse of a dictatorship often sets loose rivalries and festering emotions over past wrongs.

Might intimidation, force, and massacres work in 2014? Able to attack from the air at will, with external military aid and assistance from *Hizbullah* and probably Iran's *Quds Force,* al-Assad's military victory in western Syria can be imagined. However, a total victory is unlikely or at least delayed: some rebel militias are likely to receive supplies of sophisticated weapons to use against tanks and aircraft.

The diplomats' preferred solution of a negotiated unity government seems an impossible fantasy. Of course, diplomats should attempt to negotiate, but many participants in the war are guilty of crimes against humanity. Their hatreds and survival instincts will resist compromise, and the opposition is incapable of uniting over any compromise. It seems more certain that bloodshed will continue until either exhaustion or victory has its way.

For now, victory seems closer to the government's grasp. The opposition is failing; given the near-anarchy in some rebel held areas, including the imposition of locally-determined "Shari'a" law, foreign governments initially sympathetic to reform efforts must now wonder if a rebel victory would actually bring democracy and improve human rights.

On the emotional level, the conflict has torn many families and neighborhood friendships apart. The increasingly sectarian conflict will likely result in cleansing minority groups from villages and towns. It may also fracture Sunni Islam into moderate and militant factions. A society of cultured and hospitable people is being destroyed, life by life, and the living history of their cities, towns, and castles is crumbling. Unfortunately, it seems unlikely that the near future will offer peace any more than did the recent past.

School kids at Citadel

The Republic of Turkey

Near the mouth of the Bosporus in Istanbul survive old residences and, looming above them, the Sultan Ahmet I Mosque—the "blue mosque." Photo: Miller B. Spangler

Area: 300,948 sq. miles (779,452 sq. km.).
Population: 77 million.
Capital City: Ankara (pop. 3.5 million, est.).
Climate: Mostly hot and dry in the summer, though humid along the coasts; winters generally are wet and mild on the coasts, cooler inland and very cold in the eastern mountains.
Neighboring Countries: Greece (West); Bulgaria (Northwest); Georgia, Armenia (Northeast); Azerbaijan (East); Iran (East); Iraq (Southeast); Syria (South).
Time Zone: GMT +2 (+3 in summer).
Official Language: Turkish.
Other Principal Tongues: Kurdish; far fewer speak Arabic, Greek or Armenian.
Ethnic Background: Turkish linguistically and culturally, but physical characteristics vary. European features predominate rather than Central Asian.
Principal Religion: Islam (about 98%).
Chief Commercial Products: Cotton and textiles, mohair, tobacco, hazelnuts, raisins, sorghum, grains, meat, iron and steel, chromite, petroleum products, manufactures, including televisions, refrigerators, automobiles, and textiles.
Major Trading Partners: Germany, U.S., Libya, Russia, Iran, Switzerland and the U.K.
Currency: New Turkish Lira.
Former Political Status: Heart of the Ottoman Empire; independent.
National Day: October 23 (Proclamation of the Republic, 1923).
Head of State: Winner of the August 2014 presidential election; likely Recep Tayyip Erdoğan.
Head of Government: To be determined.
National Flag: Red field containing a large white crescent with a smaller five-pointed star between its points.
Gross Domestic Product: $851.8 billion (at current prices, 2013); $1,200 billion (Purchasing Power Parity).
GDP per capita: $15,700 (PPP).

During the early 1920s, a new nation arose on the historical peninsula of Asia Minor and the adjacent tip of Europe. The Ottoman Empire had ruled a mosaic of Greeks, Armenians, Kurds, and Turks in the territory before World War I, but faced dismemberment after its defeat. A former Ottoman general, Kemal Atatürk, led the Turkish community to seize its independence and establish a national state. Although the Turkish tribes originated in Central Asia and only 5% of the new country lay in Europe, Atatürk strove to create a modern, secular and European country to replace the religiously-inspired empire.

Geography: Besides a small European portion around the historic city of Istanbul, modern Turkey covers Asia Minor, known as Anatolia, and the mountainous region to its east. Although the nation enjoys a long coastline on the Aegean Sea, almost none of the major islands are Turkish. Instead, though often located only a few miles from Asia Minor, they belong to Greece.

Two long, narrow straits divide European from Asian Turkey. The Dardanelles leads from the Aegean Sea into the small Sea of Marmara. Vessels continuing to the Black Sea then sail up the Bosporus. For centuries, authority over the straits between the Black Sea and the Mediterranean has been important, for whatever power rules the straits influences the commercial and strategic well-being of other Black Sea states.

Apart from its long seacoasts, Turkey is a country of high elevations, and averages more than 3,500 feet above sea level. Asia Minor forms a plateau surrounded, except on the west, by mountain ranges. The highest mountains are in the eastern part of the country. A spectacular peak on the Iranian border, called *Ağri Daği* in Turkish and Mt. Ararat in English, reaches 16,945 feet. Many other mountains exceed 10,000 feet, and the plateau itself varies in elevation from 2,500 to 7,000 feet.

The heart of Asia Minor is largely desert, because mountains to the north and south block out rain-bearing clouds. In

Turkey

this region Lake Tuz has one of the highest concentrations of salt and minerals of any lake or sea. To the east, Lake Van also contains high levels of dissolved salt and no visible outlet, although underground channels may connect it to the Tigris or Euphrates. All together, many lakes comprise 3,256 square miles of the total area of the country.

Two traditionally useful rivers are the Kizil Irmak and the Sakarya, both draining into the Black Sea. The Seyhan and Ceyhan empty into the Mediterranean, after running through the fertile plain around Adana, where much of Turkey's cotton is grown. The mighty Tigris and Euphrates both originate in Turkey, but they pass through steep mountain gorges, so their usefulness was originally irrigation of the plains of Syria and Iraq. Now they serve as the basis for GAP, the Southeast Anatolia Project for agricultural and industrial development, a massive power and irrigation scheme.

Western Asia Minor generally enjoys good winter rains, as do the southern Taurus Mountains. The Pontus Mountains along the north coast have moderate rains throughout the year, especially in the spring. The eastern highlands receive abundant precipitation, but the elevation and rugged terrain makes them often not suitable for agriculture. Forests grow in these mountains and those of the north, but few trees grow elsewhere.

History: The modern Republic of Turkey rose from the ruins of the Ottoman Empire, which was defeated and dismembered at the close of World War I. Secret agreements during the war divided many areas with little regard for national feeling, and left only a very small Turkish-ruled area in northern Asia Minor. At the Paris Peace Conference, the Arab parts of the empire fell as prey to Britain and France, and Turkish-speaking provinces seemed destined for partition among Italy, Greece and Armenia as well.

To enforce their colonial claims, Greek troops occupied Izmir and moved inland, while the French sought the region around Adana. Pending a peace treaty, British forces occupied the Sultan's capital, Istanbul, while Armenians and Kurds both appealed to the Peace Conference for their own states. However, in 1920 an energetic and determined army officer, Mustafa Kemal, summoned delegates to Ankara, to save the nation. Calling themselves the Grand National Assembly, the delegates elected Kemal as its president; he later adopted the surname Atatürk. In the next months, they established an independent Turkish nation with the small railroad town deep in Anatolia as the capital.

To the astonishment of the Allies, Atatürk molded Ottoman troops and volunteers into a fervent and disciplined force. It pushed out the French and retook provinces claimed by Armenia. The Italians withdrew from southwest Asia Minor, and Britain from Istanbul. France recognized the new Turkish regime quickly, hoping to gain national advantage. Peace with Greece only followed a bitter war, worsened because in retreat the Greek troops destroyed everything and committed outrages upon Turkish villagers. Reflecting these military successes, the Treaty of Lausanne gave Turkey full sovereignty over most of the territory it now possesses.

Kemal Atatürk

In 1923, the Grand National Assembly proclaimed Turkey a republic, and under Atatürk's leadership, the Assembly voted deep changes that shook Turkish society. The office of Caliph was abolished in 1924, along with religious law courts. The 1924

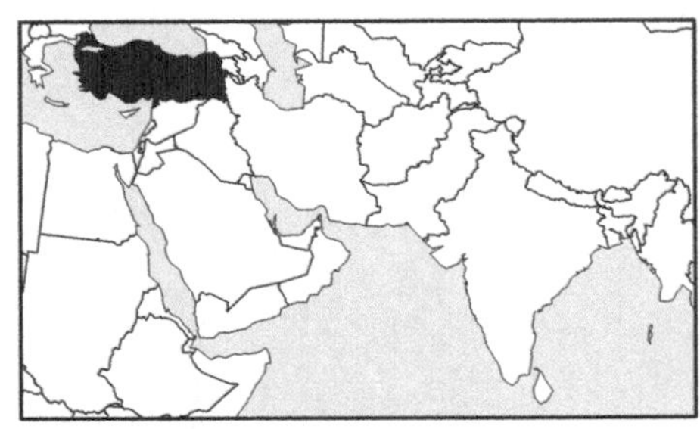

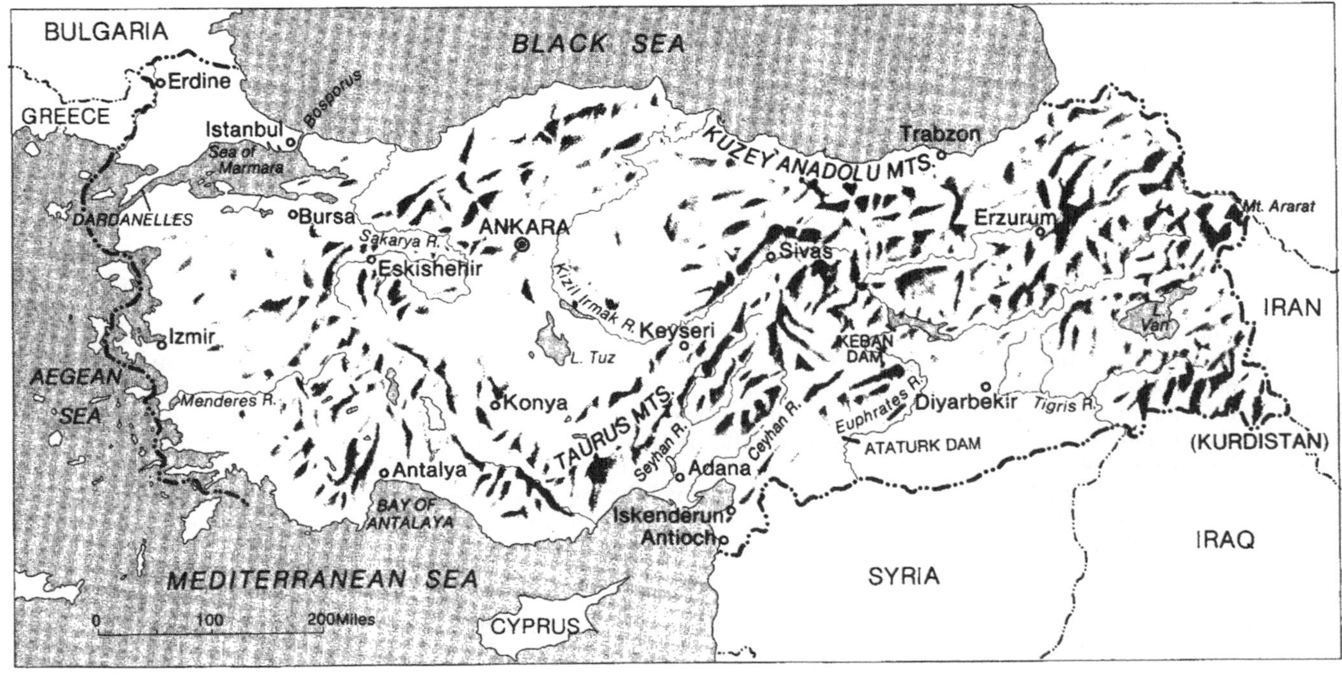

Turkey

Stone heads of gods built for King Antiochus I in southwestern Turkey over 2,000 years ago

constitution made Ankara the capital, designated the National Assembly as the center of authority and guaranteed freedom of speech, press and travel. While the document provided for a democratic form of government, in fact Kemal Atatürk ruled as a dictator. Opposition was ruthlessly crushed, particularly that by Kurds in the southeast.

The new government determined to rush Turks towards modernity. It forbad men to wear Muslim-style hats without brims. It forced people to dress like Europeans, and as far as possible, to think and act like them. The government replaced the Arabic script with the Latin alphabet, making every book and sign in the country obsolete, a process that helped purify Turkish of many Arabic and Persian loanwords. Even names changed, as Mustafa Kemal and the rest of the nation adopted the use of family names. Kemal himself became "Atatürk," Father of the Turks. The policy of secularization closed religious schools, abolished the dervish brotherhoods, and eliminated many other aspects of Ottoman culture. The Western calendar replaced the Muslim, polygamy was ended, and women received a new status. Codes of law based on European models replaced Ottoman procedures influenced by the Islamic *Shari'a*. The day of rest was moved from Friday to Sunday.

The pace of change moved rapidly in other social and economic spheres. Universal primary education was proclaimed, corruption attacked, and Atatürk committed the military to continuing reform. In subduing the Christian Armenians and Greeks, the Turkish army was ruthless (although most of the 1.5 million Armenians who perished did so during World War I). This caused almost all surviving members of these minorities to emigrate, leaving Turkey short of managerial talent and entrepreneurs.

Economically, Atatürk favored a program of industrialization behind high tariff barriers. When private industry failed to expand sufficiently during the Great Depression of the 1930s, the government created State Economic Enterprises to operate in textiles, metals, banking and other areas.

Kemal Atatürk died in 1938, recognized as the hero of his nation in his own lifetime. The National Assembly elected his close associate, Ismet Inonu, as the second president. Faced the difficult task of guiding the nation through World War II, Inonu kept Turkey neutral, but at the end of the war threats from the Soviet Union forced it to seek allies in the West. Beginning in 1947, Turkey received massive U.S. economic and military aid, given to help resist Soviet pressure, and in 1951 it joined the North Atlantic Treaty Organization.

Turkey moved cautiously toward democracy with competing political parties. The *Republican People's Party* treasured Atatürk's legacy, but in 1950 the *Democratic Party*, which appealed to the conservatism of old-fashioned landlords and little-educated peasants, won a landslide.

Dominant during the 1950s, the *Democratic Party* became authoritarian. It banned opposition political activities and plunged the country into serious debt. With the nation slipping badly, in 1960 officers seized power, since the military considers itself the heir of Atatürk's reforms. They arrested high officials and *Democratic Party* politicians, executing some, including the former prime minister. Then the military oversaw the creation of a new constitution, and after elections handed power back to the politicians.

Though it returned Turkey to formal democracy and set a precedent for a watchdog role, the military intervention did not solve the underlying political and economic problems. Indeed, some of its drastic measures created bitterness for a whole generation. A decade later, in 1971, student protests, unemployment and violence by extremist groups shook public confidence. The army forced the prime minister to resign and again took strong measures to restore law and order.

Nevertheless, by the late 1970s, protests and assassinations again shook the country. Extremists on both the Marxist left and Islamic right reinforced old communal rivalries and in 1978 unrest erupted into mob fighting in Marash, east of Adana. The Shi'a and Alevite communities, generally poorer than the majority Sunni Muslims, suffered more than 100 dead and several hundred injured. Since the Shi'a and Alevite supported the *Republican People's Party*, and the Sunnis backed the conservative *Justice Party*, heir to the dissolved *Democratic Party*, the conflict reflected socio-economic, political, and religious divisions. Despite the imposition of martial law in many regions, the toll from the violence exceeded 5,000.

Surprising almost no one, in 1980 the military seized power again and installed a governing council that took vigorous steps against terrorism. It arrested more than 10,000 suspects during the first month. Strict controls were imposed on the press, hundreds of mayors were dismissed, and taxi drivers were ordered to shave daily. Within months, violence declined and the country and even its taxi drivers looked cleaner. However, many innocent people languished in prison.

Austere, cold and imposing, the Ataturk Mausoleum in Ankara reflects the character of modern Turkey's founder.
Photo by Wayne Thompson

The Return to Democracy

Criticizing the 1961 constitution as unworkable, the military leaders drafted a new one. To encourage new leadership, it banned the previous political parties and about 100 leading politicians from political activity for ten years. Meanwhile, martial law courts punished participants in the violence, sentencing tens of thousands to prison, sometimes for lengthy terms. To little surprise, many prisoners were tortured and mistreated in ways common to Turkish prisons, such as corporal punishment, solitary confinement in a small, dark cell, or bread-and-water diets.

Two political challenges dominated Turkish political life during the 1980s and 1990s, challenging both the military and political elite. Throughout the Southeast, a major rebellion by disaffected Kurds led to the deaths of perhaps 30,000 civilians and the evictions of hundreds of thousands of others from their villages. Meanwhile, against a background of economic stagnation, the Islamic-influenced *Welfare Party* won local elections and finally came to govern Turkey—briefly.

The Kurdish Insurrection

For millennia, tough mountain tribesmen speaking Kurdish dialects have inhabited the heights and valleys where the borders of Iraq, Iran and Turkey converge. Outside East and South Asia, these Kurds form the largest ethnic group lacking independence. Kurds have rebelled against each state where they form sizable local majorities.

Today's political problems result directly from the breakup of the Ottoman Empire after World War I. Kurdish leaders claimed eastern Anatolia but failed to influence the peace settlement, and the Treaty of Lausanne brushed aside Kurdish desires for independence (see Iraq: History).

For decades, Turkey officially classified Kurds as "Mountain Turks," and manipulated their dialectic differences to avoid recognizing them as a separate national group. Kemal Atatürk and his successors rigorously crushed Kurdish revolts and suppressed any evidence of Kurdish identity. Regulations prohibited the language from use in personal names, public speeches, and at weddings and social occasions. Until 1991, no books, papers, street signs or pamphlets legally appeared in the language. Legalizing Kurdish TV broadcasts took another decade. However, the dialects remained alive, even when illegal. Cassettes in Kurdish circulated widely, and in recent years satellite broadcasts enabled programs from Europe to reach viewers.

Most Kurds traditionally lived in mountain villages, divided from others across the mountains by dialect and tribal loyalties. They received little formal education and that in Turkish, so for many reasons most Kurds tended to ignore national issues. However, some became successful

The old Galata Bridge, Istanbul, stretching across the Golden Horn

politicians and advanced to the top of national politics, like Ismet Inonu. Indeed, usually one-quarter of all members of parliament claimed some Kurdish ancestry, but such politicians frequently became assimilated, a threat that television and modernization bring to members of the middle classes. At the other extreme, many Kurds passionately desire their own schools and autonomy, or even independence.

In the 1980s, violence spread across the southeast and east, fomented by the *Kurdish Workers Party (PKK)*, a Marxist group led by Abdullah Ocalan (pronounced O-ja-lan). Financed and supported by Syria and by Kurds working in Europe, *PKK* fighters infiltrated into Turkey. The military, a largely conscript army, responded roughly to attacks by the *PKK*. On occasion it used heavy weapons within towns, and its brutal treatment of civilians often alienated the local population. By the mid-1990s, over 800 villages had been forcibly evacuated to cut off guerrillas from food and shelter.

The violence rose sharply in the 1990s. Despite innovations like winter operations, the military proved unable to crush the insurgency. It mounted large-scale invasions of alleged *PKK* bases in Iraqi Kurdistan and reported hundreds killed. In fact, alerted by the massive military buildup, most guerrillas had slipped away.

For its part, the *PKK* attacked civilians, especially Kurds who cooperated with the government. Foreign travelers became targets, even in Istanbul, as the *PKK* threatened the important tourist industry.

Turkey's laws and methods often seemed designed to provoke resentment. For example, Article 8 of the constitution prohibited separatist propaganda in any form, including calls for ethnic autonomy. It was used to convict dozens of journalists, politicians, and labor unionists on charges of sedition.

Turkish courts and the military allowed scant room for peaceful criticism. Kurdish parties faced frequent attempts to ban them from elections. Human rights activists suffered at the hands of the police, who arrested even minor employees. Yasar Kemal, one of Turkey's greatest living writers and the author of the internationally acclaimed *Memed, My Hawk*, received a suspended jail term for merely questioning policy toward the Kurds. Outside the law, a series of unsolved murders decimated journalists and leaders—including over 100 political leaders—sympathetic to Kurdish hopes.

In 1998 Turkish pressure forced Syria to crack down on *PKK* activities and expel its leader, Ocalan. This eventually led to his capture in Kenya by Turkish commandos, a tremendous boost to Turkish pride.

Turkish Republic of Northern Cyprus
Area: About 1,350 square miles.
Population: About 200,000.
Capital City: Turkish sector of Nicosia.
Location: 40 miles from the Turkish coast.
Ethnic Background: Turkish Cypriot, with immigrant mainland Turks.
Chief Commercial Products: Citrus fruits, grain, light manufactures
Trading Partner: Turkey.
Former Status: Part of the Republic of Cyprus (1960–1974)
National Day: November 15.
Chief of State: Dervis Eroglu (2010).
National Flag: A red crescent on a white field between two horizontal red bars.
GDP per capita: About $4,000.

Ethnic violence between its Greek and Turkish communities during the early 1960s marred the independence of the small island of Cyprus. A 1974 coup against the Greek Cypriot president enabled Turkey to invade and protect Turkish-inhabited villages and towns, as well as seize Greek ones in the north. The assault captured 38% of the island and divided it along the "Attila Line," to protect the Turkish 18% of the population. The two communities periodically bowed to international pressure and held talks on a settlement, but neither proved willing to compromise.

The Turkish-Cypriot Legislative Assembly proclaimed the independence of the "Turkish Republic of Northern Cyprus" in 1983. Only Turkey recognized this new state, and thus virtually all trade and travel must take place through Turkey. Rauf Denktash, formerly vice president of the entire island, became its president until retirement in 2005.

Living in Northern Cyprus has imposed great sacrifices in return for freedom from Greek control. Turkish Nicosia initially possessed no cinema or commercial art gallery and only five public telephones for its 40,000 people. Until recently, per capita incomes averaged about one-third the Greek level ($4,500 to over $13,000). Foreign investment is negligible, especially since European Union courts have allowed Greek owners to sue for their property sold to Europeans. Mainland Turkey provides almost half the zone's budget and funds all major public works. This requires use of the Turkish Lira, one of the least valued European currencies. Military forces from mainland Turkey control the local police, and journalists who question such links have been arrested on dubious charges. Moreover, immigrants from Turkey may now outnumber the Turkish Cypriots in their own territory.

During three decades of sporadic peace talks, Turkish Cypriots consistently demanded most territory north of the Attila Line, about 30% of the island, and a form of federalism that meant near-complete independence. Greek Cypriot leaders seemed more willing to compromise. However, in a bizarre turn of events, in 2003 many Turkish Cypriots rejected President Denktash's hardline objections and voted to accept the UN proposals, while the newly-elected Greek Cypriot president condemned the proposals for granting Turks too much. Thus Greek Cyprus joined the EU on terms constructed to encourage the Turks to compromise, while the Greeks refused the UN compromise themselves.

Mehmet Ali Talat won the 2005 presidential election. He desired reunification and EU membership for the entire island. In 2008, Demetris Christofias of the AKEL Communist Party, who held similar views, won the Cypriot presidency. The two agreed to reopen Ledra Street—the traditional shopping center closed since the 1964 communal troubles—and undertake talks on the many unresolved issues. Both leaders expressed a sense of urgency in supporting a federal republic of two zones and two communities, granting the smaller Turkish community political equality with the Greek one.

Time solved some problems—Cyprus uses the Euro, so control of the central bank makes little difference. However, grave problems remained, like the return of refugees, restitution of property, the future of settlers and troops from Turkey, and the constitution. The lack of progress contributed to loses by Talat's party in the 2009 legislative elections, and his defeat the next year by Dervis Eroglu, a separatist. In 2013 voters reversed themselves and made the leftwing Republican Turkish Party the largest.

Britain also closed down a Kurdish satellite channel, Med-TV. Broadcasting across Europe and the Middle East, it had advocating killings in reprisal for the capture of Ocalan.

On trial for his life, Ocalan called the *PKK* rebellion a "mistake," and ordered his followers to halt violence and adopt a peaceful political struggle. In 2000, a party congress formally adopted Ocalan's political strategy of peacefully improving the Kurdish community within Turkey. Most *PKK* fighters withdrew to Iraq, but fighting resumed in 2003, when the *PKK* demanded an amnesty for all PKK prisoners, including Ocalan, as a condition for a renewed truce.

For decades, the government's modest conciliation efforts have failed to address the underlying problems. One great obstacle to peace remains the uncompromising and strident nationalism common among Turkish officers and officials. This attitude justifies the arbitrary arrests, torture, and bureaucratic heavy-handedness that have long remained the ways of life in the Southeast. For example, arrests followed a soccer game when one team wore the red, yellow, and green stripes of the Kurdish colors.

Kurdish politicians frequently face legal challenges. The Constitutional Court dissolved political parties because of alleged links with the rebels. As many Kurds grew disillusioned by the government's failure to satisfy even modest demands, activists formed the *Peace and Democracy Party (BDP)*, and won 35 seats in the 2011 elections running as independents.

To escape this mistreatment and for better economic opportunity, about 500,000 Kurds migrate to western Turkey annually. Others flee to Iraq and join the *PKK* fighters, who launch cross-border raids of increasing severity. The total death toll from the violence exceeds 40,000.

Complying with the human rights provisions of the European Union, Parliament voted major reforms by 2004, including permission for Kurdish schools and radio broadcasts. However, attitudes in the military and government bureaucracy meant that changes came grudgingly and slowly. For example, applicants for licenses to teach Kurdish found themselves blocked by repeated technicalities, and Kurdish broadcasting by the state-owned radio and TV service only began after transmissions of such locally-insignificant languages as Bosnian. Indeed, the 30-minute weekly programs in two Kurdish dialects were not even described as Kurdish.

Following months of negotiations, in 2013 Abdullah Ocalan called for a ceasefire without conditions, arguing "the weapons should be silent and ideas should speak." Soon afterwards, *PKK* units withdrew to northern Iraq. The continuation of the ceasefire will depend on negotiations over the revised Turkish constitution. Though the Kurds no longer demand independence, it will be difficult for many Turks to accept the sort of autonomy the *PKK* desires.

Political and Economic Stagnation

Following months of negotiations, in 2013 Abdullah Ocalan called for a ceasefire without conditions, arguing that "the weapons should be silent and ideas should speak." Soon afterwards, *PKK* units began withdrawing to northern Iraq, though the withdrawal was later halted because Kurdish demands had not been addressed. The PKK no longer demands independence, but it will be difficult for many Turks to accept the sort of autonomy the *PKK* desires.

Only the patient and brave (with good lateral vision and quick reflexes) dare to drive Istanbul's Tanlabas Boulevard.

Photo: Miller B. Spangler

In response to the ceasefire, Prime Minister Erdoğan did announce major concessions over language. Cities and towns could adopt their native place names in place of Turkish ones. Non-government schools could instruct in Kurdish and foreign languages, and an ultra-nationalist oath would no longer be required of all students.

Another significant gesture was to propose a lower vote threshold for a party to enter parliament. Kurds comprise about 20% of the nation's population, but the largest Kurdish grouping, the *Peace and Democracy Party (BDP)*, regularly failed to meet the 10% threshold. Erdoğan's target of the bar set at 5% was more plausible, since *BDP* candidates received 4% of the vote in the 2014 municipal elections.

Instead, parliamentary politics continued feverishly through much of the 1990s. The decade witnessed nine governments in as many years, including one headed by Tansu Ciller, the country's first woman to hold the office. Unfortunately, political attention often focused on gaining office rather than on governing well.

The instability resulted in significant part from a culture that fostered aggressive personal ambitions by individual politicians, combined with an electoral system that encouraged parties to splinter. Rather than the "winner-takes-all" model common in the English-speaking world, Turkey had adopted proportional representation (PR). The great theoretical virtue of PR—it produces a legislature that reflects voters' preferences more accurately—sometimes becomes its great practical weakness. Winner-takes-all systems ruthlessly punish minor parties—votes for them and for the loser—are "wasted" in terms of legislative seats. As a result, the winning party usually receives a higher proportion of seats in the legislature than its share of the vote, enabling it to act more decisively. As a result, parties tend to compete for voters in the center of the political spectrum.

In the 1980s, Turkish elections had also manufactured sometimes substantial majorities, even with PR, by virtue of a law that granted the party with the most votes the votes of all parties receiving less than 10% of the total. As a result, for example, in 1987 the *Motherland Party* gained a large majority of seats in the National Assembly (292 of 450) but won only 36% of the vote.

Beyond PR, elections failed to provide good government because political opinion was deeply fractured. In 1996, for example, the Islamic *Welfare (Refah) Party* came first, though winning only 21% of the vote. On mathematical grounds alone, forming a coalition government became extremely difficult. With the *Welfare (Refah) Party* as the largest, stable coalitions became impossible. Islamist in a nation dominated by secularists for 70 years, it seemed guilty, as Tansu Ciller claimed, of "sinking the country into darkness," Six cabinets held office in just three years as civilian and military secularists attempted to keep the *Welfare Party* from office. However, to avoid possible parliamentary investigations of corruption that might implicate her, Ciller sought the safety an alliance with her ideological enemy. *Welfare's* leader, Necmettin Erbakan, became the country's first Islamist prime minister.

Erbakan clearly reoriented foreign policy toward the Islamic world. He visited Iran to sign a major gas deal, and toured Libya. However, his term was brief. When some local officials of the *Welfare Party* openly contradicted secularist traditions, the military quietly encouraged parliamentary maneuvering that collapsed the coalition in 1997. For good measure, the Constitutional Court later banned the party because it had permitted women to wear head-scarves in public buildings, encouraged Islamic schools, and kept (unproven) links with secret societies. The courts also convicted Erbakan and several other party officials, including the mayor of Istanbul, of making statements deemed too Islamist.

Bulent Ecevit's left-wing but nationalistic *Democratic Left Party* swept to first place in the 1999 elections. Though the old bonus for being the largest party no longer applied, Ecevit succeeded in forming an unlikely alliance with the right-wing *Nationalist Action Party*. Ecevit now provided stable leadership, waging a war on corruption that landed "big fish" (particularly bankers) as well as petty criminals. The police also discovered that the Turkish paramilitary group *Hizbullah* (not directly related to the Lebanese group) had murdered more than 100 secular intellectuals, Marxist Kurds, and other victims. Control over spending brought the rate of inflation below 40%. In 1999 the European Union at last accepted Turkey as a candidate for membership.

That same year, an earthquake devastated seven western provinces—the country's industrial heartland. The civil administration and the military both proved inept at rescue efforts, though better at feeding and sheltering hundreds of thousands left homeless. Despite its location on a major geological fault, Turkey had not developed specialized rescue teams. Television pictures that showed a centuries-old mosque and its slender minaret standing intact beside collapsed apartment buildings illustrated an equally serious failing: for decades, officials had failed to issue and enforce appropriate building codes.

American style still sells in Turkey
Photo by Wayne Thompson

As successor to the long-serving President Suleyman Demirel, the National Assembly elected Ahmet Necdet Sezer, chairman of the Constitutional Court. A legal scholar rather than a politician, Sezer strongly emphasized the rule of law. The changes that Sezer advocated became the more powerful because he desired reform not so much to please Europe but to benefit Turks.

When the strong personalities of President Sezer and Prime Minister Ecevit clashed seriously in 2001, stock market investors took flight. Those with money (including, allegedly, the governor of the Central Bank!) speculated against the Turkish lira, draining $7 billion from the Central Bank's reserves within hours. Overnight interest rates reached an annual rate of 5000%, and the country plunged into its worst economic recession since World War II. The GDP fell by almost 10%, and nearly a million workers lost their jobs. The rates of suicide, theft, prostitution and stress-related illness all climbed, and media experts warned of a "social explosion." Another symptom of the misery came from the 1.5 million people who canceled their cell phone contracts. Besides the government's deficit, the banking system lay at the heart of the trouble. Many banks had borrowed funds abroad and lent them for politically-important projects with little chance of business success. Saving such banks required billions of dollars, much of it from the IMF. Turkey became its largest debtor.

Under the stress, Ecevit's coalition fragmented. The *Nationalist Action Party*

Former President Abdullah Gul

opposed human rights proposals like banning capital punishment and allowing Kurdish-language TV broadcasting. Finally, members of Ecevit's own party forced early elections, hoping to catch the Islamist political forces disorganized.

Rise of the *AK Party*

After the *Welfare Party* had been declared illegal, Islamist deputies failed to unite. However, one faction formed the *Justice and Development Party* (known by its initials as the *AK Party*), under the country's most popular individual politician, Recep Tayyip Erdoğan. A former mayor of Istanbul previously convicted of inciting religious hatred by publicly quoting from a poem, and banned by the Supreme Court from running for parliament, he claimed that *AK Party* was not Islamist, but merely Islamic-rooted.

Voting day transformed Turkish politics. Not a single party from the previous parliament managed to win 10% of the national vote, and therefore, all of them, both government and opposition, failed to enter the new parliament. The victor was *AK Party*, with 34% of the popular vote and nearly two-thirds of the seats. The *Republican People's Party* captured most of the rest and formed the opposition. Coalition politics had ended. The large *AK Party* majority soon overturned the law that Erdoğan had broken, rendering him eligible to run for parliament. After a by-election victory, he took office in early 2003.

His initial challenge was the U.S. desire to attack Iraq through Turkey, long regarded in Washington as a special NATO ally, overwhelmingly Muslim but staunchly anti-Communist. However, the Turkish constitution requires parliamentary approval of any foreign troops stationed in the country, and public opinion polls showed that 90% of the population opposed an unprovoked attack on a fellow Muslim country. Business leaders feared the loss of markets and another recession. Strategists and the military worried that Iraqi Kurds might declare independence or seize Kirkuk. Despite promises of substantial U.S. aid, parliament narrowly rejected the U.S. plan.

A visionary with a proven record as an administrator, Erdoğan took office with both goals and energy. He traveled abroad—to Greece—to convince European leaders of his reformist ideas and to reassure Greeks of his peaceful intensions. He pressured Rauf Denktash, the obstinate Turkish-Cypriot leader, to accept the UN plan for peace on the island (see box).

In his first two years of office, Erdoğan guided a legal revolution in human rights through parliament. After a decade of immobilized coalitions, the *AK Party's* majority enabled it to abolish the death penalty, restrict torture by the police, and increase the media's freedom of expression. A major reform of the penal code raised protections for women, and established life sentences for perpetrators of "honor killings."

In the political domain, parliament curbed the military by making the National Security Council advisory, under civilian rather than military leadership. Military spending was even placed under parliamentary control. Political detainees, including some Kurdish militants, were amnestied.

Recognizing these long-delayed improvements in human rights, as well as Erdoğan's moderate stand over Cyprus, the EU opened talks on Turkey's admission in 2005. As expected, the talks proved difficult, both for objective reasons like the culture, size, and poverty of Turkey, as well as cultural fears about the arrival of 70 million Muslim Turks as Europeans. One particular stumbling block is the requirement that Turkey open its ports and airports to all EU members—including Cyprus—though its Greek government refuses trade with the Turkish north.

Presidential Candidate
Recep Tayyip Erdoğan

One unsettled domestic issue—at least for conservative police and prosecutors—is the prohibition on statements that "insult" the nation. For Orhan Pamuk, uttering the words "One million Armenians and 30,000 Kurds were killed in these lands" sufficed to bring criminal charges in 2005. The charges were dismissed, fortunately so, because the next year Pamuk won the Nobel Prize for literature. Three of his novels have been published in English, *The White Castle, My Name is Red,* and *Snow.*

Orhan Pamuk escaped the state prosecutors, but the deeper intolerance, plus a payment, motivated a teenager to assassinate the country's leading Armenian journalist, Hrant Dink. Although Dink had been convicted of claiming that Armenians had suffered genocide during World War I, his murder evoked a surprising outpouring of regret and sympathy from liberal-minded Turks.

Crises over Presidential Elections, 2007

Political tensions inevitably rose in 2007, when the five-year election cycle of the Grand National Assembly coincided with the seven-year term of the presidency, set to expire in May. Massive demonstrations by secularists reflected fears that the *AK Party* majority in the Assembly would enable it to select the next president. President Sezer warned that the danger of Islamic radicalism was greater than ever. The military chief bluntly stated that a committed secularist was needed in the presidential palace. Symbols matter, and many secularists abhorred the thought of a president's wife wearing a headscarf while hosting a reception in the Çankaya Palace.

Very carefully, party leaders announced their candidate just before the filing deadline, reducing time for public protests. Rather than Prime Minister Erdoğan, previously convicted of reciting an Islamist poem, the party selected Abdullah Gül, the foreign minister. His nomination lacked a two-thirds majority by a few votes on the initial ballot, but victory seemed assured with the third ballot, when a simple majority would suffice. However, the Constitutional Court insisted, on dubious legal grounds, on a two-thirds quorum for a presidential election. The third ballot therefore did not take place.

In response, Erdoğan sought to demonstrate the nation's will. He called early elections for the National Assembly. Despite the determined opposition of staunch secularists, the *AK Party* won an overwhelming triumph, capturing nearly half (48%) of all votes, and gaining an absolute majority of seats. The victory also eliminated the legitimacy of any military intervention pretending to "preserve democracy."

Two issues dominated Turkish political life during the following year. First, the National Assembly duly elected Abdullah Gül as president, meaning that the first lady attended receptions wearing a headscarf. Second, the *AK Party* formed a tactical alliance with the ultra-nationalists and amended the constitution to ban the exclusion of students from universities except for reasons stipulated by law. This protection for women wearing scarves met the aspirations of millions of party supporters, but infuriated secularists, who hold the principles of Kemalism above the constitution. The Constitutional Court soon struck down the amendment.

Democracy itself faced serious threat in 2008 when prosecutors charged that the *AK Party* had sought to undermine secularism and should be banned. Clearly, the party had attempted to abolish the universities' prohibitions on wearing headscarves and it had strengthened religious education. Many commentators expected the Constitutional Court to rule in favor of the prosecutors, but it side-stepped the political chaos that would have followed a ban. Instead, the court decided that since the party had raised human rights standards and had not acted violently, its punishment was the loss of half its government subsidy.

Long-running investigations of alleged secularist plots also threatened to provoke a military intervention. After a newspaper and a court were attacked in 2006, prosecutors charged that a shadowy group of secular extremists code-named Ergenekon had unleashed violence, to stoke unrest and provoke an army coup. Dozens of prominent secularists, including university professors, journalists, retired generals, and members of a police special operations unit were arrested. Placing retired military officers on trial in civilian court for the first time tested Turkish democracy, especially because the alleged conspirators were often prominent critics of the government.

In 2010, hundreds more military officers—including generals and admirals—were charged with participation in the "Sledgehammer Plot." They allegedly conspired to bomb two mosques in Istanbul and provoke Greece into shooting down a Turkish plane, thus creating the circumstances for a military seizure of power. Such trials confirmed the powerlessness of the former secular establishment to protect its prominent members.

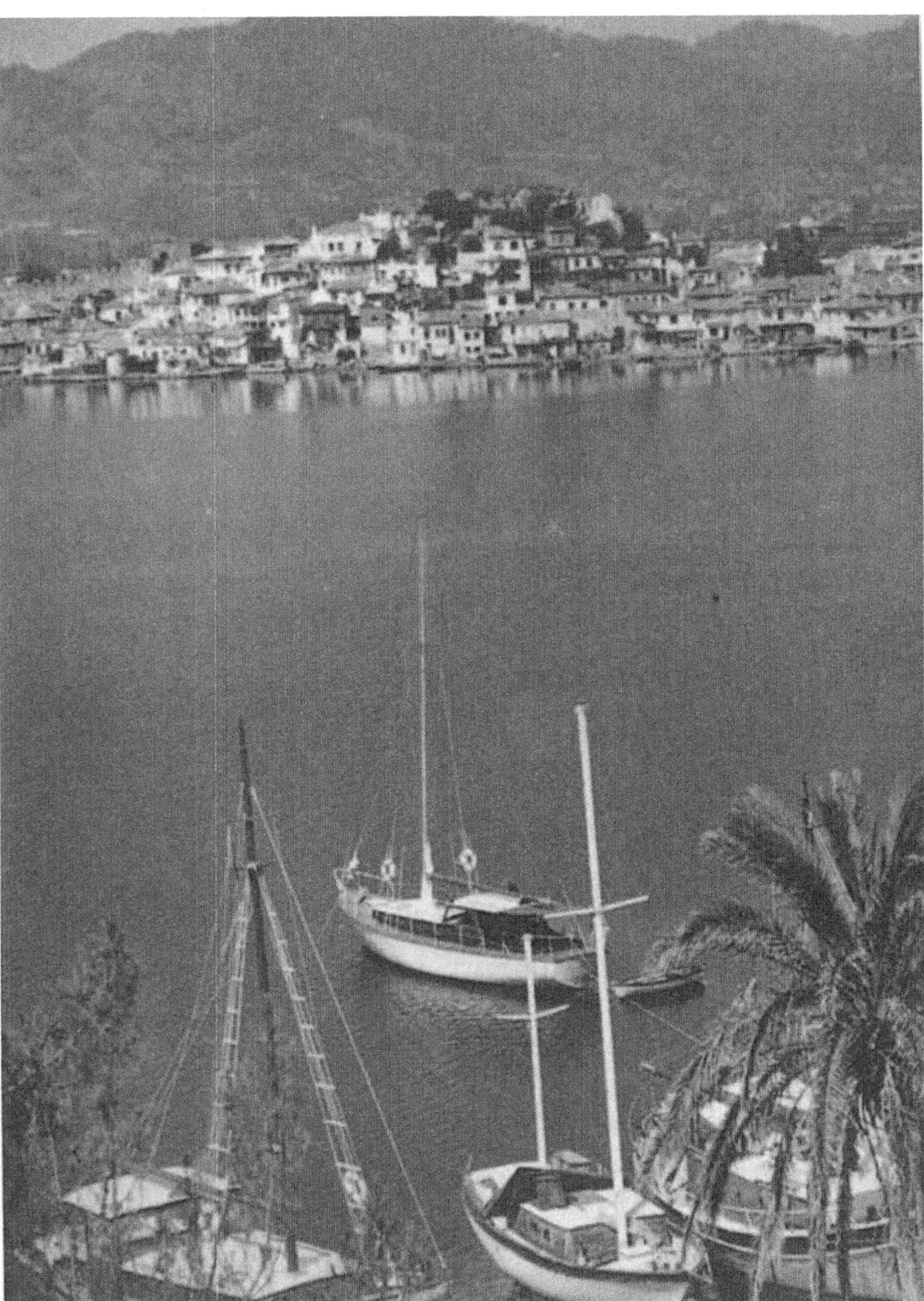

Mararias, one of the beautiful summer resorts on the Aegean Sea

Generals involved in the 1997 "postmodern coup" that overthrew Prime Minister Necmettin Erbakan were investigated, but perhaps the ultimate symbol of the changed political environment was the trial of General Kenan Evren, who led the 1980 coup d'état and served as president for six years.

As expected, the *AK Party* won a large majority in the 2011 National Assembly elections. Prime Minister Erdoğan had campaigned on both the successful past—the economic prosperity his cabinets had brought the country (see **Economy,** below)—and a vision for the future. He promised, for example, a canal *around* Istanbul, to divert much of the heavy freight and tanker traffic from the Bosporus. He also called on voters to support his quest for a new constitution that would place the military under firm civilian control.

Although Erdoğan won a historic triumph by increasing his party's share of the popular vote in a third successive election, it actually lost seats as fewer citizens "wasted" their votes on parties failing to exceed the 10% threshold. By contrast, the major opposition *Republican People's Party (CHP)* gained additional seats with its new social democratic approach. The nationalists barely survived the 10% threshold.

Because the *AK Party* failed to achieve a two-thirds majority, it lost the opportunity to establish a constitution on its own. This result probably benefitted the country: a document forged in consensus with opposition parties will likely win greater acceptance and stand the tests of time far better than one dictated by a single party. Prime Minister Erdoğan duly called for consultation with other groups.

In 2013, a decade after taking power, Recep Tayyip Erdoğan's magical political touch began to fail him. He antagonized the West by declaring "As with Zionism, anti-Semitism and fascism, it is inevitable that Islamophobia be considered a crime against humanity." International human rights organizations criticized the loss of press freedoms and reported that Turkey ranked first in the world in the number of jailed journalists. In Turkish cities, weekly rallies silently demonstrated opposition to the justice system over the convictions of so many military officers. Opposition parties and human rights advocates objected to limitations on the selling of alcoholic drinks.

The most publicized protests began when a few dozen environmentalists, many of them young and educated and including a number of women, gathered in Istanbul's Gezi Park to oppose plans to replace the park with a shopping center. When the police attempted to clear the park, the demonstrators resisted. Others across the country soon joined the protests, including activists from the opposition *Republican People's Party* and left-wing labor unions.

The Battle over Headscarves

In 2008 Turkey's Constitutional Court ruled that parliament's constitutional amendment to permit women to wear headscarves in universities conflicted with the constitutional principle of secularism. Why so great a concern over such modest pieces of fabric?

From one perspective, it is a clear issue of conscience and human rights. If a devout Muslim girl or woman wishes to enhance her modesty by wearing a scarf over her hair, should government interfere? There are more pressing national problems to address.

Opponents, some of them practicing Muslims, provide a very different perspective: the scarf announces a woman's religious persuasion, a view that a woman's attire in the 14th (Muslim) century should be based on customs from the 1st century. By a small extension, the scarf also proclaims a woman's loyalty to Islamist political parties. Political insignia do not belong in public places such as universities. Even in the individualistic West, American schools ban gang-related insignia.

Proponents of headscarves respond that women in scarves intend no criminal conduct. They may vote for any party they please: it is not a return to the brownshirts worn by Hitler's followers in Germany. Furthermore, the ban causes unnecessary grief. For example, when the mother of a wounded soldier visits him in a military hospital, she must remove her scarf.

After the Islamist-leaning prime minister approved their use in 1998, the courts and military overruled. The election of the Islamist *Virtue Party's* Merve Kavakci to parliament sharpened the issue. Parliamentary regulations did not explicitly prohibit the scarf, and some reasoned that elected representatives should be entitled to wear whatever they deemed appropriate. Secularists sharply disagreed, regarding the National Assembly as the heart of Atatürk's legacy.

Kavakci appeared wearing a scarf at parliament's opening session in 1999. Accused of violating the republic's basic secular principles, she refused to remove the offending cloth, or leave the chamber. The assembly was forced to adjourn; government came to a halt, even before the new prime minister was designated. Stripped of her Turkish citizenship, Ms. Kavakci now wears her scarf in peace, in U.S. exile.

By some estimates, the country's secular universities dismissed a quarter-million scarf-wearing women in the 1990s and following years. Because their convictions of modesty conflicted with Kemalist conceptions of secularism, these women lost the opportunity for intellectual development and career options. However, most modern societies accept that certain dress standards can be imposed. In 2005, the European Court of Human Rights sided with the ban, justifying it as "protecting the rights and freedoms of others and maintaining public order." It ruled similarly in a French case in 2014.

The ban applied primarily to government buildings, including universities and hospitals. In 2013 Prime Minister Erdoğan modified it by allowing its use by public employees, but not judges, the military, and the police.

Foreign Relations: A New Regional Role

For decades, Western nations valued Turkey as a Cold War ally and the eastern bulwark of NATO. More recently it became a military partner of Israel. However, with the Soviet threat removed and the economy developing rapidly, Erdoğan set Turkey's foreign policy on an increasingly independent course. Presenting himself as a Middle Eastern and developing-world leader, he sought to win new markets for the country's industries, as well as to influence the region. He attempted to mediate between Israel and Syria, and offered to process Iran's partially-enriched uranium for research and medical purposes.

The government also supported Turkish Islamist groups participating in the flotilla of vessels that challenged the Israeli blockade of Gaza. Vociferous criticism followed the 2010 Israeli commando raid in international waters on the Turkish vessel *Merve Marmara* that killed nine Turkish citizens. The special relationship between the two non-Arab but Middle Eastern states seemed at an end. When Israel refused to apologize, diplomatic relations weakened, and the special military alliance collapsed.

During the popular protests of the 2011 Arab Spring, Erdoğan encouraged authoritarian rulers to resign, and condemned dictators like Syria's al-Assad and Libya's Gaddafi for using violence against their own people. Turkey accepted refugees from Syria and hosted the rebels' political leadership. However, when terrorist explosions killed 46 in the border town of Reyhanli, political critics claimed that Turkey had adopted too great a role.

Erdoğan turns authoritarian

A decade after taking power, in 2013 Recep Tayyip Erdoğan's magical political touch began to fail him. He antagonized many in the West by declaring "As with Zionism, anti-Semitism and fascism, it is inevitable that Islamophobia be considered a crime against humanity." International human rights organizations criticized the loss of press freedoms and ranked Turkey first in the world in the number of jailed journalists. Opposition parties and human rights advocates objected to limitations on the selling of alcoholic drinks, and during weekly rallies demonstrators silently protested the justice system over the convictions of so many military officers.

The most publicized protests began when a few dozen environmentalists, some of them women and many of them young and educated, gathered in Istanbul's Gezi Park on the edge of Taksim Square, the heart of modern Istanbul, to oppose plans to replace the park with a shopping center, mosque, and opera house. When police attempted to clear the

A combine harvesting wheat in southern Turkey

park, the demonstrators resisted. Others protests formed across the country, joined by activists from the opposition *Republican People's Party (CHP)* and left-wing labor unions.

In contrast to other *AKP* leaders who apologized for harsh police tactics, the Prime Minister remained critical of the demonstrations and blamed a "treacherous plot" for the affair. After days of protests, he ordered police to clear Taksim Square; this was accomplished using water cannon, tear gas, and rubber bullets. Other government agencies also attempted to punish the protestors. The Turkish health ministry, for example, investigated healthcare professionals at makeshift first aid centers for acting without permission from the ministry.

The protests eventually diminished, but many observers concluded that the entire affair weakened Erdoğan substantially. His authoritarian style and the harsh handling of the protests also delayed membership negotiations with the E.U.

More serious crises followed. In December, special police units conducted spectacular raids on prominent officials and businessmen, arresting more than 50 on corruption charges. The offenses ranged from money laundering to bribery in granting construction permits on sites protected for environmental or cultural preservation. Three cabinet members' sons faced charges of accepting bribes, and the general manager of a large state-owned bank had stashed millions in cash in his home library. The entire scandal pointed to corruption surrounding the Prime Minister.

The arrests clearly took Erdoğan by surprise, but he struck back harshly. Discerning a plot by a moderate Islamist group, the Gulen movement, whose followers had infiltrated the justice ministry and police, the Prime Minister sacked the top prosecutors and police officials most involved in the investigation and arrests. Thousands of police officials were reshuffled, and new leadership was installed. A later "reform" aimed to bring prosecutors and judges under greater control by the justice ministry, clearly attacking their independence.

It seems likely that a plot did exist. The Islamic scholar Fethullah Gulen and his *Hizmet (Service)* movement had partnered with the AK Party during its rise to power. Its supporters provided many of the police and judicial appointees who proved a counterweight to the strong secularist traditions within the government. However, from his exile in Pennsylvania, Gulen came to oppose several positions adopted by Erdoğan, including his strong backing for Egypt's *Muslim Brotherhood*, the widespread arrests of journalists, and the violent police actions against the Gezi Park demonstrators. Perhaps to demonstrate the government's power, in November the education ministry also closed down the nation's entrance-exam preparation centers, many of them run profitably by *Hizmet*. The corruption scandal and arrests seem *Hizmet's* response, timed to precede both local elections and the presidential contest due in 2014.

The prime minister became even more biting in his attacks on the international conspiracy against him when an audio recording purported to be a telephone conversation between himself and his son was posted on social media. Apparently the voices were genuine, but had been spliced together to create a conversation about moving millions of Euros of cash. The recording suggested wiretapping by his enemies, and Erdoğan ordered Twitter closed (the courts later reversed the decisions). Weeks later, a release on Facebook provided the bugged recording of top politicians, military officers, and intelligence experts discussing a possible attack on Syria.

To Turkey's secularists and much of the rest of the world, Erdoğan's political future seemed gravely compromised, and opinion polls charted the public's increasing disapproval. However, public support for *Hizmet* fell even faster.

Campaign accusations of fraudulent ballots raised fears about the integrity of the 2014 local elections. Some were false; others involved the fate of the 150 million ballots printed for an electorate of only 52 million. Most pre-election claims did not prove valid—and the national vote tallies proved that *AK Party* had maintained popular support, winning nearly 43% of the vote, almost equaling the combined 44% of the *CHP* and the right-wing nationalist *MHP*. Nevertheless, in certain tight races integrity seemed compromised. For example, when the *CHP* claimed fraud in Ankara, election commissions quickly ruled there was insufficient evidence. Erdoğan quickly seized the victory to proclaim that that those who had leaked state secrets "will pay for this . . . From tomorrow there may be some who flee."

The great electoral prize of 2014 is the presidency, with a direct election for the first time replacing election by parliament. To challenge Erdoğan more effectively, the *CHP* and *MHP* selected a joint candidate, Ekmeleddin İhsanoğlu, a widely respected scholar and author. As the former Secretary-General of the Organization of Islamic Cooperation, he was hardly the typical candidate the secular *CHP* would nominate, but he had the potential to woo religious conservatives who desired change. The *AK Party*, unable to nominate the popular but term-limited Abdullah Gul, simply accepted Erdoğan's candidacy when he announced it.

Early election polls indicated Erdoğan held a 20-point lead over İhsanoğlu for a voting day after this volume's publication.

Culture: One cannot think of Turkey without thinking of Istanbul—one of the great historic cities of the world. The ancient Greek colony of Byzantium later became Constantinople, capital of the Eastern Roman Empire. It evolved into the capital and center of the Byzantine world, where ancient Hellenistic culture persisted until its capture in 1453 by the Ottomans under Sultan Mehmet II. The Ottomans renamed it Istanbul and installed their sultan in the Topkapi Saray, the Great Palace overlooking the Bosporus and Golden Horn. The spectacular mosques of Istanbul still remain places of deep reverence.

Although Ankara, located near the nation's center, is the political capital, Istanbul is the modern cultural and economic heart of Turkey. Europe's largest city, with a population approaching 12 million, it extends for miles along both sides of the Bosporus. Its great variety of people and different ways of living make it one of the world's most interesting cities.

By contrast, Ankara is a very modern city, but has the unhappy distinction of possessing some of the worst air pollution of any city anywhere. This is not the result of heavy industry, but of geography—the city lies in a natural bowl, trapping smoke and fumes.

Turkish culture today blends strong pride in ethnic heritage with a culture influenced by religion from Arabia and modern arts and ideas from Europe and North America. In many ways, Turkey is a land of two cultures.

From a country long considered overwhelmingly agricultural and rural, between 1970 and 1990 Turkey rapidly changed into a nation of city dwellers. In the cities one hears Western music and modern young women can meet male friends in a restaurant or dance in nightclubs.

Old ways die hard in rural areas, however. In many villages for both cultural and Islamic reasons the feeling is still strong that women should not attend public events with men. Women and girls do not attend the *halkevi*, "people's house," traditionally the center of social life in most villages. Likewise, in remote villages the visitor may rarely see a woman's face, but in Istanbul, Izmir, and Ankara women work in most positions they hold in Europe or America.

The Keban Dam on the Euphrates River WORLD BANK Photo

Since the founding of the Republic, educated Turks have deliberately tried to imitate the literature and drama of Europe. There is a state theater performing Western plays or plays following Western forms, but the typical Turk finds this alien. Karagoz, the shadow puppet and his friends and enemies are more to Turkish taste; both fantasy and real-life situations appear in the puppet shows. Likewise, the great majority of Turks love their own music. To the accompaniment of three or four instruments, including a lute (bazouki), a drum and perhaps a violin, a singer's folk songs tell of love, war, heartbreak or death—often in long, drawn-out and high-pitched quavering tones, using minor toned scales.

The traditions of Kemal Atatürk decree secularism, and until recently successive cabinets—if necessary prodded by the military—remained aloof or even hostile to religion. Nevertheless, today Islam lives as a vital part of the beliefs of most Turks. Religious classes returned to schools after the 1980 military coup, as part of the cultural heritage of the country. Instruction about religion was not intended as indoctrination, though sometimes it had that effect. During the 1980s the Kemalist ban on words of Arabic origin and Islamic connotation was removed, and terms and phrases last used by educated people of the Ottoman Empire now reappear in writing and on radio and television.

Education has been a primary concern of the government for decades. Elementary education is completely free, and nearly universal. The "middle schools" are similar to three-year junior high schools, while the lycée corresponds to an academic high school and is primarily intended to prepare students for university study. Only higher-ranked graduates of middle schools are able to enter the lycées.

Turkey now has dozens of universities. The oldest is Istanbul University, which traces its founding to Mehmet the Conqueror in 1453. It now enrolls over 30,000 students; the next largest is Ankara University. Another institution in Ankara offers instruction in English rather than Turkish, Middle East Technical University. Expanded with assistance from the UN, and several foreign nations, it serves other countries of the Middle East as well as Turkey.

Economy: Long famous for carpets, mohair and dried fruits, Turkey long remained a land of relatively poor traditional farmers who struggled for a living in remote villages. As recently as the 1970s agricultural products amounted to half the nation's exports.

Industry developed slowly, partly because local handicrafts suffered competition from European manufactured goods. The first major thrust of industrialization occurred only in the 1930s, sponsored by the government for political and social reasons as well as economic ones. Protected by high tariffs, regulation and other trade barriers, the factories of the State Economic Enterprises (SEEs) failed to become efficient competitors. High inflation and shortages of foreign exchange frequently halted periods of strong economic growth. The Ottoman Empire had been the political "Sick Man of Europe" in the 19th century, and for most of the 20th century, Turkey was the economic "Sick Man of Europe."

In the 1980s, Prime Minister Turgot Özal launched reforms that began to transform the economy. He freed markets, reduced tariffs, eliminated exchange controls, and removed the heavy hand of government trade restrictions. This encouraged investment by both domestic and foreign firms. Industry seized the opportunity to expand, and the resulting export-led growth transformed the stagnant economy of the late 1970s into one enjoying rapid rates of real GNP growth. Exports rose by 400% between 1980 and 1987, before inflation again damaged their competitiveness.

Özal's free market policies alleviated but failed to eliminate many traditional economic problems. Population growth at 2.5% per year absorbs a major portion of national income growth. Consequently, although many Turks work abroad, unemployment often hovered around 20%, and incomes reached just 34% of the European Union's average. Public education lags greatly, and social security is minimal (though government employees like teachers retire young). Tax revenues fell far short of requirements, creating a budget deficit regularly exceeding 10% of GNP, and the foreign debt of about $65 billion required large payments for interest and principal. Monopolies exist in tobacco, sugar, and alcohol, while regulations elsewhere discourage entrepreneurs.

Nevertheless, profitable opportunities abounded in many fields. Tourism climbed rapidly in the late 20th century, though hampered by insufficient infrastructure and sanitary facilities as well as fears of terrorism. Given beautiful scenery, a warm climate, exotic customs, and a wealth of historic locations, by 2010 the nation attracted some 32 million visitors annually.

Designing a carpet pattern, Istanbul WORLD BANK Photo

A world apart from luxury tourist hotels, the Southeast Anatolia Project (GAP) offers the possibility of improving some of the country's most impoverished areas. A complex of 20 dams, 19 hydroelectric plants, tunnels and irrigation canals, the project's expected cost will exceed $32 billion. Besides generating large amounts of electricity from the Atatürk Dam, initially the world's sixth largest, and others on the Euphrates and Tigris Rivers, the project is planned to divert enough water to irrigate some four million acres.

Several problems threaten completion of the project. The combined plans for water use by Turkey, Syria, and Iraq may drain the Euphrates dry, so armed conflict remains possible if unlikely (see "When Will the Taps Go Dry?" p. 8). Declining economic benefits, combined with rising costs, make some dams less profitable than alternative ways of generating electricity, and concerns over soil salinity, chemical pollution and water quality may limit irrigation. Critics also argue that villagers displaced by the reservoirs are often not compensated significantly, because the land may be owned by rich landlords, and the villagers are conveniently removed for their protection from the *PKK.* Thus GAP's electrification, roads and farming services may never reach the average farmer in the style of America's TVA, and the local Kurds may lose their heritage without economic gain.

The start of the Ilisu Dam near Hasankeyf on the Tigris in 2006 aroused concerns as well over the eventual flooding of an archaeological marvel, a city left undestroyed throughout the Middle Ages. Insurers later brought construction to a temporary halt, but conservationists remain concerned.

Widely-Based Prosperity Arrives under Erodğan

The first two terms of *AK Party* rule (2002–2011) witnessed a near-explosion of economic growth. Despite a population increase, *per capita incomes more than doubled* as the nation moved from recession to Chinese-style economic growth. Inflation dropped to 4%, while unemployment fell from the traditional 20% to half that. The budget deficit and foreign debt both fell as proportions of GDP, as exports soared across Europe and firms entered new markets. Once a nation of tottering banks, new regulations kept them from risky lending, and none failed during the world recession of 2008–09.

Manufacturing also boomed. Shipbuilding came to rank as fourth in the world, automobiles as sixth in Europe, and the country's firms gained a 50% share of the market for European-made color TVs. No longer are exports primarily agricultural.

While many of the successful policies were actually initiated by past prime ministers, Erdoğan and the *AK Party* deserve credit for continuing liberalization and fostering trade. Strongly supported by business interests, the prime minister personally opened export markets by including executives on his official visits abroad. Transformed from the economic "Sick Man of Europe," Turkey joined the G-20, the club of the world's twenty largest economies.

In 2005, the country celebrated the opening of a pipeline, this one nearly 1,200 miles long from Baku, Azerbaijan. It is valuable to consumers in Europe because it avoids two important difficulties: Russian control (like the other routes out of the Caspian basin), and shipping through the crowded Bosporus.

The Future: Until 2013, most European and U.S. analysts considered Prime Minister Erdoğan and the *Justice and Development Party (AK Party)* a force for effective rule in a conservative Muslim context, with free-market reforms that strengthened economic growth. After decades of political instability and crony economics, Turkey had finally realized her potential as a major regional economic and political power.

In Turkish, *"AK"* means white. But Erdoğan and his government are increasingly stained with arbitrary arrests of journalists, crony deals with property developers, and the excessive use of force against protesters. He will likely win the presidential election, but his increasing failure to distinguish between his country and himself, to consider the Gezi Park protests and the corruption scandals "coup attempts" and to threaten those who failed to rally to defend him reflects poor judgment. He is polarizing the country, and his falling popularity may eventually worry other *AK Party* leaders.

In 2012 this volume concluded "By a politician's standards, Erdoğan at 58 is a young man. Perhaps the greatest danger to his legacy is that with traditional constraints removed, he will grasp for too much power." Subsequent events verified that prediction far faster than anticipated.

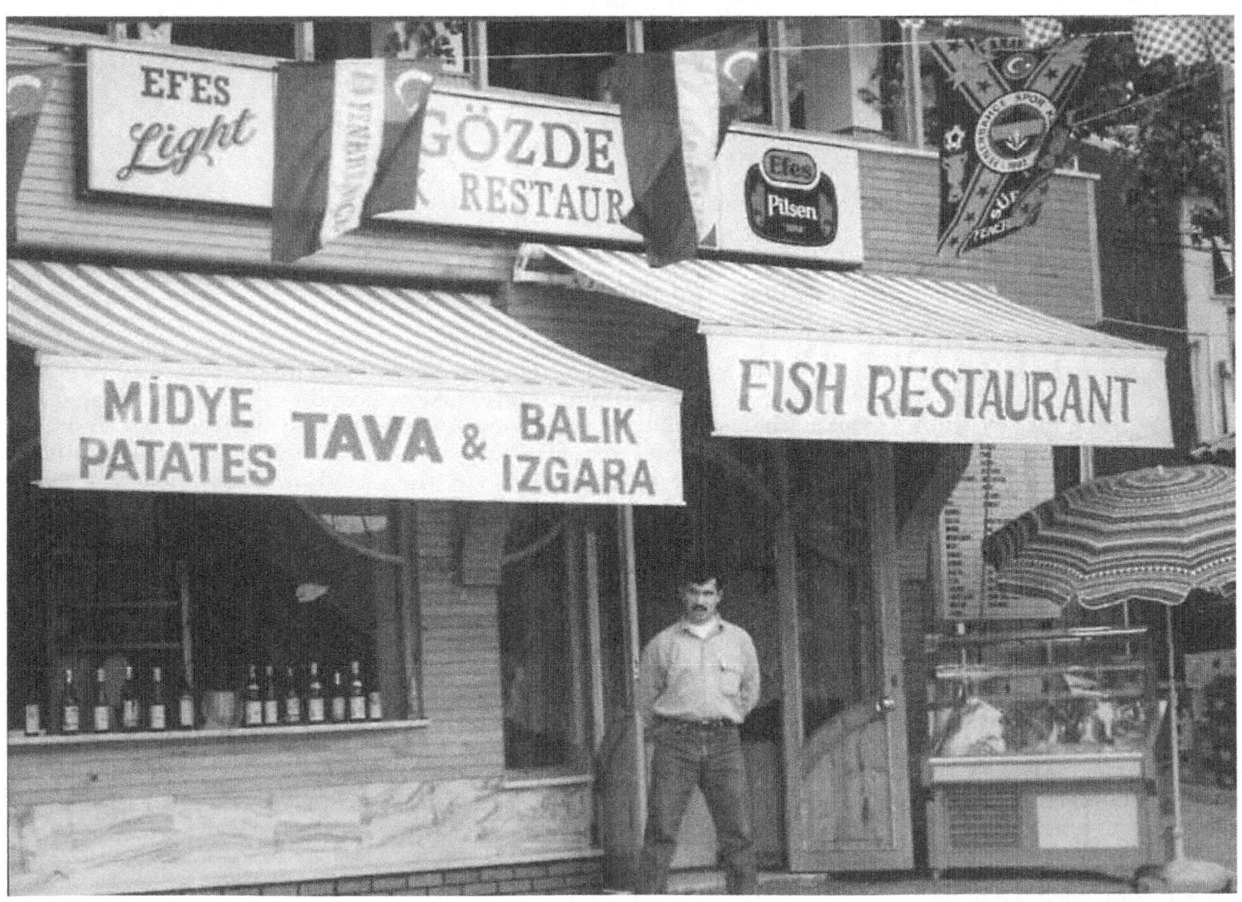

On the Bosporus near the Black Sea

Photo: Miller B. Spangler

The United Arab Emirates

The Abu Dhabi business district from a pedestrian crossover

Courtesy: Caltex Petroleum Corp. (Joe Brignolo '95)

Area: 30,000 square miles (77,700 sq. km.).
Population: 9 million (about 7 million foreigners).
Capital City: Abu Dhabi (pop. 900,000, estimated).
Climate: Extremely hot except for moderate winters. Precipitation is rare, though some rain falls in the highlands between Ras al-Khayma and Fujayra.
Neighboring Countries: Oman (Northeast and Southeast); Saudi Arabia (South and West).
Time Zone: GMT +4.
Official Language: Arabic.
Other Principal Tongues: English (widely used), Hindi, Urdu and Farsi (Persian).
Ethnic Background: Arab-speaking citizens comprise about 20% of the population, while expatriate workers from Pakistan, India and Iran compose a majority.
Principal Religion: Islam (55%; mostly Sunni; perhaps 25% Hindu and 10% Christian foreigners).
Chief Commercial Products: Petroleum, liquefied natural gas (LNG), petrochemicals, including plastic and paint, food processing, dates, machinery, boat repair and aluminum.
Major Trading Partners: Japan, Germany, U.K., U.S., Singapore, South Korea.
Currency: Dirham (= 100 fils).
Former Colonial Status: Each sheikhdom accepted British protection and control of foreign affairs, but enjoyed domestic autonomy (1892–1971).
National Day: December 2, 1971 (Independence Day).
Chief of State: Sheikh Khalifa bin Zayed Al Nahyan (Ruler of Abu Dhabi), President of the Supreme Council of Rulers.
Head of Government: Sheikh Muhammad bin Rashid Al Maktoum (Ruler of Dubai), Vice-President and Prime Minister.
National Flag: Three equal bands of green, white and black (top to bottom) are flanked at the pole by a vertical red band of the same width.
Gross Domestic Product: $412 billion (at current prices); $288 billion (Purchasing Power Parity).
GDP per capita: $31,900 (PPP).

Abu Dhabi and five smaller states along the southern limit of the Arab Gulf, plus one on the Gulf of Oman, comprise the federation known as the United Arab Emirates. Most of the land is desert and the climate hot and humid. For centuries, the inhabitants farmed or herded sheep and goats in the interior, or sought a living from fishing and pearling. A further career was piracy, especially in the extremely shallow Gulf whose sandbanks and coral reefs protected locals from strangers.

Most of Abu Dhabi (pronounced ah-bu za-bi) is low coastal plain and flat desert. In the south, imperceptibly, they become the Empty Quarter of Saudi Arabia. Their topography contrasts greatly with the rugged slopes of the Hajar mountain range that marks the border between Abu Dhabi and Oman and continues to the tip of the "Horn of Arabia." Scattered rainfall in the mountains provides several oases with water for irrigation; the largest is *Al-'Ain* in eastern Abu Dhabi. While there are no permanent rivers, several dozen dams trap runoff for irrigation or to recharge aquifers.

United Arab Emirates

Each of the seven states bears the name of its capital city, and is headed by an *Emir* ("Prince"), who uses the traditional title of *Sheikh*. The territory of Abu Dhabi is about three times as large as the other six states combined. Each state maintains considerable internal autonomy under its hereditary ruler:

Abu Dhabi (pop. 1.9 million, estimated). Sheikh Zayed bin Sultan Al Nahyan
Dubai (pop. 1.5–1.7 million, estimated). Sheikh Muhammad bin Rashid Al Maktoum; Sheikh Hamdan bin Muhammad, crown prince
Sharja (pop. 350,000 estimated) Sheikh Sultan bin Muhammad al-Qasimi
Ajman (pop. 50,000, estimated). Sheikh Humaid bin Rashid al-Nuaimi
Umm al-Qaywayn (pop. 30,000, estimated). Sheikh Rashid bin Ahmad al-Mualla
Ras al-Khayma (pop. 120,000, estimated). Sheikh Saqr bin Muhammad al-Qasimi
Fujayra (pop. 50,000, estimated). Sheikh Hamad bin Muhammad al-Sharqi

In a society developing as rapidly as this, population figures are very rough estimates at best, and the division of the population is a somewhat delicate issue. From the 180,000 inhabitants at independence in 1971, in twenty-five years the total reached *12 times* as large. (Had the U.S. population then grown that rapidly, it would now surpass China and India combined.)

Overlapping territorial claims by the various states produced a number of neutral zones, some involving more than two Emirates. They are shown darkly shaded on the accompanying map, the lack of clarity reflecting the actual identity of the territories.

History: Recent archeological discoveries show continuous habitation of the coast for the past 7,000 years, and scattered settlements in the *wadis* (desert valleys) for much of the period. One graveyard excavated in Sharja that dated about 200 B.C. included two horses and 13 camels apparently sacrificed during burial ceremonies. By 2,000 years ago, ports in the region traded as far away as India and China. Perhaps linked to trade, Christianity spread widely, attested by burials, churches, and even a monastery.

The Islamic conquest apparently brought years of substantial prosperity during the Umayyad and early Abbasid dynasties. Later constructions, however, seem mostly fortifications. After centuries of Muslim Arab settlement and sporadic Iranian incursions, in the 1500s the Portuguese seized the dominant role in the Gulf. They soon lost it to the Dutch and British, who sought freedom of commerce rather than colonies.

At the turn of the 19th century, *Wahhabi* envoys from Central Arabia incited some local sailors to attack Western commerce, hence its reputation in Europe as the Pirate Coast. Britain then intervened in local fighting, and beginning in 1820, forced treaties on the states to suppress piracy and prohibit warfare at sea. Thus the terms Trucial States or Trucial Oman came into use, though Arabs generally called it the Oman Coast.

According to treaties signed at mid-century Britain controlled foreign affairs and defense. Internal matters remained under the rulers, and little development took place. Indeed, the major events of world history had little impact, although competition from cultured pearls drove down profits from pearling and reduced the standard of living. As late as the 1950s disputes over borders or pearling rights led to skirmishes between desperately poor emirates. One continuing dispute in the 1940s and 1950s concerned rival claims by Saudi Arabia, Oman and Abu Dhabi to the Buraimi oasis.

The search for petroleum in the emirates began in the 1930s, and the later president of the U.A.E., Sheikh Zayed bin Sultan, served as a guide to one of the first exploration teams. Twenty years later, in 1958, commercial deposits were discovered, and oil production began in Abu Dhabi in 1962. Its revenues rapidly transformed the economy and society. Dubai also discovered oil, though relatively small amounts, and it deliberately developed into the region's chief trading center.

Faced with rising anti-colonialism and the high military costs of maintaining the protectorate, Britain withdrew from the Gulf in 1971. It encouraged the emirates to unite. Six formed the U.A.E., and Ras al-Khayma joined later, but Qatar and Bahrain opted for independence. The federal constitution adopted in 1971 divided responsibility for governance between federal institutions and the individual emirates. The seven sheikhs rule some internal affairs of their own states; they determine oil policy and may even possess their own military. However, responsibility for education, public health and currency belongs to the federation. Given the imposing

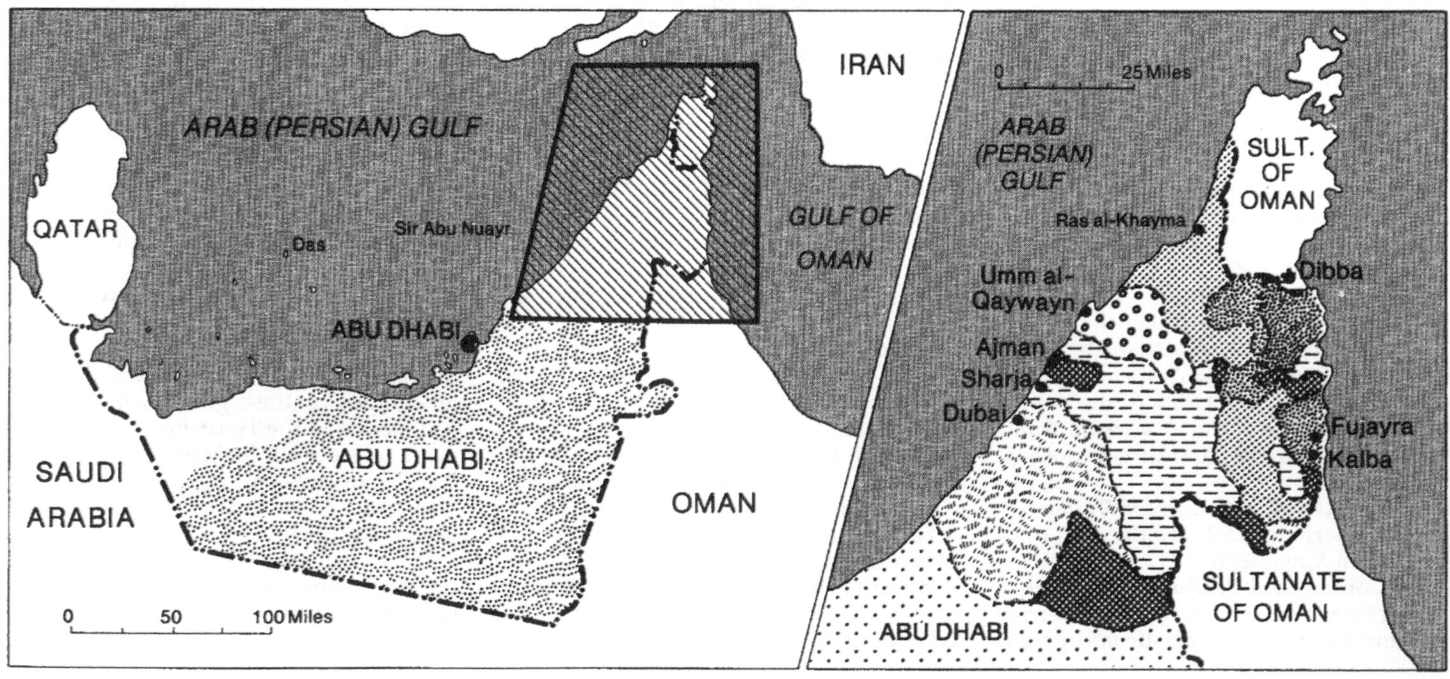

H. H. Sheikh Khalifa bin Zayed Al Nahyan, Ruler of Abu Dhabi and President, UAE

H. H. Sheikh Maktoum bin Rashid Al-Maktoum, Ruler of Dubai and Vice President, UAE

H. H. Sheikh Sultan bin Muhammad al-Qasimi Ruler of Sharja

H. H. Sheikh Humaid bin Rashid al-Nuaimi, Ruler of Ajman

H. H. Sheikh Rashid bin Ahmad al-Mualla, Ruler of Umm al-Qaywayn

H.H. Sheikh Saqr bin Muhammad Al-Qasimi, Ruler of Ras al-Khayma

wealth of Abu Dhabi, other states have tended to cooperate.

At the federal level, authority lies with the Supreme Council of Rulers. It chose as its first president Sheikh Zayed, and reelected him for seven consecutive five-year terms. The president appoints the prime minister, typically the ruler of Dubai. Something akin to a legislature exists, the Federal National Council, whose 40 members represent individual emirates; half are elected by a restricted group of voters. Abu Dhabi contains the largest population, 90% of the oil deposits, and contributes the overwhelming portion of the national budget.

The 1980s brought two difficulties. Some off-shore oil platforms were attacked during the Iran-Iraq War, disturbing commerce. After the collapse of OPEC's price

H. H. Sheikh Hamad bin Muhammad Al-Sharqi, Ruler of Fujayra

structure in the mid-1980s, oil revenues fell 40%, and an economic recession struck. By 1990, however, construction cranes again sprouted across the major cities, signaling a return to economic growth. New tourist hotels, shopping centers, commercial buildings and factories suggested that while oil continued to provide the mainstay of the economy, diversification will play an important role in the future. Currently only 70% of GDP comes from the oil sector.

To pay for the growth, the country allegedly sold more oil than its OPEC quota (see Economy). Iraq condemned the Emirates as well as Kuwait, and in 1990 the U.A.E. quickly joined the Gulf War coalition to liberate Kuwait. The conflict emphasized the presence of foreign workers in the Emirates, where a law demanding the replacement of all foreign employees of the federal civil service proved impossible to implement.

In 1992 Iran reopened an old dispute over three small but strategic islands in the Gulf, Abu Musa and the two Tunbs. Iran had contested their ownership with Sharja after Britain's withdrawal in 1971, but for two decades a working compromise allowed both countries a role. Iran's unilateral action in 1992, perhaps the hasty result of Tehran politics, aroused Arab fears. While the U.A.E. desires to settle the matter through the International Court of Justice, Iran has refused and continues to develop the islands. However, Iran is a major trading partner of Dubai, and as long as Iran seeks friendly relations with Arab states, the issue lies dormant. Meanwhile, Abu Dhabi remains a major purchaser of modern weaponry and the country hosts a major arms exposition.

As the twentieth century closed, a number of signs suggested that the seven emirates were gradually strengthening their sense of unity. In 1996 a national law replaced individual emirate rules on traffic offenses, and the next year a federal environmental law took effect. Although probably dwarfed by the (undisclosed) Abu Dhabi budget, the federal budget continued to provide funds for the economic and social development of the poorer emirates, and the rivalries of Dubai and Abu Dhabi remained friendly rather than contentious. The sense of unity seems likely to increase: younger inhabitants reportedly feel a greater loyalty to the U.A.E. than do their parents.

After several years of declining health, Sheikh Zayed of Abu Dhabi, died in 2004 at the age of 86. People from all the emirates mourned the passing of a leader they considered the generous and wise founder of the country. The succession proved swift and smooth, as Zayed's eldest son Khalifa had been appointed crown prince 35 years earlier.

Dubai's economy suffered particularly hard from the world economic recession of 2008–09, even though the emirate only indirectly depends on oil income. Wealthy expatriates found themselves unable to purchase new properties, speculators pulled out of the market, and real estate prices fell by perhaps 40%. The decline in world trade hurt trans-shipment and aluminum demand fell 30%. As local firms ran short of cash, a massive loan of $10 billion from the UAE central bank cushioned the downturn and provided cash to pay some building costs. Nevertheless, construction on many projects came to a halt. Tens of thousands of expatriates, thrown out of work with construction companies, financial firms, and elsewhere, left for home.

Like other Gulf Cooperation Council governments, the rulers of the UAE are determined to maintain control. One potential source of instability lies in the activities of human rights activists and social media activists. A potentially more violent danger might be the activity of Islamists who reject the moral authority of the government.

In 2013 the Federal Supreme Court tried 94 Islamists with alleged ties to *al-Islah*, a local group linked with the *Muslim Brotherhood*. The international media was not allowed to observe the trial, and human rights groups condemned the trial as unfair for, among other shortcomings, ignoring allegations of torture. Most of the defendants, who include human rights lawyers, professors and university students were convicted and imprisoned for multi-year terms.

The rulers' great concern with political Islam, particularly the *Brotherhood*, continued after the conviction of two-thirds of those tried. The UAE supported the coup that removed Mohammed Morsi from power in Egypt, and extended billions in financial aid. The Emirates also joined with Kuwait and Saudi Arabia in pressuring Qatar to reduce its links with the *Brotherhood*, including alleged backing provided by the Arabic broadcasts of Al-Jazeera.

Culture: The culture of the United Arab Emirates is not essentially different from that found in neighboring countries. The majority of the native Arabs, who are *Sunni*, retain a sense of their tribal backgrounds and traditions.

Women in the U.A.E. play a greater role in society than in many conservative Muslim countries. Not only are girls educated, but the government fosters adult education programs that have reduced the female illiteracy rate to around 20%. While women hold a few significant positions in the private sector, the government employs large numbers, especially in education and health care. By the 1990s, women comprised 16% of the workforce.

Modern education arrived relatively recently. In 1968, the adult literacy rate was only 21%. At independence, a decade after oil exports began, only 30,000 children attended school. By the mid-1990s, the figure had climbed to 400,000, and enrollments rose even more rapidly in high school. The construction of schools in even the most remote hamlets provides all children with the opportunity to learn; education is compulsory from the age of six.

Long a particular concern of Sheikh Zayed, who grew up when the emirates lacked a single modern school, adult education programs have proved so successful that the literacy rate reached 85% in the mid-1990s. Government policies indicate a concern with the quality of education as well as its extent.

Higher education was traditionally represented by technical colleges, several private institutions, and the Emirates University located in al-'Ain. Founded in 1978, by the early 1990s it graduated its first classes of physicians. Women comprise about two-thirds of the roughly 13,000 students, reflecting the greater likelihood that young men will study abroad.

In 2007, Dubai created International Academic City, incorporating Knowledge Village and its 20 foreign higher-education institutions, now including Michigan State University, or one university for every 20,000 inhabitants.

The Federation's Marriage Fund ranks as one of the most unusual features of a society where the state takes responsibility for the welfare of its citizens between the cradle and the grave. Realizing that marriage to a woman from the country had become prohibitively expensive for

Neat as an architect's model: housing in Dubai

Courtesy: Royal Embassy of Saudi Arabia

many of its young men, in 1994 the Federation created the Marriage Fund. The fund built special "Wedding Halls" where receptions cost far less than at hotels. The government also urged fathers to accept lower dowries, a major expense for many. It provides up to $19,000 to couples of limited income who wish to marry. In its first year the fund gave or lent nearly $100 million to 3,000 couples. By 2000 this had grown to 44,000 couples, and marriages to foreign women had fallen from 64% of total weddings to 26%.

A major purpose for the Marriage Fund is the need to increase the indigenous population. Nationals are outnumbered about four to one by foreign residents who have found work in the country. Native and immigrant Arabs together constitute no more than 40% of the population, with Indians (30%) and Pakistanis (25%) comprising major communities. Nearly 90% of the officers and men of the federation army of 40,000 are not native Arabs.

In a society with many single men, but few amusements and limited (legal) alcoholic beverages, sports attract great attention. Thoroughbred racing arouses particular passion, and the Dubai World Cup has become the world's richest horserace ($2126 million in prizes, 200711), and the stable of Sheikh Muhammad, Dubai's ruler, often leads the world in victories. Further down the social scale, one finds auto racing and even camel races, held on a special track. The Emirate's powerboat racing team led the world championship in 1995 until an accident killed its most talented driver.

Economy: Despite the relatively late development of its petroleum deposits (exports began in 1962), the oil reserves of the U.A.E. now exceed 97 billion barrels, and rank the fifth largest in the world. So vast are the deposits that with present discoveries alone, the U.A.E. can maintain its present level of exports until about the year 2099. Most deposits lie in Abu Dhabi, whose production exceeds 90% of the national total, with very modest output from Dubai and Sharja. Thus it was Abu Dhabi's oil revenues that transformed much of the country. The U.A.E. also possesses the world's fourth largest reserves of natural gas.

Historically, the U.A.E. received a fairly small OPEC quota (e.g., 1.1 million barrels per day, 1989), but partly because of agreements with oil companies, it overproduced. The collapse of Iraqi and Kuwaiti exports in 1990 provided opportunity for increased exports, and U.A.E. experts correctly predicted that increasing world demand for oil, plus declining reserves in several OPEC nations, would reduce excess supplies and render quotas relatively unimportant.

Outside the petroleum industry, the inhabitants find a variety of ways to earn a living. Agriculture remains an important source of employment, with over 20,000 farms. Currently the Emirates produce roughly half the vegetables that the population consumes—and all the dates. In fact, with over 20 million date palms—approximately five per person, yielding nearly 20 lbs. each—the country is one of the world's most important growers.

The Hajar mountain range provides Ras al-Khayma and Fujayra with water for irrigation. Besides dates and other traditional fruits and vegetables, these areas export strawberries, chrysanthemum, tomatoes and other high-value winter crops to Europe. Agricultural research stations attempt to adapt plants and animals to the demanding climate conditions, and seek plants that tolerate saline ground-water.

Rain falls infrequently in the Emirates, and several dams store the natural flow of the seasonal *wadis* for agricultural use and to recharge aquifers. By contrast, the population depends on desalinized water, and the al-Taweela plant gives Abu Dhabi the world's largest single unit in the world.

All the Emirates possess stretches of beach, some quite lengthy. Fujayra also enjoys a flourishing tourist trade based on trips to the mountains, including picturesque waterfalls. Sharja and other Emirates issue their own stamps, including some of the world's most eye-catching commemorative issues for sale to collectors.

The Amazing Success of Dubai, Inc.

Dubai ranks as the undisputed commercial center of the nation as well as the region, and symbols of its brash confidence abound. Its World Trade Center already ranked among the tallest buildings in the Middle East, but the Burj Khalifa, opened in 2010, become the world's tallest at 2,716 feet, a half-mile high, twice the Empire State Building. The city claims the world's most luxurious hotel, the Burj al-Arab; some consider it 7-Star, and rumors suggest some suites may cost $25,000 per night. Still under construction, Dubailand will become the largest entertainment complex in the Middle East—a family-style Vegas the size of Manhattan with complete theme parks, but no gambling, alcohol, or evident illicit sex.

The government aims for 15 million tourists a year by 2015. Many facilities already exist, including the Gulf's busiest airport, and a $3.7 billion subway system under construction. In 2001 the government-owned airline, Emirates, announced it would spend $15 billion on passenger jets, the largest order ever announced.

Aiming to become the home of international jet-setters, but limited by its relatively short (40-mile) waterfront, Dubai has constructed a series of artificial islands. Seen from the air, several take the shape of a palm tree, and their fronds, each over a mile long, extend the emirate's shoreline and provide the setting for planned communities of luxury homes, each with a view of the beach. Another project created islands in the shape of the world. However, the really grandiose multi-billion project, known as Dubai Waterfront, was planned to house 400,000 people on an area nearly three times the size of Washington, D.C. The coastlines of the various islands will stretch 500 miles, and feature more exclusive hotels (one, the Atlantis, underwater), more shops, and other entertainment centers. The world's largest mall, incorporating 31 hotels, will be across town.

Dubai's business model is free-trade zones in the desert, where firms with similar interest cluster together and take advantage of capitalism at its least regulated: no taxes, no tariffs, no limits on transferring funds, no visa difficulties for professionals. Media City, Internet City, several villages and parks, and recently Healthcare City often bring millions of feet of square feet of space devoted to state-of-the-art in the industry.

Obviously these projects greatly exceed the needs of Dubai's inhabitants. When planned, they made sense only because the emirate aimed for millions of visitors, and expected the population to reach two million by 2010, as wealthy retirees and business tycoons moved to a land of perpetual sunshine, negligible income taxes and unsurpassed internet service. One challenge in the future may be a struggle against drug use and other forms of hedonism, among the support staff if not the

Courtesy: Caltex Petroleum Corp. (Joe Brignolo '95)

United Arab Emirates

Its height of 2,716 feet makes the Burj Khalifa the world's tallest building, an amazing challenge to desert wind, heat, and of course, gravity.

wealthy themselves. Already, gambling, alcoholic drinks and prostitution are becoming less discrete.

Old-fashioned work also exists. The Jebel Ali Free Trade zone provides warehousing for transshipping goods through the world's largest man-made port. Over 1,000 companies use the zone, including Dubai Aluminum's smelter, one of the largest in the world, with a capacity of about 1,000,000 tons in 2009. Its accompanying electric generating plant provides almost half the city's drinking water through desalination.

Given Dubai's trade, construction almost everywhere, and growth industries like aluminum and liquefied natural gas (LNG), the Emirates enjoyed increasing economic diversity. In 2006, petroleum accounted for only about one-third of the economy, an exceptionally low proportion given the high per capita incomes. The country constantly expands its infrastructure—by some estimates, in 2007 about 20,000 building cranes were in service in Dubai, alone—and its military acquisitions provide a competitive battleground for defense contractors throughout the world, especially for big-ticket items like tanks and jet fighters.

During the years of rapid income growth, the U.A.E. gained the distinction of providing a greater percentage of national income to foreign aid than any country. Much of the funding comes from the Abu Dhabi Fund for Development. Originally established in 1971 to help poorer Arab states, the Fund by 1995 had aided some 44 countries in Asia and Africa with loans and grants surpassing $3 billion.

A view of Dubai City. The building in the foreground with the ball on top is the headquarters of the Emirates Telecommunications Corporation.

Courtesy: Caltex Petroleum Corporation
Photo by Marina Volochine

One distinct shadow hanging over the entire construction boom is the treatment of manual workers. Eager to work hard for a few years, then return home able to purchase a home and small farm, manual laborers from the Indian subcontinent and China often find themselves working in health-threatening heat (over 100° Fahrenheit), at dangerous jobs without insurance or healthcare. Pay checks sometimes come months late, and living conditions may mean 10 men to a room. However, Dubai's rulers showed some concern: after unofficial demonstrations at the Burj Dubai (renamed Burj Khalifa) project involved 3,000 workers and some violence, in 2006 the government announced that a labor union would be permitted—and even granted a right to strike. In addition, afternoon construction work was banned in the summer.

Another fundamental challenge to the business model is the 2008–09 world recession. It depressed housing prices in Dubai by about 60% as jobs disappeared and thousands of foreign professionals left. There was room to fall: apartments in Burj Khalifa had reportedly sold for $2,700 per square foot. Dubai World, the emirate's investment arm, found itself unable to pay billions of dollars of debt to its banks, and attempted to restructure $23 billion of debt after being rescued by the government. In the process, banks may lose up to 50% of the value of their loans. Dubai's total debt in mid-2010 was estimated at over $100 billion.

The Future: At its birth, the United Arab Emirates seemed the façade of a new nation, another alliance of traditional rulers hurriedly patched together by departing colonial officials. Thanks to oil, the pragmatism of Sheikh Zayed, and the dynamic entrepreneurial spirit of Sheikh Maktoum bin Rashid, the UAE enjoyed decades of growth and prosperity. The passing of both those admired rulers failed to dent the high level of economic confidence. One concern for the immediate future is the health of Sheikh Zayed's successor and the ruler of Abu Dhabi, Sheikh Khalifa bin Zayed, who suffered a stroke in early 2014.

The astounding scale of Dubai's business model made it the Hong Kong of the last decade. Then, just as its commercial rents ranked among the most expensive in the world, the world recession hit. The property bubble burst. The UAE recovered rapidly, but the IMF has already warned of another property bubble.

Should negotiations over Iran's nuclear enrichment program end successfully, the UAE, as a major trading center for the Gulf, will benefit significantly from the end of sanctions and a rapid revival of Iran's international trade.

The Republic of Yemen

The old walled city of San'a. "San'a' must be seen, however long the journey, though the hardy camel droop, leg-worn on the way" Traditional Arab poem
Courtesy: Caltex Petroleum Corporation

Area: 207,286 square miles (536,869 sq. km.).
Population: 27.5 million (estimated).
Capital City: San'a (pop. 1.5 million, est.).
Climate: Extremely hot and humid on the coastal plain, cooler in the mountains, often cold at night. Rainfall is moderate on the western slopes of the mountains and the highest peaks sometimes have snow.
Neighboring Countries: Saudi Arabia (North); Oman (East).
Time Zone: GMT +3.
Official Language: Arabic.
Other Principle Tongues: Mahri; English in school and international business.
Ethnic Background: Arab, with varying physical appearances; short and olive-skinned people in the mountains; heavy African admixture along the coast.
Principal Religion: Islam. The *Zaidi* sect of *Shi'a* Islam dominates the northern mountains; most other Yemenis are *Sunnis* of the *Shafi'i* legal school.
Chief Commercial Products: Crude oil, cotton, coffee, qat, livestock and hides, tobacco, vegetables, dried and salted fish.
Major Trading Partners: U.S., Japan, France, Germany, Saudi Arabia.
Currency: Yemeni Rial (= 100 fils).
Former Colonial Status: Ottoman Rule sporadic after the 16th century; British in the South (1839–1967).
National Day: May 22 (Union Day).
Chief of State: Abd-Rabbuh Mansur Hadi, President (2012)
Head of Government: Mohammed Basindawa, Prime Minister (2011).
National Flag: Three horizontal stripes of red, white and black.
Gross Domestic Product: $43 billion (current prices; likely an IMF over-estimate); $62.7 billion (Purchasing Power Parity).
GDP per capita: $2,400 (PPP), but 40% have daily incomes under $2.

In 1990, the Yemen Arab Republic (North Yemen) and the People's Democratic Republic of Yemen (South Yemen, or Aden) merged to form the Republic of Yemen. Although the area had never formed a unified state, the population widely felt itself "Yemeni." While the merger of traditional and marxist political cultures proved uneasy, the union continues.

Located in the southwestern corner of the Arabian Peninsula, Yemen's varied topography contrasts greatly with the flat, stony plains and sand dunes of central and eastern Arabia. In western Yemen, the geography takes the form of zones running from north to south. The first zone, the Tihama plain, lies along the coast of the Red Sea. Level, hot, and arid, the Tihama also inflicts high humidity on its inhabitants.

Some 30 miles inland steeply rising slopes mark a scenic mountain range and plateau that run from the Saudi border in the north to the Gulf of Aden. Peaks in the range reach 10,000–12,000 feet. By blocking air currents from the sea, they cause summer rains that make the western slopes the wettest region of Arabia, with precipitation averaging 15 inches yearly, and as much as 30 inches in a good year. However, there are no year-round rivers, but rather seasonal streams in the valleys, known as *wadis*.

San'a (Sanaa), the capital, lies in the interior plateau; its elevation of 6,500 feet is one of the highest of any national capital. East of the mountains, the high plateau gradually slopes down to the desert, eventually joining the *Rub al-Khali* or Empty Quarter of Saudi Arabia.

Yemen

Southern and southeastern Yemen, bordering the Gulf of Aden, endures a harsher geography. Its lonely, barren landscape of desert plateaus and jagged mountains is broken by two important valleys. In the southwest, the oases around Lahj provide much of the region's limited produce. In the east, the Wadi Hadhramut forms a narrow strip of green. Yemen also rules several islands, including the strategically important Perim Island in the Bab al-Mandab, the strait between Arabia and Africa.

History: Ancient and civilized kingdoms existed in what is now Yemen long before the time of Christ. One of the most famous was Saba, or Sheba. Near its capital, Marib, a great stone dam captured the runoff from summer rains. Honored in literature and legend, the dam contributed to the reputation of this region as *Arabia Felix* (Fertile Arabia), famous in Roman times for its trade in frankincense and myrrh. However, during the early Christian centuries rival Jewish and Christian chiefs sought to conquer the region. Foreign armies invaded, the dam failed, and its irrigation system deteriorated. Islam arrived towards the end of Muhammad's lifetime, during the seventh (Christian) century, and spread partly as a reaction against religions linked to foreign powers.

The *Zaidi* sect of Shi'a Islam (see Iran: Culture) became dominant in mountain regions during the ninth century, and its leader, styled an Imam, became the traditional ruler. The early Islamic period provided security and prosperity. The population increased greatly, and many terraces on the steep, rain-fed slopes date from that era.

In the 16th century the Ottoman Sultans lay claim to Yemen, but its remoteness and terrain ensured that it was never completely subjugated. Indeed, the Ottomans withdrew in the 17th century and the British gained influence at Mukha (Mocha) where they established a trading station, while the interior remained under the *Zaidi* Imams. The Ottomans attempted to regain the coast and more accessible regions after 1849, with limited success, and their rule ended in 1918.

The southern and eastern regions were variously held by feuding tribal chieftains for untold centuries. Britain seized the port of Aden in 1839. It became a valuable coaling station for ships plying the Egypt-

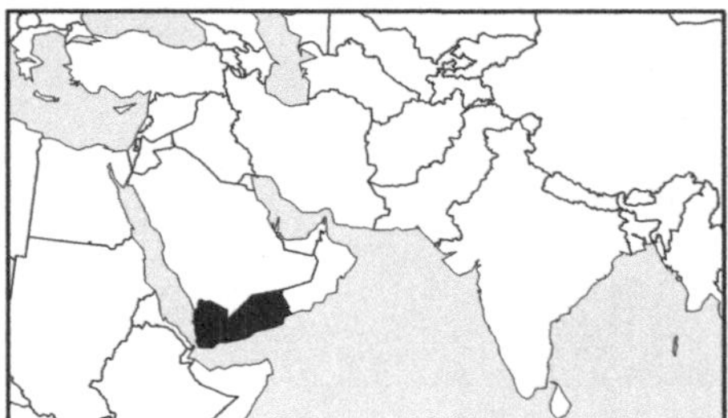

India route, but Britain took minimal interest in the interior. Between 1882 and 1914, its sheikhs and other local leaders signed treaties that ceded authority over foreign affairs to Britain in exchange for protection.

After the Ottoman Empire collapsed in 1918, the *Zaidi* ruler, Imam Yahya, tried to expand Yemen's boundaries. In the south, his expansion was stopped by Britain's defense of Aden and its hinterland. Yahya also claimed sovereignty over Asir, the coastal region to the north. Its ruler then allied with the powerful Saudi monarch, King Abd al-Aziz. After Yahya's forces attacked pro-Saudi tribes, war followed. Saudi forces routed Yahya's poorly equipped tribesmen and captured Hudaida. By the 1934 Taif Agreement, Yahya ceded Asir, although its eastern border remained undefined.

Yahya was assassinated in 1948, and the rule of his son and successor, Ahmad, followed the familiar pattern: severe and ill-informed. Few foreign "infidels" (unbelievers) were permitted to enter the country; Yemen was as isolated from the world as Tibet. The inhabitants lived much as their ancestors had a thousand years previously.

Soon after Ahmad's death in 1962, army officers inspired by Egypt's revolution against King Farouk seized control of San'a. They declared Yemen a republic, headed by Colonel Abdullah Sallal. Ahmad's son, the Imam, attempted to return

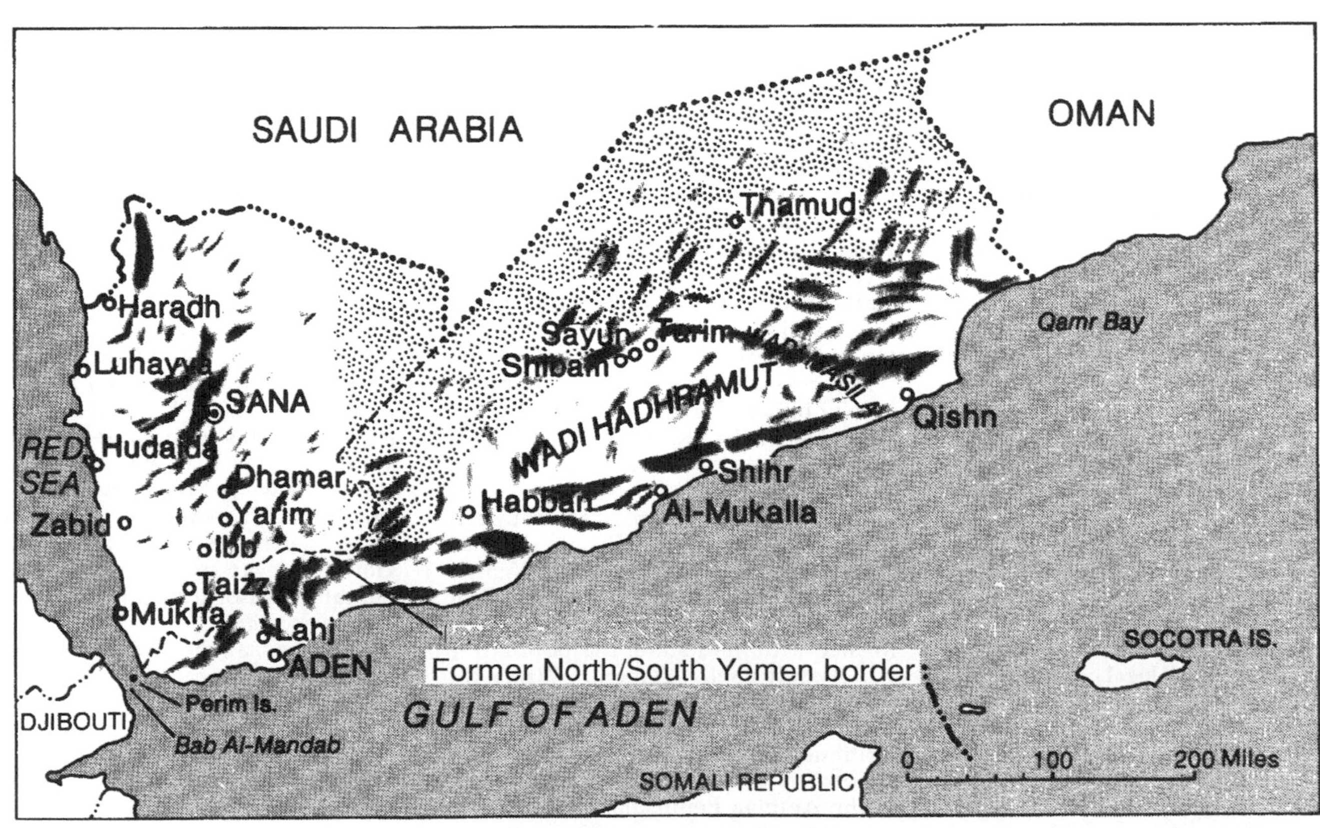

to power, but even with support from mountain tribesmen, he failed, and ultimately fled Yemen. The U.S. and the UN recognized the new republic in 1962.

Civil war followed, with bitter fighting in the winter of 1964. The Imam was supported by the Saudis; the Republic, by Egyptian troops and money. Many Yemenis desired modernization and progress under a republic, but disliked Abdullah Sallal. After Egyptian troops began withdrawing during the Arab-Israeli war of 1967, the republicans replaced Sallal with a *Zaidi* religious leader, Abd al-Rahman Iryani, who sought to unite the various republican factions and won the respect of royalist tribes by his religious prestige and political moderation. The civil war ended in 1970.

Aden Colony Becomes South Yemen

Events moved quite differently in the south. In 1937 Britain created a crown colony of the city of Aden, while loosely supervising the local rulers of the interior as long as they refrained from violence. After decades of little political development, in 1958 British officials sought to unite the various tribal leaders as a counter to growing Arab nationalism. By 1966, all the local sheikhdoms had joined the Federation of South Arabia.

Spurred by the expansion of British bases, political consciousness developed in Aden, leading to unrest and eventually terrorism. Urban nationalists sensed a British design to govern them through the two dozen tribal rulers of the Federation. After local troops mutinied in 1967, nationalists seized several of the states. Despite conflict between rival rebel groups, one Egyptian-influenced, the other the marxist *National Liberation Front (NLF)*, the federation collapsed.

In 1967 Britain withdrew from Aden, permitting the *NLF* to take control. Adopting the title People's Republic of South Yemen, the *NLF* divided the country into six states to replace the traditional principalities. But the *NLF* proved incapable of stable government. For the first three years, political alliances shifted almost continuously. In 1969, a strongly communist clique came to power, added "Democratic" to the country's title, and promised an elected People's Supreme Council. However, the elections never occurred.

In 1978, the president was overthrown and executed. Thereafter the *NLF* merged the local communist and *Ba'th* parties to form the *Yemen Socialist Party (YSP)*, but these factions plunged into open civil war in 1986. Thousands died before the defeated president fled to North Yemen with thousands of armed followers.

Though marxist and Soviet-influenced, by the late 1980s South Yemen permitted non-party candidates in local elections and then allowed opposition parties. Women's rights were among the most advanced in the entire Arab world. With the Soviet Union collapsing and the economy in shambles, the regime mended links with Arab states and sought closer relations, even unity, with Northern Yemen.

These were dramatic changes indeed. Most Arab leaders had long felt concern or even hostility about Aden's radical policies and its sponsorship of Omani rebels of the threateningly-named *People's Front for the Liberation of the Occupied Arabian Gulf*. Periodic border clashes with North Yemen occurred in the 1970s and 1981 resulted in unfulfilled agreements to unite.

The North Achieves Stability under Salih

Struggles for power also persisted in San'a. A Military Command Council took control of North Yemen in 1975. It established a degree of unity between the various factions and maintained firm central control. More important, it developed good relations with Saudi Arabia, which lent financial assistance. Stability came, unexpectedly, when Colonel Ali Abdullah Salih became president (1978).

Ali Abdullah Salih enjoying power

Photo courtesy of the White House

Despite political unrest, assassination attempts, two border wars, and a major earthquake that destroyed 200 villages, in the 1980s Salih established stable government and added democratic features to the military dictatorship. The first general election for the *Majlis al-Shura* ("Consultative Council") took place in 1988. It was widely contested, but President Salih's *General People's Congress* won the most seats. The *Muslim Brotherhood* and tribal independents also acquired significant representation.

In 1989, the leaders of the two countries again proclaimed plans for a merger. The next year public opinion in both North and South surged in favor of rapid union. Both states held elections, a rarity for the Arabian Peninsula. Trade increased between them, a consequence of greater freedom for private farmers and businessmen in the South. Surprising almost everyone, the two states merged ahead of schedule in 1990, perhaps to out-maneuver domestic and foreign opponents. President al-Attas of the South became Prime Minister of united Yemen, and a 302-member Council of Deputies included a variety of parties.

Merged, but not United

United Yemen faced grave difficulties, including the legacy of a history littered with failed merger attempts. The South's economy lay in tatters. The North's relative economic success, combined with a population four times that of the South, created fears it would dominate any union. Perhaps surprising to Americans, the North's social development lagged significantly behind that of communist-influenced Aden.

Exceptional challenges arose during the first year of union. Linked to Iraq by trade and Kuwait by aid, Yemen attempted to maintain neutrality after Iraq invaded Kuwait. As the only Arab member of the UN Security Council, however, this was impossible.

Saudi Arabia, already uneasy about miles of frontier with a united Yemen equal in national population, cut all financial aid and expelled roughly one million Yemenis. They returned to face unemployment. Other nations cut development aid, so the central bank printed money and inflation climbed. However, oil discoveries suggested reserves to support greater production.

Despite a background of high inflation and food riots, in 1993 Yemen held the first free multi-party elections of the entire Arabian Peninsula, with some 5,000 candidates for the Council of Deputies. Allegations of vote-buying and favoritism in television coverage aside, the elections were considered a broadly accurate reflection of popular opinion. However, the results also reflected strong regional differences. Salih's *General People's Congress* led the Islamic *Islah* in the north, while the *YSP* won every southern seat but few elsewhere. Nevertheless, the three parties formed a coalition government.

Personal rivalries and budget conflicts soon led to increasing hostility between President Salih and Vice President Ali

Salem al-Baidh, a southerner. As tensions mounted, clashes broke out between military units and then, in 1994, full-scale civil war. Aided by water shortages in besieged Aden and tribal and Islamist resentments against the *YSP*, Northern troops crushed the rebellion, whose leaders fled.

The war damaged further an already precarious economy. The budget deficit soared, and to meet its bills, the state turned to printing money. Inflation became so great that the government refused to release the figures, though it did devalue the *rial* by a factor of 10. Salaried professionals found their standard of living destroyed, and Yemeni university professors struck because their monthly pay of $140 equaled less than 10% of foreigners' salaries. Subsidies for wheat, flour, and oil products became unbearable burdens, but their reductions doubled prices and triggered riots. Unemployment reached 30%. Further cuts in government subsidies occurred according to the IMF-approved plan in 1996. However, some foreign aid was received as a reward.

Yemen held the first contested presidential election in the history of all Arabia in 1999. Salih won a landslide victory, in formally free voting. However, the electoral manipulation had occurred earlier. Parliament rejected all opposition nominees as candidates, so the *YSP* again boycotted the campaign, *Islah* nominated Salih as its candidate, and to meet the constitution's requirement of two candidates, one of Salih's supporters ran against him.

The country boasts some 60 million firearms, three times its population. Very few of them are hunting rifles: given their tumultuous history, men expect they will be called to fight. Law and order therefore remain sporadic. In the 1990s, tribesmen in remote areas discovered a new form of pressure politics: kidnapping foreigners to gain government projects. Tourists, petroleum workers, and even diplomats found themselves seized as bargaining chips for schools, roads, water projects and other aid. To protect the oil and tourist industries, officials typically promised to meet some demands, and gained the release of the hostages. Eventually, however, to maintain its authority, the government imposed the death penalty for kidnapping.

In 2000, suicide bombers unexpectedly maneuvered a small boat filled with explosives alongside the destroyer *U.S.S. Cole* as it refueled in Aden harbor. The subsequent explosion pierced the side of the vessel and killed nearly two dozen sailors. Though eventually blamed on Yemenis connected with *al-Qaeda*, the attack on the *Cole* raised questions about the nature of the growing Islamic fervency. Most Yemenis are poor or even impoverished. They usually hold very traditional values, and regard Western ways with suspicion. The wave of popular Islamic devotion—though not necessarily the violence—is fostered by the separate system of religious schools created by the Islamist *Islah* party when it ran the education ministry during the 1990s. The party also changed the public schools' curriculum to include a large dose of religious studies, based on books *Islah* selected. President Salih broke with *Islah* in 2001, and modified some such policies.

Rumors that the U.S. might avenge the 9/11 attacks with assaults on Yemen's Islamic extremists apparently prompted an unusually strong crackdown on Islamic militants. Scores of foreign students at Islamic study centers were expelled, and others arrested. Republican Guard and Special Forces units, commanded by the president's son, Ahmad, also attempted to extend government authority over tribal areas.

Nevertheless, popular sympathies lie with those who preach Islam rather than with the West. Tens of thousands of Yemeni veterans of the Afghan war against the Soviets sympathize with *al-Qaeda*. So do many foreign students attracted to study Islam in the religious seminaries. Anti-western bomb attacks occasionally take place in the capital and other cities, and in 2008 the U.S. embassy ordered out all non-essential staff.

Most militant Islamists come from the country's Sunni majority. However, in the distant northern province of Saada a *Zaidi* preacher, Hussein al-Huthi (or Houthi), defied the government in the *Zaidi* tradition that permits rebellion against an unjust regime. When the army attempted to enforce its control, open warfare broke out involving heavy weapons. Al-Huthi died in the fighting, but his followers continued to resist. These rebels, conservative and Shi'a rather than linked to Sunni *al-Qaeda*, may really desire to restore rule by the imams.

The Huthi rebellion again blazed into the open in 2009 when the military launched Operation Scorched Earth, eventually using air raids and heavy weapons on rebels in the provincial capital, Saada, and elsewhere. When fighting spread into Saudi Arabia, the crisis risked Iranian interference as well. A truce was finally reached in 2010, after attacks on markets, mosques, and residential areas. Hundreds or even thousands of unarmed civilians had died.

A remarkable manipulator, when a financial crisis threatened as the 2006 presidential elections approached, Salih ruled himself out of the race. Heavy subsidies had kept gasoline and diesel fuel cheap for trucks, buses, and irrigation pumps. However, the subsidy became unaffordable, and aid-giving agencies considered it a source of corruption. Two days before the cabinet cut the subsidies and tripled the price of diesel fuel, Salih announced that he would not run again.

After the price increases, violent riots shook the country, killing dozens; the army had to patrol the streets. Salih then intervened, to raise salaries, cut sales taxes, and order a small cut in fuel prices. Thus, Salih struck the pose of a caring father of the nation, in contrast to the cabinet. A carefully stage-managed convention of the *General People's Congress* nominated him for re-election.

In contrast to the staged election of 1999, opposition parties ranging from the secular *YSP* to the religious *Islah* set aside other rivalries and united behind the nomination of Faisal Bin Shamlan. A retired economist with an unmatched reputation for honesty, he attacked the country's high level of corruption and attracted wide attention. Though the battle was uneven—government officialdom knew whom to support and discretely did so—Shamlan won over 20% of the vote in the first genuinely contested presidential election in the Arab Middle East. His level of support suggested that Ali Abdullah Salih would face popular opposition to his son's automatic succession to the presidency.

Tipping Towards a Failed State

By 2009, multiple crises challenged the government.

To fight the Huthi rebellion, the military mobilized extremist Sunni groups influenced by Osama bin Laden. This informal alliance enabled some prisoners

Man on the streets of San'a

convicted of the attack on the *U.S.S. Cole* and other terrorist acts to escape, then to receive pardons for both the escape and the original crimes. However, the alliance was one-sided: the local *al-Qaeda* cell attacked Korean tourists, other foreigners and the U.S. embassy. It also renamed itself *al-Qaeda in the Arabian Peninsula*, (*AQAP*) suggesting threats to neighboring countries. For some time identified as the most active *al-Qaeda* organization, some of its local fighters organized as the *Ansar al-Shari'a (Supports of the Shari'a)* captured Zinjibar, the provincial capital of Abyan in 2011. Internationally, *AQAP* also dispatched a Nigerian to blow up a U.S. airliner en route to Detroit. His efforts failed, as did other plots, some foiled by western intelligence agencies.

Meanwhile, retired southern army officers and officials protested their meager pensions and the corrupt acquisition of land and property by northerners, fanning perceptions of discrimination. A loosely-organized, largely civilian *Southern Movement* emerged, including both former socialists and Islamic militants. Some sympathizers openly demanded succession and independence; perhaps a majority sought a federalist solution with regional autonomy. Protests led to fatalities in several southern locations,

President Salih habitually faced such crises by forming alliances with some rivals against others, while using predictions of disaster to frighten sympathetic countries into increasing foreign aid. However, the failure to keep *al-Qaeda* fighters in prison poisoned relations with the U.S., as well as Saudi Arabia and other oil states. This limited financial aid from abroad.

The underlying socio-economic crisis simultaneously deprived Salih and his government of Yemeni resources. Income from oil exports fell 75% in 2009, and output is expected to fall further. The resulting budget deficit prevented large-scale attempts to reduce unemployment, estimated at 30%. Subsidies to limit unpopular rises in food prices became too expensive. A population growing at 3.7% per year needs social services, but widespread corruption has eroded good intentions, and much of the population lacks access to medical care.

The Arab Spring in Yemen

In the weeks that followed, the demonstrations involved groups from moderate Islamists to leftists and became performance art, with music, dancing, skits, and caricatures. The head of Women Journalists without Chains, Tawakkul Karman, eloquently attacked Salih's corrupt rule and his sleazy comments about "ladies" engaging in protests. When released from arrest, she immediately returned to the podium and became a hero. She later received the 2011 Nobel Peace Prize.

Yemen Tribesmen displaying weapons during the Arab Spring

Long accustomed to deflecting dissent with promises, this time Salih could not pledge immediate prosperity. Without access to billions of dollars in foreign aid, he initially offered to leave office at the end of his term in 2013, and not to pass the presidency to his son. Simultaneously, however, he also mobilized his supporters for pro-Salih demonstrations. Some opposition leaders were arrested.

After an unprovoked attack on peaceful protestors in the square killed 45 and injured hundreds, Salih denied his forces had massacred the civilians and declared a state of emergency. Perhaps, given the murky world of Yemen's administration, Salih told the truth: the attack may have been an accident, regime sympathizers may have turned to violence without official orders, or a rival may have actually masterminded the attacks to create an outcry and force Salih from office. Demonstrators' deaths in San'a, Taizz, and other cities, and the wide range of human rights violations and abuses, including the detention, torture and killing of children reported by the UN led to resignations by some officials and even members of parliament. However, Ahmad Salih, the president's son, commanded the Republican Guard, and it dominated San'a, while nephews and other relatives led other important units. Even the defection of General Ali Mohsen al-Ahmar (Salih's half-brother), commander of an army division, failed to overthrow the president. However, rebellious tribesmen ruptured the oil export pipeline, halting the major source of government revenue.

The United States and neighboring countries initially supported Salih, but encouraged reforms. They feared that *al-Qaeda in the Arabian Peninsula* and other militant Islamists would use the chaos to organize freely. The president clearly cultivated this fear, and the military resisted feebly when Islamist militants occupied Zinjibar, the capital of Abyan in the south.

Salih's faltering rule and the violence against protesters—and his comments such as "there's an operations room in Tel Aviv with the aim of destabilizing the Arab world" that is "run by the White House"—eventually convinced the U.S. and Saudi Arabia that stability depended on his departure. The Gulf Cooperation Council negotiated with the regime and the *Joint Meeting Parties* for Salih's resignation, but Salih blocked the deal by refusing to sign it as president.

Badly wounded in an assassination attempt, Salih flew to Saudi Arabia for treatment. He continued to defy demands by opposition parties and demonstrators to transfer power to Vice President Hadi, who was powerless to halt military attacks on the demonstrators and General al-Ahmar's forces.

For months the country teetered on the brink of civil war. Salih eventually signed the GCC's proposal, but then demanded that parliament grant him and his close appointees amnesty from crimes committed in office. The election for his successor had only one candidate, his vice president, Abd Rabbu (or Abdrabbuh) Mansur Hadi. He was duly elected, and Salih left office in February, 2012, some 13 months after the protest struggle began.

Hadi inherited a nation emerging from chaos. In the north, Zaidi tribesmen of the Huthi movement continued their multi-year rebellion. Within the government,

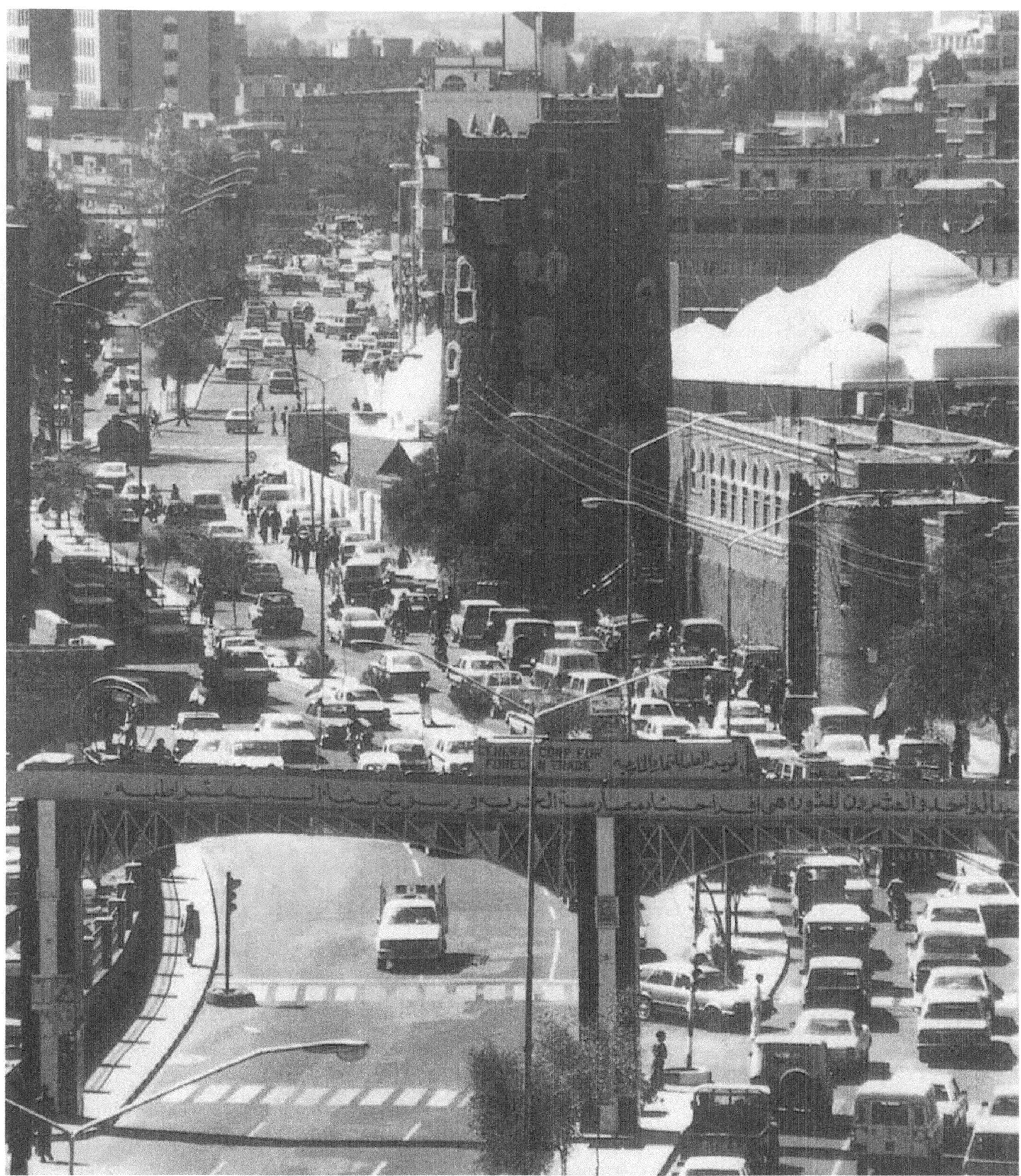

Busy downtown San'a

Courtesy: Caltex Petroleum Corporation

Salih's relatives and allies held military commands and represented rival centers of power. The new president dispatched some rivals safely abroad, as diplomats. In the south, political activists of the *Southern Movement* continued to demand autonomy or independence. More immediate threats came from Islamic extremists of the *Ansar al-Sharia,* who defeated the initial military attempts to recapture the southern city of Zinjibar. Within months, however, the military regained by the city and much of Abyan and Shabwa provinces, aided by popular disgust at the summary executions and amputations

President Abd-Rabbuh Mansur Hadi

carried out by the extremists. Nevertheless, the fighting a significant toll: in the first half of 2014 nearly 400 security forces personnel were killed.

The military's success was aided by air raids by conventional aircraft as well as drone attacks. Successful assassinations of *al-Qaeda* leaders were publicly credited to the air force, but it was widely acknowledged in Yemen that attacks on extremists, including some holding U.S. citizenship, were carried out by U.S. drones.

To tackle the demands of the Arab Spring protesters, the GCC's proposal for Salih's resignation included the calling of a National Dialogue Conference. This forum was charged with recommending policy on deep national questions and the direction of the country. These issues were debated by more than 500 representatives of widely differing groups—tribal sheikhs, urban youth activists, established political parties, women's groups, southerners, northern Zaidis, and civil society organizations. The conference completed its work in 2014, and some decisions cut to the fundamental structure of the country. An independent anti-corruption body would be established, and women's rights would be advanced by 30% representation in public office. Child marriages would be banned.

Instead of a unitary state ruled from San'a, the National Dialogue Conference voted a decentralized federal system, but unfortunately deferred specifying the regions. A presidential committee's decision to create six regions, two of them in the south, brought immediate rejection from southern activists who wished to raise the south's significance. The decision also encouraged fighting in the north, as the Huthi rebels attempted to enlarge the territory of their designated territory.

With the constitutional outline broadly agreed, the focus of concern turned to social problems, particularly hunger. Estimates indicate that ten million Yemenis, over 40% of the population, do not obtain "enough food to eat." One-third of the country's children are severely malnourished, and one quarter of women are acutely malnourished. The problem is not the physical absence of food—markets seem full. Rather, it is widespread poverty. Moreover, some 600,000 persons have been forced from their homes by the conflicts; those who escaped the fighting often lived to suffer high unemployment and inflation.

For the longer term, the growing population requires water for humans and agriculture. But the limits of sustainable pumping have been exceeded, and the water table is dropping rapidly around many cities. Yemen has been ranked as the world's most water-challenged country, and the possible solutions require dramatic transformations in lifestyles, including much less agriculture, and especially less qat.

Culture: About 70% of the population lives in the traditional style in small towns, villages or isolated clusters of houses. Until recently, most loyalties were local, mainly to the family, clan, and tribe. Devotion to the nation—as distinct from rejection of other nations—has been a rather new feeling which spreads slowly. A few people are nomads, mainly in the eastern and southern part of the country, while considerably more live in the growing cities, where the alien architecture of new buildings often clashes with the greater dignity and appeal of traditional designs.

Unfortunately many of the mud-brick skyscrapers are in danger of collapse, threatened particularly by running water and burst pipes. Foreign governments have funded a UNESCO campaign to restore San'a, paving streets and restoring portions of the *souk* (market place). However, the walled cities of Hadhramut, east of Aden and far off tourist routes despite their beauty, face the danger of buildings 500 years old collapsing.

While virtually all Yemenis are Muslims, they form two major sects. In the coastal plain and much of the settled south, inhabitants profess *Sunni* Islam and provide a center for the *Shafi'i* school. In the North, the conservative *Zaidi* sect of *Shi'a* Islam prevails, and for a thousand years until the 1962 revolution, the Imams ruled the country from the mountains.

In a uniquely Yemeni custom, every afternoon, most Yemeni men and many women gather in small social groups to chew leaves of *qat*, a tree cultivated on the terraced mountainsides. Large globs of leaves, when chewed for hours, reportedly produce a mildly narcotic effect that relaxes a person and gives a sense of contentment.

The cultivation and use of *qat* brings undesirable effects to a country seeking development. It consumes vast amounts of time, occupying most of the afternoon (the workday obligingly ends at 2 p.m.). Producing all the *qat* consumed by Yemenis provides employment for hundreds of thousands of farmers, and it is a far more profitable crop than coffee or grains. Much of the nation's limited supply of agricultural water goes to the crop.

Qat consumption is expensive, and some families spend one-fifth their in-

A potter works his trade near Aden

comes to enjoy it (and to escape giving the impression they are too poor to afford it). Though not physically addictive, it leads to a state of relaxation that discourages hard work. It may cause serious illness, and at least one study of heavy users shows a greatly increased risk of heart attacks. In 1999 President Salih announced that he was giving up the leaves, and he urged the nation to follow his example. Presumably when Yemeni adults chew the leaves, they find greater enjoyment than from any other use of their money, but given Yemen's pitiful levels of nutrition, health and education, the habit casts a long shadow over social and economic development.

Throughout Yemen, since the fall of the monarchy and the arrival of freedom from colonialism, education has taken great strides among men, though only 7% of adult women read. There are universities at San'a and Aden, and competition to enroll is fierce. The use of English in education is becoming widespread, since one of Yemen's most valuable assets is the workers which it sends abroad. In turn, they have sent badly needed money back home.

In their struggle for water, roads, schools and other projects for a better standard of living, Yemenis often formed "development associations," to pool resources for their goals. Relatively rare elsewhere in the Middle East, these community action groups involve both traditional and modern interests, and reflect a Yemeni sense that the poverty requires cooperation rather than simple competition. Unfortunately, the cooperative movement has on several occasions suffered from government attempts to take it over or politicize it.

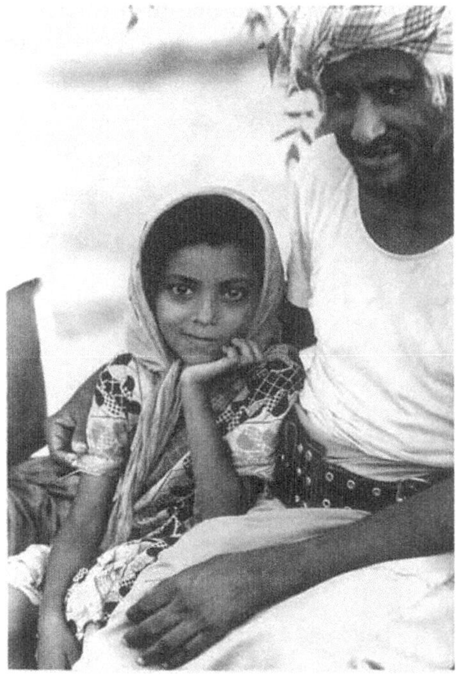

Girl with her father

Courtesy: World Bank Photo by Tomas Sennett

Economy: In terms of employment, agriculture remains at the center of the economy, especially in terms of employment. On the coast, one finds date palms and grains suitable to the hot climate. The upper slopes of the mountains, which receive good rainfall , are among the most intensively cultivated in the world. Over the centuries, farmers have built elaborate terraces with stone walls—at some places right up to the crests of the mountains.

Coffee was traditionally the important cash crop. Shipped from the old port of Mukha, it became renowned as "Mocha coffee." In recent decades, lower world coffee prices reduced production in Yemen, at the same time as production of *qat* became more profitable.

Animal herding plays an important role in the economy. Millions of sheep, goats and humped cattle are raised for milk, meat and hides. Donkeys and mules are still the most common beasts of burden as camels are not suitable in the rugged mountains, though they are far from unknown in Yemen.

It is possible that mineral deposits in commercial quantities exist in the country, but little surveying has been done thus far. Manufacturing remains in the handicraft stage; while it exhibits a high degree of skill and artistic merit, handmade products cannot supply a comfortable standard of living like machine-factory production.

Yemen is the poorest country in the Middle East, and one of the poorest in the world. Ever since the 1960s, foreign nations have provided important assistance for development, including roads, health projects and farm programs. Northern Yemen in particular proved adept at soliciting funds from rival nations, including the Soviet Union, China, the United States, West Germany and several Arab oil exporters. By contrast, its communist ties prevented South Yemen from receiving Western and Arab aid.

After oil exports commenced in 1988, the importance of foreign aid declined somewhat. By 1995 total production reached 400,000 barrels per day, and the country approved a $3 billion project to liquefy natural gas for export. However, only modest quantities of oil have been discovered, and the volume of exports is small, about 5% that of Saudi Arabia. Consequently, Yemen did not join OPEC.

Rising oil prices at mid-decade disguised the diminishing oil output, but the 75% decline in government oil revenues in 2009 reinforced fears of a possible economic collapse. Unless new discoveries are made, exports will plummet rapidly and may end as early as 2017. However, many promising geological formations have failed to yield oil, and the growing violence from *al-Qaeda* discourages foreign companies. Earnings from exports of liquefied natural gas will only partially replace oil revenues.

The Future: The decisions of the National Dialogue Conference strengthened President Hadi's authority. He has played the nation-building game with a weak hand. By his own account, "I did not take over a nation. I took over a capital where gunshots are continuous day and night, where roadblocks fill the streets. I took over an empty bank [treasury] that has no wages and a divided security apparatus and army." The National Dialogue Conference facilitated constitutional reforms, and strengthened political stability, but they did not settle the demands of two festering threats, the Huthi rebellion among Zaidi Shi'a in the north, and the *Southern Movement* in Aden.

Every socio-economic indicator of long-term success now reads "dangerous." At present rates of growth, Yemen's population will reach about 60 million by 2050. Neither sufficient water nor enough jobs will be available in such an arid and impoverished land to support that number of people. At present, about 40% of Yeminis suffer inadequate diets, and one-third of children are malnourished. The government's crumbling finances limit the opportunities for improvement, and oil exports, formerly the source of 75% of revenue, are dwindling to insignificance. Donor nations have cut foreign aid, because corruption climbed so far, so quickly.

If the government in San'a fails to assert effective federal authority, a fragmented entity remains possible, with the Zaidi north and secessionist south informally operating on their own while paying lip service to the capital. Western powers and Saudi Arabia naturally fear this outcome, because it could provide considerable operating freedom to *al-Qaeda in the Arabian Peninsula.* It should be feared as well by Yemenis of all but the most extreme persuasions, because the country's huge social challenges—youth unemployment exceeding 40%, high birth rates, corruption, poverty, budget deficits, and depleted water resources—generally require national as well as local solutions.

Given the fears of what Yemen could become—a second 1990s-style Afghanistan, or another Somalia—donor nations have great political as well as humanitarian incentives to assist a worthy government. Expect them to do so.

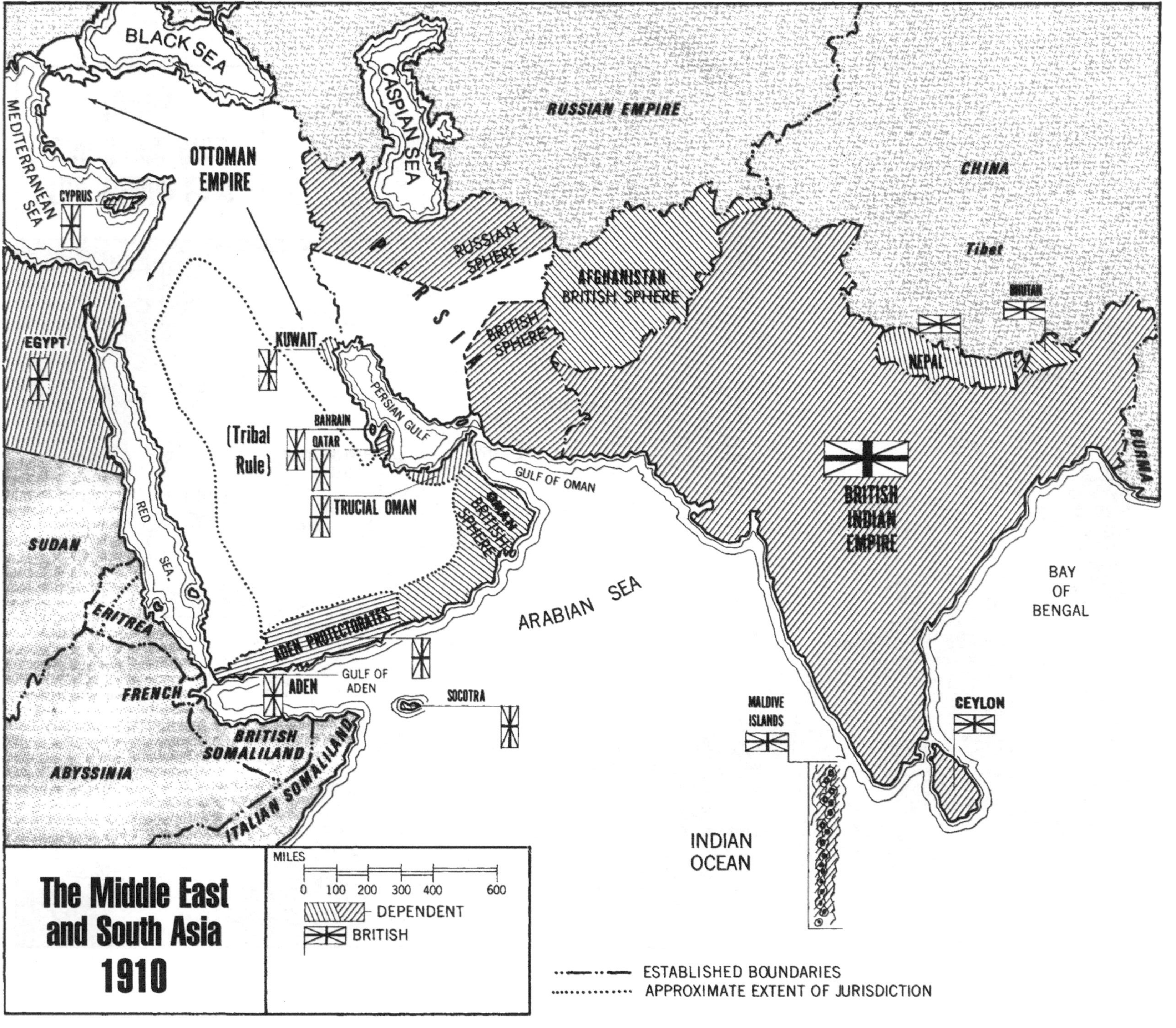

BLACK SEA
MEDITERRANEAN
SEA
CYPRUS
OTTOMAN
EMPIRE
CASPIAN SEA
RUSSIAN EMPIRE
CHINA
Tibet
BHUTAN
NEPAL
BURMA
PERSIA
RUSSIAN
SPHERE
AFGHANISTAN
BRITISH SPHERE
BRITISH
SPHERE
EGYPT
KUWAIT
PERSIAN GULF
BAHRAIN
QATAR
(Tribal
Rule)
TRUCIAL OMAN
GULF OF OMAN
OMAN
BRITISH
SPHERE
BRITISH
INDIAN
EMPIRE
SUDAN
RED
SEA
ERITREA
ADEN PROTECTORATES
ARABIAN SEA
BAY
OF
BENGAL
GULF OF
ADEN
ADEN
FRENCH
SOCOTRA
MALDIVE
ISLANDS
CEYLON
BRITISH
SOMALILAND
ABYSSINIA
ITALIAN SOMALILAND
INDIAN
OCEAN
The Middle East
and South Asia
1910
MILES
0 100 200 300 400 600
DEPENDENT
BRITISH
ESTABLISHED BOUNDARIES
APPROXIMATE EXTENT OF JURISDICTION

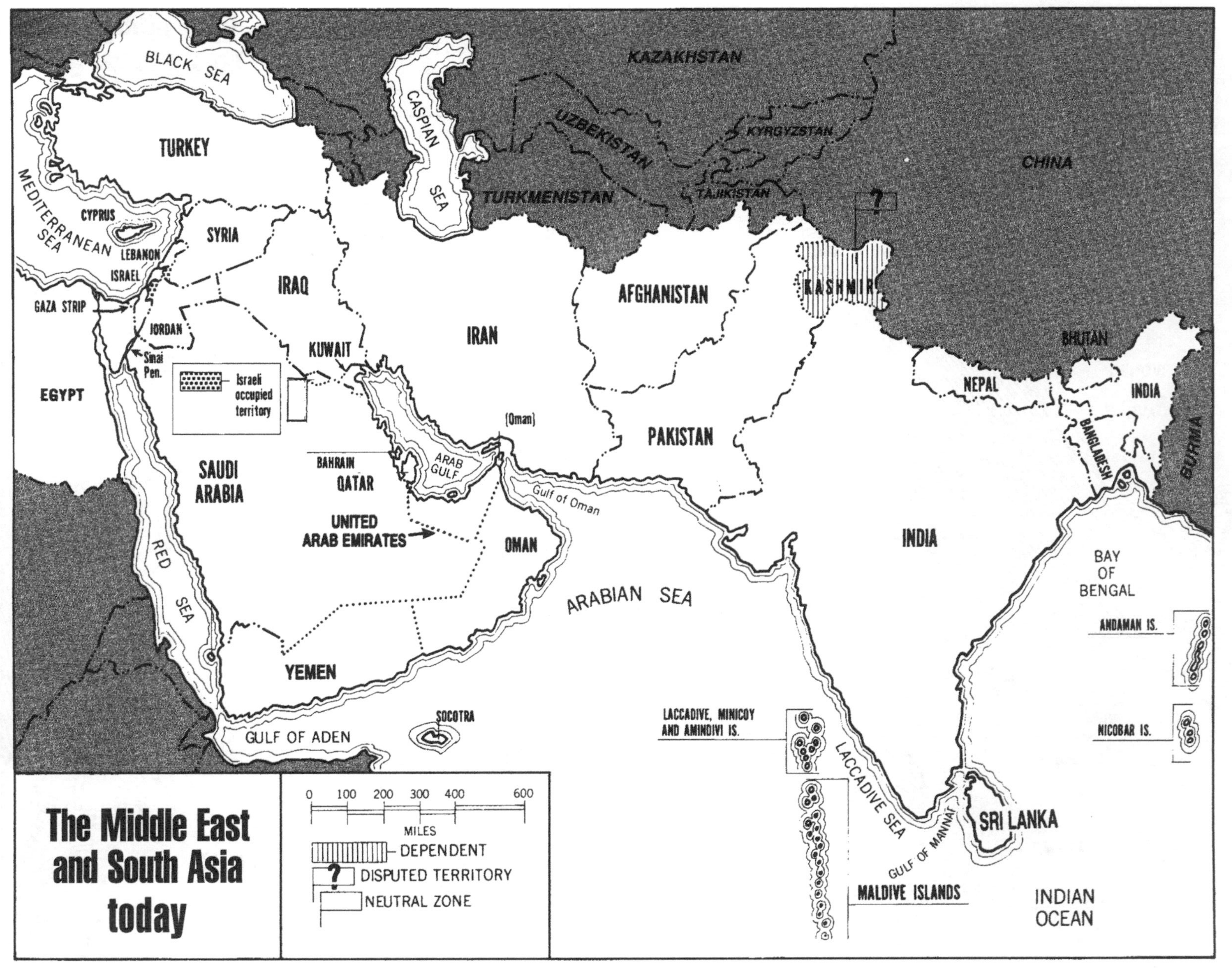

BLACK SEA
KAZAKHSTAN
CASPIAN SEA
UZBEKISTAN
KYRGYZSTAN
CHINA
TURKEY
TURKMENISTAN
TAJIKISTAN
MEDITERRANEAN SEA
CYPRUS
SYRIA
LEBANON
ISRAEL
IRAQ
AFGHANISTAN
KASHMIR
GAZA STRIP
JORDAN
IRAN
BHUTAN
Sinai Pen.
KUWAIT
Israeli occupied territory
NEPAL
INDIA
EGYPT
(Oman)
PAKISTAN
BANGLADESH
BURMA
SAUDI ARABIA
BAHRAIN
QATAR
ARAB GULF
Gulf of Oman
UNITED ARAB EMIRATES
OMAN
INDIA
RED SEA
BAY OF BENGAL
ARABIAN SEA
ANDAMAN IS.
YEMEN
SOCOTRA
LACCADIVE, MINICOY AND AMINDIVI IS.
NICOBAR IS.
GULF OF ADEN
LACCADIVE SEA
SRI LANKA
GULF OF MANNAR
MALDIVE ISLANDS
INDIAN OCEAN
The Middle East and South Asia today
0 100 200 300 400 600
MILES
DEPENDENT
DISPUTED TERRITORY
NEUTRAL ZONE

Islamic Republic of Afghanistan

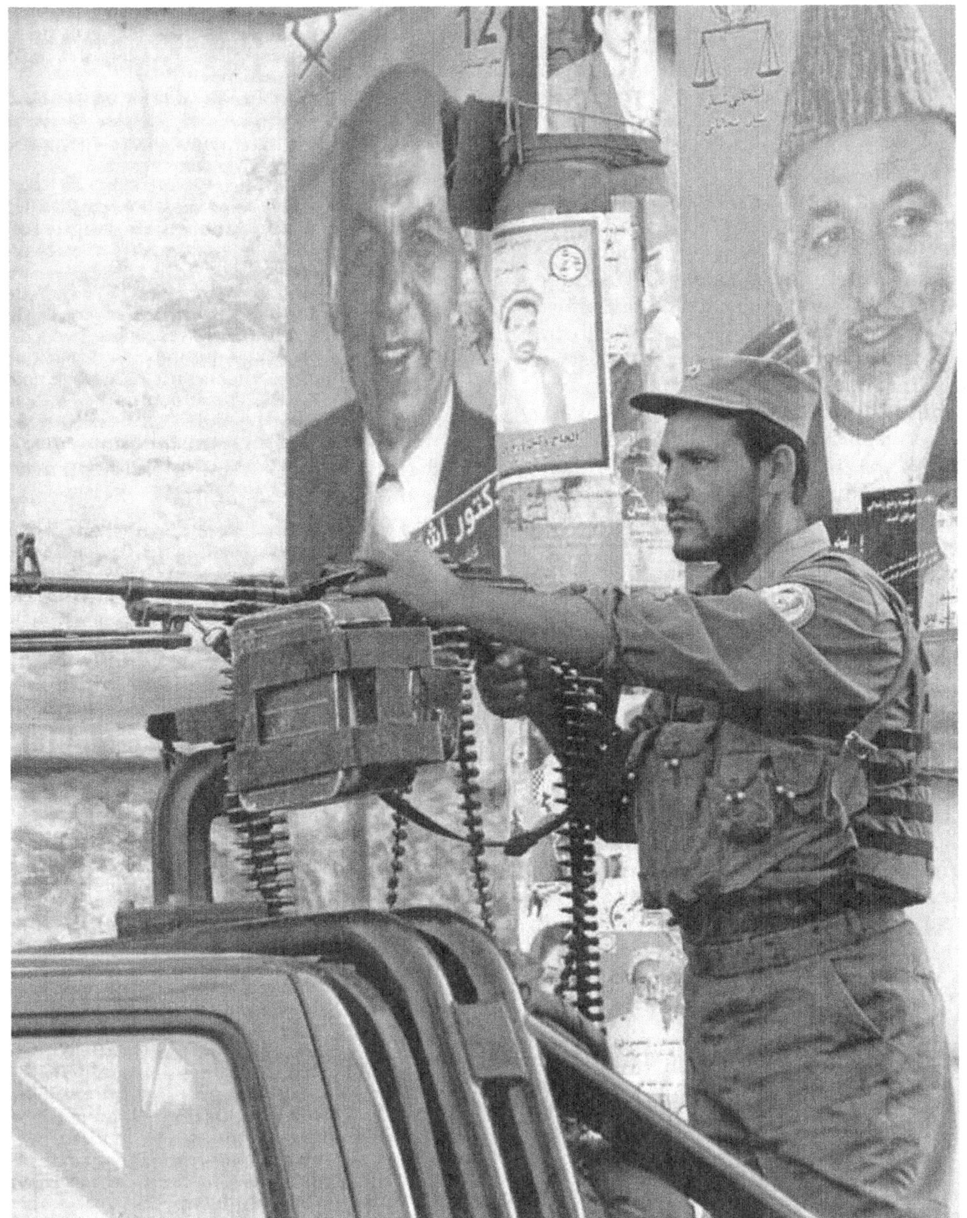

Afghan and international security forces protected voters from *Taliban* threats during the presidential election

Area: 251,773 square miles (652,225 sq. km.).
Population: Uncounted; 33 million, est.
Capital City: Kabul (pop. 3.1 million, est.).
Climate: Extremely dry, hot summers (but with cool nights); cold winters with moderate rain and snow in the mountains, scanty rain on the plain. Strong winds and dust storms are common.
Neighboring Countries: Pakistan (South and East); Iran (West); Turkmenistan, Uzbekistan, Tajikistan (formerly USSR; North); China (Northeast).
Time Zone: GMT + 41/2 hours. When it is noon in Denver, it is 11:30 P.M. in Kabul.
Official Languages: Pashtu and Dari (Persian).
Other Principal Tongues: Uzbek, Turkmen, and Baluchi.
Ethnic Background: The varied facial features reflect the characteristics of the country's invaders. Ethnic membership is mainly by language and family culture. The Dari-speaking Hazaras are distinguished from Tajiks by descent, geography, and Shi'ism.
Principal Religion: Sunni (87%) and Shi'a Islam (12%).
Main Exports: Agricultural products (dried fruit, nuts, lambskins, raw cotton, wool, grain), carpets and textiles. Opium production ranks largest in the world, with 75% of total output.
Major Trading Partners: Pakistan, Iran, Uzbekistan, Japan, Pakistan, India, and the U.S.
Currency: 1 New Afghani = 100 puls.
Former Political Status: Under British influence (1837–1919).
National Day: August 19 (traditional); May 5 (liberation of Kabul from communist rule).
Chief of State and Head of Government: TBD, President.
National Flag: Black, red, and green vertical stripes with a white emblem centered in the red containing a mosque, two flags, and sheaves of wheat (horizontally striped flags are also used).
Gross Domestic Product (GDP): $21.7 billion (current prices); $36.8 billion (PPP).
GDP per capita: $1,200 (PPP).

Afghanistan means "Land of the Afghans." Afghan in a strict sense means Pashtun or Pathan, that is, a member of any tribe speaking Pashtu, but now Afghan is applied to any citizen of this nation sometimes described as the "Turnstile of Asia."

A treeless, wind-swept land, Afghanistan's environment is hostile to human comfort and even survival, except for the short spring season when moderate temperatures and green vegetation follow winter rain and snow. Summer temperatures in the low valley of the Amu Darya (Oxus River to the ancient Greeks) often hover at 110°F. In the winter, blizzards rage in the high mountains and even at the medium elevations where most people live, temperatures may drop below zero for a few weeks. However, in the low valleys agriculture is intensively pursued, and native poplar trees abound to provide wood for rough houses.

The most striking geographical feature of the country is the complex series of mountains extending from the eastern tip for some 600 miles southwest before leveling out in the plateau near the border with Iran. Majestic peaks of the central Hindu Kush Mountains tower more than 20,000 feet above sea level, inspiring visitors, but the rugged terrain makes transportation difficult.

As a landlocked country, Afghanistan depends on transit through neighboring countries for its external trade. Most imports and exports traditionally passed through Pakistan, utilizing the railroad between Karachi and Peshawar, but depending on trucks between Peshawar and points inside the country. Another important trade route runs from Iran to Herat in the northwest, and the country's most valuable export, heroin, apparently reaches world markets through Central Asia.

Afghanistan

History: The mountains of Afghanistan form a natural divide that separates the Indian subcontinent from Central Asia to the northwest, and Iran to the west. Until modern times, the territory did not form a separate political unit. Indeed, its steep mountains and remote valleys usually felt the impact of formal government only lightly. Nevertheless, the land and its people suffered migrations, raids and conquests as a consequence of its position as the "turnstile of Asia's fate" (see Historical Background). Iranian languages were established in the region more than 3,000 years ago, and related languages have been used ever since by the majority of the population. Islam entered what had been a Buddhist land during the seventh century, and became dominant by the tenth century.

From the 14th to the 19th centuries, invaders swept across the mountains and valleys: the Mongols, followed by the plundering hordes of Timur Lang (Tamerlane), and then Babur, a Turkish chief from Central Asia who claimed descent from Timur. Babur established his capital at Kabul in the 16th century; his warriors conquered the Indus and Ganges Valleys, founding the great Mogul Empire. Meanwhile, the Safavid Empire in Iran ruled Herat and sometimes Kandahar.

After two centuries of Mogul and Safavid rule, Pashtu-speaking tribes began to exercise greater local authority, though they often feuded with one another. These tribes referred to themselves as Pashtun (*Pakhtun* was a dialectic variation), but the Persians called them Afghans, a name of unknown origin. When Safavid rule proved particularly severe and rapacious, the Afghans of Kandahar revolted and defeated the Persian army in 1711. By mid-century, Ahmad Khan Durani had proclaimed himself shah (or king) in Kandahar and seized the eastern part of the Persian empire, but his successors proved unable to create an Afghan state.

In the early 19th century, chiefs of a rival family, the *Mohammedzai,* consolidated their control over the principal centers of the country. Dost Mohammed eventually proclaimed himself Amir of Kabul and ruled as king, though it was decades later before any of his line assumed the title of shah. Dost Mohammed concentrated on controlling a smaller territory rather than overextending his forces as the previous dynasty had done. His last achievement was to drive Persian forces out of Herat.

For the next century, the two main themes in Afghan political history were the struggles between rival leaders and the interference of British Indian officials. Direct descendants of Dost Mohammed remained in power until 1978, but only by repeatedly defeating rivals—often brothers and other close relatives. Most rulers died violent deaths; power passed to brothers or cousins as often as to sons.

Between 1839 and 1919, British Indian troops periodically intervened in Afghanistan, usually in support of a rival claimant to the throne who appeared to be more agreeable to policy in Delhi. They did not always win: the First Afghan War in 1841 ended with some 4,500 British and 10,000 Indian troops massacred in the rugged mountain gorges while retreating between Kabul and the Khyber Pass.

The major motive for Britain's intervention was the desire to block Russian influence. After a century of expansion toward the Hindu Kush Mountains, by 1875 the Russian Empire nearly reached the Amu Darya—the later border of the Soviet Union. As Russian expansion continued, a new British invasion in 1878 began two years of fighting with the Afghan tribes. In the end, the new ruler, Abdurrahman, was required to put foreign relations in the hands of British authorities. Anglo-Russian rivalry in Afghanistan continued until the Tsar's government acknowledged the country to be an area of British influence.

Although the country remained neutral during World War I despite the opportunity to strike at British positions in India, in 1919 Amir Amanullah sought to gain popularity by a half-hearted attack on British India. This war lasted only a month, but ended with Britain recognizing the independence of Afghanistan in foreign as well as internal affairs.

Modernization came very slowly to the country during the first half of the 20th century, and its geographical remoteness and rigid Islam kept foreign influence to a minimum. Amanullah was forced from power after returning from an extended foreign trip and proposing reforms. His successor was assassinated in a blood feud. Family and palace intrigues dominated the first three decades of King Zahir's rule (1933-mid-1960s). However, in 1964 the king granted a new constitution that expanded the legal system beyond Islamic religious law and prohibited the king's relatives from serving as minister, chief justice or as a member of the legislature.

As a concession to an educated minority, the king allowed elections for the legislature in 1965. Political parties were not allowed, however, and the king did not permit the elected representatives to assume real law-making power, though

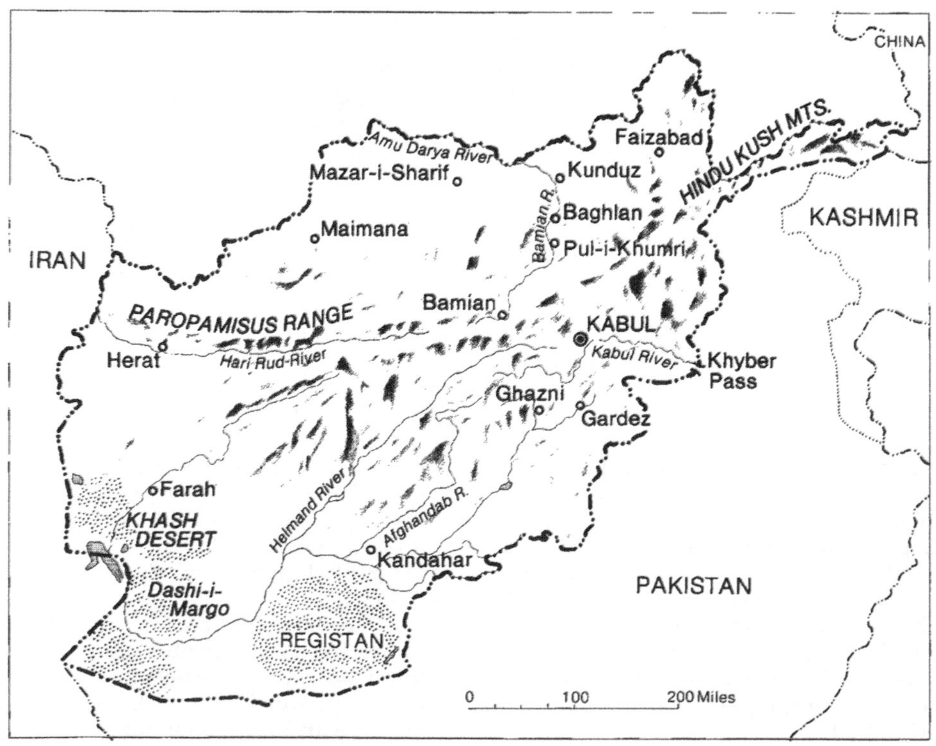

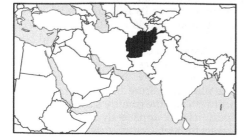

the wealthy landowners who dominated the legislature and were able protect their interests and block progressive tax laws.

Before the scheduled 1973 elections, an army coup d'etat deposed the king and abolished the constitution. It was led by Mohammed Daud Khan, the king's cousin and brother-in-law who had previously served as prime minister. He immediately proclaimed the country a republic and named himself both president and prime minister. Thus, the overthrow of the monarchy actually concentrated power in the ruling member of the Mohammedzai family.

President Daud's dictatorial rule failed to satisfy many people, and there were at least three attempts to overthrow him. To legitimize his rule, he managed his election as president in 1977 by a National Assembly *(loya jirga)*, but in 1978 a daylong battle in Kabul between communist sympathizers and loyalists ended with the deaths of thousands, including President Daud. The Communist army officers who led the coup had studied in the Soviet Union and learned the arts of political subversion along with the art of war.

Under Communist Rule, 1978–89

The victors acted in typical Communist fashion. They set up a Revolutionary Council and appointed an elderly poet and journalist as a figurehead president. The new regime rapidly formed close ties with the Soviet Union. Domestically, it adopted a red flag, and radical social and economic measures. A drastic land reform law limited an individual's maximum holding to 15 acres, Islamic schools were closed, and changes in family law conflicted with traditional Islam.

Not surprisingly, opposition surfaced, and perhaps 50,000 to 100,000 people perished during the land reforms. Resistance turned to rebellion, inspired by Islam and its religious teachers. The government sought Soviet aid to crush the widespread rebellion of the mujahidin (meaning "those who undertake jihad"), but the Soviet presence probably inflamed nationalist and Muslim opposition.

Further complicating matters, the Afghan communists were divided into two often hostile factions, *Khalq* ("Masses") and *Parcham* ("Banner"). To avert a likely defeat of communism, in late 1979 a Soviet invasion force suddenly attacked Kabul, attacking and killing the (communist) president before installing Babrak Karmal of *Parcham* as president.

Some 90,000 Soviet troops entered the struggle to defeat the mujahidin. They successfully occupied most of northern Afghanistan and the major cities of Kabul, Herat, and Kandahar, as well as the roads connecting them. However, the mujahidin, although poorly armed and divided into rival groups, operated across much of the country's rugged terrain, and won many small victories. In response, the Soviets adopted a policy of ruthless air and artillery attacks on towns and villages.

The invasion and its indiscriminate bombing and shelling turned the population into refugees. Nearly five million civilians fled the fighting, some to Iran but most to Pakistan. Their giant refugee camps, funded by Saudi Arabia, other Arab nations, and the United States, became staging bases for the mujahidin.

The Islamic resistance operated most successfully in the mountains near its supply centers in Pakistan. Another stronghold was the Panjsher Valley north of Kabul, not far from the strategic Salang highway linking the capital to northern Afghanistan. There, under the most highly regarded mujahidin commander, Ahmad Shah Masoud, the rebels withstood repeated Soviet attacks. In the west and south, other mujahidin groups fought for Herat and Kandahar, and the fighting destroyed large portions of these two historic cities.

Cruelty and inhumanity accompanied much of the fighting. Soviet forces bombed villages and dropped explosives disguised as toys in rebel areas. Soviet and Afghan troops killed hundreds of civilians in reprisal raids and tortured captured mujahidin before executing. On the other hand, some western journalists reported that rebel groups often preferred to take no prisoners and executed government supporters in newly-captured towns.

The mid-1980s Soviet policies suffered strong condemnation in the world press, even in many "non-aligned nations" that the U.S.S.R. had courted carefully for years. Moscow began to recognize that the Kabul regime remained entirely dependent on Soviet support. The military situation worsened after the United States finally provided some mujahidin with Stinger anti-aircraft missiles and other modern weapons that threatened to neutralize Soviet air power and render very difficult the supply of remote outposts.

Recognizing that Babrak Karmal had proved ineffective, in 1986 the Soviet Union forced his resignation "for health reasons." Najib Ahmadzai, then head of security in Kabul and a leading figure in *Parcham*, took control of government as the General Secretary of the Communist party. In 1987 he was elected president by a *loya jirga* (national assembly) dominated by Communists but given a smattering of legitimacy by a few tribal leaders and others.

A more flexible politician than his predecessors, Najib restored the Islamic form of his name, Najibullah, and offered political concessions, including a coalition government. However, he won over only a few inconsequential groups. By 1988, after Afghan casualties surpassed one million dead plus many millions more wounded or exiled, the Soviet leader, Mikhail Gorbachev, promised to withdraw Soviet troops and let the Afghans decide their future government.

The last Soviet troops departed in 1989 against a background of rocket attacks on Kabul and fierce fighting for several provincial cities. In the capital, crowded by over two million inhabitants, siege conditions appeared, for rebel activity often closed the Salang highway to the north and a Soviet airlift of supplies proved insufficient. Food prices rose sharply, so that the price of a large family's monthly flour—the staple food—exceeded two months' average pay. Malnutrition threatened. However, by summer the guerrillas abandoned their use of mass hunger against the regime and allowed food trucks through. Nevertheless, rocket attacks continued from the surrounding mountains and killed hundreds of people, nearly all of them Muslims and many of them children.

The stalemate at the capital reflected the country at large. The mujahidin fiercely assaulted Jalalabad, between Kabul and the Khyber Pass, but failed despite the highest casualties of the war. Similarly, in Herat, Kandahar and elsewhere the government continued to govern essentially the same cities and territory. Some officials and soldiers defected, but others fought with greater determination, fearing that capture meant death.

Victory eluded the guerrillas largely because they could not unite. Military coordination often proved weak, and separate groups made uncoordinated attacks. Personal antagonisms, ethnic rivalries, and traditional blood-feuds often overshadowed the struggle against the communist regime. In particular, the Pashtun *Hizb-i Islami*, dominant along the Pakistani border, hijacked supplies intended for its northeastern rival, Masoud's largely Tajik *Jamiat-i Islami*. Ambushes and battles broke out between them. Shi'a and Sunni mujahidin differed over their concepts of the state. Moreover the majority Sunni fractured between moderate conservatives and fundamentalists, who tended to follow Gulbuddin Hikmatyar of the *Hizb-i Islami*. In contrast, only a few mujahidin attacked the departing Soviet troops, and several groups arranged informal cease-fires with Kabul.

The disintegration of the Soviet Union in 1991 disrupted food and fuel supplies for Kabul, and the new Russian leaders desired to end an adventure that had cost more than $110 billion. The Kabul government tottered, then collapsed when Gen-

Mujahidin resistance fighters look down on a village after a Soviet aerial attack. At left are terraced crop fields.
AP/World Wide Photos

eral Abdul Rashid Dostam and his tough, Uzbek militia at Mazar-i-Sharif switched sides and formed an alliance with Ahmad Shah Masoud, the Tajik leader who had captured much of the northeast for the mujahidin. Moving quickly southwards, General Dostam's militia and Masoud's *Jamiat-i Islami* mujahidin cut the Salang highway and captured the Bagram airbase near Kabul. When Gulbuddin Hikmatyar of the *Hizb-i Islami* sent his forces to infiltrate Kabul, Dostam's militia and Masoud's guerrillas then rushed for the city, some flown by air force helicopters. Najibullah attempted to flee, but was captured, and the communist regime formally transferred power to an Islamic Afghan regime in April 1992.

Deprived of their prize, Hikmatyar's forces rocketed the city, killing and maiming the first of tens of thousands of Muslim dead by Muslim hands in the Islamic Republic. However, conditions in the capital did not reflect the country. Some areas enjoyed relative calm under the control of local warlords, and several million refugees returned from Pakistan to their often-destroyed towns and villages.

Kabul changed perceptibly under Islamic rule. Women who previously dressed in jeans and T-shirts now covered their hair and wore long black robes, some perhaps for piety; others to avoid molestation. Alcoholic beverages vanished from stores and hotel bars closed. Former officials and agents of Khad, the secret police, disappeared to avoid reprisals; some executions occurred.

Despite the creation of a Leadership Council to guide the country, politics remained confused. Amid accusations of bribery and pressure, a large council elected Burhanuddin Rabbani of the *Jamiat-i Islami* as president. However, Rabbani failed to win recognition from Hikmatyar and the *Hizb-i Islami*, and later attempts to bring Hikmatyar into the government also failed, ushering in a four-year struggle to rule Kabul. Rival mujahidin leaders made and broke alliances, all apparently to ensure that no one leader became powerful enough to rule the nation. The most cynical alliance joined Dostam and Hikmatyar, longstanding ideological and ethnic rivals, now united by resentment of Rabbani's rule over Kabul. Blockades on roads ended most travel, and the airport closed. Hundreds of thousands fled.

The Rise of the Taliban

As the nation collapsed into anarchy, a new political force inspired hope. A protest movement of religious scholars, the *Taliban* ("Students") emerged in the southern Pashtun city of Kandahar against the violence, sexual immorality and corruption of local mujahidin. Desiring to establish Islamic government under the leadership of the reclusive Mullah Omar, *Taliban* fighters ended thievery on the roads and established order.

Most *Taliban* conquests were relatively bloodless in a nation suffering great war fatigue. The *Taliban*'s superior firepower was reinforced by the mobility of their four-wheel drive pickups and the obvious faults of many corrupt mujahidin. With little fighting, the *Taliban* quickly conquered much of the Pashtu-speaking south and advanced on the capital. Briefly repulsed by Rabbani's forces, the *Taliban* rapidly conquered Herat in 1995, then launched air and missile attacks against residential areas of Kabul. In 1996 the capital fell, and Najibullah was quickly executed. Aided by Pakistani volunteers and defections among Dostam's officers, in 1998 the *Taliban* conquered the second largest city, Mazar-i Sharif, and much of the north. The opposition *Northern Alliance* led by Dostam and Masoud controlled only the Panjsher Valley and the far northeast, a

Najibullah

A windstorm sweeps down upon an Afghani sheep and camel market

Photo by Jon Markham Morrow

region lacking significant cities, plus Shi'a areas in the central mountains.

Taliban rule shocked the world. It banned television and required beards on all men, offenders who trimmed their beards too much risking their noses being cut off. To Western and even much Muslim opinion, the treatment of women defied human dignity and extended far beyond female modesty in dress. Although several hundred thousand war widows struggled to provide for their families, the *Taliban* ordered women not to work outside their homes. Later it relented for necessary tasks like nursing (for female patients only), but it demanded extreme measures to keep men from seeing women even at a distance. Even after such precautions were observed, it closed down UN-sponsored bakeries run by women. After closing universities, the *Taliban* proposed opening them for men only. It apparently desired education for girls to stop at the age of eight, and teachers caught schooling girls in homes were arrested and probably tortured.

Only three countries, most prominently Pakistan and Saudi Arabia, ever extended diplomatic recognition. Russia, India, and several Central Asian republics remained critics, sustaining the *Northern Alliance* and other opposition groups in a bleak existence.

Sanctuary for Osama bin Laden and September 11

The son of a leading Saudi construction magnate from Yemen, Osama bin Laden accepted militant Islamist ideas and joined the Afghan mujahidin to fight the Soviets. He established a loosely-organized society called *al-Qaeda* ("The Base"), and became known for criticizing Arab and Western governments. Pressured by Saudi Arabia and the U.S., he moved to Sudan in the early 1990s, where his violent diatribes against the U.S. led Sudan to ask him to leave. He returned to rural southern Afghanistan, where he established training camps.

In 1998 truck bombs at two American embassies in Africa killed hundreds. Evidence pointed to *al-Qaeda*, but Mullah Omar refused U.S. demands to hand over Osama, a "guest." UN sanctions followed in 1999 that banned most flights to the country and grounded the national airline. *Al-Qaeda* followers attacked the *U.S.S. Cole* in 2000 in Yemen. After the infamous September 11 attacks, evidence again quickly implicated bin Laden and *al-Qaeda*, and again the *Taliban* refused to hand over Osama, perhaps because on September 9, 2001 Arab suicide bombers assassinated Ahmad Shah Masoud.

On October 6, the U.S. aerial offensive began, with the usual attacks on air defenses, command centers, and communications facilities. U.S. Special Forces infiltrated Afghanistan to strengthen the *Northern Alliance* and to mark targets for smart weapons. Fearing that the U.S. would assist a *Northern Alliance* attack along the front lines, the *Taliban* had moved its troops and many Arab and Pakistani volunteers to the northern city of Kunduz before the bombing began. This left the other major cities lightly defended.

General Dostam recognized that the capture of Mazar-i Sharif would break the *Taliban's* supply line and prevent a retreat by the troops concentrated in the north. With

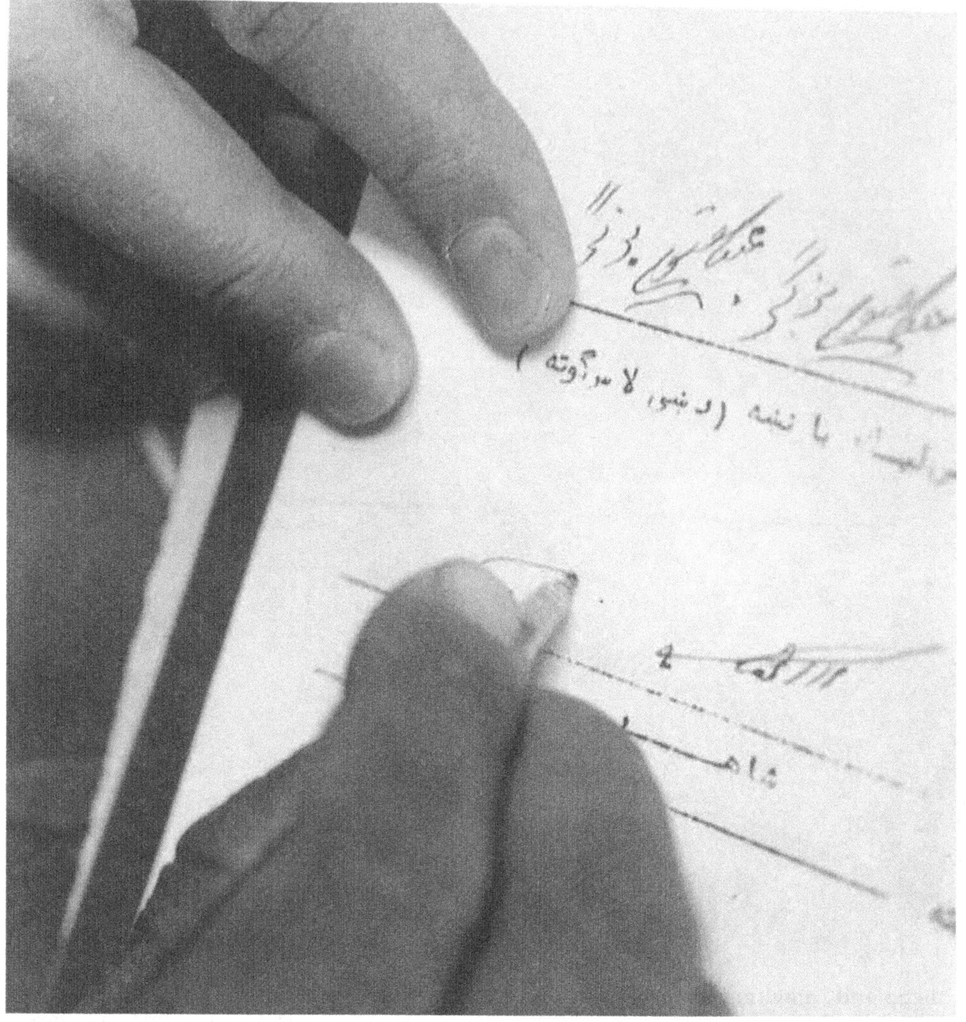

An Afghani farmer signs an application for a tractor WORLD BANK photo

U.S. air support, Dostam's forces fought bitterly for the city and won. Days later, airpower enabled the largely Tajik forces of the *Northern Alliance* to break through the *Taliban* defenses outside Kabul and enter the city, almost unopposed. Despite fears that the city might again become a battlefield between rival mujahidin, the population celebrated the *Taliban's* collapse and the legalization of music, kite flying, and education for girls.

In the south, particularly around Mullah Omar's home town of Kandahar, the *Taliban* faded more slowly. The Pashtun heartland could not be captured by the *Northern Alliance*. However, local anti-*Taliban* rivals emerged to provide ground soldiers for the conquest. In the eastern mountains of Paktia province U.S. troops and Afghan militiamen fought mopping-up operations near Gardez. Large caves in the rugged terrain had provided refuge for the mujahidin fighting the Soviets. The vast weapons stockpiles had passed to the *Taliban*, and Osama bin Laden himself had frequented the area. However, though possibly wounded, he eluded his pursuers. He would survive in Pakistan for another decade, until caught by U.S. SEALS at his home in Abbottabad in 2011.

Karzai, Warlords, and Elections

Hamid Karzai, a Pashtun of notable family, was selected by representatives of several factions at a council in Germany to serve as the provisional national leader. Civilized, thoughtful, and distinguished, Karzai persuaded wealthier nations to donate nearly $5 billion in aid. The money was critical: civil servants had not been paid in seven months, and the treasury was bare.

Hundreds of delegates, from all significant population groups and even some (appointed) women, formed a much-anticipated *loya jirga* in 2002 to select an interim ruler pending a new constitution and elections. After the aged ex-king, Zahir Shah, who came to the throne in 1933, withdrew from consideration, the *loya jirga* selected Hamid Karzai as president.

Forming his cabinet proved difficult. Tajiks from the *Northern Alliance* and other militia leaders demanded significant roles, disproportionate to their ethnic groups' shares of the population. Personal rivalries and conflicting political ideologies also complicated matters. The *Northern Alliance* eventually received the ministries of defense, finance, and foreign affairs, although gradually its members would be forced from office.

His cabinet formed, Karzai faced significant problems in actually ruling. Rather than disarm after victory, the militias remained, and their leaders often controlled their home districts. U.S. forces, initially disinterested in nation-building, worsened the problem by hiring sometimes unsavory warlords as mercenaries against suspected *Taliban* and *al-Qaeda* hideouts. For practical reasons—there were fewer American soldiers in Afghanistan than police in New York—the U.S. could not disarm the militias. In 2003 the UN-sponsored Disarmament, Demobilization and Reintegration Program at last offered militiamen money, clothes and food vouchers in exchange for weapons.

Lacking supreme authority, Karzai risked becoming little more powerful than the mayor of Kabul, protected by American bodyguards and an international security force. However, militia warlords were not all petty thugs who seized provincial capitals and forced Karzai's governors to flee. In Herat, Ismail Khan ignored Kabul's regulations and appropriated customs revenues locally, depriving Kabul of tax revenues. But he ran a fairly effective though authoritarian mini-state. Its streets were clean and paved, and opium production was minimal.

Several achievements marked Karzai's early years in office. Three million children entered school, and two million refugees returned. Aid organizations began widespread humanitarian relief. Committees drafted a new constitution that delicately managed the role of Islam. Business flourished as refugees invested funds previously held abroad, and the economy grew rapidly. The central bank issued a new currency, also called the Afghani, worth 100 times the value of the old one. The new currency conveniently ended the ability of some local rulers to print their own. Reconstruction projects repaired the Salang tunnel and the Kabul-Kandahar highway. Entrepreneurs established mobile phone systems in several cities.

The 2004 presidential election allowed the nation to render its verdict on Hamid Karzai. Karzai picked a Tajik—the brother of Ahmad Shah Masoud—to share the ticket. The voters proved highly enthu-

Then-President Hamid Karzai flanked by vice presidents Mohammed Fahim, a Tajik, and Karim Khalili, a Hazara.

siastic about the first free election, and more of them registered to vote than the probable adult population. Despite *Taliban* threats, little violence occurred, and Karzai won 55% of the vote. Significantly, Karzai's share of the vote usually reflected the Pashtun share of the provincial population, from about 90% near Kandahar in the south to only 10% in the Tajik northeast. In effect, the vote became an ethnic census.

Uniquely for the Southern Asia, the constitution reserves 25% of the seats in parliament for women. While some elected women were very traditional relatives of warlords, even a woman as outspoken as Malalai Joya won a seat. True to her reputation, she addressed the opening session of parliament and attacked the warlords among its members as criminals "with hands stained by the blood of the people."

The *Taliban* Return

In early 2005 the top U.S. general proclaimed security "exceptionally good." However, when spring returned the *Taliban* and foreign volunteers launched attacks on isolated troops, murdered aid workers, assassinated officials, harassed candidates, and destroyed schools. Techniques from the Iraqi insurgency, particularly roadside bombs and even suicide bombings, made their appearance. Anti-American activists seized on an alleged desecration of the Qur'an to stir up deadly riots. Progress in creating a national army, meanwhile, was hampered by low literacy levels, poor pay, and low compensation for soldiers killed in battle.

Trusting local intelligence sources, American forces sometimes struck hard at innocent civilians. An important convoy and several wedding celebrations were bombed, killing dozens of civilians and wounding scores. Informants wishing to settle old scores had suggested that *Taliban* suspects might be in the area, and Afghans celebrating the joyful occasion by firing into the air became the targets of missiles. By 2006, the *Taliban* cynically adopted the tactic of entering a village, attracting U.S. attention, and then withdrawing before the air strikes, which inevitably killed innocent civilians. President Karzai later protested the policy to the U.S., complaints that were repeated with increasing forcefulness. More than once, the U.S. forces denied causing civilian deaths, only later to admit some casualties.

Why, years after the ouster of the *Taliban,* have casualties climbed to hundreds per month during the summer fighting season? Why do they again dominate parts of Helmand, Zabul, Uruzgan and Kandahar provinces in the south, while enforcing rules as far north as Kunduz? In one dramatic weekend in 2008, they freed all the inmates of Kandahar prison and took over villages just a few miles outside of the city. In 2011 they attacked Kandahar again. According to U.S. intelligence estimates, the *Taliban* control 10% of the countryside to the government's 30%, with the remaining territory tribal.

Analysts suggest that a number of factors encouraged the resurgence. The U.S. and its NATO allies initially failed to occupy many rural areas. They left the south's pacification to traditional warlords who failed to impose decisions from Kabul. Over time, these warlords became corrupt as well as inefficient, so much so that NATO commanders demanded the replacement of several of them before replacing U.S. forces there.

Second, the *Taliban* retained the sympathy of many traditional Pakistanis, and found refuge in Pakistan's rugged border areas, where its units regrouped and rearmed. Elements in the Pakistani military intelligence provided more than a blind eye to *Taliban* fighters seeking refuge. Information and supplies were provided; probably weapons as well. Allies in North Waziristan received freedom to organize attacks across the border. Though publicly an ally in the fight against terrorism, on several occasions Pakistan responded to U.S. drone attacks and other operations by blocking supply convoys to Afghanistan.

Third, the Afghan government proved ineffective even in relatively safe regions. Cities desperately needed new housing, street repairs, clean water, and sewers that worked. An army of the unemployed could have provided the labor for much of the work. But between a penniless state and lavish foreign aid spent on experts' salaries and other priorities, reconstruction proved slow. Polls indicated that a majority felt that foreign aid had not benefitted them.

The poorly-trained and poorly-paid police were often both corrupt and inefficient. As a result, petty crime was common. Terrorist attacks and suicide bombings occurred frequently in Kandahar, and dramatically in Kabul, Mazar-i-Sharif, and Herat. These attacks shook confidence. Before the 2009 presidential election, the NATO secretary general publicly blasted "corrupt and inefficient" government, and demanded government action, after the blood shed and money donated by NATO members.

To no surprise, administrative failures handicapped the struggle against the *Taliban*. Some estimates suggested that in 2010, only 25% of the most important areas of the country were secure and supporting the government. The arrival of 30,000 additional U.S. troops provided increased firepower, especially in the south. However, the Afghan military is underpaid, largely illiterate, and poorly trained. While the troops are considered a vital partner to U.S. and NATO forces, they have difficulty in maintaining security in towns and villages after *Taliban* fighters have been defeated. As a consequence, a much-publicized U.S. offensive to bring security to Kandahar was delayed.

President Karzai regularly faults the U.S. and its allies for rising popular concerns about the war. After decades of fighting, many Afghans resent civilian casualties, and U.S. and allied air attacks in some recent years killed somewhere between 200 (U.S. estimates) and 600 (UN) civilians. Rates for over-all violence climbed nearly 40% in 2011. Dissatisfaction with the high casualty rate became a national issue, with 77% of respondents in a national poll condemning the bombings.

More recently, night raids on civilian homes by U.S. and NATO forces became the dominant political complaint. The military valued their effectiveness—they could "own the night" even where the *Taliban* controlled the day. But even Afghans who supported broader U.S. goals condemned the loss of innocent lives and the psychological impact when foreign troops burst into private homes, including the women's quarters.

Finally, the *Taliban* movement itself proved remarkably resilient, spreading quietly across the rural countryside, collecting taxes and attacking girls' schools when powerful enough to do so. Joining nationalist slogans to the religious, it depicted Karzai as a foreign agent and sought to create a sense of inevitable victory after the foreigners' inevitable departure. Throughout, both the *Taliban* and warlords enjoyed great profits from the opium trade.

The Challenge of Opium

For the long run, the greatest challenge to a democratic administration will be the production and trade of opium, because it funds warlords, strengthens the *Taliban*, and corrupts the government. In 2001 the *Taliban* had prohibited growing opium poppies. Under Karzai, the absence of authority encouraged many impoverished farmers to resume opium cultivation *because opium typically provides the farmer between 4 and 20 times the income of wheat* per acre.

Local theologians agree that Muslims should not consume it, though they differ as to whether producing opium for use by non-Muslims really conflicts with Islam. Regardless of theology, the presence of such quantities of highly addictive drugs has resulted in one million addicts. Proportionally, this is the highest rate in the world.

To avoid arousing anti-American feelings, U.S. forces initially did not attack opium fields or refining facilities. After rising ten-fold in 2002, opium production doubled again in 2003, almost entirely in the insecure south and west. By 2009, the UN estimated that production totaled about 7,000 tons, from 14 of the 34 provinces. Output fell in 2010, due to a plant fungal disease, but in response, prices climbed, encouraging greater cultivation, and the next year the value of output rose by 133%.

After processing into heroin, the product may be worth half the value of the legal GDP, and the *Taliban* stronghold of Helmand province produces more opium than the second-largest producing nation, Myanmar. Total world output had reached only 600 tons in 1999.

The opium trade weakens Karzai's government in many ways. It strengthens many warlords, who tax or even trade the drug. Corruption flourishes, as payoffs protect certain fields and smugglers. An internationally-funded program to pay farmers to destroy their opium crops ended up in many cases paying the warlords' supporters instead. Aerial spraying to destroy the crops upsets aid agencies, who reason that farmers would be driven to desperation if no alternative income was provided. Though costing about $1 billion annually, the eradication effort is considered a failure in many provinces. The combination of broader economic development and stricter enforcement of laws may prove the key, but achieving either, let alone both, remains beyond the reach of the Karzai administration in many southern areas.

Election Fraud Weakens Karzai

As presidential elections approached in 2009, President Karzai's popularity reached new lows, and American support for him wavered. His 40 election rivals included candidates of many viewpoints, some with ability and close contact with the U.S., a sign of increasing distrust between Kabul and Washington. However, Karzai deftly played several issues. He condemned Washington for casualties from air attacks and demanded the Supreme Court postpone the elections from April to August, a delay necessary for both security and administrative reasons.

Few of Karzai's rivals enjoyed national stature of any significance; his most serious rivals enjoyed limited support. Moreover, Pashtun voters would not likely support a Tajik or other minority candidate, and Karzai reached out to that community by carefully selecting General Mohammed Fahim, a former Tajik militia commander, as a vice presidential nominee. The president's campaign also enlisted the support of tribal leaders, officials, and others.

Although the election passed off peacefully, allegations of mass fraud quickly overwhelmed initial claims of an impressive Karzai victory (55% to 30% for Dr. Abdullah Abdullah, the former foreign minister). Fraud apparently touched the entire process, beginning with voter registration in the absence of an identification system and continuing through bribery and falsified ballots. The results plunged the country into a political and constitutional crisis, and the election commission stripped Karzai of sufficient votes to force a run-off vote. However, Dr. Abdullah then conceded, claiming that the run-off could not be free and fair.

Despite his waning popularity, Afghans recognized that President Karzai would win a fair contest against a non-Pashtun. His triumph in a corrupt election instead left him weakened internationally and domestically. When he attempted to repay political allies by appointing them to the cabinet, parliament rejected nearly 75% of his nominees. Relations with the U.S. and other nations declined, as donors threatened to halt aid to ministries run by corrupt politicians.

Fraud likewise dominated the 2010 parliamentary elections. Though hotly contested, turnout fell to 40% amid voter cynicism and Taliban intimidation in several regions. The election authorities subsequently excluded 1.3 million of the 5.6 million votes, and the new parliament included fewer pro-Karzai members.

That same year corruption allegations about Kabul Bank, the largest in the country, led first to a run on the bank, as depositors hurried to withdraw their funds, and then to a massive scandal that on a proportional basis (5% of GDP) was one of history's largest.

Both the Communists and the Taliban opposed private banks; when Ahmad Karzai came to power, the country lacked banks that would take depositors money and lend to others. At the same time, foreign governments and aid agencies expected to make payments by check. Into the commercial vacuum stepped Sherkhan Farnood, by profession a poker player, who established Kabul Bank, with very well-connected notables—including the president's brother—as major shareholders. Kabul Bank became the government paymaster for its 250,000 employees and teachers. However, it later emerged that the real purpose of the bank was to recycle deposits to just 19 people and companies. They received nearly $1 billion in loans. To hide corruption, some bank records were fraudulent and there were two sets of books indicating what borrowers owed, and really owed. Most of loans left the country and will never be repaid.

International agencies provided the funds to keep the bank in operation, but their pressures led the Afghan government to bring Farnood and several associates to justice. They were convicted, imprisoned, and their property was seized. Nevertheless, the entire Kabul Bank saga suggests a regime operating to benefit a highly favored elite.

The Withdrawal of Foreign Troops

The scheduled departure of all U.S. and NATO combat troops by the end of 2014 focused great attention on the possible consequences. Western military experts initially considered Afghan troops and police incapable of defending the government and society. Afghan units had rarely fought alone, and the *Taliban* proved able to launch guerrilla attacks in Kabul with some frequency. But in 2013 the Afghan National Army (ANA) carried out successful, large-scale operations that demonstrated effective planning and organization. Coalition casualties dropped dramatically between 2011 and 2013, but ANA casualties rose. Afghans were doing the fighting.

Logistics and military equipment seem the most challenging areas. The ANA will fight with much lower levels of technology, including limited use of air power. Unable to assert its authority over the entire territory, it might be forced to withdraw to the most important provinces that its troop can defend, resulting in the country's informal partition and *Taliban* rule over the south and east.

Reluctant to see the longest U.S. war result in the collapse of its ally, the U.S. offered to train and assist the ANA after the withdrawal. Officials from Kabul and Washington negotiated an agreement to establish the roles and conditions for the proposed U.S. training mission. However, on various pretexts Karzai refused to sign the agreement, despite a *loya jirga's* approval of it, even after the Obama administration threatened that the longer the delay in signing the agreement, the smaller would be the assistance.

Given war-weariness and indications of a military stalemate, both Afghan officials and Western diplomats sought to compromise with the *Taliban*. President Karzai summoned delegates to a special *loya jirga* to discuss options for peace. However, during a meeting with Taliban representatives, a suicide bomber assassinated Burhanuddin Rabbani, the chief government representative.

At least publicly, the *Taliban* refuse to negotiate with Kabul as long as foreign troops remain, a policy designed to shame the Karzai government. Likewise, to demonstrate its continuing importance, the Kabul government demands that it take the lead in negotiations with the *Taliban*.

The U.S. insists on several "necessary outcomes" in a negotiated peace, including acceptance of the Afghan Constitution (and its promise of women's rights) and a *Taliban* renunciation of *Al-Qaeda*. Kabul's primary concerns include an end to the fighting.

Fraudulent elections again, 2014

The withdrawal of foreign troops coincided with the election of Karzai's successor and the expected first peaceful transfer of power. Six major candidates emerged from the nomination process, a varied group ranging from highly educated professionals to former mujahidin leaders who fought the Soviet occupation. Some nominees likely worried Western aid donors as well as moderate Afghans. Abdul Rasul Sayyaf, for example, had offered Osama bin Laden sanctuary and campaigned to implement Shari'a. General Abdul Rashid Dostam, the Uzbek warlord and past king-maker, reappeared as a vice presidential candidate. Given terrorists' threats to disrupt the campaigns, each candidate received an armored vehicle and security detail.

Unlike campaigns in long-established democracies, where political parties play the major role in defining platforms and managing campaigns, in Afghanistan ethnicity, alliances and patronage networks play the major roles in efforts to win. As elections approached, President Karzai's brother, who had displayed little previous interest in politics and established few alliances, withdrew his candidacy. The experienced Dr. Abdullah Abdullah appeared as the candidate to beat.

Despite terror attacks on foreign observers, the country's election commission, and an assassination attempt on Abdullah, both rounds of the election passed relatively peacefully. The election commission reported that turnout doubled the 2009 total despite the intimidation. Moreover, the top finishers in the first round both appeared capable leaders. As expected, Abdullah placed first, with 45%; his rival in the final round was the president of Kabul University, Ashraf Ghani Ahmadzai, formerly the finance minister and an economist with the World Bank. Generally known by his first two names, he received 32% of the vote.

Days after the second round, while ballots were still being delivered to Kabul and counted, Abdullah publicly rejected any figures that might be announced. He claimed that both the Independent Election Commission and its complaints body were partisan and the counting was fraudulent. Calling on the UN to solve the problem, Abdullah withdrew his monitors from the commission's work.

Evidence later provided by the Abdullah campaign showed the commission was anything but independent and neutral. Several thousand employees had been dismissed after the first round, and successors appointed. Leaked recordings of telephone conversations captured the voice of a senior election official urging a provincial governor to "bring the sheep stuffed and not empty." He also discussed the response to an army commander's arrest of local election officials after the discovery of stuffed ballot boxes before voting actually began. The scale of the stuffing seems vast: questioning how the election commission knew so quickly the total national vote numbers, the Abdullah campaign claimed that only about six million voters actually participated, implying one million fraudulent ballots.

The election official protested his innocence and denounced the recording as a fake, but he resigned on national television. Ignoring the wider political crisis, the supposedly neutral complaints commission expressed a willingness to investigate if the recordings had been made legally. As this volume went to press, the release of the preliminary vote counts had been delayed.

In comments that elsewhere might be considered presidential for rising above the fray, Abdullah pledged to accept defeat if an honest vote count showed he had lost. But he rejected a fraudulent result, and in response election observers faulted the integrity of the process for several reasons. In some provinces the number of voters in the second round was three times that of the first. Remarkably, the many extra voters rarely spoiled their ballots, and a suspiciously high number of women cast their ballots in traditionally insecure areas.

Culture: Like many other nations of the modern world, Afghanistan does not possess a culture which is entirely distinct from that of nearby lands. This is true not only of the folkways of a mainly pastoral and agricultural society, but also of religion, art and political organization.

The ties of blood and tribe are strong. Loyalty to the extended family, clan and ethnic group often exceeds nationalism. It is considered not only a duty, but the normal way of doing things to side with cousins and other relatives or to aid them in time of need, as well as to share in the happy times of weddings, births (especially of sons) and the celebration of holidays. The most firmly implanted of all secular holidays is *No Ruz*, in honor of the first day of spring—March 21st or 22nd.

Most Afghans farm. They live in small villages, typically located on a slope at the edge of a cultivated valley. Until the civil war, many people had never traveled any distance from their birthplace, and most villages are still fairly isolated. A few nomads move frequently in search of pasturage for their sheep, goats, cattle and (in the case of a few tribes), camels.

Religion is as natural to the people of Afghanistan as the air they breathe. The name of God is invoked on every possible occasion, and political leaders can oppose the dominance of religious practices only at their peril. Though many people speak Dari, a form of Persian, most Afghans feel a general distinctness because they are Sunni Muslims, while most Iranians are Shi'a.

Women's Rights in a Patriarchal Society

During the years of *Taliban* rule, women suffered greater denials of their basic human rights in Afghanistan than in any other nation across the globe. In a form so extreme as to prevent women from looking out on the street, Islamic rules combined with traditional patriarchal values. Historically, among some classes and tribes women had often been possessions, or at best inferior humans; justice for the rape of a girl might be settled through her marrying the attacker and thus avoiding charges of adultery. Because family honor and the avoidance of shame were—and remain—higher values than a woman's happiness and safety, female victims usually found no protection from the police or relatives. Wives or daughters who attempted to escape abuse by leaving the home generally faced imprisonment, simply for absence from the family.

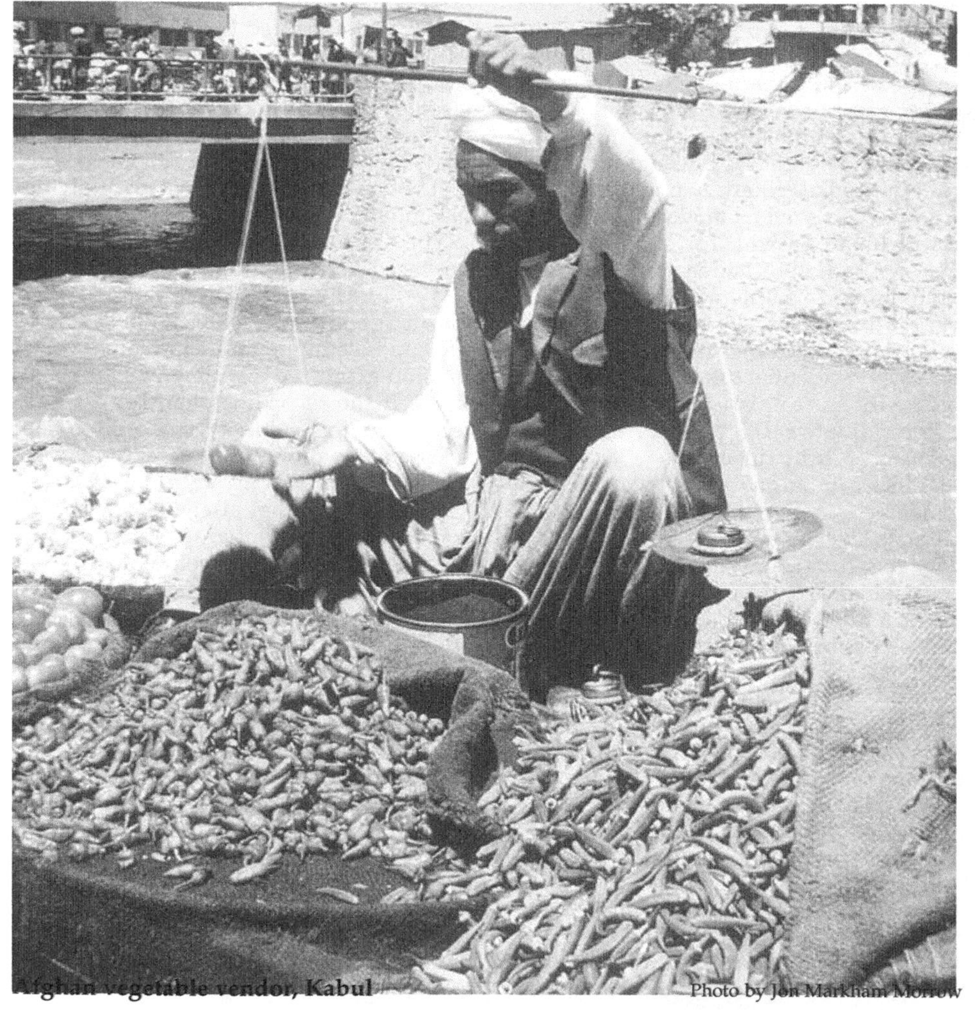

Afghan vegetable vendor, Kabul — Photo by Jon Markham Morrow

In the 1990s, the *Taliban* used the greater power of the state to enforce its regulations, including the prohibition of girls' education beyond puberty. In contrast, the Karzai administration improved the practical circumstances and legal rights of women in a number of ways. Where schools for girls could operate safely, they did. Women do serve as members of parliament, and are more active in public life. But President Karzai, perhaps fearing a backlash over granting greater freedom to women, stands accused of making compromises against women's interests. For example, he endorsed a clerical opinion that permitted husbands to beat their wives under certain circumstances.

Surprisingly, a recent poll indicated that only a minority of women fear that the country could become a worse place following the departure of international troops. The return of *Taliban* rule will clearly make conditions far worse. To quote one commander, "The rights that Islam has given to a woman, no other religion has— that she sit quietly in her home, veiled. That she take care of food and clothes for her husband."

Artistic and Cultural Expression

Literary expression largely takes the form of poetry, ranging from the intricate, elegant poems of professionals to the more direct, forceful and colorful folk poetry which displays the soul of the people. Poetry often expressed and preserved Pashtun identity and cultural values of Pashtuns, and the works of two 17th century poets, the warrior Khushhal Khan Khattak and the mystic Rahman Baba are still popular in a country where only 7% of the population enjoys electricity and poetry readings are large public events.

Especially in Pashtun areas, fundamentalist objections and suspicions often extend to all Western ideas, a view that limits education. The UN Development Report for 2005 ranked the educational system as the worst in the world. In some areas, it has not progressed since then. As few as 14% of the adult population can read and write, while until recently a high school diploma was almost unknown outside the cities and larger towns. Although the new constitution enshrines the right of education for girls, only a very few girls' high schools exist, and those who attend them often suffer threats and harassment.

Higher education, backed by the communists, suffered during the civil wars of the 1990s and essentially collapsed under the *Taliban*. During the following decade, the number of public colleges and universities climbed to 24, while 33 private institutions opened. Their combined enrollment climbed rapidly to 73,000 students—nearly twenty-fold. Since over 50,000 high school students take university entrance exams, admission is highly competitive, despite often-dilapidated facilities, shortages of faculty, and poor security.

Religion and local traditions combine with poverty and illiteracy to continue to create great hardship for women even though the worst fundamentalist regulations have been removed and women are permitted to seek employment. According to the UN, women are often condemned to lives of malnutrition, exclusion from public life, rape, violence and forced marriage. Amnesty International blames feudal customs for women being treated like property—and men suffering no consequences for abusing them. Among the most unfortunate are the tens of thousands of war widows, and young women forced into arranged marriage. Many of these girls are married before the legal age of 18, and many find their conditions desperate. Suicide attempts are on the rise. Cultural change will take longer than a new series of legal edicts.

Despite its poverty, and current cultural attitudes against the visual arts and public presentations by women, as the turnstile of Asia Afghanistan historically produced masterworks of art and decoration, variously showing Islamic, Chinese, Indian, and Hellenistic influences. Many such *objets d'art* were already gathered in Kabul's National Museum when the Soviet invasion took place in the 1970s. The Bactrian Hoard, some 22,000 pieces dating back 2,000 years and considered the "most important gold treasure ever found in Asia," was discovered about the same time.

One of the most remarkable if unlike band of heroes during the country's 30 years of conflict were a small group of museum guards and curators who hid and protected the most valuable objects in the National Museum. Some objects were apparently stored in the presidential palace, in a safe that even a notable militia leader could not blast open. Artifacts left in the National Museum suffered rocket attacks, looting, and finally the deliberate destruction of art by *Taliban* activists. Despite suffering unemployment and cases of torture, those who hid the precious objects succeeded in saving them.

The museum curators could not save from the *Taliban* two outdoor statues of the Buddha near Bamian. Carved into a cliff over 1,300 years ago, before the Muslim conquest of Afghanistan, the larger of the two statues measured about 150 feet high and ranked as the tallest standing Buddha in the world. Despite an international outcry, troops used artillery to demolish these unique relics.

Economy: The civil war inflicted suffering on some of the world's poorest people and postponed badly-needed reconstruction. Poverty stalks the land, and only a few African countries suffer worse conditions; indeed, since the ouster of the *Taliban* in 2001, the country has slipped from 117 to 181 in the UN rankings, the second lowest. The child mortality rate exceeds that of every other country. Millions of land mines still threaten. Over 100,000 Afghans, many of them children, have lost limbs; in 2005 the casualty rate averaged 100 dead or wounded per month.

Agriculture is the livelihood of the country. Yet, only 20% of the country at most can be irrigated, and less than half of that potential farm land is actually cultivated. In good years the country is self-sufficient in cereal grains, but frequent droughts require grain imports. The high price of cotton on world markets has encouraged increased its production, though of course present profits lie in opium.

The skins and wool of the Karakul sheep remain important exports in keeping with long tradition. The United States has been one of the principal purchasers, particularly of the skins of the Karakul lambs. While the wool of the mature sheep is coarse, stringy and brown, that of the newborn lambs is tightly curled and a glossy black, highly prized as a material for fur coats.

The northern part of the country has significant deposits of natural gas and a little oil. Natural gas exports to the Soviet Union were halted when the withdrawing Soviets capped the wells, but may eventually supply Uzbekistan as well as the area around Mazar-i Sharif. Mineral resources, such as iron ore and coal in the Hindu Kush Mountains, have not yet been exploited. Perhaps these and other mineral resources contributed to Soviet desires to control the country. Soviet data led American geologists to survey the country much more intensively, leading to the discovery of the largest known lithium deposits and huge veins of iron, copper, cobalt, gold and other minerals that could make Afghanistan a world mining center.

Developing such resources will prove difficult in a country with minimal roads and a single railroad line of 47 miles, linking Mazar-i-Sharif to the Uzbek border. Given these conditions, despite the U.S. military involvement and discovery of the resources, western companies often fail to invest. A Chinese company is developing one of the world's largest copper mines in Logar province at a cost of $3 billion, and other Chinese investment seems likely.

The Future: The collapse of Iraq's military and police when faced with Islamist attacks in 2014 casts a long shadow over the future of Kabul's ruling elite. Will Afghan troops fight any more successfully without their international allies? Especially if (as seems likely) much of the country considers the 2014 election results fraudulent?

Last year's volume predicted that fraudulent elections in 2014 "will spell disaster for a moderate and democratic government for many years to come. It even risks the breakdown of central government into feuding autonomous regions in the south, northwest, north, and east." That statement still stands. Should the run-off election be declared invalid and another one held? With U.S. senators insisting on a comprehensive audit of the election results (rather than the minimal 10% undertaken by the election commission), the prospects for Western aid to a fraudulently-elected president seem slim.

Even with "clean" election results, despite the blood and treasure the United States has expended, it might not achieve an Afghan regime it wants: one that protects and empowers women, meets at least minimal standards of integrity, and governs effectively.

Some *Taliban* consider time on their side with the ANA weakening without U.S. and NATO support. Naturally, this outlook provides few incentives to negotiate a peaceful compromise. Others, however, recognize the war-weariness of a nation in conflict for over 30 years. Low-lying discussions with the *Taliban* have taken place in Qatar, but the sparring for negotiating advantages is still in its early stages. As the withdrawal nears, substance may replace posturing in Qatar, while in Afghanistan battles begin to demarcate the limits of power.

Ahmad Shah Masoud, Tajik Mujahidin Leader

The People's Republic of Bangladesh

Passengers disembark from a ferry boat at Narayanganj, Bangladesh WORLD BANK Photo

Area: 55,598 square miles (143,998 sq. km.). Land appears and disappears from the rivers and Bay of Bengal.
Population: 151 million.
Capital City: Dhaka (pop. 12 million, plus suburbs).
Climate: Tropical and rain soaked; the country is subject to destructive hurricanes.
Neighboring Countries: Surrounded by India on three sides; a short border with Burma lies on the southeast.
Time Zone: GMT +6. When it is midnight in Bangladesh, it is noon in Chicago.
Official Language: Bengali.
Other Principal Tongues: English (in schools and commerce).
Ethnic Background: Over 98% Bengali, except small tribal groups in the Chittagong hills.
Principal Religion: Islam (87%) and Hinduism (11%).
Chief Commercial Products: Garments, textiles, jute, tea, rice, wheat, sugar, hides.
Major Trading Partners: U.S., India, China, U.K., Japan, United Arab Emirates.
Currency: 1 Taka = 100 paisa
Former Colonial Status: Part of British India (1765–1947) then a province of Pakistan under the name *East Pakistan* (1947–1971).
Independence Date: Proclaimed independent in March 1971; achieved in December.
National Day: December 16.
Chief of State: President Abdul Hamid (2013)
Head of Government: Hasina Wajed, Prime Minister (2009).
National Flag: A green field with a large red circle in the middle.
Gross Domestic Product: $160 billion (at current prices); $350 billion (Purchasing Power Parity).
GDP per capita: about $2,200 (PPP), but 50 million live on less than one dollar per day.

Most of the land of Bangladesh is flat, wet alluvial plain, formed over scores of centuries by three great river systems depositing their silt as they near the Bay of Bengal. Indeed these rivers, the Ganges, the Brahmaputra and the Meghna, lose their identities as their waters become mingled in a maze of waterways and swamps along the southern coast. Much of the country is less than 30 feet above sea level.

Four traditional scourges annually threaten life and property in Bangladesh. The rivers flood during the summer monsoons, covering half or more of the land. Tropical storms like Cyclone Sidr (2007)—equivalent to hurricanes—sweep in from the Bay of Bengal, strengthened by a funnel effect of the shoreline that creates high tides of salt water. Disease spread by polluted waters, and famine resulting from destroyed crops, complete the list.

Of all the countries in Asia, nature threatens humans most in Bangladesh. Bacteria flourish in the tropical climate, and the frequent floods multiply the consequences of inadequate sanitation. Dense population in a country with little industry forces landless farmers onto silt islands barely above high tide. Then floods, or even shifting river channels, destroy land and crops, threatening famine for those who cannot afford to buy food. Beyond individual and local tragedies, the statistics of overpopulation paint a grim picture for the future. Although roughly three-quarters of its people live by farming and less than 20% in urban areas, the country's population density exceeds 1,800 per square mile—far higher than the Netherlands in Europe with its employment concentrated in commerce, industry, and services.

The long-term future appears grim. Ecologists blame the worsening floods of recent years on the deforestation of the Himalaya Mountains in India and Nepal, where the great rivers of Bangladesh originate. The loss of forest increases flooding for two reasons. First, the soil retains less water, causing faster runoff. Second, the rapid runoff carries deposits of silt downstream, raising the level of river beds and diverting them. Former president Ershad declared the floods a "man-made curse," and proposed regional cooperation to end them, as well as better control of the rivers in Bangladesh. However, geologists also suspect that the river delta is simply sinking into the ocean.

Where family farms measure a few acres at best, only rice provides subsistence. Two or even three crops per year, tended with much labor and scarcely any machinery, enable the country in a good year almost to feed itself.

Unfortunately, another consequence of the same deforestation of mountain forests is seasonal drought in the west of the country. Essentially, by late winter and spring too little water flows through the region's many rivers. Shipping becomes dangerous, and irrigation canals dry up just when water is vital for young crops. One solution, the construction of dams to regulate water flow, will require years of study before construction begins, and the estimated cost exceeds $1 billion.

Geography forces the use of boat and barge for most travel and transportation. There are 3,000 miles of navigable rivers, but only about 10,000 miles of surfaced roads. The marshy ground and many rivers render road building difficult and costly. Many streams of the delta are not bridged, and ferry service causes many delays.

A small region southeast of Chittagong is located above the deltas and flood plains of the rivers. Its hills, valleys and forests make this region, known as the Chittagong Hill Tracts, the only one in the nation where virtually all the land is not used for agriculture.

History: Bangladesh and territory to the west for many centuries bore the native name *Bangla.* The region was designated by English officials as the presidency, or state, of Bengal in 1699. With the partitioning of British India and independence of India and Pakistan in 1947, the territory became East Pakistan. Although united by the bond of a common religion, the Bengalis of East Pakistan—a majority in the country—were often unhappy with government dominated by men from West Pakistan.

Dissatisfaction grew rapidly in the late 1960s, with resentment over attempts to promote Urdu, the major language of West Pakistan, and the award most foreign aid and development projects to West Pakistan. In 1970 the *Awami League* of Sheikh Mujibur Rahman pledged autonomy for East Pakistan, and won a majority of seats in elections for the National Assembly. However, General Yahya Khan, the president, prevented the National Assembly from meeting, and hence the *Awami League* from taking power. Sheikh Mujib was arrested. Uprisings then broke out in the East.

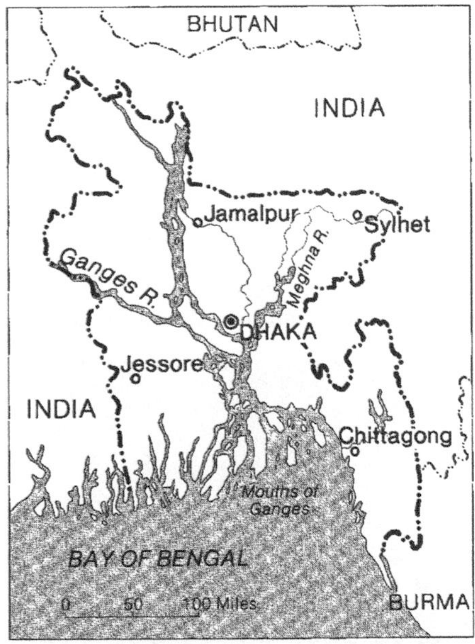

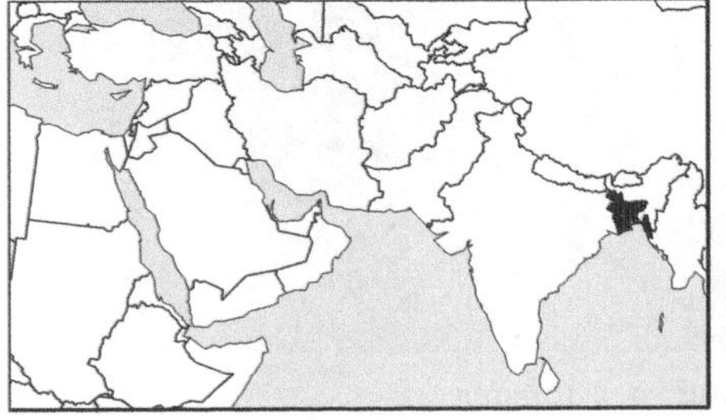

In March, 1971 Bangladesh ("The Bengal Nation") proclaimed its independence. A popular rebellion broke out, but for nine months the Pakistani occupation army repressed it, with three million Bengali deaths reported (a figure disputed by Pakistan). Millions more sought refuge across the border, and in December 1971 India attacked the Pakistani occupiers. Two weeks later they surrendered.

During 1972 the new nation and its government took form. The Indian army withdrew and massive international aid arrived for the great tasks of aiding the refugees and restoring an economy devastated by war. Months were required for the nearly 10 million Bengalis who had fled to India to return to their homeland—often to find that their homes had been destroyed.

Sheikh Mujibur Rahman dominated political life during these years. Still imprisoned in West Pakistan when independence was won, he was immediately declared president of the new nation. Freed in 1972, he received a hero's welcome in Dhaka. His first official acts were to resign as president and take the office of prime minister.

During the first years of independence, political power lay fully in the hands of Sheikh Mujib and loyal members of his *Awami League,* especially after the 1973 elections gave the party almost all the 300 seats in the National Assembly. However, those in power frequently sought personal gain. Much of the international relief sent to alleviate starvation and suffering actually enriched government officials and army officers.

Public feeling eventually turned strongly against officials over their failure to improve the conditions of the poverty-stricken masses. Even Sheikh Mujib's personal popularity melted away amidst the corruption, banditry and violent disorders. In response, he made himself a virtual dictator and used emergency regulations to censor the press rigorously and jail critics of the administration without trial.

In 1975, a group of military officers murdered Mujib and overthrew his government. They ruled only briefly, however, for soon General Ziaur Rahman seized power. No relation to Mujib, Zia at first placed a retired Supreme Court justice as president, and then assumed the title himself in 1977.

Although initially a military dictator, President Zia moved toward allowing political activity by organizing his own *Bangladesh National Party (BNP)*. Zia won the 1978 presidential election that year, but his assassination during an unsuccessful military coup in 1981 ended an era of relative stability.

Remarkably for a Muslim country, the two largest parties have been led by women. Sheikh Hasina Wajed, the daughter of Sheikh Mujibur Rahman, inherited his title, a rare occurrence in the Islamic world, and has led the *Awami League*. Her rival, Khaleda Zia, adopted the Hindu royal title of begum after the death of her husband, Ziaur Rahman. She has headed the more conservative *BNP* that her husband founded. Both women cooperated in strikes, protests and boycotts against President Ershad.

Demonstrations and riots in 1990 followed the familiar strike patterns, but this time the opposition groups jointly demanded Ershad's immediate resignation and free elections. Riots followed the reported arrests of opposition leaders, and troops fired on crowds killing dozens. When members of Ershad's own *Jatiya Party* left parliament and senior army officers refused to take control, Ershad resigned.

Bitter Two-Party Rivalry, 1991

The parliamentary election campaign of 1991, like every election since, seemed an often bitter competition between two dead men. The *Awami League* extolled Mujibur Rahman, while the *BNP* praised Ziaur Rahman. The results brought Khaleda Zia and the *BNP* an eventual majority in the 300 elected seats. The newly-elected parliament restored its prime minister to supremacy and rendered the president a figurehead, and Khaleda Zia took office. The *Awami League*, more socialist and pro-Indian, led the opposition.

The two women alternated in power for nearly all the next 16 years, except for several months immediately preceding an election, when the constitution provides for a non-partisan interim administration. Typically, the economy did well at mid-term, but as parliamentary elections approached, there were usually strident accusations of corruption, parliamentary walkouts, frequent general strikes, demonstrations, riots, and travel blockades organized by the party in opposition. These often brought the economy to a halt.

For Sheikh Hasina, one contentious issue has remained bringing to justice the plotters who overthrew and murdered Sheikh Mujib and nearly his entire family. Sheikh Hasina herself escaped death only because she was abroad; two decades later as prime minister she ordered the arrest of surviving suspects, despite a promise of immunity issued by military rulers. Finally, in 2010, five convicted plotters were hanged for the murders.

General Ziaur Rahman apparently did not participate in the plot, but once in power he sent some of the plotters abroad, and the *BNP* considered him the real hero of independence. During its years in power, the *BNP* minimized Sheikh Mujib's role, and Khaleda Zia celebrated her birthday on the day of Sheikh Mujib's death. Symbolically, Sheikh Hasina's government dismantled the pontoon bridge to Ziaur Rahman's island grave, removed his name from the airport, and closed his exhibits in the national museum.

In 2001, the less-secular *BNP* won an overwhelming victory at the polls, with its allies (including the *Jamaat-i Islami*) capturing two-thirds of the parliamentary seats. Khaleda Zia thus gained the ability to move quickly against the public's two greatest concerns: corruption and crime. However, she failed at both. Repeatedly ranked as the most corrupt nation on earth by Transparency International, Bangladesh proved particularly unable to punish high-level bribe-takers. The anti-corruption bureau operated out of the prime minister's office, and never charged prominent members of a ruling party.

Sheikh Hasina Wajed, Prime Minister

Popular discontent with crime became so great that during broad daylight mobs lynched nearly a dozen suspected criminals in the capital. Unfortunately, immediate reductions in the crime rate were unlikely, because the police were considered the most corrupt institution in the country. Crimes with particularly low rates of punishment include throwing acid at women's faces and attacks on the Hindu minority. In 2003 the prime minister ordered 40,000 troops into the cities to help police in a massive roundup of suspected criminals. However, crime levels fell only modestly, and public lynching continued despite the military's involvement.

During BNP rule, political violence was disproportionately aimed at the *Awami League*. The nation was shocked by a grenade and shooting attack on Sheikh Hasina during a political rally that killed nearly twenty people, some of them prominent party leaders. Usually, the assailants in political violence escaped capture and trial, but *Awami League* claims that the *BNP* was behind some killings proved justified by the murder conviction of some party members.

Numbering dozens of publicly identified groups, the extreme Islamist movement includes both peaceful and violent activists. Secular politicians are not their only victims: movie theaters, circuses, and other entertainments have been attacked. The *BNP* governed in coalition with the fundamentalist *Jamaat-i Islami*, and the government only cracked down

Fishing for shrimp and rock lobster

after the extremist *Jamaat-ul-Mujahideen* exploded 500 bombs across the country timed for the same hour. The same group attacked several courts and assassinated two judges—since the *Jamaat* desired to impose Shari'a Islamic law, courts were a particular target. After conviction in court, six *Jamaat* leaders were executed in 2007.

Demonstrations and general strikes began in 2006 months before the appointment of an interim administration to replace the *BNP* cabinet during the last months before elections. Faulting the outdated and allegedly falsified electoral register, the *Awami League* determined to boycott the elections, and plunged the country into chaos with violence, strikes, and transport blockades. Finally, with the *BNP* already claiming victory in uncontested races, in 2007 the president declared a state of emergency and appointed Dr. Fakhruddin Ahmad to head an interim government supervised by the military.

A former central banker, Dr. Ahmad determined create a voting system worthy of the public's faith. A massive new electoral register was ordered, complete with digital photographs and fingerprints of perhaps 90 million adults, to deter anyone from voting several times. To provide time for the registration, the election was postponed for nearly two years, and the names of 12 million fake voters were removed from the rolls.

In common with his military backers, Dr. Ahmad also sought to punish corrupt politicians and halt the destructive rivalry between the two major parties. All political activity was banned. Dozens of former cabinet members and leaders both parties found themselves under arrest, as did Khaleda Zia's son, Tarique Rahman and eventually Khaleda herself, charged with corruption. Sheikh Hasina, who was initially abroad, was arrested after her return and charged with extortion.

Country boats on a Bangladesh river

Begum Khaleda Zia

Despite the military's attempt to reform politics, during the 2009 elections the same two parties made the same promises of cheaper food, tackling corruption and reducing crime. They were headed by the same two women, both out on bail for corruption charges they considered politically motivated. Sheikh Hasina's *Awami League* and its allies won an overwhelming victory, gaining 250 of the 300 seats.

Just weeks in office, Sheikh Hasina faced a brutal revolt by troops of the paramilitary border guards, the Bangladesh Rifles, over low pay and the appointment of army officers as their commanders. Scores of officers and civilians were murdered, but the revolt failed. An investigation into its causes was promptly released publicly, and trials followed, allowing Sheikh Hasina to demonstrate the rule of law.

Failed Elections, 2014: Government accomplishments in Dhaka revolve around politics. Economic development, good government, and social improvement are lesser priorities. Because winning matters so much, violent protests and general strikes over the ruling party's alleged interference regularly marked election campaigns. To avoid this harmful conflict, parliament passed a law that a non-partisan caretaker cabinet should govern during the campaign season. However, before the 2014 elections the *Awami League* used its massive majority to overturn the law. This provoked a series of violent strikes by the *BNP* and other opposition parties. By remaining in power, the *Awami League* thus squandered effective government during the last months of a parliament and damaged the economy through the inevitable strikes.

As they had threatened, the *BJP* and other opposition parties boycotted the vote in 2014. Only 147 of the 300 seats were contested; the *Awami League* triumphed, but only 20% of eligible voters participated.

In another move whose long shadow eventually will shade the parliamentary contest, in 2010 Sheikh Hasina's government established an International Crimes Tribunal to try those who allegedly committed war crimes during the 1971 War of Independence. The tribunal was not genuinely international, and its operations did not meet international standards. Moreover, it focused narrowly on the largest Islamic party in the country, the *Jamaat-i Islami*, which had supported Pakistan at the time (see below). Eleven of its past and present leaders faced trial.

The slow pace of the trials and several death penalties handed out to party leaders suggest the possibility that the *Jamaat* may be banned, punishing it and removing a major ally of the *BJP*. Protests against the convictions turned violent as *Jamaat* supporters turned their fury on religious minorities, burning homes and temples and killing scores.

Political Parties: Four major political groups represent most political aspirations within the country. The *Bangladesh National Party* favors economic liberalization and a conservative Muslim orientation, in contrast to the traditionally socialist and pro-Indian leanings of the *Awami League*. Although discredited by revelations of corruption during Ershad's years, his *Jatiya Party* retains seats in parliament, more a collection of aspiring politicians than an ideological force.

Fundamentalist Muslims form the *Jamaat-i Islami*, founded by the radical Islamic theorist Syed Abul Ala Maududi. Its leaders' murky roles during the independence struggle remain a complication. Golam Azam, its leader in the 1990s, had opposed Bangladesh's independence, and for years he lived in Dhaka as a Paki-

Bangladesh

The bicycle-rickshaws of bustling Dhaka.

stani. Nevertheless, the party joined the *BNP* coalition in 2001. Like many other politicians, its leader was arrested on corruption charges in 2008. In 2012, Golam Azam, the current leaders, and several top members of the *Jamaat* were charged with war crimes, thus crippling the leadership of a traditional ally of the *BNP*.

Culture: For the three-quarters of the population directly involved in farming, plus the small-town merchants, craftsmen and officials, life revolves around the agricultural seasons. The typical farmer lives with his large family in a simple hut of thatch and mud built on a low mound of earth for protection against monsoon floods. Since the land is extremely fertile, a very small plot can be one man's farm. He sells the produce from his little farm at one of the small towns located on the intersections of waterways. He can afford no modern luxuries; his main entertainment is sitting with his family and friends, talking about the day's events and problems.

Reflecting the poverty of the country, only 40% of the population is literate, with the rate for women half that for men. Fortunately, widespread primary education is increasing the rate for each: roughly 75% of all children receive some formal education.

Besides vocational and professional institutes, there are several universities, the largest of them the University of Dhaka. Students clashed with police in 1992, after the government approved a law to punish those caught cheating on final exams with five to ten years in prison. Although other students recognize that widespread cheating diminishes the respectability of their degrees, 4,000 students were expelled in 2000 for cheating on the English exam required for university graduation.

Despite Bangladesh's staggering population density, it has only a handful of large cities. With the allure of a capital city's opportunities, Metropolitan Dhaka's population has passed the 12 million mark, and it consumes about half the electricity produced in the country. Ringed by rivers, the city was forced to expand upwards rather than outwards and recently experienced a building boom. Inadequate control of building permits and the illegal construction of high rises near the airport have led international aviation authorities to demand their removal. The second largest city is Chittagong, the nation's main port, with more than a million residents.

Numbering over 140 million, the country's Muslims form the world's fourth largest Muslim community, following those of Indonesia, Pakistan and India. Nevertheless, the Provisional Constitution made the nation a secular state that provides all religions with equal legal standing. Public holidays include Muslim holy days, Christmas, and various Hindu and Buddhist festivals. Islam itself shows a national coloring here, influenced by some Hindu and other ideas.

Intolerant Treatment of Women

The recent rise of fundamentalist Islamic groups has coincided with increasing intolerance. Often those who suffered were women. For example, Dhaka University re-imposed the "Sunset Law," a 1922 regulation requiring women students to return to their dormitories before darkness. The restriction, said one faculty member, was "a shield to protect the women's chastity." Outside the university, women's participation in sport has been condemned, and women swimmers were excluded from a swim meet after threats of violence. "Eve teasing," the often sexual harassment of women, has become a sport for some young men, who taunt, inflict verbal abuse, and stalk women, especially those not veiled. Fearful of reprisals and shame, victims may not report crimes to the police.

Other women suffer even worse. Some have been murdered, others driven to suicide. A few hundred women (and men) annually suffer acid attacks that disfigure their faces, usually because of land disputes against their families or by rejected suitors. Fortunately, after special fast-track courts were established to impose the death penalty on offenders quickly, the number of these assaults has fallen.

Society victimizes women in other ways. Composed of village elders and clerics, village arbitration councils designed to settle property disputes illegally ordered whippings or even stoning for several girls and women charged with sexual immorality. Other women and young girls are victimized into debauchery: according to police reports, kidnappers annually sell some 10,000 into brothels, some abroad.

Death by hanging is the sentence commonly demanded by Islamic militants for both Taslima Nasreen and Farida Rahman. The latter, a Member of Parliament, aroused the ire of fundamentalist Muslims when she noted that there would be no harm in allowing women to inherit more than the small percentage set by the Qur'an. Nasreen, a feminist whose novel of the plight of Hindus in Bangladesh became a bestseller, denied that she had proposed that the Qur'an be revised to fit the modern world. Charged with blasphemy, she overcame her legal problems, but fled the country because of threats on her life.

There are two principal dialects of the Bangla language. The old literary one is much admired but not understood by ordinary Bengalis, while the modern colloquial, understood and used by both the educated and uneducated is the country's language. It is written in a form of the *Nagari* alphabet, widely used for the languages of India.

Children fortunate enough to attend school

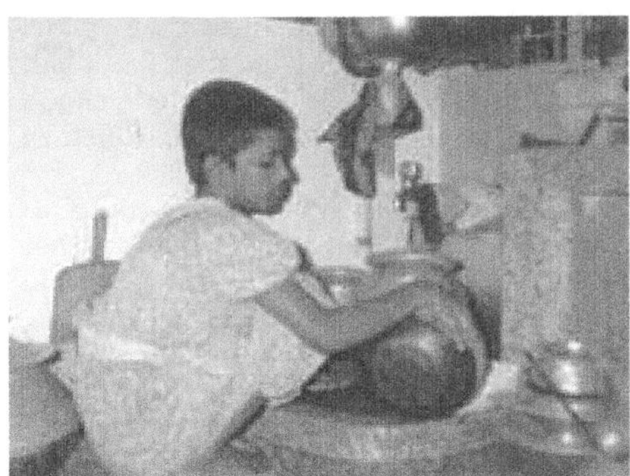

Thousands of children work as domestic help

The earliest preserved literature in Bangla dates to the 14th century. Until two centuries ago, it was only verse, intended to be recited or sung. Bangla prose began in 1800 when a missionary, with the help of native assistants, translated the Bible into that language. The vast literary outpouring of the 19th and 20th centuries included novels and drama. The short stories and poems of Rabindranath Tagore received the Nobel Prize for literature in 1913, one of the first awards for a non-European language. Besides modern approaches such as this, there remain the traditional poetry and other aspects of the rich culture of Bengal.

However flourishing, the Bangla culture is not the culture of all inhabitants. During the partition of India in 1947, thousands of Muslims from Bihar and elsewhere moved to East Bengal. Loyal to a Muslim state rather than a Bengali one, they tended to support Pakistan during the conflict in 1971. With Pakistan unable, or perhaps unwilling, to bear the cost of these two-time refugees, about 300,000 of them live destitute in camps in Bangladesh, awaiting some distant solution to their lives of desperation. A high court decision in 2008 granted citizenship to those born in the country after 1950, an important step towards greater rights and economic opportunity.

Other non-Bengalis live in the Chittagong Hills, where some local tribes practice Buddhism, Christianity or Hinduism. Violence flared in the 1970s after Bengalis moved into the area seeking land. By the mid-1990s, the scattered violence of 20 years had caused over 8,000 deaths, and thousands of tribesmen fled to India and Burma. Following a peace treaty in 1997, some 35,000 refugees returned from India, but slow implementation of the accord leaves some observers fearing renewed violence.

Economy: Even today, most Bangladeshis live on farms. Across most of the country, the climate and soil combine to produce good yields of rice, and in years without catastrophes more than 10 million tons are harvested. However, this is not enough to feed the large population, and output falls after devastating floods or cyclones. The government has made valiant efforts to increase food production—for instance by digging irrigation canals to water an extra crop in the dry season. Much food still must be imported, and paid for partly by foreign aid.

The country's traditional export crop was jute, the tough plant fiber used to make burlap and rope. When industrial nations turned increasingly to synthetic fibers, world demand for jute declined, and Bangladesh suffered falling profits and cuts in wages and employment. After continuing losses, in 2002 the government closed the Adamjee Jute Mills, at one stroke putting 19,000 workers out of work. For decades the leading source of jobs and exports, the jute industry now employs only a few thousand workers. That may represent the low point in jute's fortunes, because growing environmental concerns encourage the use of jute in packaging, rather than plastic bags, and scientists are discovering uses for the fiber in textiles and carpeting. Annual exports now exceed $1 billion.

The country's poverty results partly from misguided economic policies, past and present. Seeking to raise the standard of living by encouraging industry, early in 1972 the new country took over the businesses, banks and industries owned by West Pakistanis. It then nationalized most other foreign trade, banks and basic industry, leaving only some British tea and jute interests privately owned.

During two decades of mismanagement, few government-owned businesses ever earned a profit. Sectors like telecommunications, electricity and banking still remain inefficient under government ownership. The nationally-owned Biman Bangladesh Airlines managed its fleet of aging aircraft so poorly that it reportedly lost $80,000 on each flight to New York, owed millions of dollars for jet fuel, and could not pay for repairs on several aircraft. The airline cut routes and jobs severely in 2007 to reduce losses.

Privatization and large-scale investment by Japanese and Korean firms once seemed the best hope for economic expansion, but instead, during the 1990s employment grew in an unexpected way. Small and mostly locally-owned factories sprang up to employ growing numbers of workers to produce coats, dresses and other garments for export. To cut costs, the industry used cramped spaces, low safety standards, and inadequate wiring. Additional floors were often added, well beyond the zoning approval. Fires broke out frequently, with employees sometimes trapped by padlocked exits; 100 employees died in a factory fire in 2012.

Because Bangladeshi garments were not subject to international quotas, output often rose at 10%–20% per year. The industry is vital to exports, providing 80% of all export earnings, valued at nearly $25 billion each year. It has also improved social conditions by providing vital income for women. However, wages have remained abysmal, for some women less than $1 per day.

Touched off by dismissals at one factory, strikes over wages and safety issues broke out in 2006, and some 80 factories were set ablaze before promises were made of higher pay. Workers demanded higher wages again in 2010, up to $72 per month, still among the lowest in the world, and about one-sixth the amount necessary to house and feed a family of four. In response, the minimum wage was raised from $20 to $36 per month for a 60–70 hour week. After two years of inflation, in 2012 workers again sought higher pay.

By 2013, the Rana Plaza building collapsed, killing over 1,100 workers and injuring 2,500. It was one of the world's worst industrial disasters and focused global attention on the industry and its safety. The Rana Plaza housed several textile factories and symbolized short-

Water, water, everywhere . . . river traffic

comings that had long been denounced. For example, the top three floors violated city building codes, and the day before the collapse, cracks were visible in the walls.

Although it employed nearly four million workers in 4,500 factories, the industry clearly failed to enforce reasonable safety standards. The country's deep levels of corruption left government regulation also ineffective. Months after the Rana Plaza disaster, labor unions and many multinational companies that purchase the exports finally reached a legally-enforceable agreement to inspect the factories that produce their garments. Because the foreign firms will stand liable for later failures, they have strong reasons to ensure safety. Unfortunately for the factory workers, major U.S. importers such as Wal-Mart, Sears, and The Gap prefer a non-binding agreement with a smaller role for labor unions.

For men born to poor families—the vast majority in the country—the route to prosperity often involved working abroad, particularly in the oil states around the Persian Gulf. Some six million held jobs abroad in 2008, mostly as laborers in construction and domestic service. Unfortunately, the world recession left tens of thousands of the migrant workers without jobs, and often still owing substantial debts to the middlemen who had arranged their overseas employment

A decade ago, discoveries of natural gas, both onshore and offshore, offered hopes for potential economic benefits. However, a great dispute arose over the proposal to export the gas to India. The foreign companies involved in discovering and developing the fields desired to do so, partly to sell in a more prosperous market. However, nationalists strongly opposed such sales, arguing that with only 20% of homes connected to the electric system, there was a huge market for the gas in power plants as well as in producing fertilizer and replacing gasoline in buses and trucks.

Following the unwillingness of the government to permit exports, Shell and Unocal, the largest companies involved, sold their interests to smaller companies more willing to make risky investments. The lack of investment reduced supplies below electric generating needs by 2010, leading to daily limits on air conditioning.

One major nonpolitical issue facing the government is arsenic poison that threatens the water supply of nearly half the population. The arsenic occurs naturally in the soil, and water from deep wells drilled to deliver water with lower bacteria levels frequently carries traces of arsenic. Though not immediately fatal, the arsenic levels often cause scattered tumors and may lead to cancer; some two million people suffer from arsenic poisoning. In 2006 scientists at Rice University in the U.S. discovered that the arsenic would attach to particles of iron oxide (i.e., rust) about 1/5,000 the width of a human hair. In turn, a simple magnet could then remove the iron oxide, but it will take years to provide filters to the 25 million people who knowingly poison themselves by drinking impure water.

Roughly 50 million Bangladeshis exist below the poverty line, and their daily incomes of $1 mean they often survive on only one meal a day. As always, the poorest are usually women and children; these paid a large price when political chaos interrupted work and deterred investment. By any standard, Bangladesh remains one of the poorest nations in the world, and public health statistics illustrate the poverty. A majority of children are malnourished and stunted. Sixty percent of the population lacks access to even simple health clinics, and medical challenges abound, including some 2,000 deaths per year from rabies.

Nevertheless, there are some success stories. In the mid-1980s, children composed 40% of the workforce, a rate that officially fell below 10% by the end of the decade. In 2009, estimates suggested that about half of all children aged 6–10 attended school, though only 10% of teenagers enrolled in high school.

One reason that some families could afford to have their children studying rather than working was the Grameen Bank. Founded by Muhammad Yunus in 1976, the bank specializes in making small loans to poor individuals who have productive ideas but lack property to use as security for a loan. In 2006, when he and the bank received the Nobel Peace Prize, Yunus's microcredit program had nearly 7 million customers, the vast majority of them women who repaid their loans on time. Microcredit thus empowered those at the bottom of the social scale and stimulated a revolution of sorts.

By 2009, nearly a dozen organizations, including internationally-recognized agencies like CARE and World Vision, had made loans to some 20 million borrowers. However, the world economic crisis, natural disasters, over-borrowing, and simple bad luck left many borrowers unable to repay without selling their productive investments or removing their children from school and sending them to work.

The Future: As expected, Sheikh Hasina and her *Awami League* triumphed in an election boycotted by all significant opposition parties. She now rules with a massive parliamentary majority, but her victory lacks legitimacy in Western opinion and much of the 80% of the electorate who did not bother to vote. A few months of appointed rather than elected government would have been a small price to pay for elections considered fair by the losers.

Unfortunately for its citizens, the purpose of government in Bangladesh is to reap the benefits of office rather than pursue the national interest and development. As a result, operations such as the Grameen Bank under its founder Mohammad Yunus will attract unfavorable attention from governments suspicious of rival centers of power. Until such attitudes change, Bangladesh will not become an Asian Tiger economy, no matter how low its wages.

The country's challenges remain enormous. All prime ministers have desired to tame rising river levels, which threaten annual flooding. Two-thirds of the population lacks access to electricity, and poverty is so vast that many families depend on child labor for regular meals. The sheer magnitude of problems, competing demands from interest groups, and a fractured political system render government ineffective in taking critical decisions over energy and corruption. The pace of real change falls far behind construction of tall apartment blocks in Dhaka.

"Two women in Maijpara" Source: World Bank Photo by Chernush

The Kingdom of Bhutan

Taktsang ("The Tiger's Nest") Monastery, situated high in a cliff near Paro in western Bhutan, was destroyed by fire in April 1998. The King has called the incident a national disaster and promised to rebuild it. According to legend, Padma Sambhava—or Guru Rinpoche, as he is also known—flew here on a tiger to meditate when he was introducing Buddhism into Tibet and Bhutan from India in the 8th century A.D. The monastery was built on the site at a later date.

Photo by Edwin Bernbaum

Area: 14,812 square miles (38,364 sq. km.).
Population: 750,000.
Capital City: Thimphu (pop. 100,000, estimated).
Climate: Frigid in the high mountains, temperate with good rainfall in the central valley and extremely hot and humid with torrential rains on the south.
Neighboring Countries: India (South and East); China (North).
Time Zone: GMT +6.
Official Language: Dzongkha (Tibetan dialect), with English the language of schooling.
Other Principal Tongues: Sarchopkha, a Tibetan dialect, and Nepalese in the south.
Ethnic Background: Ngalop or Bhutanese (60%), Sharchops of Indo-Mongolian origin in the East (20%), Nepalese in the southwest (15%), and smaller aboriginal groups.
Principal Religions: Mahayana Buddhism (80%) and Hinduism.
Chief Commercial Products: Hydroelectric power, lumber and wood products, cement, fruit, rice, yaks and other livestock, woven textiles and other handicrafts.
Major Trading Partner: India.
Currency: 1 Ngultrum = 100 chetrum.
Historical Status: Independent, though subject to guidance from Britain and then India.
Date of U.N. Membership: 1971.
National Day: December 17, honoring the first king (1907).
Chief of State: Jigme Khesar Namgyal Wangchuck, the *Druk Gyalpo* ("Dragon King").
Prime Minister: Tshering Tobgay (2013).
National Flag: A rectangular field of yellow and vermillion, divided diagonally with a large white serpent-like dragon in the center.
Gross Domestic Product: $2.2 billion (at current prices); $5.6 billion (purchasing power parity).
GDP per capita: $7,500 (PPP).

A small nation squeezed between two giants, Bhutan shares the cultural of Tibet across its Chinese border, while its trade and political alignment lie with India to the south.

Geographically, Bhutan resembles Nepal—both are located on the southern slopes of the Himalayan Mountains. Bhutan's rivers rise in the Great Himalayas in the north and flow southward through intensively-cultivated valleys. The rivers all flow into India and empty into the Brahmaputra River.

This land of rugged natural beauty presents a striking contrast between the snow-clad northern peaks, the lower mountain slopes covered with woods, and the dense, lush undergrowth of the southern foothills. Deer, tigers, elephants and other wildlife live mostly in the foothills.

History: Few documentary sources provide details of the early history of this land. In the 9th century, Tibetan-speaking peoples entered the rugged mountain valleys. Followers of Mahayana Buddhism, by the 15th century they structured their society around fortified monasteries known as dzongs, and maintained links with Tibet. However, there was limited central authority the leading lama, the Dharma Raja, and raids against the expanding British East India Company ended with a treaty in 1865 that cost Bhutan territory, but gained recognition of its autonomy and a British subsidy.

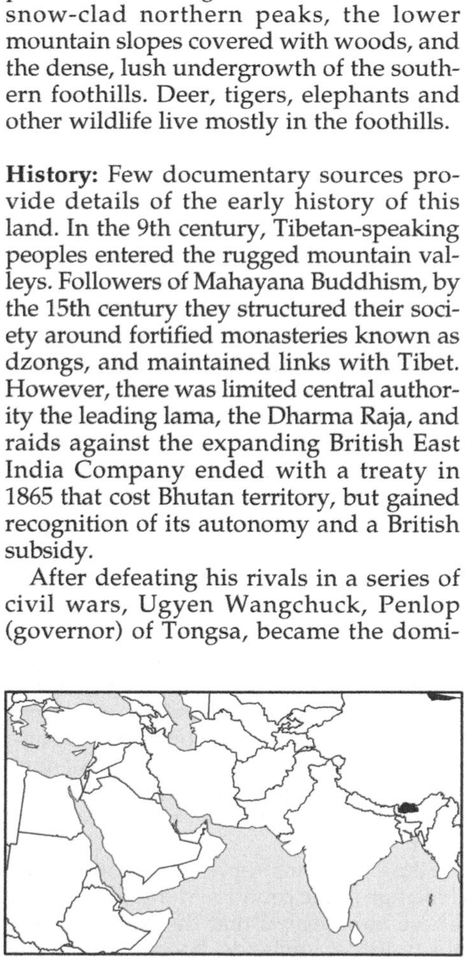

After defeating his rivals in a series of civil wars, Ugyen Wangchuck, Penlop (governor) of Tongsa, became the domi-

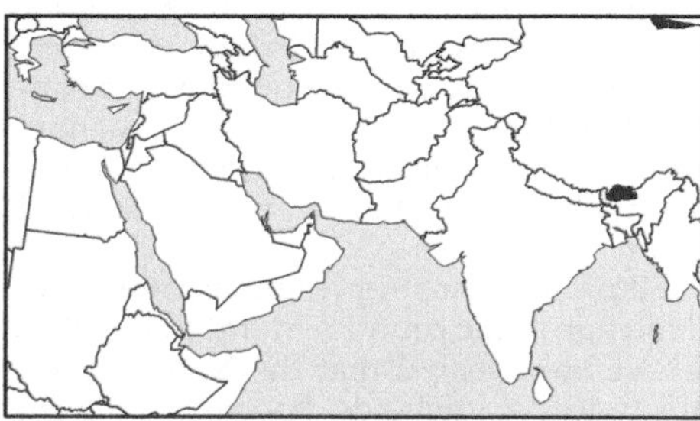

nant power, and in 1907 an assembly of lamas, chiefs and officials elected him the country's first hereditary *Druk Gyalpo*, or Dragon King. Authority since then has passed from father to son.

Britain recognized Bhutan by the 1910 Treaty of Punakha, and gained authority over its foreign affairs. Bhutan signed the treaty partly in fear of Chinese claims to its territory, based on alleged Chinese control from Tibet in the 18th century. A new treaty in 1949 with India recognized Bhutan's independence and provided free trade; it was revised in 2007 to provide Bhutan more freedom in military and diplomatic matters. India provides an annual subsidy that accounts for much government revenue.

After China claimed parts of the country in the 1950s, defense relations were strengthened with India. The border with China is not demarcated and remains closed, but Chinese troops allegedly crossed it in 2005 and built roads. Bhutan's joining the United Nations marked the nation's full independence (1971).

Until the mid-20th century, Bhutan imposed a rigid isolation upon itself, so that it remained as closed to the world as Tibet. However, when Jigme Dorji Wangchuck became Druk Gyalpo in 1952, he introduced changes. He freed slaves, ended the custom of making his subjects bow down before him with their faces on the floor, set up schools, restricted land ownership, modernized the system of land taxes and established the Tsongdu, or National Assembly.

When Jigme Dorji Wangchuck died in 1972, his 17-year-old son, Jigme Singye Wangchuck, ascended the throne. Under the new ruler the country continued its slow awakening to the modern world. In 1988, responding to public worries about the succession, the king married publicly the four sisters he previously had wed privately. The celebration distinctly echoed the king's desire to preserve Bhutan's society from outside influences: foreign diplomats were not invited.

Two changes in 1999 brought the population into direct contact with the world outside when Bhutan inaugurated internet service and lifted its ban on the corrupting influence of television. The government intended the single channel to present national arts and culture, rather than rebroadcast Hollywood or Indian programs. However, many viewers preferred to connect to cable, so when a wrestling channel and American music channels enticed too many Bhutanese, the government blocked them.

Ethnic tensions represent a continuing challenge to the country. Many ethnic Bhutanese have feared that the Nepalese minority in the lowlands, boosted by illegal Indian and Nepali migrants across poorly guarded frontiers, threatened to become a majority. In response, the monarchy classified them as aliens and vastly reduced the official estimate of population. As part of educational reforms, the required teaching of Nepali in schools was dropped.

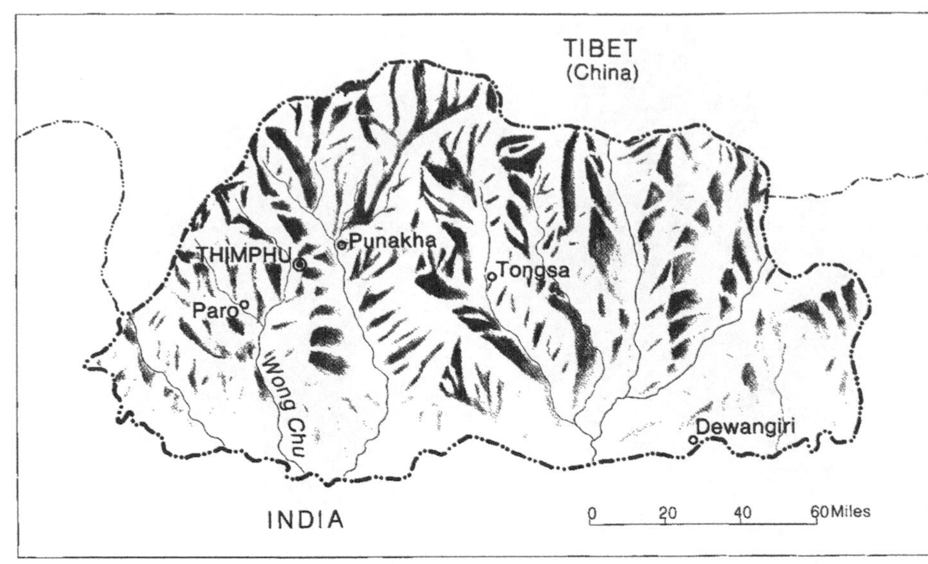

In 1990 riots and demonstrations broke out in southern Bhutan, apparently organized by the (illegal) *Bhutan People's Party* and other Nepali groups. Police and troops repressed the disturbances, and some 100,000 people sought refuge in Nepal. The king took steps to reduce tensions, including reopening schools and reappointing some officials of Nepali origin. The U.S. has offered to accept over half of the refugees, whose camps have been infiltrated by Maoists and other extremists.

In 2004 Bhutan became the only country to ban the sale of cigarettes and chewing tobacco, though smoking itself is not yet illegal. Bhutan's first ruler banned the use of tobacco in government buildings, but modern arguments for the ban revolved around economics: the government pays medical care, and can ill-afford to subsidize unhealthy habits. Health authorities also fear another social danger. The stresses and opportunities of modernization have encouraged abuse of alcohol. By one estimate 30% of hospital deaths are due to alcoholism.

Jigme Khesar Namgyal Wangchuck, the Druk Gyalpo or "Dragon King"

King Jigme Singye Wangchuck unexpectedly abdicated in 2006 in favor of his eldest son, Jigme Khesar Namgyal Wangchuck. Young and educated in the U.S. and Britain, he had won respect in the kingdom and popularity on official trips abroad. His coronation in 2008 proved a lavish affair by local standards, with thousands of foreign dignitaries and media personality. In 2011 he married a commoner, Jetsun Pema, in an elegant ceremony.

Politics: Though by tradition an absolute ruler, King Jigme Singye Wangchuck yielded additional powers in 1998 and then extended democracy with the 2005 constitution. It retains the monarch as the symbol of the state—but he or she must retire at age 65.

A fascinating mixture of tradition and modernity, the constitution was released on the web to facilitate discussion. It stresses the spiritual heritage as well as the government's responsibility to protect biodiversity and maintain a minimum forest cover of 60%. Legislative authority resides in a parliament of two houses, the elected National Assembly and the nonpartisan National Council. To answer the vexing question of political parties, the National Assembly includes two, and only two, political parties. The leader of the larger serves as prime minister.

Elections in 2007–08 determined the members of first the National Council and then the National Assembly. Two parties contested the National Assembly elections, the *People's Democratic Party (PDP)* closely linked to the queen mother, and the *Druk Phuensum Tshogpa (DPT)* or *Bhutan Peace and Prosperity Party*, headed by a commoner, Jigmi Thinley. He claimed to represent ordinary Bhutanese and became prime minister after his party won 44 of the 47 seats.

During the 2013 elections, the opposition *PDP* downplayed Gross National Happiness and attacked features like Pedestrian Day, a culturally-inspired ban on town traffic that burdened businesses. The party promised prosperity, and promised expensive items for everyone: abolishing preliminary civil service exams, benefits for the aged, a rototiller for every village, better maternity leaves, higher pay for government workers, and full employment for youth. It won a strong majority, and its U.S. educated leader, Tshering Tobgay became prime minister. India quickly restored its subsidy; it had been withheld, perhaps partly to pressure against warming relations with China.

In office and faced with a crisis over the national debt, Tobgay responded with an austerity program, promising to live at home and pool cars for cabinet use. He relaxed the ban on wearing foreign-style clothes and openly discussed economic issues like jobs and overcoming poverty. The tourist industry, the nation's largest, felt it appropriate to discuss opening the country to mass tourism.

Prime Minister Tshering Tobgay

Culture: The population is comprised mostly of hardy tillers of the soil and herders. They live in small communities scattered in the fertile valleys cut deeply into the rugged mountains of the central and southern part of the country. No one lives permanently in the high mountains of the north, while those who live in the narrow tropical fringe along the southern border lead a way of life quite different from the rest of Bhutan. Citizens are required by law to wear traditional dress; a quick trip to the pharmacy in jeans and T-shirt may result in arrest.

No real urban centers exist yet. Communities tend to cluster around a dzong, found in every major valley and settled region. A dzong was originally a great fort built on a strategic spot commanding a river. In times of war, people from the surrounding area sought refuge there. After warlords passed from the scene, dzongs came to serve as administrative centers, monasteries, or even warehouses. Many of them have prayer halls with elaborately carved interiors, walls covered with religious paintings, statues of Buddha and quarters for officials, lamas and guilds.

The new national capital of Thimphu has been constructed beside the great Tashi Chho Dzong, once the headquarters of powerful penlops. Thimphu reflects the country's determination to modernize in its own fashion. All buildings must be constructed in the traditional style, and the only traffic light was removed. However, the government provides TV broadcasts, and the newspaper, originally a public relations sheet, appears in Dzongkha, English, and Nepali.

Economy: Unlike most of the world, where the economy as measured by the Gross Domestic Product (GDP) is considered the chief measure of well-being, Bhutan values an even less precise measure, the Gross National Happiness (GNH). Given the prevailing Buddhist philosophy, this stresses inner peace and satisfaction, rather than material wealth, and a rise in the suicide rate is therefore a matter of serious concern.

Government policy encourages people to remain on the land, essentially as small-scale farmers and herdsmen who nevertheless enjoy access to electricity, simple medical care, and educa-

Capital with a difference: Thimphu has no traffic lights.

tion. While this preserves the culture and therefore GNH, the small, inefficient farms cannot compete in price with imported grains and meat. To protect its small farmers, Bhutan has not joined the World Trade Organization.

Given the topography, the small country produces a wide range of foods, ranging from rice and tropical fruits through citrus and temperate-climate vegetables. The mountain slopes provide abundant pasturage for livestock. Cattle are common up to more than 12,000 feet above sea level in summer, and yaks are grazed at even higher elevations.

Since 1961 a series of five-year plans have encouraged development, and usually stressed investment in roads, education, agriculture, health, minerals and hydroelectric power. Exports of electricity to India now provide government revenues and foreign exchange. Recent policy favored privatizing the ownership of several corporations, including the cement and insurance companies. The goal of privatization was to encourage a modern middle class, because unlike government-run corporations in most countries, these were profitable monopolies.

After building two hotels to provide lodging for foreign dignitaries attending the King's coronation in 1974, Bhutan cautiously permitted a small tourist industry to develop, and two five-star hotels were opened in 2005. Travelers may enter by one of only two ways: a difficult land route, or by regularly scheduled air service to Paro by Druk Air.

In deference to local sensitivities, temples and other holy places were closed to tourists in 1988, but the Dzongs are still accessible. In addition to cultural tours through Dzongs, town and villages, there are also organized treks along steep mountain trails to isolated mountain valleys. Added to concern about tourism's sometimes corrosive effects on culture, traditions, and values, environmentalists worry about its pollution.

To preserve its natural resources, Bhutan has banned hunting wildlife, prohibited lumbering, and provided a special route for migrating elephants. The government even warned against the cutting of young trees for use as poles for Buddhist prayer flags believed to guide the dead. However, reports of erosion and polluted water in some locations suggest that population pressure may degrade Bhutan just as it does India and Nepal.

The Future: Bhutan features one of the last national contests between preserving traditions and the modern culture of materialism and pleasure. Most societies lose this race, as television, videos, and even education corrode long-established values. In Bhutan's case, materialistic pursuits clash strongly with the personal inner peace so important to the philosophy of the country.

King Jigme and his father have stressed the country's uniqueness. Tshering Tobgay, the new prime minister, emphasizes material concerns like poverty. He and his party back changes that weaken the symbols of traditional life. Expect at least a polite clash between the two perspectives.

Farm buildings in Bhutan Photo by Richard Harrington

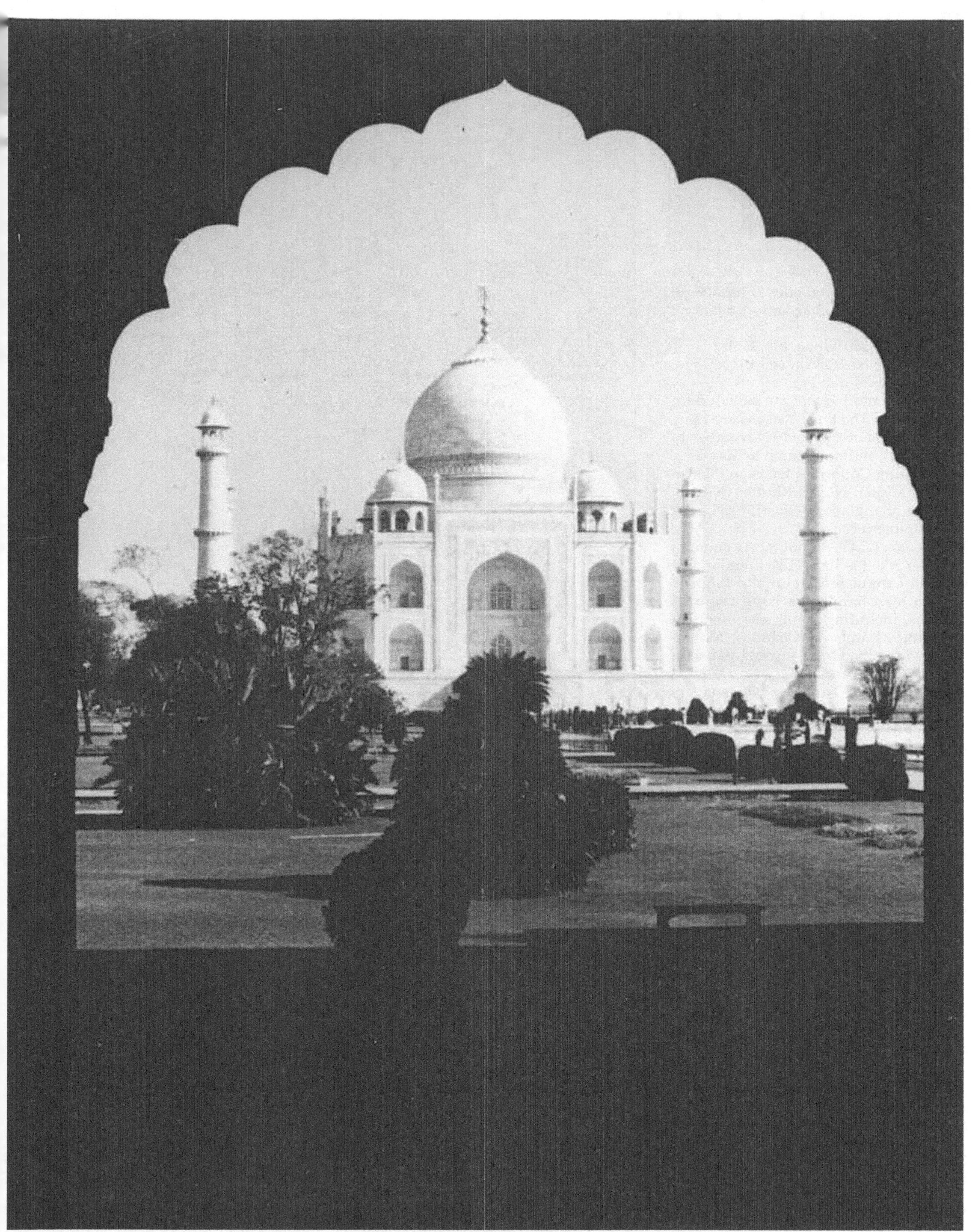

The Taj Mahal at Agra

The Republic of India

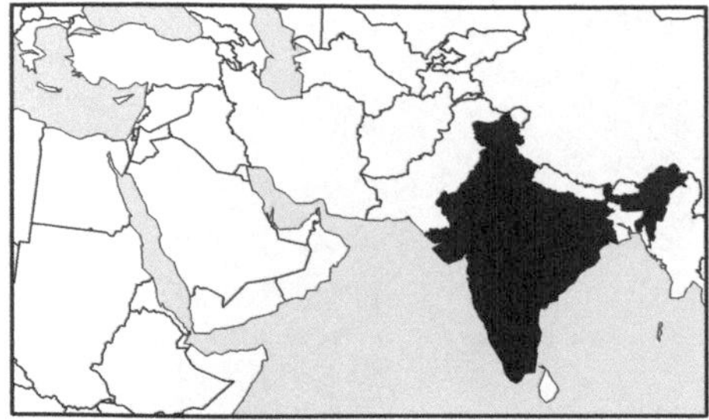

Area: 1,210,700 square miles (3,136,500 sq. km.), including Indian sector of Jammu and Kashmir.
Population: 1.260 billion, est. 2014.
Capital City: New Delhi (pop. 3 million; with Delhi, 14 million).
Climate: Tropical except for the northern mountains. The three seasons are rainy (June to October), cool (November to February), and hot (March to May).
Neighboring Countries: Pakistan (Northwest); China, Nepal, Bhutan (North); Burma, Bangladesh (East); Sri Lanka (off southern coast).
Time Zone: GMT + 5 hours. At noon, in New York, it is 10:30 P.M. in India.
Official Languages: Hindi and English. Seventeen languages have regional status, including Assamese, Bengali, Gujarati, Kannada, Kashmiri, Malayalam, Marathi, Oriya, Punjabi, Sanskrit, Tamil, Telugu and Urdu.
Other Principal Tongues: Newspapers within India are reportedly published in at least 49 languages.
Ethnic Background: Communities are differentiated primarily on the basis of language and religion; differences in physical characteristics do not generally correspond with these communal distinctions.
Principal Religions: Hinduism (84%), Islam (11%), Christianity (2%), Sikhism (0.7%), Buddhism (0.7%).
Chief Commercial Products: Textiles, clothing, gems and jewelry, steel, cement, automobiles, machinery, computer software, motorcycles, processed food, consumer appliances, coal, chemicals, and various metals.
Main Agricultural Produce and Livestock: Rice, wheat, barley, potatoes, corn (maize), cassava, bananas, coconuts, beans, mangoes, tea, coffee, tobacco, pepper, sugar cane, cattle, goats, buffalo, sheep, pigs and poultry.
Major Trading Partners: U.S., Japan, U.K., Germany, Russia.
Currency: Rupee (= 100 paisa).
Former Colonial Status: British Indian Empire (1858–1947).
National Day: January 26, Republic Day.
Chief of State: Pranab Mukherjee, President (2012).

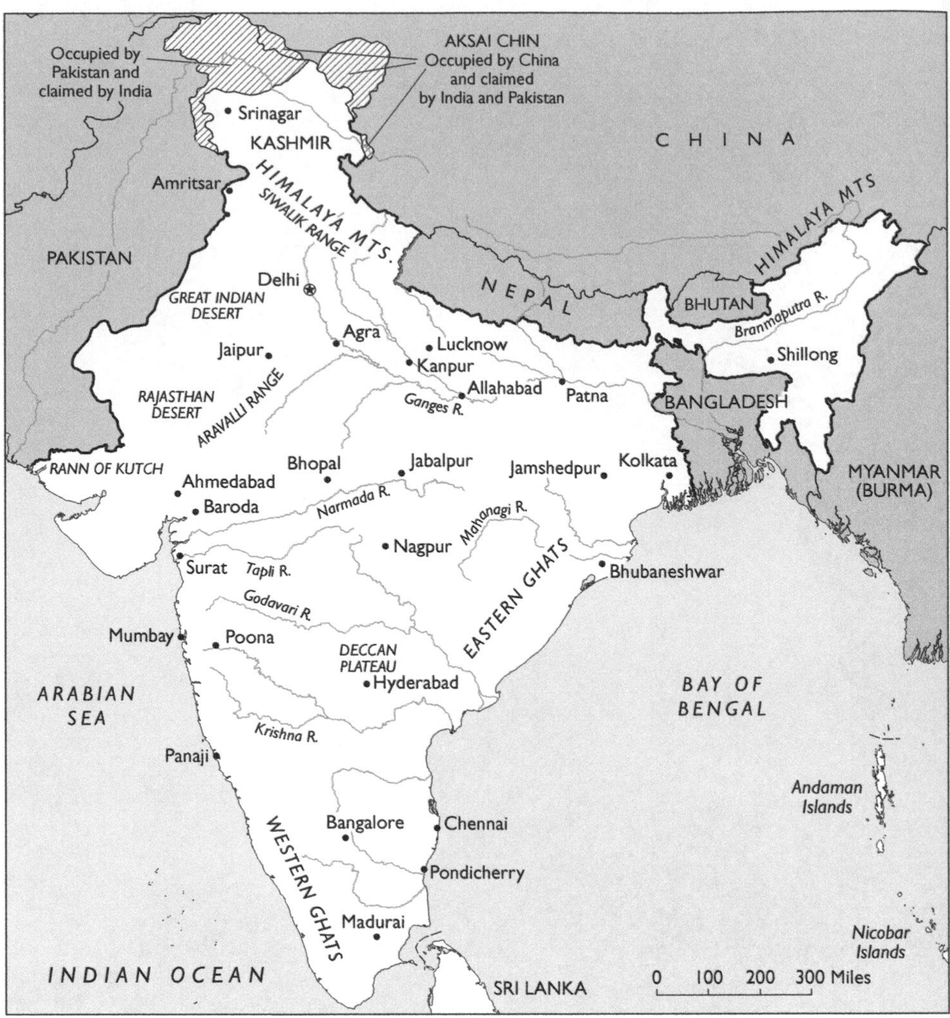

Head of Government: Narendra Modi, Prime Minister (2014).
National Flag: A tricolor with equal horizontal bands of deep saffron, white and dark green. Centered on the white stripe is the wheel of Asoka in navy blue.
Gross Domestic Product: $2,000 billion (at current prices); $5,425 billion (purchasing power parity).
GDP per capita: $4,300 (PPP).

Second only to China in population, India occupies most of the South Asian subcontinent and ranks seventh among the world's nations in area. The size of its population, combined with its historical and cultural heritage developed over thousands of years, often overwhelm the imagination and make comparisons difficult. For example, India's population exceeds that of all Africa south of the Sahara, or more than the population of all the other countries in this volume combined. Indeed, the annual growth in the number of India's citizens exceeds the population of most countries in this volume. A land of stunning contrasts in geography as well as the quality of human life, India represents a major cultural force in the modern world. In areas as diverse as religion, food, and computer software engineering, India's influence greatly exceeds its boundaries.

Three major topographical regions divide the subcontinent. On the northern borderlands tower the Himalayas, the perpetual snow and ice of their summits overlooking lesser peaks and foothills at their base. Rivers and streams from the mountains flow south to the great plain that provides a home for much of the country's population. Centered on the Ganges River, the plain is also watered by the Indus on the west and the Brahmaputra on the east. The third region is the peninsula that juts out into the ocean, a triangle of plateaus, valleys and mountains. The coastal plains around this region are moist and tropical, particularly in the narrow plain between the Arabian Sea and the Western Ghat Mountains, and densely populated.

Extreme variations in rainfall and temperatures produced great variations in vegetation. On average only a few inches

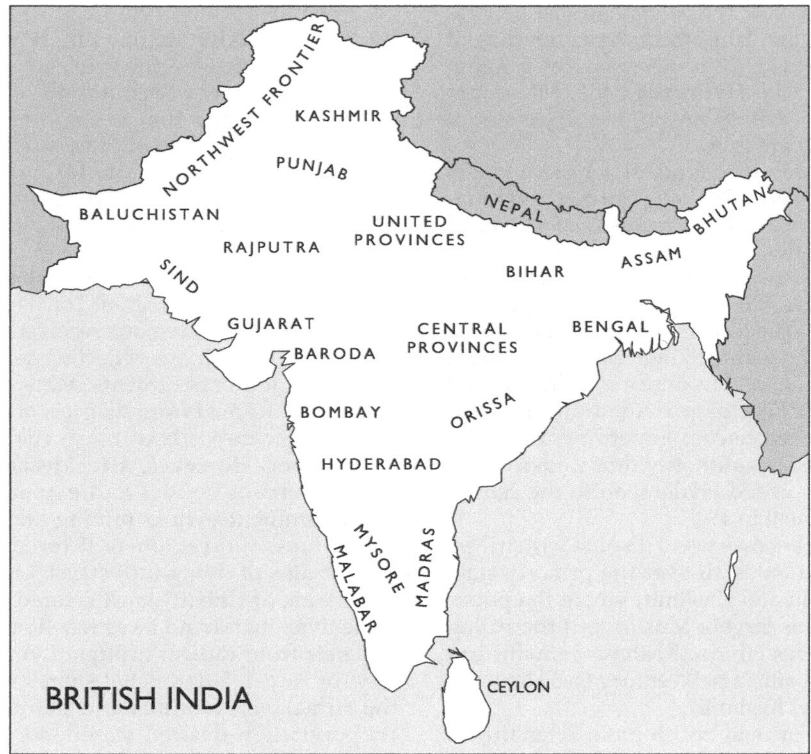

fall annually in the western desert of Rajasthan, but the record in one village of Assam approached *40 feet* of rainfall in a year. The northeast is typically the wettest region; it and the ocean side of the Western Ghats generally receive more than 100 inches of precipitation annually. Most of the rain falls during the summer, brought by the southwest monsoon. The Ganges Plain, the northwest and the coast of Tamil Nadu also receive varying amounts of winter rainfall.

The land and the climate show great contrasts—and so do the people. Religious practices vary greatly within the Hindu majority and there are also followers of a multitude of other religions. Folkways differ considerably in various parts of the country, or even between communities in the same city. Sometime allegiances to language, religion, and ethnic group threaten the unity of India. However, a functioning democracy and economic integration reinforce the national unity forged in the independence struggle against the British.

History: While India possesses a cultural tradition that extends back for several thousand years, the formation of the present nation began only with the British conquest (see Historical Background) some 250 years ago. By bringing many small states and petty princes under its rule, Britain laid the foundation for both the Republic of India and other nations in the region.

As regions fell under East India Company rule, they desperately needed reform. India was overtaxed and undereducated, with crime rampant and the arts in decay. Several Indian practices offended British opinion, from the several hundred annual burnings of widows and other ritual murders to values expressed by idol worship. However, British reforms and the seizure of several Indian states aroused both Muslim and Hindu opinion by the 1850s, especially in the north, and led directly to the so-called Indian Mutiny of 1857 (see Historical Background). Surprising the British by both its extent and its ferocity, the Mutiny drew strength from traditional groups outside the army as well as native troops from both Hindu and Muslim backgrounds. Although the rebellion was crushed, Parliament ended the East India Company's rule and replaced it with British colonial administration.

The Mutiny produced major changes. Loyal ethnic groups thereafter played greater roles in the army, and the close contact between British officers and Indian troops built traditions that remain today. Because the princes had generally remained loyal, the policy of replacing their rule in conquered territories was abandoned in favor of close contacts with them. Land reform was set aside, and the upper classes conciliated.

The Mutiny encouraged Britain to abandon the goal of Europeanizing Indians, and the emphasis turned instead to public works to make the land more productive within the empire. The spirit of imperial grandeur led, in 1877, the government to proclaim Queen Victoria Empress of India.

Two trends in India during imperial rule deserve mention. First, colonial laws and officials provided unity for a vast region previously divided by ethnic and religious groups. A single administrative and judicial system, roads, railways and postal communications aided the physical unification. Western-style education provided a new professional class with a common language, English, and greatly contributed to a sense of unity.

Second, a national consciousness distinct from religious or social feelings arose against foreign rule. Its first outward sign was the formation in 1885 of the *Indian National Congress,* which reflected the aspirations of the new professional class. In its early years, it failed to persuade the colonial rulers to recognize its demands, and it also proved unable to incite the illiterate masses, especially villagers, to any kind of action.

Though it continued to develop among the tiny minority of Indians educated in English, nationalism had no visible effect otherwise until World War I. Then a man with rare gifts of leadership, Mohandas Karamchand Gandhi, later called *Mahatma* ("Great Soul"), returned to India as an attorney experienced as a political activist in South Africa. Unrest and occasional outbursts of violence were already beginning when his public work in India began. His insight and an ability to translate nationalist ideas into terms that had meaning for the uneducated masses of Hindus enabled him to capture the leadership of the *Indian National Congress* by 1920.

Gandhi's methods appealed to the religious nature of Hindus. Rejecting violence, the weapon he used was passive resistance, a policy of non-cooperation with colonial rule. After he imposed the necessary discipline on his followers, non-cooperation became a weapon that the British could not effectively oppose. Slowly, the *Congress* demands won concessions. Indians were allowed into the Indian civil service and were granted limited local self-government.

Although *Congress* was not intended as a Hindu party, Gandhi was not able to bridge the gap between Hindus and Muslims in India, and tensions between the two communities increased. The leading Islamic party was the *All-Muslim League* led by Muhammad Ali Jinnah. Strongly focused on the interests of the Muslim community, Jinnah and his party led the move to partition India, although recent scholarship shows the crucial role played in this decision by rebuffs from Jawaharlal Nehru, president of the *Congress Party*, in 1946.

Independence and Partition

India gained independence as a dominion in August, 1947, after British officials gained agreement for a partition plan creating a separate Muslim nation (see Pakistan). The precise borders between India and Pakistan remained a British secret, lest the inevitable violence following their announcement spoil the festivities. Jawaharlal Nehru, Gandhi's chief lieutenant in the *Congress Party*, became the country's first prime minister.

Strife between Hindus and Muslims plagued the partition. In many frontier areas the population was mixed, making it impossible to divide Muslims from Hindus and others. In the end, the British chairman of the boundary commission had to rule on the borders. The most dangerous regions were the Punjab in the northwest and Bengal in the east.

In the Punjab, savage fighting erupted between the two religious communities. Fearful of strife and of becoming a minority, Hindus on the Pakistani side of the border fled toward India while Muslims on the Indian side fled toward Pakistan. Nearly four million people took part in this two-way flight. Many thousands of them were massacred on both sides. To avert further bloodshed, Gandhi toured the country, preaching peace and cooperation between the two religious groups, an activity credited with averting massacres in Bengal. However, Hindu extremists hostile to his moderation assassinated Gandhi in 1948.

Government and Politics

A new constitution in 1950 made India a fully independent republic and broke the last formal ties to Britain. The presidency is a largely ceremonial post; real power lies with the prime minister and the lower house of the legislature, known as the *Lok Sabha* or "House of the People." In contrast, the relatively powerless members of the upper house *(Rajya Sabha* or "Council of States") reflect the state governments that select them. The Prime Minister governs with the support of Parliament, and maintaining a majority in the *Lok Sabha* regularly proved difficult after the rise of regional parties prevented any party from winning a majority.

A major challenge at independence was the formation of a modern administration. Britain had often maintained the existing rulers' authority as dependents of the British Crown, and in 1947 Britain restored the rights that the rulers had lost generations earlier. Thus, the Indian government faced some 562 "princely states" ranging in size from Hyderabad (82,000 square miles, 16 million subjects) to tiny states of a few square miles.

To retain the rights of all these rulers meant chaos. By 1949, through persuasion, threats, and promises of pensions (withdrawn some 20 years later), India had been reorganized into 30 states and territories. Two cases proved especially difficult. The Muslim ruler of Hyderabad, which had a large Hindu majority, sought independence, but unrest and the alleged abuse of Hindus provided an opportunity for the central government to send in troops. His authority thus undermined, the ruler ceded Hyderabad to the central government in 1949.

The other case was a dispute with tribesmen and Pakistan over the princely state of Jammu and Kashmir, where the population was largely Muslim but the ruling family was Hindu. Kashmir remains unresolved after a half century (see Disputed Territory: Kashmir).

Boundaries in British India, often drawn by historical circumstances, frequently separated people speaking the same language. Despite occasional ethnic violence, the government altered the political map of India. Many states disappeared, and new states were created out of parts of the old. For example, Andhra Pradesh, largely Telugu-speaking, emerged from what had been Hyderabad and Madras despite desires of some for a separate Telangana state in the interior. After a campaign of fifty years, the new state of some 35 million people was finally created in 2014.

Though generally successful, the creation of ethnic states faced difficulties in the northeast, near the borders of Tibet and Burma, where many tribes in remote areas speak their own languages and are less influenced by Hindu culture. Several small ethnic groups there desired their own states, or even independence, and sometimes adopted guerrilla warfare to achieve it. The first ethnic state, Nagaland, was created in 1961. In the 1970s and 1980s, more states followed, all among India's smallest in population. Arunachal Pradesh faces an unusual difficulty: China claimed almost the entire state, based on an interpretation of Tibet's one-time borders.

Communal conflict also occurred in the Punjab between Hindus and Sikhs, who desired their own state. The country's breadbasket, it was divided in 1966, right down to the capital, Chandigarh, between the Sikh Punjab and a Hindi-speaking state of Haryana. Nevertheless, Sikh militants demanded the creation of an independent "Khalistan." In 1983 they occupied the Golden Temple in Amritsar, the focus of Sikh religious life. When Indira Gandhi ordered the army to assault the temple, many Sikhs, not all of them militants, resisted the invasion of their shrine, and heavy casualties resulted. Sikh separatism remained acute for a decade complicated by Sikh rivalries, government repression, and unfulfilled promises of justice. Only after the return of civilian rule in the 1990s did violence subside in a conflict that claimed about 20,000 lives.

Three distinctive regions received statehood in 2000, each one reflecting separate cultures or local resentments. Mineral-rich Jharkhand, formed from districts of Bihar, holds major deposits of mica, coal, iron and copper. However, after decades of Bihar's corrupt politics and exploitation by government-owned mining and steel companies, the region is littered with the remains of dying industries. Like the tribal state of Chhattisgarh created at the same time, Jharkhand faces rebellions and violence from radical groups. Lying just west of Nepal, Uttaranchal shares with it the Himalayan foothills and mountains. Its population desired statehood to address their particular problems, including land prices forced up when rich city folk purchased vacation homes in the cooler mountains.

State governments are sometimes vast, matching their populations. The people of Uttar Pradesh, for example, outnumber any two countries of the European Union. In each state, the chief minister runs the

***Mahatma* Gandhi**

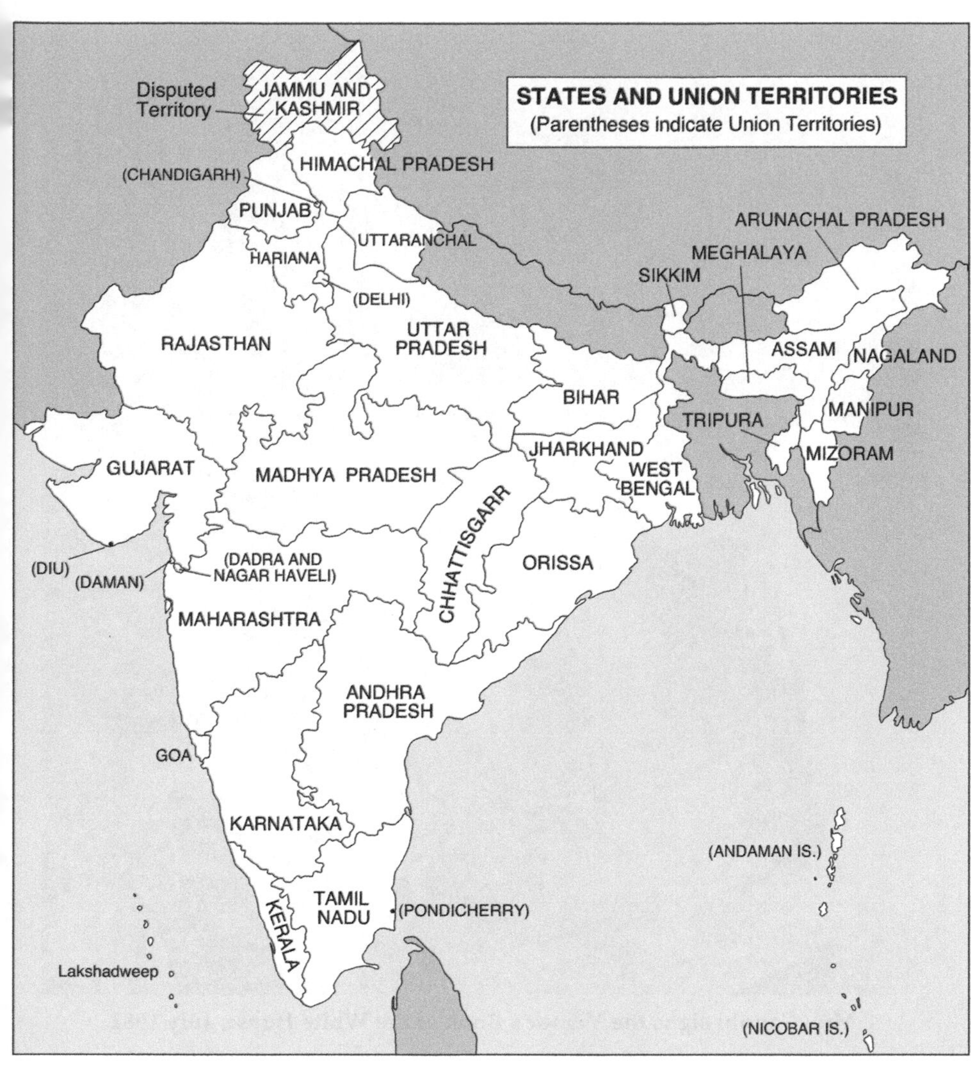

executive and is responsible to the state legislature. When a state lacks a stable government or fails to maintain calm, the president may place the state under presidential rule, usually until order is restored. Presidential rule occasionally serves to the benefit of the party ruling in New Delhi.

Nehru Sets the Country's Directions

Well before Gandhi's death, Jawaharlal Nehru had emerged as a national figure in his own right and Gandhi's successor to lead the *Congress Party* from the 1940s to the 1960s. Though an aristocrat, Nehru appeared the modern, secular socialist needed to lead India into the future. Young leftists idolized him, and by his patriotism, his integrity, and he won the hearts of the masses by his sympathy with even women and the lowest castes. Energetic, and determined, he emerged victorious from three general elections. In the words of one historian, he had a freer hand in molding policy than anyone since the Great Moguls (see Historical Background).

In domestic matters, Nehru focused on economic and social improvements, and he set the broad outlines of national policy for the next forty years. He created an Indian socialism that allowed some private enterprise but kept government ownership of heavy industry, transport, and other key sectors. A series of five-year economic plans attempted to focus on national goals; with foreign assistance, personal incomes rose despite rapid population growth. However, the richest 10% of the country enjoyed most of the benefits of economic growth; they received 40% of personal income, and enjoyed a comfortable standard of living. In contrast, most Indians remained desperately poor, some only employed at planting and harvest.

Social policy stressed equality. The constitution of the Republic abolished untouchability, and prohibited its practice. Caste distinctions in general were discouraged, and the privileged of all types—from the former princes of Indian states to rural tax collectors—came under attack. Landlords, especially powerful in an overpopulated agricultural society, found their lands distributed to the farmers by land reform. New laws provided women with equal property inheritance and alimony for divorce. Education expanded considerably, but as in many other developing countries, it grew too much at the top (university) and too little at the bottom (mass literacy and skills).

Nehru created an international reputation as a prominent leader of the nonaligned nations neutral in the Cold War who sought independence for European colonies. Nehru often suspected the motives of Western nations and sympathized with the Soviet Union. Such sympathy, however, carried practical benefits, because the rivalry of both communist and Western nations for influence in India meant that both sides provided economic aid.

India's major foreign policy concern, then as now, was Pakistan. Deep suspi-

Prime Minister Nehru with Lord Mountbatten Courtesy: Government of India

cions remained after the 1949 war over Kashmir, and an arms race began, Soviet weapons for India, American jets and tanks to Pakistan. Relations also worsened when Indian irrigation projects threatened to divert rivers flowing into Pakistan and used for irrigation there. The international community solved this problem by a technical solution, for the World Bank provided funds to Pakistan so it could utilize other rivers instead (see **When will the Taps Go Dry,** p. 8). Tension flared over Kashmir in 1965. Pakistan infiltrated irregulars first, then plunged into conventional war by an armored attack (see Disputed Territory: Kashmir). Indian forces halted the invaders, and the Soviet Union sponsored negotiations that ended the fighting. Each side withdrew to the 1949 boundaries.

India initially welcomed the Chinese communist revolution, but the Chinese conquest of Tibet in 1950 brought together the two most populated nations along a lengthy border. After the Dalai Lama fled to India to lead a moral struggle for his people, his supporters sought supplies and weapons to continue the fight. Tension increased when China constructed a road across the desolate, but strategic, Aksai Chin Plateau that India claimed as part of Kashmir. In 1962 a border war broke out, and Chinese troops defeated Indian units before withdrawing. The border dispute soured relations between the two countries for 25 years, and it encouraged China to ally with Pakistan, India's arch-enemy. Before his death in 1964, Nehru was faulted for the failure of his policy toward China, but the nation deeply mourned his passing.

Mrs. Gandhi signs the Visitor's Book at the White House, July 1982

Indira: Emergency Rule

In 1966 *Congress Party* leaders selected Indira Gandhi as party leader and prime minister. Nehru's daughter and thus long acquainted with political issues, she inherited a stumbling economy and a weak party. Mrs. Gandhi increasingly adopted socialist policies, and she nationalized the banks in 1969. The masses adored her, and provided a landslide victory in 1971. Further nationalizations followed. Mrs. Gandhi also led India into a successful war with Pakistan in 1971 that created Bangladesh, and the country conducted its first nuclear test in 1974.

By the mid-1970s, Mrs. Gandhi's programs proved less popular, and after a state court found Mrs. Gandhi guilty of election violations in 1971, she declared a "National Emergency" that invoked extraordinary powers to jail several thousand opposition leaders, censor the press, and announce drastic economic reforms. Indira's Emergency was India's closest brush with dictatorship, and the voters disapproved. *Congress* lost the next election, but in another major feature of Indian politics, a coalition of small parties failed to rule successfully. Elections returned Gandhi to power and the challenge of communal unrest. She was assassinated by bodyguards angered by the military attack on Sikh insurgents in the Golden Temple at Amritsar in 1984.

Disaster of a different sort struck Bhopal, the capital of Madhya Pradesh, that same year. Poisonous gas used to make the agricultural pesticide Sevin leaked into the atmosphere from a chemical plant owned by the Indian subsidiary of Union Carbide. The gas killed more than 6,500 people, and injured perhaps 200,000, many of them doomed to early deaths. Legal wrangles delayed settlement until 1989, when Union Carbide agreed to an Indian court's settlement of $470 million. In 1990 the government began paying the minimal compensation of $12 per month to each of the injured, and in 2004 the courts ordered payment of all remaining funds.

Religious Tensions and Economic Reform

Immediately after Indira's death, key cabinet members selected her second son, Rajiv, as prime minister, Heir to the Nehru tradition of leadership, yet in many ways a fresh face, Rajiv seized the moment of sympathy over his mother's death and called fresh elections. *Congress* emerged triumphant, winning the largest margin of victory since independence, more than 50% of the popular vote and 400 of the 542 seats in the *Lok Sabha*.

As prime minister, Rajiv began reducing the vast web of government regulations and encouraged international trade. However, Rajiv had been Indira's "non-political" son, a pilot who enjoyed a lavish lifestyle, and found government details boring. Two failures marked his rule. First, his attempt to bring peace to Sri Lanka's Tamil rebellion failed when the leading rebel force, the *Tamil Tigers*, turned against Indian troops sent to maintain peace. Second, Swedish investigators discovered secret payments to Rajiv's friends linked to the sale of Bofors field artillery

to India. "Bofors" became synonymous with corruption, and the scandal brought down his government and initiated a brief period of rule by a coalition of other parties. A *Tamil Tiger* suicide bomber assassinated Rajiv during the 1991 elections.

Destruction of the Ayodhya Mosque

Controversy over the Babri mosque at Ayodhya in Uttar Pradesh dominated Indian politics in the early 1990s. Built by the Mogul emperor Babur, the Babri mosque was holy to Muslims, but Hindus regarded it as the sacred birthplace of their god *Ram* and sought to rebuild the Hindu temple they believe preceded the mosque. Militant Hindu revival groups such as the *Vishwa Hindu Parishad* and its political ally, the *Bharatiya Janata Party (BJP)*, sought to destroy the mosque and rebuild the temple. Initially, national and state governments took extraordinary precautions to prevent violence, arresting the *BJP* leader, Lal Krishan Advani, and some 100,000 others. However, in late 1992, political maneuvering gave way to direct action. Under cover of ceremonies to construct a Hindu temple, well-organized militants attacked the dome and walls of the mosque. Ordered by the state's *BJP* government not to fire, the police stood by, and in a few hours the mosque lay destroyed, replaced by a makeshift temple.

Within hours, fighting between Muslims and Hindus spread from Ayodhya across India in the worst communal strife since independence. Days of violence claimed some 1,200 lives; thousands more were injured, most of them Muslim, and many the result of police bullets. The violence and curfews halted normal business, and losses amounted to billions of rupees. The *BJP's* parliamentary leader, L. K. Advani, was arrested, and the government banned several militant Hindu organizations, including the *Rashtriya Swayam Sevak Sangh* (the *RSS*) and the *Vishwa Hindu Parishad*, as well as two Muslim groups. Calm returned, but only slowly. Further anti-Muslim rioting in Bombay, the commercial capital, cost hundreds more lives.

After 400 sittings, 48 extensions, and 17 years in preparation, in 2009 the report of the Liberhan Commission on events at Ayodhya confirmed that the destruction of the mosque involved painstaking, premeditated preparations, and blamed both *BJP* leaders and local officials.

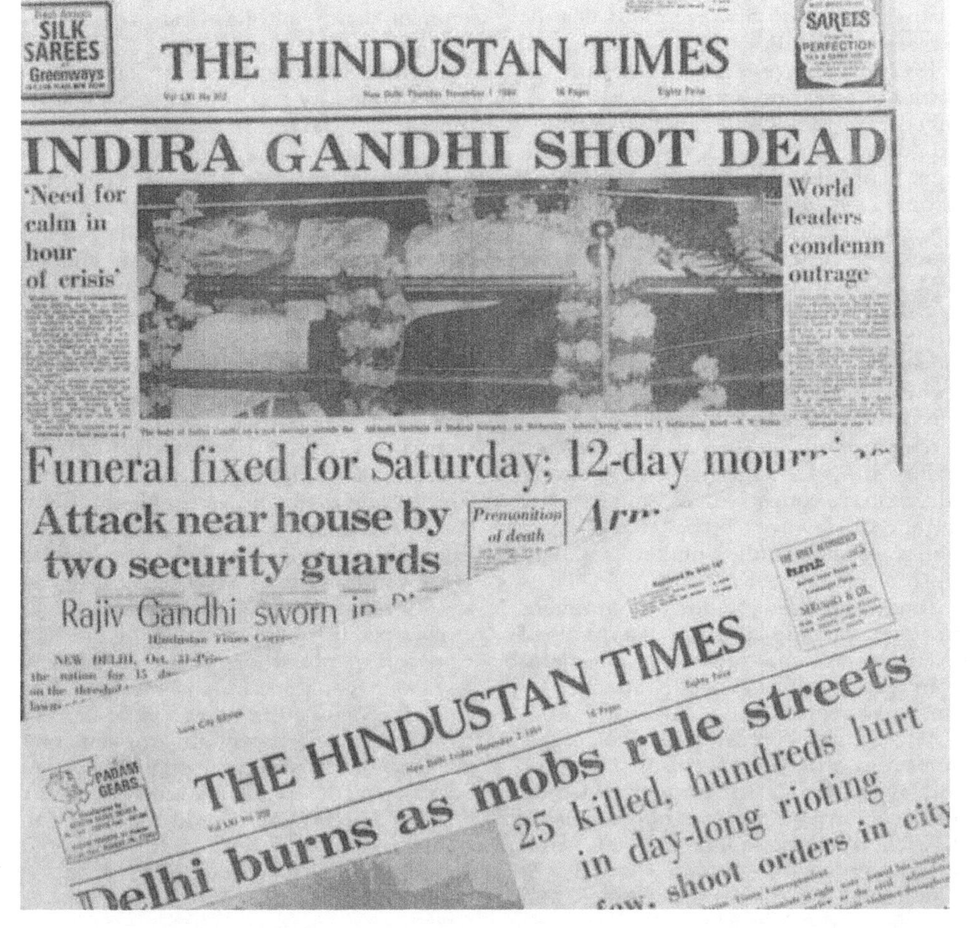

THE HINDUSTAN TIMES

INDIRA GANDHI SHOT DEAD

'Need for calm in hour of crisis'

World leaders condemn outrage

Funeral fixed for Saturday; 12-day mour...

Attack near house by two security guards

Premonition of death

Rajiv Gandhi sworn in ...

THE HINDUSTAN TIMES

Delhi burns as mobs rule streets

25 killed, hundreds hurt in day-long rioting

...few, shoot orders in city

Violence in Kashmir and Bihar

Sectarian violence flared for different reasons in Kashmir. It enjoyed a special status, with separate laws and land ownership restricted to Kashmiris, but years of political manipulation and election-rigging—most notably in 1987—destroyed any legitimacy of the state government. Its overwhelming Muslim majority probably desired an end to Indian rule, though it was divided between favoring independence or unity with Pakistan. Only force and direct control from New Delhi retained Kashmir within India. Economic development languished, and a state with some of the greatest potential for hydroelectric power actually imported most of its electricity.

In the early 1990s, Muslim protests demanded freedom from India. Armed militants took and occasionally murdered hostages, while the often non-Kashmiri police killed dozens of protestors and militants. The leading Muslim activist, Maulvi Mohammad Farooq, was assassinated, and by 1996 the death toll had reached about 20,000.

The violence was often financed and supplied by Pakistan. In 1999 Islamic fighters and Pakistani troops secretly crossed the Line of Control dividing Kashmir and established positions high on peaks overlooking Kargil on the vital highway to Leh, near the Tibetan border. To repulse the invaders, Indian troops advanced up steep slopes with little cover. It took ten weeks of determined battle, significant casualties, and world opinion to persuade Pakistan to withdraw the remaining infiltrators. Two nuclear powers had fought significant land battles without going to war, but the results might not prove as fortunate next time.

Jammu and Kashmir held state elections in 2002. This was not the exercise of civic responsibilities. Pakistani-based militants murdered moderates, and the *All-Party Hurriyat Conference*, a loose confederation of 23 separatist groups, boycotted the vote. But, the elections were sufficiently free and honest to defeat the *National Conference*, the pro-Indian party that traditionally won corrupt elections. A new coalition government released some militants, and promised to relieve the harsher regulations and police actions. It has not been entirely successful, and Human Rights Watch has faulted the Indian military for killings of suspects without trial, and Pakistan for backing the armed militants.

Confidence-building progress between Pakistan and India at mid-decade brought further hopes for improvements in Kashmir, even if its broad solution remains distant. Bus service between Srinagar, the capital of India's portion, and Muzaffarabad permitted relatives to see each other after nearly sixty years. Moreover, Kashmiris on each side of the Line of Control began to visualize new types of solutions. Moderate opposition groups even traveled the bus, and held a conference that increased the popularity of non-violent solutions. Though a settlement eluded Kashmir, the level of violence declined, but surged again in 2010–11, amid accusations of harsh treatment by the security forces.

Violence of a different nature swept portions of rural Bihar during the 1990s. Again the initial causes were political, social, and economic. The Bihar state government had failed to provide security—or schools, clinics, roads, and electricity. The chief minister, Laloo Prasad Yadav, of a low-ranking, cow-herding caste, used state jobs and contracts as sources of patronage for his supporters. Corruption charges finally forced him from office in 1997, but his illiterate wife replaced him when their party won state elections. Without economic reform and foreign investment, the level of poverty increased yearly. Signs of improvement only followed the election of a new state government in 2006, whose policies and spending on infrastructure brought signs of growth through road construction and other projects.

Political Corruption and BJP Victories

Financial scandals in the late 1990s finally ended *Congress's* role as the natural ruling party. Before the 1996 elections, investigators revealed illegal payments on an immense scale to many prominent politicians and officials. For example, a former cabinet minister kept over *36 million rupees in cash* at home. The resulting public uproar forced the resignation of the *Congress* prime minister, cabinet members and the *BJP* leader. In subsequent elections the electorate resoundingly rejected *Congress* and selected new groups like the caste-based *Samajwadi* and *Bahujan Samaj* parties, the *BJP*, or leftist alliances ranging from *Janata Dal* to the *Communist Party-Marxist*.

In 1998 the *BJP*'s moderate leader, Atal Bihari Vajpayee, dropped extreme planks of his party's platform such as laws to prohibit Muslims from practicing polygamy and successfully formed a coalition. His coalition's most remembered achievement, however, was a series of nuclear explosions in Rajasthan that stunned the world and delighted most Indians. The tests changed India's rank from "nuclear-capable" to "nuclear power." Despite Pakistan's answering nuclear tests, in the subsequent elections Vajpayee's coalition won a solid majority. It used its powers to enact economic reforms such as cutting fuel subsidies and to purchase expensive weaponry: T-90 tanks, an aircraft carrier, and jet fighters from Russia; jet trainers from Britain; a submarine or two from France; and locally-produced missiles and nuclear weapons.

Former Prime Minister Manmohan Singh

Closer Relations with the U.S.

The September 11 attacks deepened the growing friendship between the U.S. and India. Officially and popularly, India sympathized with any victim of Islamic extremists—India also was a victim, in Kashmir. However, because Pakistan shared information with the U.S. and allowed U.S. access to Afghanistan, India did not win conclusive American support. Most countries still consider Kashmir a disputed territory.

Kashmiri guerrillas launched a deadly attack on the Indian Parliament in late 2001. Prime Minister Vajpayee responded by demanding that Pakistan ban the two groups allegedly involved, *Jaish-i Muhammad* and *Laskar-i Toiba*, and generally clamp down on extremists. The army prepared for battle, and moved to the border. Fearful of the first real war between nuclear-armed antagonists, the U.S. and other nations counseled Pakistan to yield, and it did. However, brutal attacks again took place on the Indian military and non-Muslim civilians of Kashmir.

Conflict between religious communities broke out again in 2002, when a trainload of Hindu militants returning to Gujarat from Ayodhya was allegedly attacked by Muslim extremists, leaving nearly 60 dead. (A later inquiry blamed the deaths on disputes and a riot, not a terrorist attack). For days thereafter, well-organized Hindu mobs conducted a pogrom of the Muslim districts of Ahmedabad, the state capital. The mobs slaughtered about 1,500, vandalized businesses and homes, and caused many thousands to flee to refugee camps. The police failed to protect them even there.

Significantly, Gujarat was one of the few states ruled by the *BJP*. Horror at the violence led coalition parties in the national government to demand the dismissal of Gujarat's chief minister. However, nothing happened, and none bolted the coalition. Moreover, the *BJP* easily returned to power in Gujarat's state elections. Hindu militants therefore saw the religious-nationalist ideology of "Hindutva" as the key to power.

Hoping instead for victory based on the country's prosperity, Prime Minister Vajpayee called elections for 2004. A moderate, he adopted the electoral slogan "Shining India," a vague or even meaningless phrase intended to tap "feel good" sentiments after several years of rapid economic growth. *BJP* advertising showed smiling children at school, and well-dressed families relaxing. Sophisticated technology showed in campaign methods, too, with recordings from the prime minister sent to all cell-phones.

By contrast, *Congress* failed to present a slick message, and its leader, Sonia Gandhi, found herself targeted as a foreigner. However, she traveled tirelessly to speak to crowds about the many who had been left behind by "Shining India," including women, youth, and farmers.

Congress Returns to Power: The nation was stunned by an upset victory for *Congress*. It replaced the *BJP* as the largest party in parliament, and successfully sought a coalition with minor parties and a common understanding with communist and left-wing parties, the *Left Front*. Sonia Gandhi surprised the country, again, by refusing to become prime minister. Her party then nominated Manmohan Singh, the "father of economic reforms" responsible for India's rapid growth back in the 1990s. The stock market rebounded. A fitting, if unintended symbol of *Congress's* greater toleration for non-Hindus, Singh became the first Sikh prime minister just before the twentieth anniversary of the battle for the Golden Temple in Amritsar. By coincidence, the president was not a Hindu either, but a Muslim who won fame as a rocket scientist linked with the nuclear weapons program.

Hampered by the demands of 24 coalition parties plus those of the supporting *Left Front*, Singh's accomplishments proved modest. He failed to reform labor laws or to privatize poorly-run government companies. One very significant achievement was the institution of Value Added Tax (VAT), which should reduce corruption and spread the tax burden. It also should reduce the deficits of state governments, a serious concern.

Determined to spread the nation's prosperity to rural areas, Singh's alliance created the National Rural Employment Guarantee Scheme. Rather than cash welfare payments, it promoted "Growth with a Human Face" through providing a minimum of 100 days employment per unemployed household per year, often in local self-help projects that pay little over $1 per day. The scheme achieved modest results in its first year, but the cabinet deemed it effective enough, and it was extended to the entire country in 2008. Its advocates see the project providing many good things: increased economic security through higher farm wages, slower migration to the overcrowded cities, the creation of productive infrastructure, and greater independence of women.

Less successfully, the government proposed to raise the quotas in higher education for the socially disadvantaged castes from 22.5% to 49.5%. The better Indian universities already turn away many applicants, and extending the quota would exclude many middle-class students. Demonstrations against the proposal spread across the country, and even doctors and medical students went on strike against it. Nevertheless, the ruling coalition remained stable, partly because there was no alternative majority. The proposal was soon delayed by the courts.

With national elections approaching, Singh's Communist allies in the *Left Front* deserted the coalition over a nuclear technology deal with the U.S. To help develop India's energy resources, Singh had negotiated an agreement that separated India's military and civilian nuclear programs and then granted India access to civilian nuclear technology and fuel—both previously denied because India had developed its own nuclear weapons. The proposal provided significant benefits, but for ideological reasons the *CPI (Marxist)* and its allies launched popular protests against it but failed to bring Singh down with a vote of no confidence.

In late 2008 a group of gunmen came ashore in Mumbai and launched attacks on the Taj Mahal and Oberoi luxury hotels, a popular restaurant, a Jewish center, a hospital and a train station, shocking the nation and the world. Anti-terrorism police responded slowly, and nearly 200 civilians died in the suicide raid. Evidence, partly from a surviving attacker, quickly implicated the Pakistani extremist group *Laskar-i Toiba* in the attack, a group long suspected of working closely with Pakistani military intelligence. India demanded that Pakistan ban the group and arrest its leaders and other terrorists; the new civilian government moved slowly in that direction.

The World's Sixth Nuclear Power

Indian interest in atomic power began before independence, when the industrial Tata Company set up a research program. In the 1950s, the U.S., Canada and Britain all provided nuclear facilities, hoping to encourage research and generate cheap electricity. However, despite its public stand against nuclear weapons, India never signed the Comprehensive Test Ban Treaty, and it undertook the design and construction of nuclear reactors free from inspection by the International Atomic Energy Agency.

After China exploded its first atomic bomb in 1965, the scientists at the Indian Atomic Energy Commission secretly began accumulating the enriched uranium from those reactors for possible atomic bombs. In 1974, an explosion in Rajasthan proclaimed that the country was the world's sixth nuclear power, but New Delhi confirmed that its program was peaceful, though it now had the ability to explode weapons.

By the 1990s, politicians desired further nuclear tests, to illustrate the country's ability, and no doubt to enhance their own reputation. In 1998 Prime Minister Vajpayee publicly promised that India would not test weapons, but secretly authorized the five explosions that set off the South Asian nuclear arms race with Pakistan.

Military strategists who accept the legitimacy of some nuclear weapons frequently condemn India's acquisition of them. The 1974 explosion had led Pakistan to create its own bomb. Within both countries, the creation of weapons raced far ahead of designing strategies for their use, and possibly control over them. Thus, serious consideration of a hot line between the two countries only surfaced in 2004. Far from enhancing India's security, the explosions may actually increase the risk of conventional wars in South Asia. The resulting arms races for both nuclear and conventional weapons impose unnecessary suffering on populations whose average incomes reach only $400–$600 per year, but no doubt the satisfaction of citizenship in a nation armed with atomic weapons removes the pangs of hunger and stills the sorrows resulting from some of the highest infant death rates in the world.

The Mumbai attacks apparently did not influence the 2009 *Lok Sabha* election campaign, though the *BJP* attempted to cast Prime Minister Singh as weak and ineffective, controlled by Sonia Gandhi. Abandoned by its former leftist allies, *Congress* promised to spread prosperity to the poor, and ran on a record of economic growth and domestic peace. It nominated Singh (age 78) for another term, against the *BJP's* equally aged Lal Krishna Advani (81). Analysts widely predicted that neither major party would emerge with enough seats to create a strong coalition; some believed a third group of leftist and caste-based parties might even emerge strongest. Given the massive electorate of 714 million voters and over 800,000 voting centers, voting took place regionally, spread over four weeks.

Congress emerged with a remarkable win, the greatest by a single party in two decades. Its *United Progressive Alliance* gained over 50 seats, and needed only a few additional votes for a majority in parliament:

United Progressive Alliance	262
National Democratic Alliance	158
Third Front (Leftist alliance)	76
Fourth Front (regional)	27
Other Parties	20

In one respect, the gods indeed favored Singh and *Congress*. Despite the world recession, the economy grew almost as fast as China's. Indians also voted after five years of good monsoons, two months before the 2009 rains came late and sparse to the western regions of the country, but flooded the east.

The Maoist threat

In the words of the newly-elected prime minister, the Maoist insurgency had become India's greatest internal security threat. Since the 1960s, Maoist revolutionaries have considered rural India's strong caste divisions, tribal populations and great inequality of wealth fertile conditions for class warfare. Operating across state borders, they organized bands comprised of tribal peoples and Dalits for actions against the police and landowners.

Active particularly in forested rural districts of West Bengal, Chattisgarh, Bihar and Jharkhand, and Orissa, the Maoists provided a voice to tribal complaints that their lands were sold to outsiders for development projects such as bauxite and iron mines while they remained landless and poor, lacking in the schools, roads, and investment essential for prosperity. As violence escalated in 2009–10, the Maoists hijacked one train and derailed an intercity express. For its part, the government launched a massive paramilitary operation to clear large sections of forest of the Maoist threat, only for the troops to suffer a major ambush. The struggle has claimed over 6,000 lives.

Corruption Scandals Discredit Politicians

Midway through its term, corruption scandals threatened to engulf Prime Minister Singh's government. The telecommunications minister, Andimuthu Raja, a member of the coalition party *DMK*, was accused of accepting bribes to sell mobile phone licenses by directly, rather than by auction. In the process, the treasury lost perhaps $40 billion in revenues. The scandal led to the trial of Raja and several officials from cell phone companies.

India has long tolerated small gifts in return for official favors. However, these figures are large, and the telecoms scandal was quickly followed by other major allegations involving government funding or approval. Sleaze and shoddy construction practices marked Delhi's 2010 Commonwealth Games. Several top officials were arrested for corruption, including the organizing committee's director, a *Congress Party* official.

The sleaze extended to both national parties and to many regional ones. Indeed, venality seemed rife at the state level. In Tamil Nadu, the *DMK* lost state elections badly although (or because) it distributed 15 million small TV sets (a significant gift in a country where perhaps 600 million people live on less than a dollar per day). The chief minister of Karnataka, who led the state *BJP*, conducted a scam involving iron ore mines that cost more than $3 billion in revenues over five years.

Another scandal involved the transformation of a modest building for war widows in Mumbai into a 31-story complex with apartments for retired officers, officials, and relatives of the state's chief minister, a leader of *Congress*. Yet another former chief minister of Maharashtra was fined by the Supreme Court for intervening to block legal complaints against a state legislator and his family who had allegedly tortured farmers who fell behind on loans, while charging 10% interest per month. However, he initially remained in Singh's federal cabinet as industries minister.

As Elections Approach

Economic and political conditions declined well before the 2014 parliamentary elections. Economic growth fell after 2012, to little more than half its levels during the previous decade. Scores of major infrastructure projects and other government investments stalled, and the rupee lost value on the foreign exchange market. Apparent good news—the claim that the number of people living in extreme poverty had fallen from 37% of the population

Prime Minister Narendra Modi

to 22%—proved misleading. Meanwhile, inflation—symbolized by the price of onions--rose to its highest level in 20 years, harming the poor and middle classes.

As optimism about prosperity faded, public dissatisfaction with corruption increased. Social activists seized national attention with demonstrations and a series of public fasts to protest corruption. The new *Aam Aadmi Party* ("Common Man's Party) placed second in Delhi's territorial elections and briefly took power. Despite bad losses in those elections, *Congress* failed heed popular dissatisfaction. For example, when the Supreme Court ruled that convicted lawmakers must be removed from office, the cabinet proposed an executive order designed to block the ruling. The same inability to focus on critical matters was evident when *Congress* failed to select its prime ministerial candidate. Manmohan Singh announced he was stepping down, but although Rahul Gandhi managed the election campaign, he was not nominated for office.

By contrast, the *BJP* demonstrated its desire for victory. Setting aside its elderly leaders, the party nominated Narendra Modi as its candidate for prime minister, emphasizing the economic success of Gujarat under his leadership. Campaigning for prosperity rather than the *BJP*'s traditional sectarian emphasis, Modi successfully deflected concerns about his role in the 2002 Ahmedabad sectarian riots. Regional, leftist, and caste-based parties continued their traditional appeals.

Spread over many weeks for security reasons, and once again setting a world record for the number of eligible voters (814 million), the 2014 elections delivered much more than had been forecast. The *BJP* won an astounding victory: 31% of the national vote that transformed into 282 of the 543 seats in the *Lok Sabha*, only the second time in history that a party had won an absolute majority. By contrast, *Congress* retained only 19% of the popular vote. It lost 162 seats and retained only 44 MPs, making 2014 its worse ever defeat by far. For the smaller parties, small changes in shares of the popular vote could make great differences. For example, Jayalalitha's *AIADMK* 1.6% increase in the popular vote won 28 seats, while the rival *Dravida Munnetra Kazhagam (DMK)* lost 0.1% of the national vote, and every one of its previous 18 members of parliament.

Within weeks, the Modi cabinet had prepared new economic and financial measures to spur growth and reduce inflation.

Culture: India does not have an official religion; it is a land of many religions. Yet it is a Hindu nation, and that fact is in part responsible for the toleration of other religions. About 80% of the population is Hindu, but there are 140 million Muslims (over 13%) and about 20 million Christians, the third largest group. There are also many Buddhists in this land where Buddha lived in the sixth century B.C. and preached a message which emphasized the sanctity of life in all forms.

Hinduism is not merely part of a culture, it *is* a culture—not simply a religion in the normal Western sense. One example of its all-embracing nature is its rigid social order dominated by the concept of caste. Hundreds of castes exist; all Hindus belong to one of them. Caste membership comes by birth, and remains for life. Social contacts overwhelmingly occur within the caste, and marriages rarely cross caste boundaries or take place within the same sub-caste.

Each caste traditionally involved a particular occupation, and with some exceptions members of the upper castes also represented the upper economic classes. The distinctions are far more than economic, and include dietary restrictions on the higher castes as well as social discrimination against members of lower castes. For example, many Brahmins will not eat food if the shadow of an "untouchable" has passed over it.

Traditionally castes fell into four broad groups. At the top, the Brahmins (priest-intellectuals), kshatriyas (warrior-nobles) and vaishyas (businessmen) compose over one-sixth of India's population. The shudras (peasants and laborers), now politically described as the backward castes, amount to 44%.

Below all of these are the "scheduled Castes," now called Dalits. Comprising

Tibetian woman sells her wares in Kalimpong Photo courtesy of Karla Allen

over 15% of the population, before independence they faced the discrimination their title "untouchable" proclaimed, while carrying out essential but dirty and dangerous occupations like street sweeping, slaughtering animals, and disposing corpses and human wastes. Indeed, demonstrators in 2010 claimed that one million impoverished Dalits clean non-flush toilets daily, despite laws banning the practices for wages as low as $4 per month.

The Indian constitution removed legal discrimination against these unfortunates, and government programs have provided assistance. Nevertheless, upper class Hindus will not drink from a Dalit's glass, or patronize the same barbershop. Despite the constitutional protection, in practice Dalits are often banned from temples, cremation grounds, and bathing spots along riverbanks. Dalits who converted to some Christian churches found that they faced similar obstacles: they were shunned from particular pews or even churches by other Christians.

The Tragic Treatment of Women

The brutal gang-rape and murder of a 23-year-old paramedic student riding on a bus in late 2012 again heightened distress about the treatment of Indian women. Unlike Islam, Indian culture has not viewed the female form as something to cover lest men sin. However, popular culture continues a long tradition of male superiority that often devalues women. For example, the Delhi city police commissioner, facing concerns about growing numbers of rapes, responded that men were not safe either, "their pockets were picked," thus implying some sort of equivalence between the crimes.

Certainly, some women reach the top in India—in politics (a president, a prime minister, and several party leaders), business, and the professions. However, these are mostly exceptions in a country where many fail to consider a woman's life equal to a man's. The problems are worse in northern India, where entrenched patriarchal traditions, disrespect for law, police insensitivity, and uprooted migrants increase the disrespect of women.

The problems begin before birth with (illegal) sex-selective abortion of unwanted girls. Difficulties continue through childhood, when more than half of all children are malnourished, and girls typically receive less food than boys. On average, they study fewer years than boys, and as they mature, the need to provide funds for a dowry sometimes leads to prostitution.

Adolescence and maturity bring little relief. Girls very often marry young: though the legal age is 18, nearly half (44%) of all brides wed before that. Women rarely enjoy a healthy diet: in poor families mothers and sisters often forego food to give husbands and sons more. Some 60% of women are anemic.

While successful marriage may lead to joy, more women die from injuries than in childbirth, a suspicious statistic. Some 100,000 women are killed annually by fires, a fate long considered to be revenge by the in-laws for delinquent dowry payments. Widowhood on occasion ends in pressures to commit suicide.

Months after the Delhi bus rape, parliament legislated tougher punishment of sex crimes, and expanding the definition of both rape and sexual harassment.

Rituals and ceremonies are prominent in Hinduism, and these are closely related to the family, for the rites are often performed at home. The major rituals relate to birth, marriage and death. The dead are cremated with as much decorum as the family can afford in keeping with its position on the social scale. Other features of Hinduism include the rejection of worldly pleasure, belief in the soul's transmigration after death to another form of life, the sanctity of the cow and the belief in many gods.

One Hindu celebration, the Kumbh Mela, brings together more people than any other single event worldwide. The "pitcher fair" is named after drops of the elixir of immortality that fell to earth during a struggle between gods and demons. Every 12 years the alignment of the stars makes washing away the sins of the body particularly effective at the city of Allahabad, the confluence of the Ganges, the Yamuna, and the mythical (but sacred) Sasaswathi. Millions converge on Allahabad, often taking weeks to walk there, carrying everything needed on their heads. About 100 million pilgrims attended the 2013 ceremony, which was marred by a stampede as millions of bathers pressed to take trains home in an overcrowded station.

Holidays and festivals are associated with each cultural community. There are three important Hindu holidays. *Diwali*, the festival of lights, is a happy celebration commemorating the homecoming of the legendary hero Rama after he defeated the demon king Ravana. The family performs special ritual prayers in the home on this occasion. *Dussehra* has varied meanings in different parts of the country and is celebrated in various ways; in some places with great happiness, in others with more religious ritual, while for some it ends with carefree folk dancing. *Holi* is an occasion in March for noise and fun, and usually folk songs are sung at gatherings around bonfires.

Muslims celebrate the same holidays as in other countries (see Saudi Arabia: Culture) but with local variations. In addition to the religious holidays, three secular festivals are being promoted. Republic Day is celebrated on January 26, Independence Day on August 15, and *Gandhi Jayanti* (Gandhi's birthday) on October 2.

Literature and the Arts

Hindi and certain other Indian languages are descended from ancient Sanskrit. Most of the ancient literature of India was written in that language, including the early religious text *Rigveda*. Slightly later, several dramas appeared in Sanskrit; the playwright Kalidasa is the

A stroll through the market

most famous. That was the beginning of a long literary history enriched by contributions from Persia and finally Western ideas and forms. Literature flourishes in contemporary India in a number of the native languages, but there are also poems, novels and other works in English.

It is only natural when one thinks of the culture of India to think of the Taj Mahal at Agra—and this is not an isolated example of architectural opulence in this land. There are rock-cut temples and architectural monuments from as early as the time of the Emperor Asoka in the third century B.C. The most admired buildings come from the era of the Hindu-Islamic synthesis beginning in the eighth century A.D. and continuing up until a few centuries ago. The Kurb Minar at Delhi and the Adina Masjid at Ahmedabad come from early in this period; the Taj Mahal, Agra Fort and Akbar's Mausoleum, the latter at Sikandra, come from later during the rule of the Moguls (15th–16th centuries). After independence, conscious attempts to create a new national architectural style achieved success in combining elements of the past and present, particularly at Chandigarh.

Painting and sculpture, especially the latter, have an ancient history in India. The stone model for the lion of the State Seal, for instance, dates from the third century B.C. But the new generation of artists is not being limited to any tradition or time; it is boldly experimenting with great freedom.

Dancing, music and drama are three arts that in India belong together. Traditionally, plays are acted in dance to the accompaniment of music. Dancing also exists separately and is a very highly developed art with elaborate symbolism.

Modern cultural forms play an important role. The movie industry produces more full length films every year (about 800) than does any other country. Because studios in Bombay traditionally dominated the industry, it became known as "Bollywood," but most movies today come from producers in southern India, in languages like Telegu and Tamil. Most Indian movies attract the entire family: they feature little violence, frequent music and dance, and exaggerated emotional attractions. But there is no obvious sexual activity, and the finish is always "happily ever-after." Stars in the industry draw huge followings, and some transfer their talents to the political stage, on occasion becoming a state's chief minister.

Exported for many years across Asia and Africa as an alternative to the culture of Hollywood, the movie industry drew additional strength from the rapid growth of cable TV in India and satellite TV around the world. Because costs of production are relatively low, foreign distribution rights alone can sometimes meet the cost of production. However, until Indian movies are filmed in English, their audience in North America will typically be limited to expatriate Indians. The 2009 best-picture winner *Slumdog Millionaire* gave many Americans their first taste of Bollywood.

Dalits "untouchables" polishing shoes

Bombay: The Movie

A Tamil film about love against the background of the Ayodhya riots nearly caused disturbances of its own in 1995. In the interests of peace, one of India's best known producers, Mani Ratnam, portrayed a love story between a Hindu man and Muslim woman. Predictably, the strongest passion he aroused was anger, not love.

For the sake of communal harmony, Mr. Ratnam edited portions at the request of Mr. Bal Thackeray, leader of the militant Hindu party *Shiv Sena* that attacked Muslim areas during the riots. The producer also cut portions in sympathy with Muslim sensitivities, and showed newspaper headlines of the attack on the mosque, rather than the attack itself.

Despite passing India's censors, the final version of the film aroused Muslim anger by implying a similar aggressiveness between Muslim and Hindu mobs. Muslim threats of disturbances halted showing for a week in Bombay—it had appeared elsewhere. However, Mr. Thackeray, who boasted of his remote control over the newly-elected chief minister of Maharashtra, insisted that threats should not prevent its opening. Under tight security, it was released.

Regardless of its portrayal of mobs and politicians, the movie risked Muslim resentment from the start. In Islamic law, a married woman joins her husband's community. When a Muslim man marries a non-Muslim, he thereby adds to the community, an honorable action that provided a Christian wife for more than one caliph. But when a Muslim woman marries outside her faith, she effectively leaves it, an event not dissimilar to apostasy.

Television, long stagnant under a government monopoly, broke wide open with the growth of (unregulated) cable TV. Now both Indian and Western programs reach the remotest villages, brought by some 30,000–70,000 cable companies to 30 million customers, who pay modestly ($2.50–$4.00 per month) for up to 75 channels.

Independence in 1947 is a dividing line in the history of education in India. Before independence there was no mass education. Thereafter, the government tried to provide free and universal education through eight years of "basic school."

These eight elementary years provide instruction in crafts along with reading and writing. After a rapid increase in education during the last two decades, nearly all children now complete those grades, and in 2011 the government finally funded universal access to high school, though poverty and other causes discourage millions from attending. Nevertheless, nearly 30% of the population remains illiterate, and 50% of women. About half the world's illiterates are Indian.

The achievements in higher education have been comparable. There were 17 universities in 1947; by 2010 there were some 370 universities and over 7,000 colleges. However, only 12% of the 18–24 year population was enrolled, compared to over 30% in most developed economies. A panel of experts has called for 1,500 universities by 2015, but government spending on education has not increased rapidly enough to meet such lofty goals. One alternative, previously blocked by government red tape, would be to allow branch campuses of European and American institutions.

While the Indian Institutes of Technology rank with the world's best in computer sciences, elsewhere the system of education requires reform. In 2007 Prime Minister Singh claimed that two thirds of the universities and 90% of the colleges were rated "below average" (by "average" he apparently meant "reasonable quality" rather than the mathematical mean). In Singh's words, "We need better facilities, more and better teachers, a flexible approach to curriculum development to make it more relevant, more-effective pedagogical and learning methods, and more-meaningful evaluation systems." Nevertheless, it takes an act of parliament to create a university, and the lack of an accreditation process means that quality often remains murky. For example, over half of all college teachers lack a graduate degree, and 25% of university positions are vacant. Salaries are far too low to attract the vast numbers of Indian academics working abroad.

Even as it educates only 7% of its young adults, India has the largest number of unemployed graduates in the world, as well as the largest number of illiterates. The unemployed often studied in the wrong disciplines, but desire the high salaries of computer scientists, engineers, and finance majors.

Economy: With 650,000 villages and scores of bustling cities, the economy of India is marked by contrasts greater than any other nation. It is home to humanity's greatest collection of the poor—some 300 million people, one-third of all those world-wide who are so impoverished that they subsist on less than $25 per month. Nevertheless, the middle class numbers about 200 million, and the number of very wealthy may exceed the number of millionaires in the United States. The rapid economic growth of this decade may transform at least parts of the country.

Poverty Partly from Choice

The poverty is not inevitable: the land possesses good soil that is easily irrigated and large deposits of coal, iron ore, and other minerals, though insufficient oil. The conditions that produced modern poverty lay first in human reactions to the natural conditions.

Culture and regulation have kept poverty in place when economic growth could have alleviated it. Regular rainfall, good soil and tropical warmth encouraged a very large and dense population in the plains and river valleys. Society then forced the lower strata of society into poverty while some members of the nobility enjoyed vast riches. In the traditional world of religious belief and caste divisions, the mixture of poverty and riches seemed natural and inevitable. Fate, or *karma,* dictated life's difficulties. Accepting it might lead to rebirth in better circumstances.

The British conquest meant some public works, along with tariff-free imports. Factory-made textiles, machinery, and consumer goods flooded India, undercutting local craftsmen and hindering attempts to industrialize. At the same time, fewer famines and better medical knowledge helped the population grow rapidly. At independence, roughly 200 million people, half the population, lived below the poverty line.

From 12th century bronze . . .

In the first 40 years of independence, the number of impoverished grew to exceed 300 million, and economists applied the term "Hindu Rate of Growth" to the economy's performance. However, the relatively slow growth resulted not from religious culture, but from regulation, planning, and high tariffs rather than free enterprise.

Public health and other statistics give some sense of the desperate poverty of many inhabitants. Both bubonic and pneumonic plague broke out in 1994, striking initially at slums on the outskirts of cities like Surat and Bombay, where crowded

. . . to the most advanced rocketry. India's spacecraft reached the moon in 2008.

Praying in the Ganges at Varanassi, one of Hinduism's holiest spots

Photo courtesy of Karla Allen

immigrants live without clean water or sanitation. By official estimates, some 30,000 tons of waste remain uncollected daily, and in rural areas only 10% of homes have a toilet or outhouse and over 600 million people lack access to a latrine. Government efforts for better sanitation have had little impact, but the recent publicity campaign "No Toilet, No Bride" links toilets to courtship and thus may bring comfort and sanitation to those above abject poverty.

Surveys in the 1990s revealed that over 300 million people lived in households so poor no one could afford a watch, and utter poverty condemned 30% of the population to fewer than two meals per day. Very few adults will escape from that poverty except through death, and by 2010 the number in poverty had climbed to 400 million. There have been hundreds of suicides by hopelessly indebted farmers, but sales of laundry detergents and cosmetics seem to be rising among those just above the poverty line.

After drastic food shortages in the 1960s, great efforts were made to increase the country's grain production. The Green Revolution—selecting strains of rice and wheat that produce well with fertilizers and irrigation—enabled the country to feed itself in 1971 for the first time since independence. In the contest between better farming and more mouths, freeing markets in the 1990s led to still greater harvests. This progress could be halted or reverse if reports of falling water tables prove correct, or if climate change reduces the extent and reliability of rainfall.

Shanty town on a Calcutta street

For years, the seas around India abounded in fish that an efficient industry could exploit, but the lack of processing and storage facilities, as well as poor transportation, allowed the fish to swim unmolested. By the late 1980s, however, India had improved the industry, and ranked eighth in the world in annual fishing catch. Now the Indian Ocean may be over-fished, particularly near the shores.

A diamond-finishing industry began in India in the 1960s when it was discovered that low wages made it profitable to work imported diamonds that were discarded by the South African syndicate. An estimated 350,000 craftsmen in India now work in tiny sweatshops where they are paid by the piece. A socio-religious group, the *Palanpuri Jains* (from the former princely state of Palanpur), have established a worldwide network to market gems cut in India. India has become the leading exporter of cut and polished diamonds.

Seeking Rapid Economic Growth

The modern Indian economy finally "took off" in the 1990s, when Manmohan Singh, the finance minister, reduced regulation, encouraged investment by foreigners, and ended most of the industrial licensing that had handicapped Indian industry. Singh also attempted to sell state businesses, simplify taxes, and reduce them for the rich. The opposition charged that the International Monetary Fund wrote the budget, but India started, somewhat timidly, to follow the East Asian models of export-led economic prosperity.

With lower inflation, higher exports, and lower tax rates, Indian and foreign companies expanded. By mid-decade, newly-permitted foreign companies expanded telephone links and constructed power plants. Spurred partly by advertising on many new TV channels, consumers sought appliances and household items. Investment by foreign companies soared, freeing Indian funds for other purposes. Exports doubled. As the growth rate of GDP reached 7%, some commentators considered India the next Asian Tiger.

The years of rapid economic growth produced two Indias, one sometimes quite rich, the other usually oppressively poor. Economic growth failed to bring much relief to those living in poverty, especially the rural poor. Over 80% of the population continued to live on less than $2.00 (U.S.) per day, and according to the Multidimensional Poverty Index, India had more poor than Africa. At the same time, the middle and upper classes purchase flashy consumer goods and speculate in India's own hi-tech stocks.

Certain states managed to capture most of the economic prosperity, particularly

Gujarat, Maharashtra, and Karnataka in the west and south. By contrast, the vast Ganges plain across Uttar Pradesh, Bihar and West Bengal experienced virtually no improvement in personal incomes. Relatively rapid population growth also reduced the growth rate per capita.

Virtually all state governments operate in deficit, and even the best may fail to provide the necessary infrastructure or enable private firms to do so. India's airports are often a horror story. Until its recent modernization and massive new terminals, one among the world's largest, New Delhi's Gandhi International Airport had only one runway.

The country lags far behind most other Asian nations in telephone lines and internet use. To saturate the country with lines for faxes and fiber optic cables required by the flourishing software industry will cost hundreds of billions. Although the necessary funds could come from foreign investment, after decades of encouraging foreign firms to undertake projects, their annual investments fall far short of either government plans or China's level.

In the 1990s much foreign investment took the form of large, headline-grabbing projects to meet the tremendous electricity shortages. However, political interference and red tape deterred many investors from completing their projects. Indians still suffer frequent power cuts and voltage fluctuations that wear out motors, but foreign investors deserted the electricity industry after the Maharashtra failed to pay the agreed price for electricity from an American company's project. To circumvent widespread shortages, many software firms and factories generate their own power.

Other problems in the electricity sector typify the challenges facing the country as it moves from socialism to greater free markets. State-owned utilities generally produce and distribute electricity. Their operations are among the least efficient in the world and they frequently suffer power "losses" (mostly theft) of 30%. In the capital, New Delhi, losses amount to 55% of production. By contrast, the world standard is just 10%. Other challenges to an effective system include many non-metered users who pay a flat rate (perhaps 60% of all use), and politicians who promise free electricity for farmers and other special-interest groups.

In electricity and telephones, as in much else except cable TV, government control and ownership lie at the heart of most problems. Privatization efforts suffer because the law prohibits closing factories employing over 100 people, and labor unions protested a proposal to raise the limit to 1,000. States like Kerala have such reputations for leftist policies and militant trade unions that neither foreign nor Indian investment has been significant.

The Indian Institute of Science symbolizes Bangalore's long tradition of excellence in science, technology, and the arts. Today, the city's industrial skills have earned it a reputation as the Silicon Valley of India. Photo by Miller B. Spangler

Subsidies for water, electricity and cheap food consume large portions of most state budgets, and reached 10% of GDP in 2000. Moves to slash them meet intense political opposition, but they devour so many resources that little is left for education, public health (800 million people do not have access to clean water), roads, or housing.

Twenty-seven government-owned state banks dominate the banking industry, thanks to regulations that kept out private firms until the 1990s and still limit foreign banks to a minority (49%) stake. The state banks' profits have been hampered by bad loans to failing government enterprises and regulations that allow bankrupt manufacturing firms to continue operating. Political pressures mandate, loans at low

Making friends in an Indian Village

interest rates to farmers and other special interests. Reform of the financial sector is a major challenge to any government.

Success in Computer Services and Autos

The success of Indian-owned firms in the computer software industry, such as Hotmail in the U.S. and Infosys Limited in India, illustrate the potential of the country's millions of engineers, scientists, and other well-trained professionals. Software exports grew at the astounding rate of 40%–50% *per year* in the late 1990s, but rates fell after 2007. The industry employed nearly three million people in 2012 and exported products worth $70 billion, more than the country's entire exports in 2000. As many (sometimes frustrated) American consumers know, India also became the world hub for call centers and other back-office procedures such as the transcription of medical records. Local firms began these industries, but in recent years multinationals have entered. In 2006, IBM announced plans for investment worth $6 billion, so the growth of these sectors seems limited mostly by the numbers of qualified employees and the supporting infrastructure.

Until the 1980s, policy favored public transportation over private, and Indian Railways carried millions of passengers daily. So few cars were produced annually that prospective customers had to sign up and then wait years for delivery of a locally-made copy of a 1950s-era European car. A joint venture with Suzuki began to produce the Maruti in the 1980s. After Asian, European, and U.S. firms set up production in the 1990s, car sales climbed 20%–50% per year and by 2005 reached one million, growing at 10%–12% per year. There seems much room for growth: car ownership in 2012 was 1.5 cars per 100 people.

Automobile production in India mixes modern engineering and traditional construction. Among the 10 million employees in the industry there is more unskilled labor, because low labor costs make it profitable to do by hand what elsewhere is done by machine. The product mix, too, reflects the mixture of wealth and modest incomes. BMW and Mercedes now produce expensive luxury autos, while Tata Motors, a local firm, unveiled its rear-engined 33-horsepower Nano in 2008, the world's least expensive car. It costs under $2,500.

As the number of cars on the roads doubled, they quickly overwhelmed the streets and highways. Even national highways are often pot-holed, crowded, and narrow, so that aside from toll roads, few truckers can drive more than 250 miles per day while an estimated 40% of fruits and vegetables rot before reaching market. The ambitious target for new roads announced in 2010 is to complete 12 miles of road per day, 4,200 miles per year, an enormous task priced at $50 billion, with urban streets costing even more. Again, besides success in software, the dominant theme in the Indian economy for the next decade will be "Infrastructure Development," with projected spending of at least $200 billion per year.

The Future: Narendra Modi's massive victory suggests that the *BJP* is the national majority party, able to govern untroubled by demands imposed by coalition partners. By contrast, the *Indian National Congress* seems to reflect the desires of a relatively few secularists, non-Hindus communities, and long-standing beneficiaries of government policies.

However, India's government is federal and complex. Until later elections, *Congress* and its allies hold more seats in the upper house than the *BJP*, and they hold significant blocking positions in many state legislatures.

Economic reforms may well bring faster growth—but they will take time. Overshadowed initially by the emphasis on economic liberalization and growth, advocates of "Hindutva" within the *BJP* and its Hindu nationalist ally, *Shiv Sena*, could seize the opportunity to enact legislation achieving their religious-nationalist goals. Kashmir's unique constitutional arrangement as India's only Muslim-majority state might provoke the test case.

Expect a more vigorous and active role for India on the world stage, remembering that the *BJP* brought India into the nuclear arms age.

A dairy farmer in Rajasthan Source: World Bank photo by Ray Witlin

The Republic of the Maldives

Typical Maldivian boats known as Dhonis wait for passengers, Malé

Area: 115 sq. mi. (298 sq. km) of land, amid 34,500 sq. mi. (90,000 sq. km.) of water.
Population: 335,000.
Capital City: Malé (population 100,000, estimated).
Climate: Warm and humid. The annual rainfall is about 75 inches, mostly from May to October.
Neighboring Countries: India and Sri Lanka are located northeast of the Maldives.
Time Zone: GMT +5.
Official Language: Dhivehi (or Divehi; similar to Sinhala of Sri Lanka).
Other Principal Tongues: Arabic and English.
Ethnic Background: A mixture of Sinhalese, Indo-European, Arab and Negro.
Principal Religion: Islam. All citizens must be Muslim.
Chief Commercial Products: Fish (canned, dried and frozen); garments, boats, handicrafts. The export of many types of live fish and shells is prohibited.

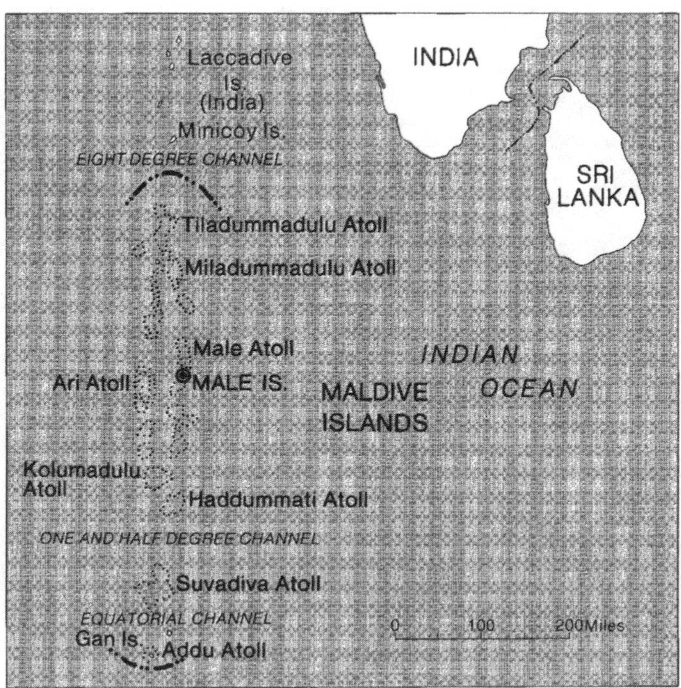

Major Trading Partners: Japan, Sri Lanka, India and U.K.
Currency: Rufiaa (1 rufiaa = 100 laari).
Former Colonial Status: Controlled by Britain (1796–1965).
Independence Day: July 26, 1965. March 29th is celebrated, as it marks the final surrender of rights by Britain in 1976.
Chief of State: Abdulla Yameen Abdul Gayoom (2013).
National Flag: A green rectangle bearing a white crescent is centered on a red field.
Gross Domestic Product: $2.4 billion (at current prices); $3.2 billion (Purchasing Power Parity).
GDP per capita: $9,600 (PPP).

Long known to Arab seamen as "Islands of the Moon," the Maldives are a string of 26 coral atolls scattered 550 miles along the top of a submarine ridge in the Indian Ocean. These atolls contain altogether almost 2,000 picturesque islets. About 200 of the larger ones are inhabited, but few of them extend even a mile in any direction. Islands rarely reach more than six feet above high tide; neither hills nor rivers exist. However, there are abundant coconut palms, white sandy beaches, and crystal clear lagoons formed by coral reefs. With hundreds of species of tropical fish and many varieties of shells and corals, the islands rank as a diver's paradise.

Located close to the equator, the Maldives experience two monsoons each year, and average about 75 inches of rain annually. Between April and October the southwest monsoon brings rain, but the dry winds of the northeast monsoon of "winter" originate in Asia and bring fair weather from December to March.

History: Straddling the sailing route between the Red Sea and East Asia, the islands were mentioned by voyagers from Rome, Egypt and China, but scholars dispute when the first settlers arrived in the islands. Discoveries by the explorer Thor Heyerdahl suggest that early inhabitants traded with ancient Egypt and Mesopotamia. Nearly nothing is known of those inhabitants, but about 2,500 years ago settlers arrived from Sri Lanka and India. Buddhism came to dominate religious life, and over the centuries sailors from Africa

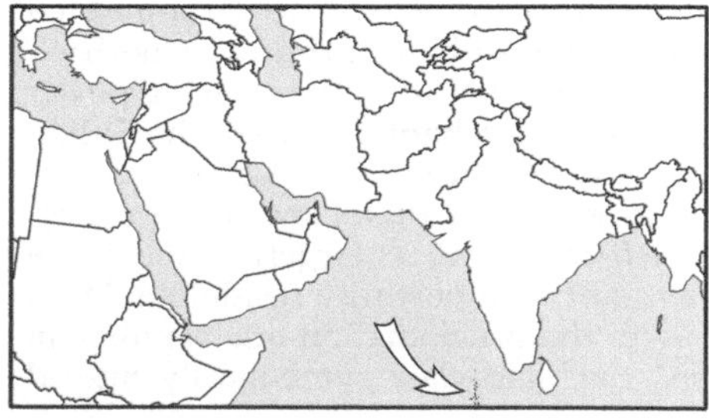

Maldives

President Abdulla Yameen (R) receives Sri Lanka's President

and Arabia joined the ethnic mix. Besides supplying vessels passing through, the Maldives exported vast quantities of cowrie shells, which became the currency in parts of Africa. From this trade, the islands earned the title "the money islands." In 1153 King Dovemi Kalaminja adopted Islam, a crucial event in the island's culture, and thereafter the kings became known as sultans.

During the following centuries, the islanders developed a unique unwritten constitution and fought off invaders, including the Portuguese in the 1500s.

Muhammad Thakurufaanu won recognition as "The Great" for liberating his country, for improving the administration, and for introducing the Thaana script to write Dhivehi. Nevertheless, under most sultans the islands remained relatively weak.

After Britain gained control of India and then Sri Lanka (1796), the dangers of invasion receded, as Britain seemed uninterested in the remote, malaria-infested islands whose chief product was dried fish. However, fearing the growing power of Indian merchants, in 1887 the Sultan sought British protection. Aside from control over foreign affairs and defense, Britain left the islanders largely to their own ways, not even posting a resident in Malé.

With the proclamation of a republic in 1953, the Maldivians symbolically entered their modern era. Although this First Republic lasted only one year, its president, Muhammad Ameen Didi, won respect for reviving Dhivehi and its literature. He reformed the system of education, improved the position of women, opened government stores to undercut foreign merchants, and also introduced strict Islamic laws. Partly to reduce the drain on foreign exchange, he banned the importation and smoking of cigarettes. Thus the Maldives became the first country to ban tobacco in the modern era, but popular dislike of such laws, as well as Didi's in-

Tasteful but too ostentatious for Nasheed: the presidential home in Malé

creasingly autocratic rule, led to his ouster and the collapse of the republic.

In 1965 a treaty with Britain provided full independence, though Britain retained—and paid for—use of an airfield and a radio communications station on Gan Island in the southernmost atoll. That same year, the Maldives became the smallest nation then received into full membership of the UN. Britain formally returned Gan Island in 1976.

A constitutional change in 1968 again established a republic. The sultan retired; his prime minister, Amir Ibrahim Nasir, won the presidency, but facing deep popular dissatisfaction, he resigned in 1978. The *Majlis*—the parliament—nominated Maumoon Abdul Gayoom, a previous cabinet minister, and a referendum approved him as president. The president serves a five-year term, and Gayoom's policies of harbor development, women's rights, and limited high-end tourism helped him win reelection every five years, as the only candidate proposed by the *Majlis*.

Tamil mercenaries hired by disaffected Maldivians attempted a military takeover in late 1988, the first invasion in four centuries. The Maldives has no army or navy, but the small National Security Service offered sufficient resistance for President Gayoom to escape his palace and request aid from friendly countries. Within hours, Indian paratroops landed; outgunned, the mercenaries eventually surrendered. The fighting awoke the nation to the need for modern defense, from radar and a trained fighting force to patrol vessels.

A prison riot of uncertain causes in 2003—torture was claimed, but denied—led to apparently spontaneous mob attacks on the parliament, the election commission, and other official buildings. More than a case of idle youths letting off steam, the riots did follow Amnesty International's accusations that the government imprisoned critics for political reasons and sometimes resorted to torture. They also preceded by just days parliament's selection of the nominee for the presidential referendum. Despite the mob's furor, the unanimous choice was a sixth term for President Gayoom, already Asia's longest-serving ruler.

In the aftermath of the violence, security forces arrested hundreds, including anyone who had been identified in pictures of the rioters. The firm hand of government blocked access to the web site of the only opposition party, the *Maldivian Democratic Party (MDP)*. Although Gayoom publicly accepted reforms, the special assembly he created to consider constitutional revision made little progress—it was twice the size of the parliament.

The 2004 tsunami centered off Indonesia wreaked vast damage to the small country: its capital city, Airport Island, and 47 other inhabited islets were flooded, and over 20 of the 87 resort islands were put out of operation. However, the loss of life reached only about 100, surprisingly low compared to seacoasts with higher land. Apparently the reefs around the islands absorbed much of the waves' power and the sea wall around Malé broke their force there. The consequence was flooding, rather than catastrophic destruction.

With world attention focused on the tsunami and its aftermath, the government had little alternative but reform. It released prisoners, and held elections for the *Majlis*. While not exactly fair—rallies, speeches and political parties were still prohibited, while the media directly or indirectly remained in government hands—the elections were free enough for candidates supported by the *MDP* (from exile) to win 18 of the 42 seats. In fairness to Gayoom, he congratulated even the *MDP* victors, and encouraged the new *Majlis* to enact reforms. It established, at least on paper, multi-party democracy, and widened press freedoms; eventually it produced a democratic constitution that Gayoom ratified in 2008.

Presidential elections fell due in 2008, and Gayoom sought a seventh term, promising the voters "dynamic years" under his trustworthy leadership. Arrayed against him, four rivals attacked his lavish lifestyle and nepotism. Strongly supported in the more traditional outer islands, Gayoom won 50% more votes than his nearest challenger, but was forced to a run-off. Supporters of the losing candidates then switched to Mohamed Nasheed of the *MDP*, and the former prisoner won the presidency.

Nasheed moved out of the presidential mansion, and planned to sell the multi-million dollar presidential yacht. He also planned to privatize the government-owned media, reform education, and restructure government. With a flair for communication, he publicized the threat of rising sea levels by conducting the world's first underwater cabinet meeting with 11 colleagues, who dove to their chairs about 12 feet below the surface. Nasheed expressed a desire to buy a new Maldivian homeland should global warming flood the islands, and also promised carbon neutrality by 2020, with electricity from solar power and virtually no use of fossil fuel.

Although Nasheed had won the presidency and global respect as a spokesman against global warming, his domestic political strength was weak. His cabinet fractured as members from other coalition parties resigned. Although winning the most votes, the *MDP* gained only one quarter of the seats in the 2009 parliamentary elections. Gayoom's supporters in the *Dhivehi Rayyithunge Party (DRP)* and their allies obstructed Nasheed's legislative goals so successfully that loyal ministers resigned in protest.

No mountains, no traffic, and short distances: no wonder they ride bicycles in Malé.

A strong unsettling force was the growing rhetoric of militant Islamism. Its sympathizers protested airline links to Israel, as well as alcohol and pork being served to tourists at resorts. The government eventually banned the links, the drinks, and the food, but did not act to enforce it. The ban did not prevent a leading member of an opposition party from claiming that Nasheed was under the influence of Jews and Christian priests in undermining Islam. On the streets, the *DRP* encouraged demonstrations blaming the president for corruption and high prices following the depreciation of the currency. For its part, the government blamed higher world prices.

As president, Waheed sought allies among parties critical of Mohamed Nasheed, even reaching out to the radical Islamic *Adhaalath Party*, which claims that music and singing are "haram" (prohibited) by Shari'a and supports the death sentence for abortion. It was also allegedly involved in a mob's destruction of the National Museum's entire collection of Hindu and Buddhist artifacts. Waheed rationalized that it was better to work with such parties rather than to exclude them. This approach alienated the more secular and liberal citizens, and it also failed to win support from traditionalists. Waheed proved an unpopular president, winning only 5% of the vote in the first round of presidential elections in 2013, and he subsequently withdrew from the contest.

Confusion and interventions marked the 2013 presidential elections demanded by Nasheed's *MDP* and the international community. With the country clearly split between supporters and opponents of Nasheed, campaigning was sometimes bitter, with strong Islamist accusations against Nasheed. The police and the Supreme Court both interfered with the election commission. One ballot was annulled, and after Mohamed Nasheed won the first round with 46% of the vote, the run-off was postponed to provide Abdulla Yameen, who had placed second, time to forge alliances. In the end, Yameen was successful. The half-brother of former president Maumoon Abdul Gayoom and candidate of his *Progressive Party of the Maldives (PPM)* won a narrow majority of 51%. In an act of statesmanship, Nasheed conceded the election.

Parliamentary elections in early 2014 confirmed the old guard's dominance of politics. The *PPM* emerged with 38 seats in the 85-member assembly; the *MDP* only 25.

Culture: All Maldivians are at least nominally Muslim, and often bear Arab names as a result. Their lives center around fishing, agriculture and a few light handicrafts. To a large extent the islanders follow strict Islamic standards of behavior, and laws prohibit drinking alcohol, Western-style dancing, possessing pornography and extra-marital sex.

Despite its geographical remoteness, few resources and relative poverty, the Maldives boast the highest literacy rate for women aged 10–45 in the Muslim world: 98%. This achievement becomes even greater considering that the English-language and modern Maldivian school systems date only to the 1960s and 1970s respectively. Not until 1979 did the government establish primary schools in every atoll, but by the late 1990s it had achieved virtually universal primary education.

For older generations, basic education took place not in a formal school, but in a Kiyavaage, a private home where children studied Dhivehi, a little arithmetic, and the Qur'an. Thereafter they could enter a Makthab or Madhurasaa, schools adapted from Islamic models. To date there is no institution of higher education in the country, though Islamic, teacher-training, and health institutes exist.

Strengthened by their education, women occupy a distinctive role in Maldivian society. Important even as rulers before Islam, in law they enjoy equal opportunities in employment, remuneration, and cultural activities. However, a 2013 government report demonstrates that in practice, women do not enjoy gender equality. Participation in the workforce is limited to traditional fields such as education, health, and agriculture, and few enjoy opportunities for advancement. Young women in particular suffer a very high unemployment rate (40%).

Partly a consequence of their lack of alternatives, girls do marry—the minimum age is 15, and most women who do not study abroad marry as teenagers. Negotiations establish the "bride price" the groom must pay, and this is retained by the woman if the marriage breaks up. Though respecting the stipulations of Islamic law regarding inheritance, Maldivian practice has allowed a woman to apply for a divorce even against her husband's desires. The divorce rate of 70% is among the highest anywhere; one consequence is that women head 47 percent of households in the Maldives, likewise among the highest rates in the world.

The Domestic Violence Act of 2012 attempted to remedy high levels of abuse and violence. Although the rates seem high (12% report sexual abuse before turning 15, and 30% of women have suffered from violence), much of the harm is inflicted by partners or within the family and not reported. When sexual morality is broken, it is also women who suffer at the hands of the law. Women are flogged; men seem to go free.

In recent decades, competition from foreign goods and modern factories closed some employment opportunities in traditional women's crafts (mat weaving and rope making, plus agriculture and fish processing). Today, women make important contributions in tourism, business and light industry. They manage companies, and practice law.

Though modernized and expanded upwards and outwards onto reclaimed land, the capital city of Malé retains a number of unusual features. Its population of about 180,000 has no buses and no dogs. With almost no crime and limited entertainment over local TV, its people enjoy socializing outdoors in the evening and weekends at the beach, where the women retain their modesty fully clothed. The relatively few tourists who actually linger enjoy the absence of hassle and a pleasant, laid-back atmosphere with the ocean always a few blocks away.

Economy: Lacking agricultural land, for centuries Maldivians turned to the ocean for fish and commerce. Until very recently, fishing was the principal livelihood for men, and shipments of dried and smoked tuna ("Maldive Fish") accounted for more than 90% of exports. Until the 1970s, fishing craft were small sailing boats, but a government program aided the fleet's conversion to diesel power. Modernization also took place in fish processing, with frozen and canned exports now accounting for over four-fifths of the total.

Many coconut palms and a few species of other fruit trees dot the islands, but agriculture is limited by the few areas of fertile soil on the tiny coral islets. The government is eager to encourage light industry, but there are few natural resources. Saudi Arabia, Japan and China have provided some foreign assistance.

Tourists began arriving in significant numbers in the 1970s, attracted by the natural beauty and cheap living. However, the islanders gained little economic benefit, and the spread of drugs, nudity and alcohol offended local society.

After President Gayoom took office in 1978, the country radically changed its approach to tourism. The jet airport opened in 1981, bringing tourists on package tours seeking relaxation, sunshine and water sports. Far different from the backpacking crowd of the 1970s, these visitors stayed at self-contained resorts on "uninhabited islands" that were taxed significantly and required to provide increasing levels of luxury. Other regulations reduced pollution, protected reefs and marine animals, and generally preserved the pristine underwater beauty for those willing to pay for it. Foreigners wishing to visit inhabited islands except the capital or a few villages on escorted trips require special permits.

One difficulty facing the Maldives is an adequate supply of clean fresh water despite the heavy annual rainfall. The rains do soak to fresh water aquifers underlying most islands, but unfortunately improper sewage facilities often pollute them. The islands' geography offers no convenient reservoirs or storage areas for potable water, and Malé uses reverse osmosis from sea water.

The Future: After two years of bitter political clashes, many citizens may desire a respite from electioneering. However, bitter rivalries will continue, given the chasm in public opinion between moderates sympathetic to the *MDP* and their opponents—loyalists to Maumoon Gayoom as well those wishing to impose Shari'a.

The tolerant ways of traditional Maldivian culture will continue to be assaulted by both the secularism of modernity and the fundamentalism of radical Islam. Public institutions are relatively weak and often fail to remedy obvious failings. There is no mechanism to monitor campaign financing, vote-buying is common, and a Supreme Court justice faces allegations of an alleged sex tape but continues in office. Meanwhile, although the *Adhaalath Party* carried only a single seat in parliament, public opinion seems susceptible to the allegations, often false, of Islamic radicals. Expect more Shari'a-influenced legislation, such as the restoration of the death penalty even for crimes committed during childhood. A cynic might think Maldivian society is unprepared for democracy.

Federal Democratic Republic of Nepal

Downtown Kathmandu

Area: 56,827 square miles (147,181 sq. km.).
Population: 28.3 million (revised estimate).
Capital City: Kathmandu (pop. about 1 million).
Climate: Very hot on the southern plains; cooler in the hills, and frigid in the high mountains on the northern border. The plains and lower slopes have heavy rainfall during the summer monsoon.
Neighboring Countries: China (North); India (East, South, West).
Time Zone: GMT +5 hours 40 minutes. When it is 1:00 o'clock in India, it is 1:10 o'clock in Nepal.
Official Language: Nepali (also called Gurkhali).
Other Principal Tongues: Gubhajius (Newari), Gurungkura, Hindi, Kiranti, Limbukura (Limbuani), Magarkura and Tibetan.
Ethnic Background: A mixture of Mongolian, Indian and Tibetan, who identify themselves as distinct communities based on language and traditions.
Principal Religions: Hinduism (about 85%) and Buddhism.
Chief Commercial Products: Woven carpets, textiles, rice, wheat, corn, millet, jute, oilseeds, cane, sugar, timber and hides.
Major Trading Partners: India (more than 50%), Japan, Germany, U.S. and Bangladesh.
Currency: Nepali Rupee (= 100 paisa).
Former Colonial Status: Limited British control, 1816–1923.
Independence Date: December 21, 1923.
Chief of State: Ram Baran Yadav, President (2008).
Head of Government: Sushil Koirala, Prime Minister (2014)
National Flag: Unusually, it consists of two red triangular pennants, one above the other, each bordered in blue. In the field of the upper is a symbolic moon, while the lower bears a symbolic sun.
Gross Domestic Product: $18.1 billion (current prices); $44.7 billion (Purchasing Power Parity).
GDP per capita: $1,600 (PPP).

Because its northern border runs along the crest of the Himalayas and its southern frontier lies on the tropical Ganges Plain, Nepal enjoys as great a geographical diversity as can be found in any small country. From an elevation of about 600 feet in the southeast to majestic Mt. Everest's 29,028 feet is a distance of little more than 100 miles by air. The entire length of Nepal from east to west is about 500 miles; at no point is it wider than 140 miles.

The strip of hot, marshy plain, averaging 30 miles wide along the southern border is called the *Tarai.* It is famed for its jungles and wildlife, though parts have been cleared. Its population and agriculture reflect those found in adjacent areas of India. While the least typical of Nepal, its agriculture is the most productive.

The slopes north of the *Tarai,* known as the *Hills,* are inhabited to an elevation of about 8,000 feet and in summer used for grazing herds to about 13,000 feet. The *Hills,* in turn, become the high mountains called the *Snows.* Some parcels of Nepali territory lie on the northern side of the crest of the Himalayas. Tibetans live there with their yaks and dzos (hybrids of yaks and ordinary cattle).

Another notable characteristic of the land is the pattern of rivers and streams flowing south from the High Himalayas to the Ganges Plain. These rivers carved out valleys with strips of relatively flat land. Surrounded by high mountains, the capital, Kathmandu, lies in the Valley of Nepal, the intensively cultivated bed of an old lake lying at an elevation of 4,500 feet and occupying about 300 square miles. The Valley of Nepal gives its name to the whole country.

History: Until the 18th century, individual cities and towns formed the basic political units. Their ruling families often descended from Hindu aristocrats who had fled from Muslim rule in India during the 14th Century. They and their retainers subjugated the mainly Mongol-Tibetan population and subsequently mixed with it.

Nepal's unity began when Prithwi Narayan rose to power in the town of Gurkha and in the 1760s completed conquest of the Valley of Nepal. Prithwi Narayan's successors, the kings of the Shah dynasty, attempted to expanded their rule, but were blocked by a large Chinese army in Tibet and defeated by the British (1815), who then controlled most of the Ganges Plain. A British resident was posted in Kathmandu, and only gradually did Nepal win recognition as lying outside India rather than forming an Indian kingdom.

After a period of instability, factional strife, and massacre under weak kings, a capable noble, Jang Bahadur, seized effective control. He retained the king—many Hindus revered him as a god—but kept him as a symbol while ruling in his name. His family, the Rana, became hereditary possessors of the office of prime minister. The Rana remained in power until the revolution of 1950–51.

An astute manipulator, Jang Bahadur balanced China and British India against each other for the benefit of Nepal. During the Indian Mutiny of 1857, he supplied Gurkha troops to fight against the rebels. The Gurkhas' courage and loyalty won British respect, and the tradition of recruiting Gurkhas for the British Empire began. Britain henceforth considered Nepal as a friendly ally and favored protected state and granted it formal independence in 1923.

India's independence in 1947 spread new ideas of nationalism and liberalism. Politically sophisticated activists from leading families who detested the Ranas' dictatorial methods formed the *Nepali Congress Party.* Influenced by the Indian party of the same name, they advocated democracy under the king.

As political tensions rose, King Tribhuvan was dismissed by the Rana prime minister and fled to India. Supporting the

Nepal

king, the *Nepali Congress* launched a revolution and gained control of parts of the country. In 1951 the alliance between King and *Congress* successfully removed the Rana family from government, and the party leader became prime minister. India and Nepal formed a special relationship that granted their citizens common rights of residence and land ownership, and promised military cooperation against any external threat.

In 1959, the *Nepali Congress* won absolute control of parliament and Bishweshwar Prasad Koirala became prime minister of Nepal's first elected government. However, King Tribhuvan had died; his son, King Mahendra quickly moved to rule rather than reign. He dismissed Koirala, arrested him, suspended parliament, and charged *Congress* politicians with corruption. All political activity was banned and the king became supreme. For the next 30 years, Nepal's kings attempted autocratic rule, sometimes with non-political elections of local councilors. This suited traditionalists, who regarded the king as the incarnation of the Hindu god Vishnu.In 1989 India blocked most trade across the border, on the pretext of fighting smuggling, but probably to punish Nepal's purchase of Chinese weapons. The Nepalese suffered greatly, finding themselves desperately short of gasoline, cooking fuel, medicine and other essentials. The weakness displayed by the royal government encouraged the *Congress Party* to join the communist-influenced *United Left Front* in protests.

When the police violently repressed the demonstrators, killing many, the shocked nation responded strikes by almost all groups, even newspaper hawkers and health workers. Unsupported even by the elite, King Birendra called for a new constitution and appointed a coalition cabinet of the *Congress Party*, the *United Left Front* and royal nominees took power. The constitution of 1990 established multiparty democracy and an independent judiciary. It thus ended absolute rule by the Shah dynasty.

Congress won an absolute majority in the subsequent elections. The party dominated politics for the next 12 years, but it failed to maintain internal discipline. Two aging veterans of the struggle for democracy in 1950, Girija Prasad Koirala and Sher Bahadur Deuba, manipulated party rules and alliances to gain office or oust each other. Certainly, *Congress* could win elections—it came second only once, defeated by the *Communist Party (United Marxist-Leninist)* of Man Mohan Adhikari in 1995. However, it could not provide stable government. Cabinets changed about yearly; politics centered on chasing office.

The parliamentary leftists failed to provide a viable alternative. A social democrat rather than a communist (despite the party's name) their leader, Man Mohan Adhikari, sought free elementary education, more funds for local governments, and tax reforms. However, his party never won a majority in parliament, and in opposition it suffered defections.

In such circumstances, politics became the rapid search for the rewards of office rather than an opportunity to serve the public good. Corruption was so rampant that cynics claimed "Governing Nepal is the art of appropriating foreign aid for personal use without getting caught." One cabinet included 37 members, one-third of the ruling *Congress Party's* members of parliament. International aid agencies and donor nations became disillusioned.

Throughout the 1990s, economic growth often stagnated, and the distribution of income became more unequal. For example, the poorest 20% of the population received less than 4% of national income, while the top 12% owned 70% of the wealth. Disillusionment with democracy spread widely.

A stubborn *Maoist* rebellion broke out in poor western districts in 1996. Partly because politicians failed to address the causes of popular distress, and partly because the police lacked the training, resources, and ideas to combat a guerrilla

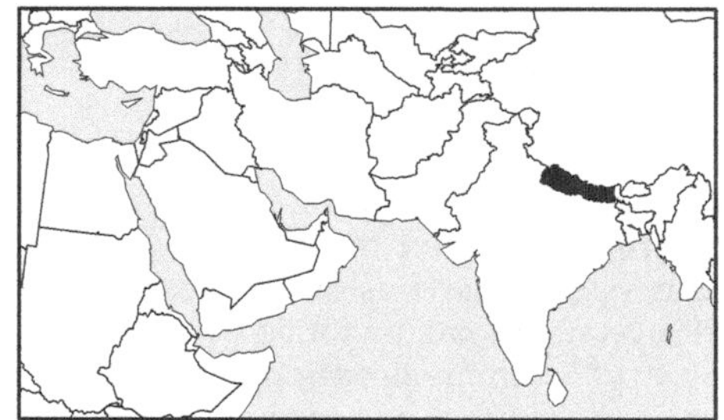

Prachanda, Maoist leader

movement, the *Communist Party of Nepal (Maoist)* gradually grew in power and destructiveness. It proved particularly adept at interfering with schools and colleges, whether by presenting programs, holding students for indoctrination sessions, or closing campuses during political strikes.

Last Years of the Monarchy

In 2001 the murders of King Birendra, his wife, and several relatives shook the nation. Crown Prince Dipendra, surviving in a coma, was declared king, but died within hours. Prince Gyanendra, Birendra's brother and perhaps the country's richest industrialist, then assumed the throne, the third king in four days. Official accounts blamed a drunken Prince Di-

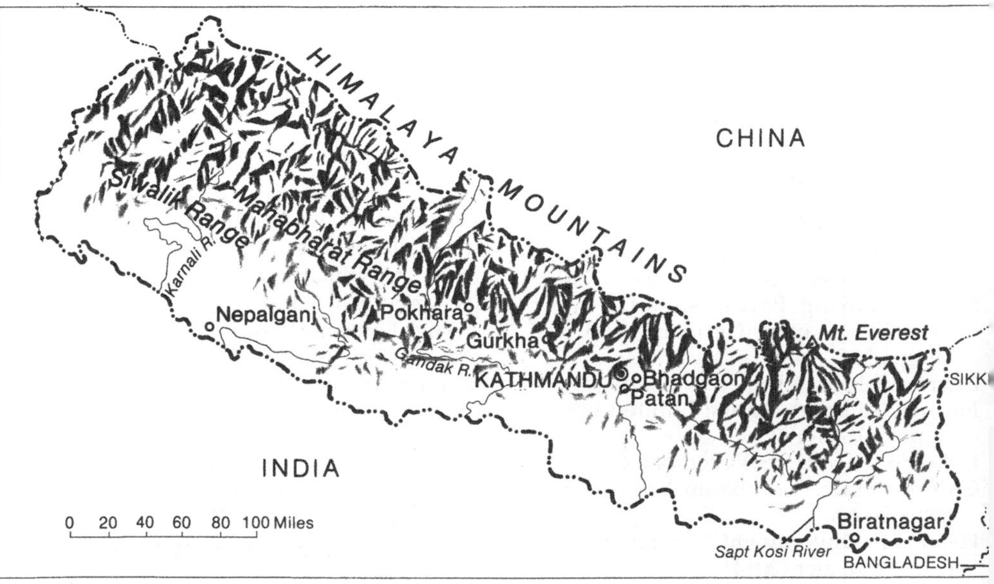

pendra for the murders, but many blamed conspiracies, and the nation hesitantly accepted King Gyanendra.

Gyanendra soon dissolved parliament and appointed his prime minister. Democracy formally ended in 2002. Few Nepalis except the politicians themselves initially seemed to care, and the king promised elections after defeating the *Maoists*. To crush the rebellion, he declared a state of emergency and ordered the army into combat. However, the rebellion spread, and sympathetic strikes shut down the capital itself. Negotiations between the monarchy and the *Maoists* failed, because the latter desired a republican constitution, a demand the king totally rejected.

The *Maoists* seemed particularly inept at public relations—even China condemned them. Bombing the Coca Cola plant in Kathmandu won grudging support from nationalists who criticized expensive foreign drinks, but discouraged foreign investment. Needing money, the *Maoists* extorted it from virtually every possible source, including tourist backpackers (asking modest amounts) and hotel owners (demanding much more). Unable to sustain their military units with volunteers, they turned to conscription, seizing several thousand children for indoctrination and military service. In response, hundreds of schools closed, and thousands of teenagers fled to India.

However, Chairman Prachanda ("majestically terrible," the adopted name of Pushpa Kamal Dahal) and his party stood for more than brutalities and bloodshed. In a country with high illiteracy and 50% of the population below the poverty line, they demanded education for all children (girls included) and an end to feudal land holding. Many of the fighters were female, and their women's organization pressed for greater rights. They also demanded a ban on alcohol, which they considered a serious social problem leading to violence within the home.

Failing to appoint a prime minister acceptable to the political parties, in 2005 the king dismissed the cabinet and took direct power. He ended freedom of the press, arrested many politicians, and tried those alleged of corruption without normal court procedures. Like the Maoists, the military and its vigilante groups committed more human rights abuses. International donors withheld aid, and demanded the restoration of democracy.

As public resentment rose, the *Maoists* declared a unilateral ceasefire and agreed to cooperate with the two major political parties, *Congress* and the *Communist Party (UML)*, for an end to "tyrannical monarchy." The political parties then initiated nationwide protests against the king's direct rule.

A solitary spot to pray at Boudnath Temple, Kathmandu. Photo courtesy of Karla Allan

While the king, apparently on his astrologer's advice, enjoyed his lakeside retreat near Pokhara, demands for a republic strengthened. Thousands of demonstrators defied prohibitions on public meetings, and attempted to march on Kathmandu. Royal officials failed to halt the protests and strikes, even with the bloodshed of shoot-on-sight curfews. After losing support among the military and even within his cabinet, Gyanendra capitulated. He recalled parliament, but the political parties, not the king, named Girija Prasad Koirala as prime minister. At Koirala's request, the *Maoists* lifted their blockade of Kathmandu.

Parliament moved rapidly to eradicate the political roles of the king. It abolished the title "His Majesty's Government," and removed his title as commander-in-chief. It stripped his image from the designs for coins and paper money, ended his freedom from taxation, and took away his power of veto. Nepal had been a Hindu kingdom. With the fate of the monarchy unresolved, the state was declared secular.

The *Maoist* cease-fire had made the protests possible, and large *Maoist* demonstrations in Kathmandu prompted the cabinet to negotiate. Prachanda and Prime Minister Koirala agreed to major changes in a Comprehensive Peace Accord in 2006. The *Maoists* entered parliament (mostly represented by women and minorities) and joined the cabinet. To reduce the danger of violent confrontation, the army was ordered to barracks, and the rebels to camps, where the UN monitored their surrender of weapons. After perhaps 13,000 deaths from the rebellion, peaceful change seemed possible, but not certain.

Ethnic conflicts rapidly replaced warfare over ideology. Speaking Indian languages rather than Gurkhali, many Madhesis of the southeastern plains felt distressed by their low level of government employment and virtual absence from the army. Protests led to riots against *Maoist* activists, killing many; the police seemed to disappear.

As expected, elections to the vital constitutional assembly involved some intimidation and even violence. The Maoist *Young Communist League (YCL)* received particular condemnation. Its 300,000 members, led by former fighters, were accused of threatening rivals, demanding payments from businesses, and forming a sort of parallel police force. The danger seemed real that Prachanda and his party leaders had unleashed a force they could not control.

Nevertheless, imperfect elections were widely preferred to strife in determining the country's future. Sensing this, the *Maoists* left the cabinet and threatened an election boycott if their two key demands were not met—proportional representation with quotas for women and underrepresented groups, and the abolition of the monarchy before the elections, rather than afterwards. The other major parties eventually yielded, and parliament approved a "federal democratic republican state" by an overwhelming majority.

The 2008 elections passed remarkably peacefully. The shock came with the results. The *Maoists* captured 220 of the 601 seats, more than the combined totals of *Congress*

Nepal

Prime Minister Sushil Koirala

(110) and the *UML* (103). The monarchy's doom was certified by the near-total defeat of royalists, and ex-king Gyanendra left the palace. Until recently a *Maoist* rebel, Prachanda became prime minister.

He recognized that he faced three tasks, the first to guide the Constituent Assembly in drafting a new constitution by 2010. Second, the economy needed relief. Third, most pressing of all, the 20,000 *Maoist* fighters idling in their special camps needed to be integrated into the National (formerly Royal) Army. This the military command fiercely opposed, even threatening to boycott athletic events that mixed soldiers and former rebels. When the president vetoed his removal of the army chief, Prachanda resigned before completing his first year of office.

The *UML* subsequently formed a coalition of 22 parties, including *Congress*. With the *Maoists* in opposition and boycotting the Constituent Assembly, fierce disagreements prevented the coalition from meeting its 2010 deadline to complete a constitution. Though the assembly's authority was extended, a fundamental gap remained between most politicians, who value law and government institutions, and the *Maoists* who saw the military as an instrument. After the 22-party coalition floundered, the *UML* and *Maoists* formed a new government, likewise considered temporary.

The government did integrate some 9,000 former rebels into the military, and dismissed more from their camps with their promised compensation. Nevertheless, popular anger and frustration with politicians grew when they failed to meet the extended deadline for a constitution in 2011. Thousands demonstrated and even the U.N. expressed concern.

At the last minute, the assembly approved a fourth year's extension of the deadline and agreed that the job would be completed. However, the Constituent Assembly could not overcome deep divisions among its members over the creation of ethnically-based states. Feeling he had no alternative, the *Maoist* prime minister, Baburam Bhattarai, dismissed the Constituent Assembly and called for elections in November 2012.

Strong opposition by other parties to holding an election with Bhattarai in office led them to reject the November date. Thanks to the winter's cold and the summer's monsoon rains, spring and fall are the only appropriate seasons for elections. Agreement on a new caretaker government led by the well-respected Chief Justice of the Supreme Court Khilraj Regmi finally enabled elections to be held in late 2013. By that time, the country lived in a formal political vacuum: it had no constitution, no elected government, no parliament, and no elected local bodies.

Ex-King Gynendra, deposed in 2008

The election results upset the *Maoists* dominance. They fell to third place, and initially alleged fraud, but local and international observers proclaimed the integrity of the vote. Voters restored the *Congress* and *Communist Party of Nepal (Marxist-Leninist)* (*UML*) to their traditional ranks of first and second largest parties in the Constituent Assembly. After attempts to establish a consensus government failed, *Congress* and the *UML* supported the appointment of the *Congress* leader, Sushil Koirala, as Prime Minister. A long-time political activist aged 75, Koirala came from a notable family: three cousins have served as prime ministers. Nevertheless, he was known for living a simple life. Koirala promised local elections in six months and a new constitution within a year. Since *Congress* accounts for only 196 of the 601 seats in the legislature, accomplishing those feats depends on both party discipline and continuing support by the *UML*.

Nepali school boys meet at Hindu Temple

Culture: Though considering themselves Nepalese, most inhabitants retain a strong loyalty to their tribe. Groups such as the Magars, Newars or Gurkhas have distinctive languages and customs; little social contact or intermarriage takes place between them. The Gurkha have enjoyed the most prestige, forming the military caste. During the political ferment in 2005–07, minority groups, whether the indigenous Janjatis or the Madhesis of the southeastern plains, pressed for greater rights.

Although in the hills and mountains the predominant physical characteristic is Mongolian, suggesting the population's origins from the north and east, religion and customs often belong to the south and west. Hinduism (see India: Culture) has been the official religion, followed by most Nepalis, though some Buddhists claim under-representation. The constitution required that the king be a Hindu and "Aryan," but in 2006 parliament declared the state to be secular.

Dancing and singing are the principal folk entertainment. Men and women usually hold such celebrations separately; it is not uncommon for young men to dress in women's clothing for the performance of certain dances. Except for simple flutes played by herdsmen, Nepalis of noble tribes will not touch musical instruments; the lowly Damais provide musicians for celebrations.

Most Nepalis are very superstitious. Women are commonly confinement away from the house and others for 10 days after the birth of a child, and exorcising evil spirits is still practiced. After a person has died, various rites are used to drive his spirit out of the house. Many superstitions relate to animals, such as the belief that keeping three cows is unlucky. If a farmer has four cows and one dies, he must either sell one or obtain another. Nepalis take astrology so seriously that astrologists were jailed for suggesting that the king's fate was "under bad stars."

Isolated and impoverished by its mountains, Nepal only slowly developed modern health and educational systems. Although most boys and half the girls receive a primary education, only about 40% of adults are literate. The leading center of higher education is Tribhuvan University, established in 1959.

Economy: An agricultural country whose inhabitants live close to the subsistence level, Nepal is one of the 10 poorest countries in the world. Its per capita income of about $300 per year reflects low levels of agricultural productivity and little industry. Manufacturing concentrates on processing local produce and simple consumer goods. The leading sectors are cotton textiles, pulp and paper, and construction.

The most productive farming region is the low-lying *Tarai,* where farmers raise two successive crops in a year. Rice is grown in the wet monsoon, other grains in the drier seasons. Level land in valleys as high as 5,000 feet above sea level are also farmed with the help of irrigation. The uplands are used extensively for grazing livestock.

Nepal's new highways, sometimes blocked by landslides as they run through the mountainous terrain, have attracted concentrations of population along them. As the main source of energy for cooking and heating is firewood, the mountains have become denuded of trees several miles on either side of these roads. The result is massive erosion, and more landslides. At the same time the women who carry the firewood in heavy baskets must climb higher and higher on the slopes to obtain their fuel.

Tourism developed at a modest rate in the 1980s but surged in the 1990s, partly because of lower airfares for European and American visitors. Before the Maoist rebellion and political upheavals, the income from tourism exceeded twice the amount earned from the traditional, but declining service of Gurkhas in the British army.

The next order of business is development of Nepal's hydroelectric power potential, optimistically estimated to exceed 83,000 megawatts. Less than 1% has been exploited, insufficient to supply the present needs of industry and homes. The government has proposed projects worth billions of dollars to foreign firms, but funding proved relatively difficult to obtain, not only because of environmental concerns. The electricity would be needed: in Nepal itself 85% of the population lack access to it, and neighboring India has tens of millions of potential consumers, though its states may be unable to pay.

The Future: The 2013 elections demonstrate that after years of turbulence Nepal's voters prefer traditional politics to revolutionary change. It is a very good omen that even though they suffered defeat, the *Maoists* acquiesced in the results. This strengthens the second Constituent Assembly as it undertakes to draft a constitution that replaces monarchy with republic, centralism with federalism, and an insurgency with routine politics.

Will 2014 witness a new constitution, or will cabinet instability prove the incompetence of politicians even without the king or revolution?

"Elderly postal delivery man in Kathmandu" Source: Mary M. Hill Forida

The Islamic Republic of Pakistan

Monumental shrine in Karachi dedicated to Mohammad Ali Jinnah, regarded as the founder of Pakistan Photo by Ray L. Cleveland

Area: Some 307,374 square miles (796,095 sq. km.), plus 32,323 square miles—83,716 sq. km.—of Kashmir.
Population: 186 million.
Capital City: Islamabad (pop. exceeds 1 million).
Climate: Generally dry, except for the mountains of the northeast; very hot except for mountainous areas.
Neighboring Countries: India (Southeast), Iran (West); Afghanistan (North); China (Northeast).
Time Zone: GMT +5.
Official Languages: Urdu, English.
Other Principal Tongues: Punjabi, Sindhi, Pashtu, Baluchi, Jatki, and Kashmiri.
Ethnic Background: Communities are distinguished by language and religion, but these divisions do not correspond to physical features. More than half the people are identified as Punjabis on the basis of language.
Principal Religion: Islam (about 95%), principally *Sunni.*
Chief Commercial Products: Textiles, rice, leather products, cotton products, tobacco, sugar.
Major Trading Partners: Japan, U.S., Germany, Saudi Arabia, China.
Currency: Pakistani Rupee (= 100 paisa)
Former Colonial Status: Part of British India (to 1947).
Independence Date: August 14, 1947.
National Day: March 23, "Pakistan Day."
Chief of State: Mamnoon Hussain, President (2013)
Head of Government: Nawaz Sharif, Prime Minister (2012).
National Flag: A large Islamic crescent and a five-pointed star in white lie within a field of green; at the pole there is a broad, vertical white stripe.
Gross Domestic Product: $240 billion (at current prices); $601 billion (Purchasing Power Parity).
GDP per capita: $3,200 (PPP).

Geographically, the heart of Pakistan is the Indus River. Tumbling from the Himalayas, the river and its tributaries traverse a vast plain stretching from the Punjab to the coast near Karachi. Irrigation from the rivers and the system of connecting canals supports intensive farming.

Southeast of the Indus Valley, the Thar Desert extends into India. This arid waste of sand and gravel receives less than 10 inches of rain per year, and supports scattered camel-breeding tribes. West of the Indus Valley, desert conditions prevail in Baluchistan, a dry mountainous region with elevations up to 11,000 feet. This thinly populated area has some irrigation and farming, but most inhabitants are Baluchi nomads who call the region Makran. The north and northwest are mountainous, including the world's second-highest peak, K-2.

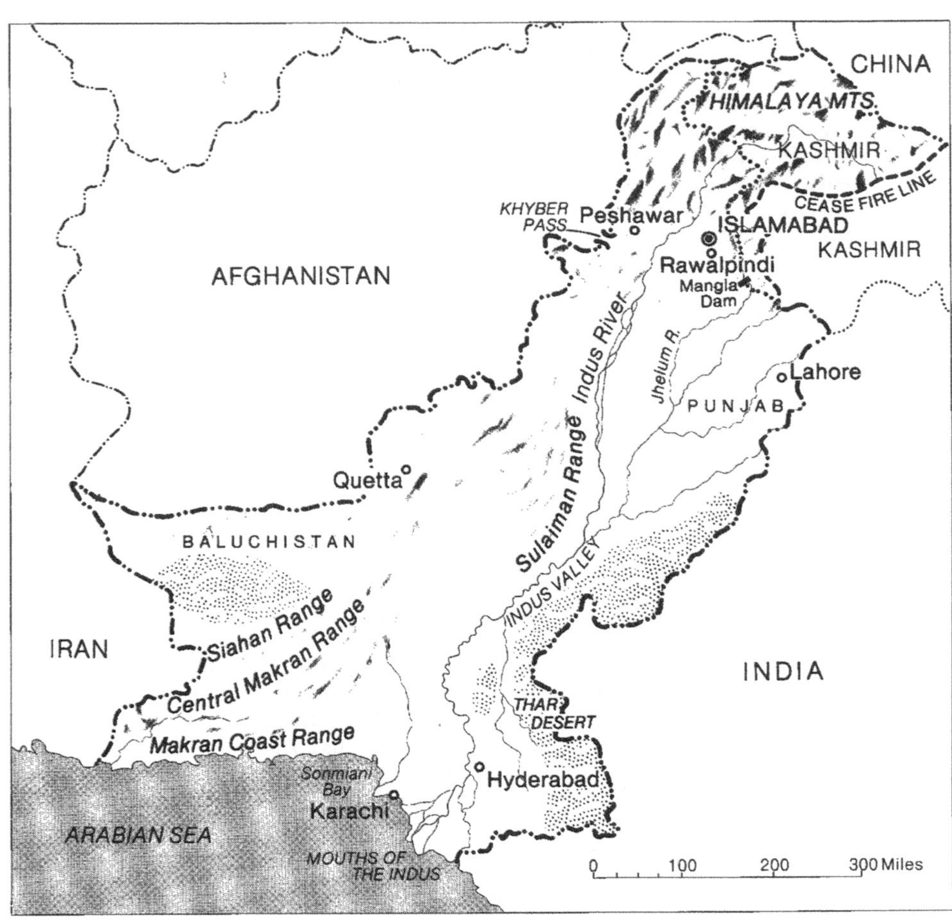

History: Before British rule in the 19th century, the territory that now comprises Pakistan had never formed a distinct political unit. Instead, various states and kingdoms ruled parts of it (see Historical Background and India: History). However, when the Indian independence movement raised the possibility of the end of British rule, Muslim leaders like Muhammad Ali Jinnah dreaded the prospect of becoming a religious minority in an India dominated by its Hindu majority. The *Muslim League of India* publicly endorsed the goal of establishing a separate state for the subcontinent's Muslims in 1940. Staunchly opposed to Hindu rule and inclined to exaggerate its potential difficulties, separatist Muslims did not foresee the problems that partition would create.

In 1947 Britain approved partition: the creation of two dominions, Hindu and Muslim. However, many Muslims lived in Hindu areas outside any possible Muslim state. Moreover, while Britain administered areas like Punjab and Bengal, and could divide them on the basis of religion, it granted the rulers of the princely states the choice of which nation to join—if either. From the partition emerged the new nation of Pakistan, the "Land of the Pure," composed of West Pakistan and East Pakistan—two areas separated physically by India (see map of India; Bangladesh was formerly East Pakistan). Ethnically fractured, and held together only by religion, Pakistan would rarely achieve national consensus over any significant secular issue.

Ethnic divisions ran deep within West Pakistan: the Land of the Pure was not uniform. More than half the population lived in Punjab, but Baluchistan and the North West Frontier Province contained sometimes-restless populations. Several rugged, Pakhtun-inhabited regions bordering Afghanistan formed, as in British times, semi-autonomous tribal areas

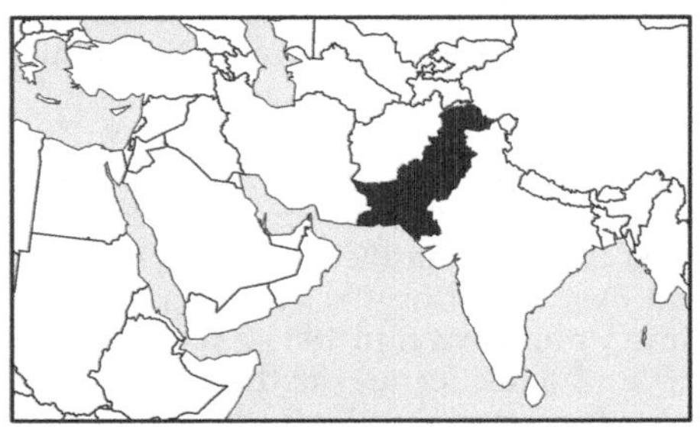

subject to tribal, not national law. Tribal leaders took decisions, influenced or manipulated by government officials posted as political agents. Participation in national political activities was prevented, and women only received the vote in the 1990s. Human rights were ignored by practices such as collective punishment and detention without trial. In 2009 the inhabitants finally gained the right to organize along political party lines rather vote for tribal leaders.

With the British withdrawal rapidly nearing, Muslim leaders hastily improvised a government in Karachi, a port city near the mouth of the Indus River. Muslims elected in 1946 to the Indian constitutional convention now sat in Karachi as the Constituent Assembly and legislature for Pakistan. Government offices had to be built from practically nothing. Civil servants proved scarce, though soldiers were plentiful, for Hindus had dominated the bureaucracy under British rule, just as Muslims had often led in the army.

Unfortunately, the new state soon lost its guiding personalities. Muhammad Ali Jinnah, the *Muslim League* leader who so strongly demanded partition based on religion, became the first governor-general, but died shortly after independence. Liaqat Ali Khan, the first prime minister and thus chief executive, was assassinated by a fanatic in 1951. Political instability became the normal course of life in Pakistan.

A massive two-way flight of Hindus and Muslims marked the actual partition. Pakistan lost many merchants and clerks while gaining large numbers of poor peasants. While Mohandas Gandhi almost miraculously averted strife in Bengal, in the Punjab militants on each side massacred hundreds of thousands. A dispute over Kashmir led to conventional war (see Disputed Territory: Kashmir), because the Hindu prince of a Muslim-majority state cast its lot with India. About 1.5 million Hindus fled East Pakistan (now Bangladesh) in 1950 for West Bengal in India, while some one million Muslims went in the opposite direction. A total of eight million people moved from one country to another.

Many Indian politicians resented the separation of Pakistan, and strained relations between the two nations proved a recurring feature until the present. A dispute over currency exchange (1949–1951) disrupted trade. Conflicts also arose over three eastern tributaries of the Indus used for irrigation in India. In a rare diplomatic achievement, this dispute was settled by treaty in 1961 (see When Will the Taps Go Dry?).

Pakistan gained United States military aid in 1954, though for much different reasons than Washington recognized. While the U.S. sought to recruit and strengthen an ally against world communism, Pakistan (which had dismissed its civilian government not long before) valued arms for possible war with its closer neighbors. Pakistan became a member first of the Southeast Asia Treaty Organization and then also of the Baghdad Pact.

From independence to the 1990s, constitutional disputes regularly marked politics. Pakistan produced few political geniuses, but many bitter rivals. The Constituent Assembly failed to determine such practical matters as whether Urdu or Bengali should be the official language. The voting strength of the Bengali—East Pakistani—members of the Assembly countered the governor-general who was from West Pakistan. After the *Muslim League* lost public support in East Pakistan in 1954, the governor-general dissolved the Assembly. Pakistani politicians and military rulers adopted many devices to manipulate the electorate and avoid the simple will of the people. Simultaneously, economic problems continued to mount, causing widespread dissatisfaction with the government.

A constitution instituted in 1956 established the Islamic Republic of Pakistan. However, elections were never held under that constitution: after just two years, a military coup d'état ended the flawed attempt at democracy. The army commander, General Ayub Khan, took the presidency himself, for a decade during which Pakistan began an inconclusive conventional war with India over Kashmir (1965).

Pakistan Falls Apart

Riots and political unrest in the late 1960s led Ayub Khan to resign, but the same political and economic problems festered under his successor, General Yahya Khan. In 1970 voters for yet another constituent assembly gave the *Awami League* of East Pakistan an absolute majority. Bengalis sensed a legal means to correct the economic and political discrimination that they believed Pakistani governments had practiced against them. However, Yahya Khan postponed the assembly and arrested Mujibur Rahman, the *Awami League's* leader. This triggered an outpouring of long-suppressed feeling in East Pakistan and resulted in its declaration of independence in 1971 as Bangladesh.

Yahya Khan's attempt to use the army to hold the two Pakistans together resulted in the destruction of whole Bengali villages and the massacre of their inhabitants. India intervened, and its army defeated the Pakistani forces and secured the independence of Bangladesh.

Alternate Military and Civilian Rule

Discredited by the defeat, Yahya Khan resigned. Zulfikar Ali Bhutto, an experienced opposition leader, became president and like nearly every Pakistani leader, he won wide initial popularity. This disappeared, however, when economic decisions and ideological differences alienated significant groups. Business leaders particularly disliked Bhutto's socialist seizure of private businesses.

Despite his socialism, Bhutto came from the landowning aristocracy of Sindh, and he dominated the Sindhi-based *Pakistan People's Party (PPP)*. The *PPP* won the 1977 elections, but the opposition accused Bhutto's government of fraud in counting votes. Riots and demonstrations led to martial law, and within weeks General Muhammad Zia ul-Haq led a military coup. He arrested Bhutto and other politicians "to save democracy for the nation."

Despite the promise of democracy, Zia canceled promised elections and banned political activity. His military regime ruled firmly, controlled the press tightly, and executed Bhutto. To foster his regime's popularity, in 1984 Zia proposed further Islamic features to the constitution and a ban on political parties. A national referendum endorsed the changes.

The Soviet Union's military occupation of neighboring Afghanistan rescued Zia's regime politically and internationally. Refugees from the brutal fighting flooded into Pakistan's border areas, burdening local society, and sometimes disturbing the peace. However, the U.S. and conservative Arab regimes, considering Pakistan a bulwark between Soviet troops and the Indian Ocean, provided weapons and funds to both the refugees and Zia's military regime.

After President Zia was killed in a suspicious plane crash in 1988, military rule collapsed. Benazir Bhutto, daughter of the executed Zulfikar, had already led agitation for democracy. Now the *PPP* quickly became the major national party, and it struck alliances with several regional parties. By contrast, the conservative *Muslim League* dominated the heavily-populated Punjab. Led by Nawaz Sharif, an industrialist, it became the fierce rival of the *PPP*.

Alternating Rule by Bhutto & Sharif

For the next 11 years, power alternated between Bhutto and Sharif. Three years in office proved long enough for each to commit enough mistakes to justify dismissal. Both Bhutto and Sharif won elections to come to power, but neither ever completed a term, their effectiveness disintegrating by the third year in office.

To generalize, Bhutto won fame and good relations in the West, but proved ineffective in domestic politics. More troubling, her husband, Asif Ali Zardari, allegedly amassed wealth from corrupt dealings and earned a reputation as "Mr. 10%." Open disputes flared between Bhutto, various presidents, and leading generals.

By contrast, Nawaz Sharif broke the tradition that reserved the office for wealthy landowners from Sindh. Sympathetic with economic freedoms, he attempted to establish the Islamic Shari'a as the highest law and adopted the death penalty for blasphemy against the Prophet Muhammad. Under the guise of fighting corruption, political opponents were arrested, most prominently Benazir Bhutto's husband.

Neither Bhutto nor Sharif brought peace of Karachi, the largest city if no longer the capital. Violence escalated there between the native Sindhis and the Muhajirs; it became an urban battle zone. The police acted brutally, but failed to contain the violence, and fatalities reached 800 in 1994 alone as factions of the splintered *MQM* attacked each other. When the violence claimed 600 lives in 1998, Sharif ordered military courts to render swift justice (three days maximum for trial, another three days for appeal, then execution). The carnage did decline, but civilian courts declared the special courts unconstitutional.

After India's nuclear tests in 1998, intense domestic pressure built up to display Pakistan's atomic weaponry. Despite strong foreign warnings and threats of sanctions, Sharif ordered tests in response. Their success propelled Pakistan into the small group of nuclear powers and won him great public applause. However, the blasts also deepened the discord with India, and brought economic punishment by foreign nations.

Perhaps reasoning they possessed an "atomic shield" against a conventional Indian attack, in 1999 Sharif and the military secretly sent Pakistani troops into Indian Kashmir to occupy and fortify positions at Kargil, overlooking India's vital road to Leh. The invaders inflicted heavy casualties on the first Indian troops sent to evict them. However, the invasion turned to fiasco when Indian successes on the battlefield and public condemnation by world leaders forced Sharif to withdraw the troops without even a face-saving gesture.

Following the humiliating withdrawal from Kashmir, Sharif proved particularly incapable. Rampant corruption flourished, and insensitive appointments antagonized public opinion. To intimidate the press, a respected journalist was beaten up. It was, after all, the third year of Sharif's term.

When Sharif attempted to dismiss the chief of staff in 1999, General Pervez Musharraf managed a bloodless *coup d'état.* He proclaimed a state of emergency, suspended the constitution, dissolved parliament and became chief executive. He promised to attack corrupt officials and make wealthy defaulters repay their loans. The public cheered, and the courts granted him three years to reform society.

Though powerful, Musharraf faced opposition. The attack on corruption moved very slowly. It also appeared mainly designed to control politicians and snared only a few. Conservative Islamists halted a proposal to reform the blasphemy law, and a strike against the new sales tax by shopkeepers weakened the new tax (they paid no income taxes, either). Suspicions mounted that the military intelligence service (the *ISI*) really ran the country.

Joining the War on Terror

After the September 11 attacks on the U.S., the government faced a dilemma. The *Taliban* regime that hosted Osama bin Laden in Afghanistan was partly a Pakistani creation. Musharraf could either acquiesce in an American attack on Islamic Afghanistan, or defy those U.S. efforts and lose any remaining international standing.

Risking assassination, Musharraf joined the war on terrorism. He permitted U.S. military flights across the country, and allowed U.S. troops to cross the border in hot pursuit. However, many Pakistanis opposed U.S. policies, and therefore Musharraf. The leaders of two Muslim parties, the *Jamaat-i Islami* and the *Jamiat Ulema-e-Islam,* called the regime illegal. After two assassination attempts in 2003 narrowly missed him, he reshuffled the high command and retired the *ISI* director sympathetic to the *Taliban.* The government also ordered the 20,000 Islamic schools to stop all military training.

Yielding to U.S. pressure, the government publicly ordered the military to root out *Taliban* and *al-Qaeda* fighters along the border with Afghanistan, a region suspected as the hiding place for Osama bin Laden. However, the critical border regions had long enjoyed autonomy as tribal agencies. In several of the Federally Administered Tribal Areas and in North West Frontier Province (now Khyber Pakhtunkhwa), attempts to establish military authority resulted in bitter skirmishes costing the lives of hundreds of soldiers in battle against fighters who knew the terrain and enjoyed local support. It may be worth noting that the most prominent *al-Qaeda* operatives were arrested in the cities, not the border areas.

The struggle against America's terrorist enemies proved difficult because of deep popular passions about local autonomy, opposition to Indian rule in Kashmir, resentment of injustice to Muslims in Palestine and elsewhere. For years, military agencies had stirred up these passions

Quality control workers inspect carpets when they come off the looms and trim excess wool
Courtesy: Caltex Petroleum Corporation

General Muhammad Zia ul-Haq

and supported the militants. Popular magazines extolled the virtues of jihad as armed struggle. Groups outlawed because of foreign pressure often reorganized quickly under new names. For example, the leader of the banned *Sipah-i Sahaba*, bailed from jail, successfully stood for parliament—and supported Musharraf's prime minister.

The war against terrorism brought benefits. Musharraf's role led many in the West to forget that he overthrew an elected government. The U.S. dropped the sanctions imposed after the nuclear tests and provided new aid. Both the Karachi stock exchange and the Pakistani rupee surged in value.

Searching for Political Stability

Though perhaps hidden at the time by the needs of government, Musharraf's later years in office became a dominated by desires to ensure control of politics. To overcome the Supreme Court's three-year limit for military rule, in 2002 a referendum was held to extend his presidential term by five years. Lavishly-funded propaganda favored the proposal, and despite a boycott by the major political parties, the result was 97.5% "Yes." This was discredited somewhat by low turnout and allegations of irregularities. The manipulation was probably unnecessary: the poor often liked the general, while the middle classes and more secular-minded citizens despaired of politicians and desired an end to the violence.

Musharraf then restored the president's power to dismiss parliament (but not directly the prime minister). He established a National Security Council of elected politicians and top military officers to review government actions. By involving the military in government, he argued, it would render the army less likely to overthrow democracy.

Before the 2002 National Assembly elections, the regime weakened opposition political parties by banning any candidate who had served two terms from taking office again. Moreover, threats of prosecution kept the most famous politicians, Benazir Bhutto and Nawaz Sharif, out of the country. While the *PPP* remained loyal to Bhutto, the *Pakistan Muslim League* split. Most of its supporters formed the *PML Quaid-i Azam (PML-Q)* that accepted General Musharraf's plans. Several Islamic parties united to form the *Muttahida Majlis-i Amal (MMA)* and concentrated their campaign against Pakistan's anti-terrorist alliance with the U.S. It placed third in the National Assembly and gained control of the border provinces of Baluchistan and the North West Frontier Province, where it began to institute Shari'a-influenced laws.

Open fighting in Baluchistan in 2005 drew attention to that poverty- and drought-stricken province. Less than 5% of the population enjoys running water, and society retains many traditional values. Baluchis list many grievances, including the exploitation of the region's natural gas and other resources with few benefits for the locals. They also fear an influx of non-Baluchis and dislike the military's presence. Nawab Akbar Bugti, the rebel leader, died fighting in 2006, reducing the organization behind the revolt but not its basic causes.

Despite its sometimes inept politics, the Musharraf administration earned respect for improved relations with India and for policies that provided faster economic growth. An attack by Kashmiri militants on India's parliament in 2001 brought the two nations close to war. However, Musharraf proved much more flexible than elected politicians. He yielded to New Delhi's demands and promised to halt infiltration across the Line of Control. He banned two extremist groups and the police arrested thousands of militants (though many soon reappeared on the streets). The *ISI* had sponsored the militants; now it encouraged them to disband.

With relations warming, despite extremists' threats a bus service began between Srinagar in Indian Kashmir and Muzaffarabad, the capital of Pakistan's portion, in 2005. Train travel followed, to Lahore.

Years of Challenge, 2007–10

When parliamentary elections and the presidential selection both fell due in 2007, political tensions rose dramatically. At least in retrospect, Musharraf repeatedly took decisions that cost him good will among the public. Desiring a new term as president after ruling for eight years, he schemed for the outgoing parliament to select the president because his supporters formed the majority. To overcome the legal roadblocks to this unusual approach, the president dismissed Chief Justice Iftikhar Muhammad Chaudhry for abuse of office.

A visionary for constitutional rule, Chaudhry turned the dismissal into a campaign for an independent judiciary. Thousands of lawyers and judges demonstrated in his support, but in Karachi dozens were killed when his supporters were attacked after the police vanished. These events weakened Musharraf's support among the modernized middle classes.

About the same time, Musharraf's support plummeted among conservative Muslims when, at a cost of 100 lives, the military crushed the Islamic extremists who had seized the Lal Masjid, the Red Mosque of Islamabad and used it as a base to attack brothels and kidnap a group of Chinese workers. Isolated by events and public opinion, Musharraf restored the Chief Justice and promised to resign from the military if he were elected president. Parliament duly selected him, but the Supreme Court delayed recognizing the decision, on grounds that it had not yet ruled on the eligibility of a presidential candidacy by the military commander.

Seeking a natural ally opposed to the militants and religious parties in the approaching parliamentary elections, Musharraf sought an accommodation with Benazir Bhutto, the *PPP* leader exiled over corruption charges. After the president granted amnesty to leading politicians with pending corruption cases, she, her husband, and Nawaz Sharif returned from exile. Bhutto's triumphal tour of the country drew large crowds, but was marred by bombings in Karachi that killed scores of *PPP* supporters.

General Pervez Musharraf

Still fearful the Supreme Court would void his presidential election while still military commander, Musharraf declared a state of emergency in late 2007. He suspended the constitution, banned political rallies, curbed the media, and dismissed the Supreme Court justices. His newly-appointed judges faithfully approved his election, and Musharraf handed over command of the army to General Ashfaq Kayani, a widely respected career soldier. Musharraf then ended emergency rule. Nevertheless, he was widely disliked, and his manipulation of the state of emergency strengthened his opponents.

Women in Pakistan

Although Pakistan elected the first Muslim female prime minister, its women rarely escape from the restrictions traditional in Iran and the Arab world. Women play so small a role in public life that some are literally invisible, uncounted even by the national census.

National statistics portray them confined to very traditional roles. Only 10% of adult women are "economically active" or employed outside the home. Over 80% of adult women are illiterate, and in rural areas the figure exceeds 90%. Male life expectancy (52 years) exceeds that for females. Only three other countries, all in the Indian subcontinent, have shared that distinction. The ratio of women to men, the lowest in the world and dropping, is 91:100. A figure this depressed suggests that the practice of purdah, or seclusion, renders some females non-persons. It also reflects high female death rates, including at childbirth. More sinisterly, an estimated 1,000 women are murdered annually for allegedly bringing dishonor on their families.

Other evidence reinforces the statistical conclusions. During Zia's rule, television and the media blamed working women for defiling society. It became questionable for women to vote, study in classes with men, and even drive. Striking deep roots in the country, such ideas remained even when a woman became prime minister. Benazir's cabinet proposed requiring women TV announcers to cover their hair.

The 1973 constitution bans discrimination, but the adoption of the Islamic Hudud Ordinance in 1979 turned legal practices strongly against female equality, especially in areas of sexuality. The maximum penalty for an adulterous spouse became death, though more commonly prison sentences were imposed, which accounted for over three-quarters of the country's female inmates. The pregnancy of an unmarried woman provided sufficient proof of her illegal sexual intercourse; no trial was necessary for a prison term. Her male partner must be identified, charged, and tried before punishment.

The law placed rape victims with a dilemma. Failure to report the rape left free the assailant—or assailants, as gang rape is not rare. However, a woman's report of rape provided evidence that intercourse took place. Conviction of rape requited the testimony of four male witnesses, usually an impossibility, but the rape victim's report to police provided evidence of her illegal sexual activity. Despite strong opposition by religious conservatives, parliament replaced these portions of the Hudud Ordinance with the Women's Protection Bill in 2006.

One recent rape case portrays the terrible plight some women face. To punish her brother, aged 12, for an alleged romantic interest across tribal lines, a rural council ordered Mukhtaran Mai to be gang-raped. Fortunate to survive the experience, she began a legal battle and related her experience to the world press. International contributions enabled this brave woman to found two schools in her village and a trauma center for women. However, when she was invited to address a human rights conference in New York in 2005, the government blocked her trip. In 2011 the Supreme Court dismissed charges against most of her assailants, for lack of evidence. She now fears for her life.

The 1984 Law of Evidence states that in financial matters, the evidence required of two men may be provided by one man and two women, thus establishing the principle of one man's testimony legally equal to that of two women. Such restrictions reflect both Islamic values and the even older customs of the sub-continent. For conservative Muslims, the Qur'an is the literal word of God, and a country's laws must fit its prescriptions, regardless of secular values or economic harm.

The greatest challenge to such a worldview comes from secular education. Pakistan ranks among the lowest in the world in the percentage of girls in elementary school, and fundamentalists intend to keep the percentage low. Thus *Taliban* gunmen seriously wounded Malala Yousafzai, a 14-year-old campaigner for girls' rights, whom they accused of "promoting secularism."

With threats like this, the next generation's women, like those of the present, will largely define themselves in the traditional roles of housewife and mother with little freedom outside the house. A recent poll of international experts by the Thomson-Reuters Foundation ranked the country as the third most dangerous for women in the world.

Benazir Bhutto's Assassination and Musharraf's Fall

As she left a political rally in Lahore in December 2007, Benazir Bhutto was assassinated. Some branch of military intelligence seems complicit, and the police at least negligent, partly because Bhutto had earlier written Musharraf that extremist suicide squads and a group of senior politicians and intelligence officials were plotting to kill her. Officially the attack was blamed on Islamic militants, but her security was clearly inadequate, and the shoddy police investigation—for example, the scene was hosed down immediately—also pointed to government failure.

Responding quickly to the death of its leader, the *PPP* transferred power to her husband, Asif Zardari. The *PPP* triumphed in the subsequent parliamentary elections, winning the most seats of any party (87). Its leaders formed a coalition with Nawaz Sharif, whose *PML-N* emerged the second largest party after campaigning about inflation, unemployment, and reinstating the Supreme Court justices. The *PPP*'s Yusuf Raza Gillani, a man of character who had served five years in jail on possibly trumped-up charges, became prime minister.

The new cabinet addressed many issues. It revised education policy, published the military budget, and righted past wrongs. The most compelling demands for change involved the fight with militants, and the restoration of the Supreme Court judges.

Because both the *PPP* and the *PML-N* had supported restoration of the Supreme Court judges, an agreement on doing so seemed within reach. However, the two parties failed to settle the matter, because their goals differed. Nawaz Sharif clearly desired Musharraf's ouster, so he hoped a restored Supreme Court would void the presidential election. By contrast, Asif Zardari apparently preferred that Musharraf remain president, because a Supreme Court decision dismissing the presidential election might also void his own pardon from corruption charges.

The crisis over the Supreme Court judges reached its conclusion in 2008. Just days before his impeachment on charges of violating the constitution, Pervez Musharraf resigned the presidency. It was, many felt, a landmark moment for Pakistan, the ouster of a former military ruler by orderly political process. The National Assembly subsequently elected Asif Ali Zardari president.

Pakistanis abroad hail SC verdict

NEW YORK, May 26: Pakistani immigrants hailed as historic the Supreme Court judgment reinstating the National Assembly and Prime Minister Nawaz Sharif, saying they were proud of the contribution of the country's judiciary to strengthening the democratic process, reports APP's special correspondent.

They said that the Nawaz Sharif government had worked for the betterment of the country and that it had achieved definite progress.

In the name of Allah, Most Gracious, Most Merciful

FOUNDED BY QUAID-I-AZAM MOHAMMAD ALI JINNAH

THE PAKISTAN TIMES

National English Daily with the largest circulation — Published simultaneously from Islamabad & Lahore

PM lauds role of Press

ISLAMABAD, May 26: Prime Minister Muhammad Nawaz Sharif has lauded Press for its outstanding commitment to democracy from the day of dissolution of the National Assembly till its restoration.

He was addressing a news conference at the Prime Minister Secretariat this evening.

Muhammad Nawaz Sharif thanked the Press for making his (Nawaz) cause its own cause.-PPI.

Regd. No. R-1 Vol. XLVII No. 108 | Islamabad, Thursday, May 27, 1993— Zilhaj 4, 1413 A.H. | Tele: No. 825893, 825766, Reporters 829297; Telex 54672 44811 (Times PK). Fax: 823467. Price Rs. 4.00

Supreme Court declares Presidential Order as *ultra vires* in a historic verdict

National Assembly, Nawaz Govt. restored

Court also dismisses review petition

By Muhammad Ilyas

ISLAMABAD, May 26: The Supreme Court of Pakistan, in a historic decision, today restored the National Assembly, the Prime Minister and his Cabinet with immediate effect.

The Court also outrightly dismissed the request on behalf of the President for suspension of the restoration order pending decision on the Review Petition which would be filed against the Court's order on Mr. Nawaz Sharif's constitutional petition.

As soon as the Court's decision became known, the corridors and vaults of the under-construction building of Supreme Court resounded with slogans of "Nawaz Sharif Zindabad" which were chanted by a large number of his supporters thronging the premises.

Mr. Shahbaz Sharif MNA, younger brother of Prime Minister Nawaz Sharif was among those present in the Courtroom when Chief Justice Dr. Nasim Hassan Shah announced the keenly awaited judgement.

(Text of SC verdict)

(See Page 5)

The National Assembly, elected in October 1990, is the 7th Assembly of Pakistan and, thanks to the Supreme Court's verdict, is the first one to be revived. Only two other Assemblies — one elected in 1962 and the other in 1970 — had their culmination under constitutional dispensation. Six Assemblies met with unnatural demise unsung and unredeemed.

Chief Justice Mr. Justice Nasim [illegible] the Supreme Court along with 10 other judges in Islamabad on Wednesday. (More pictures on Pages 3,5,12)

Pledge to work within legal framework: Cooperation of political forces sought

Nawaz vows to pursue policies with new vigour

By Maqbool Malik

ISLAMABAD, May 26: Describing the decision of the Supreme Court as historic, Prime Minister Muhammad Nawaz Sharif has vowed to work within the legal and constitutional framework and pursue his programmes with renewed vigour to propel the country out of the setbacks it had suffered in the wake of the dissolution of the National Assembly.

Addressing a crowded press conference at the Prime Minister Secretariat here Wednesday evening after the restoration of the National Assembly and his government by the Supreme Court, he observed that Pakistan suffered heavily in terms of rapid progress, foreign investment and its international image.

He asserted that his government would endeavour to bring about a new political order in the country which would be free of hypocrisy, unscrupulousness and blackmail-tronic media.

The Prime Minister went on to say that the character assassination campaign unleashed against him by the caretaker government died down in the eyes of the public as the caretaker government could not find any valid material against his government. "Had they any valid material against us, why did they not go to the courts to prove it, he questioned.

He asserted that masses did not heed the character assassination campaign launched against "me and my friends, rather they were depressed and unhappy, mourning the dissolution of the National Assembly and dismissal of my gov-

Continued on page 5 col. 2

Gen. Waheed, Admiral Saeed meet Nawaz

ISLAMABAD, May 26: Chief

Multiple crises soon tested the new regime, including a bitter dispute over demands to reinstate the Supreme Court Chief Justice. In response to forceful demonstrations and a threatened march on Islamabad, Zardari's government arrested hundreds of opposition activists, but eventually gave way and reinstated the full Supreme Court.

Predictably, the court addressed the pardon that Musharraf had granted Zardari and some 8,000 politicians, administrators and other members of the country's elite. When the court proclaimed the legislation illegal, it plunged those amnestied into legal limbo. While as president Zardari enjoyed immunity from prosecution, his popularity slumped as the nation's media became consumed with one topic: how Zardari would be replaced or sacked.

While clinging to office, Zardari accepted major changes that weakened the role of the president. He turned over control of nuclear weapons to the prime minister, and signed major constitutional changes that also ceded the power to appoint the military chiefs, judges, and the chief election commissioner. He lost the long-disputed power to dissolve parliament and to impose emergency rule on a province. The presidency became largely symbolic.

Still Struggling against Terrorism

In 2007, suicide bombers killed nearly 1,000 Pakistanis; after Iraq and Afghanistan it has suffered the most casualties in the conflict. Soldiers had also died while fighting the "War on Terror" in border regions where the *Afghan Taliban* had gained local support. Additional casualties, militants as well as unfortunate civilians, resulted from American missile strikes in those regions. Tired of the struggle, many politicians argued in favor of negotiations with the militants rather than their conquest. For its part, the *Pakistan Taliban Movement (Tehrek-i Taliban Pakistan)* argued that its struggle was with America.

In 2009 the provincial government of Khyber Pakhtunkhwa (the renamed North West Frontier Province) negotiated a truce for Swat, a beautiful, rugged region not far from Islamabad, where insurgents had fought the military to a standstill. In return for a cease-fire, the agreement released militant leaders and imposed Sharia law in Swat and adjoining regions. Human rights organizations and the international community were horrified at the victory for militancy, and the possibility of punishments such as the amputation of limbs, whipping and execution by stoning for adultery. Politicians, however, hoped that concessions over Swat and other regions would halt the extremist violence. No doubt also some intelligence and military officers preferred to see the army defend Kashmir rather than attack tribal areas.

The truce quickly failed, when militant fighters appeared even closer to the capital. Open warfare resumed between the military and *Taliban* fighters. Hundreds of thousands fled the conflict, but at least in Swat the army regained formal control, and refugees began to return to their homes. However, terrorist strikes have continued across the country, including an attack on the visiting Sri Lankan cricket team, a massive bombing of the police emergency response headquarters in Lahore, military training centers and suicide bombings in the streets. Furthermore, the insurgency threatened to spread. Impoverished areas of southern Punjab seem likely to support the *Taliban* and other groups committed to violent jihad. The region's poverty, high illiteracy, and feudal system provide the conditions where such militancy often flourishes.

Though momentarily successful in South Waziristan and some other tribal areas, the army and civilian government have not yet formulated a counter-insurgency strategy. Even when the army has controlled an area, the government has failed to reconstruct the homes, businesses, schools and offices destroyed in the conflict. It also has failed to develop civil society. Consequently, militancy and terrorism reappear given the opportunity.

Rather than occupy North Waziristan, the military has largely ceded it to Gul Bahadur, the autonomous local *Taliban* leader, who has proclaimed that his focus is liberating Afghanistan, not Pakistan. Pakistan thus allows refuge for thousands of Chechen, Arab, Kashmiri and Central Asian fighters linked to *al-Qaeda*. It also provides a sanctuary for Jalaluddin Haqqani, the Afghan militant. Given this coalition of *al-Qaeda* allies, and because the Times Square bomber trained in explosives there, the vast majority of recent drone missile strikes by U.S. forces have been aimed at North Waziristan.

In times of crisis, the deciding element is often unplanned. Pakistani public opinion about militant Islam changed perceptibly after a two-minute video showed militants flogging a screaming young girl.

Prime Minister Nawaz Sharif

Former President Asif Ali Zardari

Interviewed later on television, *Taliban* leaders awoke national concern by condemning schools, music, most entertainments, alcohol, democracy, and much else, not just in Swat, but anywhere in the country.

Other unplanned events later drove public opinion in the opposite direction. An American security contractor, Ray Davis, shot dead two young men in Lahore traffic and was subsequently identified as a CIA operative. Pakistan denied he held diplomatic immunity, and tried him for murder. However, "blood money" paid to the victims' families, a practice legal under Sharia law, resulted in his release though not the rehabilitation of U.S. prestige.

Greater consternation within the military and among the public followed the airborne raid by U.S. SEALS that killed Osama bin Laden in Abbottabad, just a mile from the Pakistan Military Academy. The successful raid, publicly acknowledge as undertaken without the military's permission or even knowledge, raised troubling questions in both countries. Pakistanis already critical of the CIA's drone attacks in border areas questioned the right of U.S. troops to attack a civilian residence deep inside the country without permission. Americans wondered aloud if the world's most sought terrorist lived so safely for so long because of covert military or intelligence assistance.

The tenuous alliance between the two nations frayed further when U.S. aircraft in Afghanistan hit a Pakistani base across the border and killed 24 soldiers. Angered by both the loss of life and the reluctance of the U.S. military to apologize (it did express deep regrets and acknowledged mistakes), Pakistan closed its borders to supplies for U.S. and NATO forces in Afghanistan. This forced supplies by land to be shipped through Central Asia.

The Turf War between the Court and the PPP

The final months of the *Pakistan People's Party* government were marked by deep struggles with the Supreme Court, agitation by militant Islamists, and tension with the military. Chief Justice Iftikhar Chaudhry had returned to the Supreme Court determined to charge politicians for their alleged misdeeds. The court began at the top: it demanded that Prime Minister Gillani ask the Swiss authorities to reopen a closed investigation of Asif Ali Zardari for corruption.

Gillani reasoned that as president, Zardari possessed legal immunity. When he therefore refused to act, the Supreme Court dismissed him from office, plunging the country into political crisis. His replacement, Raja Ashraf, was the *PPP*'s second, last-minute nominee. Six months later, the court ordered his arrest over alleged corruption when he directed the ministry of water and power. However, the evidence proved incomplete and he remained in office until a caretaker cabinet formed to supervise the elections.

Strangely, just when he sought to bring corruption charges against President Zardari, Chief Justice Iftikhar Chaudhry did not recuse himself when the court heard allegations that his own son, Arslan, had accepted millions of dollars in bribes.

The 2013 parliamentary elections aroused widespread public interest. The election turnout was the highest in 40 years, despite a *Taliban* campaign that killed mostly the supporters of secular parties. Nawaz Sharif's *Pakistan Muslim League* swept to an overwhelming victory in Punjab and gained enough seats to govern without a coalition, supported by friendly independents. Imran Khan's *Tehreek-e-Insaf* or *Movement for Justice* broke through to significance with its program of tax fairness and anti-corruption, becoming the third largest party, though not accomplishing the tsunami of reforms he predicted would wash away all the "corrupt politicians and plunderers." The *PPP*, barely escaping third place, had accomplished what no Pakistani party had ever done: to govern for its full term of office.

Taking office in a nearly-failed state, Prime Minister Sharif encouraged great expectations that he would tackle the nation's pressing problems, especially terrorism and the economy. However, the first year of his term was more remarkable for its failures, perhaps because Sharif was apparently most concerned with having Pervez Musharraf tried. Perhaps symbolizing its ineffectiveness, his administration failed so badly that the state-owned electric utility cut power to his office for unpaid bills. That literal darkness was quickly remedied, but Sharif's attempts to remove the dark cloud of terrorism brought no immediate peace.

Ignoring the military and civilian experts, he gained political support for unconditional talks with the *Pakistan Taliban*, calling that cluster of affiliated groups "stakeholders" and blaming the U.S. for Pakistan's terrorism. Some aspects seemed promising: the appointment of Mullah Fazlullah as *Taliban* leader reflected disunity within the grouping, with splits widened by competing attitudes to negotiations.

The *Taliban* used the talks as an opportunity to publicize their goals. They predictably demanded a constitution based on Shari'a, and the military withdrawal from tribal areas. Despite a halt to U.S. drone attacks, the campaign of terrorism continued, spreading further into the country's cities. Finally, in 2014 Uzbek Islamists linked to the *Pakistan Taliban* launched a brazen attack on Karachi's Jinnah International Airport, the largest in the country, killing dozens. Negotiations had proved a failure, and some analysts feared an urban insurrection (or, more correctly, insurrections), attacking and holding towns and parts of cities. The public, meanwhile, was demoralized.

A few days later, apparently at the request of Pakistan's military, the U.S. drone attacks resumed on a village known to house Uzbek fighters. Then the military launched a slow-moving campaign against North Waziristan, the tribal area with the greatest concentration of violent extremists. The assault was classic: shelling and air raids on targets, followed by a ground invasion. However, the troops moved in so long after the bombing that most civilians had fled as refugees and most terrorists had slipped away. Some, apparently, had been tipped off.

Little progress has also been achieved in reviving the economy and its interconnected problems. Electricity shortages frustrate nearly everyone, but the solution involves importing natural gas (eventually from Iran), spending billions the government does not have on generating stations, and slashing the inefficient workforce, thus alienating supporters. The empty treasury requires international loans, and thus American support, as well as tax reform. But higher taxes will inevitably hit Sharif's business supporters as well as the wealthy landowners. Meanwhile, the currency weakens.

Culture: Pakistan is a land of villages, and traditional landowners dominate society and government. The two cities of Karachi and Lahore best represent urban society. With nearly 12 million inhabitants, Karachi dominates the nation's business as the major port and industrial center. Karachi is hot, noisy, crowded and dusty; the poor are seen everywhere. Lahore is a more traditional city of about three million. Like most urban areas, both cities are crowded with picturesque but tiny stores and workshops, where handicrafts are sold directly by the artists. By contrast, Islamabad, the newly-constructed capital, was planned along modern lines.

Life in the irrigated valley of the Indus and its tributaries differs greatly that in the Thar Desert or the mountains to the northwest. In the deserts and near-deserts, camel and goatherds move continuously in search of sparse vegetation.

Though the teachings of Islam minimize class distinctions, society in Pakistan is deeply divided between a small class of wealthy landowners and millions of impoverished farm workers, some of them bonded laborers who will never escape their debts until death passes them to their children. Though the laws do not recognize a special status for the landowners, thanks to their political influence the landowners pay almost no taxes, while the urban middle classes are taxed heavily to compensate. Land reforms and the spread of education are very slowly reducing these distinctions.

For those with leisure time, soccer and cricket are popular sports. One unique local festival is Basant, the spring kite-flying festival in Lahore. Though a picturesque sight, Basant's kite-flying was often dangerous because the fliers' goal is to cut the string of rival kites. To that end, they coated strings with glass particles, creating a sometimes lethal hazard to unfortunate motorcyclists and bicyclists who caught the strings of falling kites around their necks. Banned for safety reasons in recent years, it was revived in 2007 with glass strings prohibited.

Female participation in outdoor sports has been targeted by Islamic militants, and sometimes prohibited. When women were suddenly permitted to participate in a recent one kilometer road race in Lahore, some wore the long, traditional salwar kameez (shirt plus pants), and even high heels.

The Role of Islam and Human Rights

Although it was created as a state for India's Muslims, Pakistan's early leaders avoided direct involvement in religion. However, in the mid-1970s a trend began toward enforcing Islamic practices, possibly to gain political support. Zulfikar Ali Bhutto banned alcohol and introduced Friday as the weekly day of rest, replacing Sunday (a tradition brought by Britain). (Sunday regained its status in 1997). For his part, General Zia ordered Islamic punishments: flogging criminals in public, and amputating the right hands of convicted thieves.

The lives of two boys in the mid-1990s illustrate the complicated nature of human rights. Sold by his parents at the age of four to serve as a bonded carpet weaver, Iqbal Masih worked in a factory, often shackled to a loom, until he was ten. His detailed accounts of life as a child slave brought international recognition. Reebok awarded him a "Youth in Action" tribute. However, he was shot dead while delivering food to a relative. Pakistan prohibited the employment of children in 1991, when some eight to ten million children worked in carpet factories, small industries, domestic service and agriculture. Not all are slaves, and the numbers are falling. Given family poverty, some must work to survive.

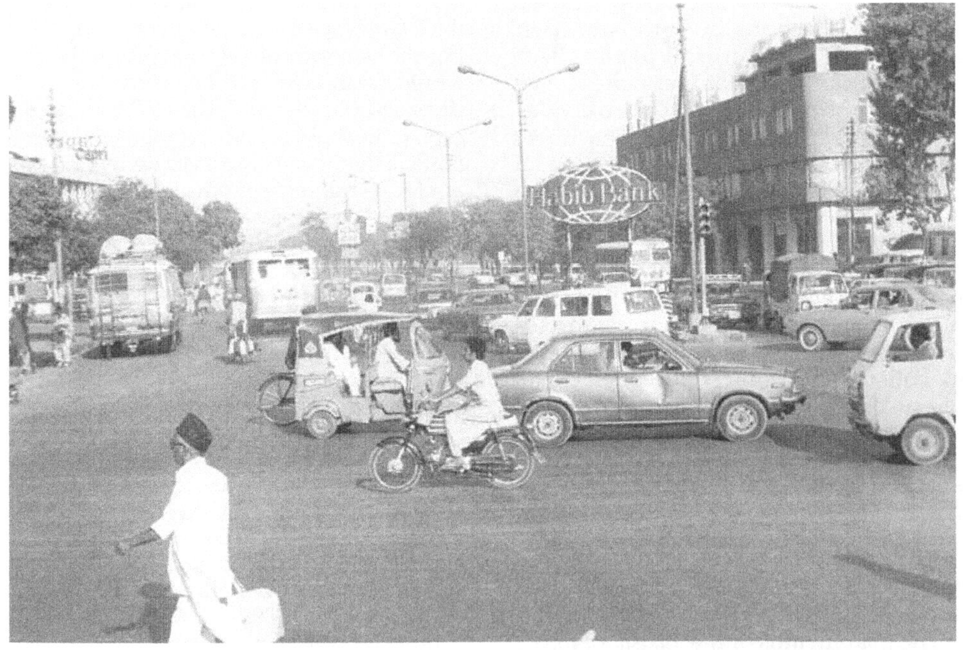

Busy intersection in Karachi Photo by Ray L. Cleveland

Mangla Dam powerhouse WORLD BANK Photo by Tomas Sennett

At the age of 14, Salamat Masih, was sentenced to death because he allegedly wrote irreverent remarks on paper thrown into a mosque. Convicted under the blasphemy laws, he and his uncle fortunately gained asylum in Germany. A third defendant was murdered, allegedly by the same imam who brought the charge of blasphemy.

Both boys were Christians, but human rights abuses are not primarily a Christian issue. Individual abuses are sometimes deadly: a mob burned alive a Muslim cleric who accidentally set a copy of the Qur'an on fire. Communal violence sheds much more blood.

Sunni militants have gunned down hundreds of Shi'a worshippers in mosques or travelling to religious festivals. In the troubled province of Baluchistan the Hazara Shi'a have suffered in particular. In early 2013, the banned *Lashkar-e Jhangvi* group carried out a double bombing that killed 89 in Quetta, most of them Shi'a. Just one month earlier its previous bombing attacks in the provincial capital killed at least 92 and led to the ouster of the chief minister.

The Ahmadiyya offshoot of Islam, considered heretical because it regards its 19th century founder as a prophet, face particular animosity. In the 1970s they were declared non-Muslims, and in the 1980s they were banned from calling their places of worship mosques and from preaching their faith. Many members of the community fled the country, but a number of worshippers were massacred in an attack in 2005.

Several factors enhance popular concern over morality and a desire to uphold an Islamic (and therefore "just") society. Widespread corruption intensifies the appeal of fundamentalist demands for Islamic purity and justice. The struggle against Indian rule in Kashmir also strengthens the appeal of political Islam. However, rival Islamic groups also manipulate the sympathies of the population. Iran and Saudi Arabia apparently subsidize *Shi'a* and *Sunni* schools that sometimes become centers for violence within Pakistan as well as across its borders.

Ignorance strengthens the appeal of groups that preach hatred based on ethnic and religious differences. Only a minority of adults can read even the simplest documents, and given the size of its population, Pakistan spends very little on education. Some ten million children never attend school; many others make only a brief acquaintance with book learning. As recently as the 1980s, children averaged only 1.9 years of schooling, compared with 2.4 in India. As always, boys attend rather more; girls, much less.

In 1998, soldiers visited every government school in Punjab. They discovered that many schools existed only on paper. Everything from teachers to exams, even repairs and sports results, had been faked. Nearly half (40%) of all teachers turned up at work only once per month, to collect their pay. To be fair, the pay hardly provided subsistence living.

The most important private system begins with rural schools and culminates in the Aga Khan University hospital and medical school. The spiritual leader of millions of *Ismaili* Muslims scattered through some 25 countries of Asia and Africa, the Aga Khan sponsors a variety of charitable works. The *Ismailis* form one Shi'a portion of Islam and accept Ismail, an eighth-century descendant of the prophet, as the seventh and last *Imam* (see Iran: Culture).

Higher education replicates the pattern, with some private colleges and universities earning excellent reputations. By contrast, the many state institutions face budgetary problems and their graduates lack respect because of widespread cheating scandals.

A rural scene in the Sindh area, Pakistan WORLD BANK Photo

Pakistan

Economy: After its creation in 1947, Pakistan made progress from an exclusively agricultural economy, but farm products still account for most of the national income. Besides the fertile soil of the Indus basin, few natural resources exist. Only minor oil reserves have been found, though substantial natural gas deposits exist in Baluchistan. Industrialization developed around local farm products, particularly cotton textiles.

In recent decades many engineers, technicians and skilled labor found employment in the prosperous states of the Arab Gulf. They sent home valuable foreign exchange, but also created severe shortages of qualified personnel in public services. The same factor has slowed the development of industry. Many lost their jobs during the 2008–09 world recession, and their return home heightened already-severe unemployment.

The valley of the Indus forms the largest canal-irrigated area in the world. Further development is being carried forward by the Indus Basin Development Fund Agreement, supported by the World Bank and several western nations. The largest irrigation projects have been the huge Mangla Dam on the Jhelum tributary and the even larger Tarbela Dam. These dams greatly increased the land under irrigation, and they supply large amounts of electricity. However, because forests in the watersheds above the dams are being stripped away, river waters have become very muddy. At the present rate of silting, the Tarbela Dam will be useful for only about 50 years.

Reacting against the dominance of industry by an alleged elite of "22 Families," Zulfikar Ali Bhutto—himself a wealthy landlord—nationalized most large private firms. By 1990 the government owned some 80% of industry. Ironically, when she won power, his daughter, Benazir Bhutto, attempted to privatize some of the same firms. The process proved both difficult and slow. Pakistani businessmen know the virtue of keeping wealth hidden, and the stock market is too small and erratic to absorb large blocks of shares. Sales to foreign investors can provide foreign exchange and managerial skills, but they risk political condemnation. Most of all, though, corruption plagues all privatization attempts.

The Bhuttos owned land. By contrast, as a businessman, Nawaz Sharif favored a flourishing private economy. His government sold a few inefficient firms, opened the stock markets to foreign capital, and loosened restrictions on foreign exchange. It reduced regulations over new machinery and factories to encourage private companies to invest. Nevertheless, the country presents many obstacles to business. The costs of borrowing are very high, and the local market frequently proves too small for an efficient scale of production. Heavy indirect taxation of industry, to compensate for the almost complete absence of taxes on the farming and retail sectors, means high-priced supplies, and the low level of education accounts for much of the low productivity per worker.

To provide the two or three million additional jobs annually for new workers requires steady economic growth. In Pakistan's case, this is threatened by poor educational achievements, a decrepit infrastructure, growing pollution and an investment climate marred by ethnic violence. On the other hand, massive investments in banking and Karachi real estate by companies in Dubai offers hope that foreign funds may someday spark faster economic growth.

For years, under Dr. Abdul Qadeer Khan, Pakistan's nuclear industry secretly worked hard, with stolen plans, to construct the centrifuges necessary to enrich uranium for nuclear weapons. The broad outlines of the industry were suspected well before the first test explosions in 1997. However, six years later the discovery of tubes for centrifuges on a vessel bound for Libya enabled investigators from the U.S. and other countries to sketch the outline of a Pakistani "cash for bombs" network. Plans, supplies, and perhaps vital materials were shipped to Libya, Iran, and North Korea. For the moment, at least, world attention has halted that export business.

The Future: Asif Ali Zardari and the *Pakistan People's Party* transferred power peacefully to an elected government, the first such transfer in the nation's history. The milestone was the more remarkable given national woes that include domestic extremism, violent ethnic rivalries, world-class corruption, policies that favor the rich, open rebellion in border areas, ever-present anxiety about India, resentment over U.S. drone attacks, and popular anger at both the U.S. and Pakistani military over the killing of bin Laden.

During his first year in office, Prime Minister Nawaz Sharif failed to utilize an effective parliamentary majority to address the nation's many ills. To date he has accomplished little, and some insiders suspect he is losing the will to govern. There are very few grounds for optimism.

Farmer inspecting a new tractor WORLD BANK Photo

The Democratic Socialist Republic of Sri Lanka

The way home from school on a rainy afternoon WORLD BANK photo

Area: 25,332 square miles (65,610 sq. km.).
Population: 20.8 million.
Capital City: Colombo (pop. 1 million, estimated); Parliament meets in Sri Jayawardenapura.
Climate: Uniformly warm throughout the year, except for comfortably cool temperatures in the higher mountains. It rains almost continuously from May to August in the Wet Zone of the southwest; elsewhere rainfall varies unpredictably.
Neighboring Countries: At its closest, India lies some 33 miles away across the Palk Strait.
Time Zone: GMT + 6.
Official Languages: Sinhala; Tamil (majority in the north).
Other Principal Tongue: English (among the educated).
Ethnic Background: The main communities identified by language and tradition are Sinhalese (73%), Tamil (19%), Moor (7%), Eurasian Burgher, and Malay.
Principal Religions: Buddhism (70%), Hinduism, Christianity, Islam.
Chief Commercial Products: Textiles and clothing, tea, rubber, rice, consumer goods, petroleum products, spices, coconuts, sugarcane, manioc and gemstones.
Major Trading Partners: U.S., U.K., Germany, Japan, India, Iraq—prewar.
Currency: Rupee (= 100 cents).
Former Colonial Status: British Crown Colony (1802–1928); self-governing British Colony (1928–1948).
Independence Date: February 4, 1948.
Chief of State: Mahinda Rajapakse, President.
Head of Government: Disanayaka Mudiyanselage "D.M." Jayaratne, Prime Minister.
National Flag: Centered on a dark crimson field with gold borders is a large gold lion in profile facing the pole and holding a sword in its right paw; at the pole are two vertical stripes, one of green and one of saffron, framed together in a gold border.
Gross Domestic Product: $71 billion (at current prices); $148 billion (Purchasing Power Parity).
GDP per capita: $7,000 (PPP).

The pear-shaped island of Sri Lanka, or Ceylon as it was first known in English, lies at the southeastern tip of India. Its climate and people resemble those of the nearby regions of India, but under the influence of Buddhism it developed a distinctive culture. Until weakened by civil war in the past two decades, Sri Lanka offered the possibility of social development—good health and education—despite relatively low incomes.

Most of Sri Lanka, including all the northern half of the island and a coastal belt around the south end, is low, flat country. The remaining one-fifth, lies above 2,000 feet in elevation, with mountains rising to peaks above 8,000 feet. These highlands force the humid summer monsoon winds from the southwest to rise, producing heavy rainfall in the southwestern quarter of the island and earning it the title "the wet zone" in recognition of its annual precipitation of 100–200 inches.

The rest of the island forms the dry zone, although its rainfall would be considered sufficient in cooler climates. Rain in the dry zone is unpredictable; it may be quite sudden and heavy, causing damaging floods that dump precious water into the ocean. Precipitation in the dry zone also comes from the northeast winter monsoon. Ground water can be raised for irrigation in most of the dry zone, from Jaffna to Batticaloa. Given the tropical cli-

Sri Lanka

Former Prime Minister
Ratnasiri Wickremanayake

mate, agriculture revolves around the patterns of rainfall rather than temperature. Wet and dry seasons replace the familiar summer and winter of temperate climates.

The two major population groups inhabit distinctly different climate zones. The Sinhalese majority is concentrated in the wet zone, while the Sri Lankan Tamils live almost exclusively in the northern and northeastern limits of the dry zone—principally on or near the Jaffna Peninsula.

History: Civilization, cities, and governments began in the dry zone of the island's north, and early ethnic conflicts remain today. Sinhalese kings had already established their capital at Anuradhapura in the third century B.C. when Buddhism gradually spread over the island and absorbed many existing religious practices. Sinhalese society skillfully designed irrigation systems and storage reservoirs to make maximum use of the dry zone's scarce water, and an impressive civilization developed.

Attracted by the prosperity of the kingdom, adventurers from India occasionally tried to seize the island, but they never succeeded in retaining it. With some interruptions, Anuradhapura remained the capital for over 1,300 years. In the 14th century a Dravidian ruler from South India succeeded in establishing a Tamil kingdom on the northern end of the island. Meanwhile, aided by improved technology, Sinhalese society had moved south into the wet zone, which had apparently remained dense jungle. By the 16th century, the Sinhalese kings ruled from Kotte, near modern Colombo.

The first European sailing vessels came from Portugal and reached Colombo Harbor in 1505. Searching for spices, the Portuguese soon built forts and by the end of the 16th century laid claim to all Ceylon. However, the highland kingdom of Kandy maintained its independence.

Superior in both business and warfare, the Dutch East India Company contested the Portuguese domination of Ceylon's trade in the 17th century. The Dutch captured Colombo in 1656, and soon controlled Ceylon's trade by holding all the ports. The Kandyan kings, who had hoped the Dutch would recognize them as rulers of the entire island, remained in control of only the interior. The last Sinhalese king of Kandy was captured and exiled in 1815, by the British.

Dutch domination noticeably influenced the island's communities. Many settlers arrived from Holland and other European countries; their descendants became known as Burghers. From their Indonesian colonies the Dutch brought soldiers and workers. Their descendants remained Muslim—the Malay are still distinct from the earlier Muslim communities who are known as Moors, using the Portuguese term for them. In a few cases the Dutch rulers moved either Tamil or Sinhalese communities to other parts of the island.

When Holland allied with France during the Napoleonic wars in the 1790s, British forces captured Ceylon and declared it a Crown Colony in 1802. It proved a success. Plantations to raise coconuts, cotton, coffee, sugar, indigo and opium flourished by the mid-19th century. When a plant disease ruined the coffee industry, tea began to replace the coffee bean. When a shortage of plantation workers developed, laborers were imported from southern India, most of them Tamils. Their descendants now form a separate community known as the Indian Tamils, and they made a strong impact on the wet zone Sinhalese regions where the tea plantations were located.

In the late 19th century a cultural reaction developed against European culture and rule. Interest in Buddhism and Hinduism revived, and strengthened in the 20th century. Renewed interest also arose in the ancient arts and literature. These movements all encouraged national feeling by restoring attachment to the period before European domination.

British officials very slowly permitted representative government on the island. In 1931 all adults received voting rights, within British rule. The constitution of 1946, with provisions to protect the Tamils and other minorities, established the legislative system. Independence came peacefully in 1948. Two political parties

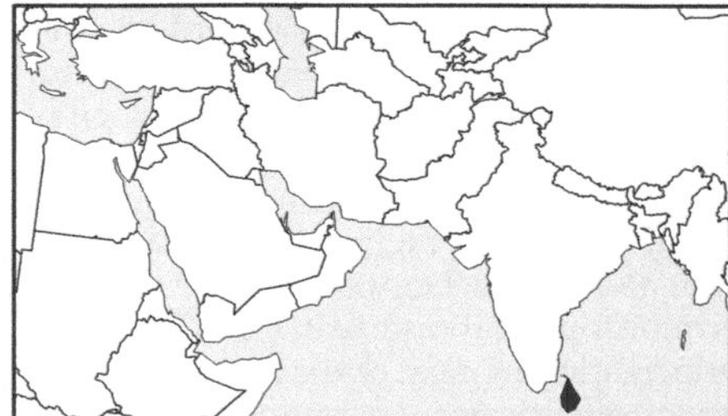

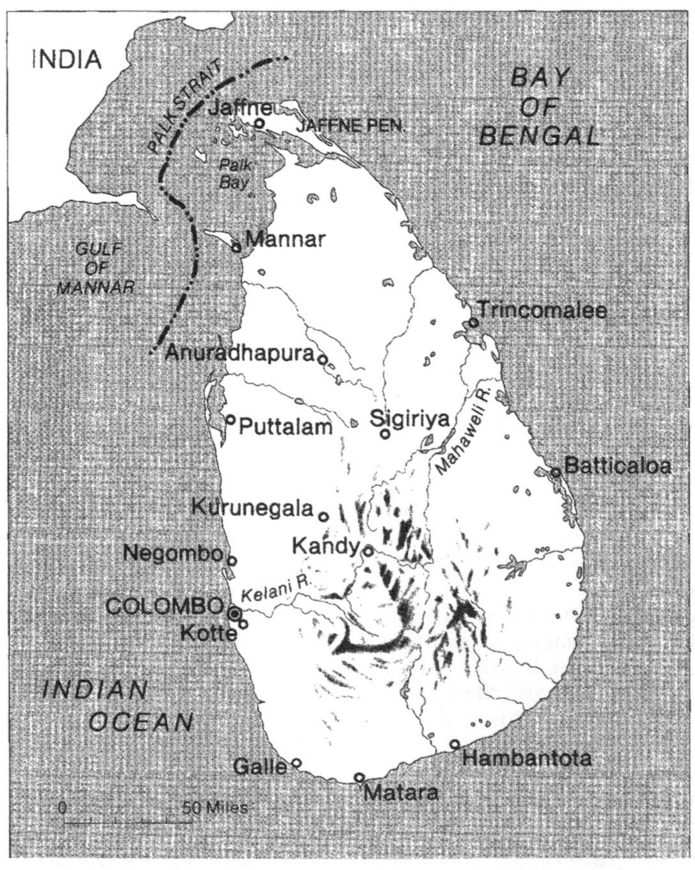

Fishermen at sea with their catamarans

have dominated Sinhalese politics ever since.

Representing the Sinhala elite, the *United National Party (UNP)* formed the first post-independence government. Its great rival, the more nationalistic *Sri Lanka* (Holy Ceylon) *Freedom Party* led by Solomon Bandaranaike took power in 1956 and enacted a number of reforms. However, it blundered by stripping English of its official status and adopting Sinhala as the only official language. Tamil was permitted "reasonable use." Violence immediately broke out in many Tamil areas. After the murder of Mr. Bandaranaike in 1959, the party was held together by his widow. She led the party to victory at the polls and became the first woman prime minister in any country.

Besides differing over Tamil rights, the two major parties clashed over economic issues, with the *Freedom Party* typically seeking a more socialist solution. Mrs. Bandaranaike again won power in 1970, but soon faced a guerrilla uprising led by the *People's Liberation Front,* known by its Sinhala initials *JVP.* At the time a communist group whose doctrines attracted many educated but unemployed young people, the *JVP* capitalized on the lack of economic development, and its Maoist-influenced uprising became violent. With foreign military aid, Mrs. Bandaranaike's government suppressed the *JVP.*

She also undertook several radical changes. Although a member of a well-to-do and influential family, she adopted socialist policies like supplying free rice, but this led to economic recession and shortages. Symbolically, a 1972 Constitution ended the nation's ties to the British Crown and changed Ceylon's name to the Socialist Republic of Sri Lanka. The presidency became largely ceremonial, while Mrs. Bandaranaike continued as prime minister.

These decisions and her style of ruling provoked opposition. Continued high unemployment and a declining economy, coupled with charges of mismanagement and corruption, led to her electoral defeat by the *UNP* in 1977.

From Ethnic Strife to War

The worst communal violence since independence swept the country in 1983, after rebels of the *Liberation Tigers of Tamil Eelam* ambushed troops near Jaffna. Seeking revenge, Sinhalese mobs (and sometimes security forces) attacked Tamils in Colombo, Kandy and elsewhere. Altogether perhaps 2,000 Tamils died, while arson left some 50,000 homeless, mainly in Colombo. Calm was not restored for more than a week. Most Tamils suspected that the country's leadership was behind the riots, and this strengthened the appeal of the *Tamil Tigers.*

Parliament then catered to Sinhalese nationalism by banning any party that advocated separatism or even autonomy. This move ended any effective Tamil representation in parliament. While Sinhalese leaders did attempt to reduce tensions and violence when convenient, the ethnic rift had become too wide to bridge with minor reforms.

As Tamil guerrilla activity increased, their terrorist acts were matched by massacres by undisciplined units of the largely Sinhalese army. By 1985 the dispute had plunged Sri Lanka into open civil war. Sinhalese leaders intended to reassert the (Sinhalese) government's rule over a united country. But to protect their cultural identity, many Tamils demanded an independent state of their own.

During the first stage of the war, Tamil guerrillas attacked the police, army units, and Sinhalese civilians in the north and east. Headed by Velupillai Prabhakaran, the *Tiger* leadership developed a disciplined ferocity among their followers, including a willingness to die for the cause. Their fanaticism, plus refuge, training and arms from the Indian state of Tamil Nadu, enabled the *Tamil Tigers* to defeat other Tamil militias and take control of the Jaffna Peninsula. In response, the (Sinhala) army and police tended to treat all Tamils as rebels, thus extinguishing moderate political viewpoints.

In 1987, Prime Minister Rajiv Gandhi of India sought to intervene, and pressured the two sides to accept a ceasefire and a small force of Indian peacekeepers to maintain order while disarming the Tamil militias. After peace was achieved, Sri Lanka would unite the northern (undoubtedly Tamil) province with the Eastern province, where Tamils, Muslims, and Sinhalese had lived in approximately equal numbers.

The agreement aroused wide Sinhalese hostility. Moreover, the *Tigers* soon stopped surrendering heavy weapons, apparently never intending to keep Gandhi's agreement. They attacked other Tamil groups and massacred hundreds of Sinhalese civilians living in the east. Facing Sinhalese accusations that India failed to defend innocent civilians, the Indian military mounted a major invasion of the *Tigers* in Jaffna. Although the Indian force rose to 50,000 troops, far outnumbering the entire Sri Lankan army of 32,000, victory proved elusive. The second stage of the war ended inconclusively, but the army replaced Indian troops in Jaffna.

The *Tamil Tigers* launched another offensive in 1990 that forced the army to abandon Jaffna fort and most of the peninsula. The *Tigers* attempted to offset the military's superior numbers and equipment with daring attacks, and increasingly depended on teenagers who entered battle with cyanide capsules, ready to prevent capture by committing suicide. In the Sinhalese heartland, the *Tigers* assassinated military commanders and politicians. A suicide bomber on a bicycle even killed President Premadasa. Although the assassin carried the cyanide capsule trademark of the *Tigers*, many suspected retaliation for the death of a Sinhalese political rival.

Elections in 1994 brought Chandrika Kumaratunga of the *Freedom Party* to power. She negotiated an extended cease-fire with the Tigers, which they again used for military purposes, this time infiltrating down the east coast as far south as Batticaloa. They then broke the cease-fire suddenly. War resumed, and the government purchased weapons abroad.

Once better-equipped, the troops recaptured Jaffna city and much of the peninsula. The *Tigers* responded with human wave attacks and truck bombs that devastated economic targets in Colombo, including the Central Bank and the port. Another bomb exploded in Kandy, at the venerated shrine housing the Buddha's tooth. It missed the precious relic but disrupted celebrations of the island's 50 years of independence.

Anticipating a truce, in 2000 the military relaxed. Again, the *Tamil Tigers* struck, concentrating on the southern tip of the Jaffna peninsula. The army's large base at Elephant Pass dominated the cause-way linking the peninsula with the mainland. Using long-range artillery, the *Tigers* shelled the camp, and then advanced to capture its water supply. When the direct assault came, the garrison vastly outnumbered the attackers, but the fort fell quickly, the greatest battlefield victory of the war until 2008–09. At the height of their power, the *Tigers* controlled about one-third of the country.

With secure access to the peninsula, the *Tigers* moved steadily towards Jaffna city and the vital airstrip nearby. Sri Lanka appealed to India, Israel and other nations for immediate military assistance to avert the city's fall and the complete defeat of 35,000 troops. Reinforced and rearmed with advanced weapons, the military halted the *Tigers'* advance just outside Jaffna city.

A dramatic suicide raid on Colombo's international airport and military airbase in 2001 significantly changed the military, economic, and political realities. The loss of eight military aircraft gutted the air force, and the army proved unable to reply with a similarly devastating attack on the *Tigers*.

Under the impact, President Kumaratunga's coalition disintegrated. The opposition *UNP* won the elections that followed, and formed a cabinet under Ranil Wickremesinghe. Taking the initiative, Wickremesinghe quickly met many *Tiger* demands. After the *Tigers* announced a cease-fire, he restored trade with the north and ended an embargo that had kept even food and medicine out of the area. Norwegian mediation arranged a "permanent" cease-fire, with detailed agreements to treat many expected problems. Then the government lifted restrictions on travel that had long been used to harass Tamil civilians The *Tigers* in turn opened highway A9, the route north to Jaffna, for the first time in a decade.

The "Permanent" Cease-fire

The cease-fire was only possible because the *Tigers* also desired a respite from warfare. Besides the evident difficulties drafting additional troops, concern over public relations also played a role. Britain and Canada had declared them a terrorist organization and, like the U.S., froze billions of dollars of the group's funds. In response, talk of self-determination and a Tamil homeland began to replace calls for independence. Velupillai Prabhakaran apologized for mistreating Muslims and expelling them from Jaffna.

The harsh living conditions within the *Tigers'* zone also encouraged the search for peace. Although perhaps 200,000 civilians had emigrated, similar numbers remained as impoverished refugees. Mines often littered roads and abandoned farmland. Many buildings damaged in the fighting had not been repaired and some schools, for example, lacked roofs, windows, and books. Lighting usually came from kerosene lamps: an entire generation grew up without electricity, never using a computer or surfing the web. Unfortunately, the *Ti-*

Village belle with a basket of mangoes

gers themselves inflicted further suffering after the cease-fire, particularly by abducting children to serve in their military.

The rapid progress of negotiations noticeably improved the living conditions of ordinary people. However, the *Tigers* refused to disarm, and demanded the immediate creation of an autonomous zone in the north and east. The *Sea Tigers* broke the terms of the cease-fire, while forced enlistment of children did the same on land. In 2003, negotiations collapsed, though fighting did not resume.

The Indonesian tsunami of 2004 hit both Tamil and Sinhalese coastal areas with great force. It killed over 30,000 and rendered hundreds of thousands homeless and jobless. The fishing and tourist industries suffered severe damage, even on the southwestern coast. International aid poured into the island, but a critical question arose of who would distribute it. The *Tigers* desired to distribute relief supplies themselves in Tamil areas, rather than permit aid agencies to operate, presumably to avert any other focus of popular loyalty. However, without government approval, the agencies could not turn over supplies to a rebel movement labeled as terrorist. Negotiations failed over this, too.

Sinhalese Politics and Strife

In amazing feats for a nation drenched in ethnic bloodshed and sometimes facing terrorist campaigns, Sri Lanka held provincial, presidential, and parliamentary elections throughout the civil war era. The two major parties, the *United National Party* and the *Freedom Party* alternated in office, but they rarely won an absolute majority in parliament. This frequently forced unstable coalitions.

National reconciliation proved elusive even within the Sinhalese community. In the late 1980s and early 1990s violence struck within the majority community. The communist *JVP* that had launched a guerrilla war in the 1970s now adopted the cause of militant Sinhalese nationalism, and launched a bloody revolt in the south. It especially assassinated members of the ruling *United National Party*. Though the *JVP* ultimately failed, the cost of victory had been high. Possibly 60,000 people had died, many at the hands of death squads. Most victims were innocent, secretly denounced by rivals or opponents.

After a vicious parliamentary campaign, in 2001 the *UNP* won an unexpectedly decisive victory on its platform of seeking peace and prosperity. After a brief constitutional crisis, the *UNP* and its allies formed a cabinet under Ranil Wickremesinghe. However, Chandrika Kumaratunga held the presidency. The daughter of Sirimavo Bandaranaike, she led the *Freedom Party*, which formed the parliamentary opposition.

Although Prime Minister Wickremesinghe showed notable sympathy with many of the Tamil demands, President Kumaratunga proved far more suspicious of the *Tigers*. Other groups wary of Tamil separatism, even within a federal Sri Lanka, included the often-mistreated Muslims, Buddhist clergy, and the militantly nationalist *JVP*. In 2004, Kumaratunga called early elections.

The *UNP* lost the elections. Wickremesinghe took credit for the cease-fire and promised voters that the emerging prosperity was the first reward of peace, but many voters felt that prosperity had reached only the rich and considered the *UNP* corrupt. Some Sinhalese voters thought the *Tigers* had gained too much from the cease-fire, while instead of supporting the *UNP*, Tamil voters chose the *Tamil National Alliance*, a front for the *Tigers*. A plurality favored the president's *Freedom Party/JVP* alliance, and gave them 105 of the parliament's 225 seats. Another party led by militant Buddhist clergy opposed concessions to the Tamils. It gained seats.

Former President Chandrika Kumaratunga

President Kumaratunga's successor as *Freedom Party* leader, Mahinda Rajapakse, won a narrow victory in the 2005 presidential elections, partly because Tamils had to vote outside *Tiger*-controlled areas. On the crucial issue of the day, the civil war, Rajapakse represented the uncompromising wing of the party and the Sinhala community. He allied with the *JVP* and the Buddhist monks' party and even rejected a federal state as a compromise solution. The president and the defense minister, his brother Gotabaya Rajapakse, determined to crush the *Tigers* rather than compromise over their demands.

The *Tigers'* leader, Velupillai Prabhakaran, played into their hands. In 2006 the *Tigers* deliberately broke the ceasefire with assassinations and attacks. The *Tigers* even bombed the country's major airbase with their small air force of prop-driven planes.

After narrowly escaping a suicide attack that left fragments near his heart, the military commander, General Sarath Fonseka, determined to defeat the *Tigers* permanently. Strengthened by arms from China, Pakistan and Russia, he, doubled the size of the army and adopted aggressive tactics at sea, destroying the *Tigers'* supply vessels far offshore. With new jets and helicopters, the air force attacked suspected *Tiger* positions ruthlessly, and on land commandos struck key defensive points.

Then the army took advantage of its much larger forces to launch multiple attacks from different directions to squeeze the *Tamil Tigers* out of the northern third of the island. From the northwestern coast and from the south, troops advanced on Kilinochchi, the *Tigers'* administrative center. It fell at the end of 2008; a few days later Elephant Pass did as well. For the first time in decades, the government controlled the entire length of the A-9 highway up the center of the island to Jaffna. Unable to obtain a ceasefire, and determined not to surrender, the *Tigers* made their last stand north of Mullaitivu on the northeast coast.

It seems clear that Prabhakaran and the *Tigers* leadership considered Tamil civilians as their ultimate trump card. Throughout the fighting in 2008 and 2009, the quarter-million civilians under their control were forced to retreat with rebel units; those seeking to flee were often shot. Hoping to win international pressure for a ceasefire, *Tiger* propaganda claimed the military inflicted large numbers of civilian casualties, many from heavy artillery even in a "No Fire" zone the army had pledged to honor. However, the military denied the claims—and both sides kept away independent reporters, so the truth also became a casualty.

In May 2009, the *Tigers* collapsed, with most of their leaders killed in the final days. Very possibly some 10,000 Tamils, most of them civilians, had died during the desperate final weeks of a battle where defeat was clearly certain.

Victory left the Sri Lankan government triumphant, politically supreme, but burdened with countless refugees, most of them ill-fed and ill-housed in strictly-

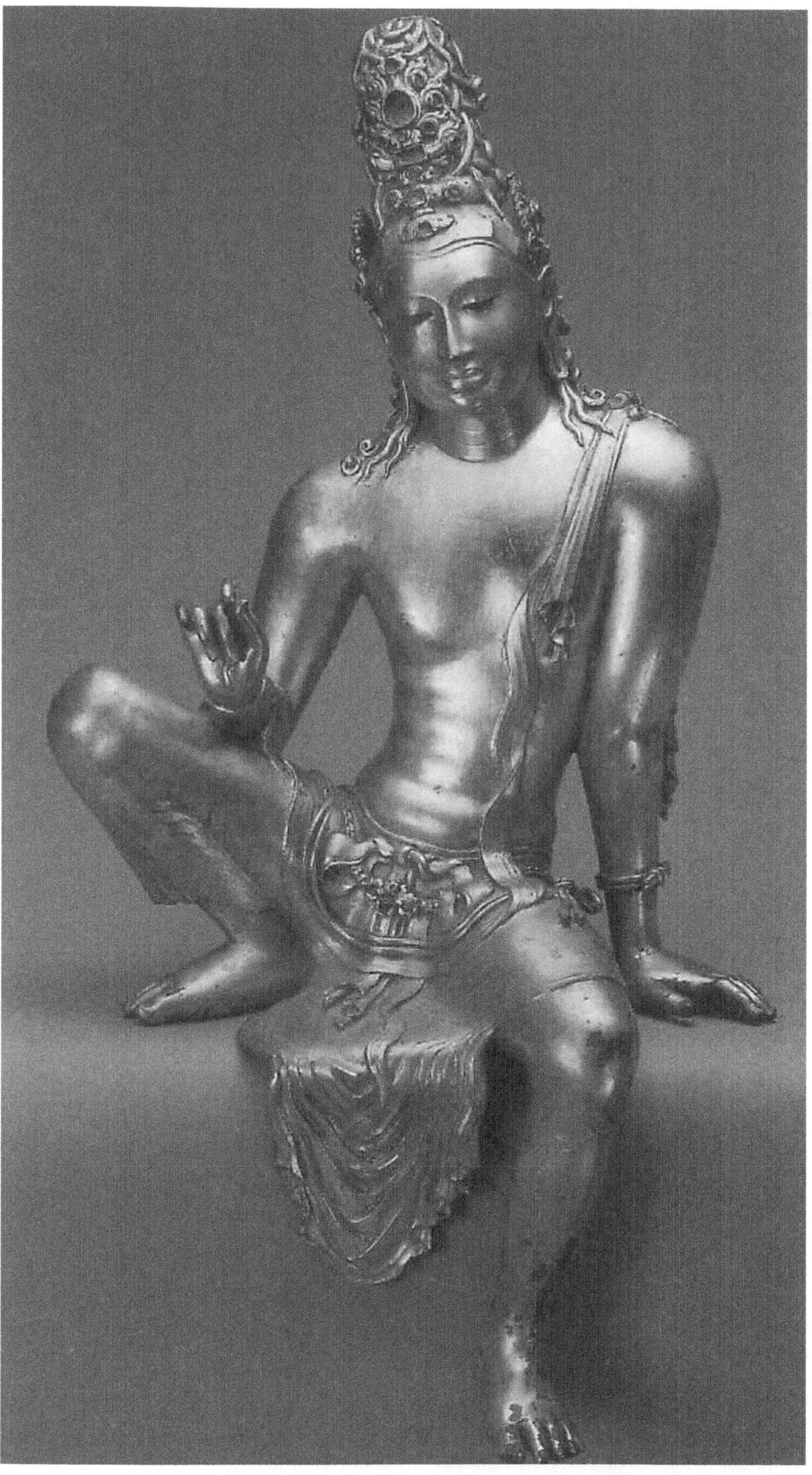

Bodhisattva Avalokiteshvara, 8th–9th century A.D., gilt, bronze and crystal in the National Museum, Colombo

controlled camps. One crucial challenge facing the government was to free and rehabilitate the refugees without providing new opportunities for any revived *Tiger* activities. A year after victory, most had returned to their often-destroyed homes and farms, but some 80,000 still remained incarcerated.

Translating military victory into political dominance, in 2010 President Rajapakse called presidential elections nearly two years early. Campaigning as the architect of a rare national victory over an insurgency, he solidly defeated the opposition candidate, Sarath Fonseka. The general who masterminded the military's final assault, Fonseka had later accused Defense Minister Gotabhaya Rajapakse, the president's brother, of ordering the execution of *Tiger* leaders as they surrendered. Weeks later, the brothers' *Sri Lanka Freedom Alliance* achieved an overwhelming victory in parliamentary elections, gaining nearly two-thirds of all seats. Human rights observers noted, however, that the media had been intimidated, and that government resources had assisted *Freedom Alliance* candidates.

Events in the following months confirmed that the Rajapakse brothers intended to rule forcefully, extend the president's powers, and disregard press freedoms. Few symbolic gestures of healing were offered to the Tamils; instead, Tamil youths were pressed into singing the national anthem in Sinhala. Their conqueror fared little better: General Fonseka was arrested on charges of conspiracy.

Given the Sinhalese pride in the *Tamil Tigers'* defeat, President Rajapakse enjoyed great domestic popularity. Parliament readily passed anti-terrorist legislation that ignored human rights, and the Sinhalese public supported statements that aggressively attacked critics of government policies. One cabinet member, for example, threatened to "break the limbs" of those who "betrayed" the country. The less fortunate critics seemed to disappear.

Upset by court rulings against the government, the government moved to impeach Chief Justice Shirani Bandaranayake on corruption charges just one year after she was appointed. Despite rulings by two different courts that the process was irregular and illegal, parliament convicted her, and the president approved the vote. At least initially, many of the nation's lawyers supported the chief justice and opposed the appointment of a former attorney general as her successor.

By 2012 the country had progressed significantly after the war. Foreign assistance provided new roads and ports, and the economy grew fairly rapidly, with GDP per capita rising by 18% between 2010 and 2012. Symbolic of the progress, the Menik

President Mahinda Rajapakse

Farm refugee camp, which had housed about 300,000 Tamils at the end of the war, was closed. In another achievement, partly because of its efforts to trace children missing from the war, the country was removed from the UN's blacklist of nations providing inadequately for child welfare.

Nevertheless, Sri Lanka remained on the defensive in several international forums. The British documentary "Sri Lanka's Killing Fields" shows apparent executions of Tamil men and the corpses of sexually assaulted women. The UN's special investigator considered the video footage authentic and evidence of human rights violations. Gradually the Rajapakse brothers shifted the government's position. Instead of claiming that the military had not killed civilians, Gotabhaya Rajapakse admitted that some soldiers may not have withstood the pressures of war. While admitting that perhaps 10,000 civilians had died, he strongly denied that genocide had occurred. Nevertheless, in 2013 the UN's Human Rights Council passed a highly critical resolution that encouraged an "independent and credible investigation" into alleged war crimes.

Culture: Culturally, modern Sri Lanka looks in two directions for its inspiration. Extremists may try to exclude one or the other of the two elements, but most people look both to the ancient culture and also to the technical advantages of modern industrial civilization. For example, some contemporary Sri Lankan artists reflect the influence of the European masters, but their works still convey the uniqueness of a native tradition.

The oldest and most famous paintings in Sri Lanka are wall frescoes of maidens at Sigiriya, the palace of a fifth-century king, Kasyapa I. The palace itself lies below a rock summit, and for decades served as a monument to Sinhalese achievements. In the 1990s, archeologists discovered the full extent of the palace gardens, the largest and most complex in Asia. Given the dry climate, the gardens required a complex system of cisterns and irrigation tunnels to maintain fountains, streams and a water garden some 300 feet long.

Much earlier architectural monuments from the past impress the visitor at Anuradhapura, for a millennium the Buddhist capital in the dry zone. Enormous domes known as stupas preserved relics, while temples and shrines were filled with stone carvings. The city's skillful engineers were masters of designing complexes of buildings complete with large bathing pools. To provide water in the dry zone, the planners laid out a series of reservoirs and aqueducts to supply not only the capital but also villages along the way. In recent years some of these water systems have been restored and put back into service with new irrigation and hydro-electric projects belonging fully to the 20th century.

Sculpture was another ancient means of artistic expression of beauty and religious feeling, as was also the ancient Sinhala poetry. Literature also took the form of grammatical studies and philosophy. Ancient literary pieces were all written in the Sinhala language, but modern literature appears in Tamil as well, as do newspapers in both languages and English.

Economy: During British rule, Ceylon tea became world-famous, and other plantations produced crops like rubber for export. These provided the income and foreign exchange to pay for imports of rice, other foods and manufactured goods. After independence, socialist politicians who distrusted international markets attempted to make the economy less dependent on foreign sales of tea and rubber. Farmers were encouraged to raise food crops for the local market, especially rice, which for some years was distributed free to all.

Today the country remains the world's largest exporter of tea. Hit by competition from East African producers, its share of the world market has fallen from about one-half to one-fifth. Many of the Indian Tamils who formed the industry's workforce were gradually repatriated, and by the late 1990s plantations provided only one-third of the crop. The rest came from 500,000 small farms that sold the green leaves to processors. In the 1990s, difficulties in two large export markets, Iraq and Russia, reduced sales and profits. Although the government removed the tea export tax in 1993, it appears that many processors and farmers face serious losses, given low world prices.

Replacing tea as the greatest export are garments and other textiles. Beginning with an investment promotion zone established beside the international airport in 1978, textile manufacturing has spread across the southern part of the country. Low wages and a literate, mostly female workforce have attracted foreign firms and joint ventures to the industry. Other

Tea pickers on a plantation near Colombo

factories now manufacture electronics components for export as well. However, in the mid-1990s workers demanded higher pay and better conditions, and struck a number of firms. Militants even held a manager hostage. This apparently surprised companies that expected little union activity. In the words of one foreign owner, "We want the government to keep industrial peace and discipline."

Hundreds of thousands of Sri Lankan women also work abroad, chiefly as maids in Kuwait and the United Arab Emirates. When Iraq invaded Kuwait, some 100,000 Sri Lankans, the vast majority of them women, lost their employment and returned home penniless. A decade later, a limited restitution should be reaching these victims of aggression, financed by the Iraqi export of crude oil.

Sri Lanka's largest single development project, in the northeast, consisted of a series of dams on the Mahaweli River, the country's largest. However, the project has become widely criticized, for a design that produced hydroelectric power instead of irrigation for the (Tamil-populated) countryside, and for construction flaws may reduce the long-term potential of the project.

With great natural beauty, a warm climate and a variety of appealing sights for visitors, tourism developed rapidly in the early 1980s, bringing in about 15% of foreign earnings. However, the *JVP* attacked tourist centers, and the twenty-six year war with the *Tigers* discouraged foreigners from visiting. In addition, the tsunami destroyed many hotels. Currently the sector is expanding rapidly, though perhaps losing some of its unique elements.

Before its wars, Sri Lanka showed one way to a relatively advanced quality of life without high incomes or large per-capita use of energy and natural resources. Compared to surrounding countries, the nation is well educated (85% adult literacy, nearly twice the rate in much richer Saudi Arabia), and its citizens enjoy average life expectancy rates of over 65 years. They also enjoy 174 non-working days a year, the likely world record. Birth rates and death rates both rank low, the courts and democracy muddle through, and the potential seems to exist for a quality of life which, though not rich, allowed the simple pleasures to be enjoyed in relative security.

Relations will be uneasy with external groups that value democracy and human rights, and even corporations sensitive about their public image. The UN seems unlikely to abandon questions about the fate of Tamil civilians caught in the final battles. Although the 2013 Commonwealth Heads of Government Meeting took place in Colombo despite calls to boycott it, and time dulls memories of past wrongs, the firm of Rajapakse & Rajapakse & Rajapakse will rarely enjoy smooth sailing in international waters.

The Future: As President Rajapakse rightly claims, Sri Lanka is a rare nation that defeated a well-armed, long-established insurgency that had held extensive territory. Given their great success, the Rajapakse brothers (president, defense minister, and presidential aide) risk overreaching themselves. Hugely popular with Sinhalese masses who feel secure in the streets for the first time in decades, they seem little concerned with media freedom, judicial independence, student protests, or incorporating the Tamils into Sri Lankan civil society.

Relations will be uneasy with external groups that value democracy and human rights, and the UN seems unlikely to abandon questions about the fate of Tamil civilians caught in the final battles. It won't always be smooth sailing. A critical indicator of the country's return as a respected member of the international community will be whether the November 2013 Commonwealth Heads of Government Meeting will take place in Colombo or not.

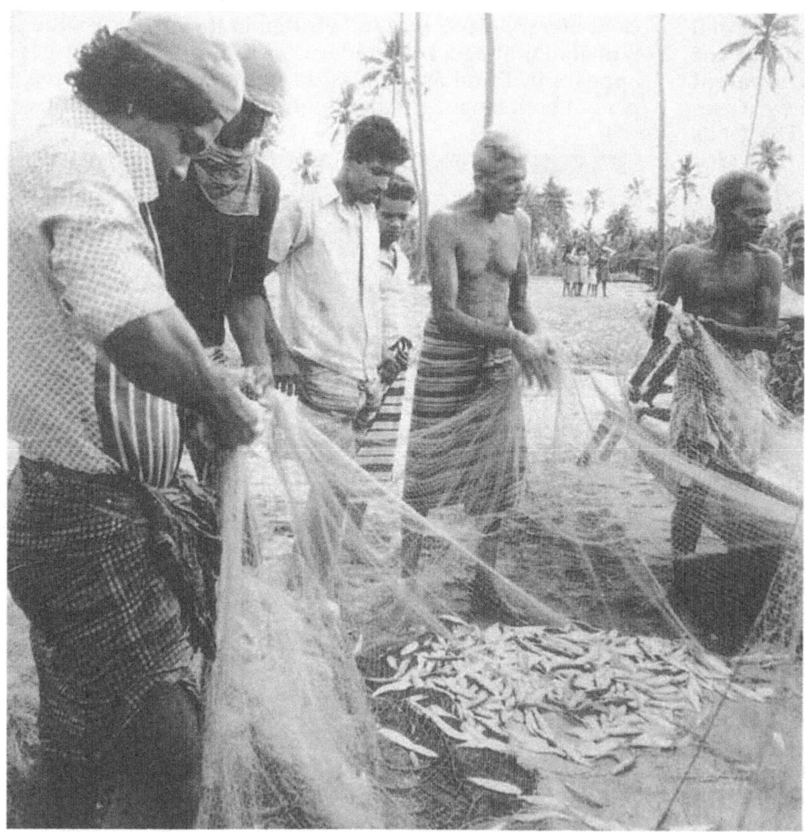

A fisherman's catch WORLD BANK Photo

Dependency of Britain

British Indian Ocean Territory

Area: About 22 square miles (57 sq. km.).
Population: Only military and support personnel.

The British Indian Ocean Territory (BIOT) consists solely of the Chagos Archipelago situated midway between East Africa and Indonesia. These wettest coral isles in the Indian Ocean, with some 145 inches of rain a year, share the same underwater ridge as the Maldives and lie 200 miles south of Gan. The BIOT was created to provide sites for British and American military installations safe from the nationalistic sentiments of independent states.

Until the BIOT was organized in 1965, the Chagos Group was a dependency of Mauritius, which received some $8.5 million in compensation for the loss. At the same time, three other island groups far to the west with little or no population—Aldabra Islands, Farquhar Group and Iles Desroches—were separated from the administration of the Seychelles and put in the BIOT.

Britain first considered the use of Aldabra for a military base, but these islands, among the last places on earth almost entirely unaffected by human settlement, contain rare birds and giant tortoises, as well as unique species of invertebrates. A determined "Save Aldabra" campaign led by the Royal Society of Britain, the U.S. National Academy of Sciences, and the Smithsonian Institution resulted rather in the leasing of Aldabra to the Royal Society as a wildlife sanctuary. Control of these three island groups was returned to the Seychelles at its independence in 1976.

In 1966 the U.S. and Britain signed a 50-year agreement for the use of Diego Garcia, the largest atoll in the Chagos group, as a joint base. The 1,800 inhabitants of this archipelago were removed by Britain to Mauritius and the Seychelles. In 1971 the U.S. Navy constructed a jet landing strip and a communications center. Later, the lagoon was dredged for use as an anchorage and the runway was lengthened. By 1988 Diego Garcia had become a major permanent U.S. base, the only one between Italy and the Philippines. Nuclear submarines can be supplied there, while warehouse ships moored in the lagoon stock enough weapons and provisions for an amphibious Marine brigade. Transient Filipino workers have been imported, because Mauritius, which claims sovereignty, withdrew its nationals working there in 1983 in support of the idea of making the Indian Ocean a "zone of peace" and keeping big-power military rivalry out.

After three decades of life in Mauritius and elsewhere, in 2000 the Chagos islanders won an appeal to the High Court in Britain that restored the islands to them. Arguing that they have not adapted successfully to living in other locations and suffer widespread poverty and distress, the islanders insisted on the right of return to Diego Garcia itself. Mauritius likewise demands sovereignty over the islands. However, returning the island to its inhabitants would violate the treaty between Great Britain and the U.S. Diego Garcia proved vital for B-52 bombers during the 1991 Gulf War, and later during fighting in Afghanistan and Iraq. In 2008 the Law Lords, Britain's highest court, blocked the islanders' return.

In 2010 the British government announced the establishment of the world's largest marine reserve, a 210,000 square mile area twice the size of Britain. One of the world's richest marine ecosystems, it hosts the Great Chagos Bank, the largest living coral and home to more than 220 coral species and 1,000 species of reef fish. The reserve further complicates the fate of the islanders because it was created without their consent it will limit commercial fishing, their traditional livelihood.

Occupied Territories

Quneitra District "Golan Heights"

Area: About 450 square miles (1,165 sq. km.)
Population: 10,000 Syrians, most of them Druze, plus 12,000 Israeli settlers (estimated).

During the 1967 Arab-Israeli War, Israel seized the southwestern portion of Syria, including its administrative center, Quneitra (or Qunaytra). For two decades the plateau provided tactical military advantages for the Syrian military, who had on occasion shelled Israeli settlements from the heights overlooking the Jordan Valley and Lake Tiberias. As Syrian troops retreated, Israeli forces rapidly occupied Quneitra district, which became known as the Golan Heights, the Hebrew term parallel to the Arabic "Jawlan."

Jolan has good rainfall, especially in the northern part, near the high mountains. Much of it is satisfactory agricultural land, though broken and stony, especially to the north, where the terrain is suitable for little more than pasturage. In addition to the Semitic tribes which had grazed their flocks in Jolan since late Roman Empire times, Shi'a and Druze villagers had established themselves on the flanks of Jabal as-Shaykh (Mount Hermon) by modern times. The main town of Quneitra was largely deserted through the first part of the 19th century, but was revived, beginning in 1873, by Chechen and Circassian refugees from the Caucasus Mountains after the Russian Empire imposed its rule on their homeland.

In the population mosaic of the Golan—typical of many parts of Syria in 1967—there were besides the Druze, Shi'a, Circassian and Arab tribes, also some Turkomans and a sprinkling of Kurds and other scattered minorities. All used Arabic in education and outside their own communities. In the fury of the Israeli invasion, thousands of these peaceful Syrian citizens fled battle scenes, while others were expelled by Israeli troops.

For reasons presumably related to Druze loyalty in Israel, the Israelis permitted only Druze villagers to resume life in the occupied zone; the Circassian, Arab and other inhabitants of the district became displaced persons, mostly around Damascus. During the 1973 October War, Syrian tank and infantry units pushed into the zone, but were eventually thrown back, and Israeli forces advanced close to Damascus. However, the greatest destruction to the town of Quneitra occurred not during warfare, but when the Israel military deliberately ransacked and destroyed buildings, including mosques and a church, before returning them to Syria according to ceasefire agreements.

By 1988 more than a score of Israeli settlements, most of them kibbutzim, had been founded in Jolan on lands owned by displaced Syrians. Some settlements are right on the narrow buffer zone, patrolled by UN observers, separating Israeli and Syrian troops. This location within easy range of Syrian guns is curious, because one of the excuses for invading and holding Jolan was to prevent Syrian artillery from shelling Israeli settlements to the southwest.

Disputed Territories

The Israeli officials who allowed the Druze to remain in Jolan may have been surprised to discover that many Druze identified themselves as Syrian Arabs and would not docilely cooperate with Israeli policies. They have protested Israeli economic measures affecting them, including high taxation without corresponding benefits. They have protested restrictions on their freedom of movement from village to village. In an attempt to disrupt them, the Israeli army has at times imposed long curfews to prevent them from carrying out their work; at other times demonstrations were forcefully broken up in confrontations where some were shot to death. When they were told they must have Israeli identity cards in order to leave their villages for any purpose, as this would have been recognition of the permanency of the occupation, they refused. After long curfews and other measures they succeeded in having the regulation relaxed.

These Druze are in a difficult position. They are obliged to cooperate to some extent with the occupation in order to survive, but not too much, lest if returned to Syrian control they might be considered collaborators.

In 1981 Israeli law was extended over occupied Jolan, and the area was added as a sub-district to the Northern District, one of the six administrative units into which the State of Israel is divided. This act, tantamount to an annexation, was denounced by the UN. Successive attempts to negotiate peace between Israel and Syria have floundered over Syria's demand for a complete Israeli withdrawal and Israel's refusal to do so.

East Jerusalem

Area: 68 square miles (175 sq. km.) form the proposed international zone recommended by the U.N. in 1947.

Population: Nearly 140,000 Muslim and Christian Palestinians, as well as a varying number of foreign residents, mostly associated with church institutions. The number of Israelis living in East Jerusalem is small but growing.

The status of the city of Jerusalem has become a signal part of the strife in the Holy Land. Old Jerusalem, with its numerous shrines, archaic buildings, narrow streets and picturesque walls (last rebuilt in the Ottoman Period), has special significance to Jews, Christians and Muslims. Because of the city's sanctity, observers sometimes overlook the non-religious factors, such as political and economic considerations involved in the present contest for control of the city.

After many generations of relatively little alteration, the 20th century brought massive changes to the city. As the British administrative center of Palestine under a League of Nations Mandate, Jerusalem saw a new city growing up to the west and north of the walled city. The new city, mostly developed for Jewish immigrants, also had modern Arab areas. Then in the plan for partition of Palestine recommended by the General Assembly of the UN in November 1947, Jerusalem was given a separate status. The plan proposed an internationally administered zone of 68 square miles, including all of Jerusalem, the town of Bethlehem to the south, and a number of nearby Arab villages. This plan, however, was not implemented by the UN Security Council and the issue was the subject of an armed contest in 1948.

When an armistice agreement was signed in 1949, the new State of Israel held the western part of the city, from which thousands of Muslim and Christian Palestinians had been forced to flee, while the Kingdom of Jordan held the remainder, including Old Jerusalem, from which several hundred Jews had been safely removed under the auspices of the International Red Cross. The proposed Jerusalem International Zone was ignored in fact—except by foreign governments, as a diplomatic nicety.

Besides forcing both Jews and Arabs from their homes, the armistice divided the city and deprived Jews of all nationalities visiting privileges to their holy places in the Jordanian sector. Two separate cities in fact came into existence, each with its own character and economy, sharing nothing except a name. Jordanian-ruled Jerusalem (Arabic "al-Quds") was conservative and native Arab in character; Israeli Jerusalem was essentially modern European. Psychologically and socially the two cities could have been more than a thousand miles apart.

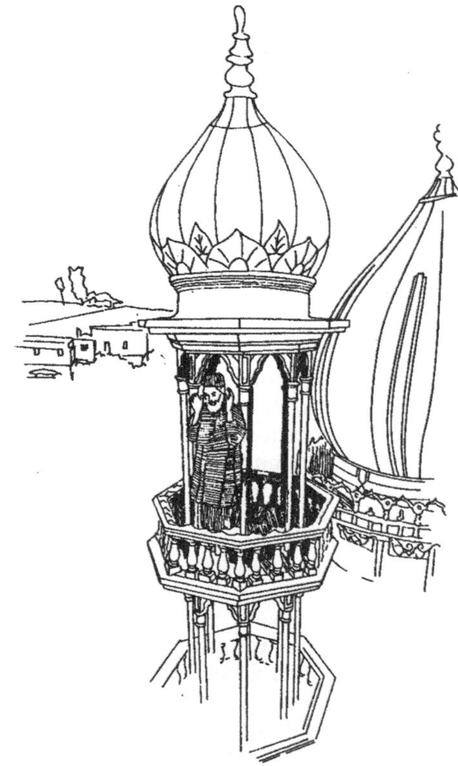

As a result of the war between Israel and neighboring Arab states in 1967, Israeli military occupation was imposed on Arab Jerusalem. East Jerusalem, as it came to be known, was joined to the municipality of the Israeli city. Israeli authorities then worked systematically to absorb the former Jordanian sector into the large Israeli city, disregarding entirely UN demands that Israel refrain from annexation of East Jerusalem.

Since its conquest of East Jerusalem, Israel has rapidly moved ahead to develop the city as part of its national territory. Homes for Israelis have been built on land seized for development, private buildings have been torn down to make way for public projects and Arab Jerusalemites who fled in 1967 have not been permitted to return to their homes. A number of prominent Arabs accused of resisting the Israeli administration have been deported to Jordan, including the former mayor of Arab Jerusalem.

Israeli spokesmen have declared emphatically that the "reunification" of Jerusalem will never be reversed and that the unified city will remain the capital of the State of Israel. Against considerable resistance, officials have encouraged the Christian and Muslim Arabs to vote in municipal elections, but have not given them Israeli citizenship (technically, they remain Jordanian citizens). They hope, in general, for deliverance from the present situation, while many Arabs and some Muslims elsewhere are determined that Old Jerusalem will be restored to Arab control.

Palestinian uprisings in the occupied territories which began at the end of 1987 magnified the division between Israeli Jerusalem and East Jerusalem. In spirit they had never been united. There have been separate areas of residence, social life and work, exemplified in the two downtowns. Christian Arabs in Jerusalem, as elsewhere in the occupied territories, have joined their Muslim fellow Palestinians as never before, having learned that the

Israelis will not show them preference as the British administration did prior to 1948. Many Arab residents of Jerusalem have torn up their Israeli identity cards, which symbolize their inferior status in the Israeli scheme. Teddy Kollak, defeated after 20 years as mayor, recognized that municipal attempts to unify the two populations failed. "Co-existence in Jerusalem," he said, "is dead."

Tensions over East Jerusalem arise almost annually, often when Jewish settlers attempt to establish or expand residences in Christian or Muslim quarters. Projects as seemingly innocuous as an archaeological park also lead to disputes when they remove Arab homes.

Kashmir

Area: 84,471 square miles (218,670 sq. km.). Of this area, 53,665 square miles (138,992 sq. km.) are controlled by India; 32,358 square miles (83,806 sq. km.) are under the control of Pakistan.

Population: About 4.8 million in the Indian zone; 1.4 million in the Pakistani zone.

The disputed territory of Kashmir, or more properly, Jammu and Kashmir, was ruled by a Hindu Maharaja, Sir Hari Singh, at the time of the partition of British India in 1947 (see India: History). The territory consisted of the districts of Jammu, Kashmir, Ladakh, Gilgit and several smaller areas, all in the northernmost part of British India. The Valley of Kashmir is one of the most pleasant parts of the entire region geographically; Ladakh, the largest district, is in the Himalayas and is mostly ice-bound.

Unrest invaded the region when British India was partitioned and the nation of Pakistan was created. The Maharaja suppressed his Muslim subjects in one area, and soon bands of plundering Muslim tribesmen were streaming toward his capital of Srinagar in Kashmir province. He fled to the city of Jammu and there signed a document on October 26, 1947 incorporating his domains into the Republic of India, although about 75% of the population was Muslim.

Indian troops were flown to Srinagar to save it from the tribesmen and to take control. Troops from Pakistan were drawn into the war which took place in the winter of 1947–48. Under United Nations auspices an agreement to stop shooting was negotiated; it became effective on January 1, 1949. The cease-fire line, which ran through the provinces of Jammu and Kashmir and then into the icy wastes of Ladakh, left India in occupation of about three-fifths of the entire disputed area.

Although the cease-fire halted open warfare, it did not bring peace, and the future of Kashmir remained undecided. Pakistan demanded a plebiscite carried out by the United Nations, but India held local elections and claimed that they served the purpose of a plebiscite—although the future of the territory was not on the ballot, and many Muslims boycotted the elections.

Kashmir remained a subject of great emotion on both sides. But outright violence was not serious until August, 1965, when Pakistan sent armed infiltrators across the Line of Control (LOC) to commit acts of sabotage and terrorism. Indian troops later crossed the LOC in three places, ostensibly to halt infiltration. Since Pakistani public opinion strongly supported fighting, its military launched a conventional invasion of Jammu with tanks and other heavy equipment in September. India responded by invading West Pakistan, near Lahore, and then farther south with a drive aimed at Karachi. Pakistan struck at India itself with attacks into Punjab and Rajasthan.

After the fighting reached a stalemate, the UN Security Council demanded a cease-fire, a decision simplified because both the Soviet Union and the United States opposed the war. The combatants complied, partly because they could not replenish their military supplies from the major powers. However, each side suspected the other of seeking further advantage, and refused to withdraw their forces from positions captured during the fighting.

In 1966 the Soviet Union invited Pakistani President Ayub Khan and Prime Minister Shastri of India to Tashkent, in the southern Soviet Union. There they were persuaded to sign an agreement for complete withdrawal behind their own borders and the 1949 LOC. Despite the withdrawal, the causes of the dispute remained. In 1999 Pakistani forces and irregulars secretly crossed the LOC and seized several peaks before being dislodged by Indian forces (see India: History). Feelings run strong in both nations, but India shows little desire to seize Pakistani Kashmir, and Pakistan's military recognizes that Indian forces are superior.

A further complication to the Kashmiri problem came when China, to facilitate road links, occupied desolate mountainous regions mapped as part of British India. One disputed zone lay in Pakistani Kashmir, but the larger occupied area, the Aksai Chin plateau, borders the Ladakh region of India. Since the 1962 India-China War, it has been occupied by China.

In the 1970s, Pakistan and China constructed the Karakoram highway to join their countries across some of the world's highest mountain ranges. The highway is 537 miles long and runs from Kashgar in China's Xinjiang province through Mintaka Pass, at an elevation of 15,000 feet in the Karakoram Range. It then continues south to Gilgit in Kashmir. At the time of its construction, the highway raised concerns not only in India, but also in the U.S. and the Soviet Union. These worries have slowly faded.

After several months of bombings and killings by a small group of Kashmiri secessionists, in 1990 police fired on a demonstration in Srinagar, killing about 50 people and marking the beginning of a popular uprising. As "freedom fighters" ambushed police, and civilians endured almost continuous curfews, talk of war mounted in New Delhi and Islamabad. Pakistan again demanded a plebiscite to allow Kashmiris to determine their own fate.

India naturally opposes any possible dismemberment, and the coalition governments in New Delhi often lack the power to make changes. Nevertheless, compromise may prove the only remaining alternative to brute force to retain Kashmir. Though the two nations negotiated a cease-fire in the Himalayan heights of Ladakh, where artillery battles had raged at a record 18,000 feet, some observers caution that popular feelings, aroused by revolt and repression, could force one weak government or the other into starting a war. The dispute promises to continue.

Regional Organizations

Gulf Cooperation Council

The rulers of Saudi Arabia, Kuwait, Qatar, the United Arab Emirates, Bahrain and Oman formed the Gulf Cooperation Council in 1981 to further their common interests, especially security and defense. Apprehensive of republican sentiments generally, and alarmed by the violent revolution in Iran and Soviet invasion of Afghanistan, the six autocracies sought to protect themselves by cooperation. While closer military contacts began, the GCC's first practical step was the formation of an Arabian free trade area through elimination of customs barriers. In 1983 it abolished tariffs on agricultural, manufactured and animal products originating in member states. Professional people were also to be allowed freedom to move between member states to work. Other joint projects related to uniformity of educational systems and expansion of educational opportunities such as the Gulf University at Bahrain.

By 1990, the GCC showed some signs of achievement and maturity. It shifted its attention from the distant problems of Israel and Lebanon to closer matters, including peace between Iran and Iraq. The organization also formed a brigade-strength joint defense force, stationed in Saudi Arabia. Although the GCC failed to deter Iraqi aggression against Kuwait, all its members supported its liberation. Until 2011, economic issues appeared most prominent. The GCC countries would benefit from a common industrial policy (to avoid duplicating expensive projects), a unified external tariff, and a similarity of subsidies and other benefits to businesses. Upset by the decision to locate the central bank in Saudi Arabia, the UAE withdrew from the proposed monetary union in 2009, and Kuwait later delayed the issuance of a euro-style single currency by the remaining members.

When anti-regime protests shook the Arab world in 2011, the focus of GCC members returned to national security, particularly the internal danger of regime change. Considering the largely Shi'a protests in Bahrain as Iranian-inspired, Saudi Arabia and the UAE dispatched military and police forces to help crush the demonstrations. Its summit conference also welcomed applications to join the GCC from Jordan and Morocco, two Sunni monarchies outside the Gulf, but with respected professional military forces.

The South Asian Association for Regional Cooperation (SAARC)

In 1985, the heads of government from seven regional nations met in conference in Dhaka and voted to establish the South Asian Association for Regional Cooperation (SAARC). Influenced by the success of alliances like the European Union and ASEAN, the founders hoped to promote economic cooperation (meaning fewer restrictions on trade), and thus reduce poverty and raise standards of living. Other objectives included better relations between countries and the creation of institutions like weather offices that could serve the entire region.

In a series of summits in the early years, SAARC's members agreed to conventions on narcotics and establishing food reserves. They adopted measures to simplify visas and travel between member nations. The Southern Asia Preferential Trading Arrangement adopted at the seventh SAARC Summit in 1993 looked forward to a regional free trade zone by 2001. Little happened immediately, but a new decision in 2005 called for the first steps in 2006, with the more developed economies of India, Pakistan and Sri Lanka abolishing all tariffs on imports from member nations by 2013.

Despite these signs of progress, trade remains limited between the seven member nations—Bangladesh, Bhutan, India, the Maldives, Nepal, Pakistan and Sri Lanka. Regulations often mean that many products are smuggled between members or shipped via other nations. In political matters, disputes between India and Pakistan often immobilized the organization. The Dhaka Declaration of 1985 forbad official discussions on contentious or bilateral issues, so SAARC is unlikely to address the most significant problems of the region. Afghanistan is expected to become a full member in 2007.

The League of Arab States

Representatives of all independent or self-governing Arab countries in the heart of the Arab world met to form the League of Arab States in 1945. The League initially included seven members, aside from Egypt all of them in Southwest Asia:

1. Egypt
2. Iraq
3. Jordan (then Transjordan)
4. Lebanon
5. Saudi Arabia
6. Syria
7. Yemen (Republic of Yemen, 1990)

Later, other nations which considered themselves to possess Arab character joined the League upon attaining political independence or soon thereafter (listed with year of adherence and, for those countries not described in this book, location):

8. Libya (1953), North Africa
9. Sudan (1956), Northeast Africa.
10. Morocco (1958), Northwest Africa.
11. Tunisia (1958), North Africa.
12. Kuwait (1961).
13. Algeria (1962), North Africa.
14. Peoples Democratic Republic of Yemen (1967–1990).
15. Bahrain (1971).
16. Oman (1971).
17. Qatar (1971).
18. United Arab Emirates (1971).
19. Mauritania (1973), Northwest Africa.
20. Somali Republic (1974), East Africa.
21. Palestine (1976).
22. Djibouti (1977), East Africa.

Djibouti, Mauritania and the Somali Republic are the only member nations in which Arabic is not the principal spoken language, though it is the main language used in schools and mosques. Djibouti has indicated its intention of making Arabic the official language and retaining French as a second language.

"Palestine" was admitted to membership by a unanimous vote in September 1976, although the Palestinian Liberation Organization then controlled no territory.

Until 1979, the League's was headquartered in Cairo on the east bank of the Nile. When Egypt signed a peace treaty with Israel considered unsatisfactory by other members, Egypt was expelled from the organization and the headquarters was moved to Tunis. Egypt rejoined the League in 1989. The League's majority condemned the invasion of Kuwait, but the sharply divided organization lost its Secretary General and returned its headquarters to Cairo thereafter. An Egyptian diplomat, Ismat Abd al-Majid became Secretary General.

Through efforts of the League, Arabic became the sixth official and working language of the UN beginning January 1, 1983. This decision was reached by the Security Council and followed a practice already common in the General Assembly. League members pay the extra expenses of the use of the additional language by the UN.

Selected Bibliography of Key English Language Sources

WEB SITES

Useful General Sites:

www.un.org (Web site for United Nations. Many links.)

www.unsystem.or (Official UN website)

http://europa.eu.int (EU server site)

www.oecd.org/daf/cmis/fdi/statist.htm (OECD site)

www.osce.org (Site of OSCE)

www.wto.org (World Trade Organization site)

www.worldbank.org/html/Welcome.html (World Bank news, publications with links to other financial institutions)

www.ceip.org (Carnegie Endowment for International Peace, using a fully integrated Web-database system)

www.cia.gov/index.html (Central Intelligence Agency)

www.odci.gov/cia (Includes useful CIA publications, such as *The World Factbook* and maps)

www.state.gov/www/ind.html (U.S. Department of State, including country reports)

http://usinfo.state.gov (U.S. Department of State)

lcweb2.loc.gov/frd/cs/cshome.html (Library of Congress with coverage of over 100 countries)

www.embassy.org/embassies (A site with links to all embassy web sites in Washington D.C.)

www.psr.keele.ac.uk\official.htm (Collective site for governments and international organizations)

http://mideastweb.org (Middle East Web Gateway resource)

http://www.palestinemonitor.org (The Palestine Monitor)

http://mfa.gov.il (Israeli Ministry of Foreign Affairs)

http://usembassy-israel.org.il (U.S. Embassy, Israel)

http://www.us-israel.org (The Jewish Virtual Library)

http://www.jpost.com (The Jerusalem Post, internet edition)

Newspapers, Journals and Television with good coverage on international affairs:

www.chicagotribune.com (Named best overall US newspaper online service for newspapers with circulation over 100,000.)

www.csmonitor.com (Respected U.S. newspaper, *Christian Science Monitor.* Named best overall US newspaper online service for newspapers with circulation under 100,000.)

www.economist.com (British weekly news magazine)

www.nytimes.com (Respected U.S. newspaper, *The New York Times*)

www.washingtonpost.com (Good international coverage)

www.foreignaffairs.org (One of best-known international affairs journal)

www.cnn.com (Latest news with external links)

www.news.BBC.co.uk (British Broadcasting Corporation site)

www.c-span.org (Includes C-SPAN International)

BOOKS

Middle East—general

Abi-Aad, Naji and Michel Grenon. *Instability and Conflict in the Middle East: People, Petroleum, and Security Threats.* New York: Saint Martin's Press, 1997.

Aburish, Said K. *A Brutal Friendship: the West and the Arab Elite.* New York: Saint Martin's Press, 1998.

Andersen, Roy R., et al. *Politics and Change in the Middle East: Sources of Conflict and Accommodation.* Upper Saddle River, NJ: Prentice Hall, 5th ed. 1997.

Anderson, Ewan E., et al. *The Middle East: Geography and Geopolitics.* 8th ed. New York: Routledge, 2000.

Bates, Daniel G., et al. *Peoples and Cultures of the Middle East.* Upper Saddle River, NJ: Prentice Hall, 2001.

Bensahel, Nora and Daniel L. Byman, eds. *The Future Security Environment in the Middle East.* Santa Monica, CA: Rand, 2003.

Choueiri, Youseff. *Arab Nationalism.* Malden, MA: Blackwell Publishers, 2001.

Cleveland, William L. and Martin Burton. *A History of the Modern Middle East.* Boulder, CO: Westview Press, 2008.

Dalrymple, William. *From the Holy Mountain: Journey among the Christians of the Middle East.* New York: Henry Holt & Company, 1998.

Deshen, Shlomo and Walter P. Zenner, eds. *Jews among Muslims: Communities in the Precolonial Middle East.* New York: New York University Press, 1996.

Dorraj, Manochehr, ed. *Middle East at the Crossroads: the Changing Political Dynamics and the Foreign Policy.* Lanham, MD: University Press of America, 1999.

Doubato, Eleanor A. and Marsha Posusney, eds. *Women and Globalization in the Arab Middle East: Gender, Economy, and Society.* Boulder, CO: Lynne Reinner, 2003.

Eickelman, Dale F. *Middle East and Central Asia.* Upper Saddle River, NJ: Prentice Hall, 1997.

Feldman, Shai. *Nuclear Weapons and Arms Control in the Middle East.* Cambridge, MA: MIT Press, 1997.

Fernea, Elizabeth W. and Robert A. Fernea. *The Arab World: Forty Years of Change.* New York: Doubleday, rev. ed. 1997.

Fisk, Robert. *The Great War for Civilisation: The Conquest of the Middle East.* New York: Vintage, 2007.

Freeman-Grenville, G.S. *Historical Atlas of the Middle East.* New York: Simon & Schuster, 1993.

Gerner, Deborah J., ed. *Understanding the Contemporary Middle East.* Boulder, CO: Lynne Reiner, 2000.

Gher, Leo A. *Civic Discourse and Digital Age Communications in the Middle East.* Westport, CT: Greenwood Publishing Group, 2000.

Gilbar, Gad G. *The Middle East Oil Decade and Beyond.* Portland, OR: International Specialized Book Services, 1997.

Gilbar, Gad G. *Population Dilemmas in the Middle East.* Portland, OR: International Specialized Book Services, 1997.

Gilsenan, Michael. *Recognizing Islam: Religion and Society in the Modern Middle East.* New York: I.B. Tauris & Company, 2000.

Glasser, Bradley L. *Economic Development and Political Reform: the Impact of External Capital on the Middle East.* Northampton, MA: Edward Elgar Publishing, 2000.

Guazzone, Laura. *Middle East Global Change: the Politics and Economics of Interdependence Versus Fragmentation.* New York: Saint Martin's Press, 1997.

Halliday, Fred. *Nation and Religion in the Middle East.* Boulder, CO: Lynne Rienner Publishers, 2000.

Hansen, Birthe. *Unipolarity and the Middle East.* New York: Saint Martin's Press, 2001.

Hawthorne, Amy W. *Democracy Deficit. U.S. Democracy Promotion Efforts in the Arab World.* Washington D.C.: Brookings, 2003.

Herb, Michael. *All in the Family: Absolutism, Revolution, and Democratic Prospects in the Middle Eastern Monarchies.* Albany, NY: State University of New York Press, 1999.

Hess, Andrew C. *Oil and Money: a Global Study of the Middle East in the Oil Era.* Chicago: Firtzroy Dearborn Publishers, 1999.

Hinnebusch, Raymond and A. Ehteshami, eds. *The Foreign Policies of the Middle East States.* Boulder, CO: Lynne Rienner, 2002.

Hiro, Dilip. *A Dictionary of the Middle East.* New York: Saint Martin's Press, 1996.

Hiro, Dilip. *The Middle East.* Phoenix, AZ: Oryx Press, 1996.

Issawi, Charles P. *The Middle East Economy: Decline and Recovery.* Princeton, NJ: Markus Wiener Publishers, rev. ed. 1996.

Jabar, Faleh A., ed. *Post-Marxism and the Middle East.* Portland, OR: International Specialized Book Services, 1997.

Kamalipour, Yahya R. *The U.S. Media and the Middle East: Image and Perception.* Westport, CT: Greenwood Publishing, 1995.

Bibliography

Kaufman, Burton I. *Arab Middle East and the United States*. Old Tappan, NJ: Macmillan Library Reference, 1996.

Kemp, Geoffrey and Robert E. Harkavy. *Strategic Geography and the Changing Middle East*. Washington, DC: Carnegie Endowment for International Peace, 1997.

Lewis, Bernard. *The Middle East: a Brief History of the Last 2,000 Years*. New York: Simon & Schuster, 1996.

Lewis, Bernard. *Multiple Identities of the Middle East*. New York: Schocken Books, 1999.

Lindholm, Charles. *The Islamic Middle East: an Historical Anthropology*. Malden, MA: Blackwell Publishers, 1996.

Link, P.S., ed. *Middle East Imbroglio: Status and Prospects*. Commack, NY: Nova Science Publishers, 1996.

Long, David E. and Bernard Reich. *The Government and Politics of the Middle East and North Africa*. 4th ed. Boulder, CO: Westview, 2002.

Maddy-Weitzman, Bruce, ed. *Middle East Contemporary Survey*. Boulder, CO: Westview Press, 2000.

Maoz, Moshe and Ilan Pappe, eds. *Middle Eastern Politics and Ideas: a History from Within*. New York: Saint Martin's Press, 1998.

Maoz, Zeev. *Regional Security in the Middle East: Past, Present, Future*. Portland, OR: International Specialized Book Services, 1997.

McKale, Donald M. *War by Revolution: Germany and Great Britain in the Middle East in the Era of World War I*. Kent, OH: Kent State University Press, 1998.

Moghadam, Valentine M. *Modernization Women: Gender and Social change in the Middle East*, 2d ed. Boulder, CO: Lynne Reinner, 2003.

Murden, Simon W. *Islam, The Middle East, and the New Global Hegemony*. Boulder, CO: Lynne Reinner, 2002.

Nawawy, Mohammed el and Adel Iskandar. *Al-Jazeera. How the Free Arab News Network Scooped the World and Changed the Middle East*. Boulder, CO: Westview, 2003.

Niblock, Tim. *"Pariah States" and Sanctions in the Middle East: Iraq, Libya, Sudan*. Boulder, CO: Lynne Rienner, 2002.

Norton, Augustus R. *Civil Society in the Middle East*. Boston, MA: Brill Academic Publishers, 1994.

Ochsenwald, William L. and Sydney Nettleton Fisher. *The Middle East: a History*. New York: McGraw-Hill, 7th. ed. 2010.

Ovendale, Ritchie. *Britain, the U.S., and the Transfer of Power in the Middle East 1945–1962*. Herndon, VA: Books International, 1996.

Owen, Edward R. *A History of Middle East Economies in the Twentieth Century*. Cambridge, MA: Harvard University Press, 1999.

Owen, Roger. *State Power and Politics in Making of the Modern Middle East*. New York: Routledge, 2000.

Peleg, Ilan, ed. *The Middle East Peace Process: Interdisciplinary Perspectives*. Albany, NY: State University of New York Press, 1997.

Pervin, David J. and Steven L. Spiegel. *Practical Peacemaking in the Middle East, Vol. 1: Arms Control and Regional Security*. New York: Garland Publishing, 1995.

Pervin, David J. and Steven L. Spiegel. *Practical Peacemaking in the Middle East, Vol 2: The Environment, Water, Refugees, and Economic Cooperation and Development*. New York: Garland Publishing, 1995.

Richards, Alan and John Waterbury. *A Political Economy of the Middle East*. Boulder, CO: Westview Press, 1996.

Rogan, Eugene. *The Arabs: A History*. New York: Basic Books, 2009.

Rubin, Barry, et al., eds. *From War to Peace: Arab-Israeli Relations, 1973–1993*. New York: New York University Press, 1994.

Saikal, Amin and Albrecht Schnabel, eds. *Democratization in the Middle East*. Washington D.C.: Brookings, 2003.

Savir, Uri. *The Process: 1,100 Days That Changed the Middle East*. New York: Random House, 1998.

Schwedler, Jillian and Deborah J. Gerner. *Understanding the Contemporary Middle East*. Boulder, CO: Lynne Rienner Publishers, 2008.

Soffer, Arnon. Translated by Mory Rosovesky. *Rivers of Fire: the Conflict over Water in the Middle East*. Lanham, MD: Rowman & Littlefield Publishers, 1999.

Tal, David, ed. *The 1956 War: Collusion and Rivalry in the Middle East*. Portland, OR: Frank Cass Publishers, 2000.

Tamini, Sargon. *Islam and Secularism in the Middle East*. New York: New York University Press, 2000.

Vatikiotis, P.J. *Middle East: from the End of Empire to the End of the Cold War*. New York: Routledge, 1997.

Viorst, Milton. *Sandcastles: the Arabs in Search of the Modern World*. New York: Random House, 1994.

Williams, Mary E. *The Middle East: Opposing Viewpoints*. San Diego, CA: Greenhaven Press, 2000.

Islam

Allison, Robert J. *The Crescent Obscured: the United States and Muslim World, 1776–1815*. New York: Oxford University Press, 1995.

Arkoun, Mohammed. *Rethinking Islam: Common Questions, Uncommon Answers*. Boulder, CO: Westview Press, 1994.

Armstrong, Karen. *Islam: a Short History*. New York: Modern Library, 2000.

Braswell, George W. Jr. *Islam: Its Prophet, Peoples, Politics, and Power*. Nashville, TN: Broadman & Holman, 1996.

Brown, L. Carl. *Religion and State: the Muslim Approach to Politics*. New York: Columbia University Press, 2000.

Butterworth, Charles E. and I. William Zartman, eds. *Between the State and Islam*. New York: Cambridge University Press, 2000.

Chebel, Malek. *Symbols of Islam*. New York: Saint Martin's Press, 1997.

Davidson, Lawrence. *Islamic Fundamentalism*. Westport, CT: Greenwood Publishing Group, 1998.

_____ . *Encyclopedia of Islam*. Boston, MA: Brill Academic Publishers, 1997.

Esposito, John L., ed. *The Oxford History of Islam*. New York: Oxford University Press, 2000.

Esposito, John L. *Political Islam: Revolution, Radicalism, or Reform*. Boulder, CO: Lynne Reinner, 1997.

Feldman, Noah. *The Fall and Rise of the Islamic State*. Princeton, NJ: Princeton University Press, 2008

Halliday, Fred. *Nation and Religion in the Middle East*. Boulder, CO: Lynne Reinner, 2000.

Hathout, Hassan. *Reading the Muslim Mind*. Plainfield, IN: American Trust Publications, 1994.

Hawting, G.R. *The Idea of Idolatry and the Emergence of Islam: from Polemic to History*. New York: Cambridge University Press, 2000.

Huband, Mark. *Warriors of the Prophet: the Struggle for Islam*. Boulder, CO: Westview Press, 1999.

Khan, Muhammad Z., translator. *The Quran*. Northampton, MA: Interlink Publishing Group, 1997.

Kramer, Martin, ed. *The Islamic Debate*. Syracuse, NY: Syracuse University Press, 1997.

Marshall, Paul, and Nina Shea. *Silenced: How Apostasy and Blasphemy Codes Are Choking Freedom Worldwide*. New York: Oxford University Press, 2011.

Memon, Ali N. *The Islamic Nation: Status and Future of Muslims in the New World Order*. Beltsville, MD: Writer's, Inc., 1995.

Moussalli, Amhad. *Historical Dictionary of Islamic Fundamentalist Movements in the Arab World, Iran and Turkey*. Lanham, MD: Scarecrow Press, 1999.

Nagel, Tilman and Bernard Lewis, eds. *The History of Islamic Theology: from Muhammad to the Present*. Princeton, NJ: Markus Weiner Publishers, 1999.

Nomani, Asra Q. *Tantrika: Traveling the Road of Divine Love*. San Francisco: Harpers, 2003. (Explores women's boundaries within Islam)

Noreng, Ystein. *Oil and Islam: Social and Economic Issues.* New York: John Wiley & Sons, 1997.

Palmer, Monte and Princess Palmer. *Islamic Extremism: Causes, Diversity, and Challenges.* Lanham, MD: Rowman & Littlefield, 2007

Renard, John. *Seven Doors to Islam: Spirituality and the Religious Life Of Muslims.* Berkeley, CA: University of California Press, 1996.

Roy, Olivier. *Globalized Islam: The Search for a New Ummah.* New York: Columbia University Press, 2006.

Van Donzel, E.J., ed. *Islamic Desk Reference.* Boston, MA: Brill Academic Publishers, 1994.

Viorst, Milton. *In the Shadow of the Prophet: the Struggle for the Soul of Islam.* Boulder, CO: Westview Press, 2001.

Zepp, Ira G., Jr. *A Muslim Primer: Beginner's Guide to Islam.* Fayetteville, AR: University of Arkansas Press, 2000.

Palestinians

Abu-Nimer, Mohammed. *Dialogue, Conflict Resolution, and Change: Arab-Jewish Encounters in Israel.* Albany, NY: State University of New York Press, 1999.

Arnon, Arie and Jimmy Weinblatt. *The Palestinian Economy: between Imposed Integration and Voluntary Separation.* Boston, MA: Brill Academic Publishers, 1997.

Ciment, James. *Palestine Israel: the Long Conflict.* New York: Facts on File, 1997.

Cragg, Kenneth. *Palestine: the Prize and Price of Zion.* Herndon, VA: Cassell Academic, 1997.

Dannreuther, Roland. *Soviet Union and Palestine Resistance.* New York: Saint Martin's Press, 1998.

Diwan, Ishac and Radwan A. Shaban. *Development under Adversity: the Palestinian Economy in Transition.* Washington, DC: The World Bank, 1999.

Farsoun, Samih K. and Christina E. Zacharia. *Palestine and the Palestinians: a Stateless Nation.* Boulder, CO: Westview Press, 1997.

Holliday, Laurel. *Children of Israel, Children of Palestine.* New York: Pocket Books, 1998.

Inbari, Pinhas. *The Palestinians between Terrorism and Statehood.* Portland, OR: International Specialized Book Services, 1998.

Jabar, Hala. *Hezbollah: Born with a Vengeance.* New York: Columbia University Press, 1997.

Kass, Ilana and Bard O'Neill. *The Deadly Embrace: the Impact of Israel and Palestinian Rejectionism on the Peace Process.* Lanham, MD: University Press of America, 1996.

Khalidi, Rashid. *Palestinian Identity.* New York: Columbia University Press, 1997.

Kimmerling, Baruch. *Palestinians: the Making of a People.* New York: The Free Press, 1993.

Mattar, Philip. *Encyclopedia of the Palestinians.* New York: Facts on File, 1999.

Nazzal, Nafez and Laila A. Nazzal. *Historical Dictionary of Palestine.* Lanham, MD: Scarecrow Press, 1997.

Peleg, Ilan. *Human Rights in the West Band and Gaza.* Syracuse, NY: Syracuse University Press, 1995.

Robinson, Glenn E. *Building a Palestinian State: the Incomplete Revolution.* Bloomington, IN: Indiana University Press, 1997.

Rouhana, Nadim N. *Palestinians in an Ethnic Jewish State: Identities in Conflict.* New Haven, CT: Yale University Press, 1997.

Shemesh, Moshe. *The Palestinian Entity, 1959–1974: Arab Politics and the PLO.* Portland, OR: International Specialized Book Services, rev. ed. 1996.

Swedenburg, Ted. *Memories of Revolt: the 1936–39 Rebellion and the Palestinian National Past.* Minneapolis, MN: University of Minnesota Press, 1995.

Toubbeh, Jamil I. *Day of the Long Night: a Palestinian Refugee Remembers the "Nabka."* Jefferson, NC: McFarland & Company, 1997.

Persian Gulf

Abdelkarim, Abbas. *Change and Development in the Gulf.* New York: Saint Martin's Press, 1999.

Baldwin, Sherman. *Ironclaw: a Navy Carrier Pilot's Gulf War Experience.* New York: William Morrow & Company, 1996.

Coughlin, Sean T. *Storming the Desert: a Marine Lieutenant's Day-by-Day Chronicle of the Persian Gulf.* Jefferson, NC: McFarland & Company, 1996.

Donnelly, Michael and Denise Donnelly. *Falcon's Cry: a Desert Storm Memoir.* Westport, CT: Greenwood Publishing Group, 1998.

Edington, L. Benjamin and Michael J. Mazarr, eds. *Turning Point: the Gulf War.* Boulder, CO: Westview Press, 1995.

El-Shazly, Nadia El-Sayed. *Gulf Tanker War.* New York: Saint Martin's Press, 1998.

Grossman, Mark, ed. *Encyclopedia of the Persian Gulf War.* Santa Barbara, CA: ABC-CLIO, 1995.

Head, William Jr. and Earl Tilford. *The Eagle in the Desert: Looking Back on the United States Involvement in the Persian Gulf.* Westport, CT: Greenwood Publishing Group, 1996.

Hutchinson, Kevin D. *Operation Desert Shield-Desert Storm: Chronology and Fact Book.* Westport, CT: Greenwood Publishing Group, 1995.

Khadduri, Majid and Edmund Ghareeb. *War in the Gulf, 1990–91: the Iraq-Kuwait Conflict and Its Implications: Views from the Other Side.* New York: Oxford University Press, 1997.

Metz, Helen Chapin, ed. *Persian Gulf State: Country Studies.* Washington, DC: U.S. GPO, 3rd ed. 1994.

Mohamedou, Mohammad-Mahmoud. *Iraq and the Second Gulf War: State Building and Regime Security.* Bethesda, MD: Austin & Winfield Publishers, 1997.

Murray, Williamson and Wayne W. Thompson. *Air War in the Persian Gulf.* Mount Pleasant, SC: Nautical & Aviation Publishing Company, 1995.

Newell, Clayton R. *Historical Dictionary of the Persian Gulf War, 1990–1991.* Lanham, MD: Scarecrow Press, 1998.

Orgill, Andrew. *The 1990–91 Gulf War: Crisis, Conflict, Aftermath: an Annotated Bibliography.* Herndon, VA: Cassell Academic, 1995.

Schwartz, Richard A. *Encyclopedia of the Persian Gulf War.* Jefferson, NC: McFarland & Company, 1998.

Summers, Harry G., Jr. *The Persian Gulf War Almanac.* New York: Facts on File, 1995.

Yetiv, Steve A. *The Persian Gulf Crisis.* Westport, CT: Greenwood Publishing Group, 1997.

Zahlan, Rosemarie Said. *The Making of the Modern Gulf States: Kuwait, Bahrain, Qatar, the United Arab Emirates, and Oman.* Reading, England: Ithaca Press, 1998.

Terrorism

Anderson, Sean and Stephen Sloan. *Historical Dictionary of Terrorism.* Lanham, MD: Scarecrow Press, 1995.

Bergen, Peter. *The Longest War: The Enduring Conflict between America and al-Qaeda.* New York: Free Press, 2011

Combs, Cindy C. *Terrorism in the 21st Century.* Upper Saddle River, NJ: Prentice-Hall, 1999.

Crenshaw, Martha and John Pimlott, eds. *Encyclopedia of World Terrorism.* Armonk, NY: M.E. Sharpe, 1996.

Egendorf, Laura K. *Terrorism: Opposing Viewpoints.* San Diego, CA: Greenhaven Press, 2000.

Gearty, Conor. *Terrorism.* Brookfield, VT: Ashgate Publishing Company, 1996.

Grosscup, Beau. *The Newest Explosions of Terrorism: Latest Sites of Terrorism in the 1990's and Beyond.* Far Hills, NJ: New Horizon Press, 1998.

Gurr, Nadine. *The New Face of Terrorism: Threats from Weapons of Mass Destruction.* New York: I.B. Tauris & Company, 2000.

Harmon, Christopher C. *Terrorism Today.* Portland, OR: Frank Cass Publishers, 1999.

Higgins, Rosalyn and Maurice Flory, eds. *Terrorism and International Law.* New York: Routledge, 1997.

Hunter, Thomas B. *The A to Z of International Terrorist and Counterterrorist Orga-*

Bibliography

nizations. Lanham, MD Scarecrow Press, 1999.

Kressel, Neil J. *Mass Hate: the Global Rise of Genocide and Terror*. New York: Plenum Publishing, 1996.

Laqueur, Walter. *The New Terrorism: Fanaticism and the Arms of Mass Destruction*. New York: Oxford University Press, 1999.

LeMesurier, Charles and Marc Arnold. *Terrorism*. London: Jane's Information Group, 1997.

Mickolus, Edward F. and Susan L. Simmons. *Terrorism, 1992–1995: a Chronology of Events and a Selectively Annotated Bibliography*. Westport, CT: Greenwood Publishing Group, 1997.

Nasr, Kameel B. *Arab and Israeli Terrorism: the Causes and Effects of Political Violence, 1936–1993*. Jefferson, NC: McFarland & Company, 1996.

Netanyahu, Binyamin. *Fighting Terrorism: How Democracies Can Defeat Domestic and International Terrorists*. New York: Farrar, Straus & Giroux, 1995.

O'Ballance, Edgar. *Islamic Fundamentalist Terrorism, 1979–95: the Iranian Connection*. New York: New York University Press, 1996.

Prunckun, Henry W., Jr. *Shadow of Death: an Analytic Bibliography on Political Violence, Terrorism, and Low-Intensity Conflict*. Lanham, MD: Scarecrow Press, 1995.

Stern, Jessica. *The Ultimate Terrorists*. Cambridge, MA: Harvard University Press, 1999.

Tanter, Raymond. *Rogue Regimes: Terrorism and Proliferation*. New York: Saint Martin's Press, 1997.

Taylor, Max and John Horgan, eds. *The Future of Terrorism*. Portland, OR: Frank Cass Publishers, 2000.

Tucker, David. *Skirmishes at the Edge of the Empire: the United States and International Terrorism*. Westport, CT: Greenwood Publishing Group, 1997.

Tucker, Jonathan B., ed. *Toxic Terror*. Cambridge, MA: MIT Press, 2000.

White, Jonathan R. *Terrorism: an Introduction*. Belmont, CA: Wadsworth Publishing Company, 1997.

Wieviorka, Michel. Translated by David G. White. *The Making of Terrorism*. Chicago: University of Chicago Press, 1993.

Water

Pachova, Nevelina I., Mikiyasu Nakayama and Libor Jansky, eds. *International Water Security: Domestic Threats and Opportunities.*

South Asia—general

Babb, Lawrence A. and Susan S. Wadley, eds. *Media and the Transformation of Religion in South Asia*. Philadelphia, PA: University of Pennsylvania Press, 1995.

Bahri, Deepika and Mary Vasudeva, eds. *Between the Lines: South Asians and Postcoloniality*. Philadelphia, PA: Temple University Press, 1996.

Baxter, Craig, et al. *Government and Politics in South Asia*. 5th ed. Boulder, CO: Westview, 2001.

Bose, Sugata and Ayesha Jalal. *Modern South Asia: History, Culture and Political Economy*. New York: Routledge, 1998.

Breton, Roland J. *Atlas of the Languages and Ethnic Communities of South Asia*. Thousand Oaks, CA: Sage Publications, 1997.

Chadda, Maya. *Building Democracy in South Asia: India, Nepal, Pakistan*. Boulder, CO: Lynne Reinner, 2000.

Dixit, J.N. *India-Pakistan in War and Peace*. NY: Routledge, 2002.

Ganguly, Sumit and Ted Greenwood, eds. *Mending Fences: Confidence and Security-Building Measures in South Asia*. Boulder, CO: Westview Press, 1996.

Hewitt, Vernon. *The New International Politics of South Asia*. New York: Saint Martin's Press, 1997.

Hossain, Moazzem. *South Asian Economic Development: Transformation, Opportunities and Challenges*. New York: Routledge, 1999.

Jalel, Ayesha. *Democracy and Authoritarianism in South Asia: a Comparative and Historical Perspective*. New York: Cambridge University Press, 1995.

Krepan, Michael L., ed. *Conflict Prevention, Confidence Building, and Reconciliation in South Asia*. New York: Saint Martin's Press, 1995.

Ludden, David. *An Agrarian History of South Asia*. New York: Cambridge University Press, 1999.

Mitra, Subrata K. And R. Alison Lewis, eds. *Subnational Movements in South Asia*. Boulder, CO: Westview Press, 1996.

Pasha, Mustapha K. *South Asia: Civil Society, State, and Politics*. Boulder, CO: Westview Press, 1999.

Peimani, Hooman. *Nuclear Proliferation in the Indian Subcontinent: the Self-Exhausting "Superpowers" and Emerging Alliances:* Westport, CT: Greenwood Publishing Group, 2000.

Schmidt, Karl J. *An Atlas and Survey of South Asian History*. Armonk, NY: M.E. Sharpe, 1995.

Schwartzberg, Joseph E. *A Historical Atlas of South Asia, 2nd Impression with Additional Material*. New York: Oxford University Press, 1993.

Synnott, Hilary. *The Causes and Consequences of South Asia's Nuclear Tests*. New York: Oxford University Press, 1999.

Tambiah, Stanely J. *Leveling Crowds: Ethno-Nationalist Conflicts and Collective Violence in South Asia*. Berkeley, CA: University of California Press, 1997.

Indian Ocean

Metz, Helen C., ed. *Indian Ocean: Five Island Countries*. Washington, DC: U.S. GPO, 3rd. ed. 1995.

Afghanistan

Adamec, Ludwig W. *Dictionary of Afghan Wars, Revolutions, and Insurgencies*. Lanham, MD: Scarecrow Press, 1996.

Adamec, Ludwig W. *Historical Dictionary of Afghanistan*. Lanham, MD: Scarecrow Press, 1997.

Cordovez, Diego. *Out of Afghanistan: the Inside Story of the Soviet Withdrawal*. New York: Oxford University Press, 1995.

Galeotti, Mark. *Afghanistan: the Soviet Union's Last War*. Portland, OR: Frank Cass & Company, 1995.

Glatzer, Bernt. *Afghanistan*. NY: Routledge, 2002.

Grasselli, Gabriella. *British and American Responses to the Soviet Invasion of Afghanistan*. Brookfield, VT: Ashgate Publishing Company, 1996.

Kakar, M. Hassan. *Afghanistan: the Soviet Invasion and the Afghan Response*. Berkeley, CA: University of California Press, 1995.

Magnus, Ralph H. and Eden Naby. *Afghanistan: Marx, Mullah and Mujahid*. rev. ed. Boulder, CO: Westview Press, 2002.

Margolis, Eric. *War at the Top of the World: the Struggle for Afghanistan, Kashmir and Tibet*. New York: Routledge, 2000.

Olesen, Asta. *Islam and Politics in Afghanistan*. Concord, MA: Paul & Company Publishers Consortium, 1995.

Pedersen, Gorm. *Afghan Nomads in Transition*. New York: Thames & Hudson, 1995.

Rais, Rasul Bakhsh. *Recovering the Frontier State: War, Ethnicity, and the State in Afghanistan*. Lanham, MD: Rowman & Littlefield, 2009

Rubin, Barnett R. *The Fragmentation of Afghanistan: State Formation and Collapse in the International System*. New Haven, CT: Yale University Press, 1994.

Rubin, Barnett, R. *The Search for Peace in Afghanistan: from Buffer State to Failed State*. New Haven, CT: Yale University Press, 1996.

Schuyler, Jones. *Afghanistan*. Santa Barbara, CA: ABC-CLIO, 1992.

Weinbaum, Marvin G. *Pakistan and Afghanistan: Resistance and Reconstruction*. Boulder, CO: Westview Press, 1994.

Bahrain

Khuri, Fuad Ishaq. *Tribe and State in Bahrain: the Transformation of Social and Political Authority in an Arab State*. Chicago: University of Chicago Press, 1980.

Lawson, Fred Haley. *Bahrain: the Modernization of Autocracy*. Boulder, CO: Westview Press, 1989.

Bibliography

Bangladesh

Baxter, Craig. *Historical Dictionary of Bangladesh.* Lanham, MD: Scarecrow Press, 1996.

Choudhury, Dilara. *Constitutional Development in Bangladesh: Stresses and Strains.* New York: Oxford University Press, 1997.

Dayal, Edison. *Food, Nutrition and Hunger in Bangladesh.* Brookfield, VT: Ashgate Publishing Company, 1997.

Heitzman, James and Robert L. Worden, eds. *Bangladesh: a Country Study.* Washington, DC: U.S. GPO, 2nd ed. 1989.

Hossain, Akhtar. *Macroeconomic Issues and Policies: the Case for Bangladesh.* Thousand Oaks, CA: Sage Publications, 1996.

Mohsin, Amena. *The Chittagong Hill Tracts, Bangladesh: On the Difficult Road to Peace.* Boulder, CO: Lynne Reinner, 2003.

Pokrant, Bob. *Bangladesh.* Santa Barbara, CA: ABC-CLIO, 2000.

Sisson, Richard. *War and Secession: Pakistan, India, and the Creation of Bangladesh.* Berkeley, CA: University of California Press, 1990.

Wahid, Abu N. and Charles E. Weis, eds. *The Economy of Bangladesh: Problems and Prospects.* Westport, CA: Greenwood Publishing Group, 1996.

Warrick, Richard A. and Q. K. Ahmad, eds. *The Implications of Climate and Sea-Level Change for Bangladesh.* Norwell, MA: Kluwer Academic Publishers, 1996.

Wood, Geoffrey D. and Iffath A. Shariff. *Who Needs Credit? Poverty and Finance in Bangladesh.* New York: Saint Martin's Press, 1998.

Bhutan

Apte, Robert Z. *Three Kingdoms on the Roof of the World: Bhutan, Nepal, and Ladakh.* Berkeley, CA: Parallax Press, 1990.

Savada, Andrea Matles, ed. *Nepal and Bhutan: Country Studies.* Washington, DC: U.S. GPO, 1993.

Zeppa, Jamie. *Beyond the Sky and the Earth: a Journey into Bhutan.* New York: Putnam Publishing Group, 1999.

Egypt

Beattie, Kirk J. *Egyptian Politics during Sadat's Presidency.* New York: Saint Martin's Press, 2000.

Boutros-Ghali, Boutros. *Egypt's Road to Jerusalem: a Diplomat's Story of the Struggle for Peace in the Middle East.* New York: Random House, 1997.

Cromer, Evelyn Baring. *Modern Egypt.* New York: Routledge, 2000.

Elkhafif, Mahmoud A. *The Egyptian Economy: a Modeling Approach.* Westport, CT: Greenwood Publishing Group, 1996.

Gershoni, Israel. *Redefining the Egyptian Nation, 1930–1945.* New York: Cambridge University Press, 1995.

Gorst, Anthony and Lewis Johnman. *The Suez Crisis.* New York: Routledge, 1997.

Harik, Iliya F. *Economic Policy Reform in Egypt.* Gainesville, FL: University Press of Florida, 1997.

Holland, Matthew F. *America and Egypt: from Roosevelt to Eisenhower.* Westport, CT: Greenwood Publishing Group, 1996.

Lucas, Scott. *Britain and the Suez Crisis: the Lion's Last Roar.* New York: Saint Martin's Press, 1996.

Meital, Yoram. *Egypt's Last Struggle for Peace: Continuity and Change, 1967–1971.* Gainesville, FL: University Press of Florida, 1997.

Metz, Helen Chapin, ed. *Egypt: a Country Study.* Washington, DC: U.S. GPO, 5th ed. 1991.

Nagi, Saad Z. *Poverty in Egypt: Human Needs and Institutional Capacities.* Lanham, MD: Lexington Books, 2000.

Sullivan, Denis J. and Sana Abed-Kotob. *Islam in Contemporary Egypt: Civil Society vs. the State.* Boulder, CO: Lynne Rienner Publishers, 1999.

Weaver, Mary Anne. *A Portrait of Egypt: a Journey through the World of Militant Islam.* New York: Farrar, Straus & Giroux, 2000.

Woodward, Peter N. *Nasser.* White Plains, NY: Longman Publishing Group, 1991.

India

Bayly, Susan. *Caste, Society and Politics in India from the 18th Century to the Modern Age.* New York: Cambridge University Press, 2001.

Bouton, Marshall M. and Philip Oldenburg, eds. *India Briefing: a Transformative 50 Years.* Armonk, NY: M.E. Sharpe, 1999.

Burke, Samuel M. and Salim Al-Din Quraishi. *The British Raj in India: an Historical Review.* New York: Oxford University Press, 1995.

Chadda, Maya. *Ethnicity, Security and Separatism in India.* New York: Columbia University Press, 1997.

Chary, M. Srinivas. *The Eagle and the Peacock: U.S. Foreign Policy toward India since Independence.* Westport, CT: Greenwood Publishing Group, 1995.

Chatterjee, Partha, ed. *State and Politics in India.* New York: Oxford University Press, 2000.

Cohen, Stephen P. *India. Emerging Power.* Washington, DC: Brookings, 2002.

Cohn, Bernard S. *Colonialism and Its Forms of Knowledge: the British in India.* Princeton, NJ: Princeton University Press, 1996.

Currie, Bob. *The Politics of Hunger in India: a Study of Democracy, Governance and Kalahandi's Poverty.* New York: Saint Martin's Press, 2000.

Dandekar, Vinayak M. *The Indian Economy, 1947–92: Population, Poverty and Employment.* Thousand Oaks, CA: Sage Publications, 1996.

Dantwala, M.L., et al., eds. *Dilemmas of Growth: the Indian Experience.* Thousand Oaks, CA: Sage Publications, 1996.

Derbyshire, Ian D. *India.* Santa Barbara, CA: ABC-CLIO, rev. ed. 1995.

Edney, Matthew H. *Mapping the Empire: the Geographical Construction of British India.* Chicago: University of Chicago Press, 1997.

Frankel, Francine R., et al., eds. *Transforming India: Social and Political Dynamics of Democracy.* New York: Oxford University Press, 2000.

Ganguly, Sumit, ed. *Understanding Contemporary India.* Boulder, CO: Lynne Rienner Publishers, 2001.

Hansen, Thomas Blom. *Saffron Wave: Democracy and Hindu Nationalism in Modern India.* Princeton, NJ: Princeton University Press, 1999.

Harrison, Selig S., et al., eds. *India and Pakistan: the First Fifty Years.* New York: Cambridge University Press, 1998

Heitzman, James and Robert L. Worden, eds. *India: a Country Study.* Washington, DC: U.S. GPO, 5th ed. 1996.

James, Lawrence. *RAJ: the Making and Unmaking of British India.* New York: Thomas Dunne Books, 1998.

Jayal, Niraja G. *Democracy and the State: Welfare, Secularism, and Development in Contemporary India.* New York: Oxford University Press, 1999.

Jenkins, Rob. *Democratic Politics and Economic Reform in India.* New York: Cambridge University Press, 1999.

Johnson, Gordon. *Cultural Atlas of India.* New York: Facts on File, 1996.

Keay, John. *India: a History.* New York: Grove/Atlantic, 2000.

Khan, Yasmin. *The Great Partition: The Making of India and Pakistan.* New Haven: Yale University Press, 2007.

Kulke, Herman and Dietmar Rothermund. *History of India.* New York: Routledge, 1998.

Maitra, Priyatosh. *The Globalization of Capitalism and Its Impact on Third World Countries: India as a Case Study.* Westport, CT: Greenwood Publishing Group, 1996.

Mansingh, Surjit. *Historical Dictionary of India.* Lanham, MD: Scarecrow Press, 1996.

Mehta, Gita. *Snakes and Ladders: Glimpses of Modern India.* New York: Doubleday, 1997.

Moorhouse, Geoffrey. *India Britannica: a Vivid Introduction to the History of British India.* Chicago: Academy Chicago Publishers, 1999.

Paz, Octavio. *In Light of India: Essays.* San Diego, CA: Harcourt Brace & Company, 1997.

Rao, C. Hanumantha and Hans Linnemann, eds. *Economic Reforms and Poverty*

Bibliography

Alleviation in India. Thousand Oaks, CA: Sage Publications, 1996.

Read, Anthony. *The Proudest Day: Indian's Long Road to Independence*. New York: W.W. Norton & Company, 1998.

Royle, Trevor. *The Last Days of the Raj*. North Pomfret, VT: Trafalgar Square, 1998.

Saberwal, Satish. *Roots of Crisis: Interpreting Contemporary Indian Society*. Thousand Oaks, CA: Sage Publications, s1996.

Sachs, Jeffrey D., et al., eds. *India in the Era of Economic Reforms*. New York: Oxford University Press, 2000.

Sanguly, Sumit and Neil DeVotta, eds. *Understanding Contemporary India*. Boulder, CO: Lynne Reinner, 2003.

Sekhon, Joti. *Modern India*. New York: McGraw-Hill, 1999.

Sidhu, Waheguru and Jing-dong Yuan. *China and India: Cooperation or Conflict?* Boulder, CO: Lynne Reinner, 2003.

Sridharan, Kripa. *The ASEAN Region in India's Foreign Policy*. Brookfield, VT: Ashgate Publishing Company, 1996.

Srinivasan, T.N. and Suresh D. Tendulkar. *India in the World Economy*. Washington, DC: Institute for International Economics, 2001.

Sugata, Bose. *Nationalism, Democracy, and Development: State and Politics in India*. New York: Oxford University Press, 1999.

Tharoor, Shashi. *India: from Midnight to the Millennium*. New York: Arcade Publishing, 1997.

Thomas, Raju G. *Democracy, Security, and Development in India*. New York: Saint Martin's Press, 1996.

Tomlinson, B.R. *The Economy of Modern India, 1860–1970*. New York: Cambridge University Press, 1993.

Vanaik, Achin. *The Furies of Indian Communalism: Religion, Modernity and Secularization*. New York: Verso, 1997.

Vohra, Ranbir. *The Making of India: a Historical Survey*. Armonk, NY: M.E. Sharpe, 2000.

Wolpert, Stanley A. *A New History of India*. New York: Oxford University Press, 3rd ed. 1989.

Wolpert, Stanley A. *Nehru: a Tryst with Destiny*. New York: Oxford University Press, 1996.

Iran

Abrahamian, Ervand. *Khomeinism: Essays on the Islamic Republic*. Berkeley, CA: University of California Press, 1993.

Abrahamian, Ervand. *A History of Modern Iran*. New York: Cambridge University Press, 2008 (paper).

Adelkhah, Fariba. *Being Modern in Iran*. New York: Columbia University Press, 2000.

Amuzegar, Jahangir. *Iran's Economy under the Islamic Republic*. New York: Saint Martin's Press, 1994.

Azimi, Fakhreddin. *The Quest for Democracy in Iran: A Century of Struggle against Authoritarian Rule*. Cambridge: Harvard University Press, 2008.

Baktiari, Bahman. *Parliamentary Politics in Revolutionary Iran: the Institutionalization of Factional Politics*. Gainesville, FL: University Press of Florida, 1996.

Bayandor, Darioush. *Iran and the CIA: The Fall of Mossadeq Revisited*. New York: Palgrave Macmillan, 2010.

Cordesman, Anthony H. and Ahmed S. Hashim. *Iran: Dilemmas of Dual Containment*. Boulder, CO: Westview Press, 1997.

Cordesman, Anthony H. *Iran's Military Forces in Transition*. Westport, CT: Greenwood Publishing Group, 1999.

Cordesman, Anthony H., Adam Mausner, and Aram Nerguizian. *U.S. and Iranian Strategic Competition*. Washington D.C.: Center for Strategic and International Studies, 2012.

Daneshar, Parviz. *Revolution in Iran*. New York: Saint Martin's Press, 1996.

Farmanfarmaian, Manucher and Roxane Farmanfarmaian. *Blood and Oil: Memoirs of a Persian Prince*. New York: Random House, 1997.

Gheissari, Ali. *Contemporary Iran: Economy, Society, Politics*. New York: Oxford University Press, 2009.

Gieling, Saskia M. *Religion and War in Revolutionary Iran*. London: I.B. Tauris, 1999.

Goode, James F. *United States and Iran: in the Shadow of Musaddiq*. New York: Saint Martin's Press, 1997.

Heiss, Mary Ann. *Empire and Nationhood: the United States, Great Britain, and Iranian Oil, 1950–1954*. New York: Columbia University Press, 1997.

Keddie, Nikki R. *Iran and Muslim World: Resistance and Revolution*. New York: New York University Press, 1995.

Mackey, Sandra. *The Iranians*. New York: NAL/Dutton, 1998.

Metz, Helen Chapin, ed. *Iran: a Country Study*. Washington, DC: U.S. GPO, 4th ed. 1989.

Moses, Russell L. *Freeing the Hostages: Reexamining U.S.-Iranian Negotiations and Soviet Policy*. Pittsburgh, PA: University of Pittsburgh Press, 1996.

Nafisi, Azar, *Reading Lolita in Tehran*. New York: Random House, 2003.

Mousavian, Seyed Hossein. *The Iranian Nuclear Crisis: A Memoir*. Washington D.C.: Carnegie Endowment for International Peace, 2012.

Peimani, Hooman. *Iran and the United States: the Rise of the West Asian Regional Grouping*. Westport, CT: Greenwood Publishing Group, 1999.

Riesebrodt, Martin. *Pious Passion: the Emergence of Modern Fundamentalism in the United States and Iran*. Berkeley, CA: University of California Press, 1993.

Sciolino, Elaine. *Persian Mirrors: the Elusive Face of Iran*. New York: The Free Press, 2000.

Walsh, Lawrence E. *Firewall: the IranContra Conspiracy and Cover-Up*. New York: W.W. Norton & Company, 1997.

Wehrey, Frederic. *The Rise of the Pasdaran: Assessing the Domestic Roles of Iran's Islamic Revolutionary Guards Corps*. Santa Monica: RAND Corporation, 2009.

Wright, Robin B. *The Last Great Revolution: Turmoil and Transformation in Iran*. New York: Alfred A. Knopf, 2000.

Iraq

Al-Hawaheri, Yasmin Husein. *Women in Iraq: The Gender Impact of International Sanctions*. Boulder, CO: Lynne Rienner Publishers, 2008.

Al-Khalil, Samir. *Republic of Fear: the Inside Story of Saddam's Iraq*. Collingdale, PA: DIANE Publishing Company, 2000.

Arnove, Anthony, ed. *Iraq under Siege: the Deadly Impact of Sanctions and War*. Cambridge, MA: South End Press, 2000.

Baram, Amatzia and Barry Rubin, eds. *Iraq's Road to War*. New York: Saint Martin's Press, 1994.

Bhatia, Shyam and Dan McGrory. *Brighter Than the Baghdad Sun: Saddam Hussein's Nuclear Threat to the United States*. Washington, DC: Regnery Publishing, 2000.

Braude, Joseph. *The New Iraq*. Boulder, CO: Westview, 2003.

Butler, Richard. *The Greatest Threat: Iraq, Weapons of Mass Destruction and the Crisis of Global Security*. New York: Public Affairs, 2000.

Clawson, Patrick, ed. *How to Build a New Iraq after Saddam*. Washington D.C.: Brookings, 2002.

Cockburn, Andrew. *Out of the Ashes: the Resurrection of Saddam Hussein*. New York: HarperCollins, 2000.

Cordesman, Anthony H. and Ahmed S. Hashim. *Iraq: Sanctions and Beyond*. Boulder, CO: Westview Press, 1997.

Danspeckgruber, Wolfgang F. and Charles R. Tripp, eds. *The Iraqi Aggression against Kuwait: Strategic Lessons and Implications for Europe*. Boulder, CO: Westview Press, 1996.

Elliot, Matthew. *Independent Iraq: British Influence from 1941–1958*. New York: Saint Martin's Press, 1996.

Fawn, Rick and Raymond Hinnebusch, eds. *The Iraq War: Causes and Consequences*. Boulder, CO: Lynne Rienner Publishers, 2006.

Grossman, Mark, ed. *Encyclopedia of the Persian Gulf War*. Santa Barbara, CA: ABC-CLIO, 1995.

Haj, Samira. *The Making of Iraq, 1900–1963: Capital, Power and Ideology*. Albany, NY: State University of New York Press, 1997.

Haselkorn, Avigdor. *The Continuing Storm: Iraq, Poisonous Weapons, and Deterrence.* New Haven, CT: Yale University Press, 1998.

Lukitz, Liora. *Iraq: the Search for National Identity.* Portland, OR: Frank Cass & Company, 1995.

Marr, Phebe. *Modern History of Iraq.* 2d ed. Boulder, CO: Westview, 2003.

Metz, Helen Chapin, ed. *Iraq: a Country Study.* Washington, DC: U.S. GPO, 4th ed. 1990.

Mohamedou, Mohammad-Mahmoud. *Iraq and the Second Gulf War: State Building and Regime Security.* Bethesda, MD: Austin & Winfield Publishers, 1997.

Musallam, Musallam A. *Iraqi Invasion of Kuwait: Saddam Hussein, His State and International Power Politics.* New York: Saint Martin's Press, 1996.

Nakash, Yitzhak. *The Shiis of Iraq.* Princeton, NJ: Princeton University Press, 1994.

Rahaee, Farhang, ed. *The Iran-Iraq War: the Politics of Aggression.* Gainesville, FL: University Press of Florida, 1993.

Shadid, Anthony. *Night Draws Near: Iraq's People in the Shadow of America's War.* New York: Henry Holt and Company, 2006

Simons, G.L. *Iraq: from Sumer to Saddam.* New York: Saint Martin's Press, 1994.

Stansfield, Gareth and Robert Lowe, eds. *The Kurdish Policy Imperative.* Washington: Brookings, 2009

Stiglitz, Joseph E. and Linda J. Bilmes. *The Three Trillion Dollar War: The True Cost of the Iraq Conflict.* New York: W.W. Norton, 2008

Israel

Arain, Asher. *The Second Republic: Politics in Israel.* Chatham, NJ: Chatham House Publishers, 1997.

Avruch, Kevin and Walter P. Zenner, eds. *Critical Essays on Israeli Society, Religion, and Government: Books on Israel.* Albany, NY: State University of New York Press, 1996.

Barkai, Haim. *The Lessons of Israel's Great Inflation.* Westport, CT: Greenwood Pub-lishing Group, 1995.

Barnett, Michael N., ed. *Israel in Comparative Perspective: Challenging the Conventional Wisdom.* Albany, NY: State University of New York Press, 1996.

Bar-On, Mordechai. *In Pursuit of Peace: a History of the Israeli Peace Movement.* Washington, DC: United States Institute of Peace Press, 1996.

Barzilai, Gad. *Wars, Internal Conflicts, and Political Order: a Jewish Democracy in the Middle East.* Albany, NY: State University of New York Press, 1996.

Ben-Ari, Eyal, ed. *Grasping Land: Space and Place in Contemporary Israeli Discourse and Experience.* State University of New York Press, 1997.

Ben Meir, Yehuda. *Civil-Military Relations in Israel.* New York: Columbia University Press, 1995.

Benson, Michael T. *Harry S. Truman and the Founding of Israel.* Westport, CT: Greenwood Publishing Group, 1997.

Bickerton, Ian J. and Carla L. Klausner. *A Concise History of the Arab-Israeli Conflict.* Upper Saddle River, NJ: Prentice Hall, 1997.

Boyarin, Jonathan. *Palestine and Jewish History: Criticism at the Borders of Ethnography.* Minneapolis, MN: University of Minnesota Press, 1996.

Bregman, Ahron. *Israel's Wars, 1947–1993.* New York: Routledge, 2000.

Buchanan, Andrew S. *Peace with Justice: a History of the Israeli-Palestinian Declaration.* New York: Saint Martin's Press, 2000.

Chesin, Amir S., et al. *Separate but Unequal.* Cambridge, MA: Harvard University Press, 1999.

Cohen, Asher. *Israel and the Politics of Jewish Identity: the Secular-Religious Impasse.* Baltimore, MD: Johns Hopkins University Press, 2000.

Cohen, Avner. *Israel and the Bomb.* New York: Columbia University Press, 1998.

Cohen, Stuart A. *Democratic Societies and Their Armed Forces: Israel in Comparative Context.* Portland, OR: Frank Cass Publishers, 2000.

Cordesman, Anthony H. *Perilous Prospects: the Peace Process and the Arab-Israeli Military Balance.* Portland, OR: Frank Cass & Company, 1996.

Corzine, Phyllis. *The Palestinian-Israeli Accord.* San Diego, CA: Lucent Books, 1996.

Dumper, Michael. *The Politics of Jerusalem since 1967.* New York: Columbia University Press, 1996.

Eban, Abba S. *Diplomacy for the Next Century.* New Haven, CT: Yale University Press, 1998.

Edelheit, Hershel and Abraham J. Edelheit. *Israel and the Jewish World, 1948–1993: a Chronology.* Westport, CT: Greenwood Publishing Group, 1995.

Evron, Boas. *Jewish State or Israeli Nation?* Bloomington, IN: Indiana University Press, 1995.

Ezrahi, Yaron. *Rubber Bullets: Power and Conscience in Modern Israel.* New York: Farrar, Straus & Giroux, 1996.

Freeman, Robert Owen, ed. *Israel's First Fifty Years.* Gainesville, FL: University Press of Florida, 2000.

Garfinkle, Adam. *Politics and Society in Modern Israel: Myths and Realities.* Armonk, NY: M.E. Sharpe, 1997.

Gilbert, Martin. *Israel: a History.* New York: William Morrow & Company, 1998.

Gilbert, Martin. *Jerusalem in the Twentieth Century.* New York: John Wiley & Sons, 1996.

HH Sheikh Rashid Bin Humaid al-Nuaimi, the deceased Ruler of Ajman

Bibliography

Goldscheider, Calvin. *Israel's Changing Society. Population, Ethnicity, and Development*. 2d. ed. Boulder, CO: Westview, 2002.

Gordon, Haim. *Quicksand: Israel, the Intifada, and the Rise of Political Evil*. East Lansing, MI: Michigan State University, 1995.

Hartman, David. *Israelis and the Jewish Tradition: an Ancient People Debating Its Future*. New Haven, CT: Yale University Press, 2000.

Hazony, Yoram. *Jewish State*. New York: Basic Books, 2000.

Hohenberg, John. *Israel at 50*. Syracuse, NY: Syracuse University Press, 1998.

Horovitz, David, ed. *Shalom, Friend: the Life and Legacy of Yitzhak Rabin*. New York: Newmarket Press, 1996.

Ilan, Amitzur. *The Origin of the Arab-Israeli Arms Race: Arms, Embargo, Military Power and Decision in the 1948 Palestine War*. Albany, NY: New York University Press, 1996.

Indyk, Martin. *Innocent Abroad: An Intimate History of American Peace Diplomacy in the Middle East*. New York: Simon & Schuster, 2009

Isserlin, Ben. *The Israelites*. New York: Thames & Hudson, 1998.

Karpin, Michael and Ina Friedman. *Murder in the Name of God: the Plot to Kill Yitzhak Rabin*. New York: Henry Holt & Company, 1998.

Karsh, Efraim, ed. *Between War and Peace: Dilemmas of Israeli Security*. Portland, OR: Frank Cass & Company, 1996.

Karsh, Efraim, ed. *From Rabin to Netanyahu: Israel's Troubled Agenda*. Portland, OR: Frank Cass & Company, 1997.

Khatchadourian, Haig. *The Quest for Peace between Israel and the Palestinians*. New York: Peter Lang Publishing, 2000.

Kop, Yaakov and Robert E. Litan. *Sticking Together. The Israeli Experiment in Pluralism*. Washington D.C.: Brookings, 2002.

Lawless, Richard I. *The Arab-Israeli Conflict: an Encyclopedia*. Santa Barbara, CA: ABC-CLIO, 2001.

Lazin, Frederick A. and Gregory S. Mahler, eds. *Israel in the Nineties: Development and Conflict*. Gainesville, FL: University Press of Florida, 1996.

Levey, Zach. *Israel and the Western Powers, 1952–1960*. Chapel Hill, NC: University Press of North Carolina, 1997.

Levran, Aharon. *Israel after the Storm: Strategic Lessons from the Second Gulf War*. Portland, OR: Frank Cass & Company, 1997.

Levy, Yagil. *Trial and Error: Israel's Route from War to De-Escalation*. Albany, NY: State University of New York Press, 1997.

Linn, Ruth. *Conscience at War: the Israeli Soldier As a Moral Critic*. Albany, NY: State University of New York Press, 1996.

Litwin, Howard. *Uprooted in Old Age: Russian Jews and Their Social Networks in Israel*. Westport, CT: Greenwood Publishing Group, 1995.

Lomsky-Feder, Edna and Eyal Ben-Ari, eds. *The Military and Militarism in Israeli Society*. Albany, NY: State University of New York Press, 2000.

Makovsky, David. *Making Peace with the PLO: the Rabin Government's Road to the Oslo Accord*. Boulder, CO: Westview Press, 1995.

Metz, Helen Chapin, ed. *Israel: a Country Study*. Washington, DC: U.S. GPO, 3rd ed. 1990.

Netanyahu, Benjamin. *A Place among the Nations: Israel and the World*. New York: Bantam Books, 1993.

Peres, Shimon. *Battling for Peace: a Memoir*. New York: Random House, 1995.

Peres, Shimon. *For the Future of Israel*. Baltimore, MD: Johns Hopkins University Press, 1998.

Peretz, Don. *The Arab-Israeli Dispute*. New York: Facts on File, 1996.

Peri, Yoram, ed. *The Assassination of Yitzhak Rabin*. Stanford, CA: Stanford University Press, 2000.

Plessner, Yakir. *The Political Economy of Israel: from Ideology to Stagnation*. Albany, NY: State University of New York Press, 1993.

Quandt, William B. *Peace Process: American Diplomacy and the Arab-Israeli Conflict since 1967*. Washington D.C.: Brookings, 2005.

Rabin, Leah. *Rabin: Our Life, His Legacy*. New York: The Putnam Publishing Group, 1997.

Rabinovich, Itamar. *The Brink of Peace: the Israeli-Syrian Negotiations*. Princeton, NJ: Princeton University Press, 1998.

Reich, Bernard. *Historical Dictionary of Israel*. Lanham, MD: Scarecrow Press, 1992.

Reich, Bernard and David H. Goldberg. *Political Dictionary of Israel*. Lanham, MD: Scarecrow Press, 2000.

Reich, Bernard. *Securing the Covenant: United States-Israeli Relations after the Cold War*. Westport, CT: Greenwood Publishing Group, 1995.

Reinharz, Jehuda. *Chaim Weizmann: the Making of a Statesman*. New York: Oxford University Press, 1993.

Rouhana, Nadim W. *Palestinian Citizens in an Ethnic Jewish State: Identities in Conflict*. New Haven, CT: Yale University Press, 1997.

Rubin, Barry, et al., eds. *From War to Peace: Arab-Israeli Relations, 1973–1993*. New York: New York University Press, 1994.

Said, Edward W. *The End of the Peace Process; Oslo and After*. New York: Pantheon Books, 2000.

Sela, Avraham. *The Decline of the Arab-Israeli Conflict: Middle East Politics and the Quest for Regional Order*. Albany, NY: State University of New York Press, 1997.

Shafir, Gershon, ed. *New Israel*. New York: HarperCollins, 2000.

Sharkansky, Ira. *Policy Making in Israel: Routines for Simple Problems and Coping with the Complex*. Pittsburgh, PA: University of Pittsburgh Press, 1997.

Sheffer, Gabriel, ed. *U.S.-Israeli Relations at the Crossroads*. Portland, OR: Frank Cass & Company, 1997.

Shindler, Colin. *Israel, Likud, and the Zionist Dream: Power, Politics, and Ideology from Begin to Netanyahu*. New York: Saint Martin's Press, 1995.

Shlain, Avi. *The Iron Wall: Israel and the Arab World*. New York: W.W. Norton & Company, 2000.

Sternhell, Zeev. Translated by David Maisel. *The Founding Myths of Israel: Nationalism, Socialism and the Making of the Jewish State*. Princeton, NJ: Princeton University Press, 1998.

Thomas, Baylis. *The Dark Side of Zionism: The Quest for Security through Dominance*. Lanham, MD: Rowan & Littlefield, 2009

Troen, S. Ilan and Noah Lucas, eds. *Israel: the First Decade of Independence*. Albany, NY: State University of New York Press, 1995.

Van Creveld, Martin. *The Sword and the Olive: a Critical History of the Israeli Defense Force*. New York: Public Affairs, 1998.

Wheatcroft, Geoffrey. *The Controversy of Zion: Jewish Nationalism, the Jewish State, and the Unresolved Jewish Dilemma*. Reading, MA: Addison Wesley Longman, 1996.

Yiftachel, Oren, ed. *Ethnic Frontiers and Peripheries: Perspectives on Development and Inequality in Israel*. Boulder, CO: Westview Press, 1998.

Jordan

Brand, Laurie A. *Jordan's Inter-Arab Relations: the Political Economy of Alliance Making*. New York: Columbia University Press, 1995.

Fischbach, Michael R. *State, Society and Land in Jordan*. Boston, MA: Brill Academic Publishers, 2000.

Lukacs, Yehuda. *Israel, Jordan, and the Peace Process*. Syracuse, NY: Syracuse University Press, 1996.

Metz, Helen Chapin, ed. *Jordan: a Country Study*. Washington, DC: U.S. GPO, 4th ed. 1991.

Piro, Timothy J. *The Political Economy of Market Reform in Jordan*. Lanham, MD: Rowman & Littlefield, 1998.

Salibi, Kamal. *A Modern History of Jordan*. New York: Saint Martin's Press, 1998.

Bibliography

Satloff, Robert B. *From Abdullah to Hussein: Jordan in Transition.* New York: Oxford University Press, 1994.

Kuwait

Anscombe, Frederick F. *The Ottoman Gulf: the Creation of Kuwait, Saudi Arabia, and Qatar, 1870–1914.* New York: Columbia University Press, 1997.

Clements, Frank A. *Kuwait.* Santa Barbara, CA: ABC-CLIO, rev. ed. 1996.

Cordesman, Anthony H. *Kuwait: Recovery and Security after the Gulf War.* Boulder, CO: Westview Press, 1997.

Crystal, Jill. *Oil and Politics in the Gulf: Rulers and Merchants in Kuwait and Qatar.* New York: Cambridge University Press, 1995.

Longva, Anh Nga. *Walls Built in Sand: Migration, Exclusion and Society in Kuwait.* Boulder, CO: Westview Press, 1997.

Smith, Simon C. *Kuwait, 1950–1965: Britain, the Al-Sabah, and Oil.* New York: Oxford University Press, 1999.

Tetreault, Mary Ann. *Stories of Democracy: Politics and Society in contemporary Kuwait.* New York: Columbia University Press, 1999.

Lebanon

Abraham, A.J. *The Lebanon War.* Westport, CT: Greenwood Publishing Group, 1996.

Abukhalil, Asad. *Historical Dictionary of Lebanon.* Lanham, MD: Scarecrow Press, 1998.

Bleaney, C.H. *Lebanon.* Santa Barbara, CA: ABC-CLIO, 1992.

Colello, Thomas, ed. *Lebanon: a Country Study.* Washington, DC: U.S. GPO, 3rd ed. 1989.

El-Solh, Raghid. *Lebanon and Arabism.* New York: Saint Martin's Press, 1999.

Harris, William. *Faces of Lebanon: Sects, Wars and Global Expansion.* Princeton, NJ: Markus Wiener Publishers, 1997.

Kalawoun, Nasser M. *The Struggle for Lebanon: a Modern History of Lebanese-Egyptian Relations.* New York: I.B. Tauris & Company, 2000.

Maasri, Zeina. *Off the Wall–Political Posters of the Lebanese Civil War.* London: I.B. Tauris,

Malik, Habib C. *Between Damascus and Jerusalem: Lebanon and the Middle East Peace Process.* Washington, DC: The Washington Institute for Near East Policy, 2000.

Phares, Walid. *Lebanese Christian Nationalism: the Rise and Fall of an Ethnic Resistance.* Boulder, CO: Lynne Rienner Publishers, 1994.

Picard, Elizabeth. Translated by Franklin Philip. *Lebanon: a Shattered Country* New York: Holmes & Meier Publishers, 2001.

Ranstorp, Magnus. *Hizb'allah in Lebanon: the Politics of the Western Hostage Crisis.* New York: Saint Martin's Press, 1997.

Schulze, Kirsten E. *Intervention, Israeli Covert Diplomacy and the Maronites.* New York: Saint Martin's Press, 1997.

Shehadi, Nadim and Dana Haffar-Mills, eds. *Lebanon: a History of Conflict and Consensus.* New York: Saint Martin's Press, 1993.

Winslow, Charles. *Lebanon.* New York: Routledge, 1996.

Zamir, Meir. *Lebanon's Quest, 1929–1939.* New York: Saint Martin's Press, 1998.

Zisser, Eyal. *Lebanon: the Challenge of Independence.* New York: I.B. Tauris & Company, 2000.

The Maldives

Metz, Helen Chapin, ed. *Indian Ocean: Five Island Countries.* Washington, DC: U.S. GPO, 3rd ed. 1995.

Nepal

Cameron, Mary M. *On the Edge of the Auspicious: Gender and Caste in Nepal.* Champaign, IL: University of Illinois Press, 1998.

Gellner, David, et al., eds. *Nationalism and Ethnicity in a Hindu Kingdom: the Politics and Culture of Contemporary Nepal.* Newark, NJ: Gordon & Breach Publishing Group, 1997.

Savada, Andrea Matles, ed. *Nepal and Bhutan: Country Studies.* Washington, DC: U.S. GPO, 3rd ed. 1993.

Oman

El-Solh, Rahbih, ed. *Oman and the South-Eastern Shore of Arabia.* Milford, CT: LPC/InBook, 1997.

Joyce, Miriam. *The Sultanate of Oman a Twentieth Century History.* Westport, CT: Greenwood Publishing Group, 1995.

Kechichian, Joseph A. *Oman and the World: the Emergence of an Independent Foreign Policy.* Santa Monica, CA: The Rand Corporation, 1995.

Pakistan

Ahmed, Samania and David Cortright, eds. *Pakistan and the Bomb: Public Opinion and Nuclear Options.* Notre Dame, IN: University of Notre Dame Press, 1998.

Blood, Peter R., ed. *Pakistan: a Country Study.* Washington, DC: U.S. GPO, 6th ed. 1995.

Burki, Shahid Javed. *Historical Dictionary of Pakistan.* Lanham, MD: Scarecrow Press, 1999.

Fair, C. Christine. *The Madrassah Challenge: Militancy and Religious Education in Pakistan.* Washington: US Institute of Peace Press, 2008

Haqqani, Husain. *Pakistan: Between Mosque and Military.* Washington: Carnegie Endowment for International Peace, 2005

Harrison, Selig S., et al., eds. *India and Pakistan: the First Fifty Years.* New York: Cambridge University Press, 1998.

Husain, Ishrat. *Pakistan: the Economy of an Elitist State.* New York: Oxford University Press, 1999.

Hussain, Jane. *A History of the People of Pakistan: toward Independence.* New York: Oxford University Press, 1998.

Looney, Robert E. *The Pakistani Economy: Economic Growth and Structural Reform.* Westport, CT: Greenwood Publishing Group, 1997.

McGrath, Allen. *The Destruction of Pakistan's Democracy.* New York: Oxford University Press, 1999.

Raza, Rafi, ed. *Pakistan in Perspective, 1947–1997.* New York: Oxford University Press, 1998.

Raza, Rafi. *Zulfikar Ali Bhutto and Pakistan 1967–1977.* New York: Oxford University Press, 1997.

Rizvi, Hasan Askari. *Military, State and Society in Pakistan.* New York: Saint Martin's Press, 2000.

Samad, Yunas. *A Nation in Turmoil: Nationalism and Ethnicity in Pakistan, 1937–1958.* Thousand Oaks, CA: Sage Publications, 1995.

Sattar, Babar. *The Non-Proliferation Regime and Pakistan: the Comprehensive Test Ban Treaty as a Case Study.* New York: Oxford University Press, 2000.

Shafqat, Saeed. *Civil-Military Relations in Pakistan: from Zulfikar Ali Bhutto to Benazir Bhutto.* Westport, CT: Westview Press, 1997.

Shah, Mehtab A. *The Foreign Policy of Pakistan: Ethnic Impacts on Diplomacy, 1971–1994.* New York: Saint Martin's Press, 1997.

Siddiqa, Ayesha. *Military Inc.: Inside Pakistan's Military Economy.* London: Pluto Press, 2007.

Talbot, Ian. *Pakistan: a Modern History.* New York: Saint Martin's Press, 1999.

Wirsing, Robert G. *India, Pakistan and the Kashmir Dispute: on Regional Conflict and Its Resolution.* New York: Saint Martin's Press, 1994.

Zaidi, S. Akbar. *Issues in Pakistan's Economy.* New York: Oxford University Press, 2000.

Ziring, Lawrence. *Pakistan in the Twentieth Century: a Political History.* New York: Oxford University Press, 1998.

Palestine National Authority

Diwan, Ishac and Radwan A. Shaban. *Development under Adversity: the Palestinian Economy in Transition.* Washington, DC: The World Bank, 1999.

Bibliography

Klieman, Aharon. *Compromising Palestine: a Guide to Final Status Negotiations.* New York: Columbia University Press, 1999.

Mattar, Philip, ed. *Encyclopedia of the Palestinians.* New York: Facts on File, 2000.

Qatar

Anscombe, Frederick F. *The Ottoman Gulf: the Creation of Kuwait, Saudi Arabia, and Qatar, 1870–1914.* New York: Columbia University Press, 1997.

Reich, Bernard and Steven Dorr. *Qatar.* Westport, CT: Westview Press, 1996.

Saudi Arabia

Cordesman, Anthony H. *Saudi Arabia: Guarding the Desert Kingdom.* Westport, CT: Westview Press, 1997.

Fancy, Mamoun. *Saudi Arabia and the Politics of Dissent.* New York: Saint Martin's Press, 1999.

Hart, Parker T. *Saudi Arabia and the United Stated: Birth of a Security Partnership.* Bloomington, IN: Indiana University Press, 1998.

Kostiner, Joseph. *The Making of Saudi Arabia, 1916–1936: from Chieftaincy to Monarchical State.* New York: Oxford University Press, 1993.

Long, David E. *The Kingdom of Saudi Arabia.* Gainesville, FL: University Press of Florida, 1997.

Metz, Helen Chapin, ed. *Saudi Arabia: a Country Study.* Washington, DC: U.S. GPO, 5th ed. 1993.

Pampanini, Andrea H. *Cities from the Arabian Desert: the Building of Jubail and Yanbu in Saudi Arabia.* Westport, CT: Greenwood Publishing Group, 1997.

Peterson, J.E. *Historical Dictionary of Saudi Arabia.* Lanham, MD: Scarecrow Press, 1993.

Vassiliev, Alexei. *The History of Saudi Arabia.* New York: New York University Press, 2000.

Wilson, Peter W. and Douglas F. Graham. *Saudi Arabia: the Coming Storm.* Armonk, NY: M.E. Sharpe, 1994.

Yizraeli, Sarah. *The Remaking of Saudi Arabia: the Struggle between King Sa'ud and Crown Prince Faysal, 1953–1962.* Syracuse, NY: Syracuse University Press, 1998.

Sri Lanka

Athukorala, Prema-Chandra and Sarath Rajapatirana. *Liberalization and Industrial Transformation: Sri Lanka in International Perspective.* New York: Oxford University Press, 2000.

Bartholomeusz, Tessa J. and Chandra R. De Silva, eds. *Buddhist Fundamentalism and Minority Identities in Sri Lanka.* Albany, NY: State University Press of New York Press, 1998.

De Silva, K.M. *Regional Powers and Small State Security: India and Sri Lanka, 1977–1990.* Baltimore, MD: Johns Hopkins University Press, 1995.

Perera, Nihal. *Society and Space: Colonialism, Nationalism and Postcolonial Identity in Sri Lanka.* Boulder, CO: Westview Press, 1998.

Ross, Russell R. and Andrea Matles Savada, eds. *Sri Lanka: a Country Study.* Washington, DC: U.S. GPO, 2nd ed. 1990.

Rotberg, Robert I. *Creating Peace in Sri Lanka: Civil War and Reconciliation.* Washington, DC: Brookings Institution Press, 1999.

Samarasinghe, S.W. and Vidyamali Samarasinghe. *Historical Dictionary of Sri Lanka.* Lanham, MD: Scarecrow Press, 1997.

Wignaraja, Ganeshan. *Trade Liberalization in Sri Lanka: Exports, Technology and Industrial Policy.* New York: Saint Martin's Press, 1998.

Wilson, A. Jeyaratnam. *Sri Lankan Tamil Nationalism: Its Origins and Development in the Nineteenth and Twentieth Centuries.* Vancouver, BC: UBC Press, 1999.

Syria

Agha, Hussein J. and Ahmad S. Khalidi. *Syria and Iran: Rivalry and Co-Operation.* New York: Council on Foreign Relations, 1995.

Commins, David. *Historical Dictionary of Syria.* Lanham, MD: Scarecrow Press, 1996.

Gelvin, James L. *Divided Loyalties: Nationalism and Mass Politics in Syria at the Close of Empire.* Berkeley, CA: University of California Press, 1998.

Hinnebusch, Raymond. *The State and the Political Economy of Reform in Syria.* Boulder, CO: Lynne Rienner Publishers, 2008.

Kienle, Eberhard, ed. *Contemporary Syria: Liberalization between Cold War and Peace.* New York: Saint Martin's Press, 1997.

Lawson, Fred H. *Why Syria Goes to War: Thirty Years of Confrontation.* New York: Cornell University Press, 1996.

Perthes, Volker. *Political Economy of Syria under Asad.* New York: Saint Martin's Press, 1997.

Quilliam, Neil. *Syria and the New World Order.* Lowell, MA: Ithaca Press, 1999.

Rabinovich, Itamar. *The Brink of Peace: the Israel-Syrian Negotiations.* Princeton, NJ: Princeton University Press, 1998.

Saunders, Bonnie F. *The United States and Arab Nationalism: the Syrian Case.* Westport, CT: Greenwood Publishing Group, 1996.

Seale, Patrick. *Asad: The Struggle for the Middle East.* Berkeley, CA: University of California Press, 1988.

Turkey

Ahmad, Feroz. *The Making of Modern Turkey.* New York: Routledge, 1993.

Abramowitz, Morton, ed. *The United States and Turkey. Allies in Need.* Washington, D.C.: Brookings, 2003.

Altunisik, Meliha Benli and Ozlem Tur Kavli. *Turkey.* NY: Routledge, 2002.

Balim, Cigdem, et al., eds. *Turkey: Political, Social and Economic Challenges in the 1990s.* Boston, MA: Brill Academic Publishers, 1995.

Balkir, Canan and Allan M. Williams, eds. *Turkey and Europe.* New York: Saint Martin's Press, 1993.

Barkey, Henri J. and Graham E. Fuller. *Turkey's Kurdish Question.* Lanham, MD: Rowman & Littlefield, 1997.

Bugra, Ayse. *State and Business in Modern Turkey: a Comparative Study.* Albany, NY: State University of New York Press, 1994.

Dadrian, Vahakn N. *Warrant for Genocide: Key Elements of Turko-Armenian Conflict.* Piscataway, NJ: Transaction Publishers, 1998.

Davison, Andrew. *Secularism and Revivalism in Turkey: a Hermeneutic Reconsideration.* New Haven, CT: Yale University Press, 1998.

Fuller, Graham E. and Ian O. Fuller. *Turkey's New Geopolitics: from the Balkans to Western China.* Boulder, CO: Westview Press, 1993.

Fuller, Graham E. *Turkey as a Pivotal State in the Muslim World.* Washington: U.S. Institute for Peace Press, 2007.

Gunter, Michael M. *Kurds and Future of Turkey.* New York: Saint Martin's Press, 1997.

Heper, Metin, et al., eds. *Turkey and the West: Images of a New Political Culture.* New York: New York: Saint Martin's Press, 1993.

Howe, Marvine. *Turkey Today. A National Divided over Islam's Revival.* Boulder, CO: Westview, 2000.

Kahveci, Erol, et al., eds. *Work and Occupation in Modern Turkey.* Herndon, VA: Cassell Academic, 1996.

Kasaba, Resat and Sibel Bozdogan, eds. *Rethinking Modernity and National Identity in Turkey.* Seattle, WA: University of Washington Press, 1997.

Kedourie, Sylvia. *Seventy-Five Years of the Turkish Republic.* Portland, OR: Frank Cass & Company, 2000.

Kedourie, Sylvia, ed. *Turkey: Identity, Democracy, Politics.* Portland, OR: Frank Cass & Company, 1998.

Kramer, Heinz. *Changing Turkey: Challenges to Europe and the United States.* Washington, DC: Brookings Institution Press, 1999.

Larrabee, F. Stephen and Ian O. Lesser. *Turkish Foreign Policy in an Age of Uncertainty.* Santa Monica, CA: Rand, 2002.

Mango, Andrew. *Turkey: the Challenge of a New Role*. Westport, CT: Greenwood Publishing Group, 1994.

Mastny, Vojtech and Craig Nation, eds. *Turkey between East and West: New Challenges for a Rising Regional Power*. Boulder, CO: Westview Press, 1997.

McDonagh, Bernard. *Turkey*. New York: W.W. Norton & Company, 2000.

Muftuler-Bac, Meltem. *Turkey's Relations with a Changing Europe*. New York: Saint Martin's Press, 1997.

Olsen, Robert, ed. *The Kurdish Nationalist Movement and Its Impact on Turkey in the 1990's*. Lexington, KY: University Press of Kentucky, 1996.

Pitman, Paul M., III, ed. *Turkey: a Country Study*. Washington, DC: U.S. GPO, 4th ed. 1988.

Pope, Hugh and Nicole Pope. *Turkey Unveiled: a History of Modern Turkey*. New York: Overlook Press, 1998.

Rittenberg, Libby, ed. *The Political Economy of Turkey in the Post-Soviet Era: Going West and Looking East?* Westport, CT: Greenwood Publishing Group, 1998.

Togan, S. and V.N. Balasubramanyam, eds. *The Economy of Turkey since Liberalization*. New York: Saint Martin's Press, 1996.

Yilmaz, Bahri. *Challenges to Turkey: the New Role of Turkey in International Politics since the Dissolution of the Soviet Union*. New York: Saint Martin's Press, 1999.

Zürcher, Erik J. *Turkey: a Modern History*. London: I.B. Tauris, 1994.

United Arab Emirates

Al-Fahim, Mohammed. *From Rags to Riches: a Story of Abu Dhabi*. New York: Saint Martin's Press, 1998.

Camarapix Staff. *Spectrum Guide to the United Arab Emirates*. Northampton, MA: Interlink Publishing Group, 1998.

Clements, Frank A. *United Arab Emirates*. Santa Barbara, CA: ABC-CLIO, rev. ed. 1998.

Yemen

Al-Madhaqi, Ahmed Nomen. *Yemen and the U.S.A.: a Super-Power and a Small-State Relationship*. New York: Saint Martin's Press, 1996.

Auchterlonie, Paul. *Yemen*. Santa Barbara, CA: ABC-CLIO, rev. ed, 1998.

Burrowes, Robert D. *Historical Dictionary of Yemen*. Lanham, MD: Scarecrow Press, 1995.

Dresch, Paul. *Tribes, Government, and History in Yemen*. New York: Oxford University Press, 1994.

CPSIA information can be obtained at www.ICGtesting.com
Printed in the USA
BVOW10s2114180814

362987BV00003BB/6/P

9 781475 812350